Israel

a travel survival kit

Neil Tilbury

Israel – a travel survival kit
1st edition

Published by
Lonely Planet Publications
Head Office: PO Box 617, Hawthorn, Victoria 3122, Australia
US Office: PO Box 2001A, Berkeley, CA 94702, USA

Printed by
Singapore National Printers Ltd, Singapore

Photographs by
Neil Tilbury (NT)
Richard Everist (RE)
Front cover: At the Western Wall (RE)
Back cover: Near Jericho (NT)

Published
August 1989

Although the author and publisher have tried to make the information as accurate as possible, they accept no responsibility for any loss, injury or inconvenience sustained by any person using this book.

National Library of Australia Cataloguing in Publication Data

Tilbury, Neil
    Israel, a travel survival kit.

    1st ed.
    Includes index.
    ISBN 0 86442 015 3.

    1. Israel – Description and travel – Guide-books.
    I. Title.

915.694'0454

The Author

Neil Tilbury was born in Portsmouth, England, where he studied hotel management. Moving up to London, he spent a few years working in the hotel and wine trades before travelling to Australia via Europe. One of the countries that he visited was Israel and, after a few months in the USA he returned there to research this guide. On completing this project he went to India to update Lonely Planet's *Kashmir, Ladakh & Zanskar – a travel survival kit*.

Acknowledgements

Grateful thanks are due to several people for their invaluable contributions to this guide. First of all I want to thank my parents for allowing me to return home to do the writing and occupy my old room (and one or two others) for more months than any of us had envisaged. In addition to their regular devoted parent roles as hotel staff, taxi drivers and laundry service, they have helped immensely with typing (Mum) and editing (Dad).

My gratitude extends to various parts of the globe for various reasons. Thanks to Steve Green and Maz Foster in Sydney; to Phyllis Solomon, Bob Posch, Brian Williams and Sam Van Syckel in New York; to Greg Porter and Sara Welchman in London; and to my brother, Mark Tilbury, who is never anywhere for long except at sea.

Travelling around Israel researching this guide I was fortunate to have met so many kind and helpful people. I am particularly indebted to the following people: Ruti Aizenberg, Uri Avnary, Shlomo Bar-Ayal, Hana, Dani and Liat Bitan, Fauzy Dahoud, Linda Deal, Basam Fiadi, Gamal Hamdi, Hamed Kashkeesh and family, Joseph Kiriati, Paula Meodovnik, Magi Nahshon, Hatem Nasif, Saleh Nasser el-Deen, Yusef S Natsheh, Irit Ovadia, Robert Rosenberg, David Shapira, Oded Shoshan and family, and Jawad Sobhi Sakallah.

I was given much help and encouragement by countless fellow travellers in Israel, and I would like to express my appreciation to all of them, especially to Tania Ben-Zion, Saskia and Leon Gorris, Mr and Mrs G Leahy, Diane Mayne, Corrie Sirota, and Tami Stuky and Tina Andesson.

For sharing their enthusiastic knowledge of the country with me, extra special thanks are due to Ilan Levy, Haim Fireshtein, Irit, Horace Richter and Keren Pardo.

Finally, I have to thank Hazel, for causing me to stay in Israel a few months longer than the two weeks initially scheduled on that first visit.

Lonely Planet Credits

Editor	Jon Murray
Cover design, design & illustrations	Margaret Jung
Maps	Graham Imeson
Typesetting	Ann Jeffree
	Gaylene Miller

Thanks to Laurie Fullerton for proofing, to Lyn McGaurr and Tom Smallman for proofing and corrections, to Peter Flavelle for map corrections and additional maps, and to Glenn Beanland for help with paste-up and illustrations. James Lyon proofed, corrected and was generally invaluable, Frith Pike compiled the indexes, Susan Weis in Tel Aviv updated the accommodation information, and Debbie Mengem-Rossdale gave sound advice.

A Warning & a Request

Things change – prices go up, schedules change, good places go bad and bad places go bankrupt – nothing stays the same. So if you find things better or worse, recently opened or long since closed, please write and tell us and help make the next edition better!

Your letters will be used to help update future editions and, where possible, important changes will also be included as a Stop Press section in reprints.

All information is greatly appreciated and the best letters will receive a free copy of the next edition, or any other Lonely Planet book of your choice.

As we went to press Israel began the process of upgrading its telephone system and eventually most phone numbers in the country will be altered.

Appreciation

Contents

INTRODUCTION   7

FACTS ABOUT THE COUNTRY History 9 – Geography 25 – Climate 27 – Flora & Fauna 27 –   9
Government 29 – Economy 30 – Population & People 31 – The UNRWA 36 –
Israel Defence Forces 37 – Religion 38 – The Arts 56 – Architecture 58 – Fashion 61 –
Festivals 61 – The Kibbutz 67 – The Moshav 69 – Kibbutz & Moshav Volunteering 70 –
Where To Find What 74 – Language 79

FACTS FOR THE VISITOR Documents & Visas 83 – Working Holidays 85 – Money 87 –   83
Costs 88 – Tourist Information 89 – General Information 90 – Media 93 – Health 94 –
Dangers & Annoyances 94 – Film & Photography 96 – Places To Stay 97 – Food 98 –
Books & Bookshops 104 – Study 106 – Things To Buy 106 – What To Bring 108

GETTING THERE Air – Overland – Sea – Departure Tax   110

GETTING AROUND Air – Bus – Train – Taxi – Driving – Hitch-Hiking – Cycling – Tours   114

JERUSALEM Old City – Jewish Quarter – Muslim Quarter – Christian Quarter –   121
Armenian Quarter – Mount Zion – The City Of David – Kidron Valley –
Hinnom Valley – Mount Of Olives – Mount Scopus – East Jerusalem – New City –
Around Jerusalem

TEL AVIV & THE SOUTH COAST Tel Aviv – Jaffa – Bat Yam – Herzlia – Holon –   201
Bnei Brak – Petah Tiqwa – Rishon Le Zion – Rehovot – Ramla – Ashdod – Ashkelon –
Around Ashkelon – Netanya

HAIFA & THE NORTH COAST Haifa – Druze Villages – Atlit – En Hod – Around En Hod –   253
Dor – Zichron Ya'acov – Caesarea – Around Caesarea – Beit She – Akko –
Around Akko – Nahariya – Around Nahariya

GALILEE & THE GOLAN Nazareth – Around Nazareth & Tiberias – Tiberias &   290
The Sea Of Galilee – Rosh Pinna – Benot Ya'acov – Jordan Bridge – Hazor –
Hula Valley & Nature Reserve – Qiryat Shimona – Tel Hai – Kibbutz Kfar Giladi –
Metulla – Hurshat Tal National Park – Tel Dan – Kibbutz Dan – Banyus –
Nimrod Castle – Mount Hermon Ski Centre – Majdal Shams & Masada –
Quneitra Viewpoint – Katzrin – Abbura Waterfall – Ya'ar Yehudiyya Nature Reserve –
Gamla – Safed – Around Safed

THE DEAD SEA Qumran – Ein Feshka – Ein Gedi – Masada – En Boqeq – Hamme Zohar –   344
Newe Zohar – Sodom

THE NEGEV Arad – Around Arad – Beersheba – Around Beersheba – Dimona –   357
Around Dimona – Kibbutz Sde Boker – En Avdat – Avdat – Mitzpe Ramon – Eilat –
Around Eilat

THE OCCUPIED TERRITORIES West Bank – From Jerusalem to Jericho – Wadi Qelt &   386
St George's Monastery – Jericho – Around Jericho – Bethlehem – Around Bethlehem –
Between Bethlehem & Hebron – Hebron – Around Hebron – Between Jerusalem &
Ramallah – Ramallah – Between Ramallah & Nablus – Nablus – Around Nablus –
Gaza Strip – Gaza – Around Gaza

INDEX Map Index   431

Introduction

One of the golden rules for successful travelling is to avoid discussing religion and politics. In Israel, however, they collide inseparably, both with each other and with virtually everything else. This is the Holy Land, and this is Palestine. Trying not to preach, condemn or promote, the broad aim of this guide is to encourage you to go and see Israel for yourself, by providing an honest and accurate account of what you will find there.

Variety and interest are two of the main ingredients required of a country to justify a visit, and Israel has to be one of the most diverse and fascinating places in the world. A land of incredible contrasts, it offers a wealth of changing landscapes, different climates, culture, history and, of course, religion. What makes Israel even more remarkable is its tiny size, perhaps

best appreciated by comparing it to the American state of New Jersey or to Belgium, which are both slightly larger, or to Tasmania, which is over twice as large. Despite being so small, Israel contains almost every type of geographical terrain: mountains, sub-tropical valleys, fertile farmland, and deserts, with a richly varied flora and fauna that makes it a paradise for nature lovers.

Israel is the Jewish Promised Land, Mohammed departed from here on his Night Journey to Heaven, and it is the land of Jesus. Jewish, Muslim and Christian pilgrims are drawn by the conviction that 'this is where it happened'. These conflicting beliefs, combined with Israel's strategic location, have made this one of the most hotly disputed areas in the world. Major wars have raged here

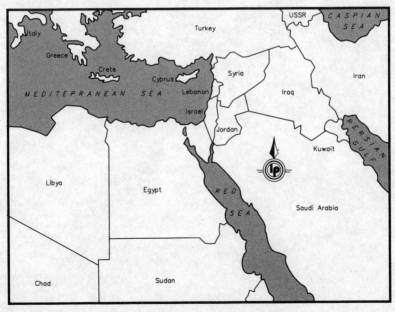

throughout the centuries: the Israelites and Canaanites, the Jews and Romans, the Muslims and Crusaders, the Turks and British, and now the Israelis and the Palestinians. In its promotion campaigns, Israel's Ministry of Tourism does an excellent job of emphasising the sandy beaches, ancient cities and biblical sites, with no mention of the real-life situation. As a result, many people enjoy themselves here without really considering local politics. Most of you, however, will realise that this is not simply a beautiful country full of friendly English-speaking people everywhere you go. Whilst the Palestine problem is tragically real and should not be minimised or ignored, it should also not deter you from making a visit here, and I have tried to illustrate the various attitudes of the locals so as to enable you to avoid any major problems.

With so much to see and do, Israel means different things to different people. Read on to discover what you can make of it all.

Facts about the Country

HISTORY

The human history of the land known today as Israel, or Palestine, goes back over 500,000 years. Due to its geographical position between Africa and Asia and on the edge of Europe, different nations have continuously moved back and forth across it, making that history somewhat complicated. Going back so far in time, getting the exact year is a matter of dispute, let alone agreeing on who descended from whom in sufficient numbers to justify today's hereditary claims. Hopefully this outline will give you a basic picture of the land's history and encourage you to find out more for yourself. One further source of information readily available is the Bible and I have included some of the main references.

The Stone Age (600,000-4000 BC)

This period is dated by part of a human skeleton found in Palestine. Then, the population lived by the numerous rivers and lakes, and while Europe suffered the Ice Age, wet and dry ages occurred here. Nomads began to settle and develop new ways of life with animal domestication and the cultivation of crops, from which evolved new skills and social organisations.

Notable remains of the Stone Age can be seen in En Avdat (Negev), Tel es-Sultan (Jericho) and Wadi Khareitun (near Bethlehem).

The Copper & Bronze Ages (4000-1200 BC)

Villages had begun to replace temporary camps, and these earliest settlements were usually near springs, due to the drier climate caused by the recession of the ice caps. The urban environment played a large part in the development of copper and bronze-making skills, but compared to other areas nearby, evolution was slow. In Egypt and Mesopotamia empires had

grown while what was to become known as Canaan was still a disjointed land.

In about 1800 BC when Abraham led a group of nomads, the Israelites, from Mesopotamia into the mountains of Canaan, the Egyptians had already held the coastal plain for several centuries. The Israelites stayed until famine forced them to move to Egypt. They remained there until around 1250 BC when Moses led the exodus. The Bible's Old Testament Books of Genesis, Exodus, Leviticus and Deuteronomy include the story of Abraham, the move to Egypt, and the exodus.

Moses failed to make it to the Promised Land but, led by Joshua, the rest of the Israelites did. It is almost certain that they did not conquer the whole land, but only took most of the mountains from the Canaanites, while the Philistines from Crete took the coastal plain. The Old Testament Book of Joshua relates to this, and the Books of Judges and Ruth deal with the social state of the land and foreign invasion attempts.

Notable remains of the Bronze Age can be seen in Arad, Jerusalem (City of David) and Megiddo. The Palestinian Arabs believe that their ancestry derives from an assimilation of the Canaanite tribes which came from the Arab Peninsula around 3500 BC, with the Philistines.

The Iron Age (1200-586 BC)

The Philistines and the Canaanites developed the use of iron and eventually controlled more of the land. This forced the Israelites to change from their loose tribal system to a centralised monarchy. Their first king was Saul (circa 1023-1004 BC), whose capital was Gev'a.

His adopted son and successor, David (circa 1004-965 BC), conquered Jerusalem, making it his capital and installing there the Ark of the Covenant, a chest believed

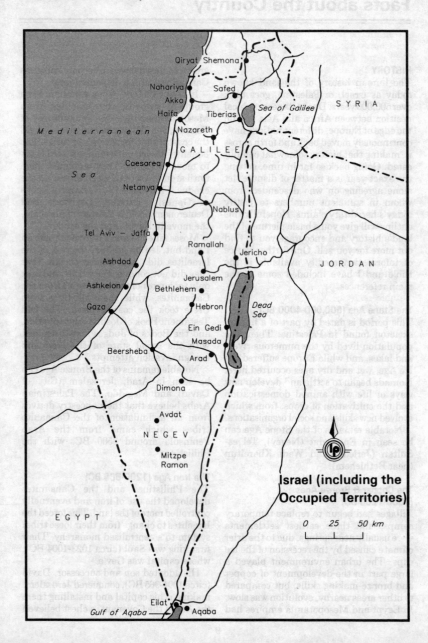

Israel (including the Occupied Territories)

0   25   50 km

to contain the stone tablets on which the Ten Commandments were written. The Old Testament Book of Samuel deals with Saul and David.

King Solomon (circa 965-928 BC) built on his father's success and is noted for his literary skills. He is believed to have written the Books of Proverbs, Ecclesiastes and the Song of Songs. Solomon's reign is often referred to as Israel's Golden Era. In about 950 BC the First Temple was built in Jerusalem.

After Solomon's death, the kingdom split in two, becoming Israel and Judah. Around 721 BC, Assyria (today Kurdistan in northern Iraq) invaded and conquered Israel and its people were scattered, becoming the Ten Lost Tribes. Judah was conquered by Babylonia about 586 BC and Jerusalem, with the First Temple, was destroyed. The Old Testament Book of Ezekiel deals with these events. Notable remains of the Iron Age can be seen in Beersheba, Jerusalem (City of David, Jewish Quarter, Kidron Valley) and Megiddo.

The Persian Period (538-322 BC)

The people of Judah were exiled to Babylonia but were permitted to return to their homeland in 538 BC by Cyrus, King of Persia, who had conquered Babylonia the year before. In a spiritual revival, Jerusalem and the Temple were rebuilt. The Old Testament Book of Zachariah deals with visions of Jerusalem's reconstruction, while the Books of Esther, David and Ezra deal with the Jews' exile and their deliverance, and Ezra and Nehemiah deal with the reconstruction of Jerusalem and the Temple.

The Hellenistic & Hasmonean Periods (332-63 BC)

The end of the Persian Empire came in 331 BC with Alexander the Great's legendary successes. When he died about eight years later, his short-lived empire was carved up by his generals. Ptolemy and Seleucus fought each other over

Palestine and eventually the Seleucids took control, uniting it with the north in 200 BC.

Since the Exile, the High Priest had assumed many of the duties previously undertaken by the king. The Seleucids needed to control this office to ensure their dominance, but the extent of their influence on religion sparked off a revolt led by the three Maccabaean brothers in 167 BC. The fight, initially for religious freedom, became a bid for political independence.

The Maccabees started the Hasmonean dynasty which extended Jewish dominance to the whole of Palestine, the Golan, and the east bank of Jordan – another Golden Era, perhaps comparable to David's and Solomon's empire. Notable remains of the Hellenistic Period can be seen in Jerusalem (Citadel, City of David, St Anne's) and Nablus.

The Roman Period (63 BC-324 AD)

Palestine became a Roman province because internal strife had reduced its effectiveness as a buffer against the Romans' enemies, but Herod the Great was given autonomy due to his commitment to the Roman Empire and his proven authority. The Romans took control around 6 AD, as after Herod's death his sons proved to be less able rulers.

Jesus of Nazareth's ministry (circa 27-30 AD) was the notable factor in an intense religious and political arena which led to the First Revolt about 66 AD. After a prolonged siege of Jerusalem in 70 AD, the Roman General Titus breached the city wall, and destroyed the Temple. The Temple's destruction made sacrificial worship impossible, and a new theory was developed: that the scattered Jewish community could only be held together by adherence to a common law. Rabbi Yohanan Ben Zakkai re-established the supreme legislative judicial body, the Sanhedrin, at Yavne; and elsewhere, for example Tiberias, centres of learning sprang up.

Over the next several centuries, the Talmud was recorded – the vast body of the Oral Law relating to all aspects of Jewish life.

Following the Temple's destruction, many Jews were sold into slavery or exiled abroad. Their descendants became the Diaspora, the Jewish communities dispersed worldwide.

Jerusalem remained central, but the emperor Hadrian decided to destroy it completely as it was a focus of renewed nationalist aspirations. This provoked the Second Revolt (132-135 AD), led by Bar Kochba. He ruled briefly but the Romans eventually defeated him, and Aelia Capitolina was built on the now levelled ruins of Jerusalem. Jews were barred from the new city and moved north to Galilee and the Golan.

Notable remains of the Roman Period can be seen in Bet Shearim, Caesarea, Gamla, Hebron, Herodian (near Bethlehem), Jerusalem (Citadel, Damascus Gate, Ecce Homo Arch, St Anne's, Temple Mount), Katzrin, Mamshit (Negev), Masada, Qumran and Solomon's Pools (between Bethlehem and Hebron).

The Byzantine Period (324-640 AD)

This period came about from the transfer of the Roman Empire's capital from Rome to Byzantium, which was renamed Constantinople in 330 AD. More importantly, in 331 AD Emperor Constantine, a recent convert, legalised Christianity and encouraged its development. Due to his policies and the subsequent consecration of sites associated with Christ's life by the churches, interest in the Holy Places was massive. Pilgrims were attracted to the Holy Land and their arrival stimulated a wide range of developments, such as the building of numerous churches and monasteries, and urban expansion. Jerusalem, for example, grew to the size it had been under Herod the Great.

Theological controversy dominated this period, but there were two serious violent episodes: The Samaritan revolt in 529 AD

and the Persian invasion in 614 AD, which resulted in the sacking of Jerusalem.

Notable remains of the Byzantine Period can be seen in Avdat, Bethlehem, Capernaum and Hammat Gader, Latrun, Mar Saba (near Bethlehem), Mamshit, Mount Gerizim and Jerusalem (Bethany, Domimas Flevit, Holy Sepulchre, St Anne's, Haram esh-Sharif).

The Early Arab Period (640-1099 AD)

The new faith of Islam, preached by Mohammed (570-632 AD), inspired the Arab invasion which ended with the surrender of Jerusalem in 638 AD. The city became a centre of pilgrimage due to its holy status for Christians under the Umayyad, Abbasid and Fatamid dynasties. In 1009 churches were destroyed in a wave of brutal persecution under Caliph Hakim. In 1071 Jerusalem was captured by the Seljuk Turks who refused to co-operate with the continuing stream of Christian pilgrims. The dispute resulted in Pope Urban II's call in 1095 for a crusade to liberate the Holy Places.

Notable remains of the Arab Period can be seen in Jericho and Jerusalem (Dome of the Rock, and excavations around the Haram esh-Sharif).

The Crusader Period (1099-1291)

Although the more flexible Fatamids managed to retake Jerusalem early in 1099, the Crusaders were already on their way and determined to rid the Holy Land of Islam. They occupied Jerusalem on 15 June 1099 and massacred all the Muslim inhabitants. Episodes of such Christian fanaticism are thought by many to have been a major cause of the inflexibility of Islam. Jewish inhabitants were also massacred on a large scale by the Crusaders.

The reign of the first Crusader king, Baldwin I (1100-1118) saw the introduction of the feudal system. This gave Palestine its most effective administration so far, taking advantage of the alms flowing in from Europe.

In 1187 Saladin (Salah ed-Din) defeated the Crusaders at the Horns of Hattin. Richard I (the Lionheart) of England led the unsuccessful Third Crusade in 1188. The Fourth to Eighth Crusades followed but recovered only some of the former territories. The end of the Crusades came with the fall of Akko in 1291 to the Bahri Mamelukes. They had already toppled Saladin's Ayyubid dynasty.

Notable remains of the Crusader Period can be seen in Abu Gosh, Akko, Belvoir, Caesarea, Hebron, Jerusalem (Bethany, Cathedral of St James, Holy Sepulchre, St Anne's, Virgin's Tomb), Latrun and Nimrod.

The Mameluke Period (1250-1517)

Palestine became a backwater due to the Mamelukes being pre-occupied with a power struggle in Egypt and their defence of Syria against Mongol attacks. Jerusalem attracted pilgrims and scholars, and also renewed Jewish settlement. In 1492 Jews were expelled from Spain and some refugees arrived in Palestine.

Notable remains of the Mameluke Period can be seen in Jerusalem (Citadel, Haram esh-Sharif and the Muslim Quarter).

The Ottoman Period (1517-1918)

Sultan Salim I led the Ottoman Turks to victory against the Mamelukes in 1517. They had taken Constantinople in 1453 and Egypt joined Palestine to extend their empire into Africa. Their second sultan, Suleiman the Magnificent, is credited with the rebuilding of Jerusalem's city walls.

These two effective administrators were followed by apparently less worthy leaders who were mostly occupied by the task of containing power struggles with Egyptian pashas. Again Palestine was relegated in terms of priority, and was under the control of pashas who are best remembered for their corrupt and violent brand of officialdom.

The country languished and local chieftains and Bedouin took advantage of the lack of law and order, carving out independent domains. Jews and Christians, particularly in Galilee, were subjected to harsh treatment. Despite this, the end of the 17th century saw an increase in Jewish immigration, due to persecution in the Diaspora. This continued slowly through the 18th century, with centres of Hasidism being set up in Safed and Tiberias by Jews from Poland and Lithuania.

The Ottoman Empire was showing signs of weakness, and the Jews, Europe and the United States all took note and jockeyed for position in the years to come – and they are still at it. In 1838 the first regular British consulate was opened in Jerusalem and became a defender of Jewish and Druze elements in Syria and Palestine. Evangelistic activities, ostensibly involving the custody of the holy shrines, often looked suspiciously like the manoeuvring of international politics. The Suez Canal, opened in 1869, speeded the rebirth of the area as a strategic crossroads. While the leading nations of the world were eyeing Palestine, so were some of the dispersed Jews, and Jewish nationalism was being revived.

Contact between the Jews in Palestine and the Diaspora had continued over the centuries, with the hope that some day all Jews would be able to meet in the Holy Land – a major part of their religious observance.

In London in 1839 a wealthy Jew, Sir Moses Montefiore, had proposed the establishment of a Jewish state, and he won some support from influential Christians in Europe. This episode is often said to have set the stage for the founding of political Zionism and the modern State of Israel.

Zionism & Arab Nationalism

The name Zionism is derived from the word Zion, the traditional synonym for Jerusalem and Israel.

In Palestine, the revival of Jewish nationalism began in 1878 with the founding of Petah Tiqwa, the first Jewish colony, by a group of native Jews from Jerusalem. The arrival of refugees in 1882 from the Russian pogroms (anti-Jewish riots and killings) and others from Rumania and Yemen expanded the movement. Many were members of the Love of Zion movement. They tended to join existing agricultural villages, or established new ones such as Rishon le Zion, Zichron Ya'acov and Rosh Pina. The new arrivals were later termed the First *Aliyah* (ascent to the Land).

In 1894, Austrian journalist Theodor Herzl published *The Jewish State*, a book outlining his idea that the only solution to Jewish persecution would be a Jewish state in Palestine. In 1897 the World Zionist Organisation (WZO) was founded at the First Zionist Conference, convened by Herzl in Basle, Switzerland.

In 1901 the Jewish National Fund (JNF) was founded to purchase land in Palestine for the Zionists. In its formative years, much of the JNF's work was land reclamation and afforestation. Once a land covered in forest, Palestine had been gradually stripped of most of its trees by successive rulers over hundreds of years. When the Zionists arrived in Palestine, much of the land was, in their opinion, suffering from neglect and exploitation. This is strongly disputed by critics who say that the Zionists exaggerated the conditions in Palestine to win support for their cause.

In 1903 came Britain's rejected offer to the WZO to found the Jewish state in Uganda. Also rejected were sites in Argentina, Cyprus and the Congo. With the swift formation of the WZO and the JNF came a well-organised programme to arrange the return of the Jews to Palestine. In 1904 came the Second Aliyah, mainly consisting of Jews escaping pogroms in Russia and Poland. Degania, the first kibbutz, was founded on the shore of the Sea of Galilee in 1909. That same year Tel Aviv, the first modern Jewish city, was established north of Jaffa.

During WW I, Britain and the Allies sought support from the Arabs and Jews to topple the Ottoman Empire. The future of Palestine was a particularly sensitive subject because of its spiritual and strategic significance. In 1916 a secret British-French agreement provided for the recognition of an independent Arab state or a confederation of Arab states, but with an international administration for Palestine to be decided after discussions with the other Allies and the Sherif of Mecca. The latter acted as the Arabs' representative, even though most were not under his political authority. This was due to his spiritual status as keeper of Islam's most holy cities. He led the Arab revolt against the Turks and the British Government assured him of their support in his plans for Arab independence.

This assurance came principally through the McMahon Letters (Sir Henry McMahon being the British High Commissioner in Egypt). The British later claimed that Palestine was excluded from such plans by virtue of subsequent discussions, but the Sherif strongly disagreed. This difference of views over the exact meaning of British Government communications was the first of many which are a major factor in the Palestine Problem.

While the British and French Governments said one thing to the Arabs and did another, the WZO made it clear that they were aiming for the creation of a Jewish state in Palestine. They pressed the British Government for support and a result was the Balfour Declaration in 1917. A statement of policy by the Foreign Secretary in a letter to Lord Rothschild, it was directed at the WZO stating that the British Government

...viewed with favour the establishment of a national home for the Jewish people, and will use their best endeavours to facilitate the achievement of this object, it being clearly understood that nothing shall be done which may prejudice the civil and religious rights of existing non-Jewish communities in Palestine or the rights and political status enjoyed by Jews in any other country.

So ambiguous is the Balfour Declaration that both Jews and Arabs have used it to back their claims. Zionists say that it shows British support for the Jewish state. Arabs say that the civil and religious rights of existing non-Jewish communities have definitely been prejudiced by the establishment of Israel, and that anyway, the establishment of a national home for the Jewish people never implied the sovereign state that Zionists had always envisaged.

Despite the propaganda value that both Zionists and Arabs place on British Government statements such as the McMahon Letters and the Balfour Declaration, many feel that as Britain had no sovereign rights over Palestine, such statements should never have been made in the first place.

The British Mandate

British policy over Palestine was far from straightforward – 'muddled' seems an appropriate adjective. Basically, the British Government needed both Arab and Jewish support in WW I. It had its eye on the Arab oilfields but did not appear to know how far its support of the Arabs should go. This led to attempts to appease both parties, and considerable confusion.

Shortly after the Balfour Declaration came the Allied victory in WW I. The British now ruled Palestine under the Mandate system. The League of Nations, a forerunner of the United Nations, devised the system to place certain territories under the 'tutelage ... of advanced nations' until such time as those same 'advanced nations' decided that they were ready for political self-determination.

In 1919, a Jewish delegation to the Peace Conference in Paris was led by Dr Chaim Weizmann. Weizmann met with Emir Feisal and they reached an agreement, of sorts, which

recognised the aspirations of both Arabs and Jews in Palestine. Zionists often refer to it as an important stage of the negotiations, but according to Arabs the agreement had always been conditional on Arab independence and so never stood a chance unless that was granted.

While the Allies were dividing up the spoils of their victory, the Third Aliyah began. Between 1919 and 1928 the Jewish population of Palestine almost tripled. The first wave (till 1923) was spearheaded by young members of the *Hehalutz* (Pioneer) movement from Russia and Poland who joined the men of the Second Aliyah to form the Histradrut, the General Federation of Jewish Labour, and the Haganah, the illegal Jewish resistance army. The Fourth Aliyah (1924-1928) brought Jews from a mainly different social background: middle-class shopkeepers and artisans, mostly from Poland where economic restrictions were being applied.

In 1921 Feisal's brother, the Emir Abdullah, invaded an area east of the Jordan River, covered by the British Mandate, and was recognised as its ruler by the League of Nations. It was renamed Transjordan, later to become the Hashemite Kingdom of Jordan after independence in 1946.

While trying to appease the WZO, representing the Jews, the British authorities in Palestine dealt with Haj Amin, Mufti of Jerusalem and head of the Supreme Muslim Council, representing the Arabs. He enjoys a reputation probably second only to Adolf Hitler for his personal and political integrity and performance. He was jailed for instigating attacks on Jews praying at the Western Wall in Jerusalem, but was later released. He then started a programme of terror and intimidation against his Arab political opponents as well as continuing his campaign of hatred and violence against the Jews. His rise to power in Palestine is said to have been a turning point in the course of Jewish-Arab relations. He is also credited with styling the Arab's uncompromising hostility to the Jewish state which many feel led to the poor public relations image from which the Arabs now suffer.

Arab acts of violence against the Jews began in earnest in 1920 and the British authorities were regularly accused by the Jews of doing little to stop them. The Jews retaliated: the Haganah fortified Jewish communities and counter-attacked. The increase in this violence seemed to be a major reason behind the British Government's restrictions on Jewish immigration. There were also fears of an unappeased Arab world backing Germany in the now imminent WW II.

In 1929 the Jewish community of Hebron was massacred by Arab extremists, the height of the violence so far. The Irgun Zvai Leumi, a Jewish underground organisation, was founded by extreme right-wing Zionists, led by Ze'ev Jabotinsky and his assistant Menachem Begin.

Due to Nazi persecution of European Jews, the Fifth Aliyah in 1933 was of the highest importance to the events in Palestine. The largest number of Jews so far made their way to Palestine, refugees from the Holocaust. It triggered off more Arab attacks against the Jewish community. The British authorities eventually arrested the extremist Arab leaders but the Mufti escaped, joining Hitler in Berlin.

Amazingly perhaps, in the face of constant harassment from the British, Jews decided to join British forces and fight against Germany in WW II as they had in WW I. They felt that the need to halt the Holocaust overruled the struggle for a Jewish state, which was therefore partially abandoned.

Not totally, though. In 1942, a conference of American Zionists adopted the Biltmore Program, thus paving the way for greater involvement of the USA in the Palestine Problem. This demanded unlimited Jewish immigration into Palestine and the establishment of a Jewish

state. The Zionists correctly forecast that after WW II Britain's role in world affairs would be greatly reduced and that the USA would become the west's major power.

As the extent of the Holocaust was realised, the Jews in Palestine embarked on a national rescue effort, although they felt hampered by the Allies' lack of enthusiasm for their cause, Britain in particular. The British did not want Jews flooding into Palestine and exacerbating the already tense racial situation. Their policy was to stop immigration, thus creating the situation of refugees from the Nazi concentration camps being turned away from Palestine by the British who had helped liberate them. This resulted in Aliyah Bet, the Jews' illegal immigration programme.

Critics claim that there were other areas of the world that the refugees could and should have gone to which did not have the powder-keg environment of Palestine. The United States is mentioned as a country which had plenty of room for refugees, yet only allowed limited numbers to immigrate, while condemning the British for not letting enough into Palestine.

In addition to the programme of Aliyah Bet, the Palestinian Jews determined to rid the country of British rule using a programme of terrorism. The Haganah and the independent Irgun and Lohamei Herut Israel all engaged in violent acts, including bomb attacks and kidnappings. In one infamous incident the Irgun, led by Menachem Begin, hanged two British Army sergeants in retaliation for Jews being executed by the authorities for terrorist activities. Many people consider today's ferocious criticism of Arab terrorism by Israelis to be somewhat hypocritical after they used similar tactics against the British. Zionists deny that their violence was terrorism, claiming that they were fighting for their ultimate survival.

Partition & The End of the British Mandate
In 1947 the UN voted to partition Palestine into an Arab state and a Jewish state with an internationalised Jerusalem. Partition was first mooted in 1937 when a British Government White Paper had proposed such a plan. It had been rejected by both the WZO and the Arabs. The Macdonald White Paper announced the British Government's decision to rescind the partition plan, including the comment that the Balfour Declaration 'could not have intended that Palestine be converted into a Jewish state against the will of the Arab population of the country'. The White Paper also announced that Palestine would become independent in 1949 as a unified state in which both Jews and Arabs would share in government.

After this, the Zionists really started to build political support in the USA and launched their terrorist programme against the British. Eventually the situation, with its complexities seemingly impossible to solve, caused Britain to prepare for the termination of its Mandate and to hand Palestine and its problems over to the United Nations. With WW II over, Palestine was the only area where British forces were still engaged in armed combat. On 18 February 1947 the British Government made the following announcement:

His Majesty's Government have . . . been faced with an irreconcilable conflict of principles. There are in Palestine about 200,000 Arabs and 600,000 Jews. For the Jews, the essential point of principle is the creation of a sovereign Jewish State. For the Arabs, the essential point of principle is to resist to the last the establishment of Jewish sovereignty in any part of Palestine . . . It is in these circumstances that we have decided that we are unable to accept the scheme put forward either by the Arabs or by the Jews, or to impose ourselves a solution of our own. We have, therefore, reached the conclusion that the only course now open to us is to submit the problem to the judgement of the United Nations.

The British had called for a special session of the UN General Assembly to deal with Palestine's future. The Arab delegation's first step was to unsuccessfully request the termination of the Mandate and the declaration of Palestine's independence.

The UN Special Committee on Palestine (UNSCOP) visited the area. It also visited refugee camps in Germany and Austria which critics claim was unnecessary, as the plight of European Jewry was a subject of world concern and not a facet of the Palestine issue. There have been accusations of Zionist propaganda during these visits, using concentration camp

Arab State (Includes Jaffa)

Jewish State

International Zone (Jerusalem)

Partition Plan 1947

LEBANON

Safed

Haifa

Tel Aviv
Jaffa
(part of Arab State)

Gaza

Jerusalem

Beersheba

EGYPT

Eilat Aqaba

survivors primed to demand refuge in Palestine.

UNSCOP fell back on the earlier British plan for partition and created more controversy by the way it divided the area between the Jews and Arabs. Understandably, debate on the UNSCOP report was intense and lengthy.

Eventually, the partition of Palestine was approved on 29 November 1947. The Partition Resolution included several elaborate safeguards for the rights of minorities, and the 'existing rights' of the area's various religions were safeguarded, and free access to the Holy Places was guaranteed. Not surprisingly, the Arab countries which had opposed the proposal while pressing the Palestinian Arabs' case declared that they would not be bound by it. The Zionists accepted it.

Violence in Palestine had risen while the UN debated the partition programme. As a result, Britain decided to terminate the Mandate and withdraw on 15 August 1948, several months in advance of the date anticipated in the UN proposal. No replacement forces were to be made available to enforce order due to a decision that the UN's planned special armed militia could not be put in place in the deteriorating security situation.

The Zionist armed forces were now being organised to be on the offensive, not only to establish control in the areas allotted to the Jewish State but to extend it into the areas designated for an Arab state. This was due to expectations, based on expert intelligence work, as well as loud rhetoric, that the Arab countries were planning to wipe out all attempts to establish the Jewish State.

In the months leading up to the British withdrawal, the Zionist and Arab forces clashed constantly. There are accounts of both sides benefiting from British arms, ammunition and even manpower, most of them undoubtedly true.

During these months many Arabs left Palestine and controversy surrounds the reasons for their abrupt departure.

Zionists claim that they left due to instructions from Arab leaders that they should temporarily vacate the area to allow Arab forces to 'rid Palestine of the Jews' and establish an independent Arab Palestine. The Arabs argue that the refugees fled Jewish military atrocities.

The War Of Independence (1948)

On 15 May 1948 the last British forces departed, ending the Mandate. On the previous day, David Ben-Gurion, the Jewish State's first Prime Minister, had proclaimed Israel an independent state. Immediately, violence from both sides mounted. Troops from Egypt, Jordan, Lebanon, Syria, Iraq and Saudi Arabia had already been infiltrating the area and the first Arab-Israeli war had started. On 26 May 1948 the Israel Defence Forces (IDF) was established, its first soldiers drawn from the various para-military units created during the Mandate.

By the end of May 1948 a ceasefire called by the UN came into effect. Israeli forces controlled the major part of Palestine, including some of what had been designated for an Arab state and also West Jerusalem. The Gaza Strip was occupied by Egypt and the rest, including East Jerusalem and Jerusalem's Old City, was occupied by Jordan, not then a UN member.

Israel was now recognised by the UN as an independent state, but not by the Arab countries and several others. Even more countries disputed Israel's decision to name Jerusalem as its capital, refusing to install embassies there and choosing Tel Aviv instead.

The UN continued in its quest to secure the 'inalienable rights' of the Palestinian people. However, Israel's alleged fait accompli of expansion beyond its pre-assigned borders, together with the Egyptian and Jordanian occupation, and the state of war between Israel and the Arab countries and the Palestinian Arabs, all contributed to its failure.

The UN's first step towards a solution

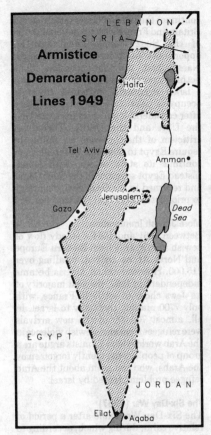

Armistice
Demarcation
Lines 1949

LEBANON
SYRIA
Haifa
Tel Aviv
Jerusalem
Gaza
Dead Sea
Amman
EGYPT
JORDAN
Eilat
Aqaba

was devastated in September 1948 by the assassination of Count Bernadotte of Sweden, the UN Mediator. Although Israel has denied Jewish involvement and resisted requests for a government investigation, men in Israeli military uniforms were witnessed committing the murder and are commonly believed to have been members of the extreme-Zionist Stern gang.

In May 1949 Israel was admitted to the UN, after a first application failed due to its non-compliance with UN resolutions. Israel has since been subjected to continued criticism for its lack of observation of UN resolutions and principles, most of which it has vigorously argued against.

Since 1950 the issue of the Palestinian Arabs' rights has been treated as a 'refugee problem' mainly by the UN Relief & Works Agency in Palestine (UNRWA). In 1967 over half the Palestinian Arabs belonging to areas in Israel or under Israeli occupation were refugees in the West Bank, Gaza Strip or neighbouring Arab countries.

Israel's Initial Development

The Zionists now set about attracting increased Jewish immigration to Israel and to plan the rapid development of their new national home. The 1950 Law of Return granted citizenship to every Jewish person requesting it. The Nationality Law (1952) allowed non-Jews to claim citizenship. By the end of 1951 the Jewish population had grown by over 750,000, with over half of them refugees from Muslim Arab countries, fleeing threatened or actual persecution.

Controversy surrounds the treatment of many of these new arrivals from the Arab countries. Many complained about discrimination by European Jews; that they were given the worst jobs or were forcibly sent to the less appealing areas of the country.

Pioneering the generally barren and inhospitable areas became a vital priority for the new country and this saw the development of kibbutzim (collective farms) and moshavim (co-operative farms). In a very short time the Jews managed to develop the infrastructure of a nation.

The massive aliyah of the initial three years after Israel's independence slowed considerably after 1952. By that time most of the Jews who had wanted to immigrate, and were able to, had done so. Then followed a new series of large numbers of immigrants, due to political events elsewhere. In 1955, aliyah from

Morocco and Tunisia was encouraged as a result of the rise in local Arab nationalism. The influx of Russian Jews into Poland caused political pressure and an increase in aliyah from there. The Hungarian uprising of 1956 caused many Jews to flee across the border into Austria, and 8680 of them made their way to Israel. After the Sinai War that year, at least 14,000 Egyptian Jews crossed the desert.

The Sinai (Suez) War (1956)

The chain of events which led to the next major war in the area varies considerably according to whose version you listen to. The Israelis claim that their actions were an outcome of the Arab policy to destroy the Jewish State, citing terrorist raids launched from the Egyptian-occupied Gaza Strip, the closure of the Suez Canal and the blockade of the Tiran Straits by Egypt which stopped Israeli shipping in those areas. Israeli forces struck back by occupying the Sinai Peninsula and the Gaza Strip.

What the Israelis consistently fail to include in their accounts of the dispute is their involvement with Britain and France, which caused the USA to lead world opinion in strong condemnation of their tactics in what became known as the 'Suez Crisis'. Britain and France, angered by the Egyptian nationalisation of the Suez Canal, which they part-owned, planned an airborne invasion of Egypt, whilst the Israelis moved overland into the Sinai and Gaza. After initial success, the refusal of the USA to bail out Britain, suffering from monetary problems due to the expense of the military operation, caused the withdrawal of British and French troops.

Some critics claim that Israel has always created pretexts for invading Arab territory and that the Suez War was yet another example. According to them, Israel planned to 'set up' Egypt so that it would enter and then lose a war. They point to an unprovoked Israeli raid on the Egyptian forces at Gaza. The argument

continues that when Nasser later angered Britain and France with his nationalisation of the Suez Canal, Israel saw an opportunity to go into battle; although Nasser had, on that occasion, done nothing against the Israelis.

Israel eventually withdrew from its occupying positions in Egyptian territory after considerable pressure from the UN, the USA and the USSR. There was criticism of these powers for failing to require Egypt to renounce its intention to continue its state of war with Israel. Instead Egypt soon closed the Suez Canal and returned to the Gaza Strip, contrary to prior assurances that it would not.

More Jewish Immigration

Between 1961 and 1964 a steady flow of Jewish immigrants from Eastern Europe and North Africa arrived, totalling over 215,000. However, when Algeria became independent in 1962, the vast majority of its Jews chose to settle in France, with only 7700 making their way to Israel. In all, almost 700,000 of the new arrivals were refugees from anti-Jewish violence in the Arab world whom Zionists argue are a group of people conveniently forgotten by the Arabs, who complain about the Arab refugee problem created by Israel.

The Six-Day War (1967)

The Six-Day War came after a period of relative calm, during which, according to Israel, the Arab countries rebuilt their military power, still with the aim of destroying the Jewish State.

There had been an increase in Arab terrorist attacks on Israel, from Syria and Egypt, and in anti-Israeli speeches by Arab leaders in the previous two years. By June 1967, Egypt again blockaded the Tiran Straits and ordered the UN peace-keeping forces out of the Sinai. With the Egyptian Army apparently moving towards Israel, the Israeli air force attacked and crippled its Egyptian counterpart still on the ground. Jordan then attacked Israel from the east, and

Syria from the north. After the six days, 5-10 June, Israel had defeated the Arabs, and occupied the Golan Heights, the West Bank region, including East Jerusalem and Jerusalem's Old City, the Gaza Strip and the Sinai Desert.

The Israeli version of the events leading up to the Six-Day War is disputed. While Israel claims that it was forced to retaliate against the mass attack of Arab forces from three countries, it is argued that Israel attempted to provoke the Arabs into starting the war, failed, and made the first strike itself. Critics claim that, despite Nasser giving the impression of wanting to destroy Israel, his speeches were merely his way of trying to improve his prestige in the Arab world, and that Israeli provocation encouraged his behaviour.

In April 1967, Nasser had been accused by his allies of hiding behind the UN peace-keeping forces instead of assisting Syria when Israel had shot down six Syrian fighter planes in Syrian air-space. This provoked Nasser into ordering the UN out and again closing the Tiran Straits to Israeli shipping. It is argued that the Israelis deliberately created this situation, and that the fuss they made about the closure of the Straits was a calculated exaggeration, as very little Israeli shipping used the area. Egypt had closed the area to Israeli shipping not to cause a major inconvenience, that was impossible, but as a gesture to appease Syria.

The argument concludes that these Israeli tactics failed to provoke Nasser into invading, and that Egyptian troops in the Sinai were actually in defensive positions, while Israeli troops were in an offensive order of battle. The Israeli forces were apparently more powerful by a big margin, due mainly to Nasser's army being involved in a five-year-old war in Yemen. It is hardly likely that he would have invaded Israel without waiting to have all his troops available, it is argued. Finally, it was the Israelis who attacked first, according to them in defence, but

according to critics, as part of an overall plan to increase the size of the Jewish State.

The most important outcome of the war was the re-unification of Jerusalem. After the 1949 Armistice, Jordan had maintained control there and refused access to the Holy Sites to all Israelis – Jews, Muslims and Christians (at Christmas and Easter, Christians were allowed access). Now Bethlehem, Hebron and Jericho, once virtually inaccessible from Israel, were just a short drive away. This really opened up the country's tourism industry, with

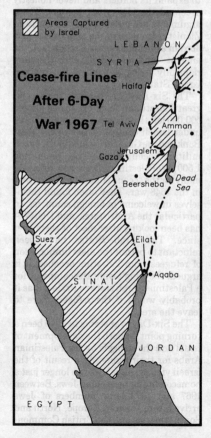

Areas Captured by Israel

LEBANON

SYRIA

Cease-fire Lines

Haifa

After 6-Day

War 1967 Tel Aviv

Amman

Gaza Jerusalem

Beersheba Dead Sea

Suez Eilat

SINAI Aqaba

JORDAN

EGYPT

Israel becoming a synonym for the Holy Land. The capture of the Golan Heights allowed the development of Tiberias and the Sea of Galilee as a major tourist attraction.

Israel has often claimed that after the Six-Day War it wanted to negotiate a peaceful settlement involving the return of the Occupied Territories. The Arab countries' stand, that there would be no peace, no negotiations and no recognition of Israel, is given as the reason for the failure of such a policy. Israel's critics say that the Jewish State has always wanted to expand its borders and never honestly accepted the UN's 1947 borders. These arguments are based largely on constant Zionist references to the area that is now Jordan as being a part of Eretz Israel, the ancient land of Israel, and therefore rightfully being a part of the modern Israeli State.

The Six-Day War brought the second great Palestinian Arab exodus as almost 500,000 left their homes, leaving 1,200,000 under Israeli control. Those in the West Bank and the Gaza Strip came under Israeli military occupation. The remaining 1,500,000 Palestinians were now refugees, many for the second time after fleeing first in the 1948 war. They often found themselves unwelcome in foreign countries, in particular the Arab States, and UNRWA has been looking after most of them ever since. The Arab States have been reluctant to permit the mass immigration of refugees from Palestine because, it is argued, they don't want the campaign for a Palestinian Arab state to fizzle out as it probably would if the refugees were to leave the area.

The Six-Day War seems to have been a turning point for both the development of Israel and the struggle by the Palestinian Arabs for their rights. As a result of the Israeli victory, aliyah was no longer just a homecoming for persecuted Jews. Between 1967 and 1972 large numbers of Jews arrived from Western Europe, North and South America and the British Common-

wealth, largely a result of the 'pull' of Israel rather than the 'push' of anti-Jewish persecution – there was an upsurge in confidence that the Jewish State was here to stay and succeed.

The War of Attrition (1969-1970) & the Yom Kippur War (1973)

The War of Attrition lasted 16 months from spring 1969 and was caused by Egyptian shelling attacks across the Suez Canal ceasefire line. Israel responded with its air force. There were also clashes with Jordan and a general increase in

Territory held by Israel during the Six-Day War until the Syrian attack on Oct 6 1973

Syrian territory held by Israel at the cease-fire of Oct 24 1973

Israeli-Syrian Demarcation Line 1949-1967

Israeli-Syrian Cease-fire Lines

LEBANON

Sidon

Damascus

Mazraat Beit Jann

Hasbaya

Sassa

Qiryat Shemona

Khan Erenbe

Jeba

Safed

Khushniye

Rosh Pina

Rafid

Ramat Magshimim

Tiberias

Yarmuk

ISRAEL

SYRIA

Jordan

JORDAN

Irbid

Arab terrorist activity. Eventually the UN and the USA managed to secure a new ceasefire agreement.

The Yom Kippur War took Israel and the world by surprise. It almost resulted in the defeat of the Jewish State although Israel has called it one of its greatest military victories. In 1973 Egypt and Syria launched simultaneous attacks on the holiest day of the Jewish calendar – Yom Kippur, the Day of Atonement (see Festivals section). With most of the totally unprepared IDF's civilian reserves and many of its regulars off-duty and in the synagogues praying, the first three days of the war almost brought an Arab victory. However, the IDF was soon fully mobilised and it took the offensive by the third day, first on the Syrian front and later in the Suez Canal area. The fighting stopped on 24 October, 18 days after it had started, with a UN call for a ceasefire.

The heavy losses sustained by Israel and the loss of face caused by its highly-rated intelligence service's failure to foresee the Arab attack had a sobering effect on the euphoria which had followed the Six-Day War. The people's confidence was affected and the Labor Party, in power since independence, was severely criticised and eventually voted out of office.

A Search for Peace

One of the effects of the shock of the Yom Kippur War was said to be a more urgent desire for peace, which made Dr Henry Kissinger, the US Secretary of State, a familiar figure with his 'shuttle diplomacy'. However, it took him until May 1974 to negotiate an agreement between Israel and Syria, after the earlier UN Middle East peace conference in Geneva concluded an agreement between Israel and Egypt.

On 21 June 1977 the new Israeli Prime Minister, Menachem Begin of the Likud Party, called for the leaders of Jordan, Syria and Egypt to meet him to end the dispute. Critics were sceptical of Begin's sincerity, claiming that he was merely appeasing the voters who had just elected

him and that his subsequent actions, including the encouragement of West Bank settlement, the Taba dispute and the question of the Gaza Strip and the West Bank in general, show that Israel was not so willing to negotiate.

President Sadat of Egypt accepted Begin' challenge and after both had broadcast messages to each other's respective populations, Sadat visited Israel on 19 November 1977. The importance of his visit cannot be over-stated – a top Arab leader, who had been previously denying the Jewish State's right to exist, was now flying there to negotiate peace. Begin reciprocated with a visit to Egypt. During the following 16 months of negotiations the US, led by President Carter, played an active role. On 26 March 1979 the historic Egypt-Israel Peace Treaty was signed by Sadat and Begin.

Unfortunately the results of the treaty have not lived up to expectations. Israel and Egypt's relationship has become known as the 'Cold Peace' and it appears that in their haste to produce the treaty, its authors neglected to include all the necessary elements to produce a genuinely peaceful solution – not that this was necessarily possible. However, Israel and Egypt are at peace, whatever its temperature, and the security situation on the Israel-Egypt border has never been so quiet. President Sadat was assassinated by Arab extremists due to his involvement in the treaty, and his successor, President Mubarak, has taken a less flamboyant course. He has tried to appease both Arab nationalists and Egypt's western allies. Meanwhile, it is now possible for travellers to visit Israel from Egypt, and vice versa – something which once would have been unheard of.

Operation Peace for Galilee (1982)

When the IDF invaded Lebanon in June 1982, the Israeli Government felt it necessary to destroy PLO bases along Israel's northern border. This was due to constant terrorism, and heavy artillery and rocket attacks against Israel. Critics of the Israeli response point to the remarks allegedly made by David Ben Gurion, Israel's first Prime Minister, and Moshe Dayan, Defence Minister in the 1960s and 1970s, that it was important for Israel to create a Christian state in Lebanon, by force if necessary.

Critics claim that Israel was violating international law and Lebanese sovereignty. For the first time, thousands of Israelis demonstrated against the military actions of their Government. Prime Minister Begin resigned while controversy raged. He gave no reason for his resignation, but it was thought to be mainly due to guilt over his decision which had cost so many Israeli lives. Those in favour of Operation Peace for Galilee point to the great reduction in terrorist activity in the area as a direct result, and argue that international law guarantees a country the right to enter foreign soil to remove an armed threat which the host country cannot control.

The PLO

The Palestine Liberation Organisation (PLO), first formed in 1964, adopted a new Covenant in 1968. Basically, it committed all Palestinians to fight for their rights due to the failure of the international community to secure their natural, as well as promised, right to an independent state. This Covenant described Israel as an illegal state, and demanded the 'total liberation of Palestine'.

This led to Israel's refusal to have any dealings with the PLO. Groups under the PLO umbrella continuously resorted to violence to focus world attention on the plight of the Palestinians, but it is strongly argued that such tactics did little to benefit the Palestinians themselves. The PLO justified the violence by quoting the UN General Assembly's affirmation of 'the legitimacy of the people's struggle for liberation from . . . foreign domination

and alien subjugation by all available means including armed struggle'.

Despite worldwide condemnation of PLO-sponsored terrorism, the international community generally recognised the Palestinian cause. In 1969 a UN General Assembly resolution recognised 'that the problem of the Palestine Arab refugees has arisen from the denial of their inalienable rights'.

As far as Israel and the USA were concerned the PLO was a totally evil organisation not deserving official recognition. At the same time, it had been admitted into the UN where it received support from several countries. This resulted in resolutions being passed in its favour, and at Israel's expense. One of the most notable of these equated Zionism with racism. The PLO also established offices in major cities just like any leading political organisation.

In 1974, the Palestinian National Council, the body which elects the leaders of the PLO, reportedly decided that their previous policy was not working, and decided to settle for a Palestinian state in the West Bank and the Gaza Strip. This would exist alongside, and not in place of, Israel. It was also decided to achieve this goal through diplomacy, not force. The PLO therefore claimed to have accepted since 1974 the existence of Israel behind its pre-1967 borders, and blamed the Israelis and their supporters for suppressing news of this policy. They claimed that the policy was ignored by the Israelis who stepped up their efforts to paint the PLO as a collection of terrorists that could not be trusted.

Certainly this was a common image of the PLO in the wake of acts of terrorism such as attacks on innocent airline passengers, and the hijacking of a Mediterranean cruise ship and the murder of one of its passengers. The PLO, however, claimed that such acts were committed by groups that they had disowned and that the Israelis knew this.

Today

Israel has mostly withdrawn from Lebanon and there has been a turn-around in the country's finances. For years Israel had high inflation, with prices going up so quickly, often daily, that the currency was replaced, and then the replacement devalued, with no halt to the rise in prices. Inspired by Mrs Thatcher's monetarist policies in Britain, the Israeli Government has now managed to reduce the inflation rate from over 500% to around 20%.

Israel's policy of 'Open Bridges' must be unique in the history of war. It facilitates trade between the occupied West Bank and Jordan, allows some reciprocal family and social visits, enables some Palestinians to attend universities in Arab countries and also allows some local Muslims to undertake the pilgrimage to Mecca. There is still a lot of criticism of the policy, one argument being that there is not as much freedom of movement as the Israelis claim.

Near Metulla, on the Israel-Lebanon border, is the 'Good Fence', where an Israeli medical clinic provides treatment, and referrals of serious cases to Israeli hospitals, for residents of southern Lebanon. Since 1976 over 220,000 Lebanese have crossed the border for medical attention courtesy of the Good Fence. Lebanese Christians and Druze are also permitted to visit relatives and hold jobs in Israel, commuting each day from Lebanon through the checkpoint.

The Breakthrough? In late 1987 the PLO-inspired *intifadeh* began in the Occupied Territories. This policy of non-co-operation and active protest resulted in a heightening of tensions, the deaths of many Arab protesters, and a great deal of unfavourable publicity for the Israelis.

In late 1988, with world opinion swinging behind him, Yassar Arafat announced that the PLO was willing to forgo the use of terrorism, that it recognised Israel's right to exist, and that it accepted UN resolutions 242 and 338.

This was a vital breakthrough, as it was these concessions that the US had demanded before it would deal with the PLO. After a few anxious days, some incredulity, and requests to rephrase the announcement, the US announced that talks with the PLO would begin.

The Israeli Government was dismayed. It claimed that the US had given in to their deadly enemy, and vowed that Israel would never deal with the PLO.

Meanwhile, Jewish settlements continue to expand in the West Bank and this adds to the complexities of the situation. The original Jewish West Bank settlers believe that this area is part of what rightfully constitutes Israel, regardless of any UN partition and various resolutions. They base their argument on biblical references and also on the military value of the area.

However, an increasing number of the Jews now living in the West Bank are not motivated by religious and/or political fervour. Rather, they are attracted by the housing available in the region which is cheaper than that available elsewhere. Most of the latest Jewish settlers in the West Bank have moved into housing developments near Jerusalem, blissfully unaware that they are living in the Occupied Territories. As Jerusalem grows, the gaps between the settlements are filled and it is easy to look at the mass of buildings as all one and the same.

GEOGRAPHY

Israel and the Occupied Territories have a total area of 27,817 square km. Part of the Asian continent, its western border is the Mediterranean Sea, to the north it is bounded by Lebanon and Syria, to the east by Jordan and to the south by the Red Sea (with views of Saudi Arabia) and Egypt. These current border lines are according to the Israel-Lebanon 1949 armistice line, the Israel-Syria disengagement line following the 1973 Yom Kippur War, and the Israel-Egypt boundary agreed to in the 1979 peace

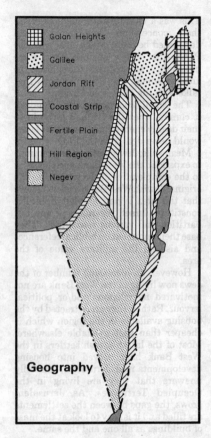

Golan Heights

Galilee

Jordan Rift

Coastal Strip

Fertile Plain

Hill Region

Negev

Geography

treaty. The task of defining the borders of Israel is impossible without upsetting someone. The described area includes the Occupied Territories, namely the West Bank and the Gaza Strip.

Coastal Plain A narrow, sandy shoreline, bordered by a stretch of fertile farmland (up to 40 km wide), runs from Rosh Hanikra in the north to the Israel-Egypt border in the south.

Mountain Ranges A series of ranges runs north to south. The mountains of the

Golan Heights and Galilee stretch southward until cut off by the Jezreel Valley. South of here are the ranges and hilly areas of Samaria and Judea in the West Bank, and the Negev. Israel's highest mountain (2766 metres) is Mount Hermon, in the Golan Heights.

Valleys The 'Rift Valley', part of the great Syrian-African Rift and the deepest valley in the world, runs the length of the country, and includes several distinct areas. The Hula Valley, between the mountains of the Golan Heights and Galilee, was once swampland, but is now a rich agricultural area with nature reserves. The Jezreel Valley, between the mountains of Galilee and Samaria is an agricultural area. The Jordan Valley runs between the mountains of Judea and Samaria in the west, and the mountains of Gilead and Moab in Jordan to the east. The northern part is an agricultural area, but the southern part is arid with limited agriculture. The Arava, a long, arid valley running from the Dead Sea to the Red Sea, is being developed for intensive agriculture.

Arid Regions The Judean Desert, between Jerusalem and the Dead Sea in the West Bank, is barren but beautiful. In the south, the Negev comprises flatlands of loess, a fine deposit of wind-blown dust and limestone, and leads the world in desert agriculture. It is the largest unspoilt area in Israel, yet is regularly left out of travellers' schedules.

Rivers & Lakes The Jordan River flows from sources in northern Galilee southward to the Dead Sea. The Sea of Galilee, at the foot of the Golan Heights, is an important source of water and, since the Golan Heights were annexed by the Israeli Government, it has become a major tourist attraction. The Dead Sea, in the Jordan Valley, is the lowest area on earth at 386 metres below sea level. It is the country's major source of minerals –

potash, bromide, magnesium – and the unique water is renowned for its healing qualities. Throughout the coastal plain, rivers flow from the mountains to the Mediterranean Sea. The most important are the Yarkon near Tel Aviv and the Kishon in the Haifa area.

CLIMATE

Climatic conditions vary considerably from region to region. In general, Israel's climate is temperate, with two seasons: winter – cold and rainy – and summer – hot and dry. Rainfall is mainly limited to between November and April, and can vary from over 1000 mm a year on Mt Hermon in the north to less than 100 mm in Eilat in the south. Most rain falls between December and February. The wettest area is Upper Galilee on the heights between Metulla and Safed. The driest areas are the southern Negev and the Arava Valley, between the Dead Sea and the Gulf of Eilat. The winter can be severe, often catching travellers with inadequate clothing. Even in the summer months a warm sweater is needed in many places as the evening temperatures drop considerably from the daytime high.

The hottest areas are those below sea level: the Jordan Valley, the shores of the Sea of Galilee, the Valley of Beit Shean, the shore of the Dead Sea and the Arava Valley. During the spring and autumn, periodic strong winds increase the temperature. Called the *hamsin* (Arabic for 50), these easterly winds were thought to blow for 50 days each year – thankfully they don't.

The widespread use of solar energy means that for much of the winter in the Jerusalem area and parts of the north there is a distinct lack of hot water and heating in some budget accommodation. The lack of sun in these areas means that returning to the hostel in the early afternoon in the hope of getting a hot shower can become part of the routine.

The climatic variations from region to region are part of what makes Israel so fascinating. For example, whilst in Jerusalem during the winter months when it is generally cold and wet, you can escape for the day by taking the bus down (literally) to Jericho or the Dead Sea, both less than an hour's ride away. After waking up in Jerusalem with the temperature at 10°C, you can change into shorts and T-shirts beside the Dead Sea in the 23°C sunshine.

Water & Irrigation

The availability of water in Israel is a major concern, due to uneven distribution of rainfall and periodic droughts. Israel leads the world in the field of irrigation, and many countries send personnel there to learn how to develop arid regions. Archaeological discoveries in the Negev and elsewhere reveal that 2000 years ago civilisations in the region used a variety of systems involving the collection and storage of rainwater.

The Jordan River, including the Sea of Galilee, is Israel's main water resource. All of the country's fresh water sources are joined in an integrated national grid. This system has increased the amount of irrigated farmland from 300 square km in 1948 to over 1600 square km today. New irrigation techniques have led to increased agricultural output, with savings of up to 50% in water use, and programmes for cloud seeding, desalinating sea water and the recycling of sewage water have been in operation for several years.

Travellers will notice the drip-irrigation system all over the country. It is used to water virtually everything from crops in the field to the plants and shrubs in town centres. Lengths of hosepipe with holes cut at set distances wind their way along the ground that needs water. Time switches, often computer linked, regulate the water flow. In arid areas, the water is mixed with chemical fertiliser to ensure efficient results.

FLORA & FAUNA

Due to its position at the junction of three

natural zones, Israel enjoys a wealth of plant and animal life, including 2500 plant types, 150 of which are found only here, 430 bird species, and 70 mammal, 80 reptile and eight amphibia species. There are nearly 300 nature reserves, covering almost 1600 square km. Some of these are major attractions for travellers and are covered in detail in relevant chapters.

Flora

Deuteronomy 8:8 describes the ancient land of Israel, with its wheat, barley, vines, fig trees, pomegranates, olive trees, and honey. These 'seven species' still flourish today, but they are just part of the country's wide range. Biblical, Roman and Crusader writings mention the now-vanished forests in the north of the country, and the Jewish National Fund's tree-planting programmes have set out to restore the county's tree population with millions of new trees.

Highlighting the range of Israel's flora and climate are wintry apple trees, Mediterranean vineyards and desert date palms, all within a few km of each other. Israel's oldest trees are believed to be in the olive groves of the Garden of Gethsemane and may have lived since the time of the Second Temple (500 BC to 70 AD).

Spring is a lovely time of year in Israel, but climatic differences mean that parts of the Israeli countryside blossom at different times. In the north, March and April see wild tulips, irises, lilies and hyacinths. In the south, the desert blooms as early as February. The Negev has lion's leaf, dandelions, groundsels and wild tulips, and in the wadies the white broom and purple irises grow.

Fauna

Like its flora, Israel's fauna is varied. The leopard, hyena, polecat, wolf, jackal, coney, porcupine, antelope, ostrich, wild boar and many reptiles can be found if you know where to look. The emblem of the Nature Reserves Authority is the ibex, a

wild goat, which can be seen in desert mountain areas where there is water. Less visible, but perhaps more interesting for its zoological classification as a relative of the elephant, is the hyrax, a sort of rock guinea pig.

Israel's skies teem with birds. Some, such as storks and swallows, rest en route to other climes; coots and ducks spend the winter; African species, such as the turtle dove, prefer the summer. As it is for certain plants and animals, Israel is the northern limit for many southern bird species, and the southern limit for many northern ones. This makes it one of the world's leading bird-watching centres.

SPNI

One of Israel's more endearing success stories is the Society for the Protection of Nature in Israel, which was founded in 1953 to safeguard the country's natural assets. Broadly stated, the aims of the SPNI are to conserve landscapes and relics of the past, to protect plant and animal life, and to protect and improve the quality of the environment.

For the traveller, awareness of the SPNI can be invaluable. The organisation's touring department, Israel Nature Trails, operates a wide range of guided tours of the many natural beauty spots in the country. These vary from a few hours to several days and are graded according to the 'hiking difficulty' involved. Most of these tours start in Tel Aviv but it is possible to join many of them in Jerusalem.

Even if you can't afford a guided tour the SPNI can be very helpful. Most of its staff are extremely knowledgeable about the country. If you fancy some wilderness wandering then they are a good source of accurate information. Unfortunately, the 30-odd years of its existence have allowed the SPNI to develop a bureaucracy of its own. This has resulted in the main offices in Jerusalem, and to a lesser extent the other branches, being staffed by a significant number of people who seem to have lost touch with the aims of the organisation. They tend to discourage travellers who wish to explore Israel alone, and are often reluctant to part with information.

Where the SPNI staff are most enthusiastic and helpful is in the 25 Field Study & Conservation Centres dotted around Israel. These FSCs are a key part of the SPNI's grass-roots programme of environmental education and practical nature conservation. Their role is nature education, nature conservation and research and data-gathering. They are situated in the different geographical regions of the country and provide hostel accommodation and study facilities (six do not provide accommodation).

Each FSC focuses on its immediate geographical area and it is the knowledge and the total involvement of the resident field instructors with their region that provides the backbone of the organisation. Once they are convinced that you are interested in seeing the real country – the varied natural beauty that is everywhere if you know where to look, they will shed the gruff Israeli exterior, open up and be extremely helpful.

Until fairly recently most of the SPNI's range of marvellous publications were only available in Hebrew, but they are in the process of being translated. It is certainly a good idea to browse through their *Israel Nature Tours* brochure to see what is offered, if only to use the information for individual hikes. The SPNI's head office (tel 02-249567) is at 13 Heleni Hamalka St, PO Box 930, Jerusalem 91008, and there you will also find a bookstore. The Tel Aviv office and bookstore is at 4 Hashfela St, Tel Aviv 6618 (near the central bus station). There are other SPNI offices in various towns.

GOVERNMENT

Israel is a secular, parliamentary and democratic republic, headed by a president. The president's powers are basically formal and he is responsible to the Knesset.

The Government, headed by the prime minister, is the main policy-making body. The first Prime Minister of Israel was David Ben Gurion (1948-1954). The Knesset is Israel's parliament, a single-chambered house of 120 members (MKs). All MKs are protected by the Act of Immunity from persecution or arrest for anything they say or do in the course of their parliamentary duties. This has resulted in several controversial incidents as certain extremist members have taken advantage of the law and entered the Haram esh-Sharif area in Jerusalem, where access is forbidden to Jews. Proceedings in the Knesset can get rather high-spirited, with MKs constantly losing their tempers: so much so that fighting is not unknown.

Political Parties

The oldest of Israel's political parties are older than the State, having been founded during the British Mandate. Despite the quadrupling of the population between 1948 and 1970, the established parties remain dominant, with new ethnic or communal groupings unable to gain substantial representation. All cabinets have been based on coalitions, and all of these had Mapai (the Labor Party) holding the central position until 1977, when a Likud (conservative/liberal) Government took office. Arab electors have shown limited support for the Knesset parties, mainly voting for individual members of the Communist and Mapai Parties.

Some smaller parties representing religious, ideological and special-interest groups have loyal, if limited, support among voters. Perhaps the most controversial party is Nat Karta, a small group of ultra-orthodox Jews based in Jerusalem's Mea Shearim district. The party's name is Hebrew-Aramaic and means 'Watchmen of the Town'. They loudly refuse to recognise the State of Israel and have even shown active support for the Palestinians, on the grounds that Judaism and Zionism (that is, political power held by Jews) are diametrically opposed. These Jews prefer to speak Yiddish, not Hebrew, and do not use Israeli currency, pay taxes or use state schools, hospitals or any other social services. They number around 120,000, which is about the same size as the kibbutz population, but they have very little influence.

The Israeli Flag & National Emblem

The design of Israel's flag is the same as that of the Zionist flag, first used officially at the First Zionist Congress, held in Basle, Switzerland, in 1897. It is based on the *tallit* (prayer shawl) with the addition of the Star of David. Israel's official emblem is the *menorah*, the ancient symbol of the Jewish people. The first description of the menorah is in the Book of Exodus, 25: 31-37 and 40. Two olive branches representing a hope for peace are included on either side of the menorah, joined by the word 'Israel' in Hebrew at the bottom.

ECONOMY

The years since independence have seen big changes in the emphasis of the country's economy, particularly during the last two decades. Investment has moved from consumer industries to the large-scale production of chemicals, plastics, metalware, electronic equipment and computers. The kibbutzim now earn almost half their income from industrial output. Israel is now a world leader in various fields, including medical electronics, fine chemicals, computer hardware and software, solar energy, agrotechnology, diamond cutting and polishing, and weapons.

Priority is given to research and development for both industry and agriculture. This has resulted in success in such diverse areas as lasers, executive jets, computerised printing techniques and the genetic cross-breeding of plants and livestock. Israel meets most of its food requirements through domestic production, and agricultural exports more than pay for the necessary imports.

Israel has successfully built on its status as the Holy Land by developing the country as a major tourist attraction. In 1985 nearly 1,500,000 tourists visited Israel, most from the USA. It is interesting to note that a large number of visitors are from the Arab countries. The vast majority of them are not tourists, but relatives of Israeli Arabs who have emigrated.

America In Israel

Everywhere you go in Israel you will be reminded of the deep involvement of the USA in the creation and support of the Jewish State. You will find many buildings, monuments, streets and parks that are dedicated to and named after leading American politicians or that have an American theme. Israel is the world's largest recipient of US aid, followed by its neighbour, Egypt. The United States has the largest Jewish community in the world, although the oft-quoted cliché, 'there are more Jews in New York than in all of Israel' is not quite true; and more visitors to Israel are from the United States than anywhere else. As the T-shirts proclaim: 'Don't worry, America – Israel's Right Behind You'.

Some Problems

So much for the good news. The bad news is that despite obvious determination, scientific and technical knowledge, and research and development programmes, the country still has to deal with the ever-increasing costs of its defence system. Without the massive financial support of the USA, it is hard to see anything but the total collapse of the Israeli economy. Defence costs aside, the lack of natural resources and the water supply problem have also taken their toll.

The subject of the economic development of the Arab sectors in Israel and the Occupied Territories is another area for dispute. A common Zionist argument is that, due to Jewish efforts, the Arabs have enjoyed economic growth, beneficial social change, and a constant rise in their standard of living. Israel's democratic system, compulsory education and the weakening of tribal and patriarchal authority have resulted in wider choices for education, employment and lifestyle. Zionists also point to the benefits of modern technology implemented since independence.

The Palestinians, meanwhile, talk about the Zionist art of rewriting history. They claim that prior to mass Jewish immigration the Palestinians were not living in the desolate, neglected country that is often described. In the second half of the 19th century, they argue, Palestinian agriculture was expanding and the area was an important exporter of agricultural products. Palestinians believe that the sudden increase in the population, caused by Zionism, created the need for higher output and used up the natural supply of water, which until then had apparently been more than adequate for the local population. Another argument is that until the Zionists received international funding they were struggling to survive in Palestine. If it takes the Zionists superior equipment and massive subsidies to live off the land, how can they condemn the local population who succeeded on their own? ask the Palestinians.

With regard to employment, Palestinians point to high unemployment and under-employment among the Arab population today. They say that this has resulted from their having to move away from areas of likely employment, and from discrimination, making only the unskilled jobs unwanted by Jews available to them.

Felafel & the Taxman
It has been said that tax evasion in Israel is more than a way of life, and I can believe it. While researching this book I was often the cause for alarm as I entered restaurants and bars, sat down, ordered, and promptly brought out my pen and note-pad. Many a guilty proprietor mistook me for a tax inspector.

Another example is the common or garden felafel. You will notice that the person serving will cut into the pitta to make a pocket for the felafel and salad. In the old days they used to do it much quicker by simply cutting off the top of the bread. They stopped doing that because tax inspectors began to count the discarded pieces of pitta, comparing their number with the receipts.

POPULATION & PEOPLE
Israel and the Occupied Territories have a population approaching 6,000,000. This includes over 3,500,000 Jews. Nearly 1,500,000 people, virtually all Arabs, live in the Occupied Territories – the West Bank and the Gaza Strip. These figures are increasing, with both the Jews and the Arabs seemingly intent on out-numbering each other. Who has the higher birth rate depends upon whom you listen to. Judging by the worried noises made by the Jewish political leaders, though, it would appear that the 'average Israeli' of today has swung towards a more materialistic lifestyle, making a large family less popular. The Arabs, meanwhile, appear to be staying with tradition and large families are still the norm.

In this guide I have generally used the terms 'Arab' and 'Palestinian' for the local Arabs, and 'Jew' and 'Israeli' for the local Jews.

Israel or Palestine?
Another problem facing the traveller is simply knowing what to call the country. To the Jews it is Israel; to the Arabs it is Palestine. You should realise the extreme sensitivities involved in the use of any words that relate to the Palestine Problem. Simply by calling Nablus by its Hebrew name, Shechem, you will annoy and upset most Arabs. Likewise, calling Hebron by its Arabic name, El Khalil, will not make many Jews very happy.

Unless you want to deliberately state your views on the political situation, you should follow a basic rule: Hebrew words for Jews, Arabic words for Arabs. Now I am not saying that you are necessarily asking for trouble if you walk up to every Arab with a big smile on your face and say 'Shalom', but you won't get a very

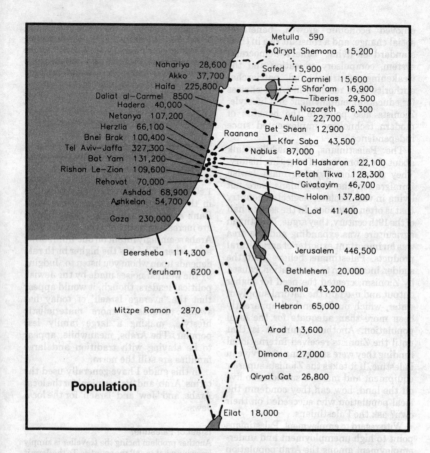

Metulla 590
Qiryat Shemona 15,200
Nahariya 28,600
Akko 37,700
Safed 15,900
Haifa 225,800
Carmiel 15,600
Daliat al–Carmel 8500
Shfar'am 16,900
Hadera 40,000
Tiberias 29,500
Netanya 107,200
Nazareth 46,300
Herzlia 66,100
Afula 22,700
Bnei Brak 100,400
Bet Shean 12,900
Raanana
Tel Aviv–Jaffa 327,300
Kfar Saba 43,500
Bat Yam 131,200
Nablus 87,000
Rishon Le–Zion 109,600
Hod Hasharon 22,100
Rehavot 70,000
Petah Tikva 128,300
Ashdod 68,900
Givatayim 46,700
Ashkelon 54,700
Holon 137,800
Gaza 230,000
Lod 41,400

Beersheba 114,300
Jerusalem 446,500
Yeruham 6200
Bethlehem 20,000
Ramla 43,200
Mitzpe Ramon 2870
Hebron 65,000
Arad 13,600
Dimona 27,000
Population
Qiryat Gat 26,800
Eilat 18,000

good price on a wooden camel – and if you want to impress a Jew with your linguistic skills, don't say 'a-halan!' Basically, it's a question of common-sense, courtesy and diplomacy.

The Jews

Between 1948 and 1952 the Jewish population more than doubled due to immigration of Holocaust survivors and Jews arriving from Arab countries. Israeli Jews are a mixed group of people with different cultures and lifestyles, despite being united in history and religion. The political and religious differences between the various communities developed over the centuries as a result of their worldwide dispersion, and have created major problems.

Ashkenazi 'Germany' in Hebrew is *Ashkenaz*, and these Jews originate from Central and Eastern Europe, mainly Germany and its neighbouring countries. They are also descendants of Ashkenazim who emigrated to North and South America, South Africa and Australia. Some of them still use Yiddish as their common language. This is a combination of Hebrew and medieval German, written in Hebrew characters. The Ashkenazim form the majority of Israeli Jews.

Sephardi 'Spain' in Hebrew is *Sephard* and these Jews are descended from those expelled from Spain and Portugal in the 15th century (although a few did arrive in Palestine from Spain earlier). After the Spanish Expulsion, many of those exiled came to Palestine, while others went to various European and Mediterranean countries, and to the New World. The Spanish Jews spoke Ladino, still in use amongst older Sephardim today. This is a mixture of Hebrew and Spanish, written in Hebrew characters. The majority of the Jews in Palestine until the 19th century were Sephardim.

Ma'aravim Loosely referred to as Sephardi, these Jews originate from Morocco, Algeria and Tunisia. These countries are to the west of Palestine and their Hebrew name means 'westerners'. Their language was a North African dialect of Arabic.

Oriental Also referred to as Sephardi, these Jews originate from various Muslim and Arabic-speaking countries. Most of them arrived in Israel relatively recently. The Yemenites come from Yemen, 'Teiman' in Hebrew, and are called *Teimanim*. Large-scale immigration of Yemenite Jews came soon after independence, when a massive air lift called 'Operation Magic Carpet' brought virtually all the community to Israel. The Iraqi Jews, suffering persecution after Iraq's army was defeated in the 1948 war with Israel, immigrated en masse. The Kurds are also from Iraq – Kurdistan, which is in northern Iraq, is ancient Assyria. Kurds first came to Palestine at the turn of the century. The Persians are from what is now Iran. Amongst them are a small group, the *Mash-hadim*, from Mashed, a holy city near Russia's border with Afghanistan. They were forced to convert to Islam in the 19th century but observed the Jewish faith in secret. There

are also Afghans, Bucharians (from Bokhara in the Soviet Union) and Cochins, from Cochin in India.

Falashas These Ethiopian Jews were airlifted to Israel from their famine-struck country in 1985. 'Operation Moses', as it was called, attracted international criticism – some said Israel should have helped all Ethiopians – and in Israel many Jews, especially Ashkenazim, found it hard to accept that these black people are really Jewish. Arguments continue about their Jewishness and whether they should go through a religious conversion ceremony, including a ritual bath. There is also concern about the cultural differences between the Falashas and their more westernised neighbours. Critics also say that the Falashas have been given poor housing in undesirable areas and are generally treated badly compared with other immigrants.

Despite presenting an image to the world of the happy Jewish State having to fight non-Jews to survive, your visit to Israel will show you that many of its Jews are also busy fighting each other. 'Two Jews equals three opinions' is an accurate cliché. With all the different cultures and temperaments which exist in Israel, the country constantly faces internal strife.

Ashkenazi Versus Sephardi This is a problem which was a feature of the Jewish race even before Israel's creation. The early Zionist pioneers and illegal immigrants were Ashkenazim. They administered the setting up of the Jewish State and later organised the mass immigration of the Sephardim from the Arab countries. The physical and cultural differences between the two groups were the cause of considerable ill-feeling, which continues to this day. Less educated, lacking good Hebrew and not as wealthy as their fellow Jews, the Sephardim claim that they were treated as second-class citizens. Today, charges of police brutality against

Sephardim suspects and the lack of Sephardim politicians are amongst the arguments for this. The controversy over the status of the Ethiopian Jews showed that being Jewish is not always enough to be acceptable to the authorities, who are predominantly Ashkenazim.

Religious Versus Secular The vast majority of Israeli Jews are not religious. Many of them follow a kosher diet, celebrate the religious holidays and have their sons circumcised, but they normally do so for traditional not religious reasons. However, a tiny religious minority wields a great deal of influence in the life of all Israeli Jews. The religious courts have exclusive jurisdiction of several areas including marriage, education, Shabbat observance, Kashrut and the question of 'Who is a Jew?' This means that Jews may only marry by the traditional ceremony, officiated by a Chief Rabbinate-approved rabbi. Rabbinical courts have exclusive jurisdiction of all matrimonial cases, including alimony and the support of children. Some people get around the law by having a civil marriage abroad. Cyprus, for geographical reasons, is the popular choice.

Shabbat observance enforced by the religious Jews results in public transport and most places of entertainment closing down – just when most people are not working and want to go out and enjoy themselves. The kosher laws are followed in many establishments by law, but more and more Jews are moving away from this diet.

Perhaps the biggest controversy is deciding how to define Jewish nationality. The religious authorities constantly refuse to recognise as Jews those converted by Reform rabbis. They also question the Jewish status of the Ethiopians and the Black Hebrews. In 1986 a particularly violent episode of the religious *vs* secular Jews conflict took place. Ultra-orthodox Jews, protesting at swimwear advertisements featuring scantily-dressed models, proceeded to set fire to bus-shelters where they were displayed. In apparent retaliation, a synagogue was set alight by a group of secular Jews. Violent clashes have occurred outside cinemas which screen films on Friday evenings. Religious Jews regularly stone passing cars and even people out walking who are not observing the Shabbat laws regarding driving and walking.

Zionists Versus Left-wingers Listing the various opposing Jewish political viewpoints currently prevailing in Israel is a lengthy task. There are major disagreements on virtually every issue. Probably the subject of defining Israel's borders and what policies should be pursued to achieve them is the major cause of disharmony. The wide range of Jewish-held views on this is often surprising and perhaps indicates why so little has been achieved in this area. Zionists and the left wing cover pretty much the whole Jewish political spectrum. Their views range from expelling every Arab from Israel and the Occupied Territories, to giving the Palestinians autonomy in their own land.

Who is a Jew?

This is often a major problem for travellers, and has nothing to do with the controversy which has inspired so many *Jerusalem Post* articles. Much more of an everyday problem is the correct identification of the local population by the tourist. Is that man with the olive skin and dark hair, wearing western clothes a Jew or an Arab? Is that lady wearing a headscarf and cardigan Israeli or Palestinian? Telling who is who by appearances is not easy. I have cringed several times in Jerusalem's Old City, having overheard well-meaning tourists asking a Muslim Arab shop keeper if he sells yarmulkas, or discussing their pro-Arab West Bank policy views with an Oriental Jew.

Israel, as I have said, is no more dangerous a place to visit than anywhere else, but do not tempt fate by making careless remarks and creating such embarrassing situations. Many of the Jews in Israel closely resemble Arabs in appearance. A large number of them were born in Arab countries where Jews lived for centuries and developed similar accents, attitudes and lifestyles. Not all Jews in Israel are white, have beards and wear yarmulkas, and not all Arabs wear kaffiyehs and carry worry beads.

The Arabs & Palestinians

Around 60% of the Arab population live in the Occupied Territories. Of the total Arab population, recent polls suggest that a vast majority consider themselves Palestinians rather than Israelis, Jordanians or Egyptians. Over 80% are Sunni Muslims, the remainder are Christians. Their common language is a Syrian dialect of Arabic.

Much controversy surrounds the origins of the Palestinians and this subject is at the heart of the Palestine Problem. A common Israeli view is that they are descended from the Arabs who invaded Palestine in the 7th century. Another is that most of them are descendants of immigrants from neighbouring countries who came to Palestine at the turn of the 19th century. Palestinians claim that their ancestry goes back beyond that and that they are a 'cumulative stock' of the many races that have lived in Palestine. This includes not just those Arab invaders, but the Canaanites who had lived here before the Jews first arrived, and the Philistines who arrived from the island of Crete circa 1200 BC.

Nearly 10% of the Arabs are Bedouins. These are tribes of traditionally nomadic people and they are Muslims. They are still mainly concentrated in the Negev, continuing to live in tents and breeding sheep, goats and camels. The Israeli Government has encouraged them to settle permanently and many have, mainly in Galilee.

The Christians

Most Christians in Israel are Arabs. The remainder mainly consist of Armenians, foreign clergymen, monks, nuns and those working for Christian organisations.

The Druze

Nearly 10% of the non-Jewish population belong to this mysterious religious sect. They live in a few villages in Galilee and on Mount Carmel. When the Israeli Government annexed the Golan Heights the Druze villages there became part of the country. These Druze are generally unhappy with being considered Israeli and have remained fiercely supportive of Syrian claims to the area. However, the other Druze in Israel are renowned for their loyalty to the Jewish State. From either side of the political fence the Druze will be among the friendliest people travellers will meet.

Small Communities

Baha'is The world centre of the Baha'i faith is in Haifa, and most of the followers in Israel live locally. Some are descended from the Baha'i leaders who were exiled to the Ottoman Empire in 1863 from Persia.

Samaritans Believed to be the smallest ethnic group in the world, there are about 600 Samaritans living in Nablus and Holon, south of Tel Aviv.

Black Hebrews This community has attracted controversy ever since the first Hebrews arrived in 1969. They number around 1200, with most of them living in Dimona. Their claim to be the most authentic descendants of the Jews exiled from Israel 4000 years ago is disputed, and they have been refused Israeli citizenship. Largely ignored by the authorities, the Hebrews are one of the understated fascinations of Israel today. This is due not only to their claims of Jewishness, but also to their communal lifestyle which incorporates such elements as a unique tofu-dominated vegetarian diet, colourful clothing, and the practice of polygamy.

Circassians An independent group in the Muslim community numbering some 4000, they originated in the Caucasian Mountains of Russia, immigrating to

Palestine in the 1890s. Mostly loyal to the State of Israel, the community is concentrated in two villages in Galilee.

Karaites A Jewish sect of about 15,000 members centred in Ramla, Ashdod and Beersheba. They reject rabbinical traditions and rulings, and have their own religious courts. After independence, the community had been reduced to only one family. Living in the Jewish Quarter of Jerusalem's Old City, they had to move due to the capturing of the area by the Jordanians. Shortly afterwards, Karaites from Egypt settled in the country and they founded the new colonies.

Meet the Israeli
The Ministry of Tourism has come up with a scheme, 'Meet the Israeli', to enable more visitors to meet Israelis at home and thus learn more about them and their lifestyle. You enquire at one of the tourist offices and they will arrange for you to have tea or coffee with an Israeli family. It usually takes a few days to find a convenient time for both you and your hosts. If you want, it is often possible to arrange a meeting with someone from a similar profession to yours, or with similar interests. (In Jerusalem enquire at the New City office at 24 King George V St, not at the Old City office).

Israelis & Children
The official IGTO brochure proudly proclaims that 'Israelis dote on children'. With about 35% of the country's population consisting of children, this should be taken as a warning. To 'dote on' means to be 'foolishly fond of', and you will soon learn that this is not necessarily such a good thing. In Israel, the sound of a screaming child is often heard. What is rarely heard is the sound of an Israeli parent telling the child to be quiet and behave. It would seem that the Israelis have decided that a laissez-faire approach to child-raising is best.

If children want to scream on the bus all the way from Tel Aviv to Tiberius, let them. If they want to eat chocolate on the bus and dribble it down the seat in front – sure, why not? If they want to run around holy places or beauty spots

and shatter the serenity and so on, it's OK. You will see many Israeli children, from tiny-tots to adolescents, behaving in ways that are obviously a result of always being allowed to do whatever they like. The term 'spoiled brat' is often applicable.

It is perhaps rather curious that the Israelis, who are renowned for their brusqueness, can at the same time be soft and tender to such a degree that a member of their younger generation can charm them and get away with behaviour that anywhere else in the world would earn the offender a 'thick ear'.

THE UNRWA
As a result of the Arab-Jewish conflict during the establishment of the State of Israel in 1948, nearly 750,000 Arabs became refugees. They headed for Arab-held areas, mostly in eastern Palestine or in what is now best known as the occupied West Bank. Many headed for the Gaza Strip, subsequently administered by Egypt, but under Israeli occupation since 1967. Other refugees went to Jordan, Lebanon or Syria. A few went further afield, mainly to the Gulf countries, Europe, Scandinavia, the USA and Australia. In 1950, when hopes for an early return of the refugees to their homes faded, the UN set up The United Nations Relief & Works Agency For Palestine Refugees. UNRWA's present task is to assist needy Palestine refugees with education, relief and health services.

As a result of the natural increases in population, there are now over 2,000,000 refugees with UNRWA. This excludes all those Palestinians who became refugees in or around 1948 but who did not register for assistance with UNRWA as they were not in need. In Israel and the Occupied Territories the number of UNRWA assisted refugees is approximately 800,000, but the number is constantly changing.

Refugee Camps
Today there are 61 UNRWA camps (West Bank 20, Gaza Strip eight, Jordan 10, Lebanon 13 and Syria 10). In and around these camps, UNRWA provides services

for those refugees registered with them, although a minority do not actually live in camps themselves. UNRWA maintains services in the camps, but they are not extra-territorial areas under UN jurisdiction – they are administered by their host country, which holds all legislative and police powers. Nor are they normally closed areas, and the inhabitants are theoretically free to move in and out of them. These movements are often strictly limited by the host government, and Israel is no exception.

Despite the significant presence of such a large number of both refugees and camps in the Occupied Territories, many visitors to Israel are unaware of their existence. This is no doubt due to their absence from most official publications and guide books. The squalor of the camps is a stark contrast to the relatively affluent conditions often only a few km away. The Arab countries opposing Israel's right to exist have continually refused to allow the Palestine refugees to integrate with them in order to keep alive the Palestinian argument. Israel, too, has refused to accept responsibility for their future.

A visit to the refugee camps is both possible and recommended although it should only be done by arrangement with UNRWA. They are not tourist attractions and unaccompanied visitors may be given a hostile reception. Hardly surprisingly, the refugee camps have become a hotbed of anti-Israel and/or anti-Jewish feeling, and terrorist activities are often organised from here. At the same time, non-Jewish visitors are normally welcome and receive extremely warm hospitality, if they present themselves correctly and sensitively. To arrange such a visit, contact the UNRWA offices in East Jerusalem or Gaza (see Jerusalem & Occupied Territories chapters).

Political Bias in UNRWA

Just as most of what you read and hear courtesy of the Israeli tourist information industry is understandably biased in favour of the State of Israel, so UNRWA and its presentation of its work is biased towards the Palestinian viewpoint. Most of UNRWA's local staff are Palestinians and the UN itself has been accused of bias because of its regular support for the Palestinian argument at the expense of Israel and the Zionists. Your visit to a refugee camp will be seen as a welcomed opportunity by Palestinians to put across their case, so rarely heard by visitors.

ISRAEL DEFENCE FORCES

Due to the Palestine Problem, and with the surrounding countries (except Egypt) still basically at war with Israel, security is the major consideration of the Jewish State. There is a constant presence of military personnel and wherever you go you will see soldiers armed with automatic rifles and machine-guns. Virtually everyone gets used to this, and to many they are a reassuring sight. Saying, 'Excuse me, could you move your gun, please?' to the young soldier sitting next to you on the bus soon becomes an acceptable part of travelling in Israel.

Established in May 1948, the IDF has developed into one of the most highly respected armies in the world. It is also one of the scruffiest, and its lack of sartorial elegance illustrates its egalitarian approach and minimalisation of the formal and ceremonial aspects of military life. Unlike most standing armies, it is a citizen's army based on the compulsory, reserve and career service of the majority of the population. Compulsory service is three years for men, two for unmarried women. Each soldier is assigned to a reserve unit upon completion of compulsory service. Men up to age 55 serve about 30 days each year, which can be increased in times of emergency. Single women are liable to reserve service up to age 34, although in practice they are exempted at around age 25. Career military service is open to any man or woman having completed compulsory service and meeting current IDF needs.

Most jobs in the IDF are said to be open to women. Certainly the Israeli women soldiers are highly noticeable, if only for the interesting interpretations of the uniform regulations which allow certain freedoms in the choice of make-up, hairstyle, jewellery and footwear.

Understandably, Arabs are not required to serve, although a small number have chosen to do so. The Druze in Galilee are highly-valued soldiers, although their Golan counterparts still support Syrian claims to that territory.

The IDF has managed to organise itself around the multiplicity of the Jewish faith. For example, it is not practical to establish synagogues suited to the various communities present in every military base. As a result, a uniform type of synagogue has emerged. Rules for the observance of Shabbat have to take into account the need for the armed forces to be on a state of permanent alert against attack, and leave is so timed that no soldier needs to travel on Shabbat. A unified prayer book tells the soldier what he must do in every eventuality according to Jewish Law. This includes the exemption of those near enemy lines from the injunction to listen to the *shofar* (ram's horn trumpet) on religious occasions if there is a danger of the enemy hearing it. Also, if during Yom Kippur a soldier feels that hunger is affecting his fighting capacity, he must break his fast. On Hanukkah, soldiers without candles or suitable oil are allowed to light the menorah with rifle-lubricating oil.

RELIGION

The religious status of this area is unique. Jews have lived here, in varying numbers, since the time of the Old Testament; Christianity began here 2000 years ago; and Muslims revere Jerusalem as their third holiest site. In addition to the 'Big Three' monotheistic faiths, Israel is today the world centre of the Baha'i faith; the

Menorah

home of the Samaritans, probably the world's smallest ethnic group; and has attracted the Black Hebrews from their exile in the USA and around the world.

Judaism

Israel is the Jewish State and as such, Judaism is the country's dominant faith. Many of the country's Jews spend most of their lives studying their faith, so don't expect to find all your questions answered in this book.

According to high Jewish doctrine, Jews are in the world to be witnesses to the claim that there is one God with whom humans can have contact: God has chosen them to act as messengers, whose task it is to pass on these details to the rest of the world. What God has said is written in the Torah, the first five books of the Old Testament. The Torah contains God's revelation to the Jews via their leader, Moses, over 3000 years ago. It contains 613 commandments, interpretations of which cover fundamental issues such as avoiding idolatry, murder and sexual abuse, and apparent trivialities such as never eating cheeseburgers, and not driving a car or making toast on Saturdays.

Judaism is an extremely complex faith, and the Torah is only the foundation of Jewish sacred literature. There are also the prophetic, historical and 'poetical' books that constitute the rest of the Old Testament. The prophetic books rank second only to the Torah in Judaism, with Isaiah the most important. It is said that without these ancient prophets, Judaism would have remained a mere tribal religion and would have been forgotten long ago. Isaiah, and also Jeremiah and Amos, stressed that God was not just for the Jews but for everyone, and that the Jews were his Priests. This point had been touched upon in the Torah but it only came to the fore in the prophetic period.

The defeat of the Jewish State and the destruction of the Second Temple around 70 AD was a major setback to the Jews. These events were believed to show either that it was no use in believing in God, or that he had to be thought of in a broader sense than before. The Jews chose the latter and many believe that this is why they have survived.

Another major written part of the Jewish faith is the Talmud, which includes the Mishnah. This great collection of writings was completed during the early centuries of the Christian era. About 2000 authors contributed towards the 63 books. The Talmud contains rabbinical interpretations of the scriptures and commentaries. Virtually every aspect of life is touched upon and it is this work that many spend a lifetime studying. In days gone by, some scholars in Eastern Europe were said to know it all by heart.

The Talmud is not the last word in Judaism. Rabbinical rulings over the years have had to be made, and they have often been the cause of much controversy. Topical areas subjected to rabbinical rulings include the use of special Shabbat elevators that religious Jews can use as they do not need to operate them and thus avoid breaking their religious law; and the complexities of dealing with Shabbat hours when flying across the International Date Line.

The primary Jewish tradition is based upon the Torah, God's commandments. Terms such as 'doctrine', 'creed', and 'theology' are now used in Judaism but they are new to it. Jewish ethics teach that people should be good citizens and act justly towards each other. The non-Jew is referred to in the original revelation to Moses, with the injunction that the Jews should behave well to the stranger in their midst. Judaism supposedly abhors violence, murder and war, but also rejects the Christian policy of 'turning the other cheek'. To Jews, killing is acceptable in self-defence.

Judaism's complexity is largely due to various individual interpretations of the Torah, and the other Jewish Written Laws. Although Judaism is non-denominational, with the same basic prayer book and identical weekly readings in use throughout the world, there have been changes in its practice and perception since the early 19th century. In Israel today, there are three main trends:

Orthodox Maintaining strict adherence to the Jewish code of life, *halacha*, this form embraces both the Written and the Oral Law.

Conservative Advocates adherence to halacha, while believing that it should be adapted to the requirements of modern life. This trend is also known as Traditional or Mesorati Judaism.

Reform Even more leeway in the adaptation process of halacha is allowed, with emphasis on the ethical aspects of Judaism and the right of the individual to choose a religious way from among the precepts of halacha.

Appearances Grasping the basics of identifying these modern trends is often made simpler by remembering the various basic dress styles of the different Jewish groups.

The most religious, pious or ultra-orthodox Jews are the Hasidim. They are a sect of Jews who follow a mystical interpretation and approach to Judaism. They originated in the late 17th century in Eastern Europe, led by the Rabbi Baal Shem Tov. They are also the most visible Jews with their black hats (on Shabbat often replaced by grand fur hats), long black coats, tieless white shirts, beards and cropped hair with *payot* (side curls). Their appearance is often a source of amusement to others but it has a special meaning to them. The Hasidic clothes are derived from the aristocracy of late medieval Poland and they wear them, regardless of the season, for two main reasons: humility, to remind them that they are less than God and to rid themselves of feelings such as vanity; and mourning, for the Temple which will be rebuilt for the return of the Messiah. The Hasidic haircut is based on the Torah's command: 'You shall not round off the hair on your temples or mar the edges of your beard' (Leviticus 19:27). The ultra-orthodox, therefore, keep their heads cropped – except for the payot – and they grow a beard.

Other Orthodox Jews grow beards and payot but do not go to such lengths as the Hasidim. These Jews will keep their hair short, trim their beards and wear more standard styles of dark suits and hats. Other Orthodox Jews are not so noticeable by their appearance, but still strictly follow the Jewish Law.

The most common sign of a religious Jew is the *yarmulka*, or *kippah* (skullcap). There is no universally recognised size for yarmulkas and you will see various styles, colours and materials used. Many interpret the covering of the head as a sign of modesty before God and an acknowledgement of his supremacy. Nowadays, covering the head is a matter of debate between those who feel it is obligatory, eg the Hasidim and other Orthodox Jews,

those who consider it necessary only for prayers and services, and those who are totally opposed to it. Some religious Jews wear a yarmulka in bed, but most do not!

Childhood & the Home By Jewish Law (Genesis 17:9-14) a boy should be circumcised on the eighth day after birth. Today, this is often performed for purely medical reasons, but the more traditional, though not necessarily religious, Jews treat it as an important ceremony with family and friends witnessing the occasion. At circumcision a boy is given a religious name by which he will be later 'called up' to the Torah. An injunction states that a boy should start his religious study from the age of three. Traditionally boys receive such an education whilst girls primarily learn how to run a home according to Jewish law. Times have changed and it is the area of the women's role that involves many of today's controversies and differences. Nowadays, most children are educated more or less alike.

Many of the major acts of Jewish worship are carried out in the home, with the parents performing a priestly role. This has a considerable effect on the child and even if in later life he/she has ceased to practise the religion, an affection for some of its aspects is often retained. The Jewish home is believed to be a main reason for Judaism's survival during the centuries of persecution.

When he reaches the age of 13, a Jewish boy becomes *bar mitzvah*. Basically, this means that he is subject to Jewish law and therefore, for religious purposes, he is an adult. On the Shabbat after his 13th birthday he reads from the Torah in the synagogue for the first time. This involves about a year's preparation and is often an emotional and noisy occasion with older relatives making their presence felt. Witnessing a bar mitzvah at the Western Wall is one of the highlights of a visit to

Jerusalem. Nowadays there is also a *bat mitzvah* ceremony for Jewish girls.

Food According to Judaism, every meal is a religious rite, as it must be *kosher*, that is, prepared in accordance with God's commandments. In the Reform tradition, the dietary laws may be treated literally or not observed at all. One attitude is that they originate from primitive taboos and are not to be regarded as God's enduring word. Some Reform Jews abstain from foods positively forbidden in the Torah but ignore the detailed rabbinical instructions that control a kosher kitchen.

Shabbat The most important meal of the week in most Jewish homes is Friday night's dinner, at the start of Shabbat. In Judaism, the 'day' begins when the sun sets. Before Shabbat starts, the house is cleaned and the dinner table is set with the best crockery and table linen. Traditionally religious fathers and sons go to the synagogue while the women prepare the meal. On his return the father blesses the children and recites from the Old Testament. To religious Jews, Shabbat is a joyful day and a time to appreciate what they have been too busy to notice during the week. No work of any kind may be carried out on Shabbat, unless it is necessary to save life.

The Orthodox maintain a particularly meticulous code which forbids writing, handling of money, and the operation of machinery of any kind. Jewish communities tend to be concentrated because religious Jews need to be within walking distance of the synagogue, as driving, using public transport and even walking too far are forbidden on Shabbat. One theory to explain the worldwide trend towards greater orthodoxy is that today's working conditions have made Shabbat observance a lot easier.

Sex & Marriage In sexual matters, Judaism has been said to advocate moderation, but to distrust total abstention.

In the past such Jewish sects as the Essenes have advocated celibacy but they were very much the exception.

Mainstream Jewish teaching places great value on married and family life. Some rabbinical authorities say that a man should not remain unmarried beyond the age of 18. Divorce under Jewish law is relatively easy, but is regarded as a failure and a tragedy in what is a central part of Judaism. Tradition says that the altar of the Temple weeps when a Jewish divorce occurs.

Orthodox Judaism is generally wary of contraception. It believes that Jews should have large families in obedience of God's command to procreate, and also to preserve Judaism, which loses large numbers every generation due to mixed marriages. If having children endangers the mother's health, contraception will be considered, as sex is considered a central part of a marriage. Abortion also is normally permitted only if there is danger to the mother's life.

Death & the Afterlife Basically, Jewish teaching says that at death the body returns to God. Traditionally, the funeral takes place within 24 hours of death, to allow mourners to quickly face the reality of the death; to conform with the interpretation of the Bible which says that the body should return to its natural course of decomposition as soon as possible; and to show respect for the deceased, as it is considered a humiliation to the dead to be unburied.

Maintaining a burial society and a cemetery to ensure that there is no distinction between the funerals of the rich and the poor is one of the highest priorities of a Jewish community. There is no cremation in traditional Judaism, because Jews believe in a physical resurrection on the Day of Judgement. Many Jews are bitterly opposed to autopsies for this reason. It is a Jewish gesture of mourning that a man rips his clothes. This puts the mark of his broken heart on his clothing and can also provide an outlet for the anguish and emotion that a mourner feels. Today this is usually expressed by a symbolic tearing of a lapel. There is no prayer for the dead, as such, but *kaddish*, a prayer that praises God, is recited on their behalf. It is the special duty of a son of the deceased to recite kaddish.

You will notice that visitors to Jewish graves place stones rather than flowers on the grave, because this is a more permanent way of showing that a visit has been made, and also involves the mourner in the act of burying the deceased, thus helping to return him to God.

Synagogues, Rabbis & Prayers The word 'synagogue' means 'meeting place'. The synagogue is not only a place for prayer. The studying of religious texts by young and old, the meetings of the Community Council and the Rabbinical Court have taken place there. Once, there would be a bakery for the special unleavened bread (*matzah*) baked once a year for Pesah, and probably a ritual bath (*mikvah*). In medieval times an annexe of the synagogue may have been used as a hostel for travellers. These days, although prayer and study are the main values which the synagogue fosters, many other community activities take place there, such as groups for youngsters, young wives and senior citizens.

Synagogues have been built in a large variety of architectural styles. As a result, it is quite often possible not to realise that there is a synagogue behind you in certain places, despite the frequent external use of Jewish symbols such as the *menorah* (seven-branched candelabra) and the Star of David.

The focal point of the interior of a synagogue, normally set in the eastern wall, is a cupboard containing one or more copies of the Torah (and sometimes the Prophets and Writings). These are written in Hebrew on parchment, by a scribe with a quill pen, and kept as a scroll on two rollers. Writing such a scroll (the *Sefer Torah*) takes over a year and because of their holiness they are treasured and revered possessions. The cupboard is known as the Holy Ark (*Aron Hakodesh*) and is covered by a curtain (*Parochet*). A light is kept burning continually in front of the Ark, in remembrance of the continual light in the Temple and as a mark of respect to the Holiness of the Scrolls. Often, above the Ark, there are representations of the two tablets of stone on which were written the Ten Commandments. These usually show the first two words, in Hebrew, of each commandment. There are often illustrations of the Western Wall and Rachel's Tomb on the synagogue's walls. In the centre of the synagogue is the reading-desk, normally on a raised platform (*Bimah*). This is sometimes at the eastern end of the synagogue in front of the Ark. On Shabbat and festivals, readings from the Torah are made from here. During the year, all the five books are read. All over the world, Jews read the same portions each week. Services can be led from here or from a small lectern standing on the floor in front of the Ark.

Sermons are delivered from the pulpit and are a relatively recent addition to the service. As in the Temple, the sexes are seated separately, often with a gallery for the women. Traditional Judaism regards this separation during worship seriously, mainly for reasons of modesty. Basically the men feel that the women's presence would distract them from their prayer. The head must be covered at all times in a synagogue.

Services are led by a Ba'al Tephilah, who leads the communal prayers which are sung or chanted. Services are not necessarily led by the rabbi. He is a religious leader and teacher, employed by his congregation, and his main task is to interpret Jewish teachings to his congregation. Any male over the age of 13 can act as prayer-leader. In Orthodox Judaism, there are still remains of the old hereditary priesthood that officiated until the destruction of the Second Temple, 2000 years ago. Any man named Cohen is likely to be a member of the old priesthood; not that the proof of such descent is available. Today a Cohen has the right to bestow certain blessings, but the loss of the Temple deprived the cohenim of their function and religious leadership passed entirely to the rabbis.

Jews should pray three times a day, in the morning, afternoon and evening, with certain additional prayers to be said on Shabbat and holidays. Wherever possible, religious Jews try to form a group of public prayer. In the Orthodox tradition, this consists of a minimum of 10 men (over the age of 13) and is called a *minyan*. There is an old saying that 10 cobblers make a minyan but nine rabbis do not. Services may be held anywhere and Jews frequently arrange informal meetings for daily services at places of work, in the home and student centres, etc.

The apparent lack of decorum in synagogue services often surprises first-time visitors. People talk to each other and go in and out of the synagogue, and children are often playing there. Jewish worship is very diverse by nature and this is all allowed during certain parts of the service.

Non-Jews & Conversion 'Are you Jewish?' is a question often asked of a stranger in the street by Jews in Israel. It is never meant to offend, although it often does when the questioner walks away if the answer is negative. Normally the questioner wants to know if the other person is Jewish in order to invite them to a synagogue, Shabbat dinner or just to engage in Judaic discussion. Critics, however, cite it as an example of Jews only caring for themselves and being impolite to non-Jews.

Jews should believe that everybody has a responsibility to be humane, moral and generally good. A clear rabbinical teaching deals with what a non-Jew must do to be saved. It includes abstaining from idolatry, blasphemy, murder, theft and incest, acting justly and not eating meat that has been cut from a living animal. Providing non-Jews comply with these Seven Laws to the Sons of Noah, they do not need to comply with the complexity of the rules given specially to the Jews. Jews are encouraged to share their view of morality but some have said that persecution over the centuries has led them to shy away from this responsibility.

Jews are traditionally horror-struck with the idea of one of them marrying a non-Jew, or following another religion. Likewise, they do not encourage conversion to Judaism. They feel that the future of the Jewish people can only be ensured by the continuity of Jewish families, and that a Jew marrying a non-Jew means the end of the line. Another common feeling is that being Jewish is very much a family experience requiring the contribution of both parents.

Conversion to Judaism is usually a slow, hard process, but it does take place. The Orthodox view is that wanting to marry a Jew is not sufficient reason for wanting to become a Jew. To them, evidence of independent religious motivation is necessary. Reform Judaism is more open and, particularly if the prospective convert does not practise another faith, marriage is often considered a sufficient reason for conversion.

Mezuzah The Torah (in Deuteronomy 6:4-9 and 11:13-21) has inspired Jews to attach a *mezuzah* to the entrances of homes, public buildings, synagogues and to the room inside.

The mezuzah is a container of wood, metal, plastic, stone, ceramic or even paper containing a parchment with the afore-mentioned references from the Torah lettered on the front and the Hebrew word *Shaddai* (Almighty) lettered on the back. Usually the container has a hole through which the word *Shaddai* can be seen, or the Hebrew letter *shin* displayed on its front.

The mezuzah may date to the period of the Jews' slavery in Egypt, as Egyptians placed a sacred document on the entrance of their houses. The word 'mezuzah' means 'doorpost' and there is some disagreement over the significance of the custom. Some people believe it protects their house, others that it protects the occupants from sinning. Another theory is that it is a reminder that worldly affairs are unimportant when compared to God. It is a common custom for Jews to kiss their fingers after touching the mezuzah as they enter and leave.

Tallit Married Orthodox men, and Jewish Conservative and Reform males past the age of bar mitzvah, wear the *tallit* (prayer shawl). On each of the four corners of the tallit are the *tzitzit* – symbolic tassles as directed by the Torah (Numbers 15:37-41). While the regular tallit is specifically for prayer, the Torah's instruction is to wear a garment with tzitzit all day. Therefore, traditional Jews wear the smaller tallit katan all day, and the larger tallit just for prayers. Despite the Torah's clear instructions about using blue cord in the tassles, most Jews use white cord. I was told that the shade of blue required came from a dye acquired from an animal which ceased to be available. The Black Hebrews and the Karaites both use blue thread in their tzitzits, though. Tying the tzitzit involves symbolic methods, as does the wrapping of the individual in the tallit. Verses from Psalms (104:1-2) are read and kabbalistic meditations follow.

Tefillin You will notice at the Western Wall and perhaps in some of the bus stations, Jewish males wrapping a leather strap around their arm and wearing a small box strapped to their head. This is *tefillin*, the result of the Jews' interpretation of instructions in the Torah (Exodus 13:1-10, 13:11-16; Deuteronomy 6:4-9, 11:13-21).

Tefillin are composed of two main parts which are worn every weekday morning during the Morning Service, Shaharit.

Jew at the Western Wall wearing the Tefillin

Tefillin shel yad is the strap wrapped around the arm and hand; and *Tefillin shel rosh* is the small box placed on the head. Both parts include a box, called a *bayit* (plural *batim*). Shel yad has one compartment and shel rosh has four separate compartments, placed tightly together. The shel rosh also has the Hebrew letter *shin* on two sides. This is seen by some as an allusion to the Ten Commandments and the patriarchs.

Enclosed in each bayit is each of the stipulated portions of the Torah, written on parchment, tightly rolled and tied with animal hair. For the shel yad, they are written on one long piece of parchment; for the shel rosh each quote is written on a separate piece and put in a separate compartment. *Giddin*, threads made from the fibres of a kosher animal's hip muscle tissue, are used to sew the bayit shut.

The shel yad binds the arm, therefore the body; the shel rosh binds the mind.

The tefillin, then, binds the whole person, mind, heart and body, together to worship God. It also reminds Jews that the mind, heart and body are to be used for good and not evil. The tefillin are a memorial to the exodus of the Jews from Egypt, a sign of where they have been, who they are and where they are heading – the permanent duty of God's service. Traditionally only men wear tefillin but some women do. They are not worn on Shabbat or holidays.

Black Hebrews This group, mainly former black Americans, believe that they are Jews, descended from the original tribe of Judah. They claim that their ancestors went into exile in Africa, and were eventually taken as slaves to the USA, the Caribbean islands and England. They do not believe that all black people are Jews. There has long been a recognised (although not by everyone) black Jewish community in the USA and Africa but the Hebrew's claims have been the cause of considerable controversy since the first of them arrived in Israel in 1969. Both the Israeli Government and the Religious Courts have refused to recognise them as Jews.

The community was founded in Chicago in the early 1960s by Ben-Ami Carter. One of their many controversial theories is that all the biblical characters, including Abraham, Solomon, and Jesus, were black. This is based on such Bible references as Daniel 7:9; The Song of Solomon 1:5; 4:1; and Revelations 2:18. Their most important belief is that they are descended from the original Hebrew Israelites and have now been called by God to return to the Promised Land. Rather than travel directly to Israel, the Hebrews, led by Carter, first went to Liberia to experience the wilderness in preparation for the Promised Land. There the community developed their principles of a vegetarian diet, and abstinence from smoking, alcohol (except their own wine) and pharmaceutical drugs, and complete isolation from the corrupting influences of the world. They learned the Hebrew language and took up wearing African clothing styles, with the women covered from head to toe and the men growing beards and wearing wool hats. Men were surnamed Ben Israel (Son of Israel) and the women Bat Israel (Daughter of Israel).

In 1967 one of the community arrived in Israel to spy out the land for Carter, rather like spies had for Moses. In 1969 four other Hebrews arrived, posing as tourists. Joining the first arrival they were given accommodation and work in Arad, then a new development town encouraging people to live there. Later that year more community members, mainly women and children, arrived and for the first time made their citizenship claims, under the Law of Return. The Government was not at all keen on the idea, but the new arrivals were given temporary visas and accommodation in nearby Dimona while their claims were investigated.

Initially the Hebrews were popular with the locals but that was all to change. A few months later, in 1970, another group arrived, claiming to be the fathers and husbands of those living in Dimona. Ben-Ami Carter was amongst this group. By now, the authorities had decided that the Hebrews were not Jews, but, apparently reluctant to break up the families, admitted the newcomers as tourists but with no housing privileges. In the following years more Hebrews arrived, mostly posing as tourists rather than returning Jews. Most were now in Dimona, with others in Arad and Mitzpe Ramon, another Negev development town desperate for residents.

In 1972, the Government decided that no more Hebrews were to be allowed into Israel, but gave no guidelines on how to distinguish members of the community from legitimate black tourists. This allowed Hebrews to avoid the ban by simply posing as tourists and pilgrims, and led to international controversy with lengthy interrogations and considerable harassment for most blacks entering Israel. At the end of 1972 the Supreme Court ruled that the Hebrews were not Jews and upheld the Government's right to deport them. However, it also suggested that those already in the country should be permitted to stay, and since then the official policy has been equally concise.

Meanwhile, locals, in Dimona in particular, complained about the over-crowded conditions and excessive noise created by the Hebrews' presence. Eventually the community was given a former absorption-centre complex originally designed as temporary accommodation for newly-arrived immigrants, and this is where most of the 1200 or so Hebrews live today.

Another reason for the controversy over the Hebrews has been the statements reportedly made by Ben-Ami Carter and other leaders. He strenuously denies much of what he has been quoted as saying over the years, accusing the media of discrimination. He has been quoted as declaring that the 'white' Jews had stolen the language, history and culture of his community, who are the 'real' Jews, and that he will eventually rule over Israel. His status as leader of the community is indisputable, but whether he is 'dictator', 'con-man', 'prophet' or the 'Prince of Peace' (all of which he has been called) is less clear.

You will see members of the Hebrew community, mainly in Tel Aviv but also in other areas, selling their home-made jewellery and other craftwork. There is also the chain of Eternity Restaurants featuring their unique tofu-dominated vegetarian food. They welcome visits to the community's home in Dimona, in order to show people their lifestyle and discuss their claims.

Messianic Jews This small group of Jews differ from the majority in that they accept Jesus Christ as the Son of God and all that he has said as written in the New Testament. They have formed their own denomination within the Christian Church as they still have major differences with some interpretations of the teachings of Jesus Christ in relation to their under-standing of the Old Testament and the status of the Jewish people.

Samaritans According to the Samaritans' fullest version of their history, the Chronicle II, they are directly descended from the Joseph tribes, Ephraim and Manasseh. Until the 17th century they possessed a high priesthood descending directly from Aaron through Eleazar and Phinehas. They claim to have lived continuously in the area and are also believed to be the world's smallest ethnic group. Prior to the publication of Chronicle II, the most widely available and decisive source of the history of the Samaritans was the Biblical account in II Kings 17.

The Samaritan priesthood dominates life in the community. These men are the sole interpreters of the law and the calendar, which is a vital part of their faith as it governs the observation of their festivals. Unlike the Jews who have the Bible and the Talmud, the Samaritans have a faith whose beliefs are relatively simple to outline. After Moses, Joshua is the only prophet to be held in high esteem. It could be said that the Samaritan doctrine is that anything not covered in the Five Books of Moses cannot be regarded as valid. They regard the Ten Commandments as nine, adding a 10th of their own stipulating the sanctity of Mount Gerizim.

The Samaritan way of life results from an interpretation of biblical laws which is usually stricter than that of the most ultra-orthodox Jews. They observe Shabbat in similar style to the Jews, and also have the same circumcision rules. During their menstrual period, women are obliged to remain separated from their families for seven days, and the men must look after them. After giving birth, a woman is considered to be unclean. If the child is a son, the period is 40 days, for a daughter, it is 80 days. The Samaritan bar mitzvah is dependent upon the individual's education and ability, not age. Marriage is the reason for more celebration than any other Samaritan ceremony. The bridegroom's family proclaims a week of celebration, starting the Shabbat before the wedding which takes place on the fourth day. Intermarriage with the Jewish community is permitted only after the High Priest is convinced that the convert will be suitable for observing the Samaritan traditions. Divorce is rare. The Samaritans bury their dead in their cemetery on Mount Gerizim.

Over the years, the Samaritans have been greatly affected by the political turmoil in the area. During the beginning of the British Mandate the Samaritan community had separated, with about half of them moving away from Nablus to Holon near Jaffa. After Israel's independence the Samaritan communities became split between Israel and Jordan. The Six-Day War reunited the two communities.

Karaites The name of this small sect means 'people of the Scriptures' but could also be interpreted as 'propagandists'. Their main characteristic is the recognition of the Scriptures as the only source of religious law, and they reject rabbinical tradition and the Oral Laws. Their name was not applied until the 9th century and the sect appears to have been formed due to a variety of factors, including the amalgamation of several rebel trends in Babylonian-Persian Jewry; the tremendous religious, political and economic fermentation in the entire East due to the Arab conquests; and social and economic grievances of the poorer classes of Jewry.

In principle, the Bible is the Karaites' sole source of creed and law, but apart from its fundamental stand on the Oral Law, Karaite creed does not differ in its essentials from that of Rabbinical Judaism.

Islam

The Arabic word *Islam* means voluntary surrender to the will of Allah (God) and obedience to his commands. Muslims prefer to use the Arabic word *Allah* whatever their nationality. Some Muslims interpret 'Islam' as meaning peace, believing that observing total obedience to Allah is the only way to achieve peace. A Muslim is a person who accepts the Islamic way of life and practises it. The three fundamental Islamic beliefs are: *Tawhid*, oneness of Allah; *Risalah*, prophethood; and *Akhirah*, life after death.

Tawhid This is the most important Islamic belief. It implies that everything in earth originates from Allah, who is the 'one and only Creator'. He is also the 'Sustainer and the sole Source of Guidance'. This belief governs all aspects of a Muslim's life. Islam views human life as a compact whole and rejects any compartmentalisa-

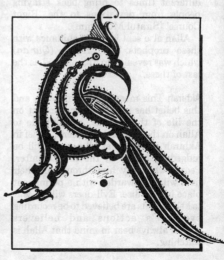

Islamic calligraphy

tion. As there is only one 'Creator and Source of Guidance', there is no scope for any partnership. Allah is neither born 'nor is anyone born of him – he has no son or daughter'. Humans are 'his' subjects. In Islam, he is 'Allah, the One'.

Tawhid brings a total change to a believer's life. It means worship of Allah, who is 'always watching', and encourages working for this supremacy in all areas of everyday life. The purpose of life is to please Allah.

Risalah It is believed that Allah gives guidance (*Hidayah*) on how to live, and Risalah is his channel of communication – the prophets and messengers. The chain began with Adam, and includes Noah, Abraham, Ishmael, Isaac, Lot, Jacob, Joseph, Moses, Jesus and lastly Mohammed. The message brought by each of them is believed to be the same. They all urged the people of their time to obey and worship Allah alone and no-one else. It was necessary to send prophets at different times to bring back straying people from deviations to the 'Right Course' (Siratul Mustaqim).

Allah also sent books of guidance with these prophets. The Koran (*Qur'an*) which was revealed to Mohammed, is the last of these.

Akhirah This means life after death and this belief has a far-reaching impact on the life of the believer, accountable to Allah on the Day of Judgement. Belief in Akhirah implies that all actions will be judged by Allah in the life hereafter. People who obey him throughout their lives will be rewarded with a permanent place in Paradise. Evil-doers will be sent to hell. Angels are believed to be recording everyone's actions and believers should always bear in mind that Allah is watching.

Five Basic Duties of Islam These are known as the pillars of Islam, and should be performed regularly and correctly with an

awareness of their relevance to practical life. This brings the Muslim's life into line with Allah's wishes. It also enables the believer to fit neatly into the system of Islam which aims at the establishment of truth and the eradication of untruth.

Ash-Shahadah, the first and most fundamental of the five basic duties, is to pronounce the first declaration of faith, the *Kalimah: La ilaha lah Muhammadur rasalul lah* (There is no God except Allah, and Mohammed is Allah's messenger).

Salah These are compulsory prayers, offered five times a day, either individually or in congregation. They are considered to be the practical demonstration of faith and to keep believers in constant touch with their Creator. This makes them conscious of the basic duty to work for the establishment of a true order in society and to remove untruth, evil and the indecent. Salah should induce qualities of self-discipline, steadfastness and obedience to the truth, making Muslims honest and courageous. The five daily prayers are:

Fajr	(dawn prayer)
Zuhr	(after midday prayer)
Asr	(late afternoon prayer)
Maghrib	(after sunset prayer)
Isha	(night prayer)

Zakah This welfare contribution is a compulsory payment from a Muslim's annual savings. The rate of payment is 2.5% on cash, jewellery and precious metals, with another rate for animals and agricultural produce. It is neither a charity donation nor a tax. Charity is optional and taxes can be used for any governmental purpose. Zakah is an act of worship and it is one of the Islamic economy's fundamental principles, designed to develop an equitable society where everyone has a right to contribute and share.

Sawm From dawn to sunset every day

during Ramadan, the ninth month of the Islamic calendar, Muslims should refrain from eating, drinking, smoking and sexual relations. It is a means of achieving self control, designed to raise a person's moral and spiritual standards above selfishness, laxity and other vices. Sawm is an annual training programme to refresh Muslims' determination to fulfil their obligation to Allah. Muslims usually end up spending more time praying than usual during Ramadan. You will also notice that they stay up later at night, too, in order to eat and socialise.

Haj This pilgrimage to the 'House' of Allah is obligatory at least once in the life of all Muslims who can afford to undertake it. It is a journey to Al-Ka'bah, in Mecca, Saudi Arabia, where the prophet Mohammed was born.

Haj symbolises the unity and equality of mankind and is the annual assembly of the Muslim community (*ummah*). It also stands as the peak of Muslims' obligatory duties as it should lay bare to them that they belong to no-one but Allah. You will often see a sign proudly displayed on the house of a Muslim who has made such a pilgrimage. Often brightly coloured, an illustration of Al-Ka'bah, in Mecca, is a central theme of the sign.

The Koran This is the sacred book of the Muslims and was sent to Mohammed through the angel Gabriel (Jibrail). It is believed to be the word of Allah. It consists of 114 *Suras* (chapters) and 6236 verses. Muslims usually learn to read it and many memorise it by heart.

The Koran has remained completely unchanged over the past 1400 years. Its teachings, principles, doctrines and directions deal with all areas of this life and the life after death. The Koran's theme basically consists of the three fundamental ideas of Tawhid, Risalah and Akhirah. Muslims believe that success in this life and in life after death depends on obedience to the Koran's teachings.

Mohammed Allah's last messenger was born in 571 AD. Mohammed first received revelations from Allah when he was 40. At that time, the people in Mecca worshipped idols and Mohammed introduced them to Islam with mixed results. He continued to preach Allah's message, gradually increasing the number of followers. Both he and they suffered persecution from the idolators, and in 622 he moved to Medina where he won acceptance as leader and eventually established the first Islamic State. The Islamic calendar begins from the day of the prophet's migration to Medina.

Within two decades most of the Arab world had been converted to Islam. They spread the faith successfully, their methods often violently ruthless. The various Arab conquerors seemed to interpret Islam in a manner matched by the Crusaders' version of Christianity. Muslims today vary considerably in their interpretation of their faith. Their common belief is that its ideology is capable of solving present day human problems and is, in fact, the only hope for this world – if it is practised faithfully.

The Sunni At an early stage Islam suffered a major split that remains to this day. The third Caliph, successor to Mohammed, was murdered and followed by Ali, the prophet's son-in-law in 656. Ali was assassinated in 661 by the Governor of Syria who set himself up as Caliph in preference to Ali's descendants. Most Muslims today are Sunnites, followers of the succession of the Caliph, while the others are Shias or Shi'ites who follow the descendants of Ali.

Sunni is the practice of the prophet Mohammed. It is contained in the *Hadith*, a collection of his sayings and actions, and actions done with his approval. You need to know the Hadith, recorded by the prophet's companions after his death, in order to understand and interpret the Koran.

Islam & the Holy Land In Islam, there are three holy places in the world: the Ka'bah, in Mecca; the Mosque of Mohammed, in Medina; and the Temple Mount, or Haram esh-Sharif, in Jerusalem – in that order of status. According to Ezekiel 5:5 and 38:12 the Temple Mount is the centre of the world, and Muslim scientists found corroboration for this view in their calculations that the area is in the centre of the fourth climatic zone, the central region north of the equator. However, it is the Koran's description of Mohammed's Night Journey (Sura 17) that has elevated Jerusalem's position. It tells of Mohammed, who was sleeping by the Ka'bah, being taken to the Temple Mount in Jerusalem by a Buraq, a winged creature. From there they rose to heaven, on the way meeting good and evil powers. In heaven they saw Abraham, Moses and Jesus with whom Mohammed prayed as their leader. Until 624 AD Muslims prayed in the direction of Jerusalem. It was then decided to face Mecca.

Jerusalem also has a special place in Muslim mysticism. Various traditions relate to the city and inspired Muslims to live in Palestine, especially in Jerusalem's vicinity. It is believed that the Crusades fostered the development of Arab literature in the area. Much of this was important for Islam and later became the principal stimulus for Muslim pilgrimages to the holy places in Jerusalem.

Sex, Marriage & Family Life Marriage is the basis of family life in Islam. Marriages are generally arranged by parents with the couple's consent. The wedding ceremony is a simple service but is surrounded by much celebration and attended by family and many friends. Islam strictly forbids the free mixing of the sexes after puberty. This means all socialising, not just pre-marital sex. Extra-marital sex is also a sin and despite what most

non-Muslims believe, there is no sexual discrimination in Islam. Husband and wife are equal partners in the family, playing their role in respective fields. Divorce is permitted but is regarded as the most abominable of legal acts. Polygamy is illegal under Israeli law, but this does not affect Muslims in the Occupied Territories – most Muslims there are monogamous anyway.

Diet Islam is not as complex as Judaism when it comes to food and drink, but Muslims are supposed to observe some regulations. They are only allowed to eat animals which are slaughtered in the prescribed manner, and not pigs, carnivorous animals, or the blood of any animal. All alcohol is prohibited.

Dress Simplicity and modesty are encouraged. Muslims are required to cover their bodies properly and decently. Men must be covered from navel to knees, and must not wear pure silk or gold. Women must cover the whole body except the face and hands. Strict Muslims insist that women cover their face when going out and when meeting strangers, although in Israel this is not often enforced. A woman's outfit must not arouse a man's base feelings, so skin-tight, transparent or revealing styles are out. Women's clothes for men and vice versa are not allowed, and neither is symbolic dress of other religions.

Non-Muslims should be aware of these dress codes and, out of respect, adhere to them when in predominantly Muslim areas. Doing so will make their presence much more welcome, and therefore much more enjoyable. Men should appreciate that wandering around Muslim areas in shorts causes offence, especially in Nablus, Hebron and Gaza.

Social Manners Islam teaches decency, humility and good manners. Muslims traditionally greet one another with the words 'As-salamu 'Alaikum' (peace be to you), and the reply is 'Wa'alaikumus salam' (peace be on you, too). The most valued virtues are keeping promises, honesty, justice, fair play, helping the poor and needy, respect for parents, teachers and elders, love for children, and good relations with neighbours. Islam condemns enmity, back-biting, slander, blasphemy, ridicule, rudeness and arrogance.

Mosques The word 'mosque' comes from the Arabic word *mesjid*, meaning a place of adoration. Most mosques have domes and minarets, making them easy to recognise. Inside, facing the holy city of Mecca, is the *mihrab* (or prayer niche), normally a round recess or alcove covered by an arch. This directs the congregation towards Mecca to honour Mohammed's birth place. The *mimbar* (pulpit) is usually nearby. The *imam* (preacher) gives the Friday sermon from here. The *Khatib* is a low, railed wooden platform where the khatib, or reader, sits to recite the Koran to worshippers sitting all around. Outside, or near the doorway, is a water tank for washing the hands, face, and feet before prayers. Prayers are said barefooted and traditionally with the head covered. There is no seating in mosques; you kneel, sit or even lie flat on the floor. Women are normally expected to pray at home but some of the larger mosques have facilities for them.

There are no professional priests attached to a mosque. The imam who gives the weekly sermon normally has a regular full-time job. The *muezzin* is the man who cries the call to prayer five times every day from the minaret. He has been largely replaced by taped recordings, hence the familiar tone, wherever you are, of what is often an unrequested wake-up call.

Not all mosques welcome non-Muslims. Sometimes a sign saying 'For Prayers Only' or similar can be seen. Do not presume that you are welcome to enter a mosque, but ask. You must always remove your shoes and in some cases leave any bags and cameras outside. After making enquiries (and not just with the mosque officials involved) I never came across a case of such items being stolen.

Christianity
The organisation of the Christian faith in Israel is often a cause of mystery and concern to western pilgrims and non-Christians alike. Certain churches have the advantage of having been established here before others. As a result, the relative standing of churches elsewhere in the world is often irrelevant here. The Greek Orthodox Church, for example, owns more than half of the Church of the Holy Sepulchre (the supposed site of the crucifixion, burial and resurrection of Jesus Christ) and more of the Church of the Nativity in Bethlehem than any other religious body. Its patriarchate has seniority in the Christian hierarchy of Israel, despite the fact that this church constitutes only a fraction of the world's Christian population and is geographically confined mainly to Greece and the Slavic

countries. The Armenian Church, established in Palestine in the 5th century, has a world congregation of only 6,000,000 but owns a third of Jerusalem's holy sites. Obscure in the church councils of the world, the Copts and Assyrians are highly visible in Israel.

Meanwhile, the Roman Catholic Church owns only 17% of Jerusalem's holy sites. You see, it only established itself here during the Crusades, making it a relative newcomer. The Protestants have even less authority, and are restricted to singing their Christmas carols in the Church of the Nativity's courtyard because they do not own any part of the building.

All this is a result of the intense rivalry between the factions of the Christian world. This is thought to have erupted in the 11th century when the eastern (Greek Orthodox) and the Latin (Roman Catholic) churches had a major row. Since then there has been a continuing struggle to exclude each other from the holy places, with the smaller churches also claiming rights.

After the defeat of the Crusaders in the 12th century, the Muslims claimed ownership of all the holy places, and sold the rights of worship to interested parties. Over the years the poorer churches were forced out. In 1757 the Turkish authorities drew up the rights of possession in nine of the most important shrines. Known as the 'status quo', it is still applicable today. But while it may outline the official position it has not ended the bitter disputes over who should have what.

The Orthodox Church The Greek Orthodox Church is the oldest ecclesiastical body in Israel, and is probably the closest successor to the original Judeo-Christian community of St James. A Greek-speaking Christian community emerged in Jerusalem in the mid-2nd century, gaining importance during the rule of Constantine when most of the holy sites were discovered. Byzantine times saw the church prosper, then decay under the Arabs. During the later Middle Ages the Orthodox Church languished, recovering under the Turks; but at the beginning of the 20th century it only numbered a few thousand. Today it has developed to be the lynchpin in the often bitter rivalry between the various churches in Israel.

The Orthodox Church is an Arabic-speaking community led by a virtually exclusively Greek-speaking hierarchy. The Orthodox patriarchate of Jerusalem is the only autonomous church in the country, with all the others being dependent to various degrees on a head office abroad.

Israel is also the home of two Russian Orthodox missions, both in Jerusalem, one representing the Moscow patriarchate, and the other the Russian Church Abroad. Both claim to be the legitimate successors of the 19th century Russian Government's mission. The Moscow mission is in possession of the green-domed cathedral in Jerusalem's Russian Compound, and other churches in Jaffa, Nazareth, Tiberias and Haifa. The Church Abroad is in charge of the photogenic onion-domed Church of St Mary of Magdalene in Gethsemane, on the Mount of Olives. Being out of communion with the patriarch of Moscow, the Church Abroad is not recognised by the Orthodox patriarch of Jerusalem. The Moscow patriarchate's Jerusalem churches are assumed to be bases for Soviet intelligence and espionage. The violent death of a Russian nun in recent years was the talk of the town.

The Romanian Orthodox patriarch is also represented by a church and small community in Jerusalem.

The Armenians Many travellers might not even know where Armenia is (USSR), let alone that it is represented by one of the Holy Land's more powerful Christian communities. By the 7th century it had 72 monasteries in Palestine, and under the Arabs and Crusaders the number increased.

Much of Mount Zion in Jerusalem is the property of the Armenian Church, and has been since the 10th century.

The beauty of the area is largely due to the Armenian buildings, constructed during the existence of the Armenian Kingdom of Cilicia. All but six of their monasteries were lost in power struggles, mainly with the Greek Orthodox. However, they managed to maintain their rights in the major holy sites. During the Mandate, they formed a prosperous community of some 5000 with their own churches, schools and culture. Due to emigration they number only about 2500 today.

The Armenian patriarchate, also based in Jerusalem, shares the Churches of the Holy Sepulchre and the Nativity with the Orthodox and Latin patriarchates. This complex system of sharing has often been the cause of violent clashes between rival members of these Christian sects.

The Syrian Orthodox & Copts The Syrians have had a bishop in Jerusalem since 1140, the Copts since 1236. Also called the Jacobites, the Syrian Orthodox are headed by an archbishop whose residence is the monastery of St Mark, in Jerusalem. The Copts, from Egypt, have a monastery upstairs at the back of the Church of the Holy Sepulchre. Both these groups celebrate Christmas at the Armenian altars in the Church of the Nativity, but otherwise they use their own small chapels in the Church of the Holy Sepulchre.

The Ethiopians From the Middle Ages until the 16th century, the Ethiopians owned chapels and altars in various holy places. Today they are confined to a ramshackle monastery on the roof of the Church of the Holy Sepulchre in Jerusalem, where they also have the chapel of St Helena, as well as a lovely church and monastery in West Jerusalem and a chapel near the Jordan River.

The Catholics The Latin patriarchate of

Jerusalem was established by the Crusaders in 1099, ceased to exist in 1291 and was re-established in 1847/8. The Latin community includes over 45 religious orders and congregations. There are around 30 female communities and several hundred houses.

Most of the Catholic religious groups were established here over the last 130 years, except the Franciscans. For more than 500 years, they were the sole body in charge of Catholic interests in Palestine and the Middle East. It was they who regained and maintained rights of worship and possession in the major holy places, established programmes for their restoration, catered for the huge numbers of pilgrims and ministered to the small Catholic communities in the country that sprang up around their monasteries and convents.

The Uniates These are the Oriental churches in communion with Rome, and they are represented in Israel by relatively small communities. The largest comprises the Melkites, who are mostly in Akko and Galilee. The next in size are the Maronites, mostly near the Lebanese border. The Chaldeans and the Syrians and Armenian Catholics are far fewer in number. All the Uniate patriarchs are based in Arab countries and the churches in Israel are controlled by patriarchal vicars as their representatives. The Uniate churches do not have any rights in the principal Holy Places.

Protestants Anglican and Prussian Lutherans arrived in Palestine 160 years ago. Missionary work among Jews and Muslims was one of their aims, but the Greek Orthodox Church was the source of most converts. The British Mandate was a particularly prosperous period of development for the Anglican church here, but by 1948 most of its English-speaking congregation had left the country. Today the Evangelical Episcopal Church is primarily Arab-speaking, and the Anglican Archbishop in Jerusalem presides over a synod made up of Egyptian, Libyan, Sudanese, Iranian and Jordanian bishops.

The Israeli Government recognised the church as a separate religious community in 1970. The Anglicans have no rights in the Church of the Holy Sepulchre, but an arrangement with the Greek Orthodox Church allows them to occasionally celebrate mass in the nearby Chapel of St Abraham. The Anglican cathedral in Israel is St George's in East Jerusalem.

The German Lutherans established schools, hospices and hospitals in Palestine. These included the Hospice of the Order of St John in Jerusalem and the Augusta Victoria Hospice (now a hospital) on Mount Scopus. Despite the considerable setbacks as a result of the German involvement in the two world wars, the Lutherans have re-established themselves as the Evangelical Lutheran Church. They are led by a prophet residing in the Church of the Redeemer in the Muristan area of Jerusalem's Old City.

There are some notable non-German Lutheran institutions in Israel. They include the Swedish Theological Institute and the Finnish Missionary School in Jerusalem, the Swedish school and hospital in Bethlehem, and the Scandinavian Seamen's Churches in Haifa and Ashdod. There are also several minor Protestant groups representing reformed Christianity. These include Presbyterians, Baptists, Pentecostalists, Quakers and Adventists.

The Church of Jesus Christ of Latter-day Saints Also known as the Mormon Church, they are often misunderstood and unrecognised as Christians. Mormons basically accept Christian beliefs but think that Christianity went astray soon after the death of Jesus Christ. The lost authority was restored to Joseph Smith, the church's founder, to whom was revealed the Book of Mormon. The Book of Mormon is a supplement to, not a

replacement for, the Bible, and it was produced to give a deeper appreciation and understanding of God's truths as revealed in the Bible.

In the last two decades of their presence in Israel, the Mormons have converted six Christians and two Jews. When in 1984 permission was given to the Mormon Church-run Brigham Young University to build a school on 2½ hectares near the Hebrew University campus on Mount Scopus in Jerusalem, loud and often vicious protests were heard from Jews. They claimed that the development posed a dreadful threat to Judaism, due to Mormon missionary work. Hasidic Jews led the demonstrations and some wealthy American Jews offered to pay the Mormons several million dollars just to cancel their plans, in addition to buying their land.

The episode has highlighted the touchy subject of whether Israel regards itself as a secular state or a Jewish theocracy which attacks minority religions. Israeli politicians were genuinely exasperated by the religious conflict, although not necessarily for the right reasons. They felt that the religious Jews were wrong to harass the Mormons because the Mormons have been among Israel's strongest supporters in Washington. It was also pointed out that Jews could hardly plead for the freedom of Jewish education and lifestyles in the USSR whilst in Israel Christians are being suppressed.

Christian Zionism & the International Christian Embassy In 1980, when the Israeli Government confirmed that Jerusalem was to remain the capital of the Jewish State, 13 countries closed their embassies in the city in protest at the decision, transferring them to Tel Aviv. These events inspired a group of Christians already living in Israel to open and operate the International Christian Embassy Jerusalem (ICEJ) in the Holy City. Before the closure of the embassies they had already finalised plans for an international Christian celebration during the Feast of Tabernacles and so there were about 1000 Christians from 23 countries gathered in Jerusalem at an opportune moment. They felt that Israel had been unfairly abandoned by the world.

The Embassy's goals are to show concern for the Jewish people, especially for Israel, as inspired by Isaiah 40:1; to remind and encourage Christians to pray for Jerusalem and Israel; to provide an information centre for Christians where they can learn about current events; to begin or assist projects in Israel for the well-being of all, regardless of race, ethnic background or religion; and to be a reconciling influence between Arabs and Jews. The ICEJ does not claim to represent all Christians. It is an embassy in as much as it represents a nation of Christian Zionists who interpret the Bible (eg Romans II) as requiring support of the Jewish people and the modern state of Israel. In fact, one of its beliefs is that Israel's borders should rightly include the area which is now Jordan. Christian Zionists consider Islam's claim of Jerusalem as its third holiest site to be highly questionable. They argue that Muslims believe in the holiness of Jerusalem chiefly because Jews and Christians do and that in practice the city has religious significance to Islam only when it is threatened or occupied by non-Muslims. The ICEJ maintains that the Koran assures Muslims that the Jews would always be smitten and abased and could never rule over them (Sura II: The Cow verse 61); therefore Jerusalem's importance to the Islamic world is not that it is the site of Mohammed's flight to heaven but that its possession by Muslims symbolises the triumph over Judaism and Christianity. They also claim that many of the Islamic stories and legends about Jerusalem originally came from Jewish converts.

The creation of the ICEJ was an immense but pleasant surprise to most Jews and, in Israel in particular, it was welcomed with emotional gratitude.

The Druze

With its name derived from al-Darazi, one of the group's founders, the Druze religion has its roots in Ismailism, a religio-political movement in the 10th century. A similarly classified group themselves, the Druze are a difficult people to understand due to the nature of their faith, which they call *Din al-Tawhid*. It includes a belief in one supreme God operating in the world through a system of cosmic principles, periodic human manifestations of this God, and esoteric interpretations of the revealed religions whose prophets (eg Moses, Jesus and Mohammed) were the bearers of esoteric truth only. The inner meaning of these prophets' missions was secretly told to a select group of Druze by an incarnation of Jethro, Moses' father-in-law. The traditional site of his grave, near Hittim, in Galilee, is a place of pilgrimage for the Druze. They have few ceremonies or rituals, and only a small number of them are actually told what the faith is all about. Despite their roots in a form of Islam, the Druze are not Muslims.

Speaking Arabic and with similar lifestyles to the Arabs, the Druze have remained a separate community by their effective prohibition of inter-marriage, the non-admission of converts, a long history of armed conflict with the many rulers and rival groups over the years and a strong sense of group solidarity. Despite this, or maybe as a result, they are renowned for their hospitality to visitors.

Baha'ism

A world religion which has established its centre in Haifa, it is named after its founder Baha'u'llah (The Splendour of God). Baha'ism developed out of the Bahi, a Muslim mystical movement founded in Persia in 1844. It teaches that religious truth is progressive, not final; that the human race is educated by God through a series of prophets who have appeared throughout history and will always appear to guide the destinies of mankind. These have already included Moses, Zoroaster, Buddha, Jesus Christ, Mohammed and also Baha'u'llah. They apparently give the world the same fundamental teachings but reveal laws and principles designed to suit the requirements of the age in which they appear.

The aims and purposes of Baha'ism include upholding God's unity; recognising the unity of his prophets; teaching the sodality of all people, regardless of culture or race; urging either the creation or selection of an auxiliary international language; and declaring that the purpose of religion is to promote peace and friendship.

The inspiration for the Bahi faith, Sayyid Ali Mohammed, was born in Shiraz, Persia, circa 1820. Accused of heresy, he was arrested and shot in 1850 for his proclamation that he was the *Bab*, the Gate to the knowledge of divine truth. His body was secretly buried by his followers in Teheran. They suffered persecution and fled to Baghdad, from where the leaders were later exiled to Cyprus (1863). Mirza Husayn Ali, the stepbrother of the Bahi's successor, proclaimed himself to be the new Bab under the name of Baha'u'llah. He was then exiled again, to Adrionople (1864) and later to Akko, which he reached in 1868, accompanied by about 70 of his family followers. He turned the faith into a universalist ethical religion and in 1899 he organised the transfer of Ali Mohammed's body to Akko from Teheran. The Baha'u'llah died in 1892 and his tomb near Akko has become a shrine and, for the Baha'is, the holiest place in the world.

Abbas Effendi became the leader of the faith under the name of Abd al-Baha (the Servant of Baha). He transferred his residence to Haifa and visited North Africa, Europe and the USA to spread Baha'ism. He also arranged for the Bab's body to be interred in a shrine in Haifa on Mount Carmel. He died in 1921 and was interred in the same shrine.

Baha'ism has since developed worldwide. One of the largest Baha'i communities is in Iran, where they suffer harsh persecution. Membership of the faith is expanding rapidly in India (now with the largest Baha'i community), Africa, South East Asia, the Pacific region and amongst the South American Indians.

THE ARTS
Popular Music
The Israeli popular music scene is such that success in the awful Eurovision Song Contest is considered a major achievement. Things are currently on the way up, however, according to local experts. As with other areas of Israeli life, the army has made its mark here. Until the 1970s, talented musicians doing their army service produced variety shows for the armed forces. Nearly all of the established artists in Israel older than 25 made their start in this way. The IDF's Chief of Staff in the 1970s disbanded the entertainment unit but in the last few years it has been reformed and the process has begun again.

The biggest problems for Israeli musicians are the small home market and the struggle to penetrate abroad, where there is little demand for their Hebrew material (translation into English is often impractical).

In addition to standard western-style 'middle of the road' music, you can hear:

Oriental Known as 'bus station music' because its popularity sprang from pirate cassettes sold in the markets around Tel Aviv's central bus station. This style was popular for years amongst Jews from the Arab countries who used to buy the cassettes in large numbers (one cassette apparently sold half a million copies). The music caught on with soldiers who took it home, and now some of the most successful artists are from this section of the business.

Underground/New Wave Several young groups are now producing this style of music. *The Penguin* in Tel Aviv is probably the best venue to see them.

Jazz This has a hard-core following and there are some live venues, mainly in Tel Aviv (see Tel Aviv Entertainment section). The quality of the performances does vary but is often excellent.

Hasidic Rock Hasidic Jews have developed an interesting blend of musical styles well-worth listening to. Hasidic rock is usually described as a combination of East European gypsy music with American bluegrass. Often performed at festivals, it can be enjoyed more regularly in Jerusalem.

International Artists With the political situation as it is, Israel has not been a regular feature on world tours by big names, but this is slowly changing. The popular venues are Ha Yarkon Park and the Mann Auditorium in Tel Aviv, Sultan's Pool in Jerusalem and the Roman amphitheatre at Caesarea.

Classical Music
Israel has long been associated with excellent classical music. This really started in the 1930s when Jewish musicians, including the best of Europe's composers, performers and teachers fled to Palestine to escape Nazism. The Israel Philharmonic Orchestra and violinist Yitzhac Perlman are world-renowned, and there are many other musicians and groups worthy of note. The major orchestras and groups perform regularly, mainly by subscription, from October to July - visitors will not always find it easy to get tickets to these concerts. The most important venues are the Mann Auditorium in Tel Aviv and Jerusalem's Binyanei HaOomah. Cultural centres elsewhere

regularly host classical concerts, and the historic settings of Caesarea's Roman amphitheatre and Akko's Crusader castle are often used.

In 1986 the Nuyha/El-Hakawati Theatre in East Jerusalem produced the first-known Arabic operetta. Their music department teaches the use of traditional Arab instruments and incorporates a recording studio.

Cinema
Israeli cinema has enjoyed international critical acclaim with films such as *Runaway Train* and *Othello*, after commercial success with lower quality productions that kept such questionable talents as Chuck Norris fed and watered. *Missing in Action, Invasion USA* and *Delta Force* are part of a massive output, still expanding, in film and video production and in distribution and cinema ownership.

Film making in what is now Israel can be traced back to the beginning of the century, when Edison cameramen came to Jerusalem to shoot footage of the local inhabitants. A series of British and Hollywood productions filmed in Israel in the '50s and early '60s, such as *Exodus* and *Cast a Giant Shadow* provided a training ground for technicians and directors. The 1964 production *Shabtei* can be said to have signalled the emergence of Israel's own film industry. Since that time, the staple diet of Israeli cinema has been the *bourekas* film. The name derives from a pastry, and is given to low budget comedies using stereotyped characters lifted from Israel's diverse population. This has usually meant an emotional, lazy and vulgar Sephardi competing with a snobbish, humourless and dull Ashkenazi.

Alternatives to the bourekas films are those by the *Kayitz* film makers, who produce more serious films, often on subjects that are typically Israeli: the early Zionist pioneers, illegal immigration, the wars, espionage, etc. As with so many industries in Israel, the small home market presents a problem, and security problems make distributors abroad reluctant to book Israeli films.

Many travellers subsidise their stay in Israel by working as film extras. Note that the pay is low, but you are fed well and it can be fun (see Employment section).

ARCHITECTURE
An Historical Legacy
Palestine's successive invaders have left a range of architectural styles.

Roman Sites such as Herodian, Masada, Hammat Gader, Caesarea, Sebastiya and the renovated Citadel in Jerusalem's Old City attest to the Romans' centuries of rule. Herod the Great's reign saw a great deal of building activity.

Crusader Examples of the Crusaders' European-style castles and fortresses include the subterranean city at Akko, the fortress at Nimrod (with later additions by the Muslims), Monfort castle in the north, Belvoir fortress in the Jordan Valley and various additions in Jerusalem's Old City such as the Church of the Holy Sepulchre.

Muslim Undoubtedly the country's most impressive remains, these are dominated by minarets, domes and arches. Classic examples include mosques such as Jerusalem's Dome of the Rock and Akko's El-Jazzar, excavations around Jerusalem's Haram esh-Sharif, Hisham's Palace in Jericho, Tokan castle in Nablus, and the older buildings in Hebron's market place.

Mameluke With more ornamentation in the stone facades, this style is distinct from the earlier Muslim period. Jerusalem's Old City has the best examples anywhere – do not miss the Muslim Quarter and the Haram esh-Sharif.

Ottoman The lengthy rule of the Ottoman Empire was marked in Palestine by a lack

of productive activity, and the architectural field was no exception. However, a marvellous example of what they were capable of is Suleiman's city wall in Jerusalem. Akko also features notable examples of Ottoman workmanship.

Israeli Architecture
To have even a basic understanding of contemporary Israeli architecture, three facts are worth knowing:

1. Judaism prohibits the use of an image, sculpture or any other visual aid for religious practice.
2. The 2000 years of the Diaspora left the Jewish people with no architectural background, as they either tried to integrate into their local culture, or kept to themselves discreetly. Even when Jews started to renew settlement in Palestine in the 19th century, they used a mixture of architectural styles from the various parts of the world they had just left.
3. The modern history of Israel has been from the very beginning an extremely hard struggle against enormous odds, and aesthetic considerations in building design rated low.

Israeli architecture could be said to have begun in the 19th century, when new settlers combined the styles of their European backgrounds with Middle Eastern influences. Examples of this can be found in Jerusalem, in the rectangle marked by Prophet (Hanavi'im) St, Ethiopia St, Harav Shemu'el Salant St and B'nai B'rith St; and in particular the Swedish Theological Institute there. Mostly, though, this architecture tended to be simple, modest and far from noteworthy.

The establishment of new neighbourhoods outside the old cities began with the construction of Mishkanot Shananim, followed by Yemin Moshe in Jerusalem in 1858. They were built at the initiative of Sir Moses Montefiore and designed by an English architect, William Edmond

Smith. Marked by the windmill designed to be a working model but rendered useless by the lack of sufficient wind, the complex has recently been restored and is one of the city's more exclusive residential areas.

The architecture of the early 20th century was influenced by the 'international' style, which considers the location of a building to be irrelevent to its design, and the socialist vision of a planned society. These combined with the Zionist ideal of a new society free from the sicknesses of the old Europe left behind by the new immigrants. Ahuzat Bait, a neighbourhood on the outskirts of old Jaffa, built in 1909 to the pattern of a European garden city, is the earliest example of these influences.

The Bezalel School of Art was founded in Jerusalem to foster a Hebrew style derived from biblical and Islamic images. Bialik House, built in Tel Aviv in 1924, is one of the finest examples of the Neo-Eastern style. Although planned in the traditional European way, the flat, unembellished facades, a staircase emphasised by the dome tower and the wooden pergolas at the balconies, give the building its Neo-Eastern image. Recently restored, it is in Bialik St, in one of the city's more attractive neighbourhoods.

During the Mandate period, the British tried to restore local tradition by studying the informal patterning of Arab building styles in villages. The main post office in Jaffa Rd, Jerusalem, (1930s) was designed in a manner similar to many Islamic and English Gothic buildings, and the Rockefeller Museum (1920s) in East Jerusalem is modelled after Islamic palaces. The Scottish St Andrew's Hospice in Jerusalem (1927) shows the architect's interest in Armenian monastery styles.

Examples of the International style of the '30s include Weizmann House in Rehovot (1936), and Hadassah Hospital (1936-39) and the Shocken Library (1936) in Jerusalem. Socialist Zionism inspired the architecture and building styles of the day. Methods of mass production and the adaptation of building blocks to the land division system were used by contractors. Unfortunately the end result was usually dreary residential development projects.

Another major influence on the Jewish architects was the Bauhaus School from Germany, and today Tel Aviv has the best examples of this style anywhere in the world. On Frishman St is the Shikun Ovdim, the best known example of the workers' neighbourhood; in it the architect Arieh Sharan created comfortable and minimalist housing. Bauhaus styles can be found all over Tel Aviv, but for the purer examples look in the area around Allenby and King George Sts.

Architecture Since Independence

Israel's independence brought massive waves of immigrants, and much more housing was required for them. The centralisation of construction work under a single authority resulted in identical housing projects throughout the country. The architecture looked bureaucratic, with minimum standards for appearance and comfort and an emphasis on the low cost and speed of construction.

Without considering basic physical and demographic factors, about 20 new towns were built. This resulted in communities with severe economic and social problems. Major segments of the many neighbourhoods built in those years did not survive the 1970s without the need for rehabilitation.

These early plans were costly failures. The majority of the population is still concentrated in the three big cities and massive residential construction work continues around Jerusalem and Tel Aviv. Beersheba, the Negev's 'capital', was planned in the 1950s with anonymous blocks built in a park. This park is nothing but arid land as the planned greenery never grew satisfactorily.

Due mainly to the rejuvenating effects

of Israel's victory in the Six-Day War, prosperity came to the country and the need to economise on building costs was no longer a major consideration. A need to break away from the 1950s image of low standards was felt, along with a wish to create a new, positive architecture. Many projects were undertaken in this period, and as a result many inexperienced architects were employed. You can see their hideous creations in many central vantage points. A rare bright point from this period is the Israel Museum in Jerusalem, which integrates a modern building with mountainous topography. The imagery is loosely based on terraced Arab villages while the forms and construction are rooted in European modernism.

While much of modern Israeli architecture is ugly, you can find attractive buildings if you know where to look. In Tel Aviv, the IBM Israel building (corner of Weizman St and King Saul Blvd) and the adjacent Asia House are worth looking at, and the Wolfson Engineering Building at Tel Aviv University is the centre of much attention. The striking Faculty of Social Studies at Beersheba University was designed for protection from the barren Negev Desert.

Jerusalem's Architecture

Jerusalem, as you will discover, is like nowhere else on earth. Local Arab construction was the basis for architectural development at the turn of the century here. Later Jewish and Christian dwellings resembled the typical Arab Mediterranean styles. Houses were generally built around a large courtyard, often with surrounding walls. Check out the Sheikh Jarrah neighbourhood for great examples of the traditional styles. Hebron Rd, between Jerusalem and Bethlehem, also features some wonderful examples of Arab housing.

Jerusalem's Christian architecture, strongly influenced by Europe, is monumental, though sometimes disappointing. The many elaborate churches

certainly had an enormous impact on the local styles which had previously been dominated by narrow lanes and simple single- and two-storey buildings with small domes and narrow windows. The Catholics initially tended to concentrate outside the Jaffa Gate area, and their buildings were constructed in styles reminiscent of the Florentine Renaissance or the later Baroque. The classic example is the renovated Notre Dame complex opposite the New Gate.

The Russian Orthodox churches command their settings, both looking out on and being seen from the Old City. The Russian Compound and the Church of Mary Magdalene on the Mount of Olives are monumental in the Byzantine style.

Many Jewish settlers wanted to be self-sufficient and not dependent on charitable funds (the primary support of the Jewish population). This had an effect on the establishment of the new neighbourhoods in Jerusalem outside the Old City. Jewish building design of this period was greatly affected by archaeological research. A Swiss missionary and amateur archaeologist, Conrad Schick, designed many buildings in Jerusalem, including Mea Shearim and the beautiful Tabor House, now the Swedish Theological Institute.

Further examples of the city's outstanding buildings include the YMCA building at 26 King David St, which is elegant and imaginative, modern but also Moorish, Romanesque and Oriental. Opposite the YMCA is the King David Hotel, which was intended to be one of the world's great hotels. The exterior is somewhat over-shadowed by the YMCA but the interior has touches of Assyrian, Hittite and Phoenician styles. The Sherover Jerusalem Theatre was designed to appear as if it had grown naturally out of the hill on which it stands, merging with the connecting terraces to create one entire piece.

Architects who design buildings for Jerusalem are under immense pressure to try to integrate their structures with the city's traditional aura. Four distinctive elements are featured: the dome, the arch, cantilevered features and the use of stone. The last is enforced by law and goes back to the time of British rule.

In Jerusalem recently, renewal has been the order of the day, in particular in the Jewish Quarter of the Old City. Mostly destroyed by the Jordanians after the 1948 War of Independence, the reunification of Jerusalem after the Six-Day War has seen construction here on a massive scale. Planning principles included making use of traditional building techniques and preserving the existing texture of buildings and narrow alleyways; allowing only pedestrian traffic in the local alleyways and using electric vehicles for public services and deliveries; grouping buildings around communal courtyards, using stepped sections which allow air and light to enter lower floors and using roofs as terraces; and incorporating archaeological findings into the new buildings, eg the Cardo. Damascus Gate, the Old City's most ornate, is one of the renovation programme's great successes. Sultan's Pool, below the Old City to the west, is now an open-air amphitheatre and one of the country's top concert venues.

FASHION

Israel has a busy fashion industry, not without its problems, but managing to achieve impressive export sales. Swimwear is the country's most successful clothing export.

It shouldn't take long for you to notice that many Israeli Jews are extremely fashion conscious. Teenage sabras (Israel-born Jews) in particular can be seen parading the streets, beaches and discos, glancing at every surface in the hope of a reflection in which to check their outfits and hairstyles. The older generation of Jews are much less fashion conscious, often wearing styles reminiscent of their native countries. Arab men wear a mixture of traditional and contemporary

styles, the younger generation turning more towards western fashions. Arab women generally wear traditional clothes, although most do not cover their faces.

Despite the hot climate, the East European furriers and leather craftsmen manage to continue their business and Israel provides excellent quality with low prices.

Newe Tzedek, in Tel Aviv, is the centre of the country's fashion trade, crammed with workshops and showrooms. Designer boutiques are centred on the city's Yermiyahu St. A textiles and fashion centre has been established in Tel Aviv to provide a meeting place for buyers, manufacturers, suppliers and other interested parties.

FESTIVALS
Jewish

The most important day to be aware of is the Jewish Shabbat, starting every Friday at sunset and lasting until sunset on Saturday. It causes most of the country's facilities to come to a grinding halt. If you are not an observant Jew, ensure that on Friday you arrive somewhere where you can spend Shabbat doing something that is not affected by the lack of transport, shops, banks and eating places. With a bit of careful planning it is possible to get the most out of every day in Israel.

The Jewish festivals and celebrations understandably dominate the Israeli scene. Although the religious purposes of these festivals are intended only for the Jews, they have a meaning for everyone and have been adopted as national holidays by the mainly secular Jewish population. The festivals are supposed to remind Jews of their duty to God and to non-Jews, and play an important part in the building of the Kingdom of God where all people recognise God as the Father and love each other.

The Jewish calendar, not surprisingly, is complex. Based on a lunar year, it has 12 months which, now named, were initially just numbered. They are: Nisan, Iyyar,

Sivan, Tammuz, Av, Elul, Tishri, Heshvan, Kislev, Tevet, Shevat and Adar. Nisan is the first month of the year, although the New Year, marked by Rosh Ha-Shanah, occurs in Tishri, the seventh month (usually around September/ October). Rosh Ha-Shanah actually marks the world's creation, a different celebration from the first month of the year. The Jewish lunar year has 354 days, so a leap month called Adar II is added seven times in a 19-year cycle to keep the discrepancy with the solar year to a minimum.

Rosh Ha-Shanah Read Leviticus 23:24, Numbers 29:1 and Nehemiah 8:2-3. Rosh Ha-Shanah is one of the two days of the Jewish calendar known as Days of Judgement or Days of Awe. The other is Yom Kippur. On these days, Jews are called upon to account to God. Purely religious in character, they are mainly celebrated in the synagogue. As for all Jewish holidays, prayer services begin the eve of the holiday and in the case of Rosh Ha-Shanah continue for two days. A special feature during the prayers is the blowing of the shofar, to remind Jews to obey God's command.

Characteristic foods eaten on Rosh Ha-Shanah include pomegranates, over which the blessing of the first fruits of the New Year is recited; apples dipped in honey or other honeyed foods to augur a sweet year; and tongue or fish heads to mark the 'head of the year', a direct translation of Rosh Ha-Shanah.

Yom Kippur Read Leviticus 16:30-31, 23:27-28, 31-32, and Numbers 29:7. Known as the Day of Atonement, it occurs on the 10th of Tishri and ends the 10 days of penitence which begin on New Year's Day. For the observant, Yom Kippur means 25 hours of complete abstinence from food, drink, sex, cosmetics (including soap and toothpaste) and animal products. The time is spent in prayer and contemplation and sins are confessed. It is the only Jewish holiday that is equivalent to Shabbat in sanctity.

This is the day where virtually everything under Jewish control comes to a stop. Children play in the empty roads, and there is no TV or radio – *everything* is closed for the day.

Sukkot & Simhat Torah Read Exodus 34:22, Numbers 28:26, Leviticus 23:34 and 36 and Deuteronomy 16:9-10 and 13. The Feast of Tabernacles and Rejoicing in the Law are celebrated in the month of Tishri (15-23). The Festival of Sukkot has both religious and cultural significance. Most Jews, religious or not, live for seven days in home-made sukkot (shelters), to remind them of the Israelites living in the wilderness after the exodus. The sukkot can be erected on the balconies of apartments and houses, in gardens and even in hotels and restaurants. The major requirement is that the roof is made only of leafy branches to enable the sky to be seen. The agricultural significance is symbolised by the 'four species' used – the palm branch, the myrtle, the willow and the citron or *etrog*. Special blessings are recited on each of these items during the holiday.

The eighth day of the Feast of Tabernacles is Simhat Torah, Rejoicing in the Law. The cycle of reading the Torah in the synagogues has just been completed and another is immediately begun, after the scrolls have been carried around the congregation in seven encirclements (*hakafot*) accompanied by singing and dancing. In Jerusalem it is great to see the *yeshiva* (religious school) students dancing towards the Western Wall carrying the Torah Scrolls. It has become the custom to hold public 'Second Hakafot' programmes on the night following Simat Torah. These are held in parks and squares with music and dancing. Check the IGTO for information.

Hanukkah Read 1 Maccabees 4:52-59, Talmud B, Shabbat 21b from the Talmud.

They tell of the eight days, starting with the 25th day of Kislev, when there is neither mourning nor fasting. Also known as the Festival of Lights, Hanukkah celebrates the triumphant Maccabaean revolt. Its symbol is the menorah, and one of its candles is lit each night. A nice part about Hanukkah is that it has inspired a tradition of eating jam (jelly) doughnuts for a week.

The 15th of Shevat (Tu b'Shevat) The Mishnah dedicated this as the New Year for Trees and it is customary to eat fruit and nuts, in particular the carob fruit. Since independence, the day has been observed as a time for tree-planting.

Purim Read the Book of Esther. Celebrated on the 14th day of Adar, Purim, the Feast of Lots, recalls the story about hunger for power, and the hatred born of the Jews' refusal to assimilate and their unwillingness to compromise religious principle by bowing before the secular authority. Despite such a serious, if highly relevant, theme, the holiday has a carnival atmosphere and can be great fun to participate in. Fancy dress is the order of the day. During the day the streets and buses are filled with proud parents taking Superman, Madonna, Michael Jackson and Rambo to and from school and the shops, while in the evening French tarts, fairies, gangsters, etc are to be seen.

Israel is a nation of non-drinkers, and Purim is their chance to make up for it. Jews are traditionally required to get so drunk that they cannot distinguish between the words 'bless Mordechai' and 'curse Haman'. The most popular of the Purim foods are Haman's Ears, or *Oznei Haman*. A fried, three-cornered pastry filled with apricots or other fruits and covered in poppy seeds, it is supposed to look like Haman's ears.

Pesah Read Exodus 12:17-18, 12:24, 26-27, 34:18. This, the Feast of Passover, is celebrated throughout the Jewish world during the month of Nisan. It recalls and relives the events in the history of the Jews in Egypt and their exodus, led by Moses. Lasting a full week, Pesah results in most of the Jewish stores (including foodstores and markets) being closed or opened for limited hours. Public transport is affected and grinds to a halt on the first and last days of the festival, no regular bread is made by Jewish bakers, and the only brewery in the country stops production.

The holiday commences with the Seder meal on the eve of the festival. During this first meal, the story of the Passover is read. Special foods are served. For example, Ashkenazim exclude rice, while Sephardim make a point of including it. *Matzah* (unleavened bread) is the principal ingredient for all Pesah dishes, as it is forbidden to eat, and even to keep, leavened products in Jewish households at this time. Jerusalem is a good place to be to see the Priests' blessings at the Western Wall during the mornings of the intermediate days of Pesah. Hundreds of white-clad *cohenim* (priests) participate.

The Samaritans celebrate their version of Pesah on Mt Gerizim near Nablus. To them this is the authentic Mt Sinai as well as the site of Abraham's sacrifice of his son, Isaac. Here they sacrifice a lamb, watched by a crowd of onlookers, as they have done for over 2500 years.

Holocaust Day (Yom Ha-Sho'ah) The 27th day of Nisan was set aside in 1951 as a day of mourning for the Holocaust victims. The occasion also serves as a reminder of the potential for similar evils to recur. Throughout Israel on this day, sirens blast to begin a period of respectful silence. It is an effective symbol, with traffic stopping, drivers and passengers getting out of their vehicles to stand to attention. On the beaches, in shops, offices, and factories and on the kibbutzim and in the streets, everything stops. Quite an experience.

Mimouna This festival takes place on the day after the last day of Pesah and has been celebrated by the North African Jewish communities for generations. In the last few years it has been reinstated to become a popular fixture on the Israeli calendar. Mimouna's exact origins are unknown. One theory is that it is an Arabisation of the Hebrew word *emunah*, meaning faith, or belief, in the coming of the Messiah and the redemption of the Jews. Certainly the theme of Mimouna is confidence in God and patience in awaiting the Messiah. It is a marvellous chance for you to experience Israeli hospitality, which traditionally excels itself on this occasion. All over the country North African Jews organise street parties and open-house celebrations. Foreigners – Jews and non-Jews alike – are warmly invited to join in. Check the IGTO for the local arrangements wherever you are. Tel Aviv's Hayarkon Park is always packed out with revellers. The festival has always symbolised friendship and brotherhood – try not to miss it.

Independence Day (Yom Ha-Atsuma'ut) On the fifth day of Iyyar (14 May) 1948 Israel became an independent state and since then the day has been celebrated by Jews worldwide. In Israel this is done with parades, concerts, picnics and fireworks all over the country.

Lag B'Omer This is a particularly joyous occasion for the Hasidim who, to many people's surprise, do know how to laugh, sing, dance and have a good time. It takes place on the 18th day of Iyyar and comes after 33 days of mourning. A special day of celebration for all Jews, it is interpreted as a rite of spring or as the day when a plague was lifted in Jewish history. Outings and bonfires are a feature of the proceedings.

The Hasidim really go to town, or rather they leave it to head north. Thousands of them pour into Meiron, up near Safed in Galilee. There is a parade ending in torchlight with singing and dancing along the way. On arrival at Meiron candles are burned on the tomb of Rabbi Shamon and

a giant bonfire is lit. Some of the Hasidim throw their clothes onto the fire and the festivities go on all night. In the morning, three-year-old boys are given their first haircuts, and the hair is thrown onto the fire.

What's it all about? For over 1700 years the site has been holy to religious Jews. When the Romans conquered Jerusalem in the second century, the Jews fled to the area around Meiron. One of them, Shimon Bar Yochai, continued to defy the Romans and was forced to hide permanently in a cave in Peqi'in nearby. There he supposedly wrote the Book of Splendour, the bible of the Kabbalists (mystic Jews).

The enthusiastic pilgrimage serves partly to recall the teachings of the Torah and celebrate it as a gift from God. The act of cutting young boys' hair and throwing it on the fire is called Halaka (Arabic for 'shaving'). This is a variation of the ancient Israelite practice, based on Deuteronomy 18:4, of offering the first fleece of a sheep to the priest.

Shavuot Read Exodus 34:22, Numbers 28:26 and Deuteronomy 16:9-10. This is the Jewish celebration of Pentecost, the Feast of Weeks. A happy harvest event, it occurs on the sixth day of Sivan and can be a particular highlight on kibbutzim and moshavim. It is often marked by plays; people dress in white clothes and eat dairy foods. In the time of the Temple, the first crop of the year would be taken there and destroyed with fire.

Fast of 17th of Tammuz This particular day marks the Roman destruction of Jerusalem's city walls and observant Jews fast during the daylight hours.

Fast of Ninth of Av (Tishah be-Av) This day is set aside to remember the destruction of the First and Second Temples. If you are in Jerusalem, check out the packed Western Wall.

15th of Av This is the Day of Love and, according to the Mishnah, the happiest day of the year. Tradition states that the woodcutters used to return to Jerusalem after working in the fields, and girls, dressed in white, would be waiting for a proposal of marriage.

Black Hebrews

Down in Dimona, you are welcome to join in the community's various celebrations during the year.

Day of Appreciation & Love On this day, around the end of February, the Hebrews set aside the time specifically to show love to one another and to exchange gifts. They celebrate in style with their own music and singers, they all dress up in fancy clothes and there's plenty to eat, especially in the way of sweets and cakes. They also enjoy their own wine.

New World Passover During May the Hebrews celebrate the second exodus from a land of captivity, when they left the USA to return to Africa. This occasion lasts for two days. On the first day they go for a picnic and have a sports event called the *Rockameera* (Merry) Games. On the second day the children perform a presentation for the adults.

Sisters' Day On this occasion in June, the women of the community display their creations in the way of fine clothes, handicrafts and vegetarian food. They perform plays and organise forums, which the men attend while also taking care of the housework and minding the children for the day.

Brothers' Day The following week, the men show what they can do. Some great jewellery, shoes and clothes are made by them.

Youth Day At the end of August the kids take over and put on a show.

Prince of Peace Music Festival Here the Hebrews celebrate with music. They play a variety of soul, jazz/funk and gospel styles, much of which they write themselves.

Quintessence Night This is an evening, in November or December, for the family to be together. Candlelight and music help create an atmosphere of love and unity and together they praise God.

Muslim

The Muslim festivals are observed with some solemnity although there are occasions of joy and happiness. The pleasure of Allah is the corner-stone of all Islamic activity and there is no concept of a festival for pleasure's own sake. Apparently the happiest occasion of a Muslim's life is to see the sovereignty of Allah established in his land. Islamic festivals are observed according to the Islamic Calendar which is based on lunar months.

The Birth of the Prophet Mohammed's birthday and a day of thanks and praise to Allah.

Lailatul Miraj This remembers the night Mohammed ascended to heaven from the Temple Mount in Jerusalem.

Ramadan For non-Muslim visitors, the major effect of this month long dawn-to-sunset fast is that the less commercial Muslim Arab areas are very quiet, with business closed. After dark, though, things liven up everywhere and the Arabs seem to be up all hours.

Idul Fitr This day is observed at the end of Ramadan. Muslims express their joy at the end of their fast by offering a congregational prayer, preferably in an open field. They should express their gratitude to Allah for enabling them to observe the fast, thus preparing them for life as a Muslim. Special dishes are prepared and it is customary to visit relatives and friends, to go out for a day trip and to give presents to children. Everyone eats a great deal.

Idul Adha Idul Adha begins on the 10th of Dulil Hijja, its most important day, and continues until the 12th day of the month. It commemorates the occasion when Allah asked Abraham to sacrifice his son, Ishmael. A lamb was sacrificed instead of the boy after Abraham had shown his readiness to obey Allah. Today Muslims offer congregational prayer on the day and follow it with a sacrifice mainly of sheep, but also goats, cows and camels. The meat of the sacrificed animal is given to needy people and to older relatives. Clothes and money are sometimes given, too.

New Year's Hejira This day recalls the migration of the prophet, Mohammed, from Mecca to Medina.

Christian

Visitors with a Christian background will often find the festivals celebrated very differently from the way they are used to. This is largely due to the domination of the unfamiliar Orthodox Churches and also the fact that Christianity is very much in third place in the religious stakes here. Christmas Day, for example (ignoring the fact, just for a moment, that it is celebrated on three separate occasions by the various denominations), is just another day for most people. Even in Jerusalem there are no highly visible signs of the great event, such as decorated trees or street lights. Simply being there is the key for most pilgrims.

Christmas Day Apart from 25 December, Christmas is celebrated on 7 January by the Orthodox and on 19 January by the Armenians. The place to go is Bethlehem for the Midnight Mass on Christmas Eve. Due to the popularity of the service, space inside the Church of the Nativity is reserved for observant Catholics. Outside in Manger Square there is a large crowd watching a Protestant choir concert with participants from around the world. The actual Midnight Mass is shown on a large video screen affixed to the police station in the square and is also broadcast around the world. It can be an extremely cold night, so do wrap up.

During the day on Christmas Eve there is a traditional procession from Jerusalem's Old City to Bethlehem. Admission into the Midnight Mass service on Christmas Eve is by ticket only. These are free and can be applied for at the Terra Sancta office in the Christian Information Centre, Old City, Jerusalem. Extra buses are arranged to cater to the crowds travelling between Jerusalem and Bethlehem. These buses run irregularly all night.

Easter Celebrated first by the Roman Catholics and the Protestants and then about two weeks later by the Orthodox Church. The Church of the Holy Sepulchre and the Via Dolorosa are the centre of events for both occasions. The Orthodox celebrations are responsible for Jerusalem's Old City being packed out with pilgrims, mainly black-clad senior citizens from Greece and Cyprus. These devout Christians are extremely keen to celebrate Easter in Jerusalem and can be seen wandering around, carrying their fold-up stools used when waiting for hours to ensure a good spot for the services, some of which are outside. Note that the same pilgrims fill many of the cheap hostels in the Old City for the weeks of Easter celebration.

Celebration of the Baptism of Jesus Christ The traditional site where John the Baptist baptised Jesus Christ is on the west bank of the Jordan River, a few km from Jericho. The area has long been off-limits for security reasons and a baptism site further up river was provided near the Sea of Galilee at Kibbutz Degania.

However, the Roman Catholics have recently been able to organise a special celebration at the revered site on the first Sunday of October. Contact the Christian Information Centre in Jerusalem for details, including transport arrangements.

Armenian Holocaust Day Every year on 24 April the Armenians commemorate their overlooked tragedy with a parade and service in Jerusalem's Old City.

Festivals & Holidays Summary

January
Epiphany (6th)
Christmas Day, Orthodox (7th)
Christmas Day, Armenian (19th)
January-February
15th of Shevat
February
Day of Appreciation & Love, Black Hebrews
February-March
Purim
March
Annunciation (25th)
March-April-May
Pesah
Easter
Mimouna
Holocaust Day
April
Holocaust Day, Armenian (24th)
April-May
Independence Day
May
Lag B'Omer
New World Passover, Black Hebrews
Ascension (8th)
Pentecost (18th)
May-June
Shavuot
June
Ramadan
Idul Fitr
Sisters' Day, Black Hebrews
June-July
Fast of 17th Tammuz
July-August
Fast of 9th of Av
15th of Av
August
Idul Adha
Brothers' Day, Black Hebrews

Dormition – Assumption
Youth Day, Black Hebrews
September
New Year's Hejira
Prince of Peace Music Festival, Black Hebrews
September-October
Rosh Ha-Shanah
Yom Kippur
October
Sukkot
Simhat Torah
November-December
Quintessence, Black Hebrews
Birthday of the Prophet Mohammed
December
Christmas Day (25th)
December-January
Hanukkah

THE KIBBUTZ

Probably the most widely known Hebrew word, a kibbutz is a community of people who live together collectively on the basis of shared ownership of the means of production, shared consumption and no direct connection between work and remuneration. Each family has its own apartment but all meals are taken together in a communal dining hall. Kibbutzim vary in size, from up to 100 members to as many as 2000. Most consist of between 300 to 800 members. Most of the kibbutzim are in the north, where the movement began.

Each kibbutz is an independent legal, social and economic entity. It is run by the general assembly, made up of all the members. This meets once a week, usually on Saturday evenings. Some large kibbutzim call general assembly meetings less frequently and use a council of 30 to 40 members for intermediate decisions. The kibbutz secretary is the highest official.

In 1927 the cultivated area of kibbutzim was less than 50 square km, of which less than 2.5 square km were under irrigation. By 1981 the cultivated area had grown to over 1500 square km, with half under irrigation. The efficiency of kibbutz agriculture is much talked about, both in Israel and abroad, and it is calculated that by the year 2000 the kibbutzim will supply over half of all the country's agricultural produce.

Today, almost every kibbutz has at least one factory, and some have three or four.

There are currently 273 kibbutzim in the kibbutz movement which is divided into several organisations along political and ideological lines. The largest component is the Labor Party-affiliated United Kibbutz Movement, with 168 kibbutzim, popularly known by its abbreviated Hebrew name Takam. The next largest is the Kibbutz Artzi, with 85 kibbutzim. It is associated with the worldwide Hashomer Hatzair Youth Movement and the left-wing Mapam and has a more strict Marxist ideology. In third place numerically are the 17 religious kibbutzim of Po'el Hamizrachi, better known as Kibbutz Dati. There are also two kibbutzim belonging to the ultra-orthodox Po'el Agudat Israel, and one belonging to Ha'ihud hahaqla'i.

History

The kibbutz movement started in Russia at the turn of the century and was inspired by Marx, Engels and, later, the Russian Revolution. Before coming to Palestine the would-be kibbutzniks got together in camps to establish a system. The early kibbutzim were strictly secular and committed to the ideal of a return to the land.

Kibbutz Degania, founded in 1910 beside the Jordan River and close to the Sea of Galilee, was the first. The early kibbutz members had to cope with extremely harsh conditions with virtually no money. Galilee at that time was dominated by malarial swamps, not the trees you see now, and kibbutz life was nothing like as organised as it is today. Right from the start there was a continuing debate about the right direction for these new communes. Some members wanted to stay as small, primarily agricultural and self-sufficient units, while others wanted to grow, include industry and integrate into a national political and economic organisation. These strong differences of opinion remain today.

The arrival in the 1930s of refugees from Nazism interrupted the debate, as the kibbutzim became absorption centres. As the Zionist leaders drew up plans for a Jewish State amidst rumours of a British partition plan for Palestine, the need to expand Jewish settlement in the country was recognised. The Negev was seen as an important area and dozens of new kibbutzim were established in remote areas. The violent reaction of the local Arabs to these new Jewish settlements inspired the formation of the Palmach, a commando-style strike force and a forerunner of the IDF.

To this day, a disproportionately large number of personnel in the officer corps, air force and commando units are kibbutz members. Similarly, this intense involvement in preparing the way for the State of Israel brought widespread participation in politics, and a disproportionately large number of Knesset members and ministers are kibbutz members.

The establishment of Israel meant transferring many responsibilities from the kibbutzim to the new government. Eventually, the progress made by the kibbutzim in agriculture led them to move into industry with the spare labour that this progress had created. By 1984, kibbutz agriculture formed 40% of the national production. Since the 1960s the 'kibbutz industrial revolution' has caused many major changes in lifestyles and economic activities. Several kibbutzim now earn most of their incomes from industry, not agriculture.

The Kibbutz Members (Kibbutzniks)

Kibbutz members represent less than 3% of Israel's population, although in rural areas they often form a third of the local inhabitants. Most of the early kibbutz members were from Eastern and Central

Europe, but today the vast majority is Israeli-born – to a greater degree than the Israeli population as a whole. Most of the arrivals over the years have come from Europe, the Americas, South Africa and Australia.

The kibbutz population is generally younger than the rest of the Jewish population, as kibbutz families have more children than others, and there is a greater absorption of young people from outside. The ratio of applicants to places available on kibbutzim varies enormously. This places the movement in a dilemma, having to decide whether to increase its growth rate by building more housing and absorbing more outsiders, which could cause financial problems, or by relying on reproduction.

The traditional family, two parents and their children, is a passing phenomenon in kibbutzim. By the time a kibbutz is 50 years old, multi-generational families are well established. Children grow up alongside grandparents and other senior relatives, not just their own parents. These complex multi-generational links are a key factor in guaranteeing communal solidarity and continuity. Close to 90% of kibbutz members live in communities that have reached at least their third generation and in which this multi-generational family style is typical.

Education & Culture

The kibbutzim have their own educational system within the framework of the national Ministry of Education, ranging from kindergarten to university level. All children born the same year are raised and educated together from the babies' house to the end of high school. Most also go on to higher education. It used to be that all children slept in separate children's quarters from their parents, but there has been a move towards having children up to high school age sleep with their parents.

Two large adult education centres have been established to cater for a wide range of the kibbutz movement's needs. A third specialises in economics, management, technology and agriculture.

It appears that the kibbutz way of life, free from most of the everyday worries about prices and income, encourages the creative energies of kibbutzniks, as the kibbutz movement's cultural productivity is impressive. This includes two orchestras, two internationally known choral groups, a dance group, a theatre group, hundreds of authors, poets, singers, composers and musicians, about 600 recognised artists and sculptors, and more recently a growing number of writers, producers, directors, camera-operators and technicians specialising in video films for television. There are four nationally distributed literary journals as well as other periodicals, including literary works, published by the movement. It owns two of Israel's leading publishing houses and is involved in a third. There are two central art galleries in the Tel Aviv area for kibbutz artists, and another four in kibbutzim. More than 70 museums have been established in kibbutzim, often specialising in the archaeology of the local area where members have taken part in excavations.

THE MOSHAV

The moshav is a co-operative village, featuring aspects of both private and collective farming. Families have their own homes, children live with their parents, and these families have individual plots of land and budgets. Capital items such as machinery are owned by the moshav, which also markets the produce and buys supplies collectively to get a better price. Approximately 5% of Israel's population live on moshavim, mainly in the Arava Valley, Jordan Valley and Negev (near Gaza), with a few on the coastal strip between Tel Aviv and Haifa, and near the Sea of Galilee.

The moshav movement began in 1921, as a blending of the ideals of the kibbutz movement with those of earlier, failed attempts at Jewish settler farming. The five principles of the moshav movement were:

1. The land belongs to the nation, not to the individual.
2. Mutual aid – members help one another, especially in developing years and when someone is sick. Today what is more important is teaming up to secure a better deal with banks and credit companies as a collective.
3. You work by yourself. This principle was followed for the first 25 years or so, but mass immigration changed all that. Most newcomers had no real farming experience and could not fit into the collective or the kibbutz system. Large numbers of the new immigrants had little choice in where they were sent, and the new country needed to develop the land, so they became farmers. The B'nai HaMoshavim (Sons of the Moshavim) organisation was set up as a result. This group of agricultural experts trained and led the newcomers but their systems did not aspire to the original moshav ideals, working well as farms but not as collectives. They often employ Arabs and foreign volunteers as cheap labour to work the land whilst they work elsewhere.
4. A collective system for selling.
5. Land and water is shared equally by the members.

Today there are over 400 moshavim in Israel. About 20 of these are collective moshavim, with some aspects similar to a kibbutz. There is no private land and no communal dining room; members have their own living quarters but all the production and income belongs to the community with profits equally divided.

As in the kibbutz movement, there has been an increase, though less dramatic, in industrial activity in the moshavim as agriculture has proved to be an insufficient means of support. The moshavim do not organise their own schools, or have as much of a community-based lifestyle as kibbutzim do.

KIBBUTZ & MOSHAV VOLUNTEERING

Many people automatically associate a visit to Israel with a spell as a kibbutz or moshav volunteer. Certainly each year sees thousands of young people from all over the world descending on the Holy Land for the experience. In reality, life as a kibbutz or moshav volunteer is often clouded by inaccurate images presented by recruitment organisations, many of which (especially those dealing with moshavim), seem to be motivated more by making a fast buck than developing the flow of milk and honey. Also, former volunteers often forget the realities of hard and/or boring work, indifferent and/or unfriendly kibbutzniks and moshavniks and other negative factors, and only talk about the more enjoyable aspects of a volunteer's life.

This results in many people arriving as volunteers and being disappointed with what they find. Before committing yourself to a volunteer programme you should study carefully what it actually involves. When it comes down to discussing which kibbutzim or moshavim are the 'best', it is difficult to recommend individual sites. Location and the type of work carried out are often less important factors than the volunteers you work with, the kibbutzniks you work for and your relationships with them. What might be a fantastic place for one volunteer may well be a living hell for another.

The kibbutz movement has changed considerably from the early days and one of those changes is the system of volunteers itself. To be accepted as a kibbutz volunteer you need to be 18 to 32, in good physical and mental health, and you will be expected to work hard eight hours a day, six days a week at whatever job is assigned to you.

Every kibbutz has agriculture as its main activity but most now have some form of light industry too. Volunteers nowadays find themselves working on production lines in factories as well as picking fruit. Another possibility is working in the services, that is the dining room, kitchen or laundry. Working with the kibbutz children is not so common because of the language barrier.

Volunteers are accommodated in separate quarters from the kibbutzniks, two or four to a room. The conditions do vary and some are extremely pleasant. Most, however, are old and/or have been poorly treated over the years by a succession of bored, frustrated and drunk volunteers.

In effect, volunteers work for their keep. The kibbutz provides the basic needs – meals, accommodation, basic toilet requisites, stationery, postage stamps, cigarettes and a small personal allowance (about US$20 per month). The facilities of the kibbutz are more or less available for volunteers to enjoy. These normally include a swimming pool and a variety of other sports facilities, a library and a cinema. The best parts of kibbutz volunteering can be the kibbutz-organised trips. These are part of the deal for volunteers and the kibbutz takes them to interesting sites around the country, often including places that most visitors would not get to see.

One of the kibbutzniks has the job of volunteer leader, and he/she is basically in charge of the volunteers, organising their work schedules, days off and leisure activities, and dealing with any problems that arise.

There is often considerable friction between volunteers and their host communities. The volunteers are there for a variety of reasons, many of which do not endear themselves to the locals. Some have come for a 'working holiday' but dislike the fact that the emphasis is more on the work aspect. Many volunteers have to start work as early as 3.30 am. Six eight-hour working days a week can be demanding, especially on those who have never done such constant manual work before or who came out to Israel expecting to be able to spend more time lying in the sun as opposed to labouring under it.

However it is boredom, rather than exhaustion, which becomes a common characteristic of the working day.

Another preconceived idea about kibbutz volunteering is that it enables you to see Israel. It doesn't. With only one day off a week plus three more per month, you will need to be on a kibbutz for several months before you get to see a significant amount of the country. Being in the countryside, kibbutzim do not make ideal tour bases, anyway. The allowance is often insufficient to pay for the drinks and extra food that are normally required on kibbutz, much less the transport, food and accommodation that has to be paid for if you leave the kibbutz on days off. A small number of volunteers are attracted by the socialist ideals of the movement and they too are often disappointed by what they find. Many volunteers are here because the alternative that they face is either poorly paid work back home, or no job at all. The vast majority of volunteers are teenagers experiencing their first time away from their own country, if not from home. No doubt the large number of young people, unsupervised for perhaps the first time, with access to alcohol and the opposite sex, and isolated from other diversions, are the main factors contributing to the volunteers' unofficial battlecry of 'hedonism rules OK'.

This is how volunteers are seen by most of the kibbutzniks, and with volunteers arriving and leaving constantly there is little motivation for the kibbutzniks to open up and be super-friendly. A volunteer usually has to prove his/her efficiency at work over a period of months rather than days or weeks to win them over. Those volunteers who are fully committed may still have problems because many of them form close relationships with kibbutzniks. The threat of intermarriage and the possibility of the couple leaving the kibbutz are enough to upset most kibbutz members.

Most volunteers do enjoy their time on kibbutzim, but would agree that it turned out to be a lot different than they had expected. Their reasons for enjoying it would probably convince kibbutzniks that they are right to be cautious about welcoming volunteers with open arms. Some kibbutzim have scrapped the volunteer programme, and there has been talk of it being scrapped everywhere. This would be highly unlikely, if only because volunteers tend to be responsible for the more unpleasant menial tasks which would not appeal to a lot of kibbutzniks these days.

There are basically four ways to go about becoming a volunteer. The first two involve contacting a kibbutz representative office in your own country. You can either join a group of about 15 people or travel as an individual. The groups fly out to Israel together, are met at Ben Gurion Airport and taken directly to the kibbutz. They normally stay on kibbutz for three months and will have had an opportunity to meet one another and hear about their kibbutz before flying out.

If you travel as an individual you do not have to arrive on a pre-set date like the group, but within a month of your allocation. You are given instructions on how to reach the Tel Aviv Kibbutz Office and a letter of introduction guaranteeing you a place. As an individual you are not met at the airport in Israel and you will not necessarily get a place on a kibbutz immediately; you may have to wait more than a day or two. You also have to pay for your own accommodation, food and travel expenses whilst waiting in Tel Aviv for placement. Try not to arrive in Israel on a Friday, Saturday or just before a Jewish festival to avoid having to wait for the kibbutz office to open.

A basic registration fee is charged (about US$35). You will usually find that the price charged by the kibbutz representatives for the air fare to Israel is more than you would pay if you shopped around yourself. If you choose to join a group you have no option but to fly with them, but as an individual you can

register and then make your own travel arrangements. To find out more, contact your nearest kibbutz representative's office:

Australia
Habonim, 1 Sinclair St, Elsternwick, Victoria 3185
Belgium
Bureau de Volontaires, 68 Ave Ducpetiaux, 1060 Bruxelles (tel 02-538 1050)
Canada
Kibbutz Aliya Desk, 1000 Finch Ave West, Downsview, Ontario MSJ 2E7
France
Agence Juive, Kibbutz Desk, 17 Rue Fortuny, Paris 17
Holland
Volunteers Desk, John Veermeerstr 22, Amsterdam
UK
Kibbutz Representatives, 1A Accommodation Rd, London NW11
Project 67, 36 Great Russell St, London WC1B 3PP (tel 01-636 1262)
Kibbutz Representatives, Harold House, Dunbabin Rd, Liverpool (tel 051-722 5671)
Kibbutz Representatives, 11 Upper Park Rd, Salford 7, Manchester (tel 061-795 9447)
Kibbutz Representatives, 43 Queen's Square, Glasgow S1 (tel 041-423 7379)
USA
Kibbutz Aliya Desk, 27 West 20th St, New York, NY 10011 (tel 212 255-1338)
New Zealand
Wellington Jewish Community, POB 27-156, Wellington 1

You can make your own way to the Kibbutz Offices in Tel Aviv to apply there in person for a place. The movement is not too keen on prospective volunteers doing this as they prefer to have everything prearranged. However, as only a few people do it this way there is a good chance of your application being successful. This is dependent not only on there actually being a space for you, but on your being able to convince the kibbutz officials that you are not going to live up to the poor image that the volunteers suffer from amongst kibbutzniks. If you are British, your chances of being accepted this way are virtually non-existent due to the large number of young Brits proving to be unable to work, rest and play. Applicants from Australia and New Zealand will have no problem as they enjoy a good reputation. There are three offices in Tel Aviv to apply to:

United Kibbutz Movement (tel 03-5452555), 10 Dubonov St, Tel Aviv. Side entrance, slightly concealed; take bus No 4 from central bus station to Ben-Yehuda St (El Al Building).
Kibbutz Artzi (tel 03-435222), 13 Leonardo de Vinci St, Tel Aviv. Take bus No 70 from central bus station (on opposite side of Petah Tiqwa St).
Kibbutz Dati (tel 03-257231), 7 Dubnov St, Tel Aviv. Only Jews accepted here, with some religious observance required.

You may have to wait a few days before an opening comes up, even if you are accepted. On the other hand, it is not unusual for kibbutz representatives abroad to be telling applicants that there are no places whilst in Israel the kibbutzim are crying out for volunteers.

The final way to become a volunteer is to apply directly to an individual kibbutz. This is not normally possible but can be done, for example if there is a desperate need for volunteers due to a crop harvest or if you have a friend who is a volunteer already and can pull a few strings with the volunteer leader.

Moshav Volunteers
Moshav volunteers need to be aged 18 to 35 and be prepared to stay on a moshav for at least five weeks. A moshav volunteer is normally assigned to an individual farmer, although some do work for more than one, according to their needs. Most volunteers are provided with separate accommodation, usually shared with other volunteers and of comparable

quality with kibbutz volunteers' quarters. A few live with the moshavniks. Most volunteers provide their own meals, rather than eating with their farmer and his family. They are paid US$260 per month for an eight-hour day, six-day working week. Overtime is often available although complaints about farmers not paying for overtime and worked days-off are not uncommon. If food is provided, the volunteers' pay is approximately halved.

A fair number of volunteers soon leave a moshav, finding the work too hard and underpaid. Those who do stick it out often look back fondly at their time spent down on the farm, despite the conditions.

The major differences between being a volunteer on a moshav as opposed to kibbutz are that the work is generally much harder and you can have more of a chance to save some money (although it is not easy for most volunteers), to do more interesting and less menial tasks (not always possible though) or to be alone, if that is what you want. Relations between volunteers and moshavniks are just as strained as those on kibbutzim. Most moshav volunteers seem to be attracted by the potential, or the urgent need, to earn some money, and many are unaware of the sometimes harsh conditions that they are letting themselves in for and the difficulties involved in saving money here. The isolation of farming communities and the lack of social activities again contribute to the pressure on volunteers to spend the small amount of money earned on drink.

There are three ways to join a moshav as a volunteer. In some countries there are moshav representatives who make arrangements for individuals. However it makes sense for prospective volunteers to make their own way to Tel Aviv, sometimes saving the best part of US$60 on what a moshav representative would charge for their services and the airfare. The official moshav movement's office is downstairs at 13 Leonardo de Vinci St (tel 03-258473). From Tel Aviv central bus station take bus No 70 on the opposite side of Petah Tiqwa St. It's open Sunday to Thursday, 9 am to 3 pm. Each volunteer has to take out a health insurance policy which includes coverage for hospitalisation. There are usually more volunteers required than are available, so as long as you present yourself as hard-working, punctual and well-behaved, you should have no problems and probably find work in a day or two.

The shortage of moshav volunteers is sometimes so bad that farmers will feel forced to go to Haifa port and offer jobs to young people as they disembark from the ferries from Greece. The other way to become a volunteer is to go direct to a moshav and ask an individual farmer. This will not endear you to the volunteers' offices in Tel Aviv and you may end up regretting not having them on your side if you have any problems.

DIAMONDS

Belgian Jews began Israel's diamond industry in 1939. Since those early days, despite occasional decline, the industry has grown. In 1985 Israel emerged as the world's leading producer of cut diamonds and over 12,000 diamond cutters were in employment.

A worldwide recession in the diamond industry in the early 1980s led to a fragmentation and restructuring of the industry here into more than 1000 small units. Before then, it had been dominated by a relatively small number of firms with large workforces.

A new feature of the Israel Diamond Exchange in Tel Aviv is the Harry Openheimer Diamond Museum. This gives a well-presented introduction to the diamond trade and is proving very popular.

WHERE TO FIND WHAT
Beaches

With the fresh water Sea of Galilee (actually a lake) and the Red-Dead-Med combination, Israel offers plenty of scope for beach life and much of it is unique. The Galilee was the main area of Jesus' ministry and, in particular, where he gave the Sermon on the Mount and walked on the water. Nowhere in the world can compare to the Dead Sea and no visit to Israel is complete without the obligatory float. Most people head for the beach at Ein Gedi but En Boqeq has sand, is cleaner and has the added attraction of those salt crystals that look like icebergs from a distance.

Due to its offensive architecture, most of Eilat's publicity photographs are taken underwater. The beautiful colours of the coral and tropical fish here combine with clear water and sand to make it a special place.

On the Mediterranean coast, Tel Aviv beach on a hot August Shabbat is packed solid. The beach here is right in the centre of things and is a major attraction. Elsewhere Herzliya, Netanya and Haifa lead the beach parade.

Sea of Galilee		p 303
En Boqeq	Dead Sea	p 348
Coral Beach	Eilat	p 376
Tel Aviv		p 200
Sidney Ali Beach	Herzlia	p 238
Netanya		p 249
Carmel Beach	Haifa	p 258

Natural Beauty Spots

Try to see the world's largest crater, Makhtesh Ramon, which offers an eerie, coloured landscape of lunar-like qualities with its various rock formations; the Dead Sea region, bordered by the Judean Desert and Jordan's Moab mountains; the Sea of Galilee, surrounded by lush hills and rich in the history of the New Testament; the war-torn Golan with outstanding views across the multi-coloured patchwork of fields in the Jezreel Valley; the Negev Desert with its hidden treasures such as En Avdat and the Valley of Zin; and the Judean Desert, including such marvellous hikes as the Wadi Qelt

Negev Desert

and a visit to Mar Saba. There is more, much more; these are just some of the highlights.

Makhtesh Ramon	Mitzpe Ramon	p 370
Dead Sea region		p 344
Sea of Galilee		p 303
Golan		p 322
Mount Tabor	Jezreel Valley	p 298
Negev Desert		p 357
Judean Desert		p 387

Springs & Waterfalls Israel has a wonderful selection of beauty spots featuring water, some of which are in the desert, others in milder climes. You can be in a desert landscape and see a trail of trees following a wadi (a dry river bed). Empty for much of the year, a sudden rainfall can cause a flash flood and a raging torrent of muddy water. In the Golan Heights, one of the three main sources of the Jordan River is Banyus. Just below, a waterfall crashes down and is a popular attraction for Israelis and tourists.

One of my favourite spots in the country is En Avdat in the Negev, between Beersheba and Mitzpe Ramon. Here you can go on an awe-inspiring walk through a stunning canyon, involving some easy but slightly energetic climbing. On the way along the wadi you see various pools of spring water, ibex (the desert animal) and trees in the middle of the desert. A waterfall (in season) finishes off the show.

Sachne, or Gan HaShlosha, south of Golan, is a beautiful park featuring a natural pool and waterfalls of warm but refreshing crystalline water. It dates back to Roman times and has managed to survive without too much commercialisation. In the Dead Sea area, two of the not so immediately obvious attractions involve fresh water, not the mineral-rich salty variety. The better known of the two, Ein Gedi, on the shore of the Dead Sea, is a natural oasis in the Judean Desert. It features two pretty waterfalls, providing a refreshing change from the heat of the area and its salty competitor across the road. Ein Feshka, a little to the north along the Dead Sea's shore, is a series of pools filled by springs.

Hopefully, the hottest water that most of you will end up in can be found back in Galilee at Hammat Gader. In the valley of the Yarmuk River a successful tourist attraction is the combination of natural hot sulphur springs with Roman ruins and a crocodile park.

Just outside Jerusalem's Old City is Hezekiah's Tunnel, a great way to cool down on a hot day. The tunnel was built to secretly bring the city's supply of water from the natural Gihon spring nearby thus avoiding the danger of the enemy tampering with it. It is now possible to slosh through the tunnel with the water coming up to your knees, or higher.

En Avdat	Negev	p 368
Banyus	Golan	p 327
Sachne (Gan HaShlosha)	Galilee	p 302
Ein Gedi	Dead Sea	p 349
Ein Feshka	Dead Sea	p 349
Hammat Gader	Galilee	p 315
Hezekiah's Tunnel	Jerusalem	p 160

Archaeological Sites

Archaeology is an extremely popular subject with the Israelis, as well as many of the country's visitors. The inspiration for this is the rich supply of excavations, the busy schedule of digging, and the extensive press coverage given to new discoveries.

Jericho is arguably the world's oldest town, and the 9000-year-old remains of Tel Jericho are one of the many archaeological highlights you can visit in Israel. The City of David, outside Jerusalem's Old City, is the site of the Jebusite city conquered by King David circa 997 BC. Remains dating from Herod the Great (37-4 BC) include Caesarea, which features a Roman amphitheatre and a Crusader port; Herodian, a palace complex; Sebastiya, including a lesser known amphitheatre and what was the showpiece of the Holy Land; and Masada, the last Jewish stronghold against the Romans, spectacularly situated on the flat summit of a mountain overlooking the Dead Sea. In the Negev, between Beersheba and Mitzpe Ramon, is Avdat, the site of the Nabateans' most impressive desert city. North of the Sea of Galilee is Gamla, site of another siege by the Romans of a Jewish city.

Tel es-Sultan	Jericho	p 394
City of David	Jerusalem	p 161
Caesarea		p 272
Herodian	Bethlehem	p 408
Sebastiya	Nablus	p 422
Masada	Dead Sea	p 352
Avdat	Negev	p 369
Gamla	Golan	p 332

Museums

Israelis thrive on their history. No doubt the need to refer to it was felt necessary to argue for the Jewish State. This should be borne in mind when you visit museums and read the understandably biased accounts of various events. Regardless of your views of the accuracy of the contents of Israeli museums, there can be no disputing their presentational quality. The Israel Museum in Jerusalem is the home of the Dead Sea Scrolls, and also houses a wide range of exhibits covering archaeology and art. The Rockefeller Museum in East Jerusalem is the original purpose-built archaeological centre of the country.

On the outskirts of Jerusalem's rapidly expanding New City is Yad Vashem, the leading Israeli Holocaust museum. Its importance to the Jews cannot be over-emphasised. The Diaspora Museum in Tel Aviv tells of the Jews' dispersion around the world and features several striking, as well as controversial, presentations of Jewish history. The nearby Ha'Aretz Museum is an extensive complex consisting of eight different museums, such as the popular Glass Museum, Ceramics Museum, Lasky Planetarium and the Museum of Ethnography & Folklore. The Tel Aviv Museum is a highlight for art lovers and includes Impressionist work by Renoir and Monet, as well as more recent pieces by Roualt, Matisse and Picasso.

The country's newest museum is an interesting addition to the scene. The Diamond Museum in the Israel Diamond Exchange complex in Ramat Gan, north of Tel Aviv, tells you virtually everything you wanted to know about the precious stones, except how to afford them.

Israel Museum	Jerusalem	p 172
Dead Sea Scrolls	Jerusalem	p 172
Rockefeller Museum	Jerusalem	p 165
Yad Vashem	Jerusalem	p 173
Diaspora Museum	Tel Aviv	p 208
Ha'Aretz Museum	Tel Aviv	p 208
Tel Aviv Museum	Tel Aviv	p 211
Diamond Museum	Ramat Gan	p 208

Holy Cities

The ultimate holy city has to be Jerusalem; no other city in the world enjoys such status. It is revered by the three major monotheistic faiths of Judaism, Islam and Christianity. The Jews also regard Hebron, Safed and Tiberias as holy. The four Jewish holy cities have been compared to the four elements: Jerusalem representing fire (the Temple sacrifices), Hebron - earth (Abraham purchased the land and the Patriarchs are buried here), Tiberias - water (the city is on the lakeside) and Safed - air (being the highest city in the country and the most spiritual as a centre of biblical and talmudic study). Hebron is also holy to the Muslims, due to the Patriarchs being buried there.

Bethlehem, the traditional birth-place of Jesus, is holy to Christians, and also, to a lesser degree, to the Jews, being the location of Rachel's Tomb. Nazareth is the traditional site of the Annunciation, where the angel Gabriel informed Mary that she had been chosen to mother the Son of God. Jesus is also believed to have lived here as a child. Haifa is the world centre of the Baha'i faith and the Baha'i Shrine is one of the country's most attractive buildings. Mount Gerizim, overlooking Nablus, is the holy centre for the Samaritans.

Jerusalem	p 121
Hebron	p 408
Safed	p 332
Tiberias	p 303
Bethlehem	p 398
Nazareth	p 290
Haifa	p 253
Nablus	p 417

Synagogues

Visiting a synagogue in the Jewish State would seem to be a logical and popular thing to do. It is for Jews, but many non-Jews do not seem to want to, or feel able to. They are, however, more than welcome to visit synagogues and doing so would undoubtedly lead to more understanding of the Jewish faith. Jerusalem is the site of the Great Synagogue, part of the Hechel Shlomo complex, the seat of the Chief Rabbinate of Israel and the Supreme Religious Centre.

In the Old City down the road, the Jewish Quarter features reconstructed synagogues of much importance: the Hurva, the Ramban and the Four Sephardic synagogues. In Safed's Synagogue Quarter (Qiryat Batei Haknesset) you can visit some of the country's more beautiful synagogues. These include the Caro, Ha'Ari, Alsheik and Abuhav synagogues. In occupied Hebron, one of the most important Jewish holy sites is the synagogue in the Tomb of the Patriarchs, the only synagogue in a mosque. One of the highlights of a visit to the Mount Scopus Campus of the Hebrew University in Jerusalem is the spectacular new Hecht Synagogue. Its architecture aside, there is that wonderful view down towards the Old City.

Great Synagogue	Jerusalem	p 170
Hurva Synagogue	Jerusalem	p 144
Ramban Synagogue	Jerusalem	p 144
Four Sephardic Synagogues	Jerusalem	p 145
Caro Synagogue	Safed	p 337
Ha'Ari Synagogue	Safed	p 337
Alsheik Synagogue	Safed	p 337

Abuhav Synagogue	Safed	p 337
Tomb of the Patriarchs	Hebron	p 410
Hecht Synagogue	Jerusalem	p 165

Mosques

Dominating the skyline to such an extent that the gold Dome of the Rock has become the Jewish State's most recognisable landmark, mosques are an integral part of the country's heritage. The Haram esh-Sharif (Temple Mount) is the site of the two most important, El Aqsa, Israel's largest, and the Dome of the Rock. The Tomb of the Patriarchs in Hebron is now a mosque and a synagogue, and is one of the few places where Arabs and Jews pray together.

In Akko, the green-domed El-Jazzar Mosque is one of the largest in Israel. Gaza has the El Jamia El Kbur (the Great Mosque) originally a church built by Queen Helena and later used by the Crusaders. In the interesting streets of Nablus' Old City is the Kabir Mosque, with its beautiful arch. Revered by Muslims as the grave of the prophet Moses, the fascinating Nebi Musa is set in a spectacular location overlooking the Judean desert.

Dome of the Rock	Jerusalem	p 140
El-Aqsa Mosque	Jerusalem	p 139
Tomb of the Patriarchs	Hebron	p 410
El-Jazzar Mosque	Akko	p 280
The Great Mosque	Gaza	p 428
Kabir Mosque	Nablus	p 420
Nebi Musa		p 389

Churches

Many of the churches which mark the key Christian sites in Israel are a source of disappointment to pilgrims, because of the uninspiring architecture and the annoying presence of souvenir salesmen. Some may be disturbed by the domination of the Orthodox Churches over the Roman Catholic and Protestant Churches. Nevertheless, for many, a trip to Israel is inconceivable without at least visiting two churches: the Church of the Nativity, in Bethlehem, traditional site of Jesus' birth; and the Church of the Holy Sepulchre in Jerusalem, the traditional but disputed site of Jesus' crucifixion, burial and resurrection. Other important churches include those on the Mount of Olives, the most popular of which is the Church of All Nations in the garden of Gethsemane.

Often overlooked in Jerusalem is the beautifully situated Church of St Peter in Gallicantu, on the eastern slope of Mount Zion. Also on Mount Zion is the Church of the Dormition, whose recently renovated interior contrasts nicely with the dominating exterior, a popular landmark. Of Jerusalem's many churches, the Crusaders' St Anne's is perhaps the overall favourite when status is disregarded. Its superb acoustics, stark interior and crypt, along with the excavations of the Bethesda pools combine to delight most visitors.

Moving to Galilee, the Church of the Mount of the Beatitudes combines biblical relevance of the highest degree with attractive architecture, surrounded by beautiful scenery. The Basilica of the Transfiguration on Mount Tabor, perhaps my favourite, is left out of many travellers' schedules.

In Nazareth, the Basilica of the Annunciation is a church which most either love or hate. Its bold but controversial architecture bothers many, although the interesting collection of murals from around the world is enchanting.

Church of the Nativity	Bethlehem	p 403
Church of the Holy Sepulchre	Jerusalem	p 152
Church of All Nations	Jerusalem	p 164
Church of St Peter in Gallicantu	Jerusalem	p 161
Church of the Dormition	Jerusalem	p 160
St Anne's Church	Jerusalem	p 146

Church of the Mount of the Beatitudes	Sea of Galilee	p 311
Basilica of the Transfiguration	Mount Tabor	p 299
Basilica of the Annunciation	Nazareth	p 294

Monasteries

Visiting a monastery in Israel can be, perhaps surprisingly, one of the highlights of your visit. Many are in dramatic locations and feature stunning architecture. The prime examples of these are at Mar Saba in the Judean Desert, St George's in the Wadi Qelt, and the Monastery of Temptation in Jericho. All three are in desert climes, with hearty walks and/or climbs for those who wish to reach them. In Abu Gosh, between Jerusalem and Tel Aviv, the Crusader-built monastery is a place where you can experience the monastic life. The monasteries at Latrun and Cremisan, noteworthy for their wines, are also in beautiful locations.

St Elijah's Monastery at Mukhraqa marks the traditional site of Elijah's biblical victory over the 450 priests of Ba'al. On the eastern side of Mount Carmel, it has incredible views across Galilee and on that proverbial clear day (presumably the day after I visit such places) you can see for miles.

Mar Saba		p 407
St George's Monastery	Wadi Qelt	p 390
Monastery of Temptation	Jericho	p 395
Abu Gosh		p 198
Latrun		p 199
Cremisan		p 405
St Elijah's Monastery	Mukhraqa	p 269

Markets

The best Oriental market is in Jerusalem's Old City. It has the best of everything in the country; history, range of products and atmosphere. In Jerusalem's New City, the Jewish market at Mahane Yehuda offers the best prices for fruit and vegetables and an atmosphere of its own. Many astute Arabs do their shopping here.

You will hear and read a lot about how wonderful the Bedouin market is on Thursday mornings in Beersheba – but not from me. I think it is a real let-down. Instead of waking up early on Thursdays, do yourself a favour and enjoy a lie-in. Then get up bright and early on a Friday morning in Jerusalem. There, the Arab sheep market outside the Old City, east of Herod's Gate, has more colour, tradition and general photogenic hubbub than you could expect (and without the commercialisation of Beersheba).

The markets of Hebron and Nablus, centres of violent resistance to Israeli-occupation by local Arabs, are the most authentic in the country. In Tel Aviv, the Carmel Market is a humid version of Mahane Yehuda. With the Oriental Jewish majority it is also noisier. Along the coast a little, the Jaffa flea market can be a good place to discover a variety of antiques and more recent bric-a-brac. Finally, Akko's small bazaar, underneath those green domes and minarets, is popular with visitors.

Old City	Jerusalem	p 136
Mahane Yehuda	Jerusalem	p 167
Friday Sheep Market	Jerusalem	p 165
Old City	Hebron	p 413
Old City	Nablus	p 420
Carmel Market	Tel Aviv	p 213
Flea Market	Jaffa	p 230
Old City	Akko	p 281

LANGUAGE

Israel's national language is Hebrew, followed by Arabic. English is widely spoken; there will nearly always be *someone* nearby who understands it. The majority of road and street signs are in all three languages. With Jews arriving in Israel from around the world, many other languages are commonly understood. French, German and Yiddish are the main ones, but also Spanish and Russian.

Most Arabs are fluent in Hebrew and English as well as Arabic. Many also speak other European languages, and hearing Arab shopkeepers switching languages as they haggle is quite impressive.

Surprisingly overlooked by the vast majority of Israel guides, museums and Israelis themselves, is the history of the national language. Hebrew is the language of the Bible. During the centuries of the Diaspora, Jews spoke the local language but continued to use Hebrew for prayer and religious study. With the rise of political Zionism in Europe in the mid-19th century, there was a growing awareness and appreciation of the ancient language. This resulted in more prose and poetry being written in Hebrew for a growing readership.

Eliezer Ben Yehuda, who arrived in Palestine from Lithuania in 1881, pioneered the everyday use of Hebrew and the coining of new Hebrew words necessary for modern life and times. One of his major achievements was the compilation of the first Hebrew dictionary. Ben Yehuda had the vision to revive and develop Hebrew (spoken by the Jews in ancient times) for a Jewish State that would otherwise have no common language. His eldest child was the first in the modern world to have Hebrew as his mother tongue. A minority of ultra-orthodox Jews bitterly opposed Ben Yehuda's work, believing that Hebrew should not be used as an everyday language. Even today there are a few who only use Hebrew on religious occasions.

The modern language contains elements of some European languages and you will hear many English words, taken where the Bible had no similar concept.

Although it is perfectly possible to survive your stay without uttering a word of Hebrew, it is always useful and polite to know a few words and phrases. Especially useful might be 'Shabbat Shalom' – the traditional Shabbat greeting.

Written from right to left, Hebrew has

א	ב	ג	ג'	ד	ה	ה' ו
V	H	D	J	G	B	A
ז	ח	ט	י	כ(כ')	כ(ך)	ל
L	Kh	K	Yi	T	H	Z
מ(ם)	נ(ן)	ס	ע	פ	פ(ף)	
F	P	'A	S	N	M	
צ(ץ)	ק	ר	ש	שׂ	ת	
T	S	Sh	R	Q	Ts	

Hebrew alphabet

22 characters. The 'ch' sound is a more gutteral version of the German 'ch' sound, and is a noticeable characteristic of the language.

HEBREW WORDS & EXPRESSIONS

Numbers

1	eh-HAD
2	SHTA-yim
3	sha-LOSH
4	AR-bah
5	cha-MAYSH
6	shaysh
7	SHEV-vah
8	sh-MO-neh
9	TAY-shah
10	ESS-er
11	eh-HAD-ess-RAY
12	shtaym-ess-RAY
20	ess-REEM
21	ess-REEM v'eh-HAD
30	shlo-SHEEM
50	v'ah-CHAT
100	MAY-ah
200	mah-tah-YEEM
300	shlosh may-OAT
500	cha-MAYSH may-OAT
1000	Elef
3000	shlosh-ET elef-EEM
5000	cha-maysh-ET elef-EEM

Days & Time

Sunday	YOM ree-SHON
Monday	YOM shay-NEE

Tuesday	*YOM shlee-SHEE*
Wednesday	*YOM reh-vee-EE*
Thursday	*YOM cha-mee SHEE*
Friday	*YOM shee-SHEE*
Saturday	*sha-BAT*
what is the time?	*MA ha-sha-AH*
minute	*da-KAH*
hour	*sha-AH*
seven o'clock	*ha-sha-AH SHEV-vah*
day	*yom*
week	*sha-voo-ah*
month	*CHO-desh*
year	*sha-NAH*

Useful Words

hello	*sha-LOM*
goodbye	*sha-LOM*
good morning	*BO-ker tov*
good evening	*erev tov*
goodnight	*lie-la tov*
see you later	*le-HIT-rah-OTT*
thank you	*to-DAH*
please	*be-va-ka-SHA*
you are welcome	*al low da-VAAR*
I don't speak Hebrew	*AH-NEE lo m'dah-BEHR ee-VREET*
do you speak English?	*ah-TAH m'dah-BEHR ang-LEET?*
money	*KES-sef*
bank	*bank*
yes	*ken*
no	*loh*
excuse me	*slee-CHA*
wait	*REG-gah*
what	*mah*
when	*mah-tiee*
where is	*AY-fo*
right (correct)	*na-CHON*

Transport

station	*ta-cha-na*
airport	*sde t'uFAH*
which bus goes to . . . ?	*EH-seh auto-boos no-SAY-ah le . . . ?*
stop here	*ah-TSOR kahn*
railway	*rah-KEH-vet*
bus	*auto-boos*
near	*ka-ROV*

Food & Accommodation

to eat	*le-eh-CHOL*
to drink	*lish-toth*
food	*OCHEL*
water	*my-im*
restaurant	*MISS-ah-DAH*
breakfast	*ah-roo-CHAT BO-ker*
lunch	*ah-roo-CHAT-ha-RYE-in*
dinner	*ah-roo-CHAT erev*
menu	*taf-REET*
egg	*bay-TSA*
vegetables	*YEH-rah-KOHT*
bread	*LECH-hem*
butter	*chem-AH*
cheese	*g'VEE-nah*
milk	*cha-LAV*
ice cream	*glee-DAH*
fruit	*pay-ROTE*
wine	*YAH-yin*
bill	*CHESH-bon*
hotel	*meh-LON*
room	*che-der*
toilet	*bait key SAY, no-chi YOOT*

Post Office & Shopping

post office	*dough-are*
letter	*mich-tav*
stamps	*boolim*
envelopes	*ma-ata-FOTH*
postcard	*gloo-yah*
telegram	*miv-rock*
airmail	*dough-are ah-veer*
how much is it?	*KA-mah zeh oh-LEH?*
pharmacy	*bait mer-kah-CHAT*
shop	*cha-NOOT*
shampoo	*ha-fee-FAH*
expensive	*ya-KAR*
cheap	*zol*

ARABIC WORDS & EXPRESSIONS

Learning the characters for the Arab numerals is useful, as much of your shopping will be done in Arab markets. Also any attempts, however unsuccessful, to speak their language will endear you to the Arabs. Note that Arabic numerals are read left to right, unlike the language, which is read right to left.

Numbers

0	*sifr*
1	*wa-had*
2	*tinen*
3	*talatay*
4	*arbaha*
5	*chamseh*
6	*sitteh*
7	*sabah*
8	*tamanyeh*
9	*taisah*
10	*ahsharah*

Useful Words

hello	*a-halan, mahr-haba*
goodbye	*salaam aleicham, ma-ah-salameh*
good morning	*sabah-al-kheir*
good evening	*masa'al-kheir*
please	*min fadlach*
thank you	*shoo-khran*
you're welcome	*afwan*
do you speak English?	*tech-kee Ingleesi?*
yes	*ay-wah*
no	*la*
where	*feen*
right	*yemine*
left	*she-mal*
straight	*doo-ree*
pardon	*sa-mech-nee*
how much is this?	*ah-desh hadah?*
tea	*schai*
coffee	*kah-wah*

Facts for the Visitor

DOCUMENTS & VISAS

The only officially required document for travellers in Israel is a valid passport. Worthwhile are International Youth Hostels Association (IYHA) and student cards. Membership of the IYHA will save you money at their hostels throughout the country. Although not the best value when competing against local privately-owned hostels, they are the only cheap accommodation available in some popular areas, such as the Dead Sea, Mitzpe Ramon and Tabgha.

The International Student Identity Card (ISIC) entitles the holder to a 10% discount on Israel's Egged buses, 50% off fares on Israel State Railways, and discounts at museums and archaeological sites. Even if signs make no mention of student discounts, produce your card and ask. Student fares offered by airlines and ferry companies are usually the same as those offered to people under 26 years of age. If you are combining your visit to Israel with one to Egypt, all the more reason to obtain an ISIC card. Egypt offers better discounts than anywhere else for cardholders.

An International Driving Permit is not normally required to hire a car in Israel.

On arrival in Israel as a tourist you are automatically allowed a free three-month visit. This will not happen if you look, act or smell as though you will not benefit the local scene, or if you are obviously looking for illegal employment. Immigration officials, especially at Haifa port, regularly send such people back on the next boat to Cyprus, or give them permission to stay in the country for only two weeks. Israel is a lousy country to arrive in if you are short of funds.

If, after your initial three month stay, you want more, you need to apply for a visa. You do this at an office of the Ministry of the Interior. Israel's bureaucracy can be infuriating, because of the attitude and performance of the civil servants. Along with the Egged bus information-desk staff who don't like people who ask questions about the buses, the bus drivers who accelerate as they see you running for the bus, and the many Arab men who are strangely affected by non-Arab women, they are about the most unpleasant side of Israel.

The process of applying for an extension of your visit involves an early start to beat the long queues, and proof that you can support yourself without needing to work illegally. Most offices open at 8 am and the queue is usually depressingly long by then.

Convincing the civil servants that you should be allowed to stay can be very hard or very easy and they extend visas for varying amounts of time; sometimes one month, sometimes as much as six months, but usually for three months. The process costs about US$10 and one passport-sized photo is required. There is no fee for citizens of Belgium, Luxembourg or the Netherlands.

The Jerusalem office, in particular, is renowned for its hostility and should be avoided – it is also extremely busy with the longest queues. The staff in the Eilat office seem to be affected by the heat and are the easiest to deal with. In Tel Aviv they are often overly officious but are virtual anarchists compared to the Jerusalemites. Elsewhere, the offices tend not to see too many tourists asking for visa extensions. This can mean either that they won't have a clue about the procedure and refuse to deal with you, or that they are really friendly and pleased to have something different to stamp, sign and shuffle from desk to desk. In Tiberias I found them to be very confused but very helpful.

Normal office hours are 8 am to noon,

closed on Fridays and Saturdays. On Mondays and Wednesdays they often open between 2 and 3 pm. The eight and a half sheqel question is: 'What happens if you try to leave Israel after overstaying the initial three month period without getting the visa?' I was told that fines are the order of the day, so it hardly seems worth the hassle of avoiding the procedure. By the way, it's OK to leave applying for your extension for a couple of weeks or so after the initial three months, so don't bother to rush to a main town if you are wandering in the wilderness somewhere when your three months is up. Offices are at:

Afulla
    2 Harav Levin St (tel 065-23890)
Akko
    2 Ha'Agara St (tel 04-911103)
Ashkelon
    Nafati Centre (tel 051-24246)
Beersheba
    Rambab St (tel 057-30460)
Eilat
    Municipality Building (tel 059-72133/6). Open Sunday 5 to 7pm; Monday to Thursday 9 am to noon; closed Friday and Saturday
Hadera
    73 Weizman St (tel 063-24795)
Haifa
    11 Hassan Shuqri (tel 04-667781)
Holon
    11 Jabotinsky St (tel 03-984181)
Jerusalem
    1 Shlomzion St (tel 02-228211)
Nazereth Illit
    Qyriat Memshala (tel 065-70510)
Netanya
    14 Remez St (tel 053-22153)
Petah Tiqwa
    40 Bar Kochba St (tel 03-911906)
Rehovot
    74 Herzl St (tel 08-25577)
Ramat Gan
    2 Bialik St (tel 03-719375)
Safed
    Government House, Jerusalem St (tel 067-31424)
Tel Aviv
    Jaffa Shalom Tower (tel 03-65194)
Tiberias
    23 Ze'evy El Hadof (tel 067-91724)

In theory, 03-916547 is the number for an information service for general enquiries, but their usual answer is that you should go to the nearest Ministry of the Interior office. Usually the kibbutzim and moshavim arrange for the visas of their foreign volunteers as a matter of course, and if you are a valued worker you should be able to get lengthy extensions.

The maximum period a foreigner is allowed to stay in Israel varies according to which official you ask. It can be one week if they don't like the look of you, or several years if the locals like you. Usually, one year is the most you can stay without pulling strings.

Israel is, of course, the venue for that popular traditional Middle Eastern card game: the Passport Shuffle. This involves trying to visit as many 'hostile' Arab countries as possible after a visit to Israel, without having to have an extra passport. This game was devised because the countries which have refused to recognise Israel also refuse to allow any nationalities into their countries if they have previously entered Israel. As a result, the Israeli immigration officers will, if you politely ask them, stamp an official piece of paper, rather than your actual passport. Remember two things, though, before you pack your kaffiyeh and head for the Gulf. If you stay in Israel longer than the initial three month period, when you extend your stay at a Ministry of the Interior office, your passport is automatically stamped, and no buts. If entering Israel from Egypt (the only Arab country that recognises the Jewish State and therefore not a problem) or vice versa, do not bother trying to have your passport saved from the stamp of Israel. It will be obvious by the Egyptian border stamp in your passport that you have entered Israel.

If you are heading for Jordan from Israel things get a little complicated, but far from impossible. (See the Getting There chapter for details).

Consulates & Embassies

There are seemingly more countries without diplomatic relations with Israel than those with. Most consulates and embassies are in Tel Aviv – see that chapter for addresses.

Both the Israel Ministry of Foreign Affairs and the Israel Embassy in London declined to give me a list of Israel's diplomatic offices overseas. Here are some, if not all, of them:

Australia
Embassy, 6 Turrana Ave, Yarralumla, Canberra, ACT 2600 (tel 062-731309)
Consulate, Westfield Towers, 300 William St, Sydney, NSW 2011 (tel 02-358 5077)

Canada
Embassy, 40 Laurier Ave West, Suite 601, Ottawa, Ontario, KIR 7T3 (tel 613-237 6450)

Great Britain
Embassy, 2 Palace Green, London W8 4QB (tel 01-937 6450)

Hong Kong
Consulate, 1121 Princess Building, Chater Rd, Hong Kong (tel 01-9378050)

Netherlands
Embassy, 47 Buitenhoff, The Hague (tel 070-647850)

Singapore
Embassy, Faber House, 7th Floor, 236G Orchard Rd, Singapore 9 (tel 2530996)

Thailand
Embassy, 31 Soi Lung Suan, Ploenchit Rd, Bangkok (tel 2526181)

USA
Embassy, 3514 International Drive NW, Washington DC 20008 (tel 202-364 5500)

This list is subject to change. Check in the country you are in to see if Israel is represented there.

WORKING HOLIDAYS

Many travellers find themselves wanting to work in Israel but many more find themselves having to, after running out of money. Indeed a sense of desperation would be required to want to work here, due to the generally appalling rates of pay and the frequent cases of employers exploiting foreign labour. This is partly because most of the work undertaken by travellers is illegal. Major exceptions include kibbutz, moshav, SPNI, religious, charity and archaeological volunteering.

Israel is not a good place to make money to continue your travelling. It can be done, but it involves a lot of very low-paid work.

As anywhere else, the catering industry employs the largest number of illegal workers. The gradual increase in the custom of tipping has meant that working as a waiter/ess in the right place can be relatively well paid. To get such work simply ask around cafés and restaurants. The larger, higher quality hotels tend not to employ foreigners. Everywhere else, though, seems to rely on illegal labour to keep their premises and their dishes clean.

Eilat, being tourist-oriented, has the most job openings, and is also a good place to get a more strenuous job such as labourer on building sites and road crews. Hang out in the Peace Café (see Eilat section) from about 5 am, when foremen arrive looking for casual workers. If you oversleep, enquire at the various building sites (mainly to the south). Again, the pay is as low as the temperature is high and Eilat's employers generally have a worse reputation for sharks than the adjacent Red Sea.

In Tel Aviv I met the nouveau riche of working travellers in Israel. They had found jobs through an employment agency which seemed to be ignorant of the employment status of foreigners. The guys I met were making successful careers in the 'we put air-conditioning in cars' business, and even earning overtime.

The best-paid job for travellers that I came across was egg collecting on Shabbat for observant Jews. This marvellous position paid about the same for one day's work as most jobs pay for a week. Finding such jobs is not easy. Check the *Jerusalem Post* (Friday's edition is the best for jobs) and also the noticeboards in Jerusalem and Tel Aviv Universities.

Other paid jobs in Israel include working in laundromats, just go in and ask; au pairing, via advertisements in the *Post* and agencies in Tel Aviv; and portering and catering work in hospitals, enquire at individual hospitals. Doing odd jobs in the hostels is popular as they provide accommodation, food and often a small allowance. Ask around the various hostels. Tel Aviv, Jerusalem and Eilat are the best places to look, but Tiberias is often overlooked and hostels there are often in need of staff.

The SPNI's Field Study Centres sometimes take volunteers, who work about six hours a day, five days a week in return for food, accommodation and a small allowance. It is probably best to enquire at the individual FSCs even if the SPNI office staff tell you that there are no vacancies. You will have to convince the staff at the FSC that you are suitable; that you are conscientious, and likely to remain for at least a couple of months. There is normally only one volunteer required by a FSC, if any, and duties would include cleaning, gardening and any odd jobs.

'Real' volunteers are also required by some religious and charity organisations. Christian hospitals in Jerusalem and Nazareth in particular use volunteer nurses. These can be trained and qualified people or those willing to assist feeding patients. In Jerusalem enquire at St Louis' French Hospital, next door to Notre Dame outside the Old City; and in Nazareth to the EMS, French and Italian hospitals. In Gaza the Ahli Arab Hospital (tel 051-863014) often requires experienced volunteer nurses. Enquire in person or write in advance to The Director, Ahli Arab Hospital, PO Box 72, Palestine Square, Gaza.

For Jews there are the many Jewish charities all over the country. These include projects in the renovation of buildings and neighbourhoods as well as hospitals, helping the elderly, and childcare.

Archaeological digs are definitely not for gold-diggers – most require that you pay to work. In January of each year the Israel Department of Antiquities and Museums, part of the Ministry of Education and Culture, publishes a list of the archaeological excavations of the coming year. You can ask for it at the Rockefeller Museum. General enquiries regarding excavations in Israel can be made to Caren Greenberg, Israel Department of Antiquities & Museums, Rockefeller Museum (tel 02-278603), PO Box 586, Jerusalem 91004.

The busy archaeological season is May to September when universities are not in session and the weather is hot and dry. No previous excavating experience is usually necessary but volunteers should be prepared to participate for a minimum of one or two weeks, depending on the individual dig. A fee for food and accommodation (varying from sleeping bags in a field to 3-star hotels) is required. Some expeditions do provide volunteers with an allowance for food, accommodation and/or travel expenses within Israel. Tourist offices, particularly the Jerusalem Old City branch, sometimes have notices displayed requesting volunteers for a dig, so remember to check there.

In recent years a popular way for travellers to pay their way in Israel, or just to have the experience regardless of their financial status, has been to work as film extras. The casting agency, Studio 91 (tel 03-220225), 91 Dizengoff St, Tel Aviv is constantly employing travellers to work as extras. Their office's location, 2½ flights above a side entrance next to the Senor Sandwich café, and the minimal pay for a 12 hour working day should remind you that Tinsel Town has not moved to the Middle East.

MONEY

A$1	= NIS 1.44	NIS 1	= A$0.70
US$1	= NIS 1.80	NIS 1	= US$0.56
£1	= NIS 3.10	NIS 1	= £0.33

The new sheqel (NIS) is divided into 100 agorot. There are coins of 1, 5 and 10 agorot, half and 1 new sheqel and notes of 5, 10 and 50 new sheqelim. The change to the new sheqel in 1985 came with other changes in monetary policies in a plan to reduce inflation. It appears to have at least partially succeeded, as the inflation rate has dropped from 500% to around 20%.

Despite the reduced inflation rate, the best place to change your money is still the Arab moneychangers, mainly in Jerusalem's Old City and East Jerusalem. Legalised by the Government, they are left over from the years of Jordanian control, and are popular with Israelis as well as travellers. Another good place to change money can be the hostel you are staying in.

Most Israelis, Jews and Arabs will talk in terms of American dollars, not sheqelim. This derives from the days when the Israeli currency constantly devalued, and adopting the American dollar was a reliable way to deal with that situation. I get the impression that no-one is confident enough in the new sheqel to drop the usage of the American dollar. Moneychangers and banks will change

most foreign currencies or travellers' cheques with British sterling and the DM often the most popular. It is always worth asking the dollar price when you are quoted a price in sheqelim – it often works out cheaper. Cash is best but small denominations of travellers' cheques will usually do. Prices in this book are quoted in US dollars.

Banking hours vary from place to place so check in advance. There will usually be someone willing to change your money wherever you are, but it may be at an unfavourable rate.

Payments made in foreign currency are free of the 15% value added tax. Purchases like ferry and airline tickets and accommodation at IYHA hostels can be made cheaper by paying in dollars or whatever. You can also get VAT refunds by presenting receipts of purchases made with foreign currency at a bank on your departure. In most private hostels, there is no difference between payment made in local and foreign currency.

Credit cards are very popular in Israel, although most low-cost establishments do not accept them. You can use American Express, Diner's Club, Visa or Mastercard/

Mastercharge cards to obtain more funds, depending on your credit status back home.

If you are unfortunate enough to run out of money in Israel, the quickest way to have some transferred from home is through Barclays Discount Bank. Ask them to send a 'Swift' message to your bank (this is a super-fast version of telex). Provided that your bank is responsive enough, or that you do not leave it to the end of the day or the working week, your money should be with you in two or three days. When you go to Barclays Discount Bank, insist that they send a Swift message and not a regular telex. If you get no joy from the clerk, ask for the manager and if he is unresponsive, call the bank's head office (which is at 103 Allenby St, Tel Aviv) on 03-643431. If you are in Tel Aviv, you should receive your money sooner as all transfers go to the main branches before being sent around the country as required.

If you are too far away to reach Tel Aviv, have the local bank telephone Tel Aviv after two days. Once the money has arrived there, it can be issued to you locally.

Alternatively, Bank Leumi will send a regular telex to your bank. They claim to take three days. Their main branch (tel 03-648311, 648162) is at 19 Herzl St, Tel Aviv.

American Express, Citicorp, Visa, Bank of America, Thomas Cook and Barclays are among the more widely recognised travellers' cheques in Israel. Always ensure that you have a record of your cheque numbers and their value kept separately in case of theft or loss. Also remember to carry your passport for ID purposes when you want to cash your travellers' cheques.

At the end of your stay you can convert your sheqelim at the airport or at the port in Haifa. You are allowed to reconvert up to US$100 in sheqels without bank receipts. If you are leaving the country to cross into Egypt and Jordan by road, you can convert your sheqelim at a regular bank (there are exchange facilities at both border crossings but they have proved unreliable in the past). Officious as ever, the clerk may demand proof that you are leaving the country, as aliens are normally unable to buy dollars in Israel. Your Egyptian or Jordanian visa and an explanation of your travel plans, if you do not have a coach ticket, ought to be sufficient.

Three Currencies

Many Arabs speak English and Hebrew as well as Arabic. When it comes to currency, they also deal three ways in Jerusalem and the Occupied Territories. Another leftover from the Jordanian days and also due to the 'open-bridge' policy allowing trade across the River Jordan between the Palestinians and the Jordanians, is the popularity of the Jordanian dinar. It is often valued more highly than the US dollar and always more than the Israel sheqel.

COSTS

Many budget travellers have labelled Israel as an expensive place to visit. Certainly, after months in Egypt or Turkey you will find yourself spending more to stay in the Holy Land. However, those arriving from Down Under, the UK, the States and most European countries, should find prices compare favourably. Of course, it is virtually impossible to say what travelling around Israel will cost you. Two people travelling at exactly the same standard can spend vastly different amounts if one travels faster than the other or cannot cook. A week lying on Tel Aviv beach will cost considerably less than a week touring the Galilee region, and living off food purchased in markets and supermarkets will save a packet compared to eating out.

From top to bottom: If you stay in luxury hotels and eat out, you can spend a great deal. There are luxury hotels and expensive restaurants a-plenty. At the other extreme, using markets and supermarkets, you can survive on less than US$15 a day. It totally depends on what you are looking for.

Tipping

I am told that once no-one tipped in Israel. Today in the more expensive tourist spots, a 10-15% tip is the norm. Unfortunately, it is frequently undeserved. Whoever serves you at your streetside café table will also expect a similar sized tip. In the more modest places, small change is normally the most that is required.

Tipping is a sore-point for many budget travellers. Basically I feel that it is wrong to go to a restaurant or bar where tipping is standard procedure and to expect to receive the service without paying a tip. Whether we agree with it or not, most waiting and bar staff are paid at a low rate, calculated with the expectation of tips. The total price at the foot of a bill is not necessarily the final amount due unless it states that service has been included. If it hasn't, and whoever served you did right, they are entitled to a tip.

Note that taxi drivers in Israel do not expect to be tipped. This is usually just as well: too often, they are rude, unhelpful and quick to overcharge.

TOURIST INFORMATION

The Israel Government Tourist Offices (IGTO) are numerous both around the world and in Israel. However, obtaining information about Israel is not achieved by staggering out of the nearest IGTO with a great pile of the latest glossy productions, as they are full of political propaganda. You need to read about the country's history, past and present, ensuring that the authors are not all from the same side of the political barbed-wire fence. IGTOs abroad include:

Austria
    Postfach 77, Vienna (tel 0222-529399)
Canada
    180 Bloor St West, Toronto (tel 416-964 3784)

Denmark
    Vesterbrogade 6C, Copenhagen (tel 129680, 119679)
Egypt
    6 Ibn el Malek, Cairo (tel 726000)
France
    14 rue de la Paix, Paris (tel 4261-0197, 0367)
Great Britain
    18 Great Marlborough St, London WIV IAF (tel 01-434 3561)
Italy
    Via Podjora 12B, Milan (tel 02-5463021)
Japan
    Kojimachi Sanbancho Mansion No 406-921, Sanbancho, Chiyoda-Ku, Tokyo (tel 238-9081/2)
Netherlands
    Wijde Kapelsteeg 2, Amsterdam (tel 020-249325)
Spain
    Gran Via 69, Madrid (tel 1-2484443)
Sweden
    Sveavagen 28-30, Stockholm (tel 08-213386/7)
Switzerland
    Bintheschergasse 12, Zurich (tel 01-2112344/5)
USA
    5 South Wabash Ave, Chicago IL 60603 (tel 312-782 4306)
    4151 Southwest Freeway, Houston TX 77027 (tel 713-850 9341)
    6380 Wilshire Blvd, LA CA 90048 (tel 213-658 7462)
    420 Lincoln Rd Building, Lincoln Rd, Miami Beach FL 33139 (tel 305-673 6862)
    Empire State Building, 19th Floor, 350 5th Ave, New York NY 10118 (tel 212-560 0650)
West Germany
    Westend Str 4, Frankfurt (tel 069-720157)
    Fontenay 1D, Hamburg (tel 040-454655)

IGTOs in Israel:

Airport
    Ben Gurion Airport (tel 03-9711485/6/7)
Akko
    Municipality Building (tel 04-910251)
Allenby Bridge (tel 02-922531)
Arad
    Commercial Centre (tel 057-98144)
Ashkelon
    Commercial Centre, Afridar (tel 051-32412)

Bat Yam
  Municipality Information Office, Derekh Ben Gurion 43 (tel 03-589766)
Beersheba
  Rehov Nordau (tel 057-36001/2)
Bethlehem
  Manger Square (tel 02-742591)
Eilat
  Retcher Commercial Centre (tel 059-72268)
Haifa
  Town: 18 Rehov Herzl (tel 04-666521/2/3)
  Port: Shed No 12 (on ship's arrival) (tel 04-663988)
Jerusalem
  New City: 24 King George St (tel 02-241281/2)
  Old City: Jaffa Gate (tel 02-282295/6)
Nahariya
  Municipality Building, Sederot Ga'aton (tel 04-922121)
Nazareth
  Casanova St (tel 065-70555)
Netanya
  Kikar Ha'Azma'ut (tel 053-27286)
Rafiah
  Israel-Egypt Transit Point (tel 051-37999)
Rosh Hanikra (tel 04-927802)
Safed
  27 Jerusalem St (tel 067-30633)
Tel Aviv
  7 Mendele St (tel 03-223266/7)
Tiberias
  8 Elhadeff St (tel 067-20992)

The performance of these offices varies considerably; some are friendly, but others suffer from the Israeli bureaucratic disease, especially the Jerusalem New City office. In Bethlehem, the seemingly delightful women regularly subsidise the taxi drivers' incomes by insisting that no bus service exists to Herodian, the popular archaeological site, when in fact a bus has always operated that route. In Tiberias, avoid the IGTO and contact Oded Shoshan as he visits the various hostels to collect bookings for his popular tour of the Golan – he is most helpful and knowledgeable. Likewise in Safed contact Shlomo Bar-Ayal, who is based in the Beit Yosef Hotel.

The IGTO has an excellent selection of free maps, although those for Akko,

Beersheba, Safed and Nahariya are not accurate or complete.

One of the best sources of information in Israel is the Christian Information Centre, near Jaffa Gate in Jerusalem's Old City. Obviously the title subject is their speciality but they are very knowledgeable in other areas too.

Volunteer Tourist Service

The VTS aims to give advice and help to tourists. Most noticeable at Ben Gurion Airport and in the lobbies of certain hotels in the evenings, they have a history of happy-ending-type stories to their credit, such as reuniting lost friends, and assisting tourists who are sick or injured.

GENERAL INFORMATION
Electricity
220 volts, 50 cycles, alternating current.

Time
Israel's recent experimental adoption of Daylight Saving Time in summer has caused controversy and confusion. It will probably continue to do so in a country where people love to argue. Israel is two hours ahead of GMT, eight hours behind Australian Eastern Standard Time, and seven hours ahead of American Eastern Standard Time.

Business Hours
Israel's business hours vary a lot due to the different religions practised. Being the Jewish State, Shabbat closes most shops, offices, and places of entertainment on Friday afternoon and Saturday. Some reopen on Saturday evening after sundown. At the same time, the vast majority of public transport grinds to a halt. Haifa, where the religious party is unable to do anything about it, and the area served by the Arab bus services, are the main exceptions. Muslim-owned businesses close on Fridays, although many stay open until midday. Christian-owned businesses close on Sundays.

Normal shopping hours are Monday to

Thursday 8 am to 1 pm and 4 to 7 pm; and Friday 8 am to 2 pm. Banking hours do vary but generally they are Sunday to Tuesday and Thursday, 8.30 am to 12.30 pm and 4 to 5.30 pm; Wednesday, Friday and eves of holy days 8.30 am to noon. In Nazareth banks are open Friday and Saturday mornings but are closed on Sundays. Post offices are generally open 8.30 am to 12.30 pm and 3.30 pm to 6 pm, except on Wednesday (8 am to 2 pm) and Friday (8 am to 1 pm); closed Saturday and holidays. In main cities and towns they may be open longer.

The effect that religious holidays have on business hours often takes travellers by surprise. It causes a lot of wasted time hanging around until the banks and shops open or the buses start running again. You need to remember to stock up on food in advance, too. Check for any holidays being celebrated during your time in Israel and be prepared.

Post

Letters posted in Israel can take at least two weeks to reach North America and Australia; only a little less to Europe. Most locals carry mail for each other when they leave the country, but you should think twice about doing so yourself unless you are *very* confident about the person who has given you the mail. It wouldn't be much fun to travel with a package that started ticking at 30,000 feet.

Poste restante seems to work well, although the post office in Jaffa Rd, Jerusalem, was found to be returning uncollected mail after only two weeks (they denied it). As in other countries, do not rely solely on the word of the clerk that the letter you are expecting has not arrived. Check under all your names, and if necessary ask to check for yourself. The system of queuing has been introduced to some Israeli post offices, but to most of the locals it's a whole new ball-game. Be firm and repel all pushers-in.

Telegram services are available in post offices. In main post offices a 24 hour service is provided, although you will often find yourself having to wake up the person on duty during the night. During the day the same old problem of queuing and pushing-in occurs.

Telephone

With the Israeli telephone system the problem seems to be archaic equipment, unlike the postal system which suffers from rude staff and a speed problem. Due to the poor equipment you can often dial even a local call and after the first two or three digits the number will be engaged. When you do get through the lines are consistently bad – a typical street scene in Israel is not complete without somebody screaming down a public telephone.

Public telephones do not take coins, but

tokens. These are called *asimonim* and are available from post offices, some hotel reception desks and from kiosks in areas where there are several public telephones (normally bus stations). Make sure that you stock up with them. For a local call, one asimon lasts for an unlimited period; long distance calls (ie requiring an area code) can use up a lot, depending on the distance, duration and time of day. Whatever, just keep dropping your asimonim into the phone and any that are unused are returned when the call is finished.

The demand for asimonim has created an industry staffed by those people Israel tends not to talk about – the Jewish tramps. They can often be seen propping up a wall in the central bus station, ankle-deep in phone tokens. Buying from them saves having to queue behind a bus-load of Israelis at the news-stand. It will hardly improve your Hebrew, though.

To phone abroad from Israel, public telephones can only be used for collect calls. Note that it is not possible to call collect to West Germany or Austria from any telephone. For collect calls elsewhere, either dial the international operator on 18 or, better still, dial 03 (if outside Tel Aviv-Jaffa) 633881 or 622881-2. These numbers are frequently busy so you need to be patient and keep trying. The rumour that there is only one international operator for the whole country is denied by the post office.

To dial direct abroad you need a private phone, otherwise go to a main post office in one of the larger towns or cities. Here you pay for a pre-set time period. Money is refunded for any unused units. Make sure that you know exactly how long your money gives you to speak, to avoid being cut off before you have finished (the voice of experience, folks). Note that Israeli currency only is accepted in post offices, including payments for international phone calls – no travellers' cheques, credit cards or US dollars. The post office facilities for international calls are not open in the evenings or during Shabbat and Jewish festivals.

Here are the area codes that you are most likely to use:

Afulla	065	Masada	057
Airport (Ben-Gurion)	03	Mitzpe Ramon	057
Akko	04	Nahariya	04
Arad	057	Nazareth	065
Ashdod	055	Netanya	053
Ashkelon	051	Negev area (most)	057
Beersheba	057	Qiryat Shimona	069
Bethlehem	02	Ramla	08
Dead Sea area	057	Rehovot	054
Dimona	057	Rishon le Zion	03
Eilat	059	Safed	069
En Gedi	057	Tel Aviv-Jaffa	03
Gaza	051	Tiberias	067
Hadera	063	Bethlehem	02
Haifa	04	Hebron	02
Herzlia	052	Jericho	02
Jerusalem	02	Nablus	053
Katzrin	069	Ramallah	02

Useful Telephone Numbers

Information 14 – this requires one asimon. The line is usually busy and a recorded message will often ask you (in Hebrew) to hold until an operator can answer your call. Unfortunately the local telephone directories are mainly printed in Hebrew.

Police 100
First Aid/Ambulance 101
Fire Service 102
Airport Information 03-9712484 (24 hour service); 03-381111 (arrivals only – taped message)

Note As we went to press, the phone system was being revamped and many numbers were set to change.

Public telephones are often out of order. If they are working they are frequently in an area noisy enough to make it impossible to hear yourself speak, let alone the poor unfortunate on the other end of the crackly line. An example is Jerusalem central bus station. Here the public telephones have been installed right next to the spot where every arriving bus screams to a halt.

Sports

Israel follows a variety of sports, with soccer, followed by basketball as the most popular. Israel Television regularly broadcasts matches from England and an Israeli fan's knowledge of the English game will often put his English counterpart to shame.

Sports centres are common, and the generous climate with the coast and Sea of Galilee encourage sporting activity. Swimming, sailboarding, sailing and water skiing are all popular.

The most noticeable sport is *matkot*, Israel's beach tennis. On any beach popular with Israelis you will frequently notice this game being played – usually very well, very loudly, and very dangerously for anyone having to cross the unmarked court to get to and from the sea.

Israel stages the 'Jewish Olympics', the Maccabiah Games. Held every four years since 1932, they attract Jewish athletes from around the world.

Betting

Israel has a national lottery and football pools, and the number of kiosks around the place show the 'sport's' popularity. Chaim Bermont, one of the country's better writers, once observed that the Israeli Jews' attitude to betting sums up their attitude to life in general. 'When they place a bet they don't hope to win; they expect to win'.

MEDIA
Newspapers & Magazines

Unless you read Hebrew or Arabic, your appreciation of the extensive Israeli newspaper scene will be limited. The *Jerusalem Post* is the only Jewish English-language daily (except Saturdays). Those unfamiliar with the Jewish press may find the limited subject matter tedious. Who is a Jew?, the holocaust, the Jewish birth rate, the lack of Zionism – these are the kind of subjects often discussed in its pages. The *Post* should be read regularly, though, as it does give an insight into the Jewish population which would otherwise be hard to achieve in a short space of time.

For decent articles and photography, look for *Eretz*, a quarterly magazine. The monthly *Israel Scene* covers the community, politics, industry and the arts, together with a bit of gossip. It is light and usually well-written, especially Chaim Bermont's witty column.

The Palestinian press has two English-language weeklies: *Al-Fajr* is the newspaper and *Al-Awda* the magazine. You will normally only see these sold in East Jerusalem, Jerusalem's Old City and towns in the Occupied Territories. Rhetorical in style, their pages provide an alternative picture to the official Israeli presentation of the Palestine Problem. A visit to the offices of the Palestine Press Services (tel 02-280557, 280147, 288896) at 10 Salah ed-Din St, East Jerusalem, is recommended to meet journalists and discuss the Palestine Problem.

Radio & Television

One of the most popular radio stations is the Army service (96FM, 1000AM). It offers a wide variety of programmes, and due to the involvement of virtually the entire Jewish population with the IDF, there is a wide audience. Kol Israel has four stations. Station A (540AM) broadcasts educational, discussion, and current affairs programmes. From 7 pm it broadcasts in 18 languages for Jews all over the world now in Israel. Station B (650AM) has easy listening, recipes, phone-ins, etc. Station C (94FM) was recently introduced to compete with the Army station. It plays mainly popular music for a younger audience. The Voice of Music (88FM) is the classical music station.

Very popular with travellers as well as Israelis is the Voice of Peace (100FM, 1540AM). Broadcasting 24 hours from a ship anchored off the coast of Tel Aviv, this station plays an excellent selection of popular music virtually non-stop. Its founder, Abie J Nathan, is a well-known peace campaigner and has led many colourful campaigns to further the cause. The Voice of Peace broadcasts do not reach beyond Haifa to the north and Beersheba to the south.

In Jerusalem a good alternative is Radio Jordan's broadcasts in English. Their schedule includes the British pop charts, and some classic BBC radio comedies. Listening to the news is a necessity of life for Israelis and news programmes in various languages can be heard frequently. On the Jewish buses the radio, if not already on, will be turned on loudly for the news.

Israel has one television station but people also tune to Jordan Television, and in the north to Syrian Television and Middle East Television, an American-run Christian station.

HEALTH

Before going anywhere abroad, you should have a travel insurance policy which covers medical expenses. Israel presents no special health problems, and there are no vaccinations required. A vaccination against tetanus is a good idea, though.

The main thing to be wary of is the hot, dry climate. Basically cover up and drink up. Wear a hat and use an effective sunscreen. Sunglasses are recommended as the glare can be intense. Drink more liquids than you think you need and carry a water canteen when out in the sun.

Water and food should not present any major problems, although a few travellers do suffer from diarrhoea. The best way to prevent it is to be cautious in the early

stages of your visit, especially when buying food on the street. In Israel, pharmacists are allowed to advise about medicines and sell many items that require a prescription elsewhere. If you need medicine when the pharmacies are closed, check the *Jerusalem Post* or the door of the nearest pharmacy for the list of those on emergency duty. You can also enquire there if you need a doctor.

DANGERS & ANNOYANCES
Safety

Israel is no more dangerous, and probably less so, than other countries. Bullets are not constantly overtaking you as you wander around the Holy Land. When violence has occurred it has almost exclusively involved only the local population. Any foreign targets have been chosen because they are Jewish, or, as has been the case in Jerusalem, because they have annoyed locals with their claims to be the Messiah. Israel's well-developed preoccupation with security has undoubtedly played a major part in making the country as safe as it is.

Another important factor is that most Arabs in the country warmly welcome foreign visitors, especially in the Occupied Territories. They see such visits as an ideal opportunity to put across their version of life in the Jewish State.

Many Israeli Jews expressed their concern for my safety when I told them that I was planning to visit the Gaza Strip, Nablus, Hebron and other 'trouble spots' in the Occupied Territories. In fact, the hospitality that I received there ranks with the best that I have experienced anywhere in the world. This is partly because these Arabs meet so few foreigners that when someone does make the effort to visit them, they are appreciative and friendly. The main reason, though, is that the Arabs are traditionally very hospitable people. Some Israelis were amazed when I told them how hospitable the Arabs had been, not only to me.

The tragedy is that because of the

REPORT SUSPICIOUS OBJECTS

"It's probably nothing..."

but what if it's something?

Report suspicious objects! Dial 100.

Palestine Problem, Arabs have killed Jews, and vice versa, and will no doubt continue to do so. This has caused both groups to perpetuate myths about the other. Basically, unless you are Jewish, or appear to be, you will have no more problems than might be expected when visiting any Arab area: embarrassingly frequent offers of tea, coffee and cigarettes, and the frequent harassment of non-Arab women. As in many countries, Americans of any religion should be extremely sensitive and diplomatic to ensure an enjoyable visit, due to their government's foreign policy. Canadians should just display their maple leaf as they always do!

Finally, always keep up to date with the current situation, and be aware of events that could affect your movements.

A Woman's Travel Survival Kit

In Israel, sexual harassment is a perennial problem for women travellers. The majority of problems will arise with Arab males. Verbal and physical abuse can

be a threat to your enjoyment of the country unless you observe the following guidelines. Israeli men are not known for their gentlemanly conduct towards women either, and women will also be constantly bothered by them.

The Islamic way of life is universally blamed for causing the average Arab male, from boy to old man, to behave like a sexual deviant. However, Christian Arabs often have similar habits. The solo male traveller usually experiences wonderful hospitality from the Arabs, but if accompanied by a woman for only a short time, he soon appreciates the problems she has to face.

On many occasions you will get the impression that a non-Arab woman is subjected to sexual harassment whatever she looks like and however discreetly she conducts herself. Sound advice, though often ignored, is that the dress and behaviour of the local Arab women should be emulated as much as possible when in the Occupied Territories or other Arab areas. Basically this means not wearing tight-fitting or revealing outer garments, and that the legs, arms, shoulders and neckline should be covered. The single act of wearing a bra will avoid countless unwelcome confrontations, and a hat or headscarf is also advisable.

Normally, it is best to totally ignore the predictable and constant come-ons. Even the most negative and impolite of responses from you may end up encouraging your would-be companion who may not understand your verbal or visual snub. A forceful slap or kick in the right place has proved an effective deterrent. Avoid general conversation, keep to short, sharp but polite sentences when necessary, and don't stop when you are approached or shouted at. Never hitch-hike alone or with only female companions.

By giving such advice, I don't want to paint a picture of Israel as a place unsafe for women. It is not, and thousands of women travellers thoroughly enjoy their visit. Common sense and an awareness of the local culture will be the key to an enjoyable visit.

Theft

This does not seem to be any more of a problem in Israel than anywhere else – nor any less. The standard precautionary measures should be taken. Always keep valuables with you or locked in a safe – never leave them in your room. Use a money belt, a pouch under your clothes, a leather wallet attached to your belt, or extra internal pockets in your clothing. Keep a record of your passport, credit card and travellers' cheque numbers separately in case tragedy occurs. It won't cure problems, but it will make them easier to bear.

Travelling on Egged's inter-city buses, you generally stow large bags in the luggage hold. This is a virtually trouble-free system, but keep valuables with you just in case. Crowded tourist spots and markets are an obvious hunting ground for pickpockets, so take extra care.

Beware of your fellow travellers. Unhappily there are more than a few backpackers who make their money go further by helping themselves to other people's. Sleeping on the beach, especially in Eilat, Tel Aviv and Haifa, is taking the risk that you will lose something worth more than the sheqelim saved by not paying for accommodation. Some things which are stolen are replaceable, albeit at a cost. Some things are not, like used film and addresses. Treat them as the valuables they are. Finally, a good travel insurance policy helps. Devote some time to shopping around – don't take the easy way out and listen to your bank or travel agent. You can save money on the policy this way, and give yourself more cover.

Drugs

The possession of drugs in Israel is a serious offence, often punished by a spell in prison. Purchasing drugs here is a risky business, as suppliers and police informers are often one and the same. Bringing drugs into the country yourself is foolhardy – the thoroughness of Israeli customs officers' searches is much talked about amongst travellers. Carrying packages for strangers is just asking for trouble.

FILM & PHOTOGRAPHY

Most types of film are available in Israel but you can buy it cheaper elsewhere. The quality of processing is not particularly high.

Photography in Israel presents no special problems. In strong sunlight, reflections can become glaring and a polarising filter is useful. Be careful when taking photographs to avoid military installations, although photographing soldiers elsewhere does not seem to cause problems. In general, people are not keen on you pointing your lens at them, particularly Hasidic Jews and Arab women. As travel posters and postcard will show, however, it is possible to wander right up to the Western Wall and snap away (but not during the Shabbat or

לפי דין תורה אסור לאדם להכנס
לשטח הר הבית מפני קדושתו
הרבנות הראשית לישראל

ACCORDING TO THE JEWISH LAW, IT IS
STRICTLĪ FORBIDEN FOR ANYBODY TO ENTER
THE TEMPLE MOUNT, OWNG ITS SANCTITY.
THE CHIEF RABINATE OF ISRAEL

IL EST FORMELLEMEIT INTERDIT, D'APRES
LA LOI JUIVE, A TOUT INDIUIDU DE PENETRER
DANS L'ENCEINTE DU TEMPLE, DÚ A SA SAINTETE.
LE GRAND RABBINAT D'ISRAEL

לתשומת לב:
כאן איזור מגורים
לא אתר תיירות
תושבי השכונה

ATTENTION!
THIS IS A
RESIDENTIAL AREA
NOT A TOURIST SITE
RESIDENTS OF THE AREA

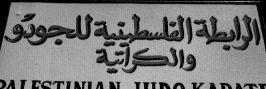

الرابطة الفلسطينية للجودّو
والكراتية

PALESTINIAN JUDO KARATE
ASSOCIATION

Jerusalem
Tel. 285906

القدس

HERE IS NO
INFORMATIO

THIS IS
A RELIGIOUS NEIGBORHOOD

PASSAGE
ONLY TO WOMEN
DRESSED
MODESTLY !

★ LONG DRESS
LOWER THAN KNEE LENGTH
NO SLACKS
★ LONG SLEEVES
BEYOND ELBOW LENGTH
★ CLOSED NECKLINE

RESIDENTS OF THE AREA

רחוב הנוצרים

طريق حارة النصارى

CHRISTIAN QUARTER RD.

ד"ר ע. פרוילין
מומחה
למחלות עור, שערות ומין
הפרעות מיניות

Dr. E. FRÖHLICH
SPECIALIST FOR
SKIN, HAIR, VENEREAL DISEASES
SEXUAL TROUBLES

a Jewish holiday). I am still amazed that photography is permitted in most of the holy sites; unless a sign says that you can't, you can.

When it comes to photography, the best time of the year to visit Israel is between November and April. This avoids the highest temperatures which create a misty haze in such places as the Sea of Galilee, Jericho and the Dead Sea region – some of the best photographic locations.

PLACES TO STAY

Israel has a wide range of accommodation with plenty of scope for both the big spenders and the budget travellers. Before you convert your money into sheqelim, remember that by paying in foreign currency you avoid the 15% value added tax. Costs rise in the high season, but the drop in visitors since the *intefadeh* means that good bargains can be struck.

Hotels

There are luxury hotels in the major cities and resorts and more are being planned. Hilton and Sheraton lead the international brigade but the Israeli company Dan has perhaps the best hotels overall. Prices for these hotels are lower than elsewhere.

Moderate Hotels

Israeli hotels are graded, from five stars down. Modestly priced hotels are found throughout the country and their quality varies considerably. In many, it pays to stand up for yourself in order to get a better price and better service. Prices in this category range from about US$35 to US$60 per night for a double room.

Bed & Breakfast

In many popular tourist areas you will find private home-owners providing accommodation. In some places they form the bulk of moderately priced rooms. They can be found by enquiring at the local tourist office, looking for signs posted in the street or in some places by simply hanging out at the bus station with

your bags. Israel Bed & Breakfast Ltd (tel 02-817001), PO Box 24119, Jerusalem, Israel 91240, is a new agency which can arrange rooms and breakfast in homes throughout Israel. Daily rates range from US$16 to US$28 per person in double occupancy and US$24 to US$40 in single occupancy.

Renting an Apartment

If you can plan a lengthy stay, this can be a comfortable way to save money on hotel and even hostel accommodation. Israel Bed & Breakfast Ltd (address above) and Homtel (tel 03-289141/2, 289503), 33 Dizendoff St, Tel Aviv, Israel, both offer private apartments and villas throughout the country. (See also Jerusalem, Tel Aviv and Eilat chapters.)

Kibbutz Guest Houses

These mainly fit into the middle price range and have swimming pools or beaches and good facilities. However, because kibbutzim are in the countryside, most are inconveniently situated for travellers relying heavily on public transport. The Kibbutz Hotels Central Office (tel 03-24611), 90 Ben Yehuda St, PO Box 3193, Tel Aviv 6130, publishes a booklet listing all their hotels, restaurants and campsites with prices, amenities and a map. You can pick it up at an IGTO or write to the organisation.

Christian Hospices

Various Christian denominations have accommodation in the vicinity of their religious sites. They are often the best value in the low to moderate price range, with cleanliness seemingly the top priority. You do not need to be a Christian to stay in one of these hospices, but you must be prepared to abide by the rules, which usually involve a strict curfew and an early start in the morning.

Hostels

Israel has 30 IYHA hostels, but it is the privately-owned hostels which offer the best value and usually the best service. Also, most IYHA hostels insist that you take breakfast, instead of allowing you to provide your own at a fraction of the cost. Non-members are allowed to use IYHA hostels at a slightly higher price. You can use a YHA card from your own country or buy one from the Israel Youth Hostels Association, 3 Rehov Dorot Rishonim, Jerusalem 91009 (tel 02-222073, 221648), or 32 B'nei Dan St, Tel Aviv (tel 03-455042). Cardholders save 10% on accommodation and food, so you should estimate how many times you would use the IYHA hostels before deciding to buy a card.

Camping

All over the country there are camping areas equipped with all the amenities but charging substantially more than most hostels. Still, there are plenty of opportunities to pitch your tent for free, just ensure that your chosen spot is not off-limits for security reasons. Camping seems to be tolerated on most public beaches. Notable exceptions include the shore of the Dead Sea and the Mediterranean coast north of Nahariya. Do be careful – theft is very common on beaches, especially in Eilat, Tel Aviv and Haifa.

FOOD

Despite loud and constant claims that Israel has an incredible variety of international cuisine due to its worldwide immigration, you'll find much of the food a great disappointment. Perhaps the great cooks from France, Italy and Switzerland were told to plant trees instead of create recipes. However, good food can be found.

Budget travellers may find that eating out on a regular basis will ruin them financially. Luckily, most hostels have a communal kitchen for guests, and so you shop in the street markets, grocery shops and supermarkets, choose from the good range of quality vegetables and fruit, and cook for yourself. Among the best places to eat out cheaply are the Egged self-service

restaurants in the main bus stations. Good, basic food costs about US$3 for a filling meal. They open for breakfast and lunch and usually close late in the afternoon. In places where there is a sizeable Arab population, there are always places to buy a filling cheap meal.

Yes, there are hamburgers and pizzas, but felafel is more popular. The popular hamburgers are those found in the South African-owned Burger Ranch chain, and MacDavid's. Pizza is very popular in Israel, but generally it is of poor quality. The best type does not imitate the style of other countries and is made by Arabs.

Although both Jews and Arabs in Israel love to sit in cafés drinking tea and coffee, people eat at home with their families. However, more and more young Jews are going out to eat dinner in restaurants and drink in bars.

Kashrut & Kosher

Kashrut is the noun derived from the adjective *kosher* which, roughly translated, means 'ritually acceptable'.

Genesis (1:29) permits all fruit and vegetables, and 'clean' animals (7:2). Basically, animals that chew the cud and which have wholly cloven hooves are clean (Leviticus 11; Deuteronomy 14). According to the Mishnah, clean birds must have a crop, a gizzard which can be easily peeled off and an extra talon. All birds of prey are forbidden. Today, those birds which are considered 'traditional' are permitted. This allows for variations according to different Jews' interpretations. Pheasant for example, is considered clean in some communities and not others. In Israel, turkey is definitely considered clean. It is on menus everywhere, often uncredited in kebabs and schnitzels in the hope that it will be thought of as lamb or veal. The Talmud directs that fertilised eggs are forbidden as are any with a spot of blood.

Only fish that have at least one fin and easily removable scales are clean. Honey is allowed despite the bee's status as a forbidden insect. The Mishnah regards it as 'transferred nectar'.

The laws of kashrut stipulate that the slaughter must be carried out by a licensed *shohet*. After slaughtering, he must examine the animal for defects which would make the animal unclean. These may be perforated organ walls, split pipes, missing limbs, missing or defective organs, torn walls or membrane covers of organs, a poisonous substance introduced into the body when mauled by another animal, shattering by a fall, and broken or fractured bones. The animal is suspended head down to allow as much blood as possible to drain out. Leviticus (7:26-27 & 17:10-14) prohibits the consumption of blood and any which does not drain out is removed by salting the meat or roasting it over an open flame.

It is forbidden to eat certain parts of clean animals, including the sciatic nerve (except on a bird), the fat attached to an animal's stomach and intestines, and the abdominal fat of oxen, sheep and goats (unless covered by flesh). The rule that the meat of an animal must not be boiled in the milk of its mother is interpreted by Orthodox Jews to mean that they cannot cook or eat meat and milk (including all dairy products) together. In order to ensure that this rule was never disobeyed unknowingly, the rabbis ruled that the separation of milk and meat must be as complete as possible. This has meant that separate utensils, dishes and cutlery must be used for dairy foods and meat. They must be stored separately and washed in separate sinks or bowls, using separate dishcloths for washing and drying. Strict observance of the Talmud means waiting up for six hours between eating milk and meat dishes. This interval varies depending on the community.

Foods which are neither milk nor meat are known as *parve* or *pareve* and should be prepared with separate utensils. Once prepared they may be used together with milk or meat. Items for sale which have

been accepted as parve by rabbi are certified on the label to ensure that mistakes can be avoided. Kosher restaurants serve either meat or dairy products, and they will not serve cheeseburgers, a cream sauce with chicken, or tea with milk in a meat restaurant.

Kosher laws greatly affect the process of winemaking. Most notably, only Orthodox Jews are permitted to touch the selected grapes and wine during production. Only when bottled and sealed can a secular or non-Jew handle the product.

Theories explaining the kosher laws include hygienic, sanitary, aesthetic, folkloric, ethical and psychological viewpoints. Reform Judaism does not insist on the observance of kashrut, and this major disagreement amongst religious Jews highlights the complexities of Judaism.

After reading that lot you have probably lost any appetite that you may have had. Here are introductions to some of the foods you will encounter in Israel for when your appetite returns.

General

The Israeli diet includes large amounts of dairy products and vegetables, because of the high price of meat. Meals commonly include salad (often tomato and cucumber), *hummus* (a paste from chick peas and olive oil) and *tehina* (a thinner paste from sesame seeds and olive oil), which is often combined with eggplant. These vary in quality from place to place and, with hummus in particular, there is much argument over who makes the best. Served spread out over a plate with pitta bread and pickles, or in a pitta sandwich, these salads are one of the cheapest meals to enjoy in a café/restaurant, and if you eat enough bread (which is often free), you will be full.

The most popular food has to be the *felafel*, and by the time they leave Israel budget travellers unable to cook for themselves will have had an overdose of this item. Felafel is ground chick peas blended with herbs and spices and normally shaped into a ball before deep frying in oil. It is most commonly served with an assortment of salads in pitta bread with tehina sauce topping it.

Like hummus, felafel inspires patrons of certain establishments to argue endlessly about whose is the best. The secret would seem to be the blend of herbs and spices (sounds like a commercial for fried chicken), the frequency with which the oil in the deep fryer is changed, whether or not any addition of breadcrumbs is noticeable and the quality of the salads and tehina. Some felafel stalls allow you to help yourself to as much salad and tehina as you like.

The most popular way to eat meat would seem to be *shwarma*, also known elsewhere as *doner kebab*. It originates from Turkey and is traditionally lamb sliced from a revolving vertical spit. In Israel, unfortunately, it is usually turkey made to taste like lamb. This is eaten along with salad and pitta or in a pitta sandwich like felafel.

Now, all of these items are popular with Jews and Arabs alike, and it is an indication of the intense friction between them that you might well hear a member of one community claim that it is their food and not the others'.

Oriental & Eastern European

Jewish food in Israel can be divided into two categories: Oriental (or Sephardim) and Eastern European (or Ashkenazi).

Oriental food was brought to Israel by the Jews from the Arab countries and is very similar to the food eaten by the Arabs. In addition to salads, felafel and shwarma, one of the most common types of Oriental food is meat cooked 'on the fire'. *Shishlik* is chunks of meat, while *kebabs* are minced meat, both on a skewer. Lamb, beef and chicken are the most popular meats used this way. Offal is also used, and restaurants serving turkey's testicles, cow's udder, spleen, heart,

kidneys and the like are increasingly popular and inexpensive.

One of the tastiest aspects of Oriental cooking is the art of stuffing vegetables and meat with rice, nuts, meat, spices and other goodies. Soups are usually made from meat stock and have a hot, spicy flavour. *Bourekas* are flaky pastry filled with either cheese, potato or spinach, and eaten as a snack.

Eastern European food is characterised by the familiar Viennese schnitzel, Hungarian goulash, and gefilte fish. Most Israelis who I have met denied enjoying the latter. Basically, it consists of ball-shaped pieces of fish heads and tails and is served chilled. Romanian restaurants, among Israel's best, are particularly good for steaks and liver. Goulash soup can be very tasty and is often a meal in itself. Stews and casseroles appear frequently on East European menus, and the 'Jewish mother's' favourite, chicken soup, must not be forgotten. *Blintzes*, which for the uninitiated are a type of pancake, are, on the whole, disappointing.

On Shabbat, most secular Jews join the religious and follow the traditional rule of no cooking. For many, this will mean eating *cholent*, a heavy stew prepared before sunset on Friday.

Palestinian

Most of the best hummus is made by Arabs, and Jews are among their best customers. Good places for this are the cheap sit-down Arab restaurants that only serve hummus, *foul* (pronounced 'fool' – beans) and, as an accompaniment, felafel. Others may also serve shwarma and shishlik and a variety of Palestinian dishes. These could include *mansaf*, rice with small pieces of lamb, nuts, lemon juice and the herbs which give this cuisine its character. This dish is a speciality of Jericho and Hebron.

Specifically from the Jerusalem area is *makluki*, an upside-down dish of rice, lamb, eggplant and other vegetables. From Nablus and the north comes *mousakan*, chicken cooked on the fire with olive oil, onions and spices, served on flat bread. *Melok* is a soup made from greens. *Kubbe* is dough stuffed with spiced lamb or beef and deep fried. It's also available in Oriental Jewish and Armenian establishments. Sometimes you will find kebabs served in a tehina sauce, or vegetables stuffed with meat, rice, nuts, herbs and spices.

In the more up-market places, *mazza*, a selection of starters, is a speciality. This includes hummus, brain salad, eggplant purée, stuffed vine leaves, olives and pickles. It can be a meal in itself.

Fish is a major menu item. Kosher laws forbid the use of shellfish, and Israeli law protects lobsters in particular. Shrimps are not protected and can often be found. Lobster is occasionally imported. Squid or calamari is popular, and the popular fresh fish are red mullet, red snapper, grouper and sole. St Peter fish from the Sea of Galilee are now farmed commercially.

Sunflower seeds and nuts are by far the most popular snack foods for Jews and Arabs alike. Everywhere you go you'll see people crunching away. You will be amazed by the way the locals can pop a fistful of seeds into their mouth, crunch, spit out the shells and chew the seeds – often talking and driving simultaneously. Pickles are also popular snacks.

Desserts & Sweets

One of the edible highlights in Israel are the Arab sweets or pastries. Usually soaked in honey and full of sugar, they cannot be good for you, but who cares? *Baklava (burma)*, toasted shredded wheat, stuffed with pistachios or hazelnuts and soaked in honey; the crumpet-like *katayeef* and *kanafe*, a contrast of cheese, wheat, sugar and honey, are the most common. A special Arab sweet treat is *moutabak*, which is cheese inside super flaky pastry covered in sugar syrup.

Palestinians are proud of their sweets and while Nablus is recognised as the top producer, with kanafe its speciality, Gaza claims to be the best. Jerusalem's Old City, though, is the place to try moutabak. *Halvah*, a kind of nougat made from sesame seeds, is popular. An original version of Turkish Delight is available, mainly in Nablus.

The Jews also have a sweet tooth and you will never be short of somewhere to dive into cream cakes and pastries. Due to the kosher laws, many of the bakers unfortunately use synthetic cream. Biscuits seem to be part of the staple diet – they are produced in large numbers by Jewish and Arab bakers.

Most Israeli ice cream will not satisfy the connoisseurs among you – too sweet and synthetic tasting. The very best brand should, however. Creamy Manalito's is made by Argentinian Jews and is available in Tel Aviv and Jerusalem. Very popular with travellers are the Eternity Restaurant's vegetable ice creams, made from calcium-rich soya bean milk.

Fruit

With its varied climate, Israel is able to produce a wide range of fruits, including oranges, apples, mangoes, guava and avocado pears. They are available at reasonable prices in the street markets and supermarkets. Israel has long been known for its vineyards, and grapes in season are very affordable.

'Sabra' is the nickname for Israeli-born Jews, derived from the cactus fruit imported to Palestine from Mexico a few centuries ago. It looks like a hand-grenade and is the inspiration for the description of Israeli Jews as tough and prickly on the outside, soft and sweet on the inside. Sold on the streets everywhere when in season, it's an acquired taste. The seeds give the locals another chance to use their unsurpassed spitting skills.

Vegetarian Food

The Eternity Restaurants in Tel Aviv, Rehovot and (possibly soon) Jerusalem, should not be missed. They produce and serve their own tofu dishes, including cream pies and hot dogs. They use no animal products whatsoever, meat or dairy, and they are cheap. The recipes have been developed by the Black Hebrew community (see Religions).

Dairy & Eggs

Milk is packaged either in plastic bags (homogenised) or cartons (sterilised, long life). Cheeses sold by weight (as opposed to the less expensive pre-packed variety) include Feta, from sheep's milk; Bulgarian, with a salty, vinegary taste; Zefat, white, round, half salty, also made with pepper or onion or garlic; Labana, a dry Arab cheese from sheep's milk, sometimes sold in oil to preserve it and also made yoghurt style; Turkish cashcavel, dry and strong, made from sheep's milk, and Balkanic yoghurt, creamy and a bit sour. The Israelis also make good versions of mozzarella, roquefort, boursin and cream cheese.

Eggs in Israel are usually terrible. The yolks are pale and the flavour is so subtle it almost isn't there. It sounds corny, but the best eggs are Arab! This is because they are free-range, while the Jewish farmers have battery hens fed on a strict diet.

Breads

Israel has a delicious selection of breads, both Jewish and Arabic. Many travellers make the mistake of assuming that the cheapest is *pitta*, the small, flat, round loaves produced by Arabs and Oriental Jews. If you are counting every agorot, then buying the subsidised Jewish standard white loaves from grocery stores and supermarkets will cost you about half the price. *Hallah*, a softer style of bread is baked for Shabbat. Jewish bakeries produce sweet breads, too. Glazed with sugar syrup, filled with currants or chocolate, they vary in quality but can be great.

Jewish Oriental bakeries produce similar breads to the Arabs. Iraqi pitta is very thin and resembles a large pancake. Arabs mainly bake pitta, and it can be thickly covered with sesame seeds or have the top sprinkled with *zarta* or *dogga*, a mixture of herbs (mainly oregano) and spices. This is served separately with pitta and bagels, which you dip into the mixture after dipping them in olive oil.

Bagels are very popular. Originally from Eastern Europe, Israeli bagels are different from most others, being crisper and drier. In Tel Aviv a softer style is produced, sprinkled with sesame seeds. A traditional way to end a night out is to visit the bagel factory and pick up a hot bagel or two. Arab bagels are similar but larger. In East Jerusalem and the Old City they are sold from carts everywhere. Be aware of the going rate and do not pay more – overcharging is common.

Other Cuisine

Israel has a small but increasing number of restaurants featuring international cuisines, including Chinese, South-East Asian, French, Italian, Indian and Mexican. Most of them are quite expensive. Worthy of special note is the very reasonably priced *Panorama Restaurant* in Tel Aviv's Astor Hotel, featuring Israeli nouvelle cuisine, said to be the start of an upward trend in the country.

Breakfast

The Israeli breakfast, traditionally salad-based, is usually made out to be something pretty special. Brochures feature photographs of buffet tables laden with what is described as 'huge selections of fresh fruits, salads and cheeses, eggs cooked various ways, yoghurt, herring, smoked salmon and endless varieties of freshly baked bread and rolls'. In reality, an Israeli breakfast will often fail to live up to such an enthusiastic description and consist of a far less exciting selection. Why the IGTO has to greatly exaggerate an item like breakfast when there are so many really good things to talk about, is beyond me.

Drinks

Tea and coffee are Israel's most popular beverages. A lover of strong tea, I find the local Jewish blends extremely weak and use two tea bags per cup. The Arabs, meanwhile, are the best teamakers anywhere. Tea is usually served in a glass. The Arabs serve it black, very sweet (tell them if you don't want sugar before it's too late) and often with mint or *maramia*, a herb which is supposedly good for the stomach. Jews serve tea black, with lemon, milk or non-dairy creamer to satisfy the kosher laws. Vegetarian restaurants usually have a range of herbal teas.

'Coffee' here means Turkish coffee. 'Nescafé' or 'nes' are the terms used for instant coffee. Espresso and cappuccino are increasingly available in Jewish establishments. Arabs and Oriental Jews often serve Turkish coffee with *'hehl*, spicy seeds which add to the flavour and aroma. Street cafés are as popular as they are in Europe. Sitting, slurping and staring at the interesting variety of people going by is a national pastime.

Soft drinks in Israel are expensive. Save a small fortune by buying cups of the *meets* (cordials) sold in cafés and by street kiosks from coolers. Freshly squeezed fruit juices are widely available at reasonable prices. Israel has its own still mineral water, Eden, produced in the Golan. The best tap water for drinking is in Safed and Rosh Pina. Most travellers have no problems with drinking the water, although in Eilat, if anywhere, you might be careful.

Tamar hindi is a traditional Palestinian soft drink, very sweet and made from dates. You'll see it sold in the Damascus Gate area of East Jerusalem by Arabs with a giant silver 'coffee pot' on their backs, wearing a belt carrying glasses strapped on in which to serve it. Although an impressive sight, the drink tastes better, or cleaner at least, from the nearby cafés. The milky-coloured drink also sold there is made from carob. Another local favourite, served hot in the winter, cold in the summer, is *sahlab*. It is made up of sahlab powder (like tapioca), milk, coconut, sugar, chopped nuts, rosewater and a glacé cherry garnish.

Beer The National Brewery Ltd controls 98% of the beer market. Starting from the bottom, price-wise, Nesher (3.8 or 4.2% alcohol) is often overlooked by travellers as it is not served in most bars or cafés. It is considerably cheaper than other products, which improves its flavour no end. Do not mistake the brown-labelled Nesher beer for the blue-labelled Nesher Malt, a dark, sweet, beer-based beverage with less than 1% alcohol. Goldstar (4.7%) is the most popular beer with travellers and until now was the only beer available on draught, as well as bottled. Maccabee (4.9%) is the Israeli favourite, considered upmarket and the only beer exported. In recent years, Budweiser (4.7 and 5%) Tuborg (5.9%) have been brewed under licence. Draught Tuborg is also available.

Beer prices vary considerably around Israel, with Eilat and Tel Aviv the cheapest places.

Wine & Spirits Although you will see several shelves in supermarkets and grocer shops lined with bottles of wine and spirits, Israelis do not drink very much. Every Shabbat and on certain holy days wine is traditionally drunk, but that is generally all. However, vines and wines existed in Israel as early as 3000 BC, making it one of the world's oldest wine-producing areas. The symbol of the Ministry of Tourism, as well as Carmel, Israel's largest wine company, depicts the two men sent by Moses to spy out the land of Canaan who carried back a bunch of grapes slung on a pole between them (Numbers 13).

The modern wine industry began in the late 19th century, when Jews from Eastern Europe made their way to Palestine. Some settled in Rishon le Zion and suffered considerable hardship in their attempts at farming. The hunger, thirst and disease that followed had not been expected in the Promised Land. Faced with defeat, they sent an emissary back to Europe to raise money. Baron Edmond de Rothschild, of the French wine family, later known as the 'Benefactor', agreed to help. He sent wine experts and business consultants to Rishon to develop the land. This aid was not limited to the immediate area, and after surveying the country and meeting other Zionist pioneers, other vineyards were developed along the coast and another winery was built at Zichron Ya'acov. In 1906 both wineries were signed over to the farmers, establishing the Societé Co-operative Vigneronne des Grandes Caves.

That co-operative is today the Carmel wine company. Originally, the co-operative's aim was to produce kosher wines for Jews worldwide, so sweet wines were developed. Soon after independence, it was decided to develop kosher table wine for a wider market. Progress has been very slow, but internationally competitive wines have been produced and improvements continue to be made.

Monfort is the second most popular wine label in Israel. Based in Netanya and named after the Crusader castle in the north, they specialised in spirits during the Mandate. They use the respected Stock label for their spirits and vermouths range under an agreement with the Italian company.

In the mid 1970s, the first vines were planted in the Golan Heights. The development there of vineyards and a winery by a co-operative of kibbutzim and moshavim has taken the industry by storm. Under the Yarden and Gamla labels, these wines have been by far the best Israel has produced. The other notable wine producers in the country are Christian monks. The Trappist monastery at Latrun, between Tel Aviv and Jerusalem, was founded in 1890. Winemaking started in 1899 when the French founders decided upon manual work as a means of support. Near

Bethlehem is the Cremisan monastery. Here the Italian Salesian monks have been making wine since 1885. Their main markets are Israel and Jordan. Note that these monasteries use the term Holy Land, not Israel, on their labels. They also both produce vermouths and fortified wines.

Although the quality of the wines and spirits in Israel can be exaggerated, they are not expensive as the fierce competition has kept prices low. In the US$2 to US$4 price range, you have a fair choice of enjoyable wines.

Arak and brandy are the best-selling Israeli spirits. *Arak* is a word of Arab origin and covers many different spirits. It is distilled from such various fermented bases as rice, palm sap, yams and dates. A regular drinker, before collapsing, managed to tell me that Israel's best brand is Alouf. Good Israeli brandies are Stock, Carmel's 777 and Carmei-Zion's Grand 41. Israeli spirits are very cheap, about US$4, and well worth taking across with you on a trip to Egypt to sell on the black market.

Whisky and vodka (Gold brand) are popular there. Vermouths and fortified wines, mainly sherry and port, are also produced locally. Other than the Stock range, their dusty state on shop shelves is more than justified. More successful are some of the Israeli liqueurs, especially Carmei-Zion's Hallelujah, a sort of Jewish Grand Marnier.

BOOKS & BOOKSHOPS

The 'average Israeli' supposedly reads 10 books a year. Every spring, Hebrew Book Week is celebrated throughout the country with open-air markets. Bookshops are plentiful, with a great many dealing in second-hand books. Steimatzky's is the largest chain of bookstores. Found everywhere, they are one of the best places for that popular travellers' pastime – glancing at the foreign newspapers and magazines.

With so many keen readers and such a

tumultuous history, Israel is the subject of more books than most countries. A list of relevant books for someone visiting Israel could easily become a book in its own right.

Politics

The ever-popular subject. Here are some titles, covering a variety of viewpoints, to give you verbal ammunition (and perhaps other ailments) for the discussions to come.

Arab and Jew: Wounded Spirits in a Promised Land by David K Shipler (Times Books, New York, 1986). The Pulitzer Prize winner and a must for anyone with an interest in the subject. The observations of the realities of Israel today are spot-on and all visitors will benefit from reading his book.

In the Land of Israel by Amos Oz (Chatto & Windus, Hogarth Press, London; Harcourt Brace Jovanovitch, San Diego, 1983). This leading Israeli writer travelled the country, discussing politics with those he met from all sections of the population.

They Must Go by Rabbi Meir Kahane (Groset & Dunlap, New York, 1981). The controversial Brooklyn-born Kahane leads Israel's *Koch* political party who advocate, amongst other things, the expulsion of all the Arabs from Israel and the Occupied Territories. Here he states his case.

From Time Immemorial by Joan Peters (Harper & Row, New York, 1984). Championed by Zionists for its conclusion that Israel's Arabs arrived more recently than is often claimed, so reducing the argument for Palestinian rights.

This Land is Our Land by Metzer, Orth and Sterzing (Zed Press, London, 1983). A study of the West Bank dispute.

My Friend the Enemy by Uri Avnery (Lawrence Hill, Westport CT, 1986). This left-wing radical, a millionaire author, publisher, and former Knesset member, visited the PLO's Yasser Arafat at the height of the war in Lebanon (to which he was opposed). This book is his account of why he went and how it went.

Jews & American Politics by Stephen D Isaacs (Doubleday, New York, 1974). A look at the USA's political and financial support of Israel.

They Dare to Speak Out by Paul Findley (Lawrence Hill, Westport CT, 1985). This former US Congressman studies the pro-Israel lobby in America.

Biographies

Tongue of the Prophets – The Life Story of Eliezer Ben Yehuda by Robert St John (Doubleday, New York, 1952). The man who revived the Hebrew language.

Herzl by Amos Elon (Holt, Reinhart & Winston, New York, 1975). The founder of political Zionism.

The Revolt – the Story of the Irgun by Menachem Begin (Nash, New York, 1977).

Ben-Gurion: Prophet of Fire by Dan Kurzman (Simon & Schuster, New York, 1983). Israel's first prime minister.

My Life by Golda Meir (Weidenfield & Nicholson, London, 1975).

Arafat: Terrorist or Peacemaker? by Alan Hart (Sidgwick & Jackson, London, 1984). Some thought-provoking conclusions.

Our Man in Damascus: Elie Cohen by Eli Ben-Hanan (Crown, New York, 1969). A fascinating account of Israel's most celebrated spy.

Travel

The Innocents Abroad by Mark Twain (American Publishing Co., Hartford CT, 1871). Still one of the best books dealing with the tourist experience in the Holy land.

Enemy in the Promised Land – An Egyptian Woman's Journey into Israel by Sana Hasan (Shocken Books, New York, 1986). Three years before Sadat, the author visited the Jewish State, and her interesting account is full of observations and experiences that illustrate the real Israel.

Jerusalem

Most visitors are captivated by this city. To get to know it better, the following books are well worth reading:

Footloose in Jerusalem by Sarah Fox Kaminker (Crown, New York, 1981). A popular guide outlining several detailed walks in the Old and New Cities.

O Jerusalem by Larry Collins and Dominique Lapierre (Simon & Schuster, New York, 1972). The most popular book with travellers in Israel, this provides a balanced look at the 1948 War of Independence and the birth of the modern State of Israel.

Jerusalem – Problems & Prospects edited by

Joel L Kaemer (Praeger, New York, 1980). An
attraction of the Holy City is its complexity,
and this book includes such chapters as 'Israeli
policy in East Jerusalem' and 'The Christian
Establishment in Jerusalem'.

For Jerusalem – a life by Teddy Kollek with his
son Amos (Random House, New York, 1978).
An insight into the administration of the Holy
City by its colourful mayor.

Religion

This is My God. The Jewish Way of Life by.
Herman Wouk (Simon & Schuster, New York,
1959).

*Wanderings: Chaim Potok's History of the
Jews* (Knopf, New York, 1978).

In the Steps of the Master by H V Morton
(Dodd, Mead, New York, 1979). A guide to the
land of Jesus.

The Orthodox Church by Timothy Ware
(Penguin, London/New York, 1975).

Islam: Beliefs & Teachings by Ghulam Sawar
(Muslim Education Trust, London, 1982).

The Druzes in Israel by Gabriel Ben-Don
(Magnes Press, Jerusalem, 1979).

Archaeology

The Holy Land by Jerome Murphy-O'Conner
(Oxford University Press, London/New York,
1986). Simply the best archaeological guide;
concise and interesting, with some deft touches
of humour.

Fiction

To be enjoyed, not believed, these are
probably the two most popular of the
countless titles with an Israeli theme.

The Source by James Michener (Random
House, New York, 1965).

Exodus by Leon Uris (Doubleday, New York,
1958).

STUDY

After a few weeks in Israel, it is not
uncommon for travellers to find that they
want to learn Hebrew. Although some will
gain a basic understanding of the language
through their day-to-day existence,
learning it properly (especially reading
and writing) will only be achieved through
study. Unfortunately, finding a place to
learn Hebrew in Israel is not easy. Most

ulpanim (language schools) cater for new
Jewish immigrants and do not seem to
encourage non-Jews. You will have to look
around to find a place. Jerusalem is a good
area because the municipality seems to
run a slightly cheaper programme of
classes. Contact the Ulpan Office,
Department of Culture, Division of Adult
Education (tel 02-224156), 11 Beit
Ha'am, Bezalel St, Jerusalem.

The Ulpan Akiva Netanya (tel 053-
52312/3), PO Box 256, Netanya 42102, is
an international school for Jews and
non-Jews and has various programmes for
learning Hebrew and Arabic. These are
expensive, though (hundreds of dollars,
folks), lasting from three to 20 weeks.
Kibbutz Ulpan is a 4½ or six month
programme for those who want to learn
Hebrew and experience kibbutz life.
Students spend half the day at work, and
the other half studying, six days a week.
Contact your nearest kibbutz office or the
Kibbutz Aliya Desk (tel 212-2551338), 27
West 20th St, New York, NY 10011, USA.

THINGS TO BUY

Israel is full of shops stocked with tacky
souvenirs for gullible tourists. To find
bargains and quality items you will need
time to shop around and patience to
haggle. Bargaining is not always the 'fun'
it is made out to be. Mostly limited to
Arab markets, it can be time consuming,
frustrating and, in general, an unwelcome
hassle. The golden rules are not to start
bargaining with a shopkeeper unless you
are really interested in buying, have a
good idea of the item's value both locally
and back home, and do not be intimidated.
Easier said than done. Do not use large
notes or travellers' cheques, as getting
change can be a problem.

Basically, the bargaining game is
played like this: the shopkeeper usually
attracts your attention and gives you a
price three to 10 times above the realistic
going rate. If you are genuinely interested
you pull a face showing disgust or
amusement at his quote, and state your

offer, saying 'Take it or leave it'. Traditionally, this should be below the amount you are willing to pay. Whatever, stick to your guns and do not be bullied, or cajoled into paying too much. Turning away from a bargaining session can often cut a price in half. A good idea is to observe the shopkeepers at work. Note how they flirt with young ladies, or bully them and the older tourists. They can also act respectfully towards potential customers.

Traditionally, Arab shopkeepers sell something cheaper early in the day, as a quick first sale means good business later. However, this line is often used to persuade customers to pay more, thinking that they are getting a bargain.

Not all your shopping needs to be done in markets. Some of Israel's best buys are luxury items from regular stores and galleries. Worth remembering is that some stores give a special discount if you pay foreign currency. Check prices elsewhere all the same as, even without a discount, they may be cheaper.

Sandals
Most travellers seem to feel that they have to buy a pair. The cheapest are in Jericho (if you bargain), not in Jerusalem's Old City. The Jewish shoe shops make better quality but at double the price.

T-Shirts
Buy from the Arabs in Jerusalem's Old City. Some good designs include the Voice of Peace, names in Hebrew and Arabic, 'Don't worry America, Israel is Right Behind You' and, if you ask for it, 'I Love Palestine' written in Arabic with the tree symbol of Palestine. Again, you can pay double elsewhere for similar shirts.

Ceramics
Some good quality ceramics in modern and traditional styles are available. Tiles and plates seem to be very popular – the Armenians are recognised as the leading craftsmen of these. The best selection is in Jerusalem's Old City, also Akko and

Jaffa. Pottery in general is widespread, and the quality varies. Hebron stands out as a place where you can see the potters at work.

Copper & Brass
They are hard to transport, but great-looking items are to be had if you have done your homework on the prices back home. Oriental coffee pots, trays and little cups, *nargilas* (hubble-bubble pipes), and various ornaments are widely available. Do shop around, and check the Jaffa flea market, Jerusalem's Old City and Mea Shearim, Nazareth and Akko in particular.

Woodwork
Olive wood is the popular material and souvenirs for all budgets are made. Most popular are crucifixes, camels, worry beads and carvings of biblical scenes and characters. Available everywhere.

Glassware
Loud claims are made about this industry in Israel but little I saw inspired me. Hebron is the recognised leader in the field, and buying there should save money.

Canework & Basketware
Gaza produces the best canework and it's sold all over the country; usually furniture, but also decorative pieces, baskets and trays. Basketware materials include rushes and raffia and are coloured with different interwoven shades.

Fashion – Leather & Furs
Leather and furs are of high quality but not cheap – just cheaper than in most other places, especially as tourists get 35% off. Begged Or ('leatherware' in Hebrew), which uses Italian and Israeli leather, is the leading house, with stores in several places. Others include D R Jordan in Tel Aviv's Dizengoff Center, and Ginette in Ha Yarkon St (corner of Yerimyahu St), Tel Aviv. For furs, check out Scharf's Furs' showroom in Talpiot, Jerusalem.

The fashion scene is centred in Tel Aviv, with Newe Tzedek being a hotbed of textile activity – workshops and showrooms. Explore this area and also Yerimyahu St where most of the boutiques are owned by designers.

Tel Aviv beach is full of sabra poseurs, many of whom will be (almost) wearing Israeli design swimwear, one of the country's more successful sports. Gottex is by far the leading name, with Gideon Oberson producing the most daring designs. You may find the prices for Israeli swimwear cheaper back home. If buying clothes in a sale, check garments thoroughly. Damaged goods are sold and there is no legal comeback.

A popular fashion accessory worldwide, but unrecognised by those wearing it, is the kaffiyeh (Arab headscarf). The black design is traditionally associated with Palestine, the red with Jordan. Other items of traditional Arab clothing can be found in the Arab markets.

Jewellery

This can range from the cheap but fashionable street variety to gold and diamonds. The Black Hebrews' handmade jewellery is some of the best and cheapest available. Jerusalem's Ben Yehuda St and Tel Aviv's Dizengoff St are the busiest street-selling zones. Yemenite jewellery is a delicate style of intricately joined metals. Heavier, massive and more roughly executed is Bedouin, Arab and Druze jewellery. Amber is one of the more commonly used stones. Religious jewellery is obviously popular.

More upmarket items, including gold, silver and precious stones, are widely available. Knowledge of this field is essential to avoid paying too much. Do not rely on the honesty of the vendor wherever you are shopping.

Things to Sell

Goods such as cassette/radios (the 'ghetto-blaster' type with detachable speakers is popular), personal stereos and cameras can be sold for a healthy profit. Sony is the most popular hi-fi make, and quality camera lenses and flashes like Vivitar are admired. Other electrical goods will not normally fetch a good price, especially in Tel Aviv and Haifa where most of the black market trade seems to operate.

I met some travellers who had arrived from Greece and Turkey with wool and leather clothing which sold like hot cakes. You will hear many fellow travellers and locals say that you can no longer succeed at the selling game. It is not true, but you must know who to sell to and where. Do not accept low offers from middle-men who want to sell your gear to someone else. Check local shop prices and sell your items at a lower but profitable rate.

WHAT TO BRING

The usual traveller's rule applies – bring as little as possible, but without having to buy too many things in Israel. Clothes and toiletries in particular can be expensive. The one thing most travellers fail to realise is how chilly Israel can be in the winter and that most summer evenings are cool enough to need a sweater. A sleeping bag is only necessary if you're going to be constantly roughing it. Hostels usually provide sheets and blankets. Also necessary are a sun hat, sunglasses, a water canteen, comfortable walking shoes (worn in but not worn out) and clothes suitable for the hot climate and for visiting religious sites. Remember that most religious sites are not open to anyone dressed immodestly. Men and women must cover their legs, shoulders, necklines and arms to the elbow. In synagogues and most other Jewish holy sites, all heads must be covered.

A small daypack is indispensable. Most travellers still opt for the backpack to carry their gear. An alternative is a large, soft but strong zip bag with a wide shoulder strap and hand grips. Not great if making several short trips or for lengthy travelling but perhaps more socially acceptable. My ideal choice is a combination of the two – the travel pack. This is a backpack with a flap which zips over the shoulder straps to turn it into a soft bag. This looks more presentable and is less prone to damage than a backpack.

Getting There

You have the choice of land, sea and air when travelling to Israel, but this can be complicated by the delicate political situation if you want to include other Middle Eastern countries on your itinerary.

AIR

Flying is now possible from more countries than ever as El Al, Israel's national airline, continues to expand its network. Competition with the increased number of charter flight operators has kept their prices low. If you are under 26 or a student you can get even cheaper deals.

Ben Gurion Airport at Lod, about 18 km east of Tel Aviv and 50 km from Jerusalem, is the country's main air terminal. Eilat Airport is used for a small number of charter flights. Bear in mind that if you arrive in Israel without a return ticket, you will probably need to show immigration officials that you have sufficient funds to leave the country or risk being given a lot less than the standard three month visa.

From the UK & Europe

Regardless of the official scheduled fares, charter flights to Israel from the UK continue to hover around the £200 mark for a 12 month open return. This can come down to as little as £160 for a 1 to 4 week return. A one-way charter ticket averages about £110. It is worth shopping around London and Manchester's cheap flight specialists for current offers. STA (tel 581 1022) at 74 Old Brompton Rd, London SW7, are regularly amongst the cheapest, as are the various Earls Court Rd cheap ticket specialists. Glance at the ads in *Time Out*, *City Limits*, *The Times* and the Sunday newspapers.

Most European countries have charter flights to Israel with considerable savings on scheduled fares: West Germany,

France, Belgium, the Netherlands and Scandinavia in particular. Prices are slightly higher than those from the UK.

From the USA & Canada

Again, charter flights offer the best deals by far but many North American travellers prefer to fly non-stop with El Al for security reasons. Consult the cheap flight advertisements in Sunday newspapers and do not rely on your local travel agent for the best deal available. Cheaper fares are around US$850 return to Tel Aviv from New York. If you have the time, combining your trip to Israel with a stopover in London, Athens or elsewhere in Europe can often be an economical option. This can involve buying a cheap return ticket to Europe and then buying another one there to take you to Israel; or you could make your way to the ferry in Piraeus, Greece, and sail to Haifa.

From Australia & New Zealand

If you are flying from Down Under you have an expensive choice, depending on the time of year you travel. Not many airlines fly direct to Israel and return fares range from around A$2000 to A$2500. Fares to other destinations in the area, especially Cairo and Athens, are cheaper, and it may work out costing you less to fly to one of these first. You could consider a round-the-world ticket which includes Israel and costs around A$2600. Again, don't believe the first travel agent's version of the best deal – shop around.

From Egypt

There are El Al and Air Sinai flights available between Israel and Egypt which will save you having an Egypt-Israel border stamp in your passport, but at a cost of around US$120.

Cheap Tickets in Israel
Although not quite as cheap as buying the equivalent tickets in Europe or North America, some Israel travel agents are at least cheaper than their competitors in the country. A few years ago, the Israeli Government put a stop to travel agents cutting the prices on air tickets, but the rule was soon ignored and you will now find special offers emblazoned on travel agents' windows, mainly in Tel Aviv and Jerusalem. Note that, despite the long queues, the Israel Student Travel Association (ISSTA) offices do not offer very competitive fares. The following agencies seem to be regularly amongst the cheapest:

GSTS, 57 Ben Yehuda St, Tel Aviv (tel 03-222261) - next to the tourist office. They also have a good selection of Lonely Planet guides.
Galilee Tours, 142 Ha Yarkon St, Tel Aviv (tel 03-221372, 230651, 220819, 225187, 203311) and 3 Ben Sira St, Jerusalem (tel 02-246858).
Mona Tours, 25 Bograshov St - at the Ben Yehuda St end - Tel Aviv (tel 03-290071, 202310, 203210).
Airtour Ltd, 32 Ben Yehuda St, Tel Aviv (tel 03-295361).

OVERLAND
To/from Egypt
Once impossible, travel between Israel and Egypt is now a thriving part of the tourist scene. For those who have the time, combining a visit to both countries is extremely popular.

In Israel, several operators provide coach services, mainly from Tel Aviv but also from Jerusalem and Eilat, to destinations in the Sinai Desert and Cairo. See the *Jerusalem Post* and the tourist offices for current prices and schedules. Alternatively, you can use local transport and cross the border on your own, taking an Egyptian bus or taxi into the Sinai or on to Cairo.

You cross the border at either Taba, near Eilat, or Rafah in the Gaza Strip, where you swap your Israeli vehicle for an Egyptian one. No Egyptian visa is required if you only visit the Sinai.

To/from Jordan
It is possible to enter Israel from Jordan, and vice versa, but you need to be diplomatic since the legal status of the West Bank depends on whether you are talking to Jordanian or Israeli officialdom. According to the Israelis the West Bank is part of Israel, according to the Jordanians it is occupied territory. The Jordanians will allow you to enter from the Occupied West Bank, but not from Israel. Therefore, you will not be allowed to enter Jordan if you have an Israeli visa (make sure your entry stamp is made on a separate document to your passport), visas issued in Israel, entry or exit stamps from the Israeli/Egyptian border (the Egyptians always enter these in your passport), or Israeli currency.

The crossing point between Israel/Occupied West Bank and Jordan is a bridge, known as the Allenby Bridge to the Israelis, the King Hussein Bridge to the Jordanians. It's an international border according to the Israelis, but not to the Jordanians. It's open for tourists Sunday to Thursday from 8 am to 1 pm, and on Fridays and eves of holidays from 8 to 11 am - allow plenty of time. On Saturdays and Israeli and Jordanian holidays the bridge is closed. In addition, the slightest political disturbance on either side can cause the bridge to close without notice for days on end.

You may find it impossible to change money at the bridge, so if you're heading to Jordan bring Jordanian dinars with you. Jordanian dinars are readily available in the West Bank and Jerusalem. They are also accepted there, so changing money is no problem if you're heading to Israel.

Absolutely no photography is allowed in this extremely sensitive area. All cameras must be empty of film - any loaded film will be confiscated.

Jordanian buses are the only vehicles allowed to take passengers across the bridge – it's not possible to walk, hitch or take a private vehicle.

Israel to Jordan You must have a Jordanian visa, best obtained at a Jordanian embassy or consulate but also issued at the Jordan-Syria border and at Aqaba. Visas are not issued at Allenby/King Hussein Bridge or anywhere in Israel.

The quickest way to get to the bridge is to take a service taxi from East Jerusalem (about US$7). Abdo Taxi & Travel Services (tel 02-283281, 286292) on the corner of Suleiman St and HaNevi'im St (behind the Faisal Hostel) in East Jerusalem, specialise in the 30-minute drive.

You can save money travelling via Jericho by bus or service taxi. From Jerusalem to Jericho catch Arab bus No 28 (US$1) from the East Jerusalem Arab bus station or Egged bus Nos 961 and 963 (US$1.50) from the central bus station in Jaffa Rd. Service taxis leave from the rank on the corner of HaNevi'im St and Suleiman St (US$2).

From Jericho to the bridge transfer to another service taxi or, if you can find one at a suitable hour, squeeze onto a Shakeen Bus. Service taxis leave from the main square by the 'Jericho Municipality' sign. Make sure that your taxi is permitted to take you right to the bridge – some will leave you short with little hope of getting another ride.

The Shakeen Bus Company's service from Hebron passes through Jerusalem and Jericho on its way to the bridge. It is difficult to know when it will arrive at any of these points, so give yourself plenty of time. From Hebron the fare is US$4, Jerusalem US$3 and Jericho US$1.30.

At the bridge there is an inspection of luggage and cameras, and a Jordanian bus takes you to the other side (JD1.500). Here you get a Jordanian permit which may have to be produced on departure or

for security checks. Service taxis and JETT buses run to Amman.

Jordan to Israel Entering Israel from Jordan presents few problems unless you are attempting to return to Israel having entered Jordan via the Allenby/King Hussein Bridge. This is technically impossible and if you don't make it you'll have to fly from Amman or cross into Egypt.

Since the West Bank is not a part of Israel (according to the Jordanians) you require a Jordanian-issued West Bank permit to enter it. This is available from the Ministry of the Interior in Amman. The issuing process normally involves some form-filling and takes three working days, but as they don't keep your passport you can use this time for more travel in Jordan.

The application form asks your religion, and it's a good idea to have one (perhaps not Judaism). You are also asked where you arrived. If you say you entered at the King Hussein Bridge you are, in Jordanian eyes, saying that you consider this to be an international border – and you won't get a permit. Try writing 'Jerusalem', or nothing at all. If the official sees the permit you received when you crossed the bridge into Jordan, your chances will plummet. Good luck!

The permit allows you a one-month stay on the West Bank. Of course once you are across the bridge you are in Israel, as far as the Israeli authorities are concerned, and are free to travel anywhere in the country. You can return to Jordan within the month so long as your Jordanian visa is still valid and your passport doesn't have an Israeli stamp in it.

From Amman, service taxis and JETT buses run to the bridge. Buses go to the Israeli check-point but taxis drop you at the foreigners terminal from where a bus crosses to the Israeli side. A tax of JD2.500 has to be paid to enter Israel.

SEA

From Greece & Italy

Thousands of travellers arrive in Israel via the ferry service from Piraeus, near Athens, while the service to Haifa from Venice still runs once a month for a diminishing few who pay from US$75 (deck) one way. The Piraeus/Haifa run is covered by several shipping lines with some stopping over in Rhodes, the others in Crete, and all stopping at Limassol in Cyprus. The cheapest tickets are US$55 (US$44 students and those under 26) for deck, US$65 (US$52) pullman seat and from US$115 (US$92) per person in a four-berth cabin. These prices are for one-way voyages in the low season. In the high season, prices go up by about 20%. Varying slightly between the different shipping companies, the high season is basically from July to the end of September. A port tax of US$12 is added for each stopover made by each passenger en route. For return voyages, 20% reductions are made (not from the student and under 26 prices).

The Piraeus/Haifa run takes about 58 hours, and the Venice/Haifa run takes over twice that time, so take plenty of food and drink for the voyage. Also, avoid sitting/sleeping downwind of the ship's funnel when up on deck; I met several soot-covered travellers disembarking at Haifa!

From Turkey

Take a ferry to Rhodes from Kusadisi and then board a Haifa-bound ferry from there (from about US$40 deck).

DEPARTURE TAX

Do not forget departure tax. It's around US$12 for most visitors, although Israeli citizens are slugged 100 to 200 sheqelim.

Getting Around

AIR

Arkia, Israel's domestic airline (which has now extended its operations to include charters to/from abroad), operates scheduled flights between Jerusalem, Tel Aviv, Haifa, Rosh Pinna and Eilat.

Prices are not really competitive with the alternative forms of public transport on the ground. You can inquire about current Arkia prices and schedules at IGTOs around the world and in Israel, as well as to the following Arkia offices:

Jerusalem
>   Klal Centre, 97 Jaffa Rd (tel 02-225888)

Tel Aviv
>   11 Frishman St (tel 03-233285)
>   Sde Dov Airport (tel 03-426262)

Haifa
>   84 Ha'Atzma'ut St (tel 04-643371)

Eilat
>   Downtown Airport (tel 059-73141)
>   New Tourist Centre (tel 059-76102)

Netanya
>   11 Ha'Atzma'ut Square (tel 053-23644)

Rosh Pinna
>   Airport (tel 069-41159)

BUS

The small size of the country and an excellent road system have combined to make bus travel the choice of public transport to be developed in Israel. Israel's bus network is dominated by Egged, the third-largest bus company in the world, after London Transport and Greyhound in the USA. Egged is a co-operative, with 5830 members and 3243 salaried employees. Together they operate 3950 buses on 3108 scheduled routes, as well as numerous special trips. Dan provides urban services in the Dan region: Tel Aviv and the immediate surrounding area.

Egged

The Egged network has a fascinating history. When the Zionist settlements were springing up in isolated areas, mainly in Galilee, a system of co-operative transport evolved to provide the vital link between them. Highways were non-existent, and the bus not only carried passengers, but also newspapers, mail, food and general supplies. The early Jewish bus driver's job is seriously compared to stagecoach drivers in the Wild West of America, and they often had one hand on the wheel and the other on a concealed gun. Perhaps this explains the common habit of today's Jewish bus driver to have just one hand on the wheel even during the most awkward manoeuvres – except that these days his other hand is busy counting his change, re-organising his various tickets, adjusting the radio to catch the latest news broadcast or popping sunflower seeds into his ever-open mouth. The pioneer days gave Jewish bus drivers a reputation of bravery and dedication and they still enjoy a status in the community above that of their peers in other countries.

Egged was formed in 1933 when four earlier co-operatives merged. The name Egged means 'linked together' and was proposed by the Jewish national poet H N Bialik to express the close bond between the new co-operative members.

A unique aspect of Egged is its national security role. Especially in the Negev region, you will often get the impression that Egged buses are glorified troop carriers, as you constantly have to wake up a dozing platoon to move their assortment of weapons and bags in order for you to get a seat. In fact, Egged's National Security Officer co-ordinates with the IDF to ensure that there is sufficient transport on busy routes, especially on Fridays, Saturday evenings after Shabbat, Sundays and before/after Jewish holidays, to enable soldiers to get to and from their bases. Often they appear to only just make it. In times of war Egged assists the IDF by acting as a back-up fleet transporting personnel and equipment.

Arab Buses

In Nazareth, East Jerusalem and the Occupied Territories, around 30 small Arab companies provide bus services. More and more, the Jewish buses tend to be of the highest quality: air-conditioned, clean, fast and modern; whilst the Arab buses, although improving, are comparatively hot, dirty, painfully slow climbing the hilly areas where they mainly operate, and on the old side. However, from their central stations in East Jerusalem to such destinations as the Mount of Olives, Bethlehem, Jericho, Hebron, Ramallah and Nablus, they are often more convenient and cheaper to use than Egged.

Costs

Israel's bus system is cheap to use, due to Government subsidies. Your longest journey is likely to be the run between Eilat and Jerusalem (four hours) or Tel Aviv (five hours), costing about US$8. ISIC holders are entitled to a discount of about 10% on inter-urban fares.

Israbus Passes Like most unlimited travel passes, their value is totally dependent on the amount of travelling done. They are valid for all Egged buses, which means all buses except those in the Tel Aviv area and the Arab network. You can be pretty certain of saving money if you get the 30-day Israbus pass, or if you plan inter-urban trips virtually every day of a seven- to 21-day period. This is not so uncommon amongst visitors to Israel and, especially if you end up using the urban buses as well, the Israbus pass certainly becomes good value.

Buying tickets is not too much of a problem – apart from the lack of smiling faces from Egged staff locked into their ticket booths and the struggle by locals to understand the rules of queuing. Being an Israbus pass holder does save you most of those minor hassles and it entitles you to discounts on certain tours, car rentals, and at some restaurants and museums.

The costs of the Israbus pass are:

Days	Cost US$	= US$ per day
7	44	6.29
14	69	4.93
21	89	4.24
30	99	3.30

The Israbus pass can be purchased at any of these Egged Tours Offices:

Afulla
Central Bus Station (tel 065-23444, 91234/6)
Ben-Gurion Airport (tel 03-971070/9) Ashdod
Shavei Zion (tel 055-51097)
Ashkelon
Central Bus Station (tel 051-29111)
Beersheba
Central Bus Station (tel 057-74341-5, 75262)
Eilat
Central Bus Station (tel 059-73148-9)
Hadera
Central Bus Station (tel 063-37722-6)
Haifa
4 Nordau St (tel 04-643131/2)
Central Bus Station (tel 04-515277/9)
Holon
47 Shenkar St (tel 03-882797, 883385)
Jerusalem
Central Reservations, 11a Hameasef St (tel 02-531286-8)
44a Jaffa Rd (Zion Square) (tel 02-223454, 224198)
Central Bus Station, 224 Jaffa Rd (tel 02-534596)
Beit Tannous, Opposite Jaffa Gate (tel 02-248144, 247783)
Nahariya
Central Bus Station (tel 04-922656, 923444/6)
Netanya
Kikar Ha'Atzma'ut 5 (tel 053-37296, 28333)
Rehovot
Central Bus Station (tel 08-452520, 452525-4)
Tel Aviv
(Head Office) 15 Frishman St (tel 03-242271-6)
59 Ben Yehuda St (tel 03-242271-6, 242132)
Kikar Namir (Atarim Square) (tel 03-283191/3, 284491)
8 Mendele St (tel 03-242271)

Tiberias
    Central Bus Station (tel 067-20474, 91080/4)

Multi-fare Discount Passes These are available on Egged and Dan urban buses. Each card is valid for a set number of single rides at a 25% saving. Another attraction is that the pass can be shared between as many people as there are rides on it so you and anyone else with you can use it. They also have no time limit. These passes are not valid for inter-urban rides, and you should calculate whether you are likely to benefit from using one, particularly a Dan pass which is basically valid only for Tel Aviv-Jaffa, Herzlia, Rehovot, Rishon le Zion and Ramla.

Return Tickets Purchasing a return inter-urban ticket can often save a considerable amount, and with the small travelling distances involved many travellers will find that it is often preferable to base themselves in one place and take a bus to visit other areas, avoiding constant packing and unpacking. Another advantage of return tickets is that there are no time limits. For example, you could buy a Tel Aviv-Beersheba return and from Beersheba wander around the Negev region at your will, later returning from Beersheba to Tel Aviv. The deal for a Tel Aviv-Jerusalem return is particularly good value and the two major cities are only about 50 minutes apart with a virtually constant flow of express buses.

Operating Hours & Frequency of Services
Overall the bus service is very good and the vast majority of locals, as well as travellers, use it. This does mean that buses fill up, especially in the rush hours which are mainly from 7 to 8 am and 4 to 6 pm Mondays to Thursdays, and most of Saturday evenings and Sundays, as a result of the Shabbat shutdown. Egged and Dan buses operate from about 5.30 am to about 10.30 pm; major routes go on until midnight. On Fridays and the eves of Jewish holidays buses run only until 3 or 4 pm. On Saturdays these buses don't run at all until sunset, or a little earlier. Some Jewish buses in Haifa and Akko (but not all of them) and the Arab buses operate every day as normal. Arab buses stop earlier, usually 6 or 7 pm.

On busy inter-urban routes, mainly to and from Jerusalem, Tel Aviv and Haifa, the buses run almost continually throughout the day. The only areas apparently lacking in a frequent bus service, although perhaps it is because there seems to be so many elsewhere, are the Dead Sea region and the Golan. The latter I can understand because of the lack of population, but the Dead Sea is such a popular destination. Yet you usually have to contend with a huge and, even by Israeli standards, impatient crowd of prospective passengers at the Jerusalem central bus station waiting for a trip down to a swim, and waiting for a bus to leave the Dead Sea region is a lengthy exercise.

TRAIN
The small passenger network of the Israel State Railways is even cheaper than the buses but, due to the location of most of the stations away from city and town centres, it is often overlooked. For ISIC holders, the train offers even better value with their 50% discount. Another advantage of the train network is that it passes through some delightfully scenic countryside, particularly the Tel Aviv to Jerusalem route, although the bus service is a lot faster.

The passenger service is limited in scope, with about three million passengers per year. The main line is Haifa/Tel Aviv Central (North) used primarily by commuters. Some trains continue to Nahariya and there is a daily train running in each direction between Haifa and Jerusalem. Despite problems with outdated equipment, the level of service and comfort is generally acceptable.

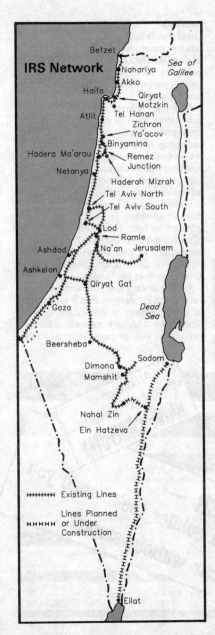

IRS Network

Betzet
Nahariya — Sea of Galilee
Akko
Haifa
Qiryat Motzkin
Atlit — Tel Hanan
Zichron Ya'acov
Binyamina
Hadera Ma'arau — Remez Junction
Netanya
Haderah Mizrah
Tel Aviv North
Tel Aviv South
Lod
Ramle
Ashdod — Na'an — Jerusalem
Ashkelon
Qiryat Gat
Gaza — Dead Sea
Beersheba
Dimona — Sodom
Mamshit
Nahal Zin
Ein Hatzeva
Eilat

ннннннн Existing Lines

ннннн Lines Planned or Under Construction

TAXI

Sherut/Service Taxi

In Israel, taking a taxi does not normally mean splurging on your own chauffeur-driven vehicle. Like its Middle Eastern neighbours, Israel is the land of the shared taxi. Most commonly called the *sherut*, the Arabs call it the service taxi, or taxi service. These are one and the same, operating on a fixed route at a fixed price which can vary from a regular weekday rate to higher rates for the late hours, Shabbat and holidays. Except for innocent airport arrivals, there is little scope for rip-off merchants with this system. Sheruts/service taxis are usually stretch-Mercedes seating up to seven passengers and you simply pay the same as everyone else. If you are uncertain about the fare, just ask locals, your fellow passengers, or check with the nearest tourist office. Regular rates are normally about 20% more than the bus, but are sometimes on a par.

Most sheruts travel between towns and cities from recognised taxi ranks. They simply drive off when they are full. This can sometimes involve waiting for six other people but you will be surprised how popular the system is, and long delays are rare. Also, what often appears to be an empty vehicle will rapidly fill up and zoom off when you climb in. The locals tend not to sit inside and wait, but stand around outside instead. You can get out anywhere along the way but you pay the same fare regardless. After dropping off a passenger en route the sherut then picks up replacement passengers wherever possible. It is interesting to witness the use of hand signals by both drivers and prospective passengers at the roadside to indicate the number of spaces available and required.

Most notably in Tel Aviv, but also in Jerusalem on Shabbat, some sheruts operate at the same price and on the same route as the local bus service, picking up/dropping off passengers as requested. On Shabbat, sheruts provide the only transport on certain major inter-city routes whilst Egged is off the road. Check what services are available to avoid being a victim of the Shabbat shut-down.

In the Occupied Territories, where the Egged service is limited to Jewish settlements rather than to general towns and places of interest, the service taxis save hours of travelling time compared to the local Arab buses.

'Special' Taxis

Drivers of 'special' (ie non-shared) taxis have a bad reputation for overcharging, unhelpfulness and being impolite. The usual 'my meter doesn't work' or 'for you, friend, special price' tricks are popular. Tourist offices display the official fare rates.

DRIVING

Good roads and small distances makes Israel a great place to hire a car. Also, in places like the Golan and the Negev, the buses do not cover so much ground and having your own car can help you to really see the area.

There are a large number of local car-hire firms as well as the international companies. Prices vary dramatically and shopping around is recommended. Be wary of initial quotes – check if insurance and unlimited distance are included. Car-hire people often do not have the cheapest advertised car available. Keep trying, and if possible book a car at least a couple of days in advance. Note that you are not allowed to take hired vehicles into the Sinai – car-hire firms have been known to keep that to themselves, letting their customers drive down to Eilat and be turned back at the border.

Unlike Israel's war-torn and dangerous image, the impression that it is a country of lousy drivers is absolutely spot-on. There seems to be a national mania for driving as fast as possible at all times,

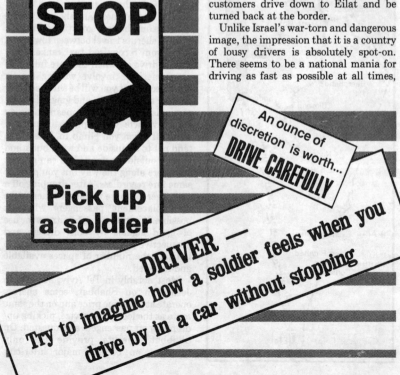

disregarding basic safety precautions such as not overtaking on bends, looking before swapping lanes and keeping a safe distance from the vehicle in front. Israel's death and injury rate due to motoring accidents is tragically high. Driving yourself can be somewhat hazardous due to the locals' antics; just keep a careful watch on the traffic and expect other drivers to do anything but the expected. The country's professional drivers are no better – they just have more practice. Over half of Egged's drivers have traffic offences (Egged's figures).

Due to the Palestine Problem, cars with Israeli registration plates are often stoned in certain areas of the Occupied Territories, so if you do hire a car it makes sense to let locals know that you are not Israeli – perhaps a flag or a sign of some sort.

Despite these conditions, having your own car in Israel is the desirable way to travel if you can afford it.

HITCH-HIKING

Hitch-hiking is always possible, sometimes easy and sometimes not, but often with the risk of danger. Not surprisingly, many Jews blame Arabs for this, but those found guilty of attacks on hitch-hikers have often been Jews and the problem seems to be more sexual than political. Therefore, women should not hitch-hike without male company. You will no doubt hear that it is unsafe for anyone to accept lifts from Arabs, and more specifically from those cars with blue registration plates (the symbol of cars owned by residents of the Occupied Territories). Even if this racist advice was correct it would be worthless, as a large number of Arabs live within Israel's borders and so drive cars with the standard yellow registration plates. This all takes us back to the issue of how safe it is to go to Israel. Again, targets of Arab hostility are mainly Israeli Jews and occasionally Jewish tourists, not every non-Arab. Hospitality is one of the things Arabs are renowned for and to condemn them all as potential murderers is a tragic error.

As you travel around Israel you will notice what seems to be a large percentage of the army hitch-hiking to and from their bases. Israelis are actively encouraged to give lifts to soldiers, so bear in mind that if you are hitch-hiking you will be last in line for a lift if there are any IDF uniforms to be seen. Note that female soldiers are forbidden to hitch-hike because of the potential danger.

Finally, remember that sticking out your thumb is not the locally accepted way to advertise to drivers that you are hitch-hiking. Here it means something more basic and impolite, although most locals recognise the foreign user's intentions. The local signal is to point to the road with your index finger.

CYCLING

Bearing in mind the mentality of most Israeli drivers, you might presume that cycling is to be considered only by those who are equally insane. On the contrary, I met numerous cyclists, many of whom had peddled across the Sinai Desert from Egypt, and none of them felt that touring Israel on two wheels was either impossible or too dangerous. To consider a cycle tour of Israel, you must bear in mind the hot climate, the frequent rainfall in certain areas at certain times, the innumerable steep hills to be negotiated (cycling from the Dead Sea up to Jerusalem is not something I am rushing to do) and, ultimately, the fact that most drivers fail to recognise your status as a road user and will not give you room as they overtake, usually tooting loudly as they pass in either direction – a very annoying habit.

Hiring a bicycle locally for a few hours is not common, but Jericho and Tiberias are places where it can be done and it is a great way to get around.

TOURS

Organised tours are big business; mainly in buses, sometimes in stretch-Mercedes and even in aeroplanes. The Ministry of Tourism ensures that prices are in line with itineraries and that the transport is up to scratch. Tours can vary between a few hours, one day, and over a week of organised sightseeing.

Egged Tours is the largest tourist carrier and they have offices in most towns (see the list under Bus). Numerous smaller companies compete for the remainder of the market. For details of tours available contact any tourist office or travel agent.

You will continually come across these tours in progress, and will benefit from listening in on a tour guide. Here is yet another area of controversy. Not the problem of freeloaders like me listening to a guide that someone else has paid for, but the law that only permits tour guides who are licensed by the Ministry of Tourism. A major exception to this rule are the various Christian church officials who lead hundreds of thousands of pilgrims around Israel. The churches maintain that their own guides are the best for their needs and that banning them would reduce the number of pilgrims. Rather than lose the good business that the Christians provide, the authorities upset the local guides by allowing the priests, vicars and monks to continue.

On the subject of tours and controversies, the Israeli guides are extremely knowledgeable about the country, its history and geography – it is often astounding how much they can tell you. However, not all of what you hear can be taken at face value. They are an important part of Israel's unofficial public relations department, and they offer an often extremely biased version of the country's political status, in ways that are so subtle you will not even notice.

Don't forget the SPNI's organised tours which specialise in taking you 'off the beaten track'. They are not cheap, but even if you can't afford them you should at least see their brochures and make your own way to the more accessible destinations featured.

Hiring an independent guide locally, either for the day or for a few hours, can be good, and you will normally get value for money. The official guides' standard of knowledge and languages is generally high, but do not get talked into hiring an unofficial guide unless they have been recommended by someone whose opinion you can trust.

Israel's diverse geography is one of its major attractions. The short distances involved in travelling around the country are made more enjoyable by the dramatic changes in scenery. Jerusalem, in the centre of things geographically as well as in every other way, is the starting or finishing point of several great trips. The roads from here down to Jericho and the Dead Sea are perhaps the best examples of sudden changes of terrain, from one type of stunning beauty to another.

The drive through the Jordan Valley from Tiberias down (or is it up?) to Jerusalem is a totally different experience. The Sea of Galilee is below sea level, and the drive from both Nazareth and Safed is unforgettable. From Safed the road winds round and down with the sea always dominating the horizon; whilst coming from Nazareth you turn a bend and suddenly it is there below you.

Another great ride is between East Jerusalem and Nablus. This passes through some of the West Bank's most scenic areas; rugged mountains and terraced valleys with olive trees and the sudden appearance of a small village in the distance. Finally, the train ride from Tel Aviv to Jerusalem winds its way through some wonderful countryside, and is a slow but cheap alternative to the Egged express bus.

Jerusalem

Population: 446,500

Jerusalem is the highly disputed capital of Israel and probably the most fascinating city in the world, as well as one of the most beautiful. It is also surely the holiest city of all – so many people have attached so much importance to Jerusalem, for so many different and conflicting reasons for so many years. The City of Peace. The City of Gold. The Holy City. In Hebrew it is *Yerushalayim*, in Arabic *El Khudz* (the Holy).

Jerusalem can be divided into three parts: the walled Old City, East Jerusalem, and the New City which rapidly continues to grow around both. The Old City is the main attraction for everyone: the religious, the historian and the more casual visitor. Within its walls you will find the holiest Jewish site, the Western Wall, part of the Temple; the third-holiest Muslim site, the Haram esh-Sharif (Dome of the Rock), from where Mohammed rose to heaven; and the most holy Christian sites of the trial of Jesus, his crucifixion and resurrection. East Jerusalem, along with the Old City, was under Jordanian control until 1967. The Old City also has the Arab markets, and in East Jerusalem you could be in any modern-day Arab town. The New City is cleaner, more modern and less exotic. However, here you will find some of Israel's leading museums, the Knesset building, and most of the city's Jewish restaurants, cafés and nightlife.

History

Jerusalem's oldest part lies on the Ophel ridge between the Kidron Valley to the east and the Tyropoeon Valley to the west, and south from the Temple Mount. A small Jebusite city was mentioned in Egyptian texts of the 20th century BC, and in 997 BC the Israelite King David conquered it. By bringing to Jerusalem the Ark of the Covenant he made the city his capital.

Under King Solomon, David's son, the city's boundaries extended to include the present day Temple Mount/Haram esh-Sharif with the construction of the Temple in 950 BC. After Solomon's death in 933 BC, the city became the capital of Judah as the 12 tribes of Israel divided. In 586 BC Jerusalem fell to Nebuchadnezer, the King of Babylon, and the city, including the First Temple, was destroyed. The people of Jerusalem were exiled to Babylonia until 583 BC when the King of Persia, Cyrus, allowed them to return. The Second Temple was constructed around 520 BC and around 445 BC the city walls were rebuilt under the leadership of Nehemiah, Governor of Judah.

The next notable stage in Jerusalem's history came with Alexander the Great's conquest of the city in 331 BC. After his death eight years later, the Seleucids eventually took over until the Maccabaean revolt 30 years later. This launched the Hasmonean dynasty who resanctified the Temple in 164 BC after it had been desecrated by the King. Jerusalem was conquered by the Romans led by General Pompey around 63 BC. In 37 BC they installed Herod the Great to rule what they called the Kingdom of Judea. The Romans resumed direct control after Herod's death, unimpressed with his son's performance, and the city was administered by a procurator. Pontius Pilate, best known for ordering the crucifixion of Jesus around 30 AD, was the fifth procurator.

About 36 years later came the First Revolt by the Jews against the Romans, but after four years of conflict the Roman General Titus triumphed. With the Second Temple destroyed and Jerusalem burnt, many Jews became slaves or exiles: it was the beginning of the Diaspora. Jerusalem continued as the capital but Emperor Hadrian decided to destroy it

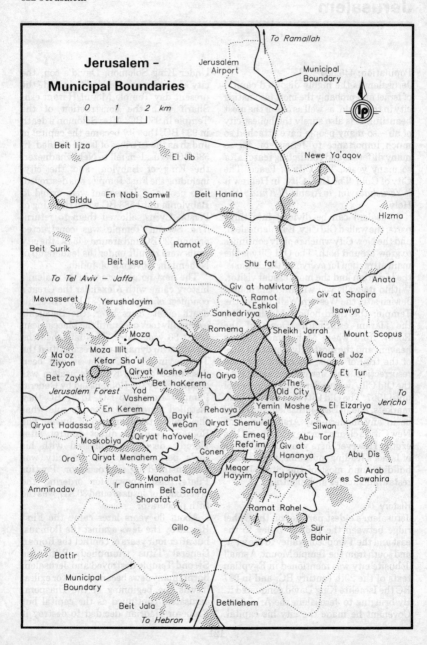

**Jerusalem –
Municipal Boundaries**

0   1   2 km

completely in 70 AD due to the threat of renewed Jewish national aspirations. This provoked the unsuccessful Second Revolt led by Bar Kochba, after which Jews were forbidden to enter Aelia Capitolina, the new city built on the ruins of Jerusalem. The Aelia Capitolina is the basis for today's Old City. In 331 AD Christianity was legalised by the Roman Emperor Constantine, and his mother visited the Holy Land in search of the Christian holy places. This sparked off the building of basilicas and churches, and the city quickly grew to the size it had been under Herod the Great. Meanwhile, the Roman Empire's capital moved from Rome to Constantinople, formerly Byzantium.

The Byzantine Empire was defeated by the Persians who conquered Jerusalem in 638, led by the Caliph Omar. In 688 the Dome of the Rock was constructed on the site of the destroyed Temple. Under the early Islamic leaders, Jerusalem was a protected centre of pilgrimage for Jews and Christians as well as Muslims, but this came to an end in the 10th century. Under Caliph Hakim, non-Muslims were cruelly persecuted and churches and synagogues were destroyed, finally provoking the Crusades 90 years later.

The Crusaders took Jerusalem in 1099 from the Fatamids who had only just regained control from the Seljuks. After almost 90 years the Latin kingdom was defeated by Saladin in 1187. During that time the area had benefited from its most effective administration so far. Under Saladin, Muslims and Jews were allowed to resettle in the city. From the 13th to the 16th centuries the Mamelukes constructed a number of outstanding buildings dedicated to religious study.

Although a Muslim academic centre, Jerusalem became a relative backwater. In 1517 the Ottoman Turks defeated the Mamelukes to add Palestine to their large empire and although they, too, are remembered for their lack of efficiency in local administration, their initial impact on the city is still much admired today. The impressive Old City walls that you see now were built by their second sultan, Suleiman the Magnificent. After Suleiman, Jerusalem's rulers allowed the city, like the rest of the country, to decline. Buildings and streets were not maintained, and corruption amongst the authorities was rife.

As a result of the Turkish sultan's 1856 Edict of Toleration for all religions, Jews and Christians were again able to settle in the city. In the 1860s, inspired and largely financed by an English Jew, Sir Moses Montefiore, Jewish settlement outside the city walls began. As Jewish immigration rapidly increased, these settlements developed into what is now the New City.

After WW I Jerusalem, which had been captured by General Allenby's forces from the Turks, became the administrative capital of the British Mandate. In these times of fervent Arab and Jewish nationalism, the city became a hotbed of political tensions. Jerusalem was always the most sought-after area of the country for both the Arabs and the Jews, and the city was the stage for much terrorism and more open warfare.

After the British withdrew from Palestine, the UN became responsible for supervising the situation. Its subsequent partition plan was accepted by the Jews, but rejected by the Arabs. Jerusalem was to be internationalised, surrounded by independent Arab and Jewish states. In the 1948 War of Independence the Jordanians took the Old City and East Jerusalem, while the Jews held the New City. Patches of no-man's land separated them and the new State of Israel declared its part of Jerusalem as its capital.

For 19 years it was a divided city and Mandelbaum Gate became the official crossing point between East Jerusalem and the New City for the few who were permitted to move between them. The 1967 Six-Day War saw the reunification of the whole of Jerusalem, and the Israelis began a massive programme of restoration, refurbishment and landscaping.

Controversy continues to surround the status of Jerusalem, and most countries maintain their embassies in Tel Aviv. According to Palestinians and other opponents of Israel, the Jewish State has no right to declare the city its capital and you would be unwise to underestimate the strength of this sentiment. There is a sincere resentment among local Arabs of what Israel has done and continues to do, regardless of the many cosmetic changes made. The Israelis, meanwhile, are determined to keep all of Jerusalem as their capital regardless of any such opposition.

Orientation

Finding your way around Jerusalem is often confusing at first. Just remember the three basic areas, Old, East and New, and concentrate on each of them separately, rather than trying to take in the whole sprawling and bewildering mass.

Old City Definitely the main attraction and easily defined, the Old City contains 20,000 people within one square km, behind solid and recently renovated walls. Seven gates give access to the fascinating narrow streets within. Jaffa Gate, at the end of Jaffa Rd, is the main entrance from the New City, while Damascus Gate does the job from East Jerusalem. These are two very important Old City landmarks: Temple Mount/Haram esh-Sharif, the site of the First and Second Temples, and now dominated by the Dome of the Rock and El Aqsa mosques and the Western Wall; and the Church of the Holy Sepulchre, marking the site of Jesus' crucifixion, burial and resurrection.

There are numerous other religious and historical sites in the Old City, plus the popular market. Some of Jerusalem's best cheap hotels and eating places are here.

East Jerusalem East Jerusalem is a compact Arab district of businesses, shops, travel agents, moneychangers, hotels and restaurants. It is easy to find your way around when you remember that the two main streets, Nablus Rd and Salah ed-Din St, form a triangle with Suleiman St which runs alongside the northern wall of the Old City. East Jerusalem's cheap hostels and eating places are easily on a par with those of the Old City, and their quality and value for money make up for the lack of attractive surroundings. This district is also important to travellers because of the two Arab bus stations and the service taxi rank.

Also in East Jerusalem are the Rockefeller Museum with its archaeological exhibits; Solomon's Quarries; the Garden Tomb, considered a possible site of Jesus' crucifixion, burial and resurrection; the Tomb of the Kings; and the Tourjeman Post Museum – a reminder of the days when this was a divided city.

New City This area is sometimes referred to as West Jerusalem, but it is no longer an accurate term due to the area's rapid expansion in virtually all directions. It is the government and commercial district and where most travellers first arrive. Your initial contact with the city is likely to be the central bus station situated towards the northern end of Jaffa Rd, one of the New City's main streets. The city centre is basically the area in and around the triangle formed by Jaffa Rd, King George V St and Ben Yehuda St (which is linked to Jaffa Rd by Zion Square).

Most of the middle and top end hotels and eating places are in this central area, along with the most popular cafés and bars. Others are nearer the Old City. Mahane Yehuda, the New City's cheap market, is just to the west of the central area. Moving further away from the centre to the west are the Knesset building, the Israel Museum, Yad Vashem, and the Hadassah Medical Center.

Other Districts Not easily slotted into the

Old, East and New categories are the Mount of Olives, Mount Scopus and the Jehoshaphat and Kidron Valleys which lie to the east and south of the Old City and East Jerusalem. On the Mount of Olives is the Garden of Gethsemane, the world's largest Jewish cemetery and, according to the Bible, the site of Jesus' ascension to heaven. To the north, Mount Scopus is dominated by the modern campus of the Hebrew University, adjacent to the Hadassah Hospital and the WW I cemetery. The Jehoshaphat Valley, between the Haram esh-Sharif and the Mount of Olives, is best known as being the site at which Jews believe that God will judge mankind after the arrival of the Messiah. The scenic Kidron Valley is the larger area between Jerusalem and Mount of Olives and leads into the adjacent Hinnom and Tyropoeon Valleys.

Information

Tourist Offices Jerusalem has two Government Tourist Information Offices. The head office (tel 241281/2) is in the New City at 24 King George V St. You would do well to avoid it unless you are desperate for help or wish to experience the Meet the Israeli scheme, as the staff were unfriendly and gave me inaccurate information. Stick to the Old City office (tel 282295/6) just inside Jaffa Gate on the left as you enter. Both offices are open Sunday to Thursday 8.30 am to 5 pm, Friday 8.30 am to 2 pm, closed Saturday.

The Municipal Information Office (tel 228844) at 17 Jaffa Rd is not so well known and therefore less busy. The staff are not always too knowledgeable, but they try. Open Sunday to Thursday 8 am to 12.30 pm, Friday 8 am to 12 noon, closed Saturday.

The Christian Information Centre (tel 287647) is at El Khattab Square, Old City, just inside from Jaffa Gate and to the right. They are very knowledgeable on their specialised subject and have a good selection of books. This is where you apply for a ticket (if you are a practising Catholic) for the Christmas Eve Midnight Mass in Bethlehem's Church of the Nativity. It's open Monday to Friday 8.30 am to 2.30 pm and 3 to 6 pm (in winter until 5.30 pm), Saturday 8.30 am to 12.30 pm, closed Sunday.

The Lifshitz Information Centre (tel 281827) is in the Cardo in the Old City's Jewish Quarter. It is run by a building company involved in the redevelopment of the traditional Jewish areas in Jerusalem, in particular the Old City's Jewish Quarter. The staff seem more interested in selling publications than giving directions. Open Sunday to Thursday 9 am to 6 pm, Friday 9 am to 1 pm, closed Saturday.

Post Offices The main post office and poste restante (tel 244745) is at 23 Jaffa Rd. The main section is open Sunday to Thursday 7 am to 7 pm, Friday 7 am to 1 pm, closed Saturday. The parcel office is on the west side of the building, down the steps from Jaffa Rd, and is open Sunday to Thursday 8.30 am to 1.30 pm, Friday 8.30 am to 12 noon, closed Saturday. Poste restante closes at noon on Fridays. After hours you can send letters, telegrams and telexes from the information desk here. During the night you'll need patience to wake up somebody, and chances are they'll speak no English.

For telegrams go around to Koresh St at the rear, open Sunday to Thursday 6 am to 10 pm, Friday 6 am to 3.30 pm, closed Saturday. Cheaper but slower is the LT (letter telegram).

There are several branches, including in El Khattab Square inside Jaffa Gate in the Old City, just up from the Christian Information Centre; and in the Jewish Quarter, east of Batei Mahse Square. Both are open Sunday, Monday, Wednesday and Thursday 8 to 10 am, 4 to 6 pm, Tuesday 8 to 11.30 am, Friday 8 to 10.30 am, closed Saturday. East Jerusalem's main post office is at the corner of Salah ed-Din St and Suleiman St, open Sunday to Thursday 8 am to 6 pm

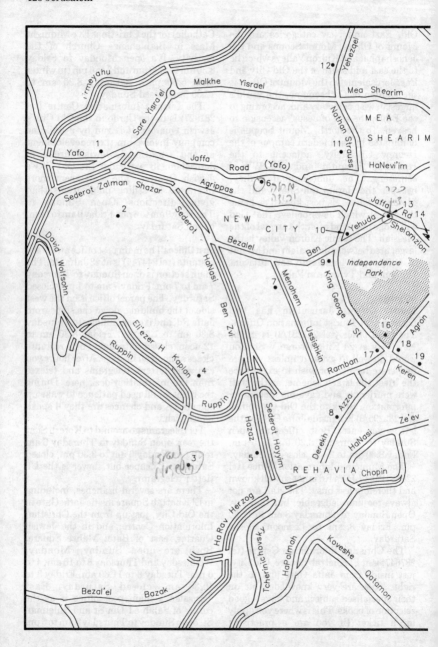

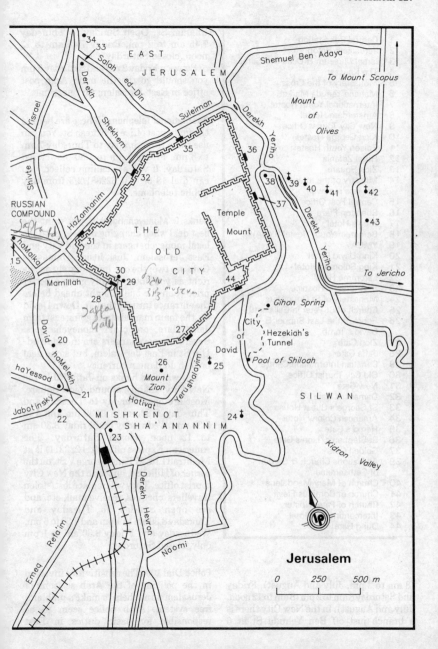

East Jerusalem

Mount
of
Olives

To Mount Scopus

Shemuel Ben Adaya

Derekh Shekhem

Salah ed-Din

Yisrael

Shivte

Suleiman

Derekh Yeriho

HaZanhanim

RUSSIAN
COMPOUND

haMalka

Mamillah

David

haMelekh

haYessod

Jabotinsky

THE
OLD
CITY

Temple
Mount

Gihon Spring

City
of
David

Hezekiah's
Tunnel

Pool of Shiloah

To Jericho

SILWAN

Mount Zion

Hativat Yerushalayim

MISHKENOT
SHA'ANANIM

Kidron Valley

Derekh Hevron

Emeq Refa'im

Naomi

Jerusalem

0   250   500 m

1	Central Bus Station
2	Jerusalem Hilton
3	Israel Museum & Dead Sea Scrolls
4	The Knesset
5	Monastery of the Cross
6	Mahane Yehuda Market
7	International Youth Hostel
8	Amsterdam Hostel
9	New City Tourist Office
10	King George Hostel
11	Edison Youth Hostel
12	Hotel Zefania
13	Zion Square
14	Ministry of the Interior (for visa renewal)
15	Central Post Office
16	Sheraton Plaza
17	King's Hotel
18	Bernstein Youth Hostel (IYHA)
19	YMCA
20	King David Hotel
21	King Solomon Hotel
22	Laromme Hotel
23	St Andrew's Hospice
24	Monastery of St Onuphrius
25	Church of St Peter in Gallicantu
26	Room of the Last Supper & David's Tomb
27	Zion Gate
28	Jaffa Gate
29	Christian Information Centre
30	Old City Tourist Office
31	New Gate
32	Damascus Gate
33	St George's Guest House
34	American Colony Hotel
35	Herod's Gate
36	St Stephen's/Lion's Gate
37	Golden Gate
39	All Nations Church & Garden of Gethsemane
40	Church of Mary Magdalene
41	Church of Dominus Flevit
42	Church of Pater Noster
43	Intercontinental Hotel
44	Dung Gate

Shamai St. Open Sunday to Thursday 7.45 am to 2 pm, Friday 7.45 am to 12 noon, closed Saturday.

Between Friday 2 pm and Saturday 8 pm you should go the the main Arab post office in East Jerusalem for telegrams.

International Telephones These are behind the main post office in Koresh St. You can use them from Sunday to Thursday 7 am to 8 pm, Friday 7 am to 1.30 pm, closed Saturday. If you are calling collect, you can dial 18 or (03) 622881/2/3 from any public telephone.

Banks & Moneychangers If you want the best deal when changing money, go to the legal moneychangers in the Old City and East Jerusalem. Just inside Damascus Gate are two; the one immediately on the right as you enter usually gives a better price than the one straight ahead before the entrance turns to the left. Down David St, the main market street going east from Jaffa Gate, are other moneychangers. Several moneychangers are in Salah ed-Din St in East Jerusalem, but some deal only in Jordanian currency.

You will find banks on Jaffa Rd in the New City, mainly around Zion Square. Most are open Sunday to Tuesday and Thursday, 8.30 am to 12.30 pm and 4 to 5.30 pm, Wednesday and Friday 8.30 am to 12 noon, closed Saturday. The American Express office (tel 222211) is at Meditrad Ltd, 27 King George V St, on the corner of Hillel St, opposite the New City tourist office. They will replace lost/stolen travellers' cheques, receive mail, etc, and are open Sunday to Tuesday and Thursday 8.30 am to 1 pm and 3.30 to 6 pm, Wednesday and Friday 8.30 am to 1 pm only, closed Saturday.

Police Dial 100. The sensitivities involved in the policing of the Arab sections of Jerusalem do not help to make a problem-free system. Arab police seem to be responsible for basic duties in East

(8 am to 2 pm, July and August), Friday and Saturday 8 am to 2 pm (8 am to 12 noon, July and August). In the New City there is a branch just off Ben Yehuda St at 6

Top: At play, Muslim Quarter, Jerusalem (RE)
Left: Mount Zion, Jerusalem (RE)
Right: Orthodox Jews contemplate layers of history at the Citadel, Jerusalem (RE)

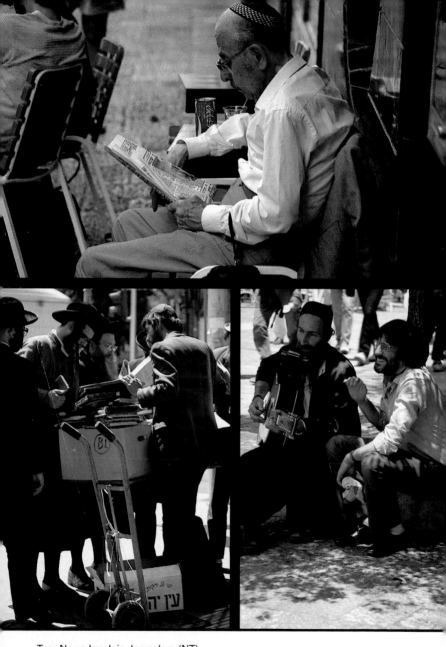

Top: News break in Jerusalem (NT)
Left: Hasidim in Mea Shearim, Jerusalem (NT)
Right: Hasidic busker and fan, Jerusalem (NT)

Jerusalem and the Old City; their station is in El Khattab Square, inside Jaffa Gate and to the right. Only go there regarding incidents within the Old City walls. For any other problems (and the Old City boys in blue will probably refer you there anyway) go to the central police station in the Russian Compound, between Jaffa Rd and HaNevi'im St in the New City. The green domes of the Russian Cathedral are a good landmark. The Lost and Found Office here deals with items lost and found in any section of the city. Open Sunday, Tuesday and Thursday 7.30 am to 4 pm, Monday and Wednesday 7.30 am to 2 pm, Friday 9.30 am to 12.30 pm, closed Saturday.

Consulates Although most countries maintain embassies in Tel Aviv for political reasons, many are represented in Jerusalem by consulates. They may well refer you to the embassy, depending on your requirements.

Austria
    8 Hoveve' Ziyyon, New City (tel 631291)
Belgium
    Sheikh Jarrah, East Jerusalem (tel 282263)
Denmark
    11 Shelomzion HaMalka, New City (tel 231122)
France
    6 Paul Emile Botta, New City (tel 231451); and Sheikh Jarrah, East Jerusalem (tel 282387)
Greece
    31 Rahel Immenu, New City (tel 633003); and Sheikh Jarrah, East Jerusalem (tel 283316)
Italy
    16 KafTet BeNovember, New City (tel 631236); and Sheikh Jarrah, East Jerusalem (tel 282138)
Sweden
    58 Nablus Rd, East Jerusalem (tel 284117)

UK
    19 Nashashiki St, New City (tel 282481); and Sheikh Jarrah, East Jerusalem (tel 282482)
USA
    18 Agron St, New City (tel 234271); and 27 Nablus Rd, East Jerusalem (tel 272681)
International Christian Embassy
    Jerusalem
    10 Brenner St, New City (tel 669823, 699389)

Society for the Protection of Nature in Israel SPNI (tel 222357) is at 13 Heleni HaMalka St. The Society's head office is in what was originally a pilgrims' hospice built by the Russian Church in the 19th century. Open Sunday 9 am to 5.45 pm, Monday, Wednesday and Thursday 9 am to 3.45 pm, Tuesday 9 am to 4.45 pm and Friday 9 am to 12.30 pm.

Student Travel ISSTA (tel 225258) is at 5 Eliasmar St, New City, across Jaffa Rd from Zion Square. Open Sunday to Tuesday and Thursday 8.30 am to 1 pm and 3 to 6 pm, Wednesday and Friday 8.30 am to 1 pm, closed Saturday.

Bookshops & Libraries Steimatzsky's carry many English-language books, magazines and newspapers. In the New City they are at 39 Jaffa Rd just east of Zion Square, and 9 King George V St, east side; in the Old City they have a shop on the Cardo.

Yalkut (tel 222786) sell second-hand books. They are at 1 Heleni HaMalka St and open Sunday to Thursday 8 am to 7 pm, Friday 8 am to 1.30 pm, closed Saturday. Also in the New City, Sefer VeSefel is upstairs at 2 Ya'Avetz St (the alley linking Jaffa Rd with Ben-Hillel St). They have a useful selection of new and used books in various languages, and a café. The Bookstop, at 6 Yosef Du Nawas St (off Jaffa Rd, east of Zion Square), New City, has new and used books and magazines. Open Sunday, Monday, Wednesday and

Thursday 9 am to 7 pm, Tuesday and Friday 9 am to 1.30 pm, closed Saturday.

In the Old City, The Bookshelf at 44 Habad St, above the Cardo in the Jewish Quarter, has used books. In East Jerusalem the Universal Library Bookstore on Salah ed-Din St has a wide selection, in particular Middle East politics and religion.

The fascinating surroundings often inspire visitors to read up on the city's history. You can find many relevant books in the British Council libraries: 31 Nablus Rd, East Jerusalem (just after the East Jerusalem YMCA), open Monday to Friday 9.30 am to 6 pm and Saturday 9.30 am to 1 pm; and on the first floor of the Terra Sancta building at the crossroads of King George V, Agron, Keren Hayesod and Ramban Sts in the New City, open Monday to Friday. Both stock English newspapers and magazines as well.

The Arab Studies Society (tel 281012) is in a side road off Nablus Rd, just before the American Colony Hotel, in East Jerusalem. The entrance is on the left side of the New Orient House Hotel. The Hebrew Union College Library, 13 King David St New City, and the Hebrew University libraries at the Mount Scopus and Giv'at Ram campuses also have good selections.

Swimming Pools Some of the luxury hotels have pools but for residents only. There are several public pools in the New City. The YMCA (tel 227111) at 26 King David St has a small indoor pool open to non-members at differing times dependent on a confusing schedule of sessions for men only, children only, members only and anybody only. The Beit Taylor pool (tel 414362) in Qiryat Yovel is open daily 9 am to 5 pm (Egged bus No 18 or 24). The Jerusalem Swimming Pool (tel 632092) on Emek Refaim St is open daily 8 am to 5 pm (Egged bus No 4 or 18). The last two charge US$1.80 Sunday to Friday but US$4.20 on Saturday.

Other For camera repairs, try Kerenor (tel 240674) at 5 Ben Yehuda St, New City.

There are a number of laundromats in the New City. Superclean Rehavia is at 26 Ussishkin St – get there on Egged bus No 19 from the city centre. Superclean Geulah, 1 Ezer Yoldot St, is the closest to East Jerusalem and the Old City. In the Mea Shearim district you walk west from the intersection of Mea Shearim and Strauss Sts and it's the first alley on the left. Bakah Washmatic is at 35 Emek Refaim, south of the centre. Take Egged bus No 4, 14 or 18, get off at the Emek Refaim post office and it's a half block further down across the street.

Camping equipment can be bought or rented from Orha (tel 226665) at 22 Nahalat Shiva in the alley off 27 Salomon St. Two-person tents cost around US$15 per week, a snorkel and mask US$8 per week.

Old City

The Old City is divided into five areas – the Armenian Quarter, the Christian Quarter, the Muslim Quarter, the Jewish Quarter and Temple Mount/Haram esh-Sharif – which in practical terms are not always so easy to define. Regardless of the current political status of Jerusalem, the Old City remains predominantly Arab.

Three of the four quarters of the Old City were never strictly defined districts or ghettos, and their boundaries changed with population shifts. The exception is the Armenian Quarter, which has remained within its boundaries . Controversy rages in particular over the status of the Muslim Quarter and the Jewish Quarter. This is due to Jews purchasing property in the Muslim Quarter to escape the overcrowded Jewish Quarter, starting in the 1830s. They seem to have peacefully co-existed with the locals for over 100 years until the Arab riots of 1936-39 forced them to leave.

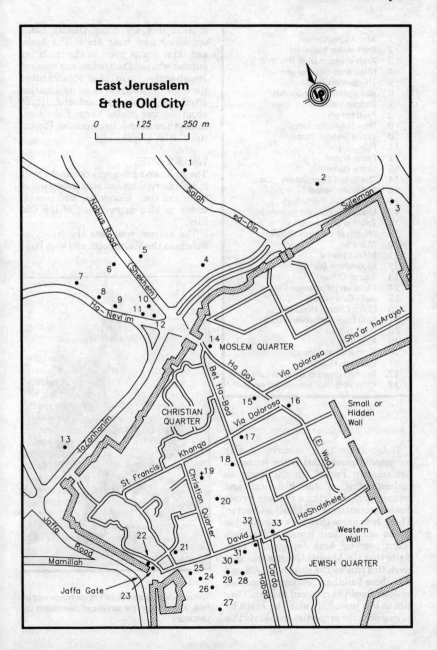

East Jerusalem & the Old City

0   125   250 m

1 Salah ed-Din
2
3
4
5
6
7
8
9
10
11
12
13

14 MOSLEM QUARTER

CHRISTIAN QUARTER

Ha Gav
Via Dolorosa
Sha'ar haArayot

15
16   Small or Hidden Wall

Via Dolorosa

Bet Ha-Bad

17

(El Wad)

Tazanhanim

Khanga

18
+19

St Francis

20

Christian Quarter

32   33

HaShalshelet

Western Wall

22

Jaffa Road

21

Mamillah

David   Cardo   JEWISH QUARTER

25   31   30
24   29   28
26   27

Habad

Jaffa Gate

23

1	Abu Ali Restaurant
2	Rockefeller Museum
3	Arab sheep market (Fridays)
4	Main Arab bus station
5	The Garden Tomb
6	Bus station (northbound)
7	Ramsis Hotel
8	Arab bakery
9	New Raghadan Hotel
10	White Sisters' Hostel
11	Palm Hostel
12	Faisal Hostel
13	Notre Dame
14	The Green Door Bakery (pizza)
15	El-Ahram Hostel
16	Abu-Shukri (hummus)
17	Linda's Restaurant (hummus)
18	Zalatino's (sweets)
19	Church of the Holy Sepulchre
20	Muristan
21	Mr A's Hostel
22	Moonshine Bar
23	Tourist Office
24	Christian Information Centre
25	Jaffa Gate Hostel
26	Christ Church Hospice
27	Blue Door (Armenian Pizza)
28	IYHA Hostel
29	Rush Inn
30	Citadel Youth Hostel
31	Lutheran Hostel
32	Rooftop views & Bedouin cafe/bar
33	Khan es-Sultan (renovated section)

Today there is a minority Jewish movement, spearheaded by the Jerusalem Reclamation Project, to encourage an understanding of the historical and geographical importance of these former Jewish properties in the Muslim Quarter. These Jews argue that Jews were forcibly driven out of their homes which were taken over by Arab 'squatters'. They claim that the Muslim Quarter was only given this title by the British in 1936 and that those buildings previously occupied by Jews should be returned to Jews. They aim to live peacefully with the Arabs by buying back the properties and slowly this is what they are doing, despite fierce opposition from most Arabs. The Arabs and other critics point to the far larger number who lost their homes as a result of Jewish aggression in the establishment of the State of Israel. For more information about the Jewish argument and details about the free guided tours of the area, contact the Jewish Reclamation Project (tel 273810, 273668).

WALLS & GATES

The walls and gates will dominate your initial impressions and your awareness of them and their history will add considerably to your appreciation of the Old City.

The current walls are the legacy of Suleiman the Magnificent and were built

Tamar Hindi – a sweet soft drink made out of fruit, and sold on the streets of Jerusalem by vendours

between 1537-1542, but have been renovated since then. The north wall was started first, followed by the east and west sides. The completion of the south wall is believed to have been delayed due to a dispute over whether or not Mount Zion should be included within the walled city. The authorities were not prepared to foot the considerable bill for extending the wall for the sake of including the Cenacle, containing the Room of the Last Supper, and insisted that the Franciscans pay for it. They had no money and so the wall excluded Mount Zion. Suleiman was angry enough to have the architects beheaded, showing perhaps that he intended his walls to honour and protect all of the city's prominent holy places.

There were six new gates in his walls and there are similarities in their style despite alterations to three of them. Jaffa, Damascus and Zion Gates still have their indirect entrances. This L-shape was designed to break the momentum of an attacking charge. Make a point of entering/leaving the Old City from all of the seven accessible gates during your stay in Jerusalem, to see as much as possible. Given official names originally, the gates' current names vary according to language and religion.

Ramparts Walk

One of the best ways to see the Old City and also its surroundings is to stroll around the ramparts. Up here you will benefit from views across the city's rooftops to East and New Jerusalem and the surrounding hills to see aspects that pass unnoticed from street level. Be careful – despite additional paving and guardrails, the stone can be slippery underfoot. Women should not go unaccompanied, due to the frequency of sexual assaults and thefts. Due to religious and security considerations, the walls around the Temple Mount/Haram esh-Sharif are strictly out of bounds.

The walk is divided into several sections: Jaffa Gate-Damascus Gate, the

Citadel-Zion Gate and Zion Gate-Dung Gate. Opening hours are Saturday to Thursday 9 am to 5 pm, and Fridays and holiday eves 9 am to 3 pm. The Citadel-Zion Gate section is open until 9.30 pm Sunday to Thursday. Tickets cost US$1.40 (students 65c) and are valid for four admissions over two days (three at the weekend), allowing you to do the walk gradually.

Finding the ramparts walk is not always easy. At Jaffa Gate access is up the stairs on the left as you enter the Old City. The Citadel stairway is on the right-hand side outside Jaffa Gate. Zion Gate's is in the gate itself, but Damascus Gate can be the most confusing. You must enter through the ancient carriage-way to the east (left) from the amphitheatre-styled plaza outside and underneath the gate, which is reached by following the steps from the west. At Lion's/St Stephen's Gate the stairway joins the walk just before it stops north of the Temple Mount/Haram esh-Sharif.

Jaffa Gate

Recently restored courtesy of South African Jewry, this was the start of the old road to Jaffa, when it was Jerusalem's port. This was the main route for traffic to and from the city. The Arabs' name for the gate is its original one, *Bab el-Khalil* (Gate of the Friend). This refers to the holy city Hebron (El-Khalil in Arabic), named after Abraham 'the Friend of God'. There used to be a wall between the gate and the Citadel but it was pulled down and the moat filled in by the Turkish Sultan Abdul Hamid in 1898 to permit Kaiser Wilhelm II and his party to ride into the city. Just inside the gate behind a wrought iron fence are two graves believed to be those of the architects beheaded by Suleiman for leaving Mount Zion outside the walls.

The Citadel – Tower of David

The Citadel's minaret and towers dominate the west wall. It is one of the country's

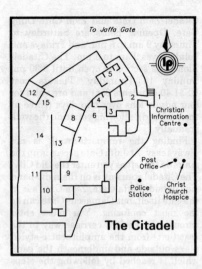

To Jaffa Gate

Christian
Information
Centre

Post
Office

Police
Station

Christ
Church
Hospice

The Citadel

most impressive restoration projects, and a major museum complex.

The Citadel stands over the site where Herod the Great built his palace in the first century BC with three towers named in memory of his friend, Hippicus, his brother Phasael and his wife, Mariamne. Excavations in the Armenian Quarter show that this palace extended almost to the present south wall. It was used by the Roman Procurators as their Jerusalem residence after Herod's death and the demise of his sons in 6 AD, and was burned by Jewish rebels in 66 AD. The towers were preserved by Titus after his victory four years later, as a monument to his troops' bravery. The Byzantines mistook this hill for Mount Zion and presumed that this was David's palace – hence the name 'David's Tower' for the one

1   A plaque by the ornamental outer gate commemorates General Allenby accepting the surrender of Jerusalem from the Ottoman Governor in 1917.
2   Leading to the entrance, the 16th century stone bridge to the barbican spans the moat, now partially filled in.
3   The angled main gate is Mameluke.
4   You enter the courtyard via this 14th century hexagonal room.
5   Climb the outside stairs to the Phasael tower's roof to get a great view of the excavations below and of the whole Old City and its surroundings.
6   These walls were built to hold the rubble Herod used to create the esplanade on which he built his palace.
7   The 2nd century BC Hasmonaean wall held the network walls to the west and had two towers.
8   This tower's orientation was altered in the Middle Ages.
9   However, this tower's original masonry is still visible.
10 Mameluke mosque.
11 A Crusader gate was here and a wall led to the middle of the north-western tower.
12 This tower's exclusively medieval foundations make it impossible to identify it with the Herodian towers, Hippicus or Mariamne.
13 The Mamelukes moved this west wall inwards.
14 Suleiman the Magnificent built the outer wall . . .
15 . . . and this gate.

previously named Phasael. The complex was then fully incorporated into the city walls but its status during the next few centuries is uncertain.

The Crusader kings of Jerusalem used it as their residence from 1128, followed by Saladin in 1187 when he took the city. The

fortress took on its present form in 1310 under the Mameluke Sultan Malik an-Nasir. The Crusader walls were retained but the old city wall which had divided the interior was levelled. The outer gateway, stone bridge and western terrace were added by Suleiman the Magnificent between 1531 and 1538. The prominent minaret was added in 1655.

In addition to the excavations, the complex includes the Museum of Modern Religious Dress, with small figures wearing examples of Jerusalem's various cultural, religious and ethnic groups. Also on display is a model of the whole city made in the 1860s. The David's Tower Multi-Screen Show in Hebrew, English, French, German, Spanish and Arabic is another attraction.

The entrance to the Citadel is just inside Jaffa Gate, around to the right as you enter the Old City, and it is open Saturday to Thursday 8.30 am to 4.30 pm, and Friday 8.30 am to 2 pm. Admission is US$2, students US$1.50.

It seems that every important historical site feels a need to put on a sound and light show. The Citadel joins the club with a production of questionable quality. However good you think the show is, you are liable to shiver all the way through it if you don't wrap up warmly – Jerusalem evenings are often surprisingly cold. The show is presented in various languages, from April to October, Saturday to Thursday evenings.

Damascus Gate

The most attractive gate and the most crowded. Its Arabic name is *Bab el-Amud* (Gate of the Column), after the column erected by the Roman Emperor Hadrian nearby. The Christians called it Damascus Gate as it marked the start of the road to Syria's capital. The Hebrew name is *Sha'ar Shechem* (Nablus Gate), as the same road passed the Jewish capital of Samaria. This is the only gate that has been excavated and the whole area has been refurbished. By the entrance to the ramparts walk is the Roman Square excavation, open daily 9 am to 5 pm for a mere 35c. A copy of the Madaba map is displayed. Found in Madaba, Jordan, it depicts Jerusalem in the Byzantine period, and it has helped archaeologists in their work locally. The museum's plaza is

View inside Damascus Gate

original, but the missing column is represented by a hologram.

Herod's Gate

This gate's official name is *Ban ez-Zahra* (the Flowered Gate), and its present name came about when 16-17th century pilgrims believed a Mameluke house, now within the Franciscan Monastery of the Flagellation, to be Herod Antipas' palace. The Crusaders first established themselves on the wall here on 15 July 1099.

Lion's/St Stephen's Gate

Although Suleiman called it *Bab el-Ghor* (the Jordan Gate), the name never stuck and it became known as St Stephen's Gate after the fall of the Crusaders in 1187, in reference to the first Christian martyr who was stoned nearby. Initially, the Christians called the present Damascus Gate by this name but the Arabs would only let Christian pilgrims leave the city by the gate facing the Mount of Olives, so the name was moved. The Hebrew name, Lion's Gate, refers to the heraldic emblems of the Mameluke Sultan Baybars, re-used by Suleiman. Legend has it that they represent the lions which would have eaten Suleiman's father if he had implemented his plan to level the city. The British removed the original back wall to allow cars to enter what leads into the Via Dolorosa, the Way of the Cross.

Dung Gate

Theories about its current name include that it resulted from the debris from the various occasions when the city was destroyed, and that the area above the wall around the gate was the local rubbish dump. Its official name is *Bab el-Magharbeh* (the Gate of the Moors) because North African immigrants lived nearby in the 16th century. The gate was widened by the Jordanians during their occupation of the city (1948-1967) to allow cars to enter. Notice the small Ottoman arch showing how the original gate was smaller.

Zion Gate

This became known as *Bab Kharet el-Yahud* (Gate of the Jewish Quarter) in late medieval times. Today the many bullet marks are signs of the fierce fighting that took place in the area during the 1948 War of Independence.

New Gate

This is the most recent gate, opened in 1887 by Sultan Abdul Humid to improve access to the Old City from the new settlements developing outside the north wall.

Golden Gate

Uncertainty surrounds this sealed entrance to Temple Mount. The Mishnah mentions the Temple's eastern gate and there are Herodian elements in the present structure. Some believe it to be where Ezekiel 44:1-3 claims the Messiah will enter the city. The gate was probably sealed by the Muslims in the 7th century to deny access to the Haram esh-Sharif to non-Muslims. It was known as the Beautiful Gate, but the Greek word for beautiful, *horain*, was

confused with the Latin word for golden, *aurea*.

A popular theory explaining why the gate was sealed is that the Muslims did it to prevent the Jewish Messiah from entering the Haram. It is said that the Muslim cemetery was put here because they believe that the Jewish Messiah will be a Cohen, who are not allowed to enter cemeteries. The Jews, however, believe that their Messiah will be a descendant of King David and will therefore be able to cross the cemetery.

MARKETS

The Old City's markets dominate the narrow streets and are one of its major fascinations. The two most direct access-points to the market areas are Jaffa Gate from the New City and Damascus Gate from East Jerusalem.

From Jaffa Gate, the main street going straight ahead and down is David St. This first section is the most touristy area of the markets. The street continues right up to the Temple Mount, becoming Bab el-Silsila St along the way. Various streets branch northwards from David St. The first is Christian Quarter Rd, full of the regular souvenir shops but with an emphasis on religious items in the immediate vicinity of the Church of the Holy Sepulchre. South-east of the traditional site of Calvary is the Muristan Market, which is usually less crowded than the other markets and specialises in leather goods, clothes and carpets. The Christian Quarter has several quiet backstreets with shops selling Christian literature and icons.

Descending along David St you come to the food markets. The huge rooms on the left, with some fruit and vegetable stalls inside, date from the Second Crusade. Heading north just past here is a narrow trio of streets, the third of which soon turns west into the second. This area is the most crowded centre of the markets, with a combination of intrigued tourists and locals shopping for everyday items such as

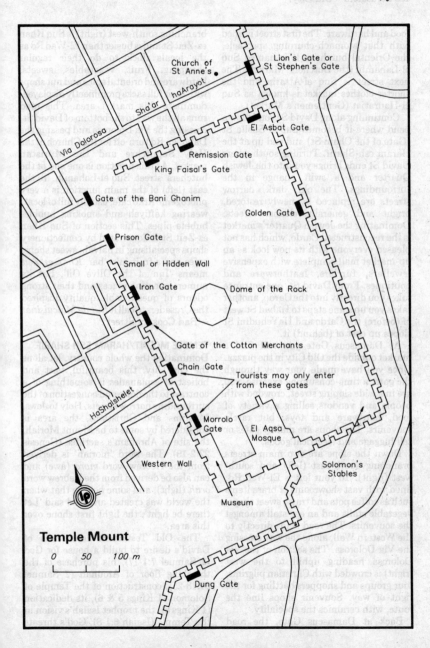

Church of
St Anne's

Lion's Gate or
St Stephen's Gate

Sha'ar
haArayot

El Asbat Gate

Via Dolorosa

Remission Gate

King Faisal's Gate

Gate of the Bani Ghanim

Golden Gate

Prison Gate

Small or Hidden Wall

Dome of the Rock

Iron Gate

Gate of the Cotton Merchants

Chain Gate

Tourists may only enter
from these gates

Morrolo Gate

El Aqsa
Mosque

Solomon's
Stables

HaShalshelet

Western Wall

Museum

Dung Gate

Temple Mount

0   50   100 m

food and hardware. The first street is lined with that stomach-churning spectacle, the Oriental butchers. It is named Suq el-Lahamin (the Butchers' Market). The next street is Suq el-Attarin and the shorter clothes market is known as Suq el-Hauratjat (Gentlemen's Market).

Continuing along David St you follow a bend where it becomes Bab el-Silsila St (Gate of the Chain St) and end up at the Haram esh-Sharif. Turning south where David St ends brings you into the Jewish Quarter and a swift change in the surroundings. The old, dark, narrow streets are replaced by newly restored, bright and generally cleaner streets. Dominating the Jewish Quarter's market is the reconstructed Cardo, which has not pleased everyone with its new look as an up-market mall complete with expensive jewellers, furriers, leatherware and boutiques. From David St, one entrance takes you directly into the Cardo, another takes you up some steps to Habad St west of (before) the Cardo and HaYehudim St slopes up east of (behind) it.

At Damascus Gate you will find a market outside the Old City in the piazza. Once you have made your way through the gate, a time-consuming exercise, you are in a wide sloping street, crowded with people and vendors selling a variety of food, hardware and toys, but rarely souvenirs. The shops are mainly cafés or sell luggage and electrical goods.

Down the slope are two main streets branching south-east (left) and south-west (right). To your left is El-Wad Rd, lined with vast showrooms of brass items such as coffee pots and trays; sweet shops, vegetable stalls and an egg stall amongst the souvenirs. The road leads directly to the Western Wall, along the way crossing the Via Dolorosa. The section of the Via Dolorosa heading uphill to the west (right) is crowded with Christian pilgrims, tour groups and shoppers battling for the right of way. Souvenir shops line the route, with ceramics the speciality.

Back at Damascus Gate, the road branching south-west (right) is Suq Khan ez-Zeit St and is busier than El-Wad Rd as the locals flock to do their regular shopping. Fruit, vegetables, sweets, hardware and oriental spice and nut shops with their full sacks prominently displayed, dominate this market area. This road runs all the way to the bottom of David St, crossing the Via Dolorosa and passing the Dabbaga Rd turn-off for the Church of the Holy Sepulchre and the Muristan market. At this junction is one end of the butchers' street, Suq el-Lohamin. To the east (left) of the main junction is a very photogenic Arab café, usually full of locals wearing kaffiyeh and smoking hubble-bubble pipes. This section of Suq Khan ez-Zeit St is dominated by confectionery shops specialising in halvah, sweet shops, cafés and a fruit juice bar. *Khan ez-Zeit* means 'Inn of the Olive Oil', but its numerous eating places and their strong odours of questionable quality inspired the Crusaders to call it *Rue de Malcuisinat* – 'Bad Cookery Street'.

TEMPLE MOUNT/HARAM ESH SHARIF

Dominating the whole country, let alone the Old City, this beautiful, vast and holiest of esplanades is something of a contrast to the noise and congestion of the surrounding narrow streets. Holy to Jews, Muslims and Christians, the area is considered by some to be Mount Moriah, the site of Abraham's sacrifice (Genesis 22:2-19). The word 'moriah' is derived from the Hebrew word *mora* (awe) and can also be derived from the Hebrew word *orah* (light), and some believe that when the world was created and God said 'Let there be light', the light first shone over this area.

The Old Testament later tells of David's desire to build a house for God (2 Samuel 7:1-17), his purchase of the threshing floor of Arounah (2 Samuel 24:18-25), construction of the Temple of Solomon (1 Kings 5 & 6), its dedication (1 Kings 8), the prophet Isaiah's vision in the Temple (Isaiah 6:1-8), God's threats regarding man's sins (Jeremiah 7:1-15), Ezekiel's vision on idolatry (Ezekiel 8), the Temple's destruction by Nebuchadnezer (2 Kings 25), the vision of the future Temple (Ezekiel 40 & 44) and its reconstruction and dedication (Ezra 4).

The New Testament mentions the Temple in its coverage of the birth of John the Baptist (Luke 1:5-25), Jesus' presentation in the Temple (Luke 2:22-28) and his parents finding him there (Luke 2:40-42), the Devil's temptation of Jesus (Luke 4:9-12), Jesus throwing the traders from the Temple (Matthew 21:12-17), Jesus meeting with the man he had cured at Bethzatha (John 5:14), Jesus teaching in the Temple (John 7:14-53), his invitation to those who had not sinned to throw the first stone (John 8:2-11), Jesus saying that the sheep hear his voice (John 10:22-39), the Jewish leaders' 'plot' against Jesus (John 11:45-53); the widow's mite (Mark 12:41-44), the prophecy of the Temple's ruin (Matthew 24:1-25), the return of the 30 silver coins by Judas (Matthew 27:2-10) and the Temple's veil torn in two (Matthew 27:52).

Temple Mount is a walled area within the Old City walls, and there are eight access gates plus the sealed Golden Gate. Although you can leave the compound by any of them, non-Muslims are only allowed to enter through two: Morrolo (Moors) Gate, just south of the Western Wall; and Chain Gate, at the eastern end of Bab el-Silsila Rd. Observant Jews do not visit the Haram because Jewish law forbids them to, as it would make them ritually unclean, due to the impurity of touching dead persons (Numbers 19:11-22).

Entrance to the area itself is free, but to visit the two mosques (highly recommended) and the museum, tickets must be purchased. Visiting hours are slightly confusing as they are based around Muslim prayer schedules, which depend on the lunar calendar. Basically, the Haram is open Saturday to Thursday 8 am to 3 pm, although those inside by

then are allowed to stay until 4 pm. During prayers (approximately 11.30 am to 12.30 pm winter and 12.30 to 1.30 pm summer), the museum shuts and entry to the mosques is for Muslims only. During the month of Ramadan the area is only open 8 to 11 am.

You are not allowed to enter the Haram unless suitably dressed, and although long robes are usually available for those with bare legs and arms, you should dress appropriately out of respect. All bags are searched on entry to the Haram and once inside you should proceed quietly in this holiest of holy places. There are patrols of plain-clothed Muslim guards, uniformed Arab police and IDF soldiers, and couples will be loudly accosted if they so much as hold hands.

In addition, certain unmarked areas are strictly off-limits and if you stray, even unintentionally, you will be lectured and perhaps even arrested. Stay away from the sides of the Al-Aqsa mosque, the Solomon's stables corner and the garden on the east side.

Tickets for the mosques and the museum are sold from two kiosks. The main one is between El Aqsa mosque and the museum, across from Morrolo Gate – the kiosk by Chain Gate is not always open. Tickets for admission to both mosques and the museum are US$3.60, students US$2.40.

El Aqsa Mosque

For the best effect, it is better to visit El Aqsa mosque first. Believed by some to have originally been the 6th century Crusader Church of St Mary converted into a mosque, it is known to Jews as *Midrash Shlomo* (School of King Solomon). Muslims maintain that it was built in the 10th century to confirm that Jerusalem is the 'furthest sanctuary' from where Mohammed began his Night Journey. Now the country's largest mosque, it is used as the main prayer mosque in preference to the Dome of the Rock.

The columns, ceiling, carpets and the

stained glass windows dominate the mosque's interior. Donated by Mussolini, the large glacial marble columns and the ceiling's paint job, courtesy of Egypt's King Farouk, were the result of the 1938-42 restoration programme. Nothing much remains from the original construction which was twice destroyed by earthquakes in its first 60 years. The impressive carpet collection is rumoured to be due to a tradition of pilgrims donating them and the level of the floor would be considerably lower without them. Saladin provided the mihrab decoration in 1187 along with what was a magnificent carved wood pulpit until 1969, when it was destroyed in a fire started by an Australian Christian fanatic who acted in the name of a 'call from on high' to restore the Jewish Temple. He believed that the Messiah would not come until he had cleared the area of the Islamic constructions.

Solomon's Stables

Turn right as you leave El Aqsa mosque, to see this south-eastern corner which is believed to be the site of the Temple's pinnacle where Jesus was tempted by the Devil (Matthew 4:5). However, this is one of the off-limits areas, so stay away. A stairway leads down to a large underground area which has nothing to do with Solomon. Twelve rows of pillars support the esplanade above, and Muslim fears of Jewish terrorist attacks on the area (attempts have been made) are the cause of the sensitivity. Access is possible to the diplomatic among you, keen enough to persuade an official of the Supreme Muslim Council to send someone with a key. The Council office is near the Ribat Ala ed-Din el-Basir building in Tariq Bab en-Nazir (Tariq Bab el-Habs) street in the Mameluke area.

Dome of the Rock

Head past El-Kas, where Muslims wash before prayers, and up the steps towards the Dome of the Rock. Also known as the Mosque of Omar, it was built between 688-691 by the Ommayad Khalif Abdul Malik ibn Marwan. Popular Arab tradition

Dome of the Rock

suggests that its purpose was to commemorate Mohammed's ascension to heaven but this is contradicted by the more recent Dome of the Ascension (Qubbat el-Miraj) nearby. A more cynical theory suggests that it was built to overshadow the Christian churches in the vicinity which were attracting Arab converts impressed by such images of power.

The mosque's design is based on mathematical dimensions related to the centre circle drawn around the rock inside. It compares with the Mausoleum of Diocletian in Split, Yugoslavia, built in 303, and in principle with 6th century churches in Syria.

Inside the mosque is the sacred rock upon which Abraham prepared to sacrifice his son, Isaac, and from which Mohammed began his Night Journey. In one corner there is supposed to be his footprint and nearby is a box containing what are believed to be hairs from his beard. The interior of the dome is masterfully covered in gold-dominated mosaics, produced by Syrian Christians. Crosses on some of the columns in the centre circle were borrowed from churches. The carved ceilings on either side of the octagon are a 13th century addition, and the Mameluke star is the dominant motif.

The cave under the rock is called Bir el-Arwah (the Well of Souls) with the voices of the dead supposedly combining with the sounds of the lower rivers of paradise as they plunge into eternity. Tradition has it that the rock marks the world's centre. After the mosque was completed, El-Malek had an inscription made, saying that he had built it and giving the date. Two hundred years later the Abbasid Caliph al-Mamun put his name to the inscription to claim credit for the construction but neglected to alter the original date.

Suleiman the Magnificent had what remained of the original mosiacs removed, replacing them with his own tiles. The

external mosaics were renewed in 1963. The prominent dome was originally gold, but this was eventually melted down to pay the caliph's debts. Now it is made of a convincing aluminium bronze alloy and is due for a minor restoration programme in the late 1980s involving a new copper base to be gilded with gold leaf.

The attractive arcades at the top of the eight stairways leading to the Dome of the Rock's esplanade are called in Arabic *maurazin* (scales). This is based on the belief that on the Last Day the scales of judgement will be suspended here to weigh the hearts of men against truth. The two on the south side are the oldest (10th century) and the newest is 15th century.

Dome of the Chain

This is the smaller version of the Dome of the Rock, sited in the exact centre of the Haram area. Mystery surrounds the reason for its construction. A popular theory is that it was a trial-run for the real thing; another is that it was the Haram's Treasury. Its name comes from the legend that Solomon hung a chain from the dome and those who swore falsely whilst holding it were struck by lightning. This perhaps confirms the treasury theory, with superstitious fear a good security system.

Mameluke Buildings

Make a point of strolling around the northern section of the Haram to admire the facades on the north and west sides. Mainly religious schools, these buildings feature some delightfully ornate stonework. The gates too, especially the Gate of the Cotton Merchants, deserve a closer inspection. The Fountain of Sultan Qaytbay is another of the city's beautiful structures over-shadowed by more illustrious neighbours. Adjacent to the Dome of the Rock, it was built by Egyptians in 1482 as a charitable act to please Allah. Interestingly its construction was supervised by a Christian master builder.

WESTERN WALL

The Western Wall (in Hebrew *Kotel Hama'aravi* or just the *Kotel*) is often referred to by non-Jews as the Wailing Wall because the Jews have traditionally come here to mourn the Temple's destruction. It is part of the retaining wall built by Herod the Great in 20 BC to support the Temple's esplanade. Look closely and you will see the different styles of bricks in the Wall. The top ones are those added by Byzantines and Muslims after the Romans had pushed out parts of the Wall that projected above the inside floor level. The original Herodian stones can be identified by their carved frames. In the south corner of the women's section smaller stones were used to fill in one of the original Temple entrances.

The Wall can be reached by foot from Dung Gate, the Jewish Quarter, or via the Arab markets on El-Wad Rd or Bab el-Silsileh St. Egged bus No 1 runs from the central bus station to Dung Gate. Access to the Wall is open to all, Jewish or not. It is open 24 hours with every access route marked by a security check-point. All men must cover their heads; complimentary cardboard yarmulkas are provided, and women may borrow shawls and leg coverings if required. Men, however, can wear shorts. Photography is permitted except during Shabbat and Jewish festivals when photography is strictly banned in the whole area, as is smoking. The Wall should be visited at different times of the day and the week to really experience its status. On Monday and Thursday mornings bar mitzvahs are held and are usually fascinating to watch, with singing and older female relatives screaming and crying.

The Wall is divided into two areas, the northern section for men, the small southern section for women. When I asked why the men had that particular end of the Wall, I was told that it was chosen by them because it received more shade from the hot sun! Day and night you will always see Hasidic Jews in their distinctive black clothes bobbing to and fro as they pray. This motion, is made in time with the prayers and becomes reflex action for most praying Jews. You will see the cracks in the Wall crammed with bits of paper containing prayers – an old tradition.

To celebrate the arrival of Shabbat there is always a large crowd on Fridays at sunset and students from the nearby Yeshiva HaKotel shuffle down to the Wall to dance and sing. During Shabbat and the Jewish festivals the Wall is a major attraction for worshippers.

Make a point of visiting the area at night, when the Dome of the Rock looms quietly behind the Wall, which is floodlit. The piazza is often the site for youth and military parades, although in keeping with the country's minimalised style of formality they are not usually very spectacular to watch.

Wilson's Arch

Situated to the north of the men's prayer section, this arch (now inside a room) carries the Street of the Chain to the Temple across the Tyropoeon (Cheesemaker's) Valley. It was once used by priests on their way to the Temple. Look down the two illuminated shafts to get an idea of the Wall's original height. Possibly Hasmonean (150-40 BC) but at least Herodian, the room's function is unknown. Women are not permitted into the room, and the site is often closed to men too, but officially it is open Sunday, Tuesday and Wednesday 8.30 am to 3 pm, Monday and Thursday 12.30 to 3 pm, and Friday 8.30 am to 12 noon, closed Saturday.

Robinson's Arch

Named after an American scholar, Edward Robinson, this is at the southern end of the Wall. It was the entrance to the passageway whereby the royal party had access from the Upper City to the Temple. Ruins of shops and stalls that supported the bridge are below the arch.

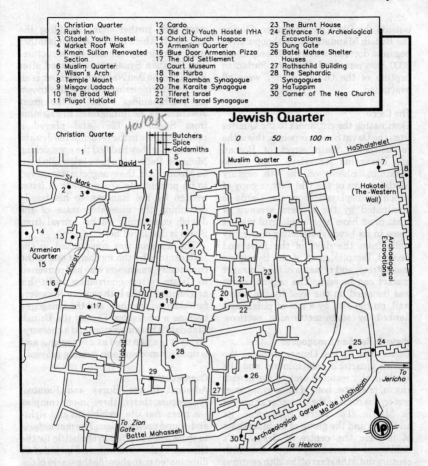

1 Christian Quarter	12 Cardo	23 The Burnt House
2 Rush Inn	13 Old City Youth Hostel IYHA	24 Entrance To Archeological
3 Citadel Youth Hostel	14 Christ Church Hospace	Excavations
4 Market Roof Walk	15 Armenian Quarter	25 Dung Gate
5 Kman Sultan Renovated	16 Blue Door Armenian Pizza	26 Batei Mahse Shelter
Section	17 The Old Settlement	Houses
6 Muslim Quarter	Court Museum	27 Rothschild Building
7 Wilson's Arch	18 The Hurba	28 The Sephardic
8 Temple Mount	19 The Ramban Synagogue	Synagogues
9 Misgav Ladach	20 The Karaite Synagogue	29 HaTuppim
10 The Broad Wall	21 Tiferet Israel	30 Corner of The Nea Church
11 Plugot HaKotel	22 Tiferet Israel Synagogue	

Jewish Quarter

JEWISH QUARTER

In the south-east sector, the Jewish Quarter stands out from the rest of the Old City due to its ongoing large-scale restoration programme. The work commenced immediately after the re-unification of Jerusalem in 1967 and it is one of the most successful building projects in the country. There are few historic monuments above ground level due to the mass destruction by the Jordanians between 1948-67 but several archaeological discoveries have been made. These tell of Jewish settlement beginning in the First Temple Period (around 1000-586 BC), continuing right through to the British Mandate (1918-48). These historical sites are used by Jews to highlight the continuity (and hence legitimacy) of the Jewish presence.

Prior to 1948, the Jewish Quarter had become a congested slum due to the growth of the Jewish population and unsatisfactory building practices. As a result of this, large numbers began to move to the Muslim Quarter and later outside the Old City altogether. During the British Mandate the local population began to decrease and by 1948 only about 2000 Jews remained. With the Jordanian capture of the Old City they were all evacuated.

The Cardo

Dominating the entrances to the Quarter from the David St access points, this is the reconstructed main street of Roman and Byzantine Jerusalem – the Cardo Maximus. Shown on the 6th century Madaba map of the Old City, a copy of which is displayed here, the Cardo is dominated by the modern versions of what must have been a colourful market place in its heyday. Remains of the city walls from the days of the First and Second Temples, part of the Byzantine main street, and remains of the Crusader market can be seen. The original street was bounded on the west by the heavy wall, on the east by a row of pillars and flanked by seven-metre-wide porticos.

Hurva & Ramban Synagogues

Dominated by the Omary mosque, the Jewish Quarter's only minaret and the symbolically restored arch of the Jewish Hurva, or Hurba, both of these synagogues rest on the ruins of the Crusader church of St Martin. The Hurva Synagogue, its additions and the group of buildings east of it were the centre of Jerusalem's Ashkenazi community from the 15th century until the start of the 20th century. 'Hurva' means 'ruins' and was the name given to the surrounding courtyard which, in 1721, was razed by Muslims who were owed a considerable amount by the Jews who lived and worshipped here and were unable to pay up. During the next 90 years the Ashkenazi community continued to live in the vicinity but without their own synagogue, leaving the ruins as they were.

The Hurva Synagogue itself was dedicated in 1864 but was destroyed by the Jordanians in 1948. Restoration work went little further than rebuilding the main arch, which may be left as it is rather than completely rebuild the structure. The Ramban Synagogue is named after Rabbi Moshe Ben Nahman. Ramban is an acronym for his name and he is also known as 'Nachmanides'. One of the great Jewish sages, he immigrated to Palestine from Spain in 1267 and played a prominent role in the return of the Jews to the city after they had fled the approaching Mongols. Believed to have originally been on Mount Zion, the synagogue was moved to its present site around 1400. A letter written by the Ramban to his family describing the miserable state of the Jewish community on his arrival from Spain is displayed here.

The minaret was constructed in the 15th century by the mother of one of the community's members who had converted to Islam after quarrelling with his neighbours. In the 16th century Jews were forbidden to pray here and the synagogue became a workshop. During the British Mandate it became a store and a cheesery. Today it is again used as a synagogue and is open for morning and evening prayers.

Quartercentre

Adjacent to the Hurva and Ramban synagogues, this is a three-in-one complex – a memorial site, exhibition and sight-and-sound presentation. The memorial is to those Jews who fell in the battle for the Quarter in the 1948 war, and includes an illuminated map showing the stages of the fighting. The exhibition features photographs taken on the day the quarter fell in 1948. The sight-and-sound presentation covers the quarter's history from the First Temple period up to the present day. Open Sunday to Thursday 9 am to 5 pm, Friday 9 am to 1 pm, closed Saturday; admission is 40c.

Old Yishuv Court Museum

This museum (tel 284636) at 6 Or HaHaim St is set up as a house, with each room showing an aspect of Jewish life in the Quarter before the destruction of 1948. Open Sunday to Thursday 9 am to 4 pm, closed Friday and Saturday; admission is US$2.20, students US$1.60.

Sephardic Synagogues

These synagogues were built by the Sephardic community at the end of the 16th century. They were built below ground level because a law at that time said synagogues could not be taller than neighbouring buildings. Destroyed by the Jordanians in 1948, they have been restored using the remains of Italian synagogues damaged during WW II. They are still used for morning and evening services. Open Sunday to Thursday 9 am to 4 pm, Friday 9 am to 1 pm, closed Saturday; admission is US$1.30, students 65c.

Shelter Houses – Batei Mahse

This was the quarter's largest square at one time and in the 19th century the site of an independent Jewish neighbourhood. The Shelter Houses were built to provide housing for the poor. During the last fortnight of the battle for the Quarter in May 1948, hundreds of Jews sheltered in the basements of these buildings as the Jewish military HQ was nearby. The area's most notable building is known as Rothschild Building A. Built in 1871 it was funded by a contribution from Baron Wolf Rothschild of Frankfurt.

Tiferet Israel Synagogue

Dedicated in 1872, this is the 'twin brother' of the Hurva Synagogue, and its tall structure, capped by a dome, was one of the Quarter's best-known landmarks until its destruction by the Jordanians in 1948. Its name means 'the Glory of Israel' and it was the largest Hasidic centre in the Old City.

Burnt House

Next to the Quarter café, this is the most impressive of the remains of the Upper City of the Second Temple era. After the Romans destroyed the Second Temple, they set fire to the Upper City and massacred the inhabitants. A sound and light show takes place here, with English programmes at 9.30 am, 11.30 am, 1.30 pm and 3.30 pm; admission is US$1.60, students US$1. It is open Sunday to Thursday 9 am to 5 pm, Friday 9 am to 1 pm, closed Saturday.

Nea Church

This was the 'New Church' built by Justinian in 543. Its southern apse projects outside the city wall and it was once the city's second-grandest church, after the Holy Sepulchre.

Wide Wall

At the western end of Tiferet Israel Rd and to the north on Plugat Hakotel Rd is the Wide Wall, remains of King Hezekiah's wide stone wall built around 701 BC. Its purpose was to protect the city from the Ashurites, against whom he had rebelled.

St Mary's of the Germans

On the north side of the steps leading to the Western Wall, this is a 12th century complex comprising a church, a hospital and a hospice. The entrance is to the church on Misgav Ladakh St, just east of the Quarter Café.

Rooftop Promenade

One of the most interesting ways to see the Old City is to climb the metal stairway on the corner of Habad St and St Mark's Rd. This takes you up onto the rooftops of the David St and surrounding markets and gives you a unique angle on the sights and sounds of the Old City. You can see the Haram esh-Sharif and the Mount of Olives to the east; East Jerusalem and Mount Scopus to the north-east; the Lutheran Church of the Redeemer's tall white tower and the domes of the Church of the Holy Sepulchre dominate the view to the north. Check out the ventilation ducts through which you can hear and see the markets below you. Visit both in the daytime and at night. In the clear moonlight, the Old City buildings are unforgettable.

MUSLIM QUARTER

Largely overlooked by visitors, this quarter covers 30 hectares in the north-eastern sector of the Old City and is its most highly populated area. The buildings tend to be dilapidated and many of the streets look uninviting, but there are a number of things well worth seeing.

St Anne's Church

Built in 1140 and generally agreed to be the best example of Crusader Architecture in Jerusalem, this church is one of Israel's most popular. Byzantine tradition claims that its crypt enshrines the site of the home of Joachim and Anne, the parents of the Virgin Mary. Next to the church are the impressive ruins surrounding the Pool of Bethesda. These were the medicinal baths where clients of the God Serapis came hoping for a miracle cure. John 5:1-18 tells of Jesus healing a man who had been sick for 38 years. The Crusaders took over the ruins of a 5th century church destroyed by Caliph Hakim. They constructed a small chapel with a stairway leading down to the northern

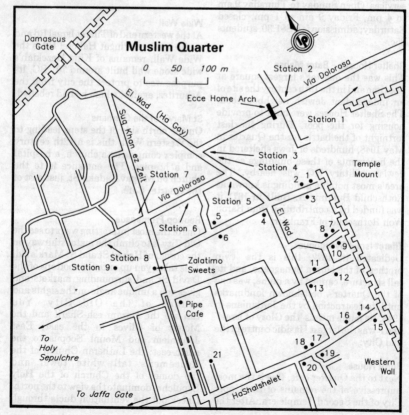

pool to allow pilgrims to venerate Jesus' miracle. Beside it they built the Romanesque church of St Anne to enshrine the Virgin's home and to serve as a chapel for a community of nuns.

Saladin turned the church into a Muslim theological school in 1192; note his inscription above the door. Successive rulers allowed the church to fall into decay so that by the 18th century it was roof-deep in refuse. In 1856 the Ottoman Turks presented the church to France in gratitude for their support in the Crimean War and it was restored to its former glory.

Apart from its architectural beauty, the church is noted for its acoustics, and a prominent sign requests that only hymns are used for sound checks. A joint in the north wall indicates a medieval extension in the bare chapel. The crypt is older than the church; note how the pillars' foundations stand out from the original shape of the caves which once formed part of Serapis' sanctuary. Open Monday to Saturday 8 am to noon and 2 to 6 pm (winter 2 to 5 pm), closed Sundays; admission is free. The entrance is marked 'St Anne – Peres Blanc'; do not use the other door marked 'Religious Birthplace of Mary'.

Via Dolorosa

This road, holy to Christians, spans both the Muslim and the Christian Quarters. Traditionally the route followed by Jesus as he carried his cross to Calvary, this road's sanctity is based on faith, not history. Its origins can be traced back to the days when Byzantine pilgrims, on the night of Holy Thursday, would go in procession from Gethsemane to Calvary along roughly the same route as today's Via Dolorosa, although there were no official devotional stops en route. By the 8th century some stops had become customary but the route had changed considerably and went from Gethsemane around the city on the south to Caiaphas' house on Mount Zion, then to the Praetorium of Pilate at St Sophia near the Temple and eventually to the Holy Sepulchre.

In the Middle Ages, with Latin Christianity divided into two camps, the situation became more complicated. One group located the Praetorium and the high priest's palace on Mount Zion, while the other placed them both north of the Temple, and so they followed totally different routes to the Holy Sepulchre. The basic reason for their conflict was simply that one group had churches on the western hill, the other on the eastern!

In the 14th century, the Franciscans devised a walk of devotion following Jesus' steps in Jerusalem. This included some of today's Stations but the starting point was the Holy Sepulchre. This became the standard route for nearly two centuries but eventually changed as a result of the enthusiasm of European pilgrims who had adapted the ceremonies according to the order of events in the gospels. Although the Christians resident in Jerusalem had also begun to follow the gospels' order of events, they had only eight Stations, whereas the Europeans

1	Muslim Supreme Council
2	Ribat Ala ed-Din el-Basir
3	Ribat Mansuri
4	Ribat Bayram Jawish
5	Turbatt es-Sitt Tunshuq
6	Serai es-Sitt Tunshuq
7	Ribat Kurd
8	Madrasa Jawhariyya
9	Madrasa Arghuniyya
10	Madrasa Muzhiriyya
11	Suq el-Qattanin
12	Hammam esh-Shifa
13	Hammam el-Ayn
14	Turba Sadiyya
15	Madrasa Tankiziyya
16	Turba Turkan Khatun
17	Turba/Madrasa Taziyya
18	Turba Kilaniyya
19	Turba Barakat Kan (Khalidi Library)
20	Madrasa/Turba Tashtimuriyya
21	Khan es-Sultan

had 14. Pilgrims arriving in Jerusalem expected to find the same as they were accustomed to back home, and the European tradition eventually caught on. The Jerusalem Way of the Cross was extended in the 18th century to include Stations within the Holy Sepulchre. However, the 1st, 4th, 5th and 8th Stations were only given their present location in the 19th century.

Today's Via Dolorosa has little to do with historical reality, as it is more likely that Jesus was condemned to death by Pilate on the other side of the city at the Citadel, next to Jaffa Gate. This was Herod's palace and where Pilate normally resided in Jerusalem. Various Bible references to the trial taking place on a platform (Matthew 27:19) and in the open (Luke 23:4, John 18:28) support this theory as the palace is known to have had such a structure. A more probable route for Jesus to have taken would be east along David St, north through the butchers' market of today, and west to Golgotha.

Stations of the Cross

Every Friday at 3 pm the Franciscan Fathers lead a procession which attracts many pilgrims, tourists and souvenir salesmen. At other times the route is often crowded with tour groups and individuals, sometimes with replicas of the cross being carried. The Stations of the Cross are often difficult to locate, despite their great importance to so many.

1st Station Inside the El-Omariyeh College whose entrance is the door at the top of the ramp on the south side of the Via Dolorosa, east of the Ecce Homo arch. Entrance is not always permitted so if you are asked to leave, however impolitely, don't be surprised. Here Jesus was tried, but there is nothing of official Christian value to see here. There is an unusual view of the Haram esh-Sharif through the windows on the upper level.

2nd Station In the Franciscan Sanctuaries of the Flagellation and the Condemnation, the Condemnation Chapel to the left is the 2nd Station. Jesus was condemned here, and the Chapel of Flagellation to the right is where he was flogged. The dome incorporates the crown of thorns and the windows of the chapel around the altar show the mob who witnessed the event. Open daily April to September 8 am to noon and 2 to 6 pm; October to March 8 am to noon and 1 to 5 pm, admission free.

3rd Station This is where the Via Dolorosa joins up with El Wad Rd and marks the spot where Jesus fell for the first time while carrying his cross. Adjacent to the entrance of the Armenian Catholic Patriarchate Hospice, the station is marked by a small Polish chapel. The street is dominated by the excavated remains of the original Roman road.

4th Station Beyond the hospice, this station marks the spot where Jesus faced his mother in the crowd of onlookers.

5th Station As El Wad Rd continues towards the Western Wall, the Via Dolorosa heads up to the west. Right on the corner, this is the spot where the Romans forced Simon the Cyrene to carry the cross. It is marked by signs around a door.

6th Station Further along the street, also on the left and easy to miss, is the place where Veronica wiped Jesus' face with a cloth. The Greek Orthodox Patriarchate in the Christian Quarter, displays what is claimed to be the cloth, which shows the imprint of Jesus' face.

7th Station This is where Jesus fell a second time and is marked by signs on the wall on the west of Suq Khan ez-Zeit St, the main market street at the top of this section of the Via Dolorosa. In the 1st century, this was the edge of the city and a gate led out to the countryside. This is part of the argument supporting the claim that the Church of the Holy Sepulchre is the genuine location of Jesus' crucifixion, burial and resurrection.

8th Station Another station easy to miss. Cut straight across Suq Khan ez-Zeit St from the Via Dolorosa and ascend Aqabat el-Khanqa. Just past the Greek Orthodox Convent on the left is the stone and Latin cross marking where Jesus told some women to cry for themselves and their children, not for him.

9th Station If final confirmation that the Way of the Cross was drawn up long after the event is required, this must be it. Come back down to where the Via Dolorosa and Aqabat el-Khanqa meet and turn right (south, and away from Damascus Gate) up Suq Khan ez-Zeit St. Head up the stairway on your right and follow the path round to the Coptic Church. The remains of a column in its door mark the spot where Jesus fell the third time.

Retrace your steps to the main street and head for the Church of the Holy Sepulchre. Inside the church are the remaining five stations.

10th Station As you enter the church, head up the steep stairway immediately to your right. The chapel at the top is divided into two naves. The right one belongs to the Franciscans, the left to the Greek Orthodox. At the entrance to the Franciscan Chapel is the 10th Station where Jesus was stripped of his clothes.

11th Station Still in the chapel, this is where Jesus was nailed to the cross.

12th Station In the Greek Orthodox Chapel, this is the site of Jesus' crucifixion.

13th Station Between the 11th and 12th Stations, this is where the body of Jesus was taken down and handed to Mary.

14th Station The Holy Sepulchre, the Tomb of Jesus. Walk down the narrow stairs beyond the Greek Orthodox Chapel to the ground floor and you will see that the Holy Sepulchre is to be found in the centre of the rotunda, which would be on your left if you were entering from outside. The actual tomb is inside the Sepulchre, beyond the initial Chapel of the Angel. Candles lit by pilgrims who make a donation dominate the small tomb, with the raised marble slab covering the rock on which Jesus' body was laid. Around the back of the Holy Sepulchre is the tiny Coptic Chapel where pilgrims kiss the wall of the tomb, encouraged by a priest who expects a donation.

Ecce Homo Arch & the Convent of the Sisters of Zion

West of the crossroads on the crest of the slope as the Via Dolorosa leads towards El Wad Rd, is an arch with a two-windowed room spanning the street. Its northern end is preserved in the Convent of the Sisters of Zion. Beneath the convent, with its entrance to the right, facing the building and around the corner, are the impressive and recently restored excavations from the Roman period. The arch is traditionally but improbably the spot where Pilate looked down at Jesus to say, 'Behold your King!'

The arch was probably the eastern gate of the city when Herod Agrippa I (37-44) extended it northwards. After the Roman victory, the wall and gate were destroyed, but the debris protected the lower section. When Hadrian replanned the city in 135 he constructed a forum on this site, leaving the original gate in the middle of the pavement. The complex had for generations been connected with Herod the Great's Antonia fortress built around 37-35 BC and named after his Roman friend, Mark Anthony. The excavations and access to the arch (not the one spanning the street) are open Monday to Saturday 8.30 am to 12.30 pm and 2 to 4 pm, closed Sundays; admission is free.

The Prison of Christ

Next door and the property of the Greek Orthodox Church, this basement chapel is supposedly the site of the cellars, cut into rock, where Jesus and the other criminals of the day were held.

Mameluke Buildings

The area surrounding the north-western wall of the Temple was never developed under the Crusaders and it was only under the Mamelukes (1250-1517) that construction really began. The religious colleges, pilgrim hospices and tombs of this period require a little exploration work to find, but the clear-cut and austere stonework of red, white and black is most attractive and worth the effort.

The information about these buildings is gathered from an ongoing British architectural survey and from inscriptions still in place which give such details as the founder's name, construction date and the building's function. Most of them are now tenements and closed to the public. However, the most interesting part of a Mameluke building is its ornate facade, normally dominated by a door with a larger recess to give extra shade and protection.

Jerome Murphy-O'Conner's archaeological guide, *The Holy Land* (Oxford University Press, 1986), covers this area in detail.

Aqabat et-Takiya

In this street is a palace, Serai es-Sitt Tunshuq (1382), which is now an orphanage. The domed tomb opposite, Turbat es-Sitt Tunshuq, was built by the palace's original owner. On the corner with El Wad Rd is the last notable piece of Mameluke architecture built in Jerusalem, the Ribat Bayram Jawish (1540), which was a pilgrim's hospice.

Tariq Bab en-Nazir (Tariq Bab el-Habs)

Like the other main routes to the Haram, this street is named after the gate at the end. In this case there are two names: Gate of

the Inspector, after the founder; and Gate of the Prison, as the Turks used Ribat Mansuri (1282), originally a hospice, as a jail. Ribat Ala ed-Din el-Basir (1267) was another hospice and the city's first Mameluke building – note the absence of coloured stones. Over by the gate is the office of the Supreme Muslim Council.

Tariq Bab el-Hadid

This street leads from El Wad Rd to the Haram's Iron Gate. Although it looks uninviting, it is worth venturing up here to see some of the most delightful Mameluke stonework, plus a hidden section of the Western Wall. Madrasa Jawhariyya (1440) was a college, and the single-storey building next door was a hospice, Ribat Kurd (1293). On the other side are two more former colleges: Madrasa Arghuniyya (1358), and Madrasa Muzhiriyya (1480) with a lovely arch. Further along is the hidden wall.

Suq el-Qattanin

Market of the Cotton Merchants. This vaulted passageway was built in the mid 13th century to provide an income for charities. The two 'Turkish' baths, Hammam el-Ayn and Hammam esh-Shifa are still in use.

Tariq Bab es-Silsila

The busy gate of the Chain St leads to one of the two access points to the Haram for non-Muslims, and becomes David St in the heart of the Old City markets. Look out for the recently restored Khan es-Sultan (1386) – a discreet entrance just up from the large 'Gali' sign leads into a courtyard surrounded by workshops.

Down towards the Haram, the Madrasa/Turba Tashtimutiyya (1382) is a mausoleum built by a top government official for himself. Further east is the Turba Kilaniyya (1352) and next door the Turba/Madrasa Taziyya (1362). The Turba Barakat Khan, on the corner opposite, is now the Khalidi Library. Continue towards the Haram to see two more tombs, the Turba Turkan Khatun (1352) and the Turba Sadiyya (1311). The open square outside the Chain Gate features the semi-domed entrance to the college Madrasa Tankiziyya (1328).

Small Wall

This site, also known as the Hidden Wall, is at the end of the last narrow passageway off Bab el-Hadid St, just outside the Haram's Iron Gate. It is marked by a small sign, visible from El Wad Rd where Bab el-Hadid St begins. This section of wall, now part of a Muslim house, is the same Western Wall that thousands of Jews flock to a few hundred metres to the south. The Arabs living here don't seem to mind the traffic of visitors and have provided an outside light on their first floor to enable Jews to read their prayers. When the Israelis took the Old City in 1967, they found that some of the stones from the Wall had been taken and used for construction work elsewhere. Note the toilet built next to the Wall but now sealed off by the Israelis.

Young Israel Synagogue

At 90 El Wad Rd, this synagogue is run by the brother of the controversial Rabbi Meir Kahane. Situated in this area it is a symbol of the discreet campaign to return certain properties in the Quarter to Jewish ownership.

CHRISTIAN QUARTER

The Christian Quarter covers nearly 20 hectares in the north-western section of the Old City, and has a population estimated at 5000. In the same way that the Mamelukes clustered their buildings around the Haram esh-Sharif, the Christians centred around the Church of the Holy Sepulchre. On higher ground than the rest of the Old City, this quarter is dominated by Christian institutions and many of its backstreets are full of grand buildings.

As you enter from Jaffa Gate, the first two streets to the north (left) – Latin Patriarchate Rd and Greek Catholic

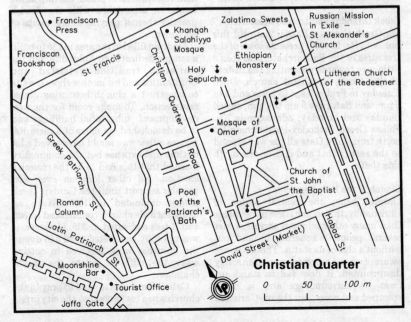

Christian Quarter

Patriarchate Rd – indicate the tone of the neighbourhood, named as they are after the offices there. They lead to St Francis St and in this area and all around New Gate, the local Christian hierarchy reside comfortably.

The Franciscans' Holy Land HQ is in St Francis St in the Monastery of St Salvador. Nearby, on Frères Rd, is the Frères College, run by the Catholic monks. In its cellar are ancient fortifications known as Goliath's Castle, dating from the 1st century Jewish revolt against Rome. On Casa Nova St are the old and new Casa Nova buildings, both owned by the Franciscans. The old building is now administrative offices but was previously the main pilgrims' hostel. Inside, a wooden doorway is carved with the names of pilgrims who had stayed here and wanted to leave a permanent reminder of their visit to the Holy Land. The low pillar near the entrance was used by them to climb onto their donkeys. The new Casa Nova building is the replacement hotel.

Greek Orthodox Patriarchate Museum

On Greek Catholic Patriarchate Rd this museum (tel 284006) presents some of the treasures of the Patriarchate, and goes a little way towards presenting the history of this locally dominant church. Open Tuesday to Friday 9 am to 1 pm and 3 to 5 pm, and Saturday 9 am to 1 pm, closed Sunday and Monday; admission is 70c. Follow Greek Orthodox Patriarchate Rd north from Jaffa Gate all the way around to the east (right) and it is on the north side (left).

Church of the Holy Sepulchre

Despite being the central shrine of Christianity, this church is less recognisable than many other religious shrines. I met several people wandering in and out without a clue of its status. Those who are aware of what it represents are often sorely disappointed. It does fail to stand out from its surroundings and is dark, cramped and noisy, but the un-Christian

behaviour of some of the monks and priests who live and pray here is the most common cause for disappointment. Many a visitor is subjected to the rudeness of these supposedly holy men as they rush around praying and blessing, pushing and bumping startled bystanders as they go by.

The church is an ugly conglomerate of different architectural styles developed over the centuries, and generally agreed to be built on the site of Jesus' crucifixion, burial and resurrection. At the start of the 1st century this was a disused quarry outside the city walls. According to John 19:17 and 41-2, Jesus' crucifixion occurred at a place reminiscent of a skull, outside the city walls and with a grave nearby. Archaeologists discovered tombs here similar to those found elsewhere and dated to this period, so the site is at least compatible with the gospel evidence. Until at least 66 AD there had been a tradition for the Jerusalem community to hold celebrations of public worship at the tomb, in accordance with the Jewish practice then of praying at the tombs of holy men.

Hadrian filled in the area in 135 to build a temple dedicated to Aphrodite, but the Christian tradition persisted and Constantine and his mother chose the site to construct a church honouring Jesus' resurrection. To make room for the new development, substantial buildings had to be demolished – a move of a mere 100 metres either way would have saved a lot of time and expense but the community insisted that this had to be the church's location. No other location ever won popular support until the Garden Tomb theory originated in 1883. Work on Constantine's church commenced in 326 and it was dedicated in 335. However, it was not fully completed until 348 due to the immense work involved in cutting away the cliff to isolate the tomb-chamber.

Caliph Omar was invited to pray in the church when his forces took the city in 638 but he refused, generously noting that if he did his fellow Muslims would have turned it into a mosque. In 1009 the church was destroyed by the Fatamid Caliph Hakim, which no doubt, would not have happened if Omar had been less considerate before. Unable to afford the major repairs necessary, the Jerusalem community had to wait until 1042 when Constantine Monomachus' Byzantine Imperial Treasury provided a subsidy. It wasn't enough to pay for a complete reconstruction of the original church, however, and a large part of the edifice was abandoned, with an upper gallery introduced into the rotunda and an apse added to its eastern side to compensate. The open courtyard stayed basically the same and this was the church that the Crusaders entered on 15 July 1099 as the new rulers of the city. They made significant alterations, absorbing the courtyard into a Romanesque church attached to the unchanged rotunda.

Therefore, the church is now a Crusader building, more or less. You will notice as you look up at the interior of the rotunda that it appears as though it is standing due mainly to the work of local scaffolders. A fire in 1808 and an earthquake in 1927 caused extensive damage, but due to the rivalry between the Christian churches it took until 1959 for the Latins, Greeks and Armenians to agree on a major repair programme. Now rumoured to be nearing completion, it has been hampered considerably by disputes between the denominations, with accusations of certain parties trying to claim ownership of areas belonging to others.

The church is locked and unlocked every day by a Muslim – the church keys have been in the possession of a local Muslim family since the days when the Arabs claimed ownership of the building and charged the Christians a fee for keeping it secure. This fee is still payable to the family but is no longer a significant amount.

The Church of the Holy Sepulchre is open daily to anyone suitably dressed – the guards are very strict and refuse entry to those with bare legs, shoulders and backs, including men or women in shorts. If you are unsuitably dressed and desperate to enter the church, ask the shopkeeper by the eastern entrance to the courtyard. Expect to pay around US$1.35 for suit hire. The church's slightly flexible opening hours are 4.30 am to 8 pm (7 pm in winter). The main entrance is in the courtyard to the south. It can be reached by two points: via Christian Quarter Rd or via Dabbaga Rd, running from Suq Khan ez-Zeit St past Muristan. Another two possible entry points are via the roof (see Ethiopian Monastery, below).

Hidden Remains of the Church of the Holy Sepulchre
The 4th century church was much larger than the present one and some interesting traces of it can be found in neighbouring buildings.

The Russian Mission in Exile Just east of the Holy Sepulchre, on the Dabbaga Rd, between the Muristan and Khan ez-Zeit markets, is St Alexander's Church, which houses the Russian mission in exile. A much-altered triumphal arch dominates the visitors' area. It once stood in Hadrian's forum, built here in 135. Through the arch and to the left at the top of the steps you can see a section of the pavement which was once part of the platform of Hadrian's temple to Aphrodite. A worn door sill is at the foot of the steps. It is often mistaken as the gate through which Jesus left the city to reach Golgotha. St Alexander's Church is only open at 7 am on Thursdays when prayers are said for Tsar Alexander III. The excavations are open from Monday to Thursday only from 9 am to 3 pm; admission is 60c, ring the bell.

Zalatino's Sweets Set back from Suq Khan ez-Zeit St just north of the stairway leading up to the 9th Station is this small

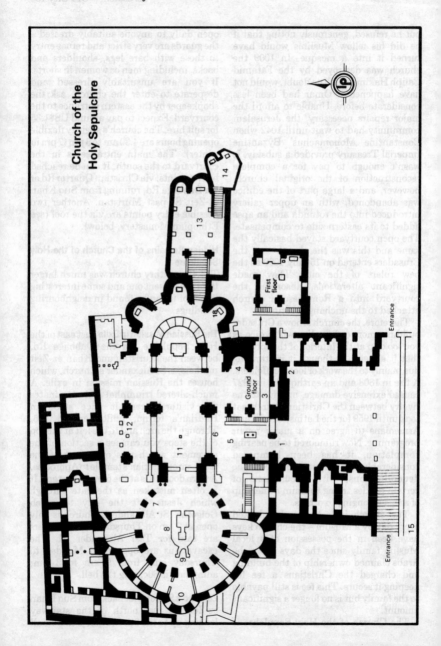

Church of the
Holy Sepulchre

1   12th century facade and entrance/exit.

2   These steps were the Crusader entrance to Calvary closed in 1187 to become the Chapel of the Franks.

3   Calvary: the 11th, 12th and 13th Stations of the Cross in the Latin and Greek Chapels. Accessible via the steep stairs on the immediate right inside the entrance, their floor is level with the summit of the block of rock left in the old quarry – you can see/touch it beneath the Greek altar marking the 13th Station.

4   In the Chapel of Adam, downstairs, a window allows you to see the rock again. One legend has it that Adam was buried below Calvary and Jesus' blood dripped through this crack to anoint him. Crusader kings were buried in this chapel and the bodies of Godfrey de Bouillon and Baldwin I lay on the two benches near the door until 1810.

5   The Stone of Unction often causes pilgrims to miss the small stairway up to Calvary, and commemorates Jesus being anointed before burial. It is not the actual stone where his body was laid out. First appearing in the 12th century, the present stone dates from 1810.

6   This wall with the paintings has no structural or major religious function but would provide a fine view of the church and create more room if demolished. It was built after the 1808 fire to support the great arch which was cracked, and was immediately festooned with Greek icons. Despite recent restoration work making the wall unnecessary, a new one was built to allow the Greeks a place to hang their icons.

7   These two columns have been left in the same damaged condition as they were after the 1808 fire, while the rest of the 11th century piers and columns were restored. Looking closely you will see that one of the two has a rim around the top while the other has a rim around the base and its taper continues in the first one. This is because the massive 4th century columns supporting the dome's drum were cut in half to be re-used to support the upper gallery added in the 11th century.

8   The tomb monument, understandably described as 'a hideous kiosk', dates only from the 19th century. The 1808 fire had destroyed the previous 11th century monument which replaced the rock tomb Hakim removed in 1009. You can queue up here to take a look inside.

9   Here you will find the Coptic Shrine at the back of the present tomb where you can see a very small section of the original (near the base).

10   This is the 4th century wall and apse, now part of the Syrian Chapel.

11   The simplicity of the 12th century Crusader church is here dominated by Greek Orthodox additions. Its upper gallery was included because of the corresponding gallery in the rotunda the previous century and is not normally found in churches of this period.

12   These two lines of different pillars were included by the 12th century architect to preserve the remains of the original colonnade on the Byzantine courtyard's north side in front of the rotunda.

13   Follow the steps down to the crypt of St Helena. The stairway walls are marked by pilgrims' graffiti – several crosses scratched into the stone.

14   Only opened in the 12th century, the crypt's north and south walls are the foundations of the 4th century basilica's nave. From this church it is believed that a narrow stairway led down to the cistern here, where the True Cross is reputed to have been found.

15   The attractive entrance to the Mosque of Omar; entrance is barred to non-Muslims.

bakery. You should come here for its excellent products, but to help pass the time waiting to be served, ask to be shown the storeroom from where you can just about see the continuation of the Hadrianic and Constantinian wall.

Unfortunately access to it has been blocked off by the recently built wall of the storeroom.

Ethiopian Monastery

Following the route to the 9th Station of the Cross, after the first left turn and as the street turns to the right, you'll see a small grey door below a green beam ahead of you. This opens onto a roof of the Church of the Holy Sepulchre. The cluster of huts here has been the Ethiopian Monastery since the Copts forced them out of their former building in one of the many disputes between the various Christian groups.

The quiet Ethiopian monks live amongst the ruins of a medieval cloister erected by the Crusaders where Constantine's basilica had been previously. The cupola in the middle of this roof section admits light to St Helena's crypt below. Access to the Church of the Holy Sepulchre is possible via two nearby points. One is through the Ethiopian Chapel (most of these monks do not speak much English but are very friendly, so ask for directions) and the other way is to go left out of the Ethiopian monastery and through the Copts' entrance.

The Mosque of Omar & the Khanqah Salahiyya

Adjacent to the Holy Sepulchre are these two mosques, and some speculation surrounds their matching minarets. To the north, the Khanqah Solahiyya is on the site of the Crusader Patriarch of Jerusalem's palace. In 1417 during its restoration a minaret was added to the roof. The Mosque of Omar was built in 1193 to commemorate the caliph's prayers in the courtyard of the Holy Sepulchre in 638, but the minaret in its courtyard was added between 1458 and 1465.

The tops of the minarets are identical in structure and materials. It is believed that they were meant to match – note that, despite the difference in ground level, a line joining their summits is absolutely

horizontal. Also it has been shown that the mid-point of a line drawn between the minarets falls roughly at the entrance of Jesus' tomb in the Holy Sepulchre. This is thought to be intentional, although the purpose is unclear. Perhaps the Mamelukes wanted to 'nullify' the Holy Sepulchre – it is the one site associated with Jesus that Muslims do not accept. Neither mosque is open to non-Muslims.

Lutheran Church of the Redeemer

Dominating the Old City skyline with its tall white tower, the present church was built in 1898 on the site of the 11th century church of St Mary la Latine. The closed northern entrance porch is medieval and decorated with the signs of the zodiac and the symbols of the months. The tower is a popular attraction, and its narrow spiral staircase leads you up to an excellent central view across the Old City and its surroundings. Open Tuesday to Saturday 9 am to 1 pm and 2 to 5 pm, closed Sunday and Monday. Admission is 65c.

Church of St John the Baptist

Jerusalem's oldest church, it stands in a hidden section of the Muristan area and is usually overlooked, having been buried by the gradual raising of surrounding street levels. However, the entrance from Christian Quarter Rd is clearly signposted. This leads you into the courtyard of a more recent Greek Orthodox monastery where a monk will usually be present to open the church for you. Originally built in the mid-5th century, it was restored after the Persians destroyed it in 614. In the 11th century the merchants of Amalfi built a new church which became the cradle of the Knights Hospitallers, using the walls of the earlier building. The present facade with the two small bell towers is a more recent addition along with a few other alterations made to ensure the building's stability.

Pool of the Patriarch's Bath

This unsightly rubbish tip was a large

reservoir believed to date from the Herodian period, but as no archaeological inspections have been made, little is known about it. A welcomed restoration project is planned for this attractive location just to the north of the David St entrance near Jaffa Gate.

Roman Column

At the quiet intersection of these four covered streets, this column is possibly the world's most distinguished lamp-post. Its Roman inscription honours Marcus Iunius Maximus, Prefect of Judea and Legate of the 10th Legion. The column was erected at the beginning of the 3rd century by one of his aides, C Domitius Sergius Honoratus. The 10th Legion was based in what is now the Armenian Quarter for over 250 years, after participating in the capture of Jerusalem in 70 AD.

ARMENIAN QUARTER

This quarter is often described as a miniature city within the Old City. With its own schools, library, seminary and residential quarters discreetly tucked away behind high walls, it is not unusual for visitors to walk straight through the quarter having seen nothing.

Armenia was the first nation to officially embrace Christianity, at the beginning of the 4th century. Its churches came under the jurisdiction of the Metropolitan of Caesarea and the country was represented in Jerusalem during the Byzantine period. An area permanently troubled by politics, the kingdom of Armenia disappeared at the end of the 4th century. This was the start of a continuing period of persecution and exile which culminated in the massacre of almost two million Armenians in 1915. The exiled community here enjoys a strong sense of unity based on their language and culture, both with strong roots in their church. Two great saints of the early 5th century, Isaac and Mesrob, are credited with the creation of the sense of national identity

which has survived these centuries of dispersal.

The Armenian Compound

About 1200 Armenians now live in what used to be a large pilgrims' hospice. It became a residential area after 1915 when refugees from the Turkish massacres settled here. Its empty, wide courtyards are a rare sight in the Old City. It is basically closed to visitors, but you can phone 282331 or ask at the entrance to the church to make an appointment for a visit.

St James (Jacques) Cathedral

The carpets, the numerous lamps hanging in the air and the use of ceramic tiles are the dominant characteristics of this ornate church built and reconstructed in honour of St James the Great, the first martyred disciple who is believed to have been beheaded on this site.

The first church to honour St James was built here by the Georgians in the 11th century. This was built on the foundations of an oratory dedicated to St Menas, an Egyptian martyr, dating from the middle of the 5th century. The Armenians, in favour with the Crusaders, took possession of the church from the Crusaders in the 12th century. They restored the church between them. With a comparable devotion to St James, the Spanish identified with the Armenians and their donations kept the Jerusalem community alive in the 15th century. With the increasingly large numbers of pilgrims, the Armenians purchased adjoining property to house them.

The 17th century porch was added when the entrance was moved. The pierced brass grilles and strange pieces of wood and bronze were used to avoid a 9th century ruling that forbade Christians to use bells. Most of the interior's structural elements date back to the Middle Ages, but the central cupola's rib vaulting is typically Armenian. The four piers were squared off in the 17th century to be

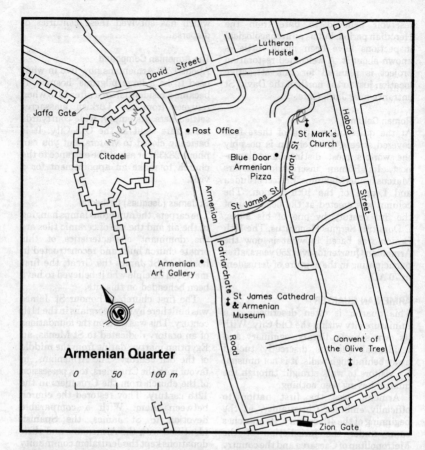

Armenian Quarter

0   50   100 m

Jaffa Gate

Citadel

museum

Post Office

Blue Door
Armenian
Pizza

St Mark's
Church

Lutheran
Hostel

David Street

Habad Street

Armenian Patriarchate Road

St James St

Ararat St

Armenian
Art Gallery

St James Cathedral
& Armenian
Museum

Convent of
the Olive Tree

Zion Gate

decorated with tiles – an Armenian speciality.

The church is only open for services, held Monday to Friday, 3 to 3.30 pm; Saturday and Sunday 2.30 to 3 pm; admission is free.

Mardigian Museum

Housed in what was a theological seminary built in 1843, with an attractive courtyard enclosed by arched colonnades on two levels, this presents an uninspiring synopsis of Armenian history. Open Monday to Saturday 10 am to 5 pm,

closed Sunday; admission is 65c. You can enter from either Armenian Patriarchate Rd or from St James' Cathedral.

Convent of the Olive Tree

Built around 1300 and a fine example of classical Armenian architecture, the site was claimed in the late 14th century to be that of the house of the high priest Annas, the father-in-law of Caiaphas (John 18:13). In the north wall a niche is claimed as the prison of Christ, an alternative to the Greek Orthodox choice on the Via Dolorosa, and in the 15th century the belief started that an olive tree outside the chapel to the north was where Jesus was tied and scourged. Nearby and part of the chapel's north-east external corner, a stone with a trimmed margin and a central cavity is believed to be the same stone mentioned in Luke 19:40 which would have cried out had the disciples not praised God.

From St James' Cathedral, cut across the compound towards the library and the Mardigian Museum, down the steps into the narrow street and through the low gateway in the far wall. It is best to visit between 8 and 9 am, although until noon you should be able to find an Armenian nun from the adjacent convent to open the chapel for you. Admission is free.

St Mark's Chapel

The centre of the Syrian Orthodox community, it also is the centre of certain traditions. The Syrian Orthodox believe it to be the site of the home of St Mark's mother, Mary, where Peter went after he was released from prison by an angel (Acts 12:12). The Virgin Mary is believed to have been baptised here, and according to some, the Last Supper was eaten here, not in the Cenacle on Mount Zion as is most popularly believed. One thing to look out for is the painting on leather of the Virgin and the Child attributed to St Luke. Its age is not known.

Open 9 am to 12 noon, Monday to Saturday, closed on Sundays; admission is free. From Armenian Patriarchate Rd head east along St James' Rd, turn north (left) onto Ararat St and the chapel is on your right, part of a convent. If the door is closed, ring the bell.

MOUNT ZION

Now meaning the part of the stern hill south of the Old City beyond Zion Gate, 'Mount Zion' in the Old Testament period referred to the eastern hill, now known as the City of David (2 Samuel 5:7). The name change came in the 4th century,

based on new interpretations of religious texts. Bordered on the west and south by the Hinnom Valley and on the east by the Tyropoeon Valley, Mount Zion has one of the city's most enchanting locations. Although now outside the city walls, the area was previously enclosed; first during the 2nd century BC. Currently undergoing an extensive reconstruction programme, this compact area contains some of the most important sites in Jerusalem.

To reach Mount Zion, leave the Old City via Zion Gate or head for Zion Gate outside the city walls from either Jaffa or Dung Gates. From the New City, Egged bus No 1 runs here from the New City via Mea Shearim and HaNevi'im St; Egged bus No 38 passes through the New City's centre.

The Cenacle of Coenaculum

Popularly thought to be the site of the Last Supper (cenacle is Greek for 'supper' and coenaculum is Latin for 'dining hall'), this is the only Christian site in Israel administered by the local government. Like so many traditions, that concerning the Cenacle is unreliable. It probably originated in the 5th century due to the other belief that it is the room where the Holy Spirit first came down on the disciples at Pentecost.

Part of the complex where David's Tomb is located, the Cenacle was a site of Christian veneration during the Byzantine period. In the Middle Ages the Franciscans acquired it but were later expelled by the Turks. Although the Israeli Government now controls the site, the Franciscans still retain a deed of purchase dated 1335. Under the Turks the Cenacle became a mosque, and Christians were barred from entering, just as Jews were kept from David's Tomb.

To get there, head south from Zion Gate, bear right at the entrance to the Franciscan monastery (double doors marked 'Custodia Terra Sancta') then take the left path when the road splits. A discrete stairway behind a door to the left leads up to the Cenacle. Many visitors mistake the first large room for the real thing, but you need to walk across this big hall to enter the much smaller room where Jesus supposedly ate the Last Supper with his disciples (Matthew 26:26-35; Mark 14:15-25; Luke 22:14-38; John 13, 14, 15, 17; I Corinthians 11:23-25; Acts 1:12-26 and Acts 2:1-4). Open daily 8.30 am to sundown, admission free. The Cenacle Chapel is open daily 8 am to 12 noon, 3 to 6 pm (winter 2.30 to 5 pm) and special services are occasionally held – contact the Christian Information Centre for details.

David's Tomb

The entrance to David's tomb is on the other side of the same building as the Cenacle. From Zion Gate head south and turn left at the Franciscan monastery door and it is on your right. There isn't a lot to see and the site's authenticity is highly disputable. However, it is one of the most revered of the Jewish holy places despite I Kings 2:10 telling of David's burial east of here within his own city. Open daily, in summer Saturday to Thursday 8 am to 6 pm, Friday 8 am to 2 pm; and in winter Saturday to Thursday 8 am to 5 pm, Friday 8 am to 1 pm. Admission is free but beware of guides forcing themselves upon you to explain away the empty spaces. Heads must be covered, and cardboard yarmulkas are provided.

Museum of King David

This museum next to David's Tomb is associated with the Diaspora Yeshiva, the adjacent Jewish school for religious study. Some rather bizarre modern art is the main exhibit. A reason for its existence appears to be to raise money for the yeshiva – donations of at least 65c are strongly encouraged. Open Sunday to Thursday 8 am to 6 pm, Friday 8 am to 2 pm and Saturday 8.30 am to 4.30 pm.

Chamber of the Holocaust

Opposite David's Tomb, this was the country's first holocaust museum. The presentation is not so lavish as that at Yad Vashem, but its chilling collection of artefacts from that terrible episode is reinforced with an amazing display of anti-Jewish propaganda produced since the Holocaust. Open Sunday to Thursday 9 am to 5 pm, Friday 8 am to 2 pm, closed Saturday; admission is free, donations requested. A slide show (75c) is given every two hours or so. Heads must be covered and cardboard yarmulkas are provided.

Church & Monastery of the Dormition

Newly restored, this beautiful church is one of the area's most popular landmarks and is the traditional site where the Virgin Mary died, or fell into 'eternal sleep'. Its Latin name is *Dormition Sanctae Mariae* (the 'Sleep of Mary'). The current church and monastery, owned by the German Benedictine order, was consecrated in 1906. It was noticeably damaged during the battles for the city in 1948 and 1967.

The church's interior is a bright contrast to many of its older and duller peers nearby. A golden mosaic of Mary with the baby Jesus is set in the upper part of the apse; below are the Prophets of Israel. The chapels around the hall are dedicated to saints: St Willibald, an English Benedictine who visited the Holy Land in 724; the Three Wise Men; St Joseph, whose chapel is covered with medallions featuring kings of Judah as Jesus' forefathers; and St John the Baptist. The floor is decorated with names of saints and prophets and zodiac symbols.

The crypt features a stone effigy of Mary asleep on her deathbed with Jesus calling his Mother to heaven. The chapels around this statue were donated by various countries. In the apse is the the Chapel of the Holy Ghost, shown coming down to the Apostles.

Open daily 8 am to noon and 2 to 6 pm. The complex also has a comfortable café

Top: Ancient olive tree in the Garden of Gethsemane. Mount of Olives, Jerusalem (RE)
Left: Mount of Olives. From the bottom – ancient tombs, Jewish graveyard, tank,
  olive grove, and church (RE)
Right: Mount of Olives (NT)

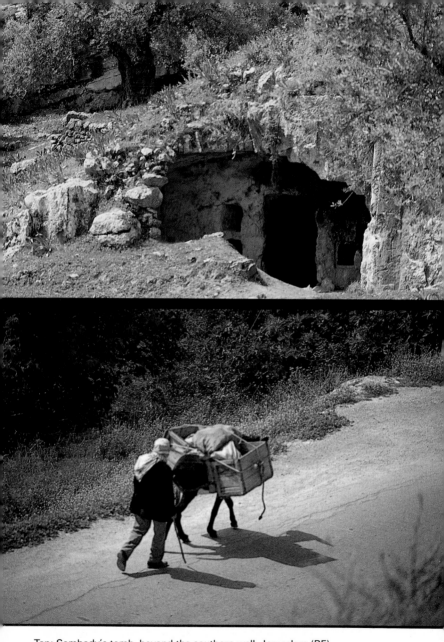

Top: Sombody's tomb, beyond the southern wall, Jerusalem (RE)
Bottom: Passing traffic, Kidron Valley, Jerusalem (RE)

serving cakes and drinks (including beer).

Church of St Peter in Gallicantu

Almost hidden by the trees and the angle of the hill's eastern slope, this church of St Peter at the Crowing of the Cock is the traditional site of the disciple Peter's denial of Jesus (Mark 14:66-72). It is also believed to be the site of the high priest Caiaphus' house, where Jesus was taken after his arrest (Mark 14:53). Archaeological findings show that a 6th century monastic church was built here.

The view from the church's balcony across to the City of David, the Arab village of Silwan and the three valleys that shape Jerusalem is reason enough to justify a visit. Open Monday to Saturday 8 to 11.45 am and 2 to 5 pm (May to September 2 to 5.30 pm), closed Sunday; admission is free. The church is reached by turning east (left) as you descend the road leading from Mount Zion down and around to Sultan's Pool.

THE CITY OF DAVID

This is the oldest part of Jerusalem, and dates back to beyond the 20th century BC and is the confirmed site of the city captured and developed by King David. The excavations are the result of work, still continuing, that started in 1850.

Gihon Spring, Pool of Shiloah & Hezekiah's Tunnel

The Gihon spring was the main reason why the Jebusites settled on the low Ophel ridge rather than choose the adjacent higher ground. *Gihon* means 'gushing', quite suitable as the spring acts like a siphon, pouring out a large quantity of water for some 30 minutes before almost drying up for between four and 10 hours. There is believed to be enough water to support a population of about 2500. The tunnel was built in about 700 BC by King Hezekiah to bring the water of the Gihon into the city and store it in the pool of Shiloah, or Siloam. Its purpose was to

prevent invaders, in particular the Assyrians, from locating the city's water supply and cutting it off (2 Chronicles 32). The tunnel's length is 533 metres (335 metres as the crow flies).

Although narrow and low in parts, you can wade through it; the water is normally about ½ metre deep. Due to the siphon effect it does occasionally rise, but only by about 15 to 20 cm.

The entrance steps leading down to the water are medieval, built due to the ground level having risen over the years. After about 20 metres the tunnel turns sharply to the left, where a chest-high wall blocks another channel which leads to Warren's Shaft which can be visited near the City of David excavations. Towards the tunnel's end the roof rises. This is because the tunnellers worked from either end and one team slightly misjudged the other's level. They had to lower the floor so that the water would flow. A Hebrew inscription was found in the tunnel, and a copy can be seen in the Israel Museum in the New City of Jerusalem. Carved by Hezekiah's engineers, it tells of the tunnel's construction.

You enter the tunnel at the Gihon spring source on Shiloah Way, down in the Kidron Valley and just south (left) of the rest house. Open Sunday to Thursday 9 am to 5 pm, Friday 9 am to 3 pm, closed Saturday; admission is free. The wade takes about 30 minutes; wear shorts and suitable footwear. A torch (flashlight) is also required, although candles are normally available from the local shop or the caretaker.

Warren's Shaft

This was built by the Jebusites to ensure their water supply during a siege. It is just inside their city's defence wall and this is possibly where Joab entered the City of David (2 Samuel 5:8, I Chronicles 11:6). About 100 metres down from the entrance to the City of David excavations, a small museum features photos of the excavation work with explanations of the water supply situation as it used to be. A spiral staircase leads to a tunnel extending into the shaft, so bring a flashlight. You can then proceed down to, or climb up from, Hezekiah's Tunnel at the bottom of the hill. Open Sunday to Thursday 9 am to 5 pm, Friday 9 am to 1 pm, closed Saturday; admission is 85c, students 65c.

KIDRON VALLEY

Apart from the wonderful views, the points of interest here are tombs. These can be reached by following the road north from the entrance to Hezekiah's Tunnel or by heading south from the Jericho Rd. The Arab village that clings to the eastern slope of the valley is Silwan. From north to south, the most prominent tombs are:

Tomb of Jehoshaphat This 1st century burial cave is notable for the impressive frieze above its entrance.

Absalom's Pillar Also dated to the 1st century, the legendary tomb of David's son (2 Samuel 15-18) is just in front of the Tomb of Jehoshaphat.

Grotto of St James or Bnei Heziv Just beyond Absalom's Pillar, this is where St James is believed to have hidden when Jesus was arrested nearby. It is probably the burial place of the Bnei Hezir's, a family of Jewish priests (Nehemiah 10:21).

Tomb of Zachariah Carved out of the rock next to the grotto with a pyramid-like top, this is where Jewish tradition believes the prophet Zachariah is buried (2 Chronicles 24:20).

Valley of Jehoshaphat

Part of the Kidron Valley, this is the area between the Haram esh-Sharif and the Mount of Olives. Joel 3:1-2 relates to it as the prophesied site of God's judgement of mankind. Jehoshaphat in Hebrew means: 'God shall judge'. Based on this, a

legend has arisen which tells of the Day of Judgement. All human beings will be assembled together on the Mount of Olives, with the Judgement Seat on the Haram opposite. Two bridges will appear across the valley between them, and everyone will have to cross either one depending on how they are judged by God. One bridge will be made of iron, the other of paper. The iron bridge will collapse and those who are sent across will die, whilst the paper bridge will hold those who were judged to be allowed to cross it and they will live eternally.

HINNOM VALLEY

Stretching east from below Mount Zion to the Kidron Valley, this was once the area for idols and child sacrifices (Jeremiah 7:31-32). Its name derives from the Hebrew *Gei-Hinnom* (Ravine of Hinnom), given to the site because of the sin and depravity practised here in ancient times.

Monastery of St Onuphrius (Aceldama)

Named after an Egyptian hermit famous for his very long beard - and for wearing nothing else! It is believed to be near to the Field of Blood which is either the land that the chief priests purchased with the 30 pieces of silver returned by Judas (Matthew 27:7-10) or the place where the repentant disciple hanged himself (Acts 1:18-19). To reach the Greek Orthodox monastery a long but scenic walk is required; either south from the Old City area or east from the New City, adjacent to the Cinemateque.

MOUNT OF OLIVES

Standing to the east of the Old City, the Mount of Olives is dominated by the world's largest Jewish cemetery and the many churches commemorating the events that led to Jesus' arrest and his ascension to heaven. The Arab village of Et Tur is on the summit - its name is Arabic for Mount of Olives.

One of the many 'musts' on a Jerusalem

visit, a trip to the Mount of Olives is best started at the top. You can walk from East Jerusalem, or take the bus to avoid what some find a strenuous walk. Arab bus No 75 runs from the station on Suleiman St.

Most of the churches and gardens are open in the morning, before closing down for at least two hours and re-opening again in the mid-afternoon. Visiting later in the day is special too: when the sun goes down you will see why Jerusalem was called 'City of Gold'.

Mosque of the Ascension

The bus often stops just outside. If not, walk south for a few minutes to reach the mosque; it's on your left. Islam recognises Jesus as a prophet and this mosque is the Crusader reconstruction of the original church built before 392. Saladin authorised two of his followers to acquire the site in 1198 and it has remained in Muslim possession since then. The stone floor bears a mark believed to be Jesus' footprint. Perhaps the reason for its unconvincing appearance today is that pilgrims in the Byzantine period were permitted to take bits of it away. Opening hours vary; admission is 65c.

Church of the Pater Noster

Continue south on the same road and on the bend is the site of the cave, also linked to his ascension, where Jesus spoke to his disciples. Queen Helena had the Church of the Eleona built - its name is a bastardisation of the Greek work *elaion*, meaning 'olives'. After the commemoration site of the Ascension was moved northwards, the cave became exclusively associated with Jesus' teachings such as that recorded by Matthew 24:1-26. Destroyed by the Persians in 614, the site later became known as the place where Jesus had taught the Lord's Prayer. This inspired the Crusaders to construct an oratory among the ruins in 1106. Based on an old tradition, attractive tiled panels display the Lord's Prayer in over 60 languages.

As you enter the gate, turn left and then right. The tomb is of Princesse de la Tour d'Auvergne who purchased the property in 1886 and built the Carmelite convent. The actual cave can be reached by going around the cloister to the left, down some stairs and through the first door on the right. Open Monday to Saturday 8.30 to 11.45 am and 3 to 4.45 pm, closed Sundays; admission is free.

Inter-Continental Hotel

Although a large gin and tonic can be most refreshing, the hotel is more renowned for its beautiful but controversial location than for its facilities and service. In front of the hotel, at the end of the road which runs along the top of the mount, is a viewing point from where many photographs of the Old City are taken. The controversy surrounding the hotel is due to it being built over part of the ancient Jewish cemetery. To the south (left), on the east side of the Kidron Valley, is the Hill of Evil Counsel. Now the site of the UN HQ, it was the residency of the High Commissioner for Palestine during the British Mandate. Going further back, it is an alternate possibility for the site of the house of Caiaphus, the high priest who paid Judas to betray Jesus.

Tombs of the Prophets

Head back up the road a little and take the path down to these tombs, now in the backyard of the nearby house, whose owner is the caretaker. Buried here are the prophets Haggai, Zachariah and Malachi who lived in the 5th century BC. Open Sunday to Friday 8 am to 3 pm, closed Saturday; admission is free.

National Cemetery & the Common Grave

This is the burial place of some of those who died in the Jewish Quarter battles of 1948.

Jewish Cemetery

The world's oldest and largest Jewish cemetery, dating back to biblical times. Its importance is based on the belief that this will be the site of the Resurrection of the Dead on the Day of Judgement when the Messiah comes (Zachariah 14:1-11).

Church of Dominus Flevit

Follow the path down to this church built by medieval pilgrims who claimed to have found the rock on the Mount of Olives where Jesus had wept for Jerusalem (Luke 19:41). In 1881 the Franciscans built a chapel nearby as the Muslims would not allow them on the site. When the existing church was built in 1954-55, excavations unearthed a 5th century monastery and a large cemetery dating back to about 1500 BC. The cemetery has since been recovered but some tombs are still visible. The view of the Dome of the Rock from the altar's window is particularly popular. Open daily 8 to 11.45 am and 3 to 5 pm; admission is free.

Russian Church of Mary Magdalene

After the splendour of its gold onions, the church's interior is disappointing, but I wouldn't want to tell that to the fierce nun who sort of welcomed me inside. She thrust a guide-sheet into my hand and ordered me to stand 'over there' and read it. Built by Alexander III and dedicated to his mother, the church is now a convent and has one of the city's best choirs. A section of the Garden of Gethsemane is claimed to be within the church's grounds. Only open Tuesday and Thursday 9 am to 12 noon and 2 to 4 pm; admission is 65c.

Church of All Nations & the Garden of Gethsemane

From the Russian church, continue down and turn right, and the garden's entrance is on the left – not at the front by the main road. Built in 1924, this church, also known as the Basilica of the Agony, was financed by various countries; hence its

popular name. It is the successor to two earlier churches. The first was built in the fourth century but was destroyed by an earthquake in the 740s. The Crusaders built an oratory in its ruins but it was abandoned in 1345 for unknown reasons. This is the popularly accepted site of the garden where Jesus was arrested (Mark 14:32-50). The garden has some of the world's oldest olive trees, but they probably do not date back to the time of Jesus. The mosaic on the church's attractive facade sparkles subtly in the evening sunlight. Open daily, April to October 8 am to noon and 2.30 to 6 pm, November to March 8 am to noon and 2.30 to 5 pm; admission is free.

Mary's Tomb

On the main road turn right, and take the stairs to the right down to this tomb. A cupola supported by columns is a memorial to Mujir ed-Din, a 15th century Muslim judge and historian. Mary was supposedly interned here by the disciples. A monument was first constructed in the 5th century but was repeatedly destroyed. The present monument is 12th-century and is owned by the Greek Orthodox Church, whilst the Armenians, Syrians and Copts have shares in the altar. Open Monday to Saturday 6.30 am to noon and 2 to 5 pm, closed Sunday; admission is free.

St Stephen's Church

This Greek Orthodox church is on the south side of the main road as it bends down and around from East Jerusalem and the Old City. Largely ignored by guides and visitors alike, it was completed in 1968. A 'modern Byzantine' church, it is near the site where Stephen, the first Christian martyr, was stoned to death. The two pleasant women who look after the church are happy to guide visitors around both the church and the chapel on the site where Stephen was slain. There are also remains of the Roman road which led from the Golden Gate down to the

Kidron Valley and an anonymous tomb cut into the rock. It is also a good place to ask questions about the Greek Orthodox Church. Ring the bell to see if anyone is in – there are no set hours. Admission is free.

MOUNT SCOPUS

With marvellous views of the city and the Judean Desert towards Jordan, a visit to this spot is well worthwhile. Mount Scopus' name is the Greek translation of the Hebrew word *hatsofim* (to look over). Its strategic location has played a decisive role in the many battles for Jerusalem over the centuries. In 70 AD the Roman legions of Titus camped here, as did the Crusaders in 1099 and the British in 1917. In the 1948 War of Independence, Arab forces attacked from here. Take Arab bus No 75 to the Augusta Victoria Hospital, or Egged buses No 4, 4A, 9, 23 or 28 to the university.

Hadassah Hospital

Noted for its architecture as well as its troubled history as an Israeli-held enclave within Jordanian-held territory before 1967.

WW I Cemetery

Buried here are soldiers from the British Commonwealth forces. Various remembrance services including ANZAC Day are held here, attended by the Mayor of Jerusalem, other local dignitaries and military personnel.

EAST JERUSALEM

Solomon's Quarries

Between Damascus and Herod's Gates, this vast cave beneath the Old City's north wall was part of a quarry that extended as far as what is now Suleiman St and the bus station. It is possible that stone from here was used to construct the Temple (I Kings 5:15-17) and that Herod the Great (37-4 BC) used it. In Jewish tradition the cave is known as *Me'arat Zidkiyahu* (the Zedekiah's Cave), because

the last king of Judah apparently used it as an escape route before being captured near Jericho by the Babylonians. The cave continues for over 200 metres beneath the Old City and offers cool refuge from a hot day, but there is little to see. Open daily 9 am to 5 pm; admission is 55c, students 30c.

Rockefeller Museum

Further east on the north side of Suleiman St, opposite the north-eastern corner of the Old City, this architectural delight is one of the leading archaeological museums in Israel. Established in 1927, its exhibits range from the Stone Age to the 18th century. The museum (tel 282251, 285151) is open Sunday to Thursday 10 am to 5 pm, Friday and Saturday 10 am to 2 pm. There are free guided tours at 11 am on Sundays and Fridays. Admission is US$3.80 but you can buy a combined ticket for this and the Israel Museum to save some sheqels. From the New City take Egged buses No 23 or 27.

Friday's Arab Sheep Market

Seeing Beersheba's touristic Bedouin market on Thursdays may seem a complete waste of time, but this early morning get-together each Friday is a most interesting spectacle. With the solid walls of the Old City as a backdrop, hundreds of kaffiyeh-clad farmers bring in their livestock to sell, and in the process provide a free show for those visitors who are not sleeping-in after a wasted day in Beersheba. Right opposite the Rockefeller Museum on the north-eastern corner of the Old City wall, just walk through the impatient traffic jam caused by the market.

Garden Tomb

Many of you will end up either participating in or witnessing earnest travellers' discussions regarding the most likely site of Jesus' crucifixion, burial and resurrection; either the Church of the Holy Sepulchre or the Garden Tomb. Certainly many find this to be the more pleasant site. As one Catholic priest was heard to say: 'If the Garden Tomb is not the true site of the Lord's death and resurrection, it should have been!' Also known as Gordon's Calvary, the site was first claimed as Golgotha by General Charles Gordon in 1883. The tomb found here, along with the hill's skull shape, convinced him of the site's authenticity.

Now owned by the Garden Tomb Association of London, the site has very friendly staff. During the summer months an interesting and often humorous free guided tour is given. Some argue that the Protestants in particular have supported the Garden Tomb theory due to the lack of their own holy site. Go and see for yourself – it's open Monday to Saturday 8 am to 12.15 pm and 2.30 to 5.15 pm, closed Sunday; admission is free. On Sunday at 9 am an inter-denominational service with singing is held, and lasts approximately 50 minutes. From Suleiman St head north along Nablus Rd and turn right on Schick St.

St George's Cathedral

This is the attractive cathedral of the Anglican Archbishop of Jerusalem, consecrated in 1898. Continue northwards along Nablus Rd and it is on the right. No set hours and admission is free.

Tombs of the Kings

Carry on northwards after St George's Cathedral to the end of Nablus Rd, turn right into Salah ed-Din St and the tombs are on the left by the corner. The first archaeologist to excavate the complex identified it as the tombs of the kings of Judah due to its majestic facade. The name has stuck, but it has since been proved that this is the 1st century tomb of Queen Helena of Adiabene, Mesopotamia. Vilnay describes it as one of the country's 'most interesting ancient burial places' but only archaeology buffs are likely to agree. Open Monday to Saturday 8 am to 12.30 pm and 2 to 5 pm, closed Sundays; admission is 65c, students 35c.

Tourjeman Post Museum

Overlooking the former Mandelbaum Gate area which was the only access point between the Jewish New City and the Jordanian Old City and East Jerusalem between 1948 and 1967, this museum is housed in an old Turkish house that the Israeli used in those days as a frontier position. A little tricky to find, it is at 1 Chail Handassa St (tel 281278). From the Damascus Gate area walk north up HaNevi'im St, turn right after the Ramsis Youth Hostel onto Chail Handassa St and it's on your left after a few minutes. Alternatively you can walk up Nablus Rd, take the road to the left of the US Consulate which takes you to the junction with Chail Handassa, Shivtei Yisrael and St George Sts. From the New City take Egged bus No 1, 11 or 27. Open Sunday to Thursday, 9 am to 4 pm, closed Friday and Saturday; admission is US$1.40.

Armenian Mosaic

Arguably the country's loveliest mosaic floor, its design features various species of birds in the branches of a vine. Laid down in the 5th-6th centuries, the colours are still incredibly brilliant. The Armenian inscription where the apse should begin in what was a mortuary chapel, reads 'For the memory and salvation of the souls of all Armenians whose names are known to God alone'. A sign referring to St Polyeuctus indicates this building just around the corner, behind the Ramsis Youth Hostel in HaNevi'im St. Open Monday to Saturday 7 am to 5.30 pm, closed Sunday; admission is free.

NEW CITY

Ammunition Hill

This was Jordan's main fortified outpost on the Jerusalem front and during the Six-Day War it was taken by the Israelis in the first major battle for the Old City. The bunker complex has been converted into a museum of the war and a memorial to the many Israeli lives lost in the fighting. Open Sunday to Thursday 9 am to 5 pm, Friday 9 am to 1 pm, closed Saturday; admission is 85c. Take Egged bus No 9, 25 or 28 and ask for *Givat Hatamoshet* (Ammunition Hill). It is in a small park east of Nablus Rd and the police HQ, and west of Levi Eshkol St (tel 284442).

The UNRWA

South of Ammunition Hill on the same side of the main road, this is the organisation's public information office. Contact Mohammed H Jarallah (tel 282451, Nablus Rd PO Box 19149) to arrange a visit to the West Bank refugee camps (see UNRWA section in Facts about the Country). Give him about 48 hours notice. Closed Saturday afternoon and all day Sunday.

Sanhedrin Tombs

Known to Christians as the Judges' Tombs, the Sanhedrin was ancient Israel's supreme court. Its 71 members sat in the Temple area and are believed to be buried in this park. Open Sunday to Friday 9 am to sunset, closed Saturday; admission is free. Take Egged bus No 2, get off at HaSanhedrin St and look for the attractive park carpeted with pebbles, acanthus leaves and fruit.

Biblical Zoo

Not far from the Sanhedrin Tombs is this zoo featuring an often ragged-looking collection of creatures whose ancestors were mentioned in the Bible. From the Sanhedrin Tombs continue south on HaSanhedrin St and turn west (right) on Bar-Ilan St. From the New City centre take Egged Bus No 7, 15 or 27. Open Sunday to Thursday 9 am to 5 pm, Friday 9 am to 1 pm, Saturday 9 am to 3 pm; admission is around US$3.80, students US$2.50. For a Saturday visit tickets must be purchased in advance due to the religious law forbidding money transactions on Shabbat.

Mahane Yehuda Market

Generally cheaper than the competition in the Old City, this Jewish food market is a fascinating hive of activity. About a km west of Zion Square between Jaffa Rd and Agrippas St, the market is an attraction in its own right even if you don't want to do any shopping. Stalls laden with fruit, vegetables, pickles, cheese, fish and biscuits line the streets along with cheap butchers, bakeries and wholesale *mahkolets* (grocery shops). On Agrippas St are several great places to enjoy meat cooked 'on the fire', open from the early evening to the early morning. The market is at its busiest on Thursday and Friday with thousands scrambling to buy the food needed for Shabbat. 'Mahane Yehuda' means 'Camp of Judah' and its streets are named after fruits.

Mea Shearim

Possibly the world's most reluctant tourist attraction, this ultra-orthodox Jewish district is the only remaining example of *shtetl* (ghetto) which existed before the Holocaust in Eastern European Jewish communities. It is just to the north of the downtown area and was established in 1875. *Mea Shearim* is Hebrew for 'one hundred gates' and is taken from Genesis 26:12, referring to Isaac farming the land and receiving a hundredfold. At one time in its formative years the district had its own defence walls with, it is said, 100 gates in them.

Walking these streets is usually an eye-opener: the residents mostly dress in 18th century East European styles. They are mainly devoted to religious study and are often financed by fellow ultra-orthodox communities abroad. Because of the intensity of the religious aspect, this is the best place in the world for buying items of Judaica. There are also many bakeries producing traditional products.

Another result of the dominant interpretation of Jewish Law here are the attitudes towards strangers. Signs proclaim 'Daughters of Israel! The Torah requires you to dress modestly' and give details of what this all means. When you visit Mea Shearim you should conform to the residents' standards in your dress and behaviour. This means that women should not wear shorts or even long trousers, but a loose-fitting skirt and long sleeves. Men should wear long trousers. Do not walk arm in arm or even hand in hand with anyone, and kissing is definitely taboo. Most ultra-orthodox Jews dislike being photographed – in fact, their interpretation of Jewish Law forbids it.

The more extreme characters have been known to stone those, Jewish and non-Jewish, who break these codes of conduct, however unwittingly. Signalled or verbal objections are more common, though. These vary from the holding of a hand to the face to avoid being photographed, to the hissing of the word 'prostitute' at a young woman whose taste in fashion does not include a shaved head, wig and scarf. Needless to say, thousands of photographs are taken each week; just be discreet and aware of the possible response to your activities. Abiding by the request to dress discreetly is not too difficult though.

Mea Shearim is a few minutes' walk from both Damascus Gate and the Jaffa Rd/King George V St junction.

HaNevi'im (Prophet) St
An important street in the New City, right on the border with East Jerusalem, it honours the prophets of Israel, many of whom lived in the city, and is lined by some important and attractive buildings. It is also a useful street for travellers, being a convenient route between the Damascus Gate area, Mea Shearim and the downtown area in the New City.

At the Damascus Gate end, by the lorry park, large numbers of Arabs gather in what is an unofficial outdoor employment agency. Every so often a car driven by an employer needing a worker for the day will cruise along, chased by job-seekers.

Ethiopian Church
Tucked away on the narrow Ethiopia St, this impressive domed construction would be a major feature in most cities, but in Jerusalem it is often overlooked. Built between 1896-1904, the church's entrance gate features the carved Lion of Judah. This emblem is believed to have been given to the Queen of Sheba, Ethiopia's queen, by Solomon when she visited Jerusalem. Open daily March to September 7 am to 6 pm, October to February 8 am to 5 pm; admission is free.

Opposite the church is the house where Eliezer Ben Yehuda lived and did much of his work on the revival of the Hebrew language. A plaque marking the house was stolen by ultra-orthodox Jews who strongly disapprove of the language's everyday use. Note the Ethiopian Consulate with its mosaic-decorated facade on your left as you descend HaNevi'im St towards the old City.

Daughters of Charity of St Vincent de Paul
On Mamillah Rd down from Jaffa Gate, this large convent is another wonderful Jerusalem building that gets lost in the crowd. The house at No 33 bears a plaque noting that Dr Theodor Herzl, the founder of political Zionism, stayed here during his visit to Palestine in 1898.

Russian Compound
Between Jaffa Rd and HaNevi'im St, and dominated by the green domes of the Russian cathedral, this area was acquired by the Russian Church in 1860. In addition to the cathedral, they constructed facilities for the many pilgrims who visited the Holy Land in large numbers until WW I. The cathedral occupies the site where the Assyrians camped in about 700 BC, and in 70 AD Roman legions assembled here during the Jewish Revolt. In front of the cathedral, the 12-metre-high Herod's Pillar is believed to have been intended for Herod's Temple.

However, it broke and was abandoned here.

Hall of Heroism In the middle of the car park in the north-west of the compound, this museum commemorates the exploits of the Jewish underground movement of the British Mandate period, which is considered by many to have been a forerunner of modern terrorism. Open Sunday to Thursday 9 am to 4 pm, Friday 10 am to 1 pm, closed Saturday; admission is US$2.

Ticho House
On Abraham Ticho St just off HaRav Kook St opposite Zion Square (tel 245068), this is the former home of Dr Abraham Ticho and his artist wife, Anna. Now part of the Israel Museum it is a popular combination of a museum, art gallery, library and café; a particular favourite with local conservative ladies. Dr Ticho, a Jew, was a leader in the field of ophthalmology and, during the British Mandate, was responsible for saving hundreds of Palestinian Arabs from blindness. Anna Ticho was an award-winning artist and Jerusalem was the major inspiration for much of her work. Included in the exhibits is Dr Ticho's study and some documents and letters of interest, in particular dealing with his work for the Arabs; his collection of Hanukkah lamps and Anna Ticho's art.

Open Sunday to Thursday 10 am to 5 pm, Tuesday 10 am to 10 pm, Friday 10 am to 2 pm, closed Saturday. The library is open Sunday to Thursday 10 am to 4 pm, Friday 10 am to noon; admission is free. The café is open Sunday to Wednesday 10 am to 11.45 pm, closed Thursday and Friday, and open on Saturday from sundown to 11.45 pm.

Bezalel School of Art
Near the King George V/Ben Yehuda Sts' junction, at 10 Shemuel HaNagid St, this is Israel's premier art school, founded in 1906. It is named after the Old Testament

artist Bezalel Ben-Ouri (Exodus 31:2-11). Next door to the main school building, at 12 Shemuel Ha Nagid St, Artists' House (tel 223653) features an art gallery, shop and a bar/restaurant. The gallery is open Monday to Friday 9 am to 1 pm and 4 to 7 pm, Saturday and Sunday 10 am to 1 pm and 4 to 7 pm; admission is free. The bar/restaurant is open daily, usually until after midnight.

Museum of the Potential Holocaust
This museum is at 31 Ussishkin St, between Keren Kayemet and Narkiss Sts, and features a display of racist propaganda, with anti-Semitism a major feature. Open Sunday to Thursday 1 to 4 pm, closed Friday and Saturday; admission is US$1.75, students US$1.50, including a guided tour. Egged bus No 17 or 19 will get you there.

Museum of Italian Jewish Art & Synagogue
At 27 Hillel St (tel 24160), on the next street parallel to and south of Ben Yehuda, down from King George V St. Open Sunday and Tuesday 10 am to 1 pm, Wednesday 4 to 7 pm; admission is 65c. Shabbat services held.

Jewish Agency Building
On King George V St (named after the British monarch reigning when the Balfour Declaration was issued in 1917), this complex is topped by a menorah illustrating the age of the State of Israel. The Jewish Agency HQ, it also houses the offices of the JNF and Keren Hayesod. During the British Mandate, this was the seat of the Jewish secondary government. On view are the Zionist Archives, the Golden Book (recording the names of donors to the cause), and occasional films. Open Sunday to Thursday 8 am to 1 pm, closed Friday and Saturday; admission is free.

Heichal Shlomo
Facing the Plaza Hotel and Independence Park at 58 King George V St, this complex

is styled along the lines of Solomon's Temple. 'Heichal Shlomo' means 'Solomon's Mansion'. The seat of the Chief Rabbinate of Israel and the Supreme Religious Centre, the emblem of the scales of justice is featured on both sides of the entrance. The Wolfson Museum here features presentations of religious and traditional Jewish life. Admission is 65c. The actual building is open Sunday to Thursday 9 am to 1 pm, Friday 9 am to noon, closed Saturday.

Great Synagogue

Next door to the Heichal Shlomo and incorporated in the complex. Attendance at a Shabbat service is recommended.

Rehavia & Komemiyut

These are amongst the city's more fashionable neighbourhoods, although the increase in the number of ultra-orthodox Jewish residents is said to be changing that. Most of the impressive properties display nameplates of the medical and legal professions. The official residence of the Prime Minister is here, on the corner of Balfour and Smolenskin Sts. Next door is the Rubin Academy of Music, and at 6 Balfour St is the Schoken Library which holds rare Hebrew prints and manuscripts. The President's official residence is on HaNassi St, near the Jerusalem Sherover Theatre and the L A Mayer Museum of Islamic Art. These neighbourhoods are basically between King George V St to the east and HaNassi Ben Zvi St to the west. Cutting through on foot to reach the Israel Museum, the Knesset building and the Monastery of the Cross, makes a pleasant stroll.

International Christian Embassy Jerusalem

At 10 Brenner St, Rehavia, this 'embassy' (tel 669389, 669823) invites everyone to watch a free video explaining the reasons for its establishment, and in particular its participation in the Feast of the Tabernacles celebrations (see Religion section in Facts about the Country). Open Monday to

Thursday 9 am to 4 pm, Friday and Saturday 9 am to 2 pm, closed Sunday.

Jason's Tomb

In Rehavia's Alfasi St this is one of the city's most interesting tombs because its history is known in detail. Built in the early 1st century BC by Jason, the head of a wealthy family, it contains two or three generations of that family. Archaeologists learned from this tomb of that era's expressions of belief in the after-life. Cooking pots, complete with food, and lighting were provided in the individual graves and some dice were found – gambling in heaven? The porch's charcoal drawings of a warship in pursuit of two other vessels indicate that Jason or a son was a naval officer. Tomb robbers had struck before the great earthquake of 31 BC destroyed it. The pyramid over the porch is a reconstruction. Before it are three courts, the nearest of which is entered by a gate. Look through the iron grille to see the burial chamber. Eight shaft-graves can be seen through the small opening on the left.

L A Mayer Museum of Islamic Art

At 2 HaPalmach St in Rehavia (tel 661291/2). A good display includes paintings, weaponry, miniatures and jewellery. Open Sunday to Thursday 10 am to 1 pm and 3.30 to 6 pm, Saturday 10 am to 1 pm, closed Friday; admission is US$2, students US$1.35. Take Egged bus No 15 from city centre.

King David St

Also called David HaMelekh, this busy road runs south from the New City centre to the railway station and has several important landmarks, including the Hebrew Union College building, the King David Hotel and the YMCA. It leads to Herod's Family Tomb, the attractive Yemin Moshe and Mishkenot Sha'ananim neighbourhoods, Liberty Bell Park and the wondrous views across to Mount Zion and the Hinnom Valley.

YMCA

The YMCA (tel 22711) is on King David St opposite the King David Hotel. The distinctive tower is open Monday to Saturday 9 am to 1 pm, closed Sunday. Admission is 65c. The soccer stadium behind the main building is the home ground for the Jerusalem team, and enthusiastic crowds attend the matches. (See also Places to Stay section.)

Herod's Family Tomb

Just south of the King David Hotel and overlooking the Old City. When archaeologists discovered it, little was found inside due to tomb robbers. Herod himself is not buried here but at Herodian, near Bethlehem.

Montefiore Windmill

A pretty landmark adjacent to Bloomfield Park and opposite Mount Zion. A museum here is dedicated to Sir Moses Montefiore, the philanthropist who financed the adjacent neighbourhood project, and deals with 'his life and his work'. Open Sunday to Thursday 9 am to 4 pm, Friday 9 am to 1 pm, closed Saturday.

Mishkenot Sha'anannim & Yemin Moshe

This is Montefiore's major contribution to modern Jewish development in the country – the first Jewish settlement outside the Old City's walls. Now beautifully renovated and a real estate agent's dream. Artists' galleries attract many visitors to the area.

Liberty Bell Park

Just across from the Montefiore Windmill an exact replica of the Liberty Bell in Philadelphia is the central point of this three hectare garden, which is used for picnics and public events.

St Andrew's Church

Alternatively known as the Scottish Church, it was built in 1927 to commemorate the capture of the city and the Holy Land by the British in WW I. Owned by the Church of Scotland, the floor features an inscription to the memory of the Scottish King Robert the Bruce, who wanted to have his heart buried in Jerusalem when he died. He arranged that Sir James Douglas would bring the heart but en route the knight was killed in Spain, fighting the Moors. The heart was recovered and returned to Scotland where it is buried at Melrose while the body is buried at Dunfermline.

House of Quality

Most noticeable here is the cable pulley stretching across to Mount Zion, which was put up in 1948 to secure a link with the Jewish forces struggling to survive against the Arabs. The House of Quality (12 Hebron St) is a showroom for goods made by local artists. Open Sunday to Thursday 10 am to 6 pm, Friday 10 am to 1 pm, closed Saturday.

Cinemateque & the Jerusalem Film Center

On Hebron Rd (tel 715398), with wondrous views across to Mount Zion, the Old City and down the Hinnom Valley, this complex houses a small museum, library and archives relating to the film industry. It's open Sunday and Monday 10 am to 3 pm, Tuesday and Thursday 10 am to 7 pm, and Friday 10 am to 1 pm. It also houses the city's best cinema and a popular restaurant with a terrace to enjoy those views.

Sultan's Pool

Now a unique amphitheatre used for a variety of concerts, this was one of the city's three major water reservoirs and the site of a cattle market.

Monastery of the Cross

Founded by King Bagrat of Georgia, it commemorates the tradition that the tree from which Jesus' cross was made grew here. Although the church is basically 11th century, various additions were made over the centuries. The Greek

Orthodox Church purchased the complex in 1685. In a valley that was once the vineyard of Jerusalem's Crusader kings, the monastery can be reached by walking through Rehavia along Ramban St, crossing Herzog St and following the path down the hillside. From the New City centre take Egged bus Nos 9, 16 or 24; from Jaffa Gate, Egged bus No 19. Get off at the first stop on Herzog St and follow the path down. Open Monday to Friday 9 am to 4 pm, closed Saturday and Sunday; admission is 65c.

Israel Museum & Shrine of the Book

This is Israel's leading museum complex, and features various facets of Jewish history in several separate museums, a sculpture garden and the Shrine of the Book, which houses some of the Dead Sea Scrolls. With specific departments dealing with archaeology, Jewish ethnography, Jewish life, Jewish ceremonial art, primitive and Israeli art, old masters and Impressionists, modern art, ancient glass and period rooms, there is a lot to see. The Billy Rose Sculpture Garden includes work by Henry Moore and Picasso.

The Shrine of the Book is a distinctive building resembling a cover of the pots in which the 2000-year-old Dead Sea Scrolls were found in caves at Qumran, near the Dead Sea in 1947. The scrolls were written by Essenes, members of a mystical, ascetic Jewish cult. They are ancient

Dead Sea Scrolls

editions of some books of the bible, and are of immense importance to Judaic scholarship.

Guided tours in English are included in the museum's admission price. Starting from the main entrance they deal with a specific area rather than the whole complex so check the current schedule for the hours and the subjects covered.

The museum is open Sunday, Monday, Wednesday, Thursday 10 am to 4 pm (Shrine of the Book 10 am to 3 pm); Tuesday 4 to 10 pm, Friday and Saturday 10 am to 2 pm. Admission is to the museum only, US$4; to the museum and the Shrine of the Book US$5, students US$2.50. Telephone 698211 or check the tourist office and *Jerusalem Post* for details of special exhibits, lectures, concerts and events. You can get there on Egged bus No 9, 17 or 24.

Knesset

A few minutes' walk from the Israel Museum and overlooking the valley in which the Monastery of the Cross sits, is *HaKirya* (the city), the government centre. Dominating the scene is the Knesset, Israel's Parliament, inaugurated in 1966. You can see the Knesset in session on Monday or Tuesday, 4 to 7 pm and Wednesday 11 am to 7 pm. The proceedings are conducted with the same standard of aggression as elsewhere, mainly in Hebrew, but occasionally in Arabic. Free guided tours of the building are held on Sunday and Thursday 8.30 am to 3.30 pm. Take your passport. Egged bus No 19 or 24.

Next to the bus stops opposite the Knesset is a bronze menorah, a gift from British supporters of the State of Israel. It is decorated with panels representing important figures and events in Jewish history.

Hebrew University

The Giv'at Ram campus of the university on Brodetsky Rd, west of HaKirya and the Israel Museum, features a strikingly designed synagogue recognisable by its white egg-shaped cupola. Other features of interest include the Academy of the Hebrew Language which displays the library and furniture of Eliezer Ben Yehuda, who was responsible for the revival of the Hebrew language. Also, the campus cafeterias provide very cheap food of very good quality. Free daily guided tours of the campus start at 9 and 11 am from the old Sherman Building. Egged bus No 24 or 28.

Model of Ancient Jerusalem

In the grounds of the Holy Land Hotel (tel 630201) on Uziel St between Herzog St and Herzl Ave, is a huge 1:50 scale model of Jerusalem as it was in 66 AD, at the beginning of the First Revolt. Open daily, summer 8 am to 5 pm, winter 8 am to 4 pm; admission is US$2.25, students US$1.75. Egged bus No 21.

Mount Herzl & Herzl Museum

Just to the north of Yad Vashem, this pleasant park is named in honour of the founder of political Zionism. He is buried here, along with his wife and parents and other prominent Zionist leaders. Nearby are the graves of the late Prime Ministers Levi Eshkol and Golda Meir, and of Ze'ev Jabotinsky who founded and led the Revisionist movement and was the spiritual leader of the Irgun and Menachem Begin. Further on lies a cemetery for Jewish soldiers killed in battle locally.

The Herzl Museum (tel 531108) includes a replica of Herzl's Vienna study, library and furniture. Open Sunday to Thursday 9 am to 6.15 pm, Friday 9 am to 1 pm, closed Saturday; admission is free. Egged bus No 13, 18, 20, 23, 24 or 27.

Yad Vashem

On the Mount of Remembrance by the edge of the beautiful Jerusalem Forest with pretty views towards the village of En Kerem, this is Israel's major memorial to the victims of the holocaust. Yad Vashem (tel 531202) means 'a place and a

name', or 'a monument and a memorial', taken from Isaiah 56:5.

From the main road, follow HaZikkaron Rd to the entrance. Next to the car park is a café, administration offices and Archives building featuring the most complete library dealing with the Holocaust.

Avenue of the Righteous Gentiles Leading off to the left, this and the surrounding gardens are a memorial to the non-Jews who risked their lives to save Jews. The trees bordering the avenue bear plaques in remembrance of certain individuals.

Remembrance Hall is a sombre construction with a mosaic floor inscribed with the names of the 21 largest Concentration and Death Camps. Men's heads must be covered here and cardboard yarmulkas are provided. On Holocaust Day (see Festivals & Holidays section in Facts about the Country), the Martyrs and Heroes Remembrance Day Assembly is held here, attended by the President of Israel and other national leaders.

Pillar of Heroism A 21-metre high memorial to honour the resistance fighters. Bordering the path leading here are inscriptions carved into stones which record their various acts of bravery.

Museum A comprehensive and harrowing presentation of the events of the Holocaust. You could easily spend many hours here, taking in the many photographs, documents, artefacts and other effects which bring home the realities faced by the Jews.

Art Gallery Do not miss this often wonderful but always poignant collection of work produced under some of the most unbearable conditions imaginable.

Hall of Names Containing over three million pages of testimony by Holocaust victims who have registered here.

Garden of the Children of the Holocaust
Simply that: a tragic area in remembrance of the child victims.

Valley of the Destroyed Communities
Commemorating the European Jewish communities that were wiped out during WW II, this memorial is under construction nearby.

Yad Vashem is open Sunday to Thursday 9 am to 4.45 pm, Friday 9 am to 1.45 pm, closed Saturday; admission is free. Take Egged bus No 13, 17, 18, 20, 23, 24 or 27.

Hadassah Medical Centre
Often confused with its namesake on Mount Scopus, this, the Middle East's largest medical centre, is famous for its synagogue featuring the Chagall Windows. These abstract stained-glass designs depict the 12 tribes of Israel based on Genesis 49 and Deuteronomy 33. Four of the current windows are replacements for those damaged during the Six-Day War. Three other windows still contain bullet holes.

Beautifully situated to the south-west of Jerusalem, the Centre overlooks the village of En Kerem and the surrounding green hills. The Bernice & Nathan Tanneabaum Tourist Reception centre is open Sunday to Thursday 8 am to 3.45 pm, Friday 8.30 am to 12.30 pm, closed Saturday. Admission is US$2.50, students US$1.50, which includes a guided tour (held every hour on the half hour). Egged bus No 19 or 27.

Kennedy Memorial
South of the Hadassah Medical Centre and about 11 km from the city centre, this memorial to John F Kennedy sits atop Mount Orah. Egged bus Nos 20 and 50 stop a good 30-minute walk away.

En Kerem
Now enveloped by the expanding New City whose ugly apartment blocks threaten to blot out the landscape, this picturesque village is dominated by attractive churches commemorating the traditional birthplace of John the Baptist and by the surrounding terraced slopes of the valley. A visit to this village with its narrow streets and alleyways can be pleasantly combined with a walk in the adjacent Jerusalem Forest.

There are some cafés in the village but although OK for a drink or snack, they are pricey for below-average meals. Most travellers bring a packed lunch from Jerusalem.

Church of St John Owned by the Franciscans and built over the grotto where St John was believed to have been born (Luke 1:5-25, 57-80). Steps lead down to the grotto with its remains of ancient structures and a Byzantine mosaic. Open March to September, Monday to Saturday 8 am to noon and 2.30 to 6 pm; October to February, Monday to Saturday 8 am to noon and 2.30 to 4 pm, closed Sunday. Admission is free. It's on the street to the right of the main road.

Church of the Visitation Also Franciscan and built on the traditional site of the summer house of Zacharias and Elizabeth, visited by St Mary (Luke 1:39-56). Note also the ancient cistern and, in an alcove, the stone behind which John supposedly hid from Roman soldiers. Upstairs is the apse of a Crusader church. Open daily 9 am to noon and 3 to 6 pm. Admission is free, and you'll find it on the street to the left of the main road, opposite that leading to the Church of St John. The spring which gives the village its name is nearby. The wall bears the words of the prophet Isaiah, 'Ho everyone who thirsts, come to the waters' (Isaiah 55:1).

Russian Church & Monastery Higher up the steep slope, this monastery (tel 222565, 654128) can only be visited by appointment.

Getting There & Away To reach En Kerem you can go direct from the New City by Egged bus No 17 (every 20 to 30 minutes) or take No 5, 6, 18 or 21 to the Jerusalem Forest. Get off at the Sonol petrol station on Herzl Blvd, continue walking in the same direction and take the first right onto Yefe Nof and the second left, Pirhe Hen, to enter the forest. Head for the Youth Centre in the middle of the forest and from there the village is visible most of the way. You can also reach En Kerem by walking down the slope from the Hadassah Medical Centre (from the stop for Egged bus No 19).

Kibbutz Ramat Rachel

This kibbutz, its name meaning 'the Height of Rachel' (referring to Jacob's wife whose tomb is in nearby Bethlehem), is conveniently situated for those who want to visit a collective farm. Telephone 715712 for details about guided tour schedules. The kibbutz also operates a guest house. Egged bus No 7.

TOURS

The huge number of places of interest in Jerusalem and the wealth of history that surrounds them make an organised tour a good idea. This can be as an introduction to the city, or to give you a more detailed awareness of certain areas.

Coach Tours

A marvellous introduction to the city but flexible enough to be a great way to get around and visit the major sites is Egged Tours' Route 99, the Circular Line. This service takes you on a comfortable coach to 34 of the major sites, with basic commentary in English provided by the driver. A single-tour ticket at US$1.30 allows you to enjoy the complete trip, and a one-day ticket at US$5 is valid for a day's unlimited travel on the Circular Line, enabling you to get off at each stop. A similar two-day ticket costs US$6.50. Operating Sunday to Thursday 9 am to 5 pm, Friday 9 am to 2 pm, with no service

on Saturday, the bus leaves Jaffa Gate on the hour, but you can board at any of the stops. It's a continuous circular route, you eventually finish at the stop where you started.

Other Jerusalem tours are offered by Egged Tours, including an aeroplane tour. Pick up their brochure from one of the Egged Tours offices. Details of other operators' coach tours can be found at the tourist offices and travel agents.

Walking Tours

SPNI These tours are mainly hikes in the surrounding countryside but some cover unusual and interesting routes within the city.

Walking Tours Ltd Offers in-depth tours of the Old City and its surroundings, including the City of David, the Jewish Quarter and the Mount of Olives. Lasting about 3½ hours, they cost around US$9, students US$6, including site admission fees. Details from the tourist offices.

Archaeological Tours & Seminars Offers various specialised Old City tours including the City of David, preceded by a short seminar. Altogether they last about two hours at US$5; three tours cost US$12.50. Details from the tourist offices.

Free Walking Tours Every Saturday at 10 am the Municipal Tourist Office organises a free walking tour to a specific site in the city. Meet outside the office at 32 Jaffa Rd. Unfortunately such a free tour on a Saturday in Israel inevitably attracts a large crowd so, although the guides are well informed, you will often have to struggle to hear them.

The Sheraton Jerusalem Plaza Hotel (tel 228133), on King George V St, corner of Agron St, offers free walking tours most days of the week, which are open to non-residents. The two-hour tours often start a sherut-ride away. Meet in the hotel lobby

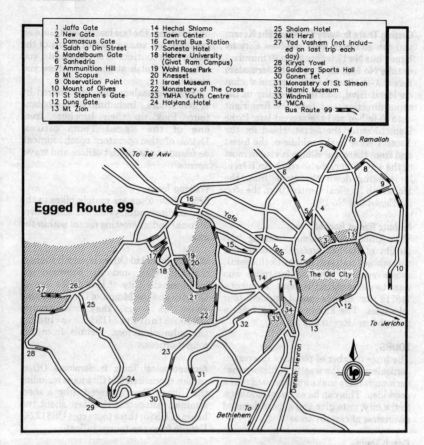

1 Jaffa Gate	14 Hechal Shlomo	25 Shalom Hotel
2 New Gate	15 Town Center	26 Mt Herzl
3 Damascus Gate	16 Central Bus Station	27 Yad Vashem (not includ-
4 Salah a Din Street	17 Sonesta Hotel	ed on last trip each
5 Mandelbaum Gate	18 Hebrew University	day)
6 Sanhedria	(Givat Ram Campus)	28 Kiryat Yovel
7 Ammunition Hill	19 Wohl Rose Park	29 Goldberg Sports Hall
8 Mt Scopus	20 Knesset	30 Gonen Tet
9 Observation Point	21 Israel Museum	31 Monastery of St Simeon
10 Mount of Olives	22 Monastery of The Cross	32 Islamic Museum
11 St Stephen's Gate	23 YMHA Youth Centre	33 Windmill
12 Dung Gate	24 Holyland Hotel	34 YMCA
13 Mt Zion		Bus Route 99

Egged Route 99

at 9 am. The King Solomon Hotel (tel 241433), on King David St across from the Montefiore Windmill, also offers free guided walking yours – check with reception for details. These three-hour tours usually start at 9.15 am in the lobby.

Jeffrey Seidel, an Orthodox Jew from Chicago, now living in the Old City, represents Ohel Avaraham, an organisation committed to giving young Jews a fresh awareness of being Jewish. Concerned by the increase in young Jewish assimilation, he organises free walking tours of Jewish sites in the Old City's Jewish and Muslim

Quarters, now expanding to include the City of David excavations. Non-Jews as well as Jews are most welcome to meet in the Western Wall piazza, by the ragged palm tree adjacent to the walkway leading to the Haram esh-Sharif, at 3 pm Sunday to Tuesday and Thursday. On Saturday the tour starts an hour before sunset with no tour on Wednesday or Friday. The tours are informed, friendly and cover Jewish aspects of the area which are often neglected. To encourage young Jews to consider the religious aspects of Jewishness, Jeff arranges free Shabbat dinners for them with local religious families and encourages them to stay at his organisation's free hostels in the Jewish Quarter (see Accommodation). He also tries to interest them in attending a yeshivah. Because of the aims of the programme, only the tours are offered to non-Jews. You can find Jeff, that is if he doesn't find you, rushing around the Western Wall piazza approaching all the young people to find Jews for his programme. Asking, 'Are you Jewish?', he tries not to offend those who aren't, but this is hard. You can telephone on 532131 Ext 3242.

Individual Guides

Hiring your own guide, especially if there are two or more of you, is affordable and beneficial. You will almost certainly be approached by prospective guides, especially around Jaffa Gate and in the Haram esh-Sharif. Official guides (who carry ID) are always very knowledgeable and usually able to pass on the relevant information. Unofficial guides can be less pompous and more flexible than their official rivals. However, hiring them can be dodgy as you have no real guarantee of satisfaction until it is too late. Always check to see if their language skills are adequate and that they seem to know what they are talking about.

A major problem when using a guide (but not for the guides) is that most visitors can be told anything about most sites. For example, one young boy insisted to me that the Notre Dame building outside New Gate was the Knesset!

PLACES TO STAY

Jerusalem offers a wide range of accommodation in a variety of surroundings, and there are some real bargains available. You can choose between the unique and colourful Old City, which offers the country's cheapest hostels and some middle range hospices and hotels; East Jerusalem, with cheap hostels and middle range hospices and hotels right outside those Old City Walls; and the New

City, where most of the luxury and middle range hotels are to be found, as well as a few hostels.

The best location to stay really depends on your requirements. The Old City and East Jerusalem are most convenient for the major sites nearby, and the Arab bus stations and service taxi rank are there. However, most hostels and hospices have strict curfews, and being at least a good 20-minute walk from the New City's downtown nightlife, they are not suitable for those who want to stay out late. Wherever you stay and whatever you pay, if you plan to stay a week or more ask about reduced rates. You will normally be successful, but if you don't ask, you don't get.

Many of the cheaper places don't officially put their prices up for the high season, and even where they do I've listed the low season price – the lack of visitors since the *intefadeh* means fierce competition for guests and lower prices.

The Old City streets have always been slightly uncomfortable for women after dark, and now with the Arab uprising everyone should be a little wary there. Many of the shops and restaurants open erratically, and some of the hotels may have closed down. Those listed were defiantly open in mid-1989.

Rooms & apartments

Bed and Breakfast in a private home, or renting a room or an apartment are options taken by many travellers (see also the Accommodation section in Facts for the Visitor).

Staying in an Israeli home helps you to see the Israeli way of life close-up and, as with apartments, it can work out better value than a three star hotel. Those with less money to spend should still consider finding an apartment if they intend spending two months or more in Jerusalem. If you look around you should be able to pay less rent than you would in a hostel, and you have privacy and independence.

To find a cheap room or studio, or

someone who needs an extra person to share an apartment, scan the *Jerusalem Post* (especially the Friday edition). *Kol Ha'ir*, a Hebrew paper, is probably the best source for such places. It's in Hebrew so get a friend to translate it. The stall holders in Mahane Yehuda market often know somebody with a room to rent, and keep your eyes open for small signs in shop windows announcing a room to let. The noticeboards at the two campuses of the Hebrew University, at the Israel Center at the corner of Strauss and HaNevi'im Sts, at the Hameshek vegetarian restaurant on Shlomzion St and at the Sefer VeSefel bookstore and café on Ya'Avetz St can also be good places to look.

Two services offer listings (in English) of properties for rent. *She'al*, 21 King George V St (tel 224456/7) is open Sunday to Thursday 8.30 am to 1 pm and 4 to 7 pm, Friday 8.30 am to noon, closed Saturday. *Dehaf Ltd*, 43 Jaffa Rd by Zion Square (tel 223941, 226335), is open Sunday to Thursday 9 am to 7 pm. *Room Renting Ltd* (tel 633563) offers various standards of rooms and apartments by the night or for longer periods. Call in the afternoons and early evening except on Shabbat.

Places to Stay – bottom end

Old City Most of the Old City's budget accommodation is found near Jaffa and Damascus Gates which is convenient as they are the main access points and are well served by buses. Egged bus Nos 1, 3, 13, 19, 20 and 80 go to Jaffa Gate from the central bus station. No 27 takes you to the Arab station near Damascus Gate. Once you have learned the way to your accommodation, it is often quicker to catch a bus to Jaffa Gate than to take the No 27 for the longer route to Damascus Gate.

Christ Church Hospice (tel 282082), al-Khattab Square, PO Box 41037. From Jaffa Gate bear right (after the Citadel), up past the Christian Information Centre to the post office on the corner on your left.

The hospice entrance is next door on the site of Herod the Great's palace gardens. Owned and run by the Anglican Church (British), it has pleasant staff and is very clean, quiet and comfortable. Good facilities include spotless bathrooms, laundry sinks, and a comfortable lounge with a piano and books. There are no cooking facilities. The private courtyard boasts the Middle East's oldest Anglican church, consecrated in 1849. Dorm beds are US$9 with a good, substantial breakfast included. Singles/doubles are US$25/27 per person. Dorms are closed 2 to 4 pm, and there's an 11 pm curfew. Lunch is available for around US$4 and dinner for US$5.

Petra Hotel (tel 282356), is at the start of David St, on the left as you enter from Jaffa Gate. The generally unpleasant Arab management surprised everyone by cleaning the place up, but don't be fooled by the attractive balconies and the view across to the Dome of the Rock. During the winter months the cold really penetrates every corner and all year round the management forget to smile but often remember to overcharge. There's a nice reception area with a TV lounge, but lousy cooking facilities. Beds in rooms crowded with about eight beds cost US$4, with some singles/doubles from US$6/9, with breakfast. Midnight curfew.

Citadel Youth Hostel (tel 286273), St Mark's Rd. It's past the Rush Inn, on the same side. This is one of the best hostels in Jerusalem. It has friendly management (sometimes too friendly) and is clean and comfortable, with a small lounge, a kitchen, and access to the roof, with one great room over-looking the Old City. Dorm beds are US$4, singles US$16, without breakfast. Midnight curfew.

Lutheran Hospice (tel 282120), St Mark's Rd, PO Box 14051. Just past the Citadel Youth Hostel on the opposite side. Spotless, excellent facilities, kitchen, beautiful garden with views of the Holy Sepulchre – all ruined by extremely unpleasant staff. Dorm beds are US$4 and singles/doubles with breakfast cost from US$28 per person. Closed 9 am to noon and a strict 10.45 pm curfew.

New Hashimi Hotel (tel 284410), 73 Suq Khan ez-Zeit St. From Damascus Gate bear right up Suq Khan ez-Zeit St and it's on your left. It's quite pleasant and quiet in this busy market area but ask the old man not to play his music too loudly in the morning. There's a comfortable lounge but no kitchen. Dorm beds are US$4, singles/doubles US$6/10. Breakfast costs US$1.75 and there's a flexible midnight curfew.

Al-Arab (tel 283537), Suq Khan ez-Zeit St. From Damascus Gate bear right up Suq Khan ez-Zeit St and it's on your left just before the New Hashimi Hotel. Not a very nice place, and there's no kitchen. Dorm beds are US$3.50 and singles/doubles are US$30 per person. Midnight curfew, but I never saw anybody staying here.

Armenian Catholic Patriarchate Hospice (tel 284262), El-Wad Rd between the 3rd and 4th Stations of the Cross. From Damascus Gate bear left along El-Wad, and it's on your left just after the Via Dolorosa. It's quiet, clean, but sombre and uncomfortable, with no kitchen or lounge. The miserable staff make you feel as though you're at boarding school. Dorm beds are US$5 and doubles start at $US20. Closed 1 to 3 pm. Curfew 10 pm.

Al-Ahram Youth Hostel (tel 280926), El-Wad Rd. From Damascus Gate bear left along El Wad Rd and it's on your right, opposite the Via Dolorosa and the 3rd Station of the Cross. This popular hostel has generally on-the-ball Arab staff who do a good job. It's comfortable, clean enough, and has a lounge, TV, music, a roof terrace and a kitchen. Free tea is often forthcoming. Dorm beds are US$4, or less for a comfortable mattress out on the roof terrace. Singles/doubles with shower cost US$15 per person. Midnight curfew.

East Jerusalem 'Hostel Row' is at the first stretch of HaNevi'im St across from Damascus Gate and opposite the service taxi rank. These hostels are some of the best in Jerusalem – they need to be as the many travellers who stay here have to contend with the noise created by Arab men hanging around the adjacent wholesale stores at all hours, watching kung fu and wrestling videos played at full volume. The summer months see the annual water melon market set up across the road, an all-night affair with more noise and cheap water melons.

Faisal Youth Hostel (tel 282189), 4 HaNevi'im St. This place is very popular and right outside Damascus Gate, which can be seen from the terrace. It's Arab-owned but run by a succession of American, European and/or British Christian stalwarts who keep it fairly clean and friendly. However, for religious reasons no unmarried couples are allowed. There's a lounge and dining area, and a kitchen with cheap tea and coffee. The large dorms have painfully deformed beds at US$5; opt for a mattress on the floor or the terrace which costs less anyway. The few double rooms usually fill quickly for about US$14. Midnight curfew.

New Raghadan Hostel (tel 282725), 10 HaNevi'im St. A very comfortable, easygoing, basically clean place with a pleasant manager. There's a large lounge with soft chairs, a kitchen and a washing machine. The balcony and the new rooms being built on the upper floors have interesting views of the Old City. Dorm beds cost US$4.50, and singles/doubles are US$9/14. Curfew 11 pm, but keys are issued for late night revellers.

Gethsemane Youth Hostel (tel 283127), Mount of Olives. Follow the road up past All Nations Church and the Garden of Gethsemane, bear right past the souvenir shop/café and it's on the right. Run by a religious Muslim family, it's basic and clean, with a kitchen. It would appeal mainly to those who like the location – a steep walk to the Old City but a short walk to the view over the Old City at sunrise. Dorm beds are US$4. Curfew 11 pm.

New City If an early curfew stops you from enjoying the New City's after-dark goings-on, then stay here. However, the uninspiring surroundings, higher prices and inferior facilities encourage most travellers to opt for the Old City and East Jerusalem. Bear in mind that between the busy periods of Christmas, Pesach/Easter and the peak summer months, the New City hostels engage in 'Price Wars' and substantial reductions are made. As soon as your Egged inter-urban bus lands at the central bus station, you will probably be approached by fellow travellers touting for the hostels, so check the current prices. Just a few of the cheaper New City hotels include:

Savoy Hotel (tel 283366), 5 Ibn Sina St, leading off past the post office. There's a dorm at US$10 and basic, no-frills rooms cost from US$12/20 for singles/doubles, with breakfast. There's a 15% discount for students.

Zefania Youth Hostel (tel 286384, 272709), 4 Zefania St. Egged bus No 27, 35 or 39 from central bus station, or No 4 or 9 from the New City Centre. Get off by the Zion orphanage and Zefania St is on the left. Someone on the bus will know where you want to get off. It's in the ultra-orthodox Jewish district of Mea Shearim, so staying here requires some understanding of the surroundings. Although the hostel staff are not ultra-religious, you are expected to dress 'modestly' - no shorts, bare shoulders, etc. You should dress like that in this area anyway, so it's no big deal. The Zefania is clean enough but tatty and untidy. It's large, with fridges everywhere, new bathrooms and radiators, TV, radio, pay-phone and a run-down kitchen. They sell tea, coffee, beer and soft drinks. You can walk to the New City in 15 minutes, and to Damascus Gate in 20. Dorm beds are US$4, singles US$12, doubles US$18, with lower rates for more than three nights. No set curfew.

King George Hostel (tel 223498), 15 King George V St. Between Jaffa Rd and Ben Yehuda St. It's in the middle of the downtown area, 15 minutes' walk to Jaffa Gate. Take Egged bus No 7, 8, 9, 10, 14 or 31, and get off at first stop on King George V St. This is Jerusalem's hippy/psychedelic haven - or so its reputation goes. It's cramped and dirty but a lot of people like it. Beer and snacks are available, and there's a kitchen and washing machines. Prices vary considerably from time to time, with dorms around US$4.50 and a small room (sleeps up to three) US$18. There's an extra charge for sheets, but the filthy mattresses are free.

International Youth Hostel, 35 Ussishkin St. Egged bus No 17 stops outside. This hostel is in a nice neighbourhood and is quite comfortable, with a TV lounge, kitchen, and roof terrace. It's west of the downtown area so there's a good 20-minute walk to Jaffa Gate. Dorm beds are US$4, and a mattress on the roof terrace costs less. Curfew 12.30 am.

Sisters of the Rosary Convent (tel 228529), 14 Agron St, PO Box 54. Egged bus No 7, 8 or 14 to the Plaza Hotel and walk down Agron St, it's on the right. Run by friendly local nuns, this is a spacious, basic but adequate place to stay, in lovely quiet surroundings. It's 10 minutes' walk to Old City and downtown area. Dorm beds are US$10, singles/doubles US$20/30. There are some triples. Breakfast costs around US$4, lunch or dinner US$8. Curfew 10 or 10.30 pm.

Bernstein Youth Hostel - IYHA (tel 228286), 1 Keren Hayesod St at the junction of Agron/King George V/Ramban. Egged bus No 7, 8 or 14. This place has good facilities and is clean, but not very friendly and is often busy with Israeli school groups. Walk to Jaffa Gate and to the downtown area in 12 minutes. Dorm beds for members are US$10, non-members US$11. Closed 9 am to 5 pm. Curfew 11 pm.

Hotel Nogah (tel 681888), 4 Bezalel St. Ask for Mr Kristal. Take Egged bus No 7, 8, 9, 10, 14 or 31 to King George V St, get off near Ben Yehuda and walk north one block. It's behind the tourist office and alongside the Bezalel School and Artists' House on the right. This clean, comfortable and quiet place has good facilities – kitchen and utensils. Doubles are around US$20. Guests get their own front door key.

Hotel Eretz Israel (tel 245071), 54 King George V St. Egged bus No 7, 8, 9, 10, 14 or 31. It's just before the large white Plaza Hotel and the house with the facade covered in wheels; note the 'Hotel' signs. An elderly Orthodox Jewish couple (who are a little blunt) do a good job in keeping a clean, quiet, comfortable guest house, popular with older Jewish visitors. No unmarried couples are allowed. There's a fridge but no kitchen. Singles/doubles are around US$22/28, but bargain hard. There's no set curfew but you are expected in by midnight at the latest.

Geffen Hotel (tel 224075, 225754), 4 HaHavazelet St. Take any downtown bus to Zion Square: it's on your left as you walk along by 42 Jaffa Rd towards the Old City. It's clean but sparse, with pleasant management, a kitchen, lounge, TV and radio. Singles/doubles are around US$22/28. No curfew.

Hotel Caplan (tel 224591), 1 HaHavazelet St, down from the Geffen Hotel near Zion Square. Basic but clean, with singles/doubles for US$20/28. No curfew.

Louise Waterman Wise Hostel – IYHA (tel 423366), 8 Pisyah Rd, Bayit Gegan. Egged bus Nos 18 or 20 to Mount Herzl – about 30 minutes by bus from downtown. Midnight curfew – don't miss the last bus at about 11.15 pm. This hostel has a good reputation, and is in a lovely building near a forest on the outskirts of Jerusalem. There's a kitchen but no utensils. Members US$10, non-members US$12, with breakfast. They also serve dinner, and it's good food for an IYHA hostel.

En Kerem Youth Hostel – IYHA (tel 416282), off Ma'ayan St. Egged bus No 17 to En Kerem, last stop. Turn left on Ma'ayan St and follow the path. There's

gorgeous scenery here in the Jerusalem hills. Members US$8, non-members US$10. Extra for breakfast, lunch or dinner. No curfew but the last bus is at about 11.15 pm.

Mitzpe Rachel (tel 717621, 715712), Kibbutz Ramat Rachel. Egged bus No 7. It's worthwhile staying here for a day or two in pleasant surroundings to see a kibbutz. Facilities include pool, tennis, lounge. Good food, too. Dorm beds in the kibbutz guest house are around US$10.

Places to Stay - middle
Old City In this price range are some very good deals at Christian hospices. Some hotels are also included here, with most of the accommodation found near Jaffa Gate. Expect to add 15% tax to most of these prices.

Notre Dame de Sion Ecce Homo Convent (tel 282445), 41 Via Dolorosa. From Damascus Gate bear left along El Wad Rd, turn left onto Via Dolorosa and it's on your left just after the first turning. It's very clean, with a study area and kitchen, but there are only double rooms at around US$30 with breakfast. Closed 10 am to noon, 10 pm curfew.

Casa Nova Pilgrims' Hospice (tel 282791), 10 Casa Nova St, PO Box 1321. From Jaffa Gate take the second left, Greek Catholic Patriarchate Rd, and follow it until it becomes Casa Nova St. The hospice is on your left with St Francis St up on the right. Run by the Franciscans with some officious Arab staff, it is clean, with vaulted ceilings and massive marble pillars in the dining room. The food is great and the rooms, mainly twins with bathrooms and central heating, are pleasant. The Hospice is often full with European pilgrims. Singles/doubles are US$28/46. Breakfast costs US$5 and there's an 11 pm curfew.

Greek Catholic Patriarchate Hospice (tel 282023), St Dimitri's Rd. From Jaffa Gate take the second left, Greek Catholic Patriarchate Rd which becomes Dimitri Rd, and the hospice is on the right on the bend. It's a bit unfriendly, but perhaps not if you're Greek. You get basic, comfortable rooms at US$25/36 for singles/doubles, with breakfast. Lunch costs US$4.50 and dinner US$5. Curfew 11 pm.

Gloria Hotel (tel 282431/2), Latin Patriarchate Rd. From Jaffa Gate take the first left and it's on the right. It has large, quiet, modernish rooms, with nice views across the Citadel from the dining room. Singles/doubles cost from US$25/44, with bathroom, breakfast included. No curfew.

East Jerusalem There are numerous hotels in the area, because before 1967 this was where all the pilgrims to the Old City would stay. Most of the accommodation is on or around Salah ed-Din St. Your typical modern Arab hotel here has spacious public areas which are usually ominously bereft of people and dominated by plastic surfaces. The decor is often garish. Like the Israeli Jews, the Palestinians don't provide good service or smile often enough (although some will say, 'What is there to smile about?'). On the whole, considering the facilities and the central location, you do get good value. Unless stated otherwise, all rooms have private bath and/or shower. Prices can vary between peak and quiet periods.

St George's Hostel (tel 283302), 20 Nablus Rd, PO Box 19018. Part of the St George's Cathedral compound, where Nablus Rd meets Salah ed-Din St. Take Egged bus No 27. A 10-minute walk to Herod's or Damascus Gate, and 15 minutes to the New City downtown area, this has to be one of the best accommodation deals around. The 'hostel' tag is inappropriate – it's a delightful cloistered building around an attractive garden, and is peaceful, clean and comfortable with a friendly English warden. Comfortable rooms, most with private bathroom cost US$22/44 for singles/doubles, with breakfast. Ask about the rates for full and half board.

YMCA East-Aelia Capitolina Hotel (tel 282375), 29 Nablus Rd. Just past the US Consulate (bear right) and it's on the left. The decor is dowdy but there are good facilities, including squash, tennis, and a swimming pool. From here it's an eight minute walk to Herod's or Damascus Gate. Singles/doubles US$30/50, with breakfast.

Pilgrims' Palace Hotel (tel 284831). Adjacent to the bus station on Suleiman St, so rooms on that side are noisy. Overlooking the city walls between Herod's and Damascus Gates, it's plain and dull but clean enough. Singles/doubles cost from US$33/45, with breakfast. Lunch or dinner costs US$8.

Rivoli Hotel (tel 284871), Salah ed-Din St. At the corner of Suleiman St, this place has adequate rooms, a nice lounge and TV rooms. Singles/doubles are US$20/32, with breakfast. Lunch or dinner costs US$8.

New Metropole Hotel (tel 283846), 8 Salah ed-Din. This is a popular place for Muslim and Christian Arab pilgrims to stay. There are views of Mount Scopus, the Mount of Olives and the Rockefeller Museum from the pleasant roof garden. Comfortable rooms with good facilities and air-conditioning cost US$20/30 for singles/doubles, with breakfast.

Capitol Hotel (tel 282561), Salah ed-Din St, opposite the Lawrence Hotel. Well-equipped rooms with balconies face the Mount of Olives. There's air-conditioning, and a bar. It's popular with tours from Europe. Singles/doubles cost from US$30/40, with breakfast. Great value.

Lawrence Hotel (tel 282585), 18 Salah ed-Din St. Basic singles/doubles are US$20/30, with breakfast.

Christmas Hotel (tel 282588), Salah ed-Din St. North of the cinema and on the corner on the right. It's clean and comfortable, with singles/doubles at US$25/40, with breakfast.

Mount of Olives *Astoria Hotel* (tel 284965), Shemuel Ben Adaya St. On the lower slopes of the Mount of Olives towards Mount Scopus, this hotel is isolated due to poor bus service. Arab buses Nos 75 and 42 go past from the Suleiman St station but not as often as you'd like. It's a typical modern Arab hotel – adequate. Singles/doubles are around US$30/40.

New City The New City's middle-priced hotels are mostly found in three main areas: near the Old City; in or within easy walking distance of the downtown area; and in the area around the Knesset and the Israel Museum. Most are new and have a long way to go, with management and staff tending to reflect the popular image of the Israeli's brash, unsmiling first impression. Most of these hotels serving meals have kosher kitchens. Add 15% tax and expect higher in the high season and on Jewish holidays.

Included in the middle range more for its style than its price is the *Har-Aviv Hotel* (tel 521515), 16 Bet Hakerem St. South of the central bus station and west of the downtown area, Egged bus No 6, 16 or 17. All the rooms in this small, quiet, pension-style hotel have a terrace. It's family operated and great value with singles/doubles costing from US$15/30, with breakfast. Take Egged bus No 20 to the downtown area from Herzl Blvd.

St Andrew's Hospice (tel 717701), PO Box 14216. In a lovely location near Bloomfield Park, overlooking Mount Zion, the Old City and the Hinnom Valley. You can take Egged bus No 5, 7, 8, 21 or 30 and it's near the train station. Belonging to the Church of Scotland, it has a friendly Scottish country house atmosphere – very comfortable and peaceful. It costs around US$25 per person in singles or doubles. Dinner, US$8, is not available on Sunday. It's popular, good value and recommended. About 12 minutes' steep walk to Zion or Jaffa Gates, and 20 minutes' walk to the downtown area.

St Charles Hospice (tel 637737), 12 Lloyd George St, PO Box 8020. Off Bethlehem Rd to the south of the Old City in the German Colony district, Egged bus No 4, 14, 18 or 24. This German-run hospice offers clean, sparse but comfortable and peaceful surroundings and is usually full. Some rooms don't have private bathrooms. US$23 per person in singles or doubles, with breakfast.

Notre Dame of Jerusalem Center (tel 289723/4/5), Paratroopers' Rd, PO Box 20531. Opposite New Gate. Egged bus No 23 stops right outside. This majestic and newly renovated Roman Catholic complex features a guest house with facilities more reminiscent of a good three star hotel, which is how it is graded. It's ideally situated between the Old and New Cities and has one of Jerusalem's best kitchens. The service is haphazard, and often rude, but most people think it's worth suffering. Singles/doubles cost from US$32/44, with breakfast.

YMCA (tel 227111), King David St, opposite the King David Hotel. Egged bus No 7, 8, 21 or 30. This is probably the best-looking YMCA in the world. Attractive grounds, basic but comfortable rooms and free use of the pool, squash, tennis and gym facilities make it a bargain (if you use them). Six minutes' walk to Jaffa Gate, 12 minutes' walk to the downtown area. It is interesting to note that this is the only YMCA whose clientele is predominantly Jewish. Singles/doubles cost from US$27/45, with breakfast.

Menorah Hotel (tel 242860, 223311), 24 King David St, next door to the YMCA. Very new, comfortable and friendly, with strictly kosher cuisine, a Shabbat elevator and a synagogue. Singles/doubles cost from US$27/40, with breakfast.

Windmill Hotel (tel 663111) is at Menedele St, in the desirable Talkieh district, 15 minutes' walk to Old City, 25 minutes to the downtown area. This is a popular, modern hotel catering for religious Jews with a strictly kosher restaurant and coffee shop, a Shabbat elevator and synagogue. Singles/doubles are US$50/60, with breakfast.

King's Hotel (tel 247133), 60 King George V St. Opposite the Plaza Hotel and 12 minutes' walk to Jaffa Gate and to the downtown area. This is an underrated quality hotel, and it's in a good location adjacent to the Great Synagogue. Singles/doubles are US$55/67, with breakfast.

Ron Hotel (tel 223471/2), 42 Jaffa Rd. Opposite Zion Square in the centre of the downtown area, this nice, basic place has echoes of elegance and days gone by. It's comfortable and good value. Singles/doubles cost from US$30/40, with breakfast.

Tirat Bat Sheva Hotel (tel 232121), 42 King George V St. A pleasant strictly kosher place with good facilities and very nice rooms with balconies. It's good value at US$45/60, with breakfast.

Jerusalem Tower Hotel (tel 222161), 23 Hillel St – the street parallel with Ben Yehuda St, just down from the tourist office. Good facilities for US$50/65, with breakfast.

Sonesta Jerusalem (tel 528221), 2 Wolfson St. A new hotel within easy walking distance of the central bus station, the Knesset, Israel Museum and university. Singles/doubles cost from US$68/80, with breakfast.

Knesset Tower (tel 531111), 4 Wolfson St. Next to the Sonesta and also new. Singles/doubles are US$52/65, with breakfast.

Places to Stay – top end
Jerusalem's luxury hotels are mainly in the New City – the Old City has no four or five star accommodation. Add 15% tax to these prices, all of which are low season. In the high season they rise by about 20%.

On the slopes of Mount Scopus, overshadowed by the controversial Mormon school complex, the new *Hyatt Regency Jerusalem* is the latest addition to the local hotel scene. Most of Israel's new hotel rooms are being built in Jerusalem, and the competition has resulted in many empty luxury rooms, so look out for bargain deals in the *Jerusalem Post* or shop around.

Inter-Continental Jerusalem (tel 282551) is on top of the Mount of Olives, with the classic view over the whole city. Singles/doubles cost from are US$85/95.

American Colony Hotel (tel 282421, 285171), 1 Louis Vincent St, Nablus Rd, East Jerusalem. Once the home of a Turkish pasha, it's now a luxury hotel with real atmosphere and class – possibly the only one in the country. Many prefer it to the more recognised King David Hotel. It has great architecture, a lovely swimming pool and gardens. The rooms vary in quality but the prices reflect this and are good value. It offers non-kosher food, including an excellent buffet every Saturday lunchtime. Singles/doubles cost from US$65/85, with breakfast.

King David Hotel (tel 221111), 23 King David St. Opposite the YMCA, the architecture of which overshadows it, this hotel has views across to the Old City. Traditionally the country's top hotel, it seems to be taking its reputation for granted: the facilities are here but the service and the food are disappointing for this level. Despite this you may well meet the British Prime Minister or the King of Nepal in the elevator. Singles/doubles start at US$150/170, with breakfast.

King Solomon Hotel (tel 241433), 32 King David St. A modern hotel overlooking the Old City and boasting the city's only kosher Japanese restaurant. Singles/doubles cost US$95/110, with breakfast.

Laromme Jerusalem Hotel (tel 697777), 3 Jabotinsky St Overlooking Liberty Bell Park and the Old City, this new El Al-owned hotel is gaining an excellent reputation and is highly rated. There's a synagogue and a Shabbat elevator. Singles/doubles cost from US$65. Prices double in the high season, but you get a free breakfast then.

Moriah Jerusalem Hotel (tel 232232),

39 Kerem Hayesod St. Behind the YMCA and within easy walking distance of the Old City and the downtown area, this modern hotel allows two children to share a double room with their parents and is, therefore, popular with families. Singles/doubles cost US$50/70 with breakfast. Double that for the high season.

Sheraton Jerusalem Plaza Hotel (tel 228133), 47 King George V St. Overlooking Independence Park, the upper floors have views across the whole city. Very central and within pleasant walking distance of both the downtown area and the Old City, there are Shabbat clocks and elevators, and the kosher restaurants include the ultra-expensive Cow on the Roof. Singles/doubles cost from US$95/125.

Jerusalem Hilton (tel 536151), Giv'at Ram. Between the central bus station and the Knesset, this is the usual Hilton set-up, including a health club. They have singles/doubles from US$65/75, with breakfast.

PLACES TO EAT
Old City

At first it might seem to be impossible to find a decent place to eat in the Old City, but not only is it possible, there are in fact some of the best examples of the specialities of the region available, most of them within the reach of a low budget, even if a minor splurge is required.

Also in the Old City, are various food stalls and shops to choose from. Pitta bread and bagels are sold everywhere, from carts and shops – check the going rate, as they are often overpriced. In particular, you can buy bread/bagels at the bottom of the slope as you enter from Damascus Gate and at the end of David St, next to the Cardo.

Unfortunately, while the *intefadeh* continues, you may find that many Old City cafés and restaurants open erratically or not at all. The opening times given here may no longer apply.

Felafel The Old City's felafel is disappointing. Because of this, stick with the cheapest place, a stall down on the right from Damascus Gate, where it costs about US$1. At the very bottom of the slope and straight ahead with the two main streets passing to the left and right of it, is a place where better felafel is sold for a little more.

Hummus Two of the world's best examples of hummus can be enjoyed here, both along the Via Dolorosa. By the 5th Station of the Cross, where the Via Dolorosa turns west (right), *Abu Shukri* is opposite at 63 El Wad Rd. Long-established and with a world-wide reputation as the place to enjoy the best hummus, this simple, clean place is busy. On Saturdays Israelis often form a queue. Continue up the Via Dolorosa towards Suq Khan ez-Zeit St and on the left near the top is *Linda's Restaurant* which many feel produces hummus of equal quality. You pay about US$2.50 for a plate of hummus with pitta and maybe olives or onions. For a little more, ask to have your plate of hummus served with pine nuts, meat and fancy garnish. Both restaurants are open daily, 8 am to 6 pm.

Pizza From Damascus Gate take the small street to the east (left) as you head for El Wad Rd. A little further and on the left is the *Green Door* bakery. Here, in a cavernous room dominated by the traditional oven, the other Mohammed Ali bakes for the neighbourhood. For travellers, his version of the pizza is a popular attraction. He will also use any ingredients that you care to bring along and he and his son work every day 4 am to 11 pm.

In the Armenian Quarter is the *Armenian Ararat Pizza Bakery*, also known as the *Blue Door*. From Jaffa Gate turn right across El Khattab Square and up Armenian Patriarchate Rd, left down St James' St, left on Ararat St and it's on the left behind the unmarked blue door, next to the Ararat Grocer. Run by a friendly Armenian couple, Hagop and Nver Meveshian, the Blue Door is only open Wednesday 11 am to 9 pm and Saturday 11 am to 5 pm and the sole product is *lahmoajin* (Arabic for 'meat dough'), known as Armenian pizza. It consists of minced lamb mixed with peppers, tomatoes, herbs and spices spread over a pitta bread base and costs only 80c.

Restaurants/Cafés *Abou Seif*, from Jaffa Gate on the left past the tourist office, is perhaps the best value sit-down restaurant in the Old City. Closed Sunday, it is open every other day for breakfast through to 9 pm, sometimes later. They have various Middle Eastern dishes, such as salads and stuffed vegetables, at around US$1.50 apiece, so you can eat well quite reasonably.

In the Jewish Quarter, just up from the Western Wall on Tiferet Yisrael St, the self-service *Quarter Café* (upstairs) has good, reasonably priced kosher food in pleasant surroundings, with a great view across to the Dome of the Rock and the Mount of Olives. You can get salads from US$3 and main meals, such as moussaka, from US$4. It's open Sunday to Thursday 8 am to 6.30 pm, Friday 8 am to 3 pm, closed Saturday.

In the Christian Quarter, the nicely furnished *Yerevan Armenian Restaurant* on Frères Rd is more expensive, but provides a pleasant change from the usual. The use of herbs and spices make the chicken, kubbe and the Armenian pizza taste pretty good. It's in a quiet backwater near New Gate. From Jaffa Gate take the second left up Greek Catholic Patriarchate Rd and follow the road up to the left, passing Francis St on the right. Around US$12 for a set three course meal.

At the *Lark Hotel Restaurant* just

down the street on Latin Patriarchate Rd, similar Armenian fare is served for about the same price.

On Suq Khan ez-Zeit St, just north of the Holy Sepulchre turn-off, is a juice bar serving carrot and orange juice all year round and others in season.

Sweets On Suq Khan ez-Zeit St, you cannot avoid gazing at the honey-soaked delights of the many Arab pastry shops. However, due to the competition it can take some time for items to sell, and at up to US$1 a time you don't want to end up with anything but a fresh pastry.

For this reason, but also because it is highly rated by the Arabs for a special treat, try *Zalatino's*, just back from the stairs leading up to the 9th Station of the Cross. This unremarkable looking little bakery produces some of the city's best pastry. Its adored speciality is the rich moutabak made to order by Abu Ali Hawash, the baker here for over 20 years. Super light pastry is kneaded and rolled over and over with a fresh cheese filling and served straight from the traditional oven with hot sugar syrup. Other sweets are available, but this is what people wait for – sometimes for over 30 minutes due to the made-to-order system. While you are waiting, ask to see the hidden parts of the Holy Sepulchre, read this book or simply sit and watch the master at work. Quite filling, a single portion is often enough for two, at about US$1.35. Open daily until the pastry is all used – usually by 11.30 am.

Bars To get to the friendly *Moonshine Bar* take the first left from Jaffa gate up Latin Patriarchate Rd and it's on the left. Owned by Rafi Kamar, a retired international banker now happily realising an ambition to run his own bar, it is my favourite place serving beer in the Old City: a clean, comfortable respite from the surrounding hubbub.

Opposite the steps leading up to the rooftop promenade on Habad St, on the corner between David St and St Mark's Rd, the *Bedouin Tent* is a popular hangout for the Old City's hostel residents with its cheap bottled beer and taped music. Open daily till late.

East Jerusalem

On HaNevi'im St, just north of the New Raghadan Hostel, a popular Arab bakery is open long hours producing delicious pitta bread and bagels. The cheaper cafés are uninviting; the cleanest and cheapest is next to the New Raghadan Hostel. In the evenings you can buy delicious felafel and offal from a noticeably clean cart parked either on the corner of Nablus Rd and Suleiman St or by the steps of the Damascus Gate piazza.

Potato chips/crisps are not quite what springs to mind on the subject of local food, but the *City Grocery*, 13 Salah ed-Din St sells the most divine plain salted potato chips/crisps.

Something of a cult amongst hummus freaks is the *Abu Ali* restaurant. Although less than spotless, it is busy with local Arabs who eat lunch early, from 11 am, and has its Jewish regulars, too. Hidden away off Salah ed-Din St, head north from Herod's Gate and turn right at the sign for 'Ibrahim Dandis'; it's downstairs on your left, opposite the offices of the Palestinian Press Service. Open daily 6 am to 4.30 pm. Tasty and inexpensive main meals are also served - simply wander into the kitchen and point out what you want from the various meat, rice and vegetable dishes kept hot on top of the stove. This is a typical Arab working man's eating place - no frills and very cheap. Prices are lower than anywhere else I ate in Israel, but they varied each time I went. Ordering soft drink along with the food never seemed to make the bill more expensive, nor did asking for more pitta. Bank on US$3 for hummus and the works, but it'll probably be less.

For a more expensive meal, East Jerusalem provides Jerusalem's best Arab restaurants and Friday nights can be

busy with most Jewish competitors closed for Shabbat. The *Philadelphia Restaurant* (tel 289770), 9 Az-Sahar St off Salah-ed Din St is one of the best. Named after Amman as it was known in ancient times, it specialises in mazzas, the traditional appetisers, as well as grilled lamb dishes. A full meal costs about US$12, but individual dishes are less and the mazzas can be a meal on their own.

Another top restaurant is the *Petra* (tel 283655), 11 El-Rashid St, the next street east of Salah ed-Din St. Here an excellent set dinner costs about US$15.

The *National Palace Restaurant* in the hotel of the same name is a little more expensive, but is recommended. The food is wonderful, with mansaf the speciality served on Fridays. About US$15 a head.

The *American Colony Hotel* provides good food in delightful surroundings. Very popular is the Saturday lunchtime buffet - good value at about US$15.

New City

Jerusalem's New City has a vast number of eateries, many of which blend into an indistinguishable mass of establishments providing coffee and cakes, hummus and salad, felafel, pizza, shishlik, Ashkenazi fare or local interpretations of international styles. Amongst a depressingly high number of mediocre places, there are some cheap options of high quality which are well worth the experience.

The Mahane Yehuda market is where you can buy the cheapest food. To save even more, learn to bargain and go along just as the market closes (about 7.30 to 8.30 pm Sunday to Thursday, and 3 to 4 pm Friday) when prices are lowest. Closed on Saturday.

Elsewhere in the New City, the basement supermarket in the Hamashbir department store on King George V St on the corner of Ben Yehuda St has a good selection of bread and dairy products at regular prices as well as other items not necessarily found in cheaper environments. Other convenient supermarkets are on

Jaffa Rd between Strauss St and Zion Square and there is a Supersol, on the corner of Agron and King George V Sts, next to the Plaza Hotel.

Felafel Perhaps the best felafel in Israel can be had at the *Yemenite Felafel*, 48 HaNevi'im St. Open Sunday to Thursday 10 am to 7 pm, Friday 10 am to 2 pm, closed Saturday. From King George V St head up Strauss St and bear right on HaNevi'im St. This mecca of felafel is on the left opposite the Russian Compound with a marvellous view of the green-domed Russian Cathedral at the end of the narrow street opposite.

Most New City felafel is sold on King George V St between Jaffa Rd and Ben Yehuda St. Just follow the trail of tehina, salad and squashed felafel balls on the pavement.

Shwarma Many of the places selling felafel also have shwarma. None of them really inspires a recommendation, but you will find the busiest of them on the corner of King George V and Agrippas Sts. Most use turkey instead of lamb, and they are likely to carve you fat instead of meat – if you are not happy with your portion, walk away and try the next place.

Hummus Available in most Oriental restaurants, the following enjoy particularly good reputations for hummus: *Ta'ami* (no English sign), 3 Shammai St parallel with and to the south of Ben Yehuda St – ignore the rude owner who seems to dislike foreigners; *Queen's*, second on left from Jaffa Rd on Heleni HaMalka St – Elvis Presley is the apparent inspiration here; and *Rahmo*, in the area of the Mahne Yehuda market, on the corner of Ha'Armonium St, off Agrippas.

Pizza Very popular here, with several outlets in the downtown triangle – but the quality doesn't seem to justify the enthusiasm of the Israelis and the

Americans (who should know better with their superior products back home). For me, the best of a poor bunch is *Pizza Ami* on HaHistadrut St, to the left as you walk up Ben Yehuda St. This choice is largely influenced by the fact that it remains open when the Ben Yehuda St cafés close at midnight and the other pizzerias have long since been hosed down for the night.

Cafés These literally line the downtown streets, and attract their own clique of local regulars. When busy they are all as bad as each other, with inefficient service and even basic items such as coffee often of questionable quality.

However, some cafés enjoy a reputation of quality and appeal to certain types. Often talked about is the *Atara* at 7 Ben Yehuda St. This is the traditional literary hang out, but on a busy evening you will not notice any difference between here and the the other equally congested cafés. *Finzi's*, further up on the same side just below Ben-Hillel St, seems to stand out too. Jerusalem's mayor has been known to bring guests here for coffee. However, a major factor in its popularity is that it's the only place serving draught beer on Ben Yehuda St.

Another café of note is the *Rimon* on Luntz St, which leads off to the right from Ben Yehuda St near Zion Square. The *Ticho House* café, in the museum and library complex at 7 Harav Kook St across from Zion Square, is very popular. This, and all of the cafés mentioned, offers basic hot dishes and salads as well as a wide range of cakes, ice cream and beverages.

As well as the European-style street cafés, Jerusalem has some alternatives. In the Nahalat Shiva neighbourhood, built in 1891, are two places with a bohemian ambience. The *Chocolate Soup*, 6 Rivlin St, serves coffee, herbal teas and milkshakes, and its menu features 'Pink Floyd' – strawberries and lemon juice, crepes and that chocolate soup, made from milk, cocoa, fruit, oats, sugar, vanilla and chocolate sauce. At 12 Yoel Salomon St, the *Tea House* is popular with local young hippy types who sit cross-legged on cushions and choose from the range of 30 herbal teas, blintzes and other desserts. Open Sunday to Thursday and Saturday 7 pm to 2 am. Closed Friday.

At 17 Yoel Salomon St, the *Harmony House* is a record store with a café where you can sit down and order while plugged into a cassette of your choice playing over your headphones – about US$2 per cassette. Also in Nahalat Shiva is *Don't Pass Me By Tea & Pie*, near the bus stop on Jaffa Rd opposite MacDavid's. This casual teahouse with its pie speciality attracts a regular young clientele.

Sefer VeSefel (meaning 'Mug & Book'), the bookstore on Ya'Aretz St, has a café noted for its ice cream, noticeboard and magazine collection, although efficient service has yet to be introduced. The *Artists' House* at 12 Shemuel HaNayid has a pleasant café away from the mainstream – also popular for its bar and for meals, it is a pleasant spot for coffee or tea and stays open till late every night. The *Domino* at 6 Hillel St is a recent and popular addition to the scene. Open till 2 am every night.

Another late-night spot is the 24 hour *Home Plus* on Harkenos St. A few years ago such a thing as an all-night café in the Holy City would have been unthinkable. Don't waste your money on the food – the vast menu means that quality is lost in the battle against quantity – but it is a popular meeting place with free newspapers, a bar and pleasant surroundings.

Away from the downtown area is the *Cinemateque* café (see Entertainment) with its wondrous location. It is also one of the few places open on a Friday evening.

Restaurants A great and inexpensive area to eat meat is along Agrippas St south of Mahane Yehuda. Perhaps the best of the small grilled meat specialists is *Abu Shabi* at No 46. Owned by a Turkish Jew

with Arab staff from Hebron, you simply look in the fridge and choose from various skewered meats and offal which are then grilled 'on the fire' and served with tehina, vegetable salad and pitta. Beer and wine are available. Each skewer costs US$2.50, salad US$2.50. Open Sunday to Thursday 5 pm to 3 am, closed Friday, Saturday from sundown to 3 am.

At 12 King George V St, the *Marvad Haksamin* (Magic Carpet) is always busy and provides a variety of inexpensive Oriental dishes such as hummus, tehina with eggplant, soups and grilled meats and stuffed vegetables from US$4. You can spend more on steak, liver and chicken. It's open all day Sunday to Thursday and lunchtime Friday, closed Friday evening and Saturday.

For good authentic Yemenite food at low prices, try *Ruchama* at 3 Ya'Avetz St opposite Sefer VeSefel. Dishes include Oriental salads, soups, *showie* (a Yemenite meat speciality), and *melawach* (a traditional Yemenite pancake, savoury or sweet). Open Sunday to Thursday, 11 am to midnight, closed Friday, Saturday sunset to midnight.

A busy lunchtime favourite is *Hen*, 30 Jaffa Rd, across from the main post office (no English sign, next to two pastry shops). Israel's President Chaim Herzog is rumoured to have eaten here as well as me – and I don't blame him. Good, basic Oriental favourites again – salads, soups, stuffed vegetables and grilled meats. You can eat well on less than US$4 or spend more. Open Sunday to Thursday 9 am to 6 pm, Friday 9 am to 3 pm, closed Saturday.

At 3 HaHistadrut St, to the right going up Ben Yehuda St, is *Sova*, a very cheap and busy self-service restaurant. The food won't win prizes but it will suit a low budget. Stews, casseroles and gefilte fish are usually on the Ashkenazi-type menu. Normally open Sunday to Thursday 11 am to 4 pm, and for dinner on Friday and Saturday. However it was closed when I was last in Jerusalem, opening only for private functions, so maybe it is no longer the cheapest New City restaurant.

For less traditional food such as spaghetti, steaks and hamburgers, *Eddie's* on Ben Yehuda St (on the right as you go up below HaHistadrut St) offers choices for around US$5.

Poondak HaHalav, 17 Bezalel St (the continuation of Ben Yehuda St across King George V St) on the left, has a good self-service salad bar (one serve only, so pile it on, folks). They also feature savoury and sweet blintzes for about US$4. A nice place, open Sunday to Thursday noon to midnight, closed Friday, Saturday sunset to midnight.

Perhaps one of the unlikeliest places to look for good food is *Notre Dame*, opposite New Gate. The complex features a coffee shop, but its main restaurant is the place to go for some excellent food and pleasant, if basic, surroundings. It's open to non-residents every day for lunch and dinner, when a set menu is featured at about US$8.

On Rivlin St next to the Tavern, *La Belle* is a pleasant restaurant with French-style food at about US$12 per person. Open Sunday to Thursday 7 pm to late, Saturday 8 pm to late, closed Friday.

The *Domino*, at 6 Hillel provides a wide variety of salads and hot dishes in the US$10 bracket and is very busy.

For Hungarian food, try the *Europa*, upstairs at 48 Jaffa Rd, opposite Zion Square, around US$15 for a full three-course meal. Open Sunday to Thursday noon to 9.30 pm, closed Friday and Saturday.

Opposite the Home Plus on Harkenos St is *HaTorif* (the Pie House). It's usually busy, serving meat and vegetarian pies and salads at about US$10 per person. Next door is *Mandy Tachi*, a good Chinese restaurant. A decent spread will cost about US$15 per person. *Tain-Lee-Chow* next to the Kings Hotel and opposite the Plaza Hotel on King George V St is also good.

For Italian food, but nothing too special, try *Alla Gondola*, 14 King George V St, opposite HaHistadrut St; *Mamma Mia*, 18 Rabbi Akiva St – head along the street opposite the Jerusalem Tower Hotel on Hillel St and turn right before the end; or *Mamma Leone*, 5 Hillel St. You can enjoy pasta, seafood and other dishes for between US$7 to US$15. All open for dinner Sunday to Thursday and Saturday, closed Friday.

Restaurants – expensive *Cohen's Restaurant* (tel 225020) at 3 Yeshiyahn St, with its unobtrusive entrance next to the kitchen door on Belilius St and adjacent to the Edison Youth Hostel, is the hiding place for perhaps Israel's top chef. He is certainly the most idiosyncratic. Michel Cohen lovingly prepares a wide range of exquisite food including exotically stuffed vegetables, fruits and meats (beef, lamb, chicken, brain, kidneys, pigeon), fish, soups, roasts and desserts. The surroundings and service are both understated and basic.

More than living up to a chef's reputation as a difficult and hot tempered character, Cohen does not open for regular hours, but only when he feels like cooking. Making a reservation doesn't even guarantee that when you turn up dinner will be prepared for you. The regular clientele include Prime Ministers, past and present, and wealthy customers have Cohen send food abroad to them. (Having said that, politicians and the wealthy are not always the best example to follow.) If you can afford it, you should risk the possible inconvenience of being turned away. Prices vary but you can spend US$20 to US$60 per person plus wine.

At the corner of HaHistadrut and King George V Sts, *Fink's Bar-Restaurant* (tel 234523) is another largely hidden treasure, although it too has its sizeable band of enthusiastic regulars. Opened in 1933, it became the favourite watering-hole for British military and police officers during the Mandate, and Jewish underground fighters would frequent the bar to hear the gossip. Later, politicians took over, followed by the journalists. Now Fink's is the traditional hangout for journalists both local and from around the world who have been sent to Israel over the years to cover the various wars and political events.

The place is notable not only for its well-stocked bar and consistently excellent Austro-Bavarian food, but for the atmosphere of bonhomie and quiet professionalism found nowhere else in Israel, and so rarely abroad. You can sit at the bar for a drink or to try the speciality, goulash soup, described as a 'Jewish ploughman's lunch', or opt for a full dinner and choose from a wide range of meats, fish and desserts, along with the extensive wine list. With less than a dozen places at the bar and only five tables, the place soon fills up and reservations are advisable. US$20 and way up, plus wine. Open Saturday to Thursday 7 pm till late, closed Friday.

More recognisable as a restaurant of quality is the less personable *Mishkenot Sha'ananim* (tel 225110, 244696) below the Montefiore Windmill. Here, French cuisine is combined with a few Moroccan appetisers in plush surroundings, across from the floodlit walls of the Old City. An extensive wine list adds to the attractions offered on the menu. A set lunch menu is about US$20, eating à la carte starts from US$25, increasing to unprintable prices when you look at the vintage claret selection. Closed Friday.

Vegetarian & Health Food *Eternity* plan to open a restaurant in Jerusalem, but until they do, the number one vegetarian eatery is *Hameshek*, 14 Shlomzion St. The menu features soups, salads, grains, pastas and some scrumptious cakes. Very popular and not expensive, from US$3 to US$8 for a good feed. Open Sunday to Thursday noon to 10 pm, Friday 11 am to 3 pm, closed Saturday.

Alumah Natural Food Restaurant, 8 Ya'Avetz St (the narrow alley linking Ben-Hillel to 49 Jaffa Rd) is a pleasantly decorated restaurant, and has a no-smoking policy; unheard of in Israel. It serves soups and salads (US$3), main dishes – grains and casseroles (US$4.50) – and a choice of desserts, herbal teas and grain coffees. Open Sunday to Thursday noon to 10 pm, closed Friday and Saturday.

Along Ezrat Yisrael St, to the right off Jaffa Rd above Strauss St, is *Bhole Baba*, a reasonably priced vegetarian and dairy restaurant serving soups and salads, blintzes, quiches and pizzas and various cakes and desserts. Open 10 am to 10 pm Sunday to Thursday, closed Friday sunset to late Saturday, but the hours vary.

Calling all peanut butter addicts, the country's finest can be found at the health food shop at 76 Jaffa Rd (between Strauss St and Mahane Yehuda).

Bakeries The district of Mea Shearim in particular has many bakeries producing the various types of bread, cakes and biscuits so popular with the locals. A favourite treat is to go along late in the evening and pick up a sticky bun or three, perhaps a chocolate-filled one as well for variety and another with currants – and don't forget the biscuits. Convenient to the downtown area is the bakery on Peri Hadash St. Go up Strauss St from Jaffa Rd, take the first left along HaNevi'im St, right along Yeshayahu St and it's just down from the Edison Cinema on the left, by the musical instrument shop. On Thursday this and other bakeries are open all night to meet the demand for Shabbat.

For bourekas, try the bakery that makes nothing else, next to the Yemenite Felafel at 48 HaNevi'im St, opposite the Russian Compound. Open Sunday to Thursday 6 am to 7 pm, Friday 6 am to 2 pm, closed Saturday.

La Lavanaise, Baguette et Croissant on the right along Jaffa Rd heading towards Mahane Yehuda from Strauss St, is a bakery and café producing those light French delights.

Ice Cream Jerusalem's creamy *Manalitos* branch is on Ben Hillel St, between Ben Yehuda and King George V Sts, the softer *Carmel* is on King George V St, away from the street to the right of the Hamashbir department store opposite Ben Yehuda St. At 51 Jaffa Rd, just below the King George V/Strauss Sts crossroads is the small kiosk of *Uri's* with its popular soft variety. The café at *Kefer VeSefel*, the bookstore upstairs at 2 Ya'Avetz St, serves home-made ice cream, along with chocolate brownies and other delights.

Bars Very popular with tourists and with an ever-growing Israeli market, Jerusalem's bars have played a considerable part in changing the face of the city's social life. Now it is possible to drink in a variety of establishments until the early hours seven nights a week. Most of the bars call themselves pubs and are open from lunchtime.

Scandals, at 8 Dorot Rishonim St, around to the left from Luntz St, off Ben Yehuda St near Zion Square, is often the quietest of these – check to see if they still have their 'Happy Hour' reductions 5.30 to 7.30 pm. *Champs*, on Yoel Salomon St by Zion Square, plays videos and is usually very busy in the evening. Around on Rivlin St is the equally popular *Tavern*. These three pubs have the cheapest draught beer in the New City.

Just across from the Tavern, and starting at the other end from 31 Jaffa Rd, near the Shlomzion St junction, is the 'Little Street of Pubs' – a narrow alleyway which is packed with revellers on good nights. The *Yard, Little Pub, La Lo's Pub* and *Pini's Pub* serve the (often literally) heaving masses. The food here won't win any prizes or save you any money, and the beer is often served short and in bad condition in the slightly less than half-litre glasses.

Back on Rivlin St, the *Pump* is a new and slightly upmarket bar serving draught and bottled beers, and various basic dishes. On Ben Yehuda St all the cafés do well selling bottled beer, with *Finzi's* the only one boasting the draught product but also charging more than the pubs already mentioned. The *Domino* at 6 Hillel St also charges more than the minimum but you are given plenty of free olives or popcorn. The *Artists' House* at 12 Shemuel HaNagid is also a popular drinking spot, open till late.

To cater for those pangs of hunger which befall most drinkers when they leave a bar late at night, the *Kiosk* next to the Tavern serves hot dogs and sandwiches till the bars are emptied.

ENTERTAINMENT

Q *What is the best part of Jerusalem's nightlife?*
A *The road to Tel Aviv!*

Although most Tel Aviv residents will insist that this old joke still applies, Jerusalem has changed considerably in the last few years. Be sure to read the *Jerusalem Post*, in particular the Friday edition, for the comprehensive list of events. Also check at the tourist offices for any special events or regular happenings, some of which will not be featured in the *Post*. Finally, you can dial 241197 after 6 pm for a recorded message, in English, telling you about some of the evening's events.

Throughout the year, Jerusalem is a major venue for special events, in particular national celebrations of Jewish festivals (see Festivals & Holidays in Facts about the Country section) and the Israel Festival. Usually held sometime during May-June, this is a three-week programme of cultural events featuring music, theatre, and dance in outdoor historical sites such as the Citadel, Sultan's Pool and the Mount Scopus amphitheatre, as well as in more conventional surroundings.

Top: Russian Orthodox Cathedral, Russian Compound, Jerusalem (NT)
Left: Western Wall and the Dome of the Rock at sunset (NT)
Right: The Citadel, Old City, Jerusalem (NT)

The eye of the storm – peace in the gardens of Temple Mount, Jerusalem
(RE – top, NT – bottom)

In the Old City, the ramparts walk between Zion and Jaffa Gates is open Sunday to Thursday until 9.30 pm and the sound and light show at the Citadel is performed in the evenings between April and November.

On Mount Zion, *Asaf's Cave* (tel 716841) at the Mount Zion Cultural Center, adjacent to David's Tomb, is the regular venue for the *Diaspora Yeshiva Band* who perform their widely appreciated brand of Hasidic rock in a mixture of Yiddish, Hebrew and English. Check for the current schedule and admission charge.

The Nuzha/El Hakaurati Theatre in East Jerusalem (tel 280957, 288189), Abu Abiyde St off Salah ed-Din St behind the Tombs of the Kings, is the Palestinian cultural centre. Plays, musicals, operettas and folk dancing are performed here in Arabic, often with an English synopsis.

The Hebrew University on Mount Scopus has regular folk dancing at the *Baraton Club* (tel 882670), usually on Wednesday and Saturday evenings at 7.30 pm. Take Egged bus No 9 or 28.

The American Colony Hotel (tel 282421) often has live jazz in its cosy cellar bar. Check there or in the *Jerusalem Post* for details.

Evenings in the New City see most people head for the downtown area to promenade, sit outside cafés (however cold it may be) and people-watch. Ben Yehuda St is the main drag for this activity which reaches its peak on Saturday night, after Shabbat. The pedestrianised street is also busy with buskers, artists and jewellery sellers. A more scenic walk would be along King David St, past the floodlit YMCA and King David Hotel and the Montefiore Windmill to enjoy the views of the Old City, Mount Zion and St Andrew's Church.

Cinema

Films from the US and Europe show up in Israel fairly soon after release, usually in the original language with Hebrew and French or English subtitles. The quality of the cinemas, in terms of comfort and sound and picture clarity, is often low, but they are not too expensive. The *Jerusalem Post* lists the current programmes and schedules but does not give you the cinemas' addresses. These are the city's main cinemas:

Cinema 1 (tel 415067) Qiryat HaYovel, out past Mount Herzl en route to the Hadassah Medical Center. Take Egged bus No 18 from King David St or Jaffa Rd – it's a circular route so you can catch it in either direction.

Cinemateque (tel 712192) Hebron Rd, shows a variety of classics, avant garde, new wave, and off-beat films. It's a membership cinema, but usually a sufficient number of tickets is available just before the performance. The complex of the cinema, café, archives and museum is tucked below Hebron Rd, down from St Andrew's Church and the railway station.

Eden (tel 223829) 5 Agrippas St, half a block on the left from King George V St.

Edison (tel 224036) 14 Yeshayahu St, from the crossroads with King George V St and Jaffa Rd, head up Strauss St, left onto HaNevi'im St, then right on Yeshayahu St and it's on your right, on the corner of Belilius St.

Habira (tel 232366) 19 Shamai St, one block south-east of and parallel to Ben Yehuda St.

Kfir (tel 242523) 97 Jaffa Rd, in the Klal Building, or *Merkaz Klal*, between King George V St and Mahane Yehuda on the left.

Orna (tel 224733) 19 Hillel St near the Jerusalem Tower Hotel on the street south of and parallel with Ben Yehuda St and down from the tourist office.

Or-Gil (tel 234176) 18 Hillel St, near the Jerusalem Tower and the *Orna* cinema.

Orion (tel 222914) Shamai St, one block south-
east of, and parallel to Ben Yehuda St.

Ron (tel 234704) 1 Rabbi Akiva St, opposite the
Jerusalem Tower on Hillel St.

Semadar (tel 633742) 4 Lloyd George St, in the
German Colony, three blocks south of the
railway station. Take Egged bus No 18
heading east along Jaffa Rd or King David
St, and get off just after the station.

The Jerusalem Hilton, the Israel Museum
and the Jerusalem Sherover and Tzavta
theatres show films occasionally. Check
the *Jerusalem Post* for details.

Theatres

Most of the theatre is performed in
Hebrew, with occasional foreign language
productions.

Jerusalem Sherover Theatre (tel
667167), 20 David Marcus St, Rehavia.
This modern complex features the classics
and modern works. It is also the home of
the Jerusalem Symphony Orchestra and
the Israel Chamber Ensemble.

Khan Theatre (tel 721782), David
Remez Square across from the railway
station entrance. In a converted and
refurbished Ottoman Turkish caravanserai,
this complex features mainly Hebrew
plays in its theatre, but the popular club
has a nightly show of Israeli folksingers
with the audience joining in with the
singing and dancing. Egged bus Nos 6, 7, 8
or 30.

Tzavta (tel 227621), 38 King George V
St, behind the car park on the right from
Ben Yehuda St, opposite the start of
Independence Park. This small music-
theatre club often features productions in
English, and visiting entertainers are
invited to audition for unscheduled
performances. Tickets are often very
affordable at US$2 to US$5.

Little Theatre, Jerusalem Hilton (tel
536151), opposite the central bus station,
presents plays in both English and
Hebrew.

Music

For classical music lovers there is usually
a quality concert to enjoy in Jerusalem.
Binyanei Ha-Oomah (tel 222481) opposite
the central bus station and adjacent to the
Jerusalem Hilton, is home to the Israel
Philharmonic Orchestra and also stages
other musical events.

Used for classical performances and
also for folk dancing are the *YMCA
Auditorium*, King David St, opposite the
King David Hotel, and the *International
Cultural Center for Youth* (ICCY) (tel
664144/6, 630900, 669838) 12A Emek
Refaim St in the German Colony, south of
the city. Take Egged bus No 4, 4A, 14 or
18. Here, the Pa'amez Teyman Folk Lore
Ensemble presents Israeli folk dances,
Yemenite, Hasidic and Arabic traditional
dances, Israeli folk singing and Khalifa
Arabic drummers. Sing along, dance
along. Tickets are sold at the door and at
many hotels. *Little Theatre*, Jerusalem
Hilton, occasionally holds musical events.

For regular jazz music but with a
variety of visiting acts performing rock,
blues, country and folk, the *Pargod
Theatre* (tel 228819, 231765), 94 Bezalel
St should not be missed. In particular,
Friday afternoons feature a free jazz jam
session 1.30 to 5.30 pm. A US$3.50 cover
charge applies most evenings. Tzavta also
has musical performances from time to
time.

Penny Lane (tel 858202), 29 HaNevi'im
St, entrance through the car park from the
Russian Compound, is a pleasant bar-
restaurant with live jazz or blues music
most evenings. The food and service are
mediocre, but the music can be
worthwhile.

The *Israel Center*, 10 Strauss St on the
corner of HaNevi'im St, features musical
concerts, in particular Hasidic rock.

Discos

Neither of Jerusalem's two commercial
discos win prizes, but you might be
tempted if you are a dance addict and
enjoy 'getting down' anywhere.

J & B Dance Club is on the 3rd floor of the Klal Building in Jaffa Rd, halfway between King George V St and Mahane Yehuda. It's open from 9 pm to 2 am and has a laser-light show. Free admission for women on Tuesdays, otherwise there's a cover charge of around US$4.

At the Zion Square end of Yoel Salomon St is *Amadeus*, (formerly the Star Club), full of Israeli teenagers, mainly 14 to 17.

What to do on Shabbat in Jerusalem

'Shabbat Shalom' in Jerusalem for the unobservant Jew and non-Jew is no longer a password to boredom. Jerusalem offers several options to enable you to make full use of the day. Wherever you decide to go you can be sure that carloads of Israelis will be doing the same, equally enthusiastic to escape the confines of the Shabbat laws. Daytime options include:

Old City & Surroundings For most of the Old City, Mount Zion, the Mount of Olives and East Jerusalem, Shabbat is just another day, with markets and most cafés and attractions crowded with Israelis and visitors as well as Arabs. The Western Wall is the destination of thousands of observant Jews, and the Jewish Quarter is completely shut down for the day. Be sure to see the crowds, the singing and the dancing that welcomes the Shabbat on Friday at sunset, or visit a synagogue.

West Bank Thanks to the Arab bus network and service-taxi system, a popular way to spend Shabbat is to head for Bethlehem, Jericho, Hebron, Ramallah or Nablus. Again, many Israelis do the same. Today is also as good a day as any to enjoy the stunning scenery on the Wadi Qelt and Mar Saba hikes (see Jericho and Bethlehem). Sheruts run from the New City to Tel Aviv.

Dead Sea This is only a couple of hours drive away, and many people take an Egged bus down on Friday before the shutdown to enjoy the sea, the nature reserve at Ein Gedi or to climb Masada.

New City Most of the Jewish cafés and restaurants close early on Friday afternoon, along with most businesses, offices and shops. The New City becomes a ghost town as buses fill up and traffic jams become the norm. An increasing number of entertainment places have begun to open on Friday nights, much to the annoyance of observant Jews. Most of the bars on and around Rivlin St, and *Scandals*, the *Domino* and the *Artists' Club* are all open and very popular. The 24-hour *Home Plus* calls it a day and closes for Shabbat. Further out, the Cinemateque café is open as usual.

East Jerusalem The quality Arab restaurants attract a lot of Jews on Friday nights, and the Old City's *Moonshine* and *Bedouin Tent* bars remain open for an affordable beer.

GETTING THERE & AWAY

Jerusalem is a busy crossroads for the Egged and Arab bus networks. The popular sherut/service taxi services makes the city a convenient base from which you can take advantage of the small distances involved, and visit many places of interest.

Coming from the north you can either take the Jordan Valley route, via Tiberias, Bet Shean and Jericho, to enter Jerusalem from the east (on the same road that you would use coming from the Dead Sea and Allenby/King Hussein Bridge), or you can take the less arid but perhaps more scenic route over the mountains, passing Jenin, Nablus and Ramallah. From places in the west, such as Tel Aviv, Haifa and Ben-Gurion Airport, you enter the New City via a steady climb up into the Judean Hills, on the four-lane highway Weizmann Blvd. It soon changes to become Jaffa Rd with the central bus station to the left. From the south you enter via Beersheba, Hebron and Bethlehem.

Bus

Egged The Egged central bus station on Jaffa Rd is where most people first arrive. Buses here connect to all the major areas in the country. Always busy, the inter-urban buses arrive in and depart from the main concourse, with the city buses operating from stops outside on Jaffa Rd and Zaiman St, reached by an underground walkway. Although the inter-urban buses usually fill up, you need only make reservations a day in advance for the Eilat bus. Buses for the Dead Sea are always busy and seem to operate independently of the official timetable. The rule is to make as early a start as possible.

For information, you can try phoning 551703. The left-luggage office is on the opposite side of Jaffa Rd from the central bus station, open Sunday to Thursday 6.30 am to 7 pm, Friday 6.30 am to 3 pm, closed Saturday. The charge is 80c per item per day.

Arab Buses The Arab buses run from two stations in East Jerusalem. Their schedules are not to be relied upon, but the last Arab buses usually leave the station by 6.30 pm. The main station is on Suleiman St, between Nablus Rd and Salah ed-Din St.

The other station is on Nablus Rd, just up from Damascus Gate, on the left. Here, services operate to/from the West Bank north of Jerusalem, mainly Ramallah (No 18 – 35c) and Nablus (No 23 – US$1.35). Some Egged buses also run from this station.

Taxi

Sheruts/service taxis make an affordable alternative to the buses. In the New City regular services include:

Tel Aviv
HaBirah (tel 224545), 1 HaRav Kook St, opposite Zion Square
Kesher-Aviv (tel 227366), 12 Shammai St, south east of and parallel to Ben Yehuda St. Daily US$2.80 per person, Friday and Saturday US$4.25.
Ben-Gurion Airport
Nesher (tel 231231), 21 King George V St, at the corner of Ben Yehuda St. US$5 from the office, US$8 to be picked up from your hostel/hotel, reserve in advance.
Haifa & Eilat
Yael Daroma (tel 226985), Shammai St, next door to Kesher-Aviv. Reservations normally necessary.

In East Jerusalem, on the corner of HaNevi'im St and opposite Damascus

Egged Buses

to	fare	time	frequency
Tel Aviv	US$2.90	50 minutes	at least every 10 minutes
Haifa	US$5.50	two hours	at least every hour
Eilat	US$10	4½ hours	a night service and 3 daytime runs
Dead Sea – Qumran	US$3	50 minutes	
– Neve Zohar	US$4.30	2½ hours	
Ben Gurion Airport	US$2.75	40 minutes	express at least every hour.

Arab Buses

to	fare	time	frequency
Bethlehem (No 22)	45c	20 minutes	every 15 minutes
Mount of Olives (No 75)	45c	10 minutes	every 30 minutes
Bethany (No 36)	45c	10 minutes	every 30 minutes
Jericho (No 28)	US$1.75	45 minutes	every 20 minutes
Hebron (No 23)	US$1.75	1 hour	every 40 minutes

Gate, the service taxi rank is where you arrive from/depart for Arab towns on the West Bank and in the Gaza Strip. Some approximate fares:

to	fare	time
Bethlehem	90c	15 minutes
Jericho	US$2.20	30 minutes
Hebron	US$1.75	40 minutes
Ramallah	US$1.25	20 minutes
Nablus	US$3.75	1¼ hours
Gaza	US$5.75	1¾ hours

These service taxis operate daily and regularly until about 5 pm, after which time the service becomes less dependable with fewer passengers to fill the vehicles.

Train

Jerusalem's railway station is in David Remez Square, south of the Old City on the edge of the New City's German colony. This is the end of the line running from Haifa via Tel Aviv, and one train only runs per day in each direction, except on Saturday when there are no trains.

Trains depart from Jerusalem at 4 pm Saturday to Thursday, and they arrive in Tel Aviv shortly after 6 pm. They continue on to Haifa, arriving at 7.30 pm. On Fridays the train departs from Jerusalem at 11 am.

The fare to/from Tel Aviv is about US$2.20, Haifa US$3.75. The ISIC discount is 25%. Egged bus Nos 5, 6, 7, 8 and 21 run between the railway station and the New City. To reach the Old City it is perhaps just as easy to walk as it is to take a bus to the start of Jaffa Rd.

Air

Arkia flights depart from the airport at Atarot, north of the city. These connect directly with Eilat and Rosh Pinna, with further connections to Haifa and Tel Aviv. There are no flights on Saturday.

Hitch-hiking

For Tel Aviv, stand on Weizmann Blvd down past Yermeyahu St and queue up behind the usual IDF pla[toon] with pointed fingers.

For Jericho and the Dead Sea, it's hardly worth the time and effort involved. You really need to take an Arab bus from East Jerusalem to get past the Mount of Olives and tooting taxi drivers. Get off along the Jericho Rd near Bethany or stay on the bus until you are on the fast stretch of road where the main bulk of Jewish traffic joins from the New City.

For Eilat, aim for Bethlehem, Hebron and Beersheba; stand on Hebron Rd by the railway station.

GETTING AROUND

Airport Transport Buses, sheruts and 'special' taxis run from Ben Gurion Airport. The trip takes about 45 minutes and costs about US$3 by bus (to the Central Bus Station) and US$8 by sherut to your hotel.

Local Transport Egged buses are the cheapest public transport, unless three or more people take a taxi. These are the main Jerusalem routes and destinations:

Bet HaKerem	6, 16, 17
Damascus Gate	27
Dung Gate	1, 38
East Jerusalem	23, 27
En Kerem	17
German Colony	4, 14, 18, 24
Israel Museum	9, 17, 24
Jaffa Gate	3, 13, 19, 20, 30, 80
King George V St	7, 8, 9, 10, 14, 31
Knesset	9, 24, 28
Mea Shearim	1, 4, 9, 27, 35, 39
Mount Scopus	9, 23, 26, 28
Mount Zion	1, 38
Railway Station	5, 7, 8, 21, 30
Yad Vashem	13, 17, 18, 20, 23, 24, 27, 39, 40
Zion Square	4, 18, 22

At the central bus station, look above the main exit to see a display of all the destinations, routes and the location of the relevant bus stops.

AROUND JERUSALEM
Avshalom Stalagmite & Stalactite Cave

The stunning Avshalom, or Absalom's, cave is some 20 km west of Jerusalem along the road from En Kerem. The predominance of limestone in the region has caused these geological formations, which are floodlit for effect and a popular attraction. The pleasant scenery en route from Jerusalem is almost worth an excursion itself.

There is only one bus to the cave: Egged No 913 leaves Jerusalem central bus station Sunday to Friday at 9.30 am, returning at noon. Egged Tours offer two half-day guided tours to the cave, each for around US$18.

Shoresh Junction

West of this junction on the Jerusalem-Tel

Jerusalem – Mt Zion covered with snow

Aviv highway, the road descends into a gorge. On both sides you can see the rusted remains of vehicles that were part of the Jewish supply convoys attacked by the Arabs during the 1948 siege of Jerusalem. Some have been daubed with red paint and inscriptions, and they form a memorial to the Jews who were killed here.

Abu Gosh

This peaceful and picturesque Arab village 13 km from Jerusalem off the main highway to Tel Aviv is significant because it is the site of Biblical Kiriath-Jearim (Town of Forests) where the Ark of the Covenant was located for 20 years until David moved it to Jerusalem (I Chronicles 13:5-8). The village is known from the time Joshua conquered it. Sheikh Abu Gosh once charged a toll on the caravans of pilgrims passing through on the way to Jerusalem. Before the new highway by-passed the village it was a popular beauty spot for Israelis, but now it sees far fewer visitors.

Two interesting churches can be seen here. Notre Dame de l'Arche (Our Lady of the Ark of the Covenant) was built in 1924 and is a local landmark, with its statue of St Mary carrying the baby Jesus. It belongs to the French Sisters of St Joseph of the Apparition, and they believe that it stands on the site of Abinadab's house where the Ark was kept (I Samuel 7:1).

Ring the bell at the door of the adjacent building if no-one is about and the church is closed. The church is built on the same site as a larger Byzantine church, and you can see its mosaic floor inside and out. Reach the church from the top of the hill overlooking the village and facing Jerusalem. Turn right coming out of the Caravan Restaurant and up the hill. Open daily 8 to 11.30 am and 3.30 to 6 pm, admission free.

The Crusader Church & Monastery is one of the country's best preserved and most attractive Crusader remains. It was built about 1142 and destroyed in 1187.

Used for many centuries as an animal shelter, it was acquired in 1859 by the French Government, who placed it under the guardianship of the French Benedictine Fathers. Since 1956 it has belonged to the Lazarist Fathers. In the subterranean section of the building is a small spring. It is believed that the monastery stands on the remains of a Roman castle. A stone from it is displayed in the church and bears an inscription of the 10th Legion, a renowned Roman unit stationed in Jerusalem in the 1st century.

This is the monastery where you can apply to stay in the small hostel (separate accommodation for six men and two women) and experience first hand the monastic life-style. There are eight monks and nuns here. Telephone 342798 to be a monk, 343622 to be a nun, or come here to enquire. The complex is next door to the mosque, so look for the minaret in the valley. The sign outside reads: 'Eglise de Croisse – Crusaders' Church'. Ring the bell to enter. Open Monday to Wednesday, Friday and Saturday 8.30 to 11am and 2.30 to 5.30 pm, closed Sunday and Thursday; admission is free, donations requested.

Place to Eat The *Caravan Restaurant* is halfway between the two churches/monasteries and next to a bus stop. You can eat well and cheaply on hummus or stuffed vine leaves or spend more on meat and dessert whilst enjoying the view across the village towards Jerusalem.

Getting There & Away Abu Gosh is most conveniently reached from Jerusalem with Egged bus No 85 or 86 which leaves every two hours, sometimes more frequently, from the central bus station.

Latrun

About halfway between Jerusalem and Tel Aviv lies Latrun, with its popular wine-producing monastery with views of many biblical sites: Emmaus, Ayalon, Bethoron, Gezer, Modin, Lydda and Sorec. Also nearby is Canada Park, one of the results of the tree-planting programme initiated by the Jewish National Fund. Latrun means 'Home of the Good Thief' – it is believed to have been the home of one of the thieves crucified with Jesus.

A modern highway cuts through the area, and to the west (the left hand side heading towards Tel Aviv) is the attractive Latrun Monastery, and to the east (the right hand side) is Canada Park and the ruins of the Emmaus church.

In the 1948 War of Independence, the Arabs closed the road here, thus cutting off supplies to Jerusalem. It was not until the Six-Day War that the Israelis took Latrun.

Going further back in time, the area has seen its fair share of conflict. Greeks and Romans, Arabs and Crusaders and the British and the Ottoman Turks have all passed through en route to the Holy City.

Latrun Monastery Founded in 1890 by the French Trappist Order of monks as a contemplative monastery, it is now widely renowned for its wine, as well as its lovely location, architecture and gardens.

The winemaking started in 1899. The monks reclaimed and cultivated the land and planted olive groves, grain fields and vegetable gardens as well as the vineyards. In the rocky areas pine trees and cypresses were chosen. In WW I the monks were expelled by the Turks, but they were able to return and in 1926 the present monastery was constructed.

Visitors are welcome to enjoy the gardens, the architecture and to buy the wine, spirits, vermouths and the olive oil produced here. The shop by the gate is open Monday to Saturday 8.30 to 11.30 am and 2.30 to 4.30 pm, closed Sunday.

Emmaus Church Above ruins rises the monastery formerly belonging to the Beit-Haram Brothers, but now functioning as the French Prehistorical Research Centre. The church was built to commemorate the Christian tradition that this is where Jesus appeared to two of his disciples after his resurrection (Mark 16:12-13, Luke 24:13-31).

Canada Park One of the country's many beautifully forested areas, you can wander around and picnic just on the edge of the occupied West Bank. You can find a well-preserved Roman bath near the church, dating from around 640. Various water holes, conduits and the remains of an amphitheatre are also to be found in the park. A sign overlooking the Ayalon Valley warns of the security situation in 'Judea and Samaria'.

Getting There & Away Latrun can be reached most easily by bus from Jerusalem. Egged bus Nos 433 or 403 pass by every 30 minutes. From Tel Aviv only one bus (in the morning) passes through, although you can change at Ramla where there are frequent connections. Remind the driver that you want Latrun before he flies past.

Tel Aviv & the South Coast

Tel Aviv - Jaffa

TEL AVIV (Population 323,400)
Tel Aviv, which now includes the old Arab town of Jaffa within its municipal boundaries, is Israel's largest metropolis and its financial and business centre. Tel Aviv is often a disappointment at first glance, particularly if your point of entry is the central bus station with its crumbling buildings, filth, strange characters and general air of confusion. Initial impressions often convince people that the city is ugly, tasteless, noisy and chaotic. However, given a little time, some patience and a knowledge of where to go, Tel Aviv has much to offer the traveller.

Unfortunately, the inhabitants of Tel Aviv have a habit of comparing their city to New York. Apart from being self-defeating, this tends to mask the uniqueness of Tel Aviv's own attributes: its collection of cafés, bars and restaurants, attracting cliques of colourful and interesting regulars; the diverse backgrounds of its inhabitants, with so many countries represented in a population of less than a third of a million; and the general scope available for having a good time. All in all, Tel Aviv's brief history makes its current size and capabilities nothing short of remarkable. Additional attractions include the vast beaches, the markets, parks and museums. Make a point of reading Robert Rosenberg's 'Tel Aviv, Tel Aviv' column in the *Jerusalem Post* for accurate and amusing insights.

Tel Aviv is the cultural and entertainment capital of Israel as well as its business centre. With the exception of the *Jerusalem Post*, all the newspapers are published here, as are most books. Tel Aviv is also the base for industry and the political parties.

Despite being a 30-minute drive from Jerusalem, many residents of Tel Aviv rarely visit the Holy City. Mostly non-religious, they see Jerusalem as boring, inconveniently situated and basically not worth a visit. They prefer their modern city's hedonistic lifestyle without the shackles of centuries-old traditions that dominate the capital. In Tel Aviv there is a recognised black market area, red light district, transvestites and a constant parade of would-be beautiful people posing furiously as they check out the competition on the beach, on the pavements and in the popular cafés and bars. It's hardly surprising, therefore, that the two cities are so separate.

History

The first modern Jewish city, Tel Aviv's history is brief but full of incident and rapid development, a reflection of the dynamism of activist Zionism. Compared to Jerusalem and its lengthy history of foreign dynasties and religions, Tel Aviv is a modern short story of Jewish drive and ambition coupled with town planning blunders.

It first developed as a long narrow strip along the coast stretching north of Old Jaffa to the Yarkon River. Conditions in Jaffa in the late 19th century were cramped and unsanitary, and, with the city walls destroyed by the Turks, many inhabitants started to move north.

The minority Jewish community established two small districts: Newe Tzedek (1886) and Newe Shalom (1890). In 1906 with assistance from the Jewish National Fund, the Ahuzat Bayit group purchased 12 hectares to build a Jewish quarter north of Newe Tzedek. These 60 families (about 250 people) were led by Meir Dizengoff who foresaw a town of 25,000.

With the English garden city in mind,

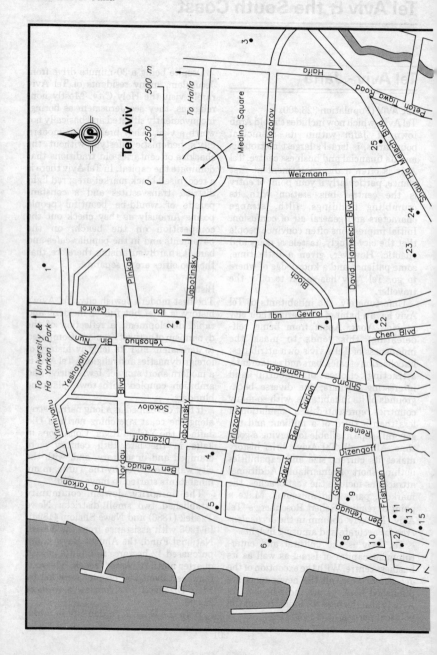

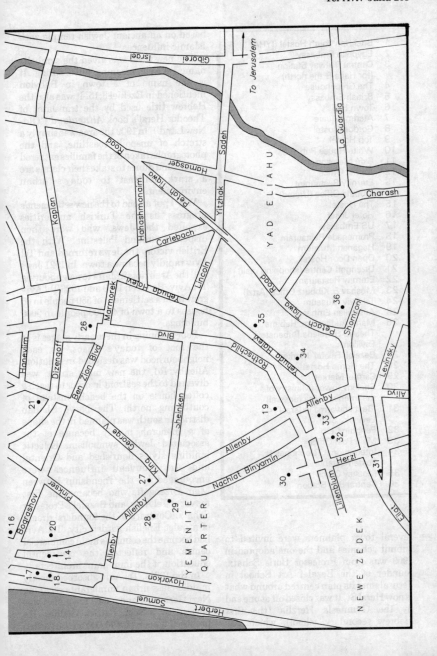

1	Bnei Dan Youth Hostel (IYHA)
2	Egyptian Embassy
3	Central Railway Station (for Haifa & the north)
4	The Greenhouse
5	British Embassy
6	Town Hall
7	Atarim Square
8	Gordon Hostel
9	Top Hostel
10	White House Pub
11	Café Mersand
12	Tourist Office
13	Eternity Restaurant
14	Kibbutz Office (United)
15	The Hostel
16	Hotel Josef
17	US Embassy
18	Promenade Restaurant
19	Haganah Museum
20	Open Door Hostel
21	Dizengoff Centre (shopping mall)
22	Eternity Restaurant
23	Moshav & Kibbutz Office (Artzi)
24	Tel Aviv Museum
25	Australian Embassy
26	Mann Auditorium, Habima Theatre & Helena Rubenstein Pavilion
27	Bezalel 'Felafel' Market
28	The Home Hostel
29	Carmel Market
30	Shalom Tower (Ministry of the Interior – visa renewal)
31	'Best shwarma in Israel', 41 Levinsky St
32	Penguin Club
33	Main Post Office
34	International Telephones & Poste Restante
35	Moshav Office
36	Central Bus Station

based on an ancient Jewish temple with Islamic influences.

The new town was given the symbolic name Tel Aviv, meaning 'hill of spring'. It is the name of a town in Babylon mentioned in Ezekiel 3:15. It was also the Hebrew title used by the translator of Theodor Herzl's book *Altneuland* ('Old-New Land'). In 1909 the area was simply a stretch of unspoilt coastline, and the photographs taken of the families gathered on the sand dunes to stake their claims are a stark contrast to today's urban environment.

WW I put an end to the new settlement's progress as the Turkish authorities expelled the Jews, who were then dispersed around Palestine. With the British victory the Jews returned and Tel Aviv rapidly became a town. In 1921 Jews fled the Arab riots in Jaffa to neighbouring Tel Aviv. Between 1909 and 1926 Tel Aviv grew from a settlement of 550 people in 65 houses to a town of 40,000 people in 3000 buildings.

Poor planning in these early stages is at the root of today's chaos, as each neighbourhood was designed in isolation. Allenby Rd, the new main street, was diverted to the seafront in order to reach a coffee house on the beach, instead of continuing north. The Newe Shanan district in south was planned in the shape of a menorah merely because of the associated Jewish symbolism. Eclectic building styles flourished and Oriental and Art Nouveau influences were encouraged by the friendship between Meir Dizengoff, who became the first mayor of Tel Aviv, and Bezalel's Professor Schatz. Contrary to the founders' dream of a quiet English garden city, Tel Aviv had become the country's main commercial centre and reflected the continental education of the immigrant architects.

In the 1930s, Tel Aviv absorbed mostly middle-class urban immigrants escaping Nazi Germany, and a new town plan was devised by a Scot, Patrick Geddes. He proposed housing for 70,000 on the garden

several town planners were invited to submit schemes and the one adopted in 1909 was from Professor Boris Schatz, founder of the Bezalel Art School in Jerusalem. His plan centred around what is now Herzl St. It was closed off at one end by the Gymnasia Herzlia (the first Hebrew secondary school), which was city model with little commercial activity. Streets were to run east-west towards the sea and Ben Yehuda and Dizengoff, the two main streets, were to run north. Lanes, leading to public areas, divided large apartment blocks. When put into practice, these plans were altered: spaces between the buildings and the public areas were decreased and commercial activity was allowed.

The 1936 Arab riots in Jaffa were a catalyst for the building of a port in Tel Aviv to reduce Jewish dependency on Jaffa's port. This was a major step in Tel Aviv's commercial development. Widespread use of the International style of building made the city a centre of modern architecture in the 1930s. The designs of Bauhaus, Le Corbusier and Mendelsohn were dominant at this time and their influence is still evident today.

Tel Aviv was bombed by Italian and Vichy planes during WW II but largely escaped serious damage. It played host to about two million Allied troops though, and become a centre of the Zionist resistance against the British anti-immigration policies. In 1948 as the British pulled out, Jewish forces attacked Jaffa and after some bloody fighting most of the Arab population fled.

The early years of Israel's independence saw Tel Aviv struggling in an economic crisis with the population swelling from 195,000 in 1946 to 345,000 in 1951. The city expanded east towards the Ayalon River and north across the Yarkon River in the 1950s. Large-scale public building housed the mass influx of new immigrants, but overcrowding was still common. Yad Eliyahu and HaTiqwa are examples of these building policies. Ramat Aviv, north of the Yarkon River, however, was planned with open space and large green areas.

Most of the city's public buildings were constructed in the 1960s during the economic boom and an American influence resulted in the profusion of tall buildings uncommon in this Mediterranean setting.

With the drift towards the suburbs, the population of Tel Aviv dropped from 400,000 to 329,000 during the '60s.

The economic crisis of the early 1970s halted public investment in building and the private sector took over, financing a spate of commercial and office buildings, shopping centres and apartment towers. The buildings of the 1980s are very different again, although the overall effect of dullness has continued. After its boundaries merged with the surrounding towns in the 1960s, Tel Aviv basically stopped expanding.

The city is now the centre of a metropolis – people commute to Tel Aviv from the suburbs and surrounding towns for work and entertainment.

Orientation

Tel Aviv-Jaffa is a large urban sprawl of connecting suburbs, such as Ramat Gan, Bnei Brak, Petah Tiqwa, Bat Yam and Holon, set on a coastal plain. Most of your time will be spent in Tel Aviv's six km long and one km wide central city area based on four main streets. These mostly run parallel to the sea. From the seafront east they are: HaYarkon, Ben Yehuda, Dizengoff and Ibn Gevirol Sts. These streets run virtually the entire length of the central city area, from the northern tip bordered by the Yarkon River, with HaYarkon and Ben Yehuda extending down as far as Allenby Rd and the Yemenite Quarter; Dizengoff leading east from Dizengoff Square at a virtual right-angle to join Ibn Gevirol, which in turn continues south to intersect with Petah Tiqwa and Eilat Sts. Allenby Rd is a fifth major street which runs in from the seafront, intersecting with Ben Yehuda St and later King George St on its way towards the central bus station area, but stopping before it gets there.

Street numbers run from the seafront to the east, and from south to north. They are posted at most street corners, either on signs or on the sides of buildings.

Most of the major facilities and

attractions, including hotels and hostels in all price ranges, can be found within the central city area. Not far away, the Tel Aviv University campus, the Diaspora and Ha'Aretz Museums and HaYarkon Park are to the north, the central railway station is to the east, and to the south are the railway station for Jerusalem, the Newe Tzedek neighbourhood and Jaffa. The Dan bus system provides cheap connections between all of these areas, and it is possible to walk to many of the places of interest.

Information

Tourist Information The IGTO (tel 223266/7) at 7 Mendele St, between HaYarkon and Ben Yehuda Sts, is open Sunday to Thursday 8.30 am to 5 pm, Friday 8.30 am to 2 pm, closed Saturday.

Post Offices & International Telephones The main post office is at 132 Allenby Rd, on the corner of Yehuda HaLevi St, and is open Sunday to Thursday 7 am to 8 pm, Friday 7 am to 2 pm, closed Saturday. The poste restante is two blocks east at 7 Mikve Yisrael St – bear right as you cross Allenby St to Yehuda HaLevi St. This is also the international telephone office, and is open Sunday to Thursday 8 am to 6 pm, Friday 8 am to 2 pm, closed Saturday.

Banks & Moneychangers Due to the current stability of the sheqel, Tel Aviv's black market area is a lot quieter than it used to be. Go to the corner of Allenby and Yehuda HaLevi Sts, outside the main post office, to see the sleazy-looking characters whispering illegal transactions out of the sides of their mouths. Most of their tourist business is done by buying goods, rather than moneychanging. Selling to them is unlikely to get you a fair price, but changing money will save you the banks' charges. However, unlike Jerusalem's legal Arab moneychangers, these guys do not accept travellers' cheques – they want cash only. The other

hangouts for the touts are Lilienblum St and between the Ramada Hotel and Atarim Square on the seafront.

Banks are most easily found on Allenby, Ben Yehuda and Dizengoff and normally open Sunday to Tuesday and Thursday, 8.30 am to 12.30 pm and 4 to 5.30 pm, Wednesday and Friday 8.30 am to 12 noon, closed Saturday.

The American Express office (tel 294654) is at Meditrad Ltd, 16 Ben Yehuda St. It's open Sunday to Tuesday and Thursday 8.30 am to 1 pm and 3.30 to 6 pm, Wednesday and Friday 8.30 to 1 pm, closed Saturday.

Police Dial 100. The central police station and the lost and found office is on the corner of Yehuda HaLevi St, three blocks east from Allenby on the right. From the central bus station, cross Petah Tiqwa Rd, head north, take the first left and it's on the left after two blocks.

Airlines For charter flight queries, contact a travel agent.

Aerolineas Argentinas
    5 Shalom Aleichem St (tel 650505)
Air Canada
    7 Moshev Ben Ezra St (tel 247976)
Air France
    32 Ben Yehuda St (tel 292333)
Air Sinai
    114 HaYarkon St (tel 246038)
Alitalia
    98 Dizengoff St (tel 244141)
American Airlines
    32 Ben Yehuda St (tel 203335)
Arkia
    Dov Airport (tel 426262)
    11 Frishman St (tel 233285)
Austrian Airlines
    17 Ben Yehuda St (tel 653535)
British Airways
    59 Ben Yehuda St (tel 229251)
Canadian Pacific
    1 Ben Yehuda St (tel 652163)
Capitol Air
    11 Frishman St (tel 236006)
Cathay Pacific
    3 Mapu St (tel 249217)

Delta Airlines
    32 Ben Yehuda St (tel 290972)
Eastern Airlines
    3 Mapu St (tel 249216)
El Al
    32 Ben Yehuda St (tel 641222)
Iberian Airlines
    14 Ben Yehuda St (tel 290976/7)
Iceland Air
    119 Rothschild Blvd (tel 201481)
KLM
    35 Ben Yehuda St (tel 652520)
Lufthansa
    75 HaYarkon St (tel 653041)
Luxair
    119 Rothschild Blvd (tel 201481)
Olympic
    13 Idelson St (tel 294381)
Pan Am
    9 Frishman St (tel 247272)
Qantas
    1 Ben Yehuda St (tel 652163)
Republic Air
    29 Allenby St (tel 200636)
SAA
    5 Shalom Aleichem St (tel 651844)
Sabena
    72 HaYarkon St (tel 654411)
SAS
    32 Ben Yehuda St (tel 292233)
Swissair
    41 Ben Yehuda St (tel 243350)
Tower Air
    78 HaYarkon St (tel 659421)
Turkish Air
    5 Shalom Aleichem St (tel 652333)
TWA
    74-76 HaYarkon St (tel 651212)
United Airlines
    117 Ben Yehuda St (tel 247224)
Varig
    5 Shalom Aleichem St (tel 650567)

Embassies & Consulates The Egyptian
Consulate (tel 224152; visa information
464151) is at 54 Basel St, just off Ibn
Gevirol St. It's open Sunday to Thursday
9 to 11 am for visa applications, closed
Friday and Saturday. Return between
noon and 1 pm the same day for collection.
At 11 am they close regardless of any
queue of applicants, so it's best to arrive as
early as possible just in case.

Tourist visas, valid for one month, cost

about US$25 but must be paid for in
Israeli currency. Nationals of Cyprus,
Finland, Norway, Sweden, USA, USSR,
West Germany and Yugoslavia only pay
about US$15. One photo is required.

An easy way to get there is to take Dan
bus No 5 and get off by the police station
on Dizengoff St. Walk east along Basel St,
the embassy is near the end on the
right.

Unless stated otherwise, all of the
following embassies and consulates in Tel
Aviv are closed on Saturday and Sunday.
Several of them maintain separate offices
for passport and/or visa enquiries.

Argentina
    112 HaYarkon St, open Monday to
    Thursday 8 am to 12 noon, Friday 8 to 11 am
    (tel 297949)
Australia
    37 King Shaul Blvd, open Monday to Friday
    8 to 11 am (tel 250451)
Austria
    11 Herman HaKohen St (off Frishman St
    between Reines and Shlomo Hamelekh
    Sts), open Monday to Friday 9 am to
    12 noon (tel 246186)
Belgium
    266 HaYarkon St, ring for opening hours (tel
    454164)
Canada
    220 HaYarkon St, open for general enquiries
    Monday to Thursday 8 am to 4 pm, Friday
    8 am to 1 pm (tel 228122)
Denmark
    23 Bnei Moshe St, open Monday to
    Thursday 8 am to 2 pm, Friday 8 am to 1 pm
    (tel 440405)
Finland
    2 Ibn Gevirol St open Monday to Friday 10
    am to 12 noon (tel 250527)
France
    Embassy, 7 Habbakuk St, open Monday to
    Friday 8 to 11.30 am (tel 454224)
Great Britain
    Embassy, 292 HaYarkon St, open Monday
    to Friday 8 am to 2 pm (tel 249171)
Greece
    35 King Shaul Blvd, open Monday to Friday
    10 am to 12 noon (tel 259704). Diplomatic
    Representatives only – the consulate is in
    Jerusalem

Italy
    Asia House, 4 Weizmann St, open Monday,
    Wednesday and Friday only, 9 am to
    12 noon (tel 264223)
Japan
    Asia House, 4 Weizmann St, open Monday
    to Thursday 9 am to 4 pm, Friday 9 am to
    3pm (tel 257292)
Netherlands
    Asia House, 4 Weizmann St, open Monday
    to Thursday 9 am to 12.30 pm, Friday 9 am
    to 12 noon (tel 257377)
South Africa
    2 Kaplan St, open Monday, Tuesday,
    Thursday 9 to 11.30 am, Wednesday 9 to
    11 am and 2 to 3 pm, Friday 9 to 11 am (tel
    256147)
Spain
    Embassy in Jerusalem, no representative in
    Tel Aviv
Sweden
    Asia House, 4 Weizmann St, open Monday
    to Friday 10 am to 12.30 pm (tel 258111)
Switzerland
    228 HaYarkon St, open Monday to Friday 9
    to 11 am (tel 546445)
USA
    61 HaYarkon St, open Monday to Friday
    8 am to 4 pm (tel 654338)

Student Travel ISSTA (tel 247164) is at 109
Ben Yehuda, corner Ben-Gurion Blvd and
is open May to September, Sunday to
Tuesday and Thursday 8.30 am to 6 pm,
Wednesday and Friday 8.30 am to 1 pm.
October to April, Sunday to Tuesday and
Thursday 9 am to 1 pm and 3 to 6 pm,
Wednesday and Friday 9 am to 1 pm.
Closed Saturday.

Bookshops Steimatzsky's at 103 Allenby
Rd is Israel's largest bookshop. There is
another branch on Dizengoff between
Frishman and Gordon Sts. Quality
Books, 45 Ben Yehuda St has second-
hand paperbacks. Pollack's, 36 King
George St, buys and sells second-hand
books.

Libraries The British Council Library (tel
214211) is at 140 HaYarkon St, opposite
the Ramada Hotel. It has a reading room
with English newspapers and magazines

and is open to all, Monday to Thursday 9 am
to 1 pm and 4 to 7 pm, Friday 9 am to 1 pm,
closed Saturday and Sunday. The
reference library upstairs is open Monday,
Tuesday and Thursday 10 am to 1 pm and
4 to 7 pm, Friday 10 am to 1 pm, closed
Sunday, Wednesday and Saturday. The
Australian Embassy has a library which
includes books on the subject of Israel,
and newspapers and magazines from
home. Open Monday to Thursday 8 am to
4 pm, closed Friday to Sunday. The
central public library is on King Shaul
Blvd adjacent to the Tel Aviv Museum.

Camera Repairs Atarim-Video & Camera
Repairs (tel 280532), Atarim Square, shop
No 352; Dorel (tel 651254), 44 Nahalat
Binyamin St; Bendak Zui (tel 657495), 56
HaYarkon St; Camera (tel 650376), 36
Allenby Rd; Hadar (tel 615343), 112
Allenby Rd; Pe'er Laboratories (tel
293689), 18 Ben Yehuda St.

Laundromats There are laundromats at 51
Ben Yehuda St, 45 Bograshov St, and 13
Allenby St. Open Sunday, Monday,
Wednesday, Thursday 8 am to 7 pm,
Tuesday and Friday 8 am to 1 pm, closed
Saturday.

Camping Equipment Lametayel (tel 286894),
Dizengoff Centre. Open Sunday to
Thursday 9.30 am to 7 pm, Friday 9.30 am
to 1 pm, closed Saturday.

Harry Openheimer Diamond Museum
The most recent addition to the country's
range of popular museums, the Harry
Openheimer Diamond Museum (tel
214219) is in the Diamond Exchange
complex, at 1 Jabotinsky St, north-west of
the city in the suburb of Ramat Gan. The
exhibits are thoughtfully presented and
include working models, a film and a
succession of lavish exhibits on loan.
Open Sunday to Thursday 10 am to 4 pm,
closed Friday and Saturday; admission is
around US$2.50, students US$1.75. Take
Dan bus No 51, 68 or 69 from the Petah

Tiqwa Rd stop across from the central bus station and HaNegev St.

Tel Aviv University

North of the Yarkon River, in Ramat Aviv, the university campus features some striking modern architecture and its departments cover the widest spectrum of all the country's universities, including fine arts, humanities, history, Jewish studies, law, medicine, the sciences, engineering, business and film-making.

Diaspora Museum

Beit Hatfusot (tel 425161), gives an interesting account of the diversity of Jewish life and culture in exile. Traditions, rituals and holidays among different Jewish communities are presented in an elaborate and innovative way, using techniques such as film, murals, slides, models, a computer and the clever chronosphere. The museum is unusual in that it is more concerned with reconstructing a way of life than with displaying treasures or artefacts from the past. There is a lot to see. It's open Sunday to Tuesday and Thursday 10 am to 5 pm, Wednesday 10 am to 7 pm, closed Friday and Saturday; admission is US$3, students US$1.50. The chronosphere multi-screen audio-visual display costs a little more. Take Dan bus No 25 from Jaffa, the west side of Carmel Market, Allenby Rd between Magen David Circle and Moshavot Square, King George and Reines Sts on the corner of Frishman St (near to Dizengoff Circle), or near to the IYHA hostel; or No 27 from the central bus station. Get off at the university, either Matatia Gate No 2 or Frenkel Gate No 7.

Ha'aretz Museum

About one km south west of the university campus (follow Ha'Universita St), this impressive complex consists of 11 small museums constructed around an archaeological site, Tel Qasile. The complex is open Sunday, Monday, and Wednesday to Friday 9 am to 1 pm, Tuesday 9 am to 1 pm and 4 to 7 pm, and Saturday 10 am to 1 pm. Admission is US$2, students US$1.35. The museums include:

Tel Qasile Excavations & Pavilion This mound was probably first settled by the Philistines in the 12th century BC. Three of their temples have been unearthed, as well as some of their town. There are also a few Crusader remains to be seen. In the pavilion is a collection of artefacts found at the site.

Glass Museum This museum houses one of the world's finest and most valuable glass collections, which traces the history of glassmaking.

Kadman Numismatic Museum Housing a collection of ancient coins and also some displays of some pre-coinage currencies.

Ceramics Museum Deals with the history of pottery, its development over the centuries and its religious significance. The collection includes Gaza and Akko styles of Ilbriq pottery.

Nechustan Pavilion Features some of the finds from excavations of the ancient copper mines at Timna – the legendary King Solomon's Mines.

Man & His Work Pavilion A collection of ancient tools.

Folklore Pavilion Jewish religious arts, ethnic costumes, ceremonial objects and a Florentine synagogue's benches, pulpit and ark.

Alphabet Museum The most recent addition, showing the history of the development of alphabets and writing.

Lasky Planetarium In the prominent domed building.

HaYarkon Park & River

The Yarkon River divides the coastal plain into the Sharon Plain to the north and the Shephela, the lowland plain to the south. In biblical times the river marked the border between the tribes of Ephraim and Dan. In the 1950s, water from here was siphoned off to irrigate the Negev Desert. The Reading Power Station's chimney on the western side of the river is a useful landmark.

The park's green expanse offers an alternative to the traffic noise and the beach parade, but the ugly electric pylons stop it from becoming too appealing. This is the site for outdoor concerts, either in the Wohl Amphitheatre or, for bigger events, on the larger grass expanse.

It is possible to take a boat trip along the river or hire your own rowing boat, although the water is dirty and the surroundings unspectacular.

Beaches

One of Tel Aviv's main attractions is its lengthy stretch of white sand to which thousands of Israelis flock in good weather, with incredible scenes of over-crowding on Shabbat. The beaches are within easy walking distance of most accommodation, eating places and shops. Bear in mind, however, that drownings are a tragically regular occurrence due to a combination of the strong undertow and reckless swimmers over-estimating their capabilities. Theft is a more widespread problem so try not to take any valuables with you when you go to the beach. The most crowded area is between the Hilton in the north and Opera Square to the south where Allenby Rd starts.

When the sun is out (and it usually is) the beaches are a sort of Israeli Copacabana, with all the local poseurs on parade. In the mornings, before the sun rises over the north of the city, a hardy group of old-timers congregate to swim and exercise; later in the day the beaches are dotted with people playing *matkot* (Israeli beach tennis). As the evening approaches, fishing takes over, especially to the north of the marina and to the south of the West Beach.

Religious Beach North of the Hilton Beach and before the old harbour is a stretch of beach reserved for religious bathers who want to be able to swim in a more modest style. On Sunday, Tuesday and Thursday only women are permitted to use the area and it is a good place for any woman, Jewish or not, to enjoy a swim or to sunbathe without the constant attention of the amorous Israeli male.

Atarim Square Also known as Namir Square, this ugly concrete jungle houses a complex of shops, offices, hotels, cafés, restaurants, bars, a cinema, a nightclub and a car park. Straddling HaYarkon St, it links Ben-Gurion Blvd with the beach. The landmarks are, from north to south, the Carlton, Marina, Plaza and Diplomat hotels.

London Square This garden between HaYarkon St and Herbert Samuel Blvd opposite Bograshov St was built in 1940 and was dedicated to the citizens of London in recognition of their courage during the blitz attacks of the Battle of Britain.

West Beach & Charles Clore Park South of the failed dolphinarium complex, this beach is a popular site for Israeli families to camp and enjoy a barbecue. The café/restaurant on the beach is a popular late-night spot, often with enthusiastic dancing in the open air.

HaYarkon St

Running the length of the downtown beaches and named after the river, this street houses Tel Aviv's luxury hotels and several embassies. As you head south the street becomes decidedly shabby, eventually entering the city's red light district, which has definitely seen better days. Dominating the southern end of HaYarkon St, where Allenby Rd starts, is Opera Square and the Israel Opera building, the home of the Israeli parliament before it was moved to Jerusalem.

The bizarre-looking apartment building at 181 HaYarkon, across from the beach north of Atarim Square, is the subject of much critical comment, with its western facade festooned with sculptured designs.

Check out the other side to see the tree mural incorporating the design of the building.

Independence Park (Gan HaAtzmaut), between the Hilton and Carlton hotels is a gay hangout at night.

Ben Yehuda St

Named after the man credited with the revival of the Hebrew language, this street was populated mainly by German Jews, who were among the most stubborn opponents of his ideas for a modern Hebrew. Many of the children of these people now run the local shops while the older generation can be seen sitting and reminiscing outside the cafés here and on Dizengoff St. When they first arrived, HaYarkon was just a path for the Arabs' camels, and Dizengoff had not been built.

Ben Gurion's House

At 17 Ben Gurion Blvd, on the seafront between Ben Yehuda St and Atarim Square, is the former house of Israel's first Prime Minister, David Ben Gurion and his wife, Paula. Maintained more or less as it was when they lived here, the small rooms are simply furnished and contain part of Ben Gurion's library of some 20,000 books as well as his correspondence with political leaders. The house (tel 221010) is open Sunday to Thursday 8 am to 2 pm, Monday and Thursday 5 to 7 pm, Friday 8 am to 1 pm, Saturday 11 am to 2 pm; admission is free. It is worth stopping on your way past one day, if only to practise your French and read Ben Gurion's letter to Charles de Gaulle, written in 1964, predicting that in 10 to 15 years Russia would be a democratic country.

Old Cemetery

On Trumpeldor St, east of Ben Yehuda, this is where many victims of the 1921 and 1929 riots lie buried, as well as the Zionist leaders Max Nordau, Ahad Ha-Am, Haim Arlosoroff, Shemaryahu Levin, the poets H N Bialik and S Tchernichovsky, and the first mayor of Tel Aviv, Meir Dizengoff.

Dizengoff St

Named after the city's first mayor (1910-37), this is Tel Aviv's prime street for people-watching and window shopping. On Shabbat and Jewish festivals, in particular Purim, the street is closed to traffic and is used as a children's playground and an extra seating area for the local cafés.

Along the length of Dizengoff St are some of the country's top cultural centres, such as the Mann Auditorium and the Habima and Cameri theatres.

Dizengoff Centre This multi-level shopping centre crosses the street, both above and below ground level, and has slowly developed into one of Israel's prime retailing areas. It houses cafés, two cinemas and several interesting shops.

Dizengoff Square & Fountain Officially named Tzina Square after the first mayor's wife, this is the raised circular plaza dominated by a modern water fountain. It was designed by Ya'acov Agam, a leading Israeli artist whose most prominent local work prior to this was the paint job on the Dan Hotel. Called 'Fire and Water', a flame periodically shoots up above the fountain while the coloured structure spins round with jets of water playing to the sound of recorded music. I think it looks awful, but it certainly attracts a lot of attention. The area immediately north of here is Dizengoff's most crowded, particularly on Saturday evenings after Shabbat. At the northern end of the street is a more upmarket area of shops, cafés and restaurants covering HaYarkon, Ben Yehuda and Yeshayahu Sts as well, known collectively as 'Little Tel Aviv'.

Tel Aviv Museum

Part of an attractive modern development

9:30   6957361

including the Law Courts and the municipal central library, the Tel Aviv Museum (tel 257361) is at 27 King Shaul Blvd. It's a large museum and it takes a few hours to see it all. Displays include paintings by Impressionists such as Renoir, Pissaro, Monet and Duffy, and Post-Impressionists such as Picasso, Kokoschka, Roualt and Matisse. Films and special exhibits are often featured, so call by or check the *Jerusalem Post* and the tourist office for the current schedule. Open Sunday to Thursday 10 am to 2 pm and 5 to 9 pm, Saturday 11 am to 2 pm; closed Friday. The admission price (US$2, students US$1.55) includes access to the Helena Rubenstein Pavilion. Take Dan bus No 18 from Trumpeldor, Ben Yehuda to Allenby; No 28 or 70 from the central bus station; No 32 from Allenby Rd, Ben Yehuda and Bograshov Sts.

Jabotinsky Institute

A historical research organisation, featuring a museum (tel 287320) which presents the history and activities of the National Resistance Movement, founded and led by Ze'ev Jabotinsky. The several departments show his political, literary and journalistic activities, and also the creation of the Jewish Legion in WW I, the para-military force of the Revisionist Movement and their illegal immigration programme. The museum is at 38 King George St on the 1st floor of the Institute. As no signs are in English it can be difficult to find. Open Sunday, Tuesday and Thursday 10 am to 6 pm, Monday and Wednesday 10 am to 1 pm and 6 to 8 pm, Friday 10 am to 1 pm, closed Saturday; admission is free.

Gan Me'ir

Sandwiched between King George and Tchernichovsky Sts, this lovely small shaded park offers a pleasant respite from the heat and noise. Designed by Abraham Karavan in the mid-1930s and also named after the first mayor, it is now threatened by plans for an underground car park,

deemed necessary to cope with the needs of Golan and Globus's new cinema development.

Allenby Rd

A Tel Avivian comparison is made here with New York's Wall St and Lower East Side. Forget it. Once Tel Aviv's main fashionable artery, it is now overshadowed by Dizengoff although it still houses the city's main market places – the Boursa (stockmarket) and the Carmel Market.

Opened in 1917, the street was named in honour of the British general who captured Palestine from the Turks. At that time the immediate area was basically an expanse of sand, but it soon became the heart of the commercial and social district. The bright lights and fancy shops are now found elsewhere but the major Israeli banks still have their main offices on or around Allenby, with 'bargain basement' shops as neighbours. Beyond the southern end is the central bus station with its cheap shops and stalls.

Allenby starts on the seafront in Opera Square and curves eastward through the decaying red light district to intersect with Ben Yehuda and Pinsker Sts to form Mograbi Square.

Heading sharply south from here, Allenby takes in the biggest and oldest bookstores; often you will see books sold from carts on the pavement.

Magen David Circle This busy junction is named after the six-pointed Magen David (Star of David) and is so-named because it is the point where six streets (King George, Allenby, Ben Yehuda, Sheinken, Ha Karmel and Nahalat Binyamin) intersect. Freelance painters and decorators hang around the King George St side of the circle hoping for some work.

Great Synagogue On the corner of Allenby Rd and Ahad Ha'am St, the synagogue, built in 1926, is the domed building with stained glass windows. It is one of the few obvious signs of Jewish religion in the city.

Bialik St

With its attractive buildings, this small street running north off Allenby Rd near the corner of Ben Yehuda, is one of Tel Aviv's much-overlooked backwaters. The street is named after Haim Nachman Bialik, Israel's national poet and the man behind the renaissance in Hebrew literature.

Reuven Rubin House At No 14 (tel 658961), on the right as you head from Allenby, is the former residence of the artist Reuvin Rubin, and you can see an exhibition of his work and his private collection of photographs and furnishings. Open Sunday, Monday, Wednesday and Thursday 10 am to 2 pm, Tuesday 10 am to 1 pm and 4 to 8 pm, Saturday 11 am to 2 pm, closed Friday; admission is 70c.

Bialik House At No 22 is Bialik's former home, which has now been converted into a small museum. It contains memorabilia connected with his life and work, along with occasional temporary exhibits. It's open Sunday to Thursday 9 am to 7 pm, Friday 9 am to 1 pm. Admission is free.

Museum of the History of Tel Aviv-Jaffa At No 27, by the side of the circular fountain at the end of the street, this museum (tel 653052) has photographs, models, a film (in English) and documents relating to the city's history. It's badly presented, which is unusual for an Israeli museum. Open Sunday, Monday and Wednesday to Friday 9 am to 1 pm, Tuesday 4 to 7 pm, closed Saturday; admission is around 90c, students 75c.

Carmel Market

Tel Aviv's loud and crowded market is between Allenby Rd, on Magen David Circle, and HaYarkon St, cutting into the Yemenite Quarter. From Allenby, the main market street is Carmel St, and you need to push your way past the first few metres of clothing and footwear stalls to be totally immersed in the atmosphere. This is probably best achieved by heading for the southern end where the fruit, vegetables and, in particular, poultry are bandied about to great effect. When in form, the stallholders have an amusing sales patter, singing songs to promote their goods and often joining in with one another.

For a change of pace, each of the narrow side streets specialises in a particular range of items, one favouring dry goods, another dried fruit, nuts and spices sold from

Street salesman, Tel Aviv

sacks. As usual, good prices are to be had as the market closes, and it's at its busiest in the pre-Shabbat rush.

On the other side of Allenby is the Bezalel Market, between King George and Tchernichovsky Sts, specialising in eat-as-much-as-you-can felafel and also an extension of the cheap clothes market.

Yemenite Quarter

Basically between Allenby Rd and the sea, Kerem Hatemanim (the Yememite Quarter) is one of the oldest areas of the city. Its crumbling buildings house some of the city's best eating places, mainly in the middle price range but it's also possible to eat well here for less.

Rothschild Blvd

Named after the Jewish family of financiers in recognition of their support for the Zionist cause, the promenade of this pleasant boulevard is shaded along its entire length and is one of the city's more attractive places for a stroll. The boulevard goes from just south of Herzl St to Habima Square close to the theatre of the same name, the Mann Auditorium and the Helena Rubenstein Pavilion.

Founders' Monument Ornamented on one side with a bas-relief and inscribed on the other side with the founders' names, the monument illustrates the development of Tel Aviv in three phases:

(i) 1909-10 – Jewish workers starting to build on the sand
(ii) 1910-18 – the Gymnasia Herzlia building, Tel Aviv's first major construction flanked by the first water tower and the residence of Meir Dizengoff
(iii) Tel Aviv today – the harbour, built in 1936 and an important factor in the Jewish struggle against Arab opposition, the Habima Theatre, Bialik House and modern apartment blocks in the background.

Independence Hall On 14 May 1948, Ben Gurion declared the establishment of the State of Israel from this hall at 16 Rothschild Blvd (tel 653942), then part of the old Tel Aviv Museum and previously Meir Dizengoff's home. Open Sunday to Friday 9 am to 1 pm, closed Saturday; admission is 90c, students 75c.

Haganah/IDF Museum At 23 Rothschild Blvd this museum (tel 623624) is the former home of General Eliyahu Golomb, one of the founders of the military organisation whose history is recorded here. The Haganah became an integral part of the IDF and exhibits mainly deal with its development over the years. Open Sunday to Friday 9 am to 3 pm, closed Saturday; admission is 90c, students 75c.

Habima Square

Linking Rothschild Blvd with Dizengoff and Ibn Gevirol, this is the centre of Israel's cultural scene.

Helena Rubenstein Pavilion Around the corner from the square at 6 Tarsat Blvd (tel 287196) and part of the Tel Aviv Museum, this small museum features temporary exhibits by guest artists, both Israeli and foreign. Open Monday to Thursday 10 am to 1 pm and 5 to 7 pm, Saturday 11 am to 2 pm, closed Friday. Admission is sometimes free depending on the exhibit, but a Tel Aviv Museum ticket is good for here, too.

Habima Theatre Now Israel's national theatre (tel 283742), the original company was founded in Moscow in 1918 by Stanislavsky and in 1928 it moved to Palestine and changed its name to Habima, meaning 'the stage'. The group presented the first Hebrew translations of works by Shakespeare, Molière, Shaw and O'Neill. All performances are in Hebrew and simultaneous translation earphones are sometimes available.

Mann Auditorium With a capacity of 3000,

the Mann Auditorium (tel 295092) is the country's major concert venue and home of the Israel Philharmonic Orchestra. The complex includes a pleasant garden, ponds and an exterior mural.

White Gallery On the corner of Rothschild Blvd and the square, this attractive complex combines a café/restaurant and a bookshop dealing with such matters as health and spiritualism.

Nahalat Binyamin St

'Never mind the price, feel the quality'. This is the old textile and haberdashery centre, which is now being rejuvenated. The name of the suburb, meaning 'Inheritance of Benjamin', dates back to 1912 when the poor artisans who settled here were looking for financial backing to build their houses. The Jewish National Fund was told that the suburb would be named after Benyamin Herzl, and the Rothschilds were told it would be named after Baron Benjamin de Rothschild.

Whoever ended up footing the bill, you can still see that a lot of money must have been spent, as here are some of the architectural delights of Tel Aviv. Look up to see the fancy balconies and balustrades, in particular No 8, Degel House; No 15, Levy House; No 16, Rosenberg House; No 27, the Norda Hotel; and the Palatin Hotel on the corner of Ahad Ha'am St.

Shalom Tower

Herzl St was the new city's first main road and the centre of the social scene. Look out for photographs of it 70 years ago to see how it started. At the top of the street was Tel Aviv's first building, the Gymnasia Herzlia, built in 1909. As the first secular, Hebrew-language secondary school, the Gymnasia became a symbol of Jewish development, acting as a cultural and economic stimulus for the community and attracting many students from abroad, who were accommodated in nearby hostels. The Gymnasia has now been demolished and Israel's tallest building, the Shalom Tower, built in 1959, now stands in its place.

The Shalom Tower includes a post office branch, supermarket/department store and the Ministry of the Interior's offices. For desperate tourists there is a terrible wax museum which tries to depict events and characters in Israeli history but fails dismally – about the only convincing piece in the whole place is Moshe Dayan's eyepatch. More worthwhile is a visit to the top floor observatory with its views of the city and, on a clear day, beyond. Admission to the observatory is US$2.75, the wax museum US$3.20, or to both US$4. Open September to May, Sunday to Thursday 9 am to 4.30 pm, Friday 9 am to 1.30 pm. October to April, Sunday to Friday 9 am to 6.45 pm. Closed Saturday.

Merkaz Mis-hari

At the southern end of Allenby Rd, dominated by Levinsky and Matalon Sts, is the wholesalers' market area, which dates back to 1925. Tel Aviv had previously relied entirely on its supplies from Jaffa but the problems between the Arab and Jewish communities put a stop to that. Most of the shops here are mini-warehouses crammed with an assortment of goods including toys and souvenirs and there are a number of good places to eat.

Newe Tzedek

One of the first quarters to be built in the new city in 1887, this area, south-west of Allenby Rd and the Shalom Tower is a delightful maze of narrow streets full of lovely old buildings of grand design. It was allowed to decay, became adopted by the textile industry which filled its northern streets with workshops and fashion showrooms, and is now 'in', and much renovation work is being carried out. Well worth a casual wander, it has a theatre, cafés, restaurants and perhaps the city's best example of an old-style bagel factory.

Manshiye

An old Arab district largely destroyed during the 1948 War of Independence, it lies at the southern end of the Carmel Market.

The Clock Tower
of Jaffa

Hassan Baq Mosque

Now being renovated under the auspices of the Ministry of Religious Affairs with criticism from some Jews. Its minaret was used by Arab snipers during the war.

Industry House

Part of a striking modern complex which is the first in a planned series of developments which will fill the now vacant stretch of coastline between Tel Aviv and Jaffa.

Etzel Museum

South of the West Beach along South Herbert Samuel Esplanade, in an attractive smoked-glass reconstruction within the stone shell of an older building, this museum (tel 657180) presents a mainly photographic history of the Jewish victory against the Arabs in Jaffa in April 1948. Open Sunday to Thursday 8 am to 4 pm, Friday 8 am to 1 pm, closed Saturday; admission is 70c.

Yad Eliyahu

This district east of the central bus station, across the busy dual carriageway, was established in 1946 by Jewish veterans of the British Army. It was named in memory of Eliyahu Golomb, one of the Haganah's commanders.

HaTiqwa

To the south of Yad Eliyahu, this district's name means Mount Hope. It was established in 1852 by a group of American Seventh Day Adventists. Only five years later they were forced to disband the colony after being stricken by disease, or attacked by Bedouin (reports vary). The area is now a depressed Sephardic neighbourhood. Its cheap meat restaurants and Iraqi bakeries are popular and well worth a visit.

Art Galleries

Opening hours vary, but Tel Aviv's many galleries are often open short periods of time, say 10 am to 1 pm and 5 to 8 pm.

Alef (tel 239932), 36 Gordon St; Israeli ceramics, silver, glass, enamel, embroidery and weaving.

Angel Gallery (tel 225637), 26 Gordon St; Israeli art.

Camera Obscura (tel 298291), 57 Allenby Rd; photography school gallery exhibiting work by students and top photographers.

Christies' (tel 204727), 2 Habima Square; regular exhibitions.

Dervish (tel 227906), 7 Gordon St; folklore from various countries, wood, ceramics, carpets.

Dvir (tel 232003), 26 Gordon St; Israeli art.

Gordon Gallery (tel 240323), 95 Ben Yehuda St; leading Israeli gallery with a twice yearly auction in the WZO Building on Kaplan St.

Julie M Gallery (tel 295473), 7 Glickson St; Israeli art.

Kibbutz Art Gallery (tel 232533) 25 Dov Hoz St; all work produced by kibbutzniks.

Sara Kishon (tel 225069), 31 Frug St; Israeli art.

Sara Levy (tel 450202), 10 Pineles St; Israeli art.

Proza Dizengoff Central; 2nd floor bookshop with exhibits by art students.

E Rosenfeld Gallery (tel 229044), 147 Dizengoff St; pleasant owner, top Israeli artists' work with regular exhibitions.

Stern Gallery (tel 246303), 30 Gordon St; Israeli art.

Tel Aviv University Mexico Building; exhibitions to inspire the art students here.

Safari Park

This 100 hectare African animal reserve in Ramat Gan will only appeal to the desperate and easily pleased. Open October to May Sunday to Thursday 9 am to 3 pm, Friday 9 am to 2 pm, June to September Sunday to Thursday 9 am to 6 pm, Friday 9 am to 2 pm. Closed Saturday. Dan buses Nos 30, 35 and 40 go there but you're only allowed to enter in closed vehicles.

Tours

Egged Tours offer a variety of guided tours of Tel Aviv-Jaffa and surrounding places of interest. They start with a half-day tour of Tel Aviv-Jaffa at around US$18 and a full day tour at US$35, so they are not

exactly cheap. Coaches leave from here to other areas of the country as well.

Places to Stay

Virtually all hostel and hotel accommodation in Tel Aviv is found in or around Ben Yehuda, HaYarkon and Dizengoff Sts and Allenby Rd. All these locations are within a few minutes' walk of the beaches, popular shopping and eating places and nightspots; a brisk walk or a cheap bus ride should put you within easy reach of most other places of interest.

A Dan bus No 4 or 5 from the central bus station will get you to the general area. When choosing a place to stay bear in mind that rooms facing the street are likely to be extremely noisy.

There are some rooms and apartments available as well as regular hostels and hotel rooms. A few are listed here, but check also with Homtel and Israel Bed & Breakfast Ltd (see Places to Stay in the Facts for the Visitor chapter).

The lack of visitors has affected Tel Aviv, and you might be able to bargain your way out of high season prices. Remember the 15% tax in more expensive places.

Places to Stay – bottom end

During the past couple of years several cheap new hostels have opened and some of the cheaper hotels have introduced dorm-style rooms. The fierce competition is good news for those on a budget since many establishments are offering lower prices and an improved range of facilities. You are likely to be approached by hostel touts at the central bus station.

Mash House (tel 657684), 4 Trumpeldor St. Take Dan bus No 4, get off at the first stop on Ben Yehuda St, continue in the same direction and turn left on Trumpeldor St. Just across from the beach, this is a great set-up with comfortably furnished studio apartments suitable for up to three people. Two apartments share a kitchen and bathroom. The owners are very friendly and their prices are good value, especially for a stay of one week or more. They take singles, but it's usually filled with people taking whole apartments at around US$40 a night. They're cheaper in the winter and much less rented by the month.

The Hostel (tel 287088), 60 Ben Yehuda St, Dan bus No 4. This place is not so good and it's on the 4th floor with no lift. It's clean enough, with a kitchen. Dorm beds are US$5.50, rooms $US17. Midnight curfew. Further along, the *Top Hostel* (tel 237419,237807) is at 84 Ben Yehuda St. Take Dan bus No 4, get off at the third stop on Ben Yehuda St, and the hostel is just south of Gordon St. Use the side entrance and take the elevator to the top floor. There's a nice bar and a kitchen. Dorm beds are US$6, doubles US$18. Closed 10 am to 1 pm, curfew 1 am.

Hotel Josef (tel 280955), 15 Bograshov St. Take Dan bus No 4, get off at the second stop on Ben Yehuda, continue walking in the same direction, turn right onto Bograshov and it's on the left. A nice and clean place, with a pleasant lounge-bar area but crowded dorms. The kitchen is closed to guests in the morning, which is inconvenient for those who don't want to pay for the over-priced breakfast. Bar and food prices are generally too high for a budget hostel. Dorm beds are US$7.50. Closed 10 am to 1 pm, curfew 1 am.

Gordon Hostel (tel 229870), 2 Gordon St, above the Terminal café. On the seafront and on the corner of HaYarkon, this hostel is in a noisy spot. It has pleasant rooms, kitchens and balconies, and a roof area. Dorm beds are US$6.75. No curfew.

The Greenhouse (tel 235994), 201 Dizengoff St. Take Dan bus No 5. Ultra clean and well furnished; you may consider it worth the few extra dollars. There is a lounge and kitchen, and everything is in good condition. Dorm beds are US$8.50 and doubles US$18. Lovely double apartments are US$28, triple or quad US$38. Closed 10 am to 2 pm. No curfew.

Bnei Dan Youth Hostel – IYHA (tel 455042), 32 Bnei Dan St. Take Dan bus No 5, get off on Yehuda HaMaccabi St, walk north two blocks, and it's across from the Yarkon River. Although a quiet place, it's inconveniently located to the north of most places of interest. The rooms can be stuffy and cramped, and there are no cooking facilities, although you can get standard IYHA food. There's a dorm or various sized rooms from US$18, breakfast included. Closed 9 am to 5 pm. Flexible 11 pm curfew.

There are a number of small hotels in the depressing red light zone and, despite recent attempts to clean the place up, many travellers will still find this area less than appealing. There's no curfew at the *Sandi Hotel* (tel 653889) which has singles/doubles for US$13/22. The *Bell Hotel* (tel 654291), 12 Allenby Rd has singles/doubles for US$25/35 with breakfast; the *Migdal David Hotel* (tel 656392), 8 Allenby Rd is slightly cheaper but without breakfast; the *Monopol Hotel* (tel 655906), 4 Allenby Rd has singles/doubles for US$20/28; and the *Hotel Eilat* (tel 655368), 58 HaYarkon St has singles/doubles for US$20/34.

Nordau Hotel (tel 621612), 27 Nahalat Binyamin St. Take Dan bus No 4 and get off by the Carmel Market. In a lovely domed building in the heart of an architecturally interesting area, the hotel is unfortunately rather grubby. No kitchen facilities. Singles are US$13 and doubles are just US$16 to US$22, all with shower. No curfew.

HaGalil Hotel (tel 655036), 23 Bet Yosef St. Take Dan bus No 4, get off at the fifth stop, cross over to 56 Allenby Rd, cut through the wide walkway and it's ahead of you on the corner of Hillel HaZaken St. A pleasant enough hotel: clean and comfortable. There's no kitchen but a fridge and tea/coffee-making facilities are available. Singles are US$16, doubles from US$25. No curfew, ask for a key.

Tamar Hotel (tel 286997), 8 Gnessin St. Take Dan bus No 5 and get off on

Dizengoff near Frishman St. Walk east along Frishman, first left, first right and it's on the left. In a pleasant, quiet residential area in the city centre, this converted functionalist-style house has an endearingly brusque owner. It's clean and comfortable but but the rooms are stuffy and there are no kitchen facilities. Singles begin around US$15, doubles US$20, some with shower. No curfew.

Places to Stay - middle

Unless stated otherwise, prices include breakfast and private bathrooms. All these prices are subject to a 15% service charge and may increase dramatically in high season. Most of these hotels are modern and uniformly anonymous with standard furnishings and no curfews.

Europa (tel 657913), 42 Allenby Rd. Take Dan bus No 4, get off after Carmel Market. This is an older hotel, with private showers but shared toilets. It's clean but sparse, above a busy shopping street. Singles/doubles from US$18/25. Breakfast extra.

Hotel Moss (tel 651656), 6 Nes-Ziona Sts, between Ben Yehuda and HaYarkon Sts. Dan bus No 4, get off at the first stop on Ben Yehuda St, continue walking in the same direction, turn left onto Idelson St and Nes-Ziona is on the right. A pleasant hotel in a quiet location; a definite step up. There's a bar, coffee shop and dining room - good value. Singles/doubles are US$30/40.

Sinai Hotel (tel 652621), 11 Trumpeldor St, between HaYarkon and Ben Yehuda Sts. Dan bus No 4, get off at the first stop on Ben Yehuda, turn left onto Trumpeldor. A better class hotel with good facilities, bars, a coffee shop, a dining room and a pool. Singles/doubles from US$60/70. *Hotel Imperial* (tel 657002, 657672, 656492) is at 66 HaYarkon St, down from the Sinai Hotel on a noisy corner, but it's good value and has a bar. Singles/doubles are US$35/45.

Ora Hotel (tel 650941), 35 Ben Yehuda St. Take Dan bus No 4, get off at the second stop on Ben Yehuda. A pleasant hotel with a bar and breakfast room. Singles/doubles from US$34/47.

Park Hotel (tel 651551), 75 HaYarkon St, adjacent to the US Embassy, overlooking the sea. Good facilities here. Singles/doubles from US$46/58. Nearby, the *Maxim Hotel* (tel 653721) at 86 HaYarkon St, overlooks the sea near the corner of Bograshov St. Singles/doubles from US$26/40. Also overlooking the sea is the *Astor Hotel* (tel 223141) at 105 HaYarkon St. Their restaurant features Israeli nouvelle cuisine. Singles/doubles cost US$42/65.

Basel Hotel (tel 244161), 156 HaYarkon St, across from Atarim Square. A higher class hotel with a pool. Singles/doubles from US$77/90. Near the Basel is the *Florida Hotel* (tel 242184), 164 HaYarkon St, across from Atarim Square, south of Ben-Gurion Blvd. Singles/doubles are US$35/48.

Shalom Hotel (tel 243277, 249444), 216 HaYarkon St, north of the British Embassy and across from the Hilton. The Stagecoach Restaurant dominates the entrance to this hotel. Singles/doubles from US$36/52.

Grand Beach Hotel (tel 241252), 250 HaYarkon St, entrance on the corner of Nordau Blvd. A grand-looking place with singles/doubles from US$55/85. The *Hotel Armon HaYarkon* (tel 455271-3) at 268 HaYarkon St is a small, smart, friendly place. Singles/doubles at US$40/50. A higher class place is the *Hotel Tal* (tel 455281) at 287 HaYarkon St, with singles/doubles from US$50/60.

Adiv Hotel (tel 229141), 5 Mendele St, down from the tourist office between Ben Yehuda and HaYarkon Sts. This hotel has a popular self-service restaurant. Singles/doubles are US$40/58.

Dizengoff Square Hotel (tel 296181/5), 2 Zamenhof St, beside Dizengoff Square, formerly the Commodore Hotel. With nice rooms and public areas, this hotel is good value. Singles/doubles are from US$30/42.

You could also try the *City Hotel* (tel 246253), 9 Mapu St, between Ben Yehuda and HaYarkon Sts, where singles/doubles are US$45/55; or the *Ami Hotel* (tel 249141) at 4 Am Israel St. It's half a block back from Atarim Square. Singles/doubles from US$40/52.

Places to Stay – top end

Tel Aviv's luxury hotels contribute to the ugliness of the city's seafront with their standard reinforced-concrete block profiles. Prices are subject to a 15% service charge and seasonal variation.

Dan Panorama (tel 663311), 10 Y Kaufman St. Formerly the Astoria Hotel, but taken over by Dan who have made improvements although they still struggle with its isolated location south of the main beaches and the downtown area. Singles/doubles are from US$85/100, breakfast extra.

Yamit (tel 651111), 79 HaYarkon St. Adjacent to the US Embassy. A new luxury apartment hotel offering great value with good reductions for long stays. It has a bar, pool, restaurant, cafés, and a nightclub. Spacious and tasteful suites from US$125.

Dan Tel Aviv (tel 241111), 99 HaYarkon St. The first luxury hotel built here, and recently renovated. You get a pool, health club, jacuzzi and shops. Singles/doubles from US$115/130, breakfast included.

Tel Aviv Sheraton (tel 286222), 115 HaYarkon St. Facilities here include a pool, health club, nightclub, piano bar and synagogue. Singles/doubles from US$115/130.

Tel Aviv Hilton (tel 546 4444), Independence Park. The northernmost of the luxury hotels, this place has a good reputation. There's a pool, health club, tennis and water sports. Singles/doubles from US$150/165.

Ramada Continental (tel 296444), 121 HaYarkon St. Although you get an indoor pool, health club, piano bar, etc, the comparative cheapness is reflected in the standard of accommodation. Singles

US$47 to US$56, doubles US$54 to US$72, breakfast included. Also slightly cheaper are the *Diplomat Hotel* (tel 294422), 145 HaYarkon St, where two children can share their parents room free of charge and singles/doubles cost from US$70/80; the *Plaza Tel Aviv* (tel 299555), 155 HaYarkon St, with singles/doubles from US$70/80; and the good value *Carlton Hotel* (tel 291291), at 10 Atarim Square, with singles/doubles from US$65/100.

Places to Eat

Tel Aviv's city centre has an incredible number of fast food outlets serving unnatural-tasting versions of foods such as shwarma, felafel, pizzas, hot dogs, hamburger and ice cream. Since many of these establishments serve over-priced, mediocre food you would do well to resist the temptation and save your sheqelim for the few establishments that offer quality and value for money.

The Carmel Market is the cheapest place for fresh fruit and vegetables. Of the supermarkets, Supersol (open till 10 pm) on Ben Yehuda, between Gordon and Mapu Sts, and the Co-op at Dizengoff Square are reasonably cheap. The country's best cheese shop is Shomorn at 88 Nahalat Binyamin St, between Levinsky and Matalon Sts, in the Merkaz Mishari wholesalers' district. The best fishmonger is The Four Fishermen, 169 Ben Yehuda St, on the corner of Jabotinsky St; the cheapest is in Jaffa, on the corner of Yefet St up past Said Abulafiah & Sons bakery.

Felafel Tel Aviv's felafel is average at best, often consisting largely of breadcrumbs. Most popular, (probably because you can eat as much of the extras as you like) are the self-service stalls around the Bezalel Market, off Allenby Rd across from the Carmel Market, between King George and Tchernichovsky Sts; and the *Camp David* stall at Dizengoff and its competitor around the corner opposite the cinema.

Hummus & Shwarma The best places for hummus are in Jaffa, but if that's too far, try the Yemenite Quarter. Don't settle for the inferior shwarma available in Atarim Square, Allenby Rd, Ben Yehuda St and Dizengoff – Israel's best shwarma is sold at the *Poondak Levinsky*. See the Cheaper Restaurants section for details.

Breakfast Definitely not to be missed is the breakfast buffet at the *Adiv Hotel's* self-service restaurant at 5 Mendele St (near the tourist office). From 7 to 10 am daily you can eat yourself silly for about US$3 with a selection of food which almost lives up to the lavish descriptions of the Israeli breakfast. Eat as much fish, eggs, cheese, olives, salad and bread, and drink as much coffee and tea as you like. You will pay the same price elsewhere and end up with little more than one cup of coffee and a couple of croissants or a sandwich.

Cafés Tel Aviv's many cafés are not normally renowned for good and/or cheap food, but for pleasant surroundings, a pavement seat from which to people-watch, or as a trendy meeting place. Among them, however, are some that are particularly worth checking out for various reasons.

One of the cheapest Tel Aviv cafés, which also serves some of the best coffee and home-made cakes in town, is *Espresso Mersand* on Ben Yehuda, at the corner of Frishman St. It is close to the tourist office and most hostels and hotels, and attracts a unique collection of regulars. These include bohemian types, journalists, actors and models, and elderly German Jews or, more derisively, 'Yekkes'. The latter, who are known for their formality and highly developed sense of propriety, come in the morning and sit outside, passing comment on everything that happens. The owner's estranged wife runs another café, the *Capri* (no English sign), opposite City Hall in Malchei Israel Square, on the

corner of Chen St. This is a popular daytime hangout for transvestites.

Among the more popular 'smart' cafés on Dizengoff, *Acapulco*, on the busy corner of Frishman St, stands out, and serves good coffee and basic food. The food at *Cherry*, on the corner of Ben-Gurion Blvd is better, the salads in particular – although a US$4 minimum is the norm.

For cheaper fare, do as the Australian Embassy staff did (prior to their transfer to new premises) and eat at the *Eilat Buffet*, on Ben Yehuda at the corner of Arlosoroff St. The food is basic but decent and cheap. The same is found at the wonderfully named *Sandwich House Hannah*, 191 Ben Yehuda, between Nordau and Jabotinsky Sts.

Handy for the beach, but only for beverages (the food is over-priced), is the *White House* on HaYarkon St between Frishman and Mapu Sts.

Another of the Tel Aviv cafés with a clientele of character is the *Kassit*, at 117 Dizengoff, between Gordon and Frishman Sts. This is the long-established bohemian hangout whose past customers have included Frank Sinatra and Harry Belafonte. Today you might rub shoulders with Israel's retired actors, comedians and musicians. A US$6 set meal is served and you can eat decent basic Ashkenazi food from about US$3.50.

Nargila on Mendele St is an all-night café, serving good cheap Yemenite food. It closes at about 7 am, as does the one on the seafront along Herbert Samuel Esplanade, south of Trumpeldor St.

Vegetarian The unique tofu-dominated food at the two *Eternity* restaurants, 60 Ben Yehuda, south of Mendele St, and 6 Malkhei Israel Square, opposite City Hall, is well worth a try. Even avid meat lovers should at least sample the vegetable shwarma (US$2), cheaper and perhaps more enjoyable than the real thing. Other dishes include vegetarian hot dogs, tamali, tofuafel, barbeque twist burgers, cheeses, yoghurts, ice cream and shakes. Prices here are good and the food is very tasty – US$5 to eat well. Open Sunday to Thursday, 9 am to 11 pm, Friday 9 am to 3 pm, Saturday sunset to midnight.

Ice Cream The *Eternity* restaurants' popular all-vegetable ice cream should be tried. As well as tasting good, it isn't fattening!

There are two *Manalitos* branches. Strangely, they're on the same stretch of Ibn Gevirol, albeit on opposite sides, between King Shaul Blvd, Kaplan and Marmorek Sts. Also on Ibn Gevirol, on the corner with Hanevi'im St, is *Lagushka*, a café serving its popular yoghurt-style ice cream. *Carvel* are expanding and now have a branch in Ramat Aviv, near the university.

Bakeries Downtown Tel Aviv has a lot of places selling a variety of cakes and pastries. Opinions vary considerably about the best, many of which are also cafés. *Espresso Marsand's* selection of home-made delights are among the cheapest as well as the tastiest – they are on Ben Yehuda, at the corner of Frishman St. The *Kapulsky* bakeries at 166 Dizengoff, next to the Cherry café, on the corner of Ben-Gurion Blvd and also at 37 Allenby Rd, on the corner of Tchernichovsky St are also top contenders.

Tel Aviv's bagels are something of a tradition and you will see them being sold on the beach and on the streets later in the day and at night. Going along to the bakery to watch them being made is a popular way to round off an evening. Perhaps the most interesting bakery is at 11 Pines St in Newe Tzedek. From the Shalom Tower, follow Montefiore St to the south-west, turn left onto HaShachar St, veer right to the end of the block, right onto Yavniel St, turn left at the second stop sign, and the bakery is along the second street on the left.

The traditional Iraqi bakeries along Etsel St in the HaTiqwa district are interesting to see with the large wafer-thin pitta being baked in the unusual-looking ovens.

Restaurants – cheap In Merkaz Mis-hari at 41 Levinsky St, *Poondak Levinsky* (no English sign), is a Turkish-owned workers' restaurant patronised by the local wholesale merchants. It is surprisingly pleasant, clean and friendly, and offers a good range of excellent and inexpensive food. The shwarma (US$3) is the main event: tender lamb with beef and with a few pistachio nuts inserted in it for extra flavour. Also on the menu are hummus, *ishkambe* (sheep's stomach soup), meat and offal grilled 'on the fire', steaks, salads and oriental sweets and draught beer. You can sit down or take away, and it's open Sunday to Friday, lunchtime only.

The Yemenite Quarter features a number of inexpensive eating places – mainly the family run, basic working man's type, serving simple Oriental delights such as hummus, spicy meat soups and meat and offal grilled 'on the fire' (US$5 plus). Popular are *Zion Gamliel*, 12 Peduyim St, *Shimon's*, on the corner of Peduyim at 28 Yiche St, and *Oved's* on the corner of Peduyim and Nahali'el Sts.

Inexpensive Oriental food is also available in the run-down HaTiqwa neighbourhood, south-east of the central bus station. Etsel St is full of popular eateries and traditional Iraqi bakeries. Israelis flock here to eat. Meat and offal grilled 'on the fire' are the speciality along with the usual hummus, tehina and vegetable salads and soups. The area has two of the best value restaurants around. *Aziz* (no English sign – tel 370911), 6 Etsel St, is open Sunday to Thursday from lunchtime till 1 am, Friday lunchtime only, and Saturday sunset to 1 am. They serve grilled cow's udder, lamb and chicken heart and shashlik, US$2 per skewer; turkey's testicles US$2.50, and goat's liver US$5. Dessert and coffee are served on the house. More presentable (and therefore arguably less authentic) and also very popular, is *Yehuda Avazi* (tel 973979), 54 Etsel St. They open at 11 am and serve until 6 am. The prices here are slightly higher than at Aziz, but you can still eat well from US$5. Wine and beer are served in both restaurants. Dan bus No 16 starts from Allenby Rd and stops at the beginning of Etsel St. Otherwise it's a 15-minute walk from the central bus station. Head south along Har-Ziyyon St, left onto Levinsky, cross the main highway to Haganah Rd and it's on the right eventually.

The *Adiv Hotel's* self-service restaurant is open daily and serves a popular set lunch/dinner consisting of soup, salad, main course and dessert for US$5. It's down from the tourist office on Mendele St.

Another bargain is the Austro-Bavarian *Restaurant Vienna*, 48A Ben Yehuda, with its entrance on the side of a passageway just north of Bograshov St. Open daily 11.30 am to 3 pm, it serves a set four-course lunch for US$6, with waitress service. You can order à la carte to spend less – about US$4 for a main dish such as wiener schnitzel.

Naknikiot Hakikar in Dizengoff Square serves inexpensive Ashkenazi food such as chopped liver (US$1.60), gefilte fish, soup with kreplach (US$1.80) and cholent (US$4).

Further north and serving better food of the same style is *Batia* at 197 Dizengoff, on the corner of Arlosoroff St. Main courses such as goulash, roast beef and schnitzel cost about US$3.75. Draught beer is served, too. This place is particularly popular with the university's film students.

The bohemian *Kassit* café/restaurant, 117 Dizengoff St between Gordon and Frishman Sts, serves basic but filling Ashkenazi food. A set meal costs US$5 for soup, salad and main course, or you can order individual dishes to spend less.

A cheap Chinese restaurant is the *Long Sang*, at 13 Allenby Rd (near the seafront) with a US$7 set menu and individual dishes for about US$4.50. The Szechuan and Cantonese food isn't bad for the price. Another good cheapie is at the corner of Dizengoff and Frishman Sts.

Restaurants - more expensive Tourist brochures for Tel Aviv glibly attach 'gourmet' and 'quality' tags to many restaurants, but if you are tempted by their enthusiastic recommendations you are likely to be disappointed. Fortunately, among the large number of anonymously identical places providing, at best, average food with poor service for inflated prices, are some very good and even excellent exceptions.

Some of the middle range restaurants are not totally out of reach for those on a budget who want to treat themselves or just have one course such as a really good salad or dessert. For either of these, or for a terrific yoghurt soup, try the *Promenade* (no English sign) on Herbert Samuel Esplanade, just to the north of Trumpeldor St. It doesn't look any better than its neighbouring rivals, but it is one of the city's best eating places. Not only are most of the dishes made from scratch on the premises, but they are served politely and in pleasant surroundings. A wide range of dishes are available, from soups and salads to various meat dishes, fish and desserts – all of a high standard. Depending on how much and what you eat, an average bill will come to about US$8 to US$15 per person. Open daily.

With such items as tomato soup with arak and St Peter's fish in papaya sauce, the *Panorama Restaurant* (tel 238913, 223141) in the Astor Hotel, 105 HaYarkon near Frishman St, serves Israeli *nouvelle cuisine*. This sincere attempt at serious, quality cookery and presentation involves various and unusual combinations of fresh local ingredients. While quite a few of the dishes prove unsuccessful, the restaurant is good value at about US$15 per person. Open daily.

For some of the country's best meat, eat at the *White Hall*, 6 Mendele St, between HaYarkon and Ben Yehuda Sts (and between the Dan Hotel and the tourist office). Here you can enjoy decent steaks and burgers and a salad bar from about US$10 – excellent value. Open daily.

Also good for meat are the city's two best Romanian restaurants. At 8 Malchei Israel Square (opposite City Hall), the *Romanesc Restaurant* (tel 265581) serves a variety of delicious specialities of the country, such as grilled meats, liver and goulash. Run by an older couple, the small room is usually full by 8 pm, so arrive well before then. Closed Friday evening. *Restaurant Alpin* (tel 658412), 56 HaYarkon St, corner of HaYarden St, serves more of the same in an equally efficient fashion. Open daily, noon to midnight. In either restaurant you can eat for US$8 to US$20.

For good French cuisine at a reasonable price, *L'Entrecote* (tel 230726, 834453), 195 Ben Yehuda by Nordau Blvd, serves a set three course menu for about US$16. Closed after lunch Friday until Saturday dinner.

The Chimney (tel 235125), 2 Mendele St, corner of HaYarkon St, serves good French-style food in pleasant surroundings. It attracts many diners from the adjacent Dan Hotel. About US$8 to US$15 for one.

Further north at 265 Dizengoff on the corner of Yermiyahu St, *Pirozki* (tel 457599) is a popular Russian restaurant. In attractive surroundings, the specialty here is *pirozkis* (soft dough pasties with various savoury or sweet fillings). Good salads and desserts are also served. About US$8 to US$15 for one. Open daily till after midnight.

The Yemenite Quarter houses several upmarket versions of the workers' restaurants already mentioned. These serve the familiar meat, offal and salad specialities in more expensive surroundings. Two of the best (and most expensive) are

the *Zion* (tel 657323), 28 Peduyim St, and *Shaul's Inn* (tel 653303), 11 Elyashiv St. You can eat very well in the Zion for about US$20, while at Shaul's Inn you'll save by avoiding the higher priced downstairs section. Both are closed Friday evenings and Saturday lunchtime, otherwise open until midnight.

Out of the proliferation of places specialising in blintzes, the most highly rated is *Shoshana & Uri's Hungarian Blintzes* (tel 450674), 35 Yermiyahu St, east of Dizengoff St. About US$5 for the savoury, US$4 for the sweet. Open Saturday to Thursday, 6 pm to 1 am, closed Friday.

The *Café Piltz Restaurant* (tel 652778, 657021), 81 HaYarkon St, adjacent to the Yamit Hotel, is a 1930s dinner-dance spot – a traditional Tel Aviv favourite. The French-style food and service do not usually live up to the nostalgic popularity of the place, but you can spend an enjoyable evening here, dancing the old-fashioned Israeli way to the Piltz Orchestra on Monday, Thursday, Friday and Saturday evenings. About US$25 per person.

One of the best Chinese restaurants is the *Red Chinese* (tel 448405, 440325), 326 Dizengoff, where Ben Yehuda ends. Open daily for lunch and dinner. About US$10 to US$20 for Szechuan and a few Thai dishes.

The first Chinese restaurant to open in Tel Aviv was *Mandy's Singing Bamboo* (tel 451282, 458785), 317 HaYarkon, north of HaSira St. It's still highly rated and priced similarly to the Red Chinese. Opposite, at 300 HaYarkon, on the corner of HaSira St is *Little Tel Aviv* (tel 450109). This place, decorated with cinema posters, has been constantly in and out of fashion since it was opened by the same team responsible for the Singing Bamboo, namely Raafi Shauly and Mandy Rice-Davies. She achieved notoriety as one of the London call-girls (the other was Christine Keeler) who played a major role in the Profumo Scandal which brought

Top: Ethiopian monk & rooftop cell, Church of the Holy Sepulchre, Jerusalem (RE)
Left: The bell tolls for . . .? Church of the Holy Sepulchre (RE)
Right: The faithful gather at the Church of the Holy Selpuchre at Easter (RE)

Top: Shabbat on the beach in August, Tel Aviv (NT)
Bottom: A Haifa felafel stall (NT)

down the British Conservative Government in the early 1960s. She later married Shauly, an Israeli entrepreneur, and they opened various Mandy's Chinese restaurants and the two Cherry cafés in Tel Aviv. Shauly was also behind Le Club nightclub on HaYarkon and the failed dolphinarium. They have since divorced, but their flamboyant public image is still attached to their establishments today.

Little Tel Aviv serves a variety of dishes from salads, burgers, steaks, pasta and chilli, to crêpes, gateaux and ice cream. Daily specials are often the best value. You can spend between US$7 and US$30 depending on what and how much you eat. There's live music Thursday to Saturday nights, and it's open daily till 12.30 am, later on Saturday.

Restaurants - expensive *Keren à la carte*, 15 Ibn Gevirol, near Marmorek St, provides a high standard of French-style food based on the recipes devised by American Keren Hendler. The food is some of the best in the city. You'll spend about US$35 per person. It's open Sunday to Thursday 12 noon to 4 pm and Saturday to Thursday 7 pm to 12 midnight, closed all day Friday.

Another of Tel Aviv's top restaurants is *Yin Yang* (tel 621833), 64 Rothschild Blvd, serving excellent Chinese cuisine. It is owned and run by Israel Aharoni, an Israeli who once taught juvenile delinquents on a kibbutz but, attracted by South-East Asia, ended up in Taiwan learning the language and the cuisine. He has published a Chinese cookery book in Hebrew and his restaurant has become widely recognised as the country's best in its category. About US$15 to US$35 per person. Open for lunch Sunday to Friday, dinner every night.

Two other restaurants serving French cuisine are worth trying. *The Casba* (tel 442617, 449101), 32 Yermiyahu St near the corner by Dizengoff, has been awarded the Israeli 'Four Forks' culinary award for the past 20-odd years. It's open Sunday to Friday for lunch and dinner, closed Saturday. *Le Versailles* (tel 655552), 37 Geula St, on the edge of the Yemenite Quarter, is a more recent addition to the scene and it's open daily. Both cost from about US$25 per person.

Entertainment
Crowds of locals and visitors are out people-watching after dark, especially around Dizengoff Square and the seafront. The bars, cafés and restaurants fill up, and people also go down to visit Old Jaffa. For more organised activities, pick up a free copy of the leaflets *Events in the Tel Aviv Region* and *This Week in Israel* from the tourist office. The *Jerusalem Post* also carries details of current entertainment in its Friday *Metro* supplement.

Cinema Many of the major cinemas show English-language films sub-titled in Hebrew. Foreign-language films are also shown in some of the smaller cinemas.

Cinemateque 1 HaArka'a St (tel 258200), part of the membership chain showing a variety of classics, avant garde, new wave, off-beat, etc. A few tickets for non-members are sold just before the performance

French Cultural Institute 111 HaYarkon St (tel 236470), occasionally shows French films

German Institute 4 Weizmann St, occasionally shows German films

Paris 106 HaYarkon, opposite the Dan Hotel (tel 236605). Pick up the *Pariscope* leaflet listing the large variety of usually interesting films shown in this popular cinema

Tel Aviv Museum 27 King Shaul Blvd (tel 261297)

Theatre Most of the theatre is performed in Hebrew, with occasional foreign-language productions.

Habima Theatre Habima Square, between Rothschild Blvd and Dizengoff St (tel 283742)

Cameri Theatre 101 Dizengoff St, entrance on
Frishman St (tel 222995)
Neve Tzedek Theatre 6 Yehieli St, Newe
Tzedek (tel 651241)

Music A range of styles is performed in a
variety of settings.

Mann Auditorium Habima Square (tel 295092,
290613), between Rothschild Blvd and
Dizengoff St. Home to the Israel
Philharmonic, it stages a wide range of
concerts
Wohl Amphitheatre HaYarkon Park is used for
outdoor concerts
Beit Lessin 34 Weizmann St (tel 256222). The
venue for some of Israel's best jazz – open
Sunday from 9.30 pm and often during the
week, too. Rock and folk music are
occasionally performed
Gordon's Pub Gordon St, between Ben Yehuda
and Dizengoff St. Jazz on Monday and
Tuesday evenings
Red Bar 213 Dizengoff St (tel 247867).
Jazz on Tuesday, Friday and Saturday
evenings
Trumpeldor Trumpeldor St, between Herbert
Samuel Esplanade and HaYarkon St.
Occasional jazz in this popular bar
Zavta Club 30 Ibn Gevirol St, downstairs
in the London Ministore Passage on the
corner of King Shaul Blvd. Folk, jazz, blues,
rock and classical.
ZOA House 1 Daniel Frisch St (tel 259341),
corner of Ibn Gevirol St has occasional
performances of plays, folk singing and
other concerts – and celebrates Israeli and
American holidays

Dance Israel's dance groups perform
regularly in Tel Aviv, at such venues as
the Mann Auditorium and the Cameri
Theatre. The *Bat-Dor Theatre*, downstairs
in the London Ministore Passage on the
corner of King Shaul Blvd and Ibn
Gevirol, is the home of the Bat-Dor
Modern Dance Company.

Discos Tel Aviv is the only place in Israel
with a well-supported, albeit limited,
selection of discos. Like the bars, they go
in and out of fashion very quickly, so ask
around.

The cheapest place to dance is the
Samba, a weekly (usually Thursday)
Latin American evening organised by
some Brazilian Jews who just love to
dance. They play their collection of tapes
from home over a not-too-brilliant sound-
system in a variety of venues such as the
West Beach. They charge about US$4.

The *Colosseum* is in the large circular
building spanning HaYarkon St in
Atarim Square. Originally a supermarket, it
now boasts the best light show and sound
system in town. It attracts a mainly young
(14 to 18) crowd and plays commercial
pop. Entrance charges vary between
US$5 to US$12 from night to night and
include varying numbers of 'free' drinks.
Tuesdays are free for women. Drinks are
not too expensive – beer US$1.60, soft
drinks 95c, local spirits US$2.50, imported
US$4.75. Thursday is for men over 25 and
women over 20.

The *Penguin Club*, 43 Yehuda HaLevi
St, between Allenby and Nahalat Binyamin
St, attracts new wave/punk characters
and features live acts on Friday and
Saturday and often during the week, too.
It's a little expensive: entrance US$8, soft
drinks US$1.50, beer US$2.50, local
spirits US$4, imported US$5.

Another relatively established disco is
Liquid which recently changed venues
and then closed down due to problems
with licensing. Ask around for its current
location.

The *Cinerama* complex on Petah
Tiqwa Rd, away from the downtown area
is said to be the Middle East's largest
disco! Formerly a circus hall, it also acts as
a concert venue but only time will tell if
the much talked about millions of dollars
of investors' money was well spent.

Sirocco, 44 Emeq Yisrael St, south from
Newe Tzedek, was once the place to go.

Nightclubs Some of the luxury hotels have nightclubs, such as *Herbie Sams* at the Yamit and *Reflections* at the Sheraton, with dancing in the *Beach Bar* at the Grand Beach.

Several nightclubs provide more authentic local entertainment and will not be fully appreciated without some knowledge of Hebrew or a companion to interpret. Mind you, the live music and singing are often good enough to enjoy without understanding a word of it and are sometimes in languages other than Hebrew. Turkish nightclubs, once limited to Bat Yam, have recently opened with much success in Tel Aviv. *Mifgash Allenby* is near the main post office on the corner of Allenby and Yehuda HaLevi St. Behind a greasy café, a curtain leads to a room crowded with tables where Turkish singers perform to enthusiastic diners, led by Avi Cohen who hails from Bat Yam and is perhaps the leading Turkish 'bus station singer'. Open every night, this popular club charges from US$12.50 for dinner – you may be able to get in without having to eat as they don't see many foreigners.

Visit the *Happy Casserole*, 344 Dizengoff St where more 'bus station superstars' have the primarily Sephardic crowd dancing on the tables. The 'Little Tel Aviv' area often features great live music and dancing at some of the bars.

Bars Tel Aviv's bars are extremely popular, especially late in the evening and towards the end of the week. Thursday night sees most Tel Avivians crowd their favourite watering holes, while on Friday and Saturday night hordes of suburbanites from such places as Bat Yam and Holon arrive. Although most of the bars attract regulars from a particular social group or profession, it is often difficult to suggest specific places because the bar that is the 'in' place this month can be 'out' the next. Most of the places listed have established their popularity over some time and

should still be in business when you get there.

The cheapest draught beer can usually be found at the *White House* and the *Goulash Corner*, neighbours on HaYarkon St, on the corner of Frishman St. Popular with travellers, they are close to the beach and the hostels. The *White House*, next door to the Labour Party HQ, attracts a large number of young Israelis and features a large photograph of David Ben-Gurion on the wall. The *Goulash Corner* is primarily a restaurant but the lack of customers for its over-priced Hungarian food prompted the proprietor to compete with the *White House* and sell cheap draught beer.

Down on the West Beach (by Charles Clore Park, south of the dolphinarium), the popular *West Beach Restaurant* is open 24 hours – Israelis often pack the tables that overlook the sea and drink all night long.

The *Boiling Box* at the Riviera Hotel, HaYarkon St, corner of Allenby, is filled by Tel Aviv's new wave/punk crowd, although they don't normally arrive until midnight. Rock videos are played loudly – open late.

On Trumpeldor St, across from the Concorde Hotel between HaYarkon St and Herbert Samuel Esplanade, *Trumpeldor* is an attractively-styled bar/restaurant with indoor and outdoor tables, open late and with occasional live jazz.

Near to The Home hostel, *Ibgi's* bar/restaurant on Hillel HaZaqen St on the corner of Alsheikh St, west of Allenby Rd bears the name of its film director owner and attracts a crowd drawn largely from the film world and its admirers. *Tzela Beera*, 226 Ben Yehuda, near Nordau Blvd, is the established hangout for Israel's film industry crowd, often with top fashion models putting in an appearance.

Bonanza is the bar/restaurant on Trumpeldor St, to the east of Ben Yehuda St. This is the regular haunt of former

Jewish underground and IDF officers and possibly arms dealers as well. During the week in the evenings, and on Shabbat during the day, these old warriors meet to drink, eat, reminisce and sing. On a good night, the place fills with the sounds of ad lib but heartfelt renditions of Edith Piaf classics and Zionist pioneer songs to piano accompaniment, as older couples dance in the old-fashioned way. Not to be missed.

In a backstreet behind Dizengoff Square, through the alley by the Nakniot Hakikar restaurant, hide two late-night bars, *Long John Silver's* and *The Backyard*. Also staying open late is the *Terminal*, on the corner of Gordon and HaYarkon.

Shoftim, on the corner of Ibn Gevirol and Shoftim Sts, is an old favourite with Israeli intellectuals, lawyers, and left-wing types. Further south on Ibn Gevirol is *Satalla*, recently opened and attracting a younger crowd. It takes its name from an Egyptian goddess and is a play on the Hebrew word *sutul*, which means 'stoned'. Both open till late.

At 213 Dizengoff, by Jabotinsky St, the *Red Bar* is another left-wing, bohemian spot, with live jazz and poetry readings on some evenings. *The Den*, on Ben Yehuda on the corner of Jabotinsky St, is more pub-like, with cheaper draught beer and a dart-board.

In 'Little Tel Aviv', where HaYarkon, Ben Yehuda and Dizengoff join up with Yermiyahu St, several popular bars operate among the up-market restaurants and designer boutiques. *MASH* (More Alcohol Served Here) and *BBC* (Bernie's Bottle Club) are popular with English travellers. On the lower level of Atarim Square the *Blue Anchor* plays heavy metal videos and also attracts a large British contingent who presumably miss the refinements of home. The nearby *Gypsy* has more of the same.

JAFFA

In Hebrew, it's *Yafo*, which is believed to be derived from either *yafé*, meaning beautiful, or the name of Noah's son, Japheth, who established the town after the flood. The Greeks called it *Joppa*, as does the Bible. This is the place where Hiram landed the Lebanese cedars for Solomon's Temple, and where the Old Testament Book of Jonah tells of Johah's experiences with God and a whale. It was under Solomon that Jaffa became the nation's seaport and today it is believed to be the world's oldest working harbour.

Archaeologists have dug up remains here dating from the 18th century BC, making it one of the oldest cities in the world. The Egyptians conquered the place in 1468 BC by hiding in large, clay pots carried into the local market. Under Herod the Great, Caesarea became the main port, but Jaffa later returned to its pre-eminent position.

During the 12th century Jaffa underwent a particularly turbulent period: the Crusaders lost the city to Saladin, but then regained it under Richard the Lionheart, only to lose it to Saladin's brother, who slaughtered 20,000 Christians in the process. After the Mamelukes conquered Jaffa in 1267 it remained in Arab hands, except for a brief period under Napoleon, until Allenby defeated the Turks in 1917.

By 1840 a wave of Jewish immigrants had settled in Jaffa and by the turn of the century, the town had become a gateway for the large-scale immigration of European Jews, many of whom founded colonies in the surrounding areas.

The first few decades of the 20th century were marked by mounting antagonism between the Jewish and the Arab communities of Jaffa and in 1929, 1936 and 1939 anti-Jewish rioting broke out. After the terror and hostility of the struggle for Jaffa in the 1948 War of Independence and in the wake of the Irgun's victory, most of the Arab population fled the town, leaving behind their homes and possessions.

Today Jaffa is dominated by Old Jaffa,

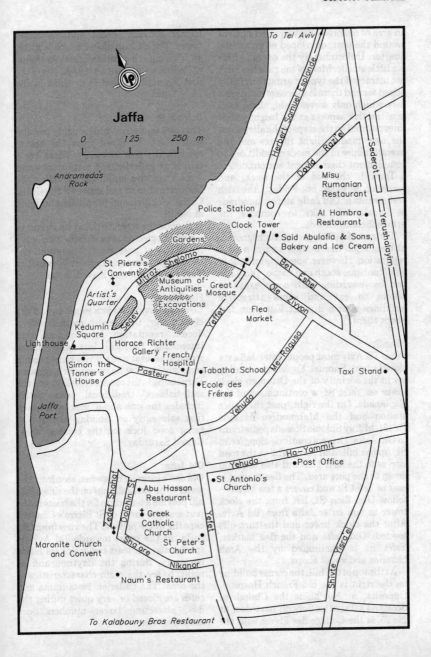

Jaffa

0   125   250 m

To Tel Aviv

Anaromeda's Rock

Herbert Samuel Esplanade

David Raziel

Sederot

Yerushalayim

Misu Rumanian Restaurant

Police Station

Clock Tower

Al Hambra Restaurant

Gardens

Said Abulafia & Sons, Bakery and Ice Cream

St Pierre's Convent

Mifraz Shelomo

Bet Eshel

Artist's Quarter

Museum of Antiquities

Great Mosque

Excavations

Ole Zivyon

Flea Market

Segev

Kedumin Square

Yeffet

Lighthouse

Horace Richter Gallery

French Hospital

We-Ragusa

Taxi Stand

Pasteur

Tabatha School

Simon the Tanner's House

Ecole des Fréres

Jaffa Port

Yehuda

Ha-Yammit

Yehuda

Post Office

Zedef Shahaf

Dolphin St

Abu Hassan Restaurant

Greek Catholic Church

St Antonio's Church

Shivte Yisra el

Maronite Church and Convent

Sha are

St Peter's Church

Nikanor

Naum's Restaurant

To Kalabouny Bros Restaurant

an area of restored alleyways and gardens around the port, developed as an artists' quarter. Unfortunately the overall effect is a little sterile. Most of the galleries have not attracted the type of artists originally hoped for and there is a sense of emptiness here which only serves to highlight such unattractive aspects as the bright yellow lines painted on the steps of the alleyways, the ugly modern light fittings and the overall failure of the modern additions to complement their ancient surroundings.

Towards the end of the week, and reaching a peak on Friday, the fish restaurants of Old Jaffa attract hundreds of Israelis who like to compare the atmosphere to Greece.

The rest of Jaffa is pretty much ignored, although the flea market enjoys a good reputation. However, spending an hour or so to continue south and east of Old Jaffa can be rewarding with some excellent places to eat and some attractive buildings with a distinct European feel about them.

Yefet St

From Tel Aviv most people enter Jaffa via the Herbert Samuel Esplanade, ending up in the vicinity of the Ottoman clock tower on Yefet St, a continuation of the Esplanade. On the right, past the police station and the Mahmudiye Mosque (1812), Mifray Shlomo St leads pedestrians to Old Jaffa. Drivers continue along Yefet St, up the hill, and turn right as the road curves to the left. This will also take you down to the port area. The flea market is east of Yefet St and covers a few blocks – follow Olei Zion St, left from the clock tower as you enter Jaffa from Tel Aviv. After the clock tower and the turn-offs towards Old Jaffa and the flea market, Yefet St is dominated by the Arab bakeries and sweet shops.

At the top of the hill, the corner building on the right is the old French Hospital. Opposite, at No 23, is the Church of Scotland's Tabatha School; next door at No 25, is the College des Fréres with the

former convent school and its round tower. The St Antonio's Church is at No 49. This church commemorates Anthonio of Padua, a 13th century monk, one of the first Franciscans and their saint in the Holy Land.

Dolphin St

This pleasant street runs roughly parallel with Yefet St, down from the bridge towards the port entrance. There are a couple of galleries and restaurants and some attractive buildings, including the Maronite church and convent, the Greek Catholic church and the pillared building at No 19.

Beyond the street to the south stretches a much neglected area of Jaffa with some reminders of past glory. The grand old red-roofed houses were built by wealthy Turks in Italian and French styles.

Flea Market

Covering several streets south-east of the clock tower, this Jewish market with a decent reputation for antiques and interesting Oriental bits and pieces requires several visits if you want to shop seriously, as new items regularly appear. Bargaining is the order of the day, and the stall-holders' traditional sales patter includes the one about making a quick first sale early on Sunday morning to bring good luck for the coming week. Closed Saturday.

Old Jaffa

Old Jaffa looks its best when seen from the water – the old buildings on the side of the hill provide a backdrop for the boats in the port and the tower of St Pierre's Convent caps the whole picture. The view from Old Jaffa up the coast towards Tel Aviv is spectacular. At least two visits are really necessary, during the daytime and at night, to see the main characteristics of the area. The galleries, restaurants and cafés are closed or very quiet during the day, attracting larger numbers once darkness falls.

Museum of Antiquities of Tel Aviv-Jaffa (tel 825373), 10 Mifraz Shelomo St. This building was a Turkish administrative and detention centre but its vaulted ceilings and archways are now home to a display of local archaeological discoveries. Facing the view up the coast to Tel Aviv, it's on the left across the paved courtyard coming up from the clock tower, or on the right as you walk down from Kedumim Square and St Pierre's Monastery. It's open Sunday to Friday 9 am to 1 pm, Tuesday 4 to 7 pm, also Saturday 10 am to 1 pm; admission is 90c, students 75c.

Ha Pisga Gardens Behind the museum, this grassy area has a small amphitheatre with a panorama of the Tel Aviv seafront as its backdrop. Excavations nearby have uncovered Egyptian, Israelite, Greek and Roman remains. The bizarre white sculpture on one of the hills, neo-Mayan in style, depicts the fall of Jericho, Isaac's sacrifice and Jacob's dream.

Kedumim Square A footbridge connects the gardens to Kikar Kedumim, Old Jaffa's reconstructed centre dominated by restaurants, clubs and galleries. This was where the city's first Jewish hostel was established in 1840. It included two *mikvot* (ritual baths) and a synagogue. Libyan Jews have re-opened the synagogue – it's on Mazal Dagim St, heading up to the left as you come down the steps from Kedumim Square and across from Simon the Tanner's House. Also in the square is another archaeological site showing remnants of a 3rd century BC catacomb.

St Peter's Monastery This orange-painted Franciscan church was built above a medieval citadel on one side of Kedumim Square. It is open for Sunday prayers.

Simon the Tanner's House This is the traditional site of the house where the Apostle Peter was staying when he received divine instruction to preach to non-Jews (Acts 9:32-43) after he had brought Tabitha back to life. It's at 8 Shimon HaBurski St at the bottom of the narrow alley leading down to the right at the foot of the southern steps of Kedumim Square. In the courtyard you can see a well, supposedly used in Peter's day, and a stone sculptured coffin from the same period. Muslims later converted it into a wash-stand to use before praying at the mosque, which was built on the site in 1730. Now a private house, it is officially open daily 8 am to 7 pm; just ring the bell and see if anyone answers. Admission is 70c. Along this narrow alley, which continues north to the other side of St Pierre's Convent are various galleries, a Greek Orthodox church, and an Armenian convent.

Galleries The central gallery area is south of the square and gardens along Mazal Dagim and Mazal Arieh Sts. Mostly open in the evenings, the Horace Richter Gallery attracts the most attention.

Israel Experience Loudly promoted, this modern complex comprises a series of 'multi-media computerised techniques' to present Israel to the masses. The masses choose to stay away. Admission is US$6, students US$4.

Port & Andromeda's Rock This is one of the oldest known harbours. It was mentioned by Hiram, King of Tyre, in conversation with Solomon (2 Chronicles 2:15) and referred to in Jonah 1:3. For centuries this was where pilgrims to the Holy Land first arrived en route to Jerusalem and it was Palestine's main port. Beyond its walls are the remains of the blackened rocks, the largest of which is named after Andromeda, the Greek mythological figure saved from being sacrificed to the Sea Monster by Perseus. Reconstruction of the port and the dredging of the approaches resulted in the rock being damaged.

Tour Every Wednesday a free guided

walking tour of Old Jaffa is organised by the Association for Tourism, Tel Aviv-Jaffa. Meet by the clock tower at 9.30 am, the tour ends at about noon.

Places to Eat

I wouldn't advise buying the Arab sweets displayed so prominently on the corner of Mifraz Shlomo St. Their turnover is far from prolific and so they are usually stale. The regular supply of car exhaust fumes no doubt plays a part in their condition.

On to much better things and something of a legend: *Said Abulafiah & Sons* (tel 834958, 812340) at 7 Yefet St. It's the furthest bakery past the traffic lights up from the foot of the hill. This was Jaffa's first bakery and from its establishment in 1880 it did good business catering for the nearby mosque, police station and the French Hospital. Now, with the family's fourth generation working here, the bakery is busier than ever with Jewish and Arab customers coming from miles around.

The main attraction is their version of the pizza, developed from a traditional Arab recipe of cracking a couple of eggs on top of pitta bread and baking it in the oven. The Abulafiah bakers were the first to retail it and soon added the tomato, mushrooms, cheese and olives. The place really caught on with Israelis and many 'copy-cat' bakeries have opened. Right next door and further down the street, almost identical looking bakeries struggle to compete while the crowds choose to swarm around the original. The central bus station in Tel Aviv also has several pizza bakeries but none of them come close to tasting as good as Abulafiah.

As well as the 'special pizza', regular items include 24 varieties of bread, such as pitta coated in either sesame seeds, or *za'atar* (spices) and olive oil, Iraqi, Arab and Persian breads, and *zambuska* (a type of pastry filled with Bulgarian cheese or potatoes). Zambuska are often split open and an egg baked in its shell (*hamim* – making it brown when shelled) is stuffed

inside and sliced up. The secret of Abulafiah's success is apparently their policy of using only good-quality ingredients and the custom of still burning wood in the now gas-fired ovens to get a better flavour – whatever it is that they do, theirs is easily the best. This wonderful business is open Monday to Saturday from about 5 am right up to 2 am or even later. They are closed on Sunday, a good day for the competition down the street. Prices are good too, about US$1.30 for the 'special pizza'.

Abulafiah recently took up making ice cream too, which has proved very popular as well. Quite a contrast to the heat of a bakery, the ice cream is made next door in over 20 flavours. Gum is used in the recipe, giving it a stretchy consistency.

Two of the best eating places in Jaffa are of the cheap Arab sit-down variety, specialising in excellent hummus. *Kalabouny Brothers* is at 132 Yefet St – continue past Old Jaffa and it's on the right just before the Hapoalim Bank on the corner, (no English sign). It's open from early in the morning till 4 pm, and serves hummus, foul, salad, chips, pitta and coffee; all for about US$4.50. At 1 Dolphin St, *Abu Hassan* (no English sign) does more of the same, less the chips.

On the same street, *Andy's 13½ Gallery* features a café in pleasant surroundings.

Misu, 7 Raziel St (turn left before the clock tower), is a cheap Romanian restaurant, open for lunch only, Monday to Friday, closed Saturday and Sunday. Sparse surroundings but excellent value and great food, with kebabs, sauerkraut, pitta and beer. The interesting menu also includes a cheap type of caviar as well as hummus, liver, steak and sheep's stomach.

The main culinary attraction in the area is fish and the approach to Old Jaffa off Mifraz Shlomo St has several outdoor restaurants, some of which also serve meat grilled 'on the fire'. Although extremely popular with Israelis, I wasn't impressed by the food, service or prices.

Chez le Beau Shebti was one of the most highly praised places that I came across, but a meal of fish with salad, pitta and beer/wine comes to about US$23 per person. You can eat much better for less in Tel Aviv.

Younes on Kedem St (you can see it from the end of Dolphin St) serves a wide range of meats, fish, salads and desserts in clean surroundings. Traditional, basic Oriental food in pleasant surroundings.

Il Patio is a small restaurant at the southern end of Dolphin St serving home-made pasta and some delicious cakes. About US$20 per person.

South of Old Jaffa overlooking a secluded beach, another highly-rated outdoor fish restaurant is *Raulf's*. Follow Kedem St down from Dolphin St. It's some distance and probably too far to go without transport. About US$20 per person.

Israel's best restaurant is probably *Al Hambra* (tel 834453), 30 Jerusalem Blvd, which is a continuation of Hamered St from Tel Aviv. This serves mainly French cuisine at suitably high prices, from about US$40 per person.

In Old Jaffa, *Toutoun* (tel 820693), 1 Mazal Dagim St, is also a very good French-style restaurant, a definite step up from most rivals. About US$25 per person.

Entertainment
Michel's Aladdin (tel 826766), 5 Mifraz Shlomo St, on the right as you walk up from the clock tower, is a popular Oriental nightclub in an 800 year old building that was originally a Turkish bath. Live Oriental music is played here and is usually of a very high standard. Free entrance during the week, US$3.75 Friday, US$6 Saturday, including a 'free' drink. Closed Sunday. Well worth a visit.

Further up the hill and in Kedumim Square and Netiv Mazalot St are other, more expensive clubs of dubious quality.

The *Hamam Theatre* (tel 813261) adjacent to the museum, is another former Turkish bath. It is now a venue for a variety of musical acts and plays.

The *Harimta Theatre/Café*, 8 Mazal Dagim St, features jazz and plays, although admission prices are not cheap.

Beki's, on Magoza St where the daylight hours see the Jaffa flea market, is a Turkish nightclub with good Turkish food and music. It costs US$50 per couple with dinner and wine – Friday and Saturday only.

On the corner near David Raziel St, *Halleluya* is a plush Greek-style Oriental nightclub with singers – very popular with locals who must have more money than their appearance would suggest. Dinner costs about US$60 per couple. Open till dawn.

Nearby, behind the police station, is *Ariana*, similar in style to Halleluya but less grand. Entrance US$8, food and drink is served.

What to do on Shabbat in Tel Aviv-Jaffa
Unlike in Jerusalem, many cafés, bars and restaurants in Tel Aviv-Jaffa are open on Friday nights and are very busy. As most shops and businesses rush to close early on Friday, many people hang out at their favourite café before the sun goes down.

'Little Tel Aviv', (the northern end of HaYarkon, Ben Yehuda and Dizengoff), Dizengoff Square and Old Jaffa are the busiest spots in the evening, along with the seafront. Charles Clore Park, by the West Beach, plays host to out of town visitors with their tents, barbecues and, occasionally, their guitars, bongos, ouds and tambourines. Cinemas are also open – the *Paris* puts on a special programme of film classics.

On Saturday, if the weather is fine, the beaches are packed solid. Despite the beautiful open countryside close by, large numbers of Israelis can be seen picnicking on the small grass area near the central railway station, surrounded by busy traffic.

All the city buses grind to a halt, but the

minibus sherut service runs between Ben Yehuda and Allenby and Mercedes sheruts operate to Jerusalem and Haifa. The other available public transport is the United Services bus No 90, running from the Panorama Hotel, along Allenby, Ben Yehuda, Bograshov, Dizengoff, Reiness and Arlozoroff Sts to Herzlia up the coast.

The only place to buy provisions during Shabbat is the mini-market in Atarim Square, open till about 5 pm – prices are high, so stock up in advance from cheaper sources early on Friday.

Cheap eating places that stay open include the *Adiv Hotel's* self-service restaurant for breakfast, lunch and dinner; and the *Vienna* at 48A Ben Yehuda and *Batia* at 197 Dizengoff, corner of Arlosoroff St for traditional Jewish Shabbat dishes such as cholent and kreplach soup. The *Kassit* café/restaurant, 117 Dizengoff, is also open throughout Shabbat.

In Jaffa, Abulafiah's bakery stays open until 2 am on Saturday morning and opens again at 5 am.

Getting There & Away
With Ben Gurion Airport close by, Tel Aviv-Jaffa is often the visitor's first stop. Just about in the centre of Israel's Mediterranean coast, the city is a popular choice as a base from which to visit other places in this small country.

The highway to the north leads to Haifa and Galilee, to the south, Ashdod, Ashkelon, Gaza and the Negev. The busy highway to the east leads to Jerusalem.

Air Arkia flights depart from the Sde Dov Airport, north of the Yarkon River and the Reading Power Station. These connect directly with Eilat and Rosh Pinna, with further connections to Haifa and Jerusalem. No flights on Saturday.

Bus The central bus station, shared by Egged and Dan, is a confusing set-up spread over several streets, having long

outgrown its original site. See the map for the location of the major routes.

Buses to Jerusalem depart at least every 10 minutes, and the trip takes 50 minutes and costs US$2.90. Departures for Haifa are every hour, more often at peak times, and the one-hour trip costs US$3. You can catch a bus for the US$4.25, 1½ hour trip to Beersheba at least every 10 minutes. There is one night bus and four day buses for the five-hour, US$10 trip to Beersheba.

Taxi Sherut services operate from Salomon St, across from the central bus station to the suburbs, Jerusalem (US$2.90) and Haifa (US$3.50). On Saturday they leave from Moshavot Square on Allenby and cost about an extra 20%. Service taxis to Gaza leave from Jaffa (one hour, US$5) on Yefet St south of St Antonio's Church (take Dan bus No 10 from Allenby).

Train Tel Aviv has two railway stations. The Central railway station (tel 254271) is for Haifa and the north and is at the junction of Haifa Rd, Arlosoroff St and Petah Tiqwa Rd. Trains run almost every hour between 6 am and 8 pm except on Saturday.

The service between Jerusalem and Haifa stops at the South railway station (tel 922676) on Kibbutz Galuyot Blvd to the south of the city (see Jerusalem chapter for the timetable).

Hitch-hiking For Haifa and the north, stand on Haifa Rd north of the Yarkon River. For Jerusalem and the south, stand either by the junction in front of the south railway station or at the intersection of HaMesilla and Golomb Ludvipol Rds.

Getting Around
Airport Transport United Tours bus No 222 provides an excellent service between the city centre and the airport, departing every hour. For information you can try phoning 432414. The left luggage office is on Finn St and is open Sunday to

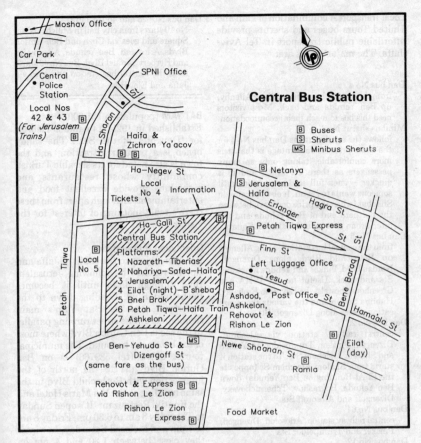

Central Bus Station

Legend:
- B Buses
- S Sheruts
- MS Minibus Sheruts

Moshav Office
Car Park
Central Police Station
Local Nos 42 & 43 (For Jerusalem Trains)
SPNI Office
Ha-Sharon St
Haifa & Zichron Ya'acov
Ha-Negev St
Local No 4
Tickets
Information
Ha-Galil St
Petah Tiqwa
Local No 5

Central Bus Station
Platforms:
1 Nazareth-Tiberias
2 Nahariya-Safed-Haifa
3 Jerusalem
4 Eilat (night)-B'sheba
5 Bnei Brak
6 Petah Tiqwa-Haifa Train
7 Ashkelon

Netanya
Jerusalem & Haifa
Erlanger
Hagra St
Petah Tiqwa Express
Finn St
Left Luggage Office
Yesud
Bene Baraq St
Ashdod, Ashkelon, Rehovot & Rishon Le Zion
Post Office St
Hamaala St
Ben-Yehuda St & Dizengoff St (same fare as the bus)
Newe Sha'anan St
Eilat (day)
Ramla
Rehovot & Express via Rishon Le Zion
Rishon Le Zion Express
Food Market

Thursday, 6 am to 5.45 pm, Friday 6 am to 2.45 pm, closed Saturday. The charge is 80c per item per day.

From the starting point opposite the passenger terminal, the bus travels to: the Panorama Hotel, on Herbert Samuel Esplanade, via Hatayashim Rd; the Central railway station; Weizmann St (for the YMCA hostel); and three stops on HaYarkon St – corner of Nordau Blvd, corner of Arlozorof St (for the Greenhouse hostel and the Hilton, Marina and Shalom hotels), and near the Diplomat Hotel (for the Plaza, Ramada, Sheraton,

Basel, and City hotels, and the Gordon hostel.

Going out to the airport, the bus picks up passengers at the Panorama Hotel, in HaYarkon St south of Allenby Rd (near the Riviera Hotel), north of Shalom Aleichem St (opposite the Yamit Hotel), 104 HaYarkon (opposite the Dan Hotel), 144 HaYarkon (opposite the Diplomat Hotel), 196 HaYarkon (opposite the Hilton), 248 HaYarkon (near the Grand Beach Hotel), Weizmann St (corner of Pinkas St), Central railway station, and Hatayashim Rd.

Local Transport A combination of Dan and United Tours buses and sheruts provide affordable public transport in Tel Aviv-Jaffa. The major routes are:

Dan bus No 4
  from the central bus station, along Allenby, up Ben Yehuda and back. Most visitors need this bus to reach their accommodation
Minibus sherut No 4
  follows the same route as Dan bus No 4 for the same price. Its advantage is that it is more comfortable, taking only as many passengers as there are seats; and it is quicker – once full it doesn't stop until someone wants to get off. It also operates on Shabbat (when the price doubles), between the northern end of Ben Yehuda and the inter-urban sheruts at Moshavim Square
Dan bus No 5
  from the central bus station, along Allenby, up Rothschild Blvd, along Dizengoff, Nordau Blvd, Pinkas and Yehuda Maccabee Sts and back. Useful for the IYHA and Greenhouse hostels, the Egyptian Embassy, Habima Square and the various shops and eating places along Dizengoff St
Dan bus No 20
  central railway station via Alosoroff, Dizengoff, Pinsker, Trumpeldor, HaYarkon and Shalom Aleichem Sts. To the station it starts from Shalom Aleichem St (opposite the El Al Building on Ben Yehuda) down Ben Yehuda, Bograshov, Tchernichovsky, Dizengoff and Alosoroff Sts
Dan bus No 64
  central railway station, Arlosoroff, Dizengoff, Pinsker and Trumpeldor Sts
Dan bus No 12
  Carmel Market, Nahalat Binyamin St, Rothschild Blvd and Ibn Gevirol
Dan bus No 32
  via Weizmann St, King David Blvd, Ibn Gevirol, Bograshov and Ben Yehuda Sts and Allenby Rd
Dan bus No 41 (to south railway station)
  goes between Levinsky St near the central bus station to the south railway station, just off Ludvipol St
Dan bus No 25 (to Jaffa)
  goes from Tel Aviv University and the Diaspora and Ha'Aretz Museums to Jaffa, via Yehuda Maccabee, Ibn Gevirol, Frishman and King George Sts and Allenby

Dan bus Nos 25 and 46 (to Jaffa)
  No 10 starts from city hall in Malchei Israel Square and goes via Chen and Ben-Gurion Blvds, Arlosoroff, Ben Yehuda, Allenby Rd and Herbert Samuel Blvd. Bus No 46 starts from the central bus station and goes via Jaffa and Elat Rds.

BAT YAM (population 131,200)
Established in 1925, its name is Hebrew for 'Daughter of the Sea'. The sandy beach is a popular attraction, and the town is also noted for its sizeable Turkish community whose restaurants and nightclubs provide excellent food and entertainment, although apart from these there's really nothing of interest for the visitor.

Orientation & Information
Bat Yam is just to the south of Jaffa and can be reached by following Jerusalem Blvd through Jaffa until it becomes Rothschild Blvd. Leading down to the waterfront, this is Bat Yam's main thoroughfare. The street running parallel to the sea is Ben Gurion Blvd where most of the hotels can be found. The municipal tourist office (tel 589766) is on Ben Gurion Blvd just to the north of the intersection with Rothschild Blvd in the same building as the Via Maris Hotel and the Kontiki Restaurant. It's open Sunday to Thursday 8 am to 6.30 pm, Friday 8 am to 1 pm and is closed Saturday. In winter they close between 1.30 and 4 pm on Monday and Wednesday.

Places to Stay
All of Bat Yam's hotels are quite expensive – from around US$40/55 for singles/doubles – and are along Ben Gurion Blvd facing the sea, from Rothschild Blvd at the northern end to the last hotel at the southern end. All rooms have showers, some have bathtubs, and prices include breakfast.

Via Maria Hotel (tel 860171), 43 Ben Gurion Blvd, is a simple seaside hotel, near the tourist office. A few doors down

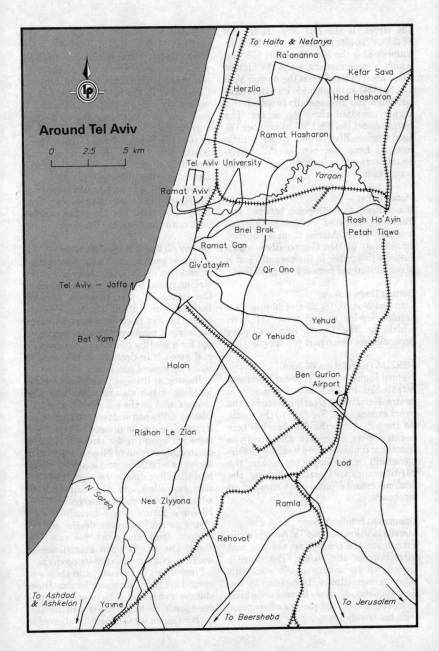

Around Tel Aviv

0   2.5   5 km

To Haifa & Netanya

Ra'ananna

Kefar Sava

Herzlia

Hod Hasharon

Ramat Hasharon

Tel Aviv University

N Yarqon

Ramat Aviv

Rosh Ha'Ayin

Petah Tiqwa

Bnei Brak

Ramat Gan

Giv'atayim

Qir Ono

Tel Aviv – Jaffa

Yehud

Bat Yam

Or Yehuda

Holon

Ben Gurion Airport

Rishon Le Zion

Lod

N Soreq

Nes Ziyyona

Ramla

Rehovot

To Jerusalem

To Ashdod & Ashkelon

Yavne

To Beersheba

the street, is the *Bat Yam Hotel* (tel 864373, 871646) at 53 Ben Gurion Blvd. At number 81 is the *Kfir Hotel* (tel 598639), which is more modern, while the highest rated hotel in Bat Yam is the *Armon Yam* (tel 582424) at number 95; its rooms have balconies and are generally fitted out to a higher standard than the others. The *Sarita Hotel* (tel 589183), at number 127 Ben Gurion Blvd seems to be a little isolated from the rest of the hotels, restaurants and cafés but it enjoys a good reputation.

Places to Eat

It's difficult to distinguish between Bat Yam's highly-rated Turkish restaurants and nightclubs. Among them is *Taverna Istanbul* at 61 Ben Gurion Blvd, which features live music in the evenings and is about US$20 per person for a good feed.

Getting There & Away

Dan bus Nos 10, 18, 25 and 26 provide a regular service to and from Tel Aviv, which is five to 20 minutes away depending on which part you are going to.

HERZLIA (population 66,100)

Named in memory of Theodor Herzl and established in 1924 as an agricultural centre, Herzlia was greatly affected by the rapid expansion of Tel Aviv to the south. As the city grew, the fine beaches here became more accessible and luxurious homes for diplomats and wealthy Israelis were built on the slopes overlooking the Mediterranean. Herzlia Pituah, the seafront area, becomes quite crowded on weekends.

Orientation & Information

Herzlia is 16 km north of Tel Aviv. Herzlia Pituah and the beaches are the only real attraction for the visitor. The town is dominated by luxury hotels and with many foreign diplomats residing in the neighbourhood, the beaches (which charge admission) are particularly popular with the trendy set.

Basel St, Shalit Square and the seafront is the area to head for – the Sharon Hotel in among various cafés, bars and restaurants, is the major landmark and the beach stretches out from it in both directions. To the north and just a short walk away is Sydney Ali Beach, which is free and is often less crowded than surrounding beaches. Sharon Beach is next to the Sharon Hotel, Dabush Beach is near the Daniel Hotel and Accadia Beach is to the south by the Accadia Hotel. Coming in by bus, get off by the Green Door home and garden store or at the Sharon Hotel for the Sydney Ali or Sharon beaches. For the other beaches wait until the Accadia Hotel stop.

Sydney Ali Beach & the Caveman

The free beach boasts a unique attraction in addition to the sand, cliffs and nearby Roman ruins. Nissim Kahalon, known as the 'caveman', has built an amazing house in the cliffside above the beach, where he has lived for about 10 years. Formerly a plasterer, Nissim decided to opt for a healthy lifestyle in the open air and eventually decided on this spot to build his bizarre complex.

Relying as little as possible on regular building materials, he used bits and pieces found on the beach such as empty bottles, driftwood and tyres and mixed his 'cement' using sand, seawater and ash from his wood fire for strength. He has created his version of Noah's Ark, which serves as a bedroom and a pigeon house, topped off by a dinosaur sculpture. He has also tunnelled into the cliff to take advantage of the natural air conditioning. Nissim's future plans include a new 'flying saucer' bedroom design and an octopus sculpture above his café. He would also like to open a small school teaching sculpture using waste products.

Nissim can be persuaded to show you around his home, although he sometimes charges a small fee. The interior is a real eye-opener. He had to battle with the local authorities for some time to be allowed to stay, and he has only recently had electricity connected. He makes a living from his café, which does good business despite the steep prices. His lush garden is irrigated by the waste water from the bathroom. The wooden tables and benches on the café terrace are made from wood found nearby and are varnished using oil washed up on the beach. The palm leaves were donated by his affluent neighbours along the cliff-top.

The deserted Sydney Ali mosque gives the beach its name. Apollonia, a Roman port, is a few hundred metres to the north but the few remains are not really worth a special trip. The Crusaders built battlements here, but they too are now rubble. Nearby you might find pieces of Roman glass from an ancient glass factory.

To reach Sydney Ali Beach, head north from the Sharon Hotel along Galei Thelet St, turn left along the dirt path just before the US Embassy residence, right along the clifftop, past the army installation, continue down the slope and turn left down the road to the beach – it's just over a 15 minute walk. Kahalon's cave is about 100 metres north of the entrance.

Places to Stay

Expensive hotels dominate and there is no budget accommodation. Prices, which include breakfast, vary between summer and winter.

The *Eshel Inn* (tel 052-570208), across from the Sharon Hotel provides one of the cheapest deals. Singles US$30 (winter), US$35 (summer), doubles US$35 and US$40. Another cheaper hotel is the *Mittlemann* (tel 052-72544), 13 Basel St, near Shalit Square with similar prices.

At 29 Hamapilim St, the *Cymberg Hotel* (tel 052-572179) is an attractive villa with a pleasant garden, lawn and veranda. A nice, peaceful place with only 11 rooms. Hamapilim St is two blocks north of Shalit Square, running parallel with Basel St.

The *Tadmore Hotel* (tel 052-572321), 38 Basel St, is staffed by hotel trainees and

the service here can be rather assertive. Singles US$42 to US$65, doubles US$70 to US$80.

Out of the luxury hotels, the *Daniel* (tel 052-544444), dominates. It quotes from the Bible – Daniel 1:19 – in its advertising and boasts an indoor pool, Dead Sea baths and a host of other facilities including a health and beauty spa. Lavish throughout, probably more so than any other Israeli hotel. Singles US$70 to US$123, doubles US$85 to US$144, suites from US$300.

The *Dan Accadia* (tel 052-556677) to the south has a pool, piano bar and synagogue with singles US$70 to US$123, doubles US$85 to US$145.

The *Sharon* (tel 052-575777) has singles for US$55 to US$95, doubles for US$65 to US$105.

Places to Eat

You can try the *Caveman's* fish and/or salads which are surprisingly tasty, although not cheap (US$6 to US$18). On Saturday the *Dabush* restaurant is a popular hangout for the 'in crowd'. Good food, too, such as couscous and stuffed vegetables. It's the restaurant on the left of the Daniel Hotel's towers; the others nearby are also good.

Getting There & Away

United Tours bus No 90 leaves Tel Aviv from the Panorama Hotel and passes along Allenby, Ben Yehuda, Bograshov, Tchernichovsky, Dizengoff, Arlosoroff and Weizmann Sts. The ride costs about US$1 and takes under 40 minutes. The bus runs throughout Shabbat, making Herzlia a popular Saturday outing.

HOLON (population 137,800)

This town was named for the barren sands on which it was established in 1935 (*hol* is Hebrew for 'sand'). Dominated in its formative years by Polish textile workers immigrating from Lodz, Holon soon became an industrial city, turning out goods such as metals, leather and nylon as well as textiles. Despite the industrialisation of the area, gardens, parks and tree-lined streets give the city a pleasant look. Holon is also notable for its tiny Samaritan colony.

BNEI BRAK (population 100,400)

This Orthodox Jewish community was established in 1924 by Warsaw Hasidim. Joshua 19:45 mentions Bnei Brak as a city of the Dan tribe and during the Roman period it became a home to many famous sages of Israel and a centre of Hebrew study. Today the new city, with its numerous yeshivot, has once again become a centre for religious study. A sign of its status is the busy sherut service between here and Mea Shearim in Jerusalem.

PETAH TIQWA (population 128,300)

Petah Tiqwa is Hebrew for 'Gate of Hope' and it was the first Jewish agricultural settlement in Palestine – it's referred to as *Em Hamoshavot* (Mother of the Moshav). Jews from Jerusalem founded a moshav here in 1924 and were faced with considerable hardship in the initial stages of development, relying heavily on financial support from Baron Benjamin Edmond de Rothschild. A stone archway honours his contribution to the town.

RISHON LE ZION (population 109,600)

Meaning 'first in Zion', Rishon Le Zion was founded by Russian Zionists in 1882. After battling with agricultural problems and disease for five years, the settlers were given financial assistance by Baron Benjamin Rothschild – his first direct involvement with Zionism in Palestine. The vineyard and cellars that he helped establish are still among the town's major attractions.

Orientation

Coming south-east from Tel-Aviv, the Carmel winery on Herzl St is just to the south of both the Egged and the Dan bus stops. Dan bus No 19 will drop you off on the corner of Herzl and Rothschild Sts

and Egged will drop you off a little further down on Herzl St.

Carmel Winery

Telephone 942021/8 to arrange a guided tour of the winery, with a brief explanation of Carmel's history and the vinification process and a tasting session to finish. Admission is 90c.

Getting There & Away

Get here on a Dan bus No 19 from Tel Aviv, which leaves from Shalom Aleichem St, between HaYarkon and Ben Yehuda (across from the El Al Building) and is the most convenient bus from the hostels and hotels. Egged bus Nos 200 and 201 leave from the central bus station. Many visitors follow a visit to the winery with a visit to the Weizmann Institute in nearby Rehovot.

REHOVOT (population 70,000)

This quiet town is best known for the Weizmann Institute of Science. Established in 1890 by Polish Jews, *Rehovot* means 'expanses' and the name was taken from Genesis 26:22 to symbolise the community's aims to expand the Zionist settlements in Palestine.

Weizmann Institute of Science

This world-renowned centre was named after Israel's first President, Chaim Weizmann, on the occasion of his 70th birthday in 1944. He was a leading research chemist, and the institute was established to provide facilities for research and study in the sciences. A free slide show explaining the Institute's activities is shown in the Wix Auditorium at 11 am and 3.15 pm, Sunday to Thursday. Closed Friday and Saturday. There is a pleasant 80 hectare garden.

Visitors' Section In Room 102 (tel 08-483597) of the Stone Administration Building (the first building on the left as you enter via the main gate), you can ask about the institute and pick up a variety of brochures. Phone in advance for a guided tour.

Weizmann House Follow the road away from the main gate and eventually bear right to reach the tombs of Weizmann and his wife, Vera, and the lovely house they lived in. Designed by the renowned architect Eric Mendelsohn, it was built in 1937 on this site because of the views across to the Judean hills in the direction of Jerusalem. Outside the house is the Lincoln limousine presented to Weizmann by Henry Ford II. One of only two ever made, the other was given to US President Truman. Open Sunday to Thursday, 10 am to 3.30 pm, closed Friday and Saturday; admission is US$1. From the house you can leave the institute's grounds via the side gate, and follow Hanasi Harishon St back to Herzl St; the bus stop for Tel Aviv is on the right.

Places to Eat

The pleasant self-service *Estate Restaurant* just inside the gate near Weizmann House provides cheap food and drink: main

meals, snacks, hot and cold drinks and beer.

Eternity, 192 Herzl St, serve their vegetarian delights, and *Carvel*, 176 Herzl St, have the popular American ice cream. Various other inexpensive felafel shops and cafés are here, too.

Getting There & Away

Egged bus Nos 200 and 201 leave frequently from Tel Aviv central bus station (US$1.25, 40 minutes), or you can pick up these buses at the Rishon Le Zion bus station (90c, 10 minutes).

RAMLA (population 43,200)

The only town in Israel that was founded and originally developed by Arabs, Ramla was an important crossroads between Damascus, Baghdad and Egypt, with the Jaffa-Jerusalem and the Haifa and Galilee-Beersheba roads converging here. It also has two railway lines running either side of it: Tel Aviv-Jerusalem and Haifa-Ashkelon.

Established in 716 by Caliph Suleiman, its name was derived from the Arabic word *aml* (sand). Until the arrival of the Crusaders in the 11th century, Ramla was the country's capital. In the Middle Ages it served as the first stop on the pilgrims' route from Jaffa to Jerusalem, and a small number of Christians have always lived there. After the 1948 War of Independence the Arab majority were forced to flee and were soon replaced by Jewish immigrants from various countries.

One of Israel's more attractive towns, Ramla is characterised by its pleasant stone buildings and streets lined with eucalyptus trees imported from Australia.

Orientation

The bus from Tel Aviv terminates at the bus station off Herzl Blvd, the main road; the four major sights of interest lie just to the north of this point.

Great Mosque

The Great, or Omari, Mosque (tel 08-

225081), was converted from a Crusader church. The white minaret can be seen to the west from the bus station, near the market. Open Sunday to Thursday 8 to 11 am, closed Friday and Saturday. Donation requested.

Church & Hospice of St Nicodemus & St Joseph Arimathea

Further north along Herzl Blvd, to the left, the clock-faced, square tower is a recognisable landmark. Turn left at Bialik St, and the entrance is through the first gate on your left. Ring the bell and one of the four monks living here will let you in.

According to Christian tradition, Ramla is the site of Arimathea, the home town of Joseph who arranged Jesus' burial with Nicodemus (John 19:38-39). Owned by the Franciscans, the church was originally built in the 16th century, although most of it was completed in 1902. Napoleon stayed in the church during his unsuccessful campaign against the Turks. If you ask, one of the monks will usually show you Napoleon's chambers. Open Monday to Saturday 8 to 11.30 am, closed Sunday; admission is free, donations accepted.

Tower of the 40 Martyrs

This was built in the 14th century as the minaret for the Jamal el Abias Mosque, which was built in the 8th century and has since been destroyed. It is sometimes referred to as the White Tower.

To reach it, continue north of the church along Herzl Blvd, turn left on Danny Mass St, and it's at the end on the left. Apparently in the morning a guard is on duty to let you in, but I never saw him. No doubt the view from the top would be worth the climb, although I imagine the steep stairway is not in good condition.

Pool of St Helena

On the other side of Herzl Blvd and further north, set in pleasant gardens, this 8th century reservoir is on the right of Hayanah St. To reach the water, enter the small building next to the blue and white murals. Named after the mother of the Roman Emperor Constantine, it is known as the Pool of El Anazia in Arabic and Breichat Hakeshatot, the Pool of Arches, in Hebrew. It was built for Harun el-Rashid, of *A Thousand and One Nights* fame.

British War Cemetery

About two km outside Ramla to the east, members of the British forces who defeated the Turks in 1917 are buried.

Getting There & Away

Best visited from Tel Aviv, Egged buses Nos 411, 451, 452 and 455 all leave from the central bus station on Newe Sha'anan St. The fare is US$1.25 and it takes about 35 minutes. There are also regular express buses from Jerusalem. The Ramla bus station fronts onto Herzl Blvd.

ASHDOD (population 68,900)

Along with Gath, Gaza, Ekron and Ashkelon, Ashdod was one of the five great Philistine cities and an important cultural and religious centre.

The Greeks settled here, calling it Azotus, but they were conquered by the Maccabees in about 147 BC. An Arab village, Isdud, was later established here and the mound or *tel* which marks the site is about five km out of modern Ashdod. In the 1948 War of Independence, the Egyptian Army was forced back after a decisive battle nearby and some have drawn parallels between the Jewish victory and Isaiah 19:16-17. In the aftermath of the fighting the local Arab population was forced to leave the area.

The modern city of Ashdod was established in 1957 on what was desert sand by the seashore. It has developed quickly into a major port: its deep water harbour has taken much work from Haifa and caused the closure of Tel Aviv's port. The navy's nautical school is here. Other industries based in Ashdod include cosmetics and textiles plants and a power plant which provides about half the country's supply of electricity.

Ashdod also serves as a major absorption centre for new Jewish immigrants.

Orientation & Information
A 'planned' city, Ashdod has little of interest for most people, dominated as it is by modern-style buildings, industrial sites and earnest attempts at gardening. The beaches are pleasant enough, and you can camp here – there are showers and no-one seems to mind.

Avi Haisman of the Bureau of Public Relations (tel 055-52301), on the 7th floor of the municipality building next to the bus station, is very helpful but there's not a lot he can tell you. The post office is on the main street, Shavei Tzion, and a Steimatzsky bookshop is next to the bus station where there are a few uninspiring eating places.

Fatamid Fortress
Unfortunately, only a small part of this pre-Crusader fortress remains and it is no longer very impressive. Known in Arabic as *Quleat El-Mine* (Fortress of the Port), the site was believed to be relatively recent until excavations unearthed bits of ceramic pottery. An early Arab document tells of Byzantine ships, which at the time were involved in trying to recapture Palestine, docking here to sell Muslim prisoners back to their families. As the ships were sighted off the coast, smoke signals were sent up from the fortress here to let the families know. They would then collect their valuables to barter with the captors. You can still see portions of the four towers. Take local Egged bus No 5 south and tell the driver where you want to go. The remains are now at the end of a row of houses on the city's outskirts.

Yaffa Ben-Ami Memorial Hill
From the top of the hill you have a good view of Ashdod and its surroundings. According to Muslim tradition, these ruins mark Jonah's tomb. He is believed to have settled in the area after his encounter with the whale.

Flea Market
If you happen to be in Ashdod on a Wednesday, you could take a look at the flea market on Lido Beach, which lasts all day.

Places to Stay
Apparently included on Israel's master plan for tourist development, Ashdod currently has only two hotels, both somewhat expensive for what they provide, and both on Nordau St. The *Miami* (tel 08-560573) and the *Orly* (tel 08-521587) are both priced the same too: singles/doubles cost from US$35/50, breakfast included. All rooms have private bathrooms.

Places to Eat
Nowhere in particular stands out. *Felafel King* next to the post office, or buying provisions at the supermarket, usually win by default.

Getting There & Away
Tel Aviv is the nearest main centre; Egged buses run direct, and often continue to Ashkelon. You can also reach Ashdod from Beersheba and Jerusalem.

ASHKELON (population 54,700)
Popular with many Israelis for its sandy beaches and national park, Ashkelon can be difficult for the budget traveller as it has no cheap accommodation.

Another major absorption centre, Ashkelon has a large community of Jews from North Africa, but there are also *olim* (new immigrants) from various countries around the world attending orientation classes during their first three months of residency in Israel.

Ashkelon's history involves a multitude of conquerors: the Philistines, the Israelites, the Greeks, the Romans, the Crusaders and the Muslims.

1	Ancient Mosaic
2	Roman Tomb
3	Shulamit Gardens Hotel
4	King Shaul Hotel
5	Ashkelon Hotel
6	Samson Gardens Hotel
7	Information Office
8	Post Office
9	Police Station
10	Rest House
11	Camping Site
12	Crusader Ruins
13	Crusader Wall
14	Municipality Building
15	Courthouse
16	Hospital
17	Bus Station
18	Stadium
19	Histadrut House
20	Railway Station

Under the Philistines, Ashkelon flourished, becoming one of the country's five major cities, its most important port, and an important caravan stop along the Via Maris, the famous trade route between Syria and Egypt. It was also the centre of their culture and the stronghold of anti-Israelite feeling.

Under the Romans many grand buildings were constructed and Ashkelon is believed to be the birthplace of Herod the Great, who seems to have been particularly keen to embellish his home town. Ashkelon was also an important

town to the Muslims, who called it the 'Bride of the East'. Before the town was finally destroyed by Sultan Baybars in 1270, Ashkelon was the scene of several major battles between Muslims and Crusaders.

In the early 19th century an English aristocrat, Lady Stanhope, led excavations here, looking for gold and silver treasures rumoured to be buried in the area. Later diggings were carried out by the British Palestine Exploration Fund in the 1920s. Although a few foundations of various buildings, statues and columns were uncovered, the ruins of ancient Ashkelon have yet to be found. The few items that were uncovered were mainly used for building houses around Jaffa and Akko.

Orientation

Situated 56 km south of Tel Aviv, Ashkelon is not a large town, but its various neighbourhoods are quite spread out and each one has retained its own identity. Arriving by bus you will go through the old Arab town of Migdal and the industrial area of Ramat Eshkol, before reaching the bus station in the new commercial centre, Afridar. This suburb was built in 1952 by a South African development company with the proceeds of donations from South African Jews. Nearby are the residential suburbs Barnea, Zion Hills and Samson. You will need to use the local buses to get about.

Information

Tourist Office The Tourist Office (tel 051-32412), is in the Afridar Centre. As usual, it seems that the quietest tourist offices have the most pleasant and knowledgeable staff. Open Sunday to Thursday 9 am to 1 pm, Friday 9 to 11.30 am, closed Saturday.

Post Offices The main post office and international telephones are on Herzl St in Migdal. Open Sunday to Thursday 8 am to 7 pm, Friday 8 am to 3 pm, closed Saturday. There are branches in the Afridar centre, Samson and near the bus station in the civic centre.

Other The Discount Bank is on Ben-Gurion St, two blocks west of the bus station, open Sunday to Tuesday and Thursday 8.30 am to 12.30 pm and 4 to 5 pm, Wednesday and Friday 8.30 am to 12.30 pm, closed Saturday. Other banks are in Migdal, Afridar and Samson.

There is a laundromat (tel 051-23431) at Herzl St, Migdal. Open Sunday to Thursday 7 am to 1 pm and 4 to 7 pm, Friday 7 am to 1 pm, closed Saturday.

The police station (emergency tel 100, information 34222/24144) is on the corner of HaNassi and Eli Cohen Sts between Afridar and the bus station.

Byzantine Church & Mosaic Floor

These 5th to 6th century Byzantine church ruins were uncovered in Ashkelon's newest neighbourhood, along with the nearby mosaic floor of the same period. Marble pillars and capitals lie around on the ground. The church is within walking distance from the city centre, but you can also take local bus No 5 to Barnea from either the bus station or the Afridar Centre. Get off at Jerusalem Blvd and walk half a block to Zui Segal St. Bus No 4 stops one block further south on the corner of Jerusalem and Bar Kochbar Sts.

Afridar

Here you'll find a courtyard containing two interesting old Roman sarcophagi. It's open Sunday to Friday 9 am to 2 pm, closed Saturday; admission is free.

Migdal

The shabbier old town has more character than the rest of Ashkelon. Prior to the 1948 War of Independence it was inhabited by Arabs who were brought here by the Turks to work on Lady Stanhope's excavations. Most of them were forced to flee to the Gaza Strip where many now live in refugee camps.

In today's Ashkelon, Migdal is the main shopping quarter, with a fruit and vegetable market on Monday and Wednesday and a produce, clothing and jewellery market on Thursday. You will also find some of Israel's cheapest felafel here. The market is off Herzl St, just past Tzahal St, down a narrow passageway to the left. Local bus No 4, 5 or 7 will take you to Migdal, or you could walk. A pleasant half hour stroll along the road running through an open field will bring you to the market.

National Park

This national park (051-36444) attracts large numbers of Israelis at weekends and holidays with its seaside location. It is dominated by excavations, as it is on the site of 4000-year-old Canaanite remains buried under the ruins of their successors' cities.

From the entrance at the north of the ancient city, the road passes through the 12th century Crusader city wall which can be traced all the way round the site. In the south-western corner, the Tower of Virgins and the Tower of Blood have collapsed onto the beach. At the base of the cliffs are part of the sea wall with its granite columns protruding to the north of the towers. These were used for bonding purposes.

The site's oldest section is between the two parking lots. Piled one on top of the other in the eroded cliff-face are strata from the Middle Bronze Age (beginning circa 2000 BC) to the Roman period. These can be clearly seen from the beach.

The ruins of two Crusader and one Byzantine church are here but all are unimpressive. The open-air auditorium was possibly a well, referred to in records dated 560.

A quadrangle, in the centre of the park, marked by Roman columns probably dates to the 2nd century, although it is often associated with Herod the Great. The columns are only partly visible because the excavators were obliged to replace the earth. The original floor level has been preserved in a small section at the southern end and here you can see various parts of the building which have been collected. These include three major pillar reliefs: two of Nike, the winged goddess of victory on a globe supported by Atlas, and one of the goddess Isis with the child god Horus. Made of Italian marble, they date back to sometime between 200 BC and 100 AD.

Outside the park, to the north, take the first left after the main intersection. At the top of the cliff, after the road turns to the right there is a Roman tomb with places for four bodies, believed to have been built for a wealthy Hellenistic family in the 3rd century. Inside is a well-preserved fresco depicting Greek mythological scenes. Open Sunday to Friday 9 am to 1 pm, Saturday 10 am to 2 pm, admission free.

Beaches

The national park's beach at the southern edge of the town has a grass lawn and the ruins. Delilah Beach is after the holiday village's beach, facing three islands within wading and swimming distance. Barnea Beach attracts the town's wealthier residents. For nude bathing, head for the North Beach. As with the whole Israeli Mediterranean coast, watch out for the strong undertow here.

A few km south of Ashkelon is Kibbutz Zikim. Nearby you can see the floating dock where tankers unload their oil. Unfortunately, they are responsible for the tar which often washes ashore – they illegally wash out their holds with sea water instead of using the more expensive chemicals.

Places to Stay

Camping is the only really cheap way to stay in Ashkelon. You can usually camp with no hassles in the national park or on the beaches if you are discreet. However, watch out for your valuables and do not camp on the kibbutz's beach. It is unsafe for women to camp alone. An official camping ground is adjacent to the national park. There are also bungalows. Despite above average prices, the camping ground is usually full on weekends and holidays.

Renting a private room can be the cheapest deal outside of canvas-dwelling. Contact the tourist office, although sometimes prospective landlords will approach you at the bus station. Rooms vary in quality, and the prices are around US$15 to US$25 per person per night.

Bargain hard, and see the room and facilities before agreeing to anything. Wandering around looking for a room can take forever, as most of these places are in Migdal and are unmarked.

Hotels include the *Ashkelon Hotel* (tel 34188), 7 South Africa Blvd is about 15 minutes' walk from the beach. Singles/doubles are US$20/27, with shower or bath. From the tourist office walk through the National Gardens and turn left on South Africa Blvd. The *Samson Gardens* (tel 34666), 38 Hatamar St has singles/doubles from US$25/40, breakfast included. More expensive is the *King Shaul Hotel* (tel 34124, 34128), 23 HaRakefet St.

Places to Eat

Migdal is the cheapest area to eat in. Some of the country's cheapest felafel is sold on Herzl St under the AGAG sign. At the intersection with Tzahal St a small shop serves tasty Moroccan sandwiches. *Nitzahon*, across the street near the post office, has Ashkelon's best selection of grilled meat and the stuffed cabbage is great – you can eat well here from about US$4. There are a few inexpensive Moroccan places in the area worth trying.

The Egged self-service restaurant at the bus station provides the usual excellent value for money, and the supermarket, two blocks west, provides various types of sandwiches – open Sunday and Monday 9 am to 7 pm, Tuesday to Thursday 9 am to 8 pm, Friday 8 am to 2 pm, closed Saturday.

Entertainment

If you decide to stay, the local nightlife involves a few bars, people-watching, a cinema, the beach and the national park. *Bayit Hakfari* (Village House), next to the clock tower in Afridar Square, is a pub popular with young Israelis.

The *Esther Cinema* (tel 22659), in Givat Zion usually shows English language films. Check with the tourist office for the current schedule of events, which normally includes a few winter concerts.

Delilah Beach often sees tourists and residents alike gathering to drink beer and eat steak or pizza. The civic centre on Hanassi St holds a disco on Saturday night (small admission fee). Also on Saturday night in the national park, *Bustan Hazeytim* (Olive Grove), features dancing, folksinging and sometimes magicians.

Getting There & Away

Ashkelon can be reached by Egged bus No 300, 301 or 311 from Tel Aviv (1¼ hours). It can also be reached by bus from Beersheba and Gaza.

Getting Around

You have to rely on the town's bus network to get around Ashkelon. For the beach, take No 13 – but only in July and August; Nos 3 and 9 will take you to within walking distance of the park behind the beach; Nos 4, 5 and 7 will take you to Zefania Square in the centre of Afridar – No 5 continues to Barnea and all serve Migdal.

AROUND ASHKELON

Kibbutz Yad Mordehai

Established in 1943 and named after Mordechai Anilewicz, a commander of the Jewish Resistance in the Warsaw Ghetto uprising against the Nazis, this kibbutz features a statue of the defiant Anilewicz, grenade in hand. Over the hill to the left of the kibbutz entrance is another monument to ferocious resistance – a rather bizarre reconstruction of the battle which took place on this site during the 1948 War of Independence. The scene shows how the kibbutzniks withstood the Egyptian Army's attack for five days, allowing precious time for Jewish forces to regroup in Tel Aviv. A few months later the kibbutz was recaptured by the Israelis.

There is also a museum which has exhibits illustrating the Jewish Resistance during the Warsaw Ghetto uprising, the Jewish community's life in Poland, and major local incidents of 1948. Open Sunday to Thursday 8 am to 4 pm, Friday 8 am to 2 pm, closed Saturday; admission is US$1, students 80c.

Egged bus No 19 runs between Ashkelon and Yad Mordechai – Sunday to Thursday at 12 noon, 2.45 and 6 pm, Friday at 12 noon and 4.15 pm. The last return bus from the kibbutz is at 3.10 pm (12.40 Friday) so visitors need to take the noon bus from Ashkelon (75c).

Qiryat Gat (population 26,800)

A rapidly growing industrial town at the heart of the Lachish region, Qiryat Gat lies about 22 km east of Ashkelon and can be reached by bus from there and also from Tel Aviv or Jerusalem. Established in 1954, it is named after the Biblical town of Gat which is believed to have stood nearby at Tel Gat, the hill to the north-east. This was a major Philistine city and the birthplace of Goliath. The excavations here have been discontinued and there is little to see in the town. There are some nearby sites of archaeological interest.

Beit Guvrin & Tel Maresha

Surrounding Kibbutz Beit Guvrin is a fascinating series of some 4000 caves, hidden by cacti and fig trees. There are also two archaeological sites nearby – Beit Guvrin and Tel Maresha.

Coming from Qiryat Gat, remnants of a Crusader castle can be seen by the roadside. The turn-off for the site is to the left from the kibbutz, beside a large tree. After a few metres the road forks. To the left is Beit Guvrin and to the right, about two km along, is the circular road leading to Tel Maresha.

The kibbutz is built on the site of a deserted Arab village, Beit Jibrin (House of Gabriel). Opposite is the remains of the ancient town of Beit Guvrin, which was an important town during Roman times. It is mentioned in Talmudic literature of the 3rd and 4th centuries and the Crusaders ruled here in the 12th century. Remains from a 3rd century synagogue, Crusader artefacts and Greek objects of art from Beit Guvrin are on display at Jerusalem's Rockefeller Museum, and Byzantine mosaics found here are now in the Israel Museum, Jerusalem.

Among the ruins at Tel Maresha is the apse of the 12th century Crusader church of St Anna. *Sandhanna*, the Arabic name for Maresha is derived from this.

It is the caves, though, that attract the most interest. Some of them are natural, created as water carried away the soft limestone; others, however, are thought to have been made by the Phoenicians as they dug for limestone to be used in the construction of the port of Ashkelon between the 4th and 7th centuries. During the Byzantine period the caves were used by monks and hermits. St John is said to have been one of those who carved crosses and altars out of the limestone here.

The easiest caves to explore are those west of Tel Maresha – you can see tracks leading from the road. Check each interesting hole in the ground that you see. Some of the caves have elaborate staircases with banisters leading down below ground level. The rows of hundreds of small niches suggest that they were used for raising small domesticated doves used in the worship of Aphrodite by the Sidonian colony between the 3rd and 1st centuries BC.

There are two burial tombs to the east of Tel Maresha, built by the Sidonians and dating from the 3rd to the 2nd century BC.

Public transport to the area is limited. Egged bus No 11 runs twice a day from Qiryat Gat, 8 am and 5 pm (8 am only on Friday). Some of the Qiryat Gat-Hebron buses also pass by. Although there is no official stop, the driver will let you off in front of the kibbutz if you ask him.

Tel Lakhish

Between Beit Guvrin and Qiryat Gat, Tel Lakhish is archaeologically more important but visually less interesting than Tel Maresha. Lakhish was a fortified city before Joshua's conquest (Joshua 10:31). With its strategic location at the intersection of the road to Egypt and the approach to Jerusalem, many battles were fought nearby in ancient times. Nine levels of settlement have been revealed by excavations, but with the most interesting artefacts now displayed in museums in London and Jerusalem, there is little to see at the site itself. Lakhish is not on any major public transport routes – by bus you will need to get off on the Qiryat Gat-Beit Guvrin road and walk/hitch the two km.

NETANYA (population 107,200)

Netanya is both a popular seaside resort, famous for its good sandy beaches and quiet atmosphere, and the capital of the Sharon district; a major industrial centre specialising in diamonds, citrus-packing and, with the country's only brewery, beermaking. Fortunately, the industrial sector of the city has been kept apart from the seafront, making Netanya an attractive city.

Named after Nathan Strauss, an American philanthropist, Netanya was established in 1929 as a citrus growing centre, soon developing as a holiday resort. In the early 1940s the British used it as a convalescent centre for the Allied armed forces. Now aimed at an older clientele, there are limited facilities for budget travellers, but those who choose to stay can enjoy a great climate, lovely surroundings and free entertainment almost every day during the summer.

Orientation

Quite a large place, Netanya is easy to get to know. The main coastal highway, Haifa Rd, links the city to Tel Aviv and Haifa. From Tel Aviv, you pass the railway station on your right just before the big intersection with Herzl St, Netanya's main east-west thoroughfare. The bus station is on Herzl St, six blocks to the west where Herzl meets Weizmann and Benyamin Blvds. A further six blocks bring you to Atzma'ut (Independence) Square, the downtown area by the sea. The tourist office, eating places and shops are all in this area and the hotels are nearby.

Information

Tourist Offices The Government Tourist Information Office (tel 27286), on the south-western corner of Atzma'ut Square, is open Sunday to Thursday 8.30 am to 2 pm and 4 to 7 pm, Friday 8.30 am to 2 pm, closed Saturday. The staff are very helpful, friendly and generally on-the-ball. The Municipal Tourist Office, on Lion Square, east of Atzma'ut Square on Herzl St, is open Sunday to Thursday 9 am to 1 pm and 5 to 7 pm, Friday 9 am to 1 pm, closed Saturday. Its role is only to help with finding accommodation for tourists rather than to give general information.

Post Office The Post Office (tel 051-41109), is at 59 Herzl St with branches in Atzma'ut Square and at 15 Herzl St. Open Sunday to Tuesday and Thursday 7.45 am to 12.30 pm and 3.30 to 6 pm, Wednesday 7.45 am to 2 pm, Friday 7.45 am to 1 pm, closed Saturday.

Other Banks can be found along Herzl St. There is a laundromat at 28 Smilansky St, near the corner of Remez St (south of Herzl St). The police emergency telephone number is 100.

Beaches

Netanya's 11 km of free sandy beaches are the basis of the city's 'Riviera' label. The seven lifeguard stations dotted along the beach are an indication of how strong the currents are. The Qiryat Sanz Beach in the north is for religious Jews with separate bathing times for men and women.

Diamond Cutting Factories

A free audio-visual programme is put on to attract potential buyers at the

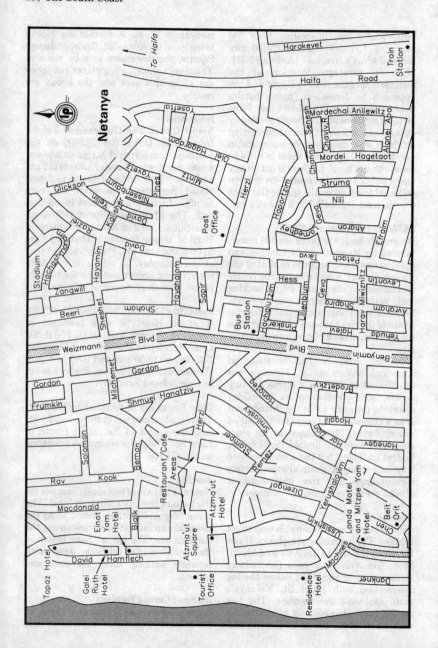

commercial NDC showrooms at 90 Herzl St (tel 34730, 34624) and 31 Benyamin Blvd (tel 22233). You can also see diamonds being cut and polished. Other free factory tours are put on at Osco Jewellery Ltd (tel 40555), 8 Shoham St, one block north of the bus station; and at Diamimon (tel 41725, 91182), Atzma'ut Square.

Citrus-Packing Houses

Enquire at the tourist office between January and March about visits to a citrus-packing house.

Places to Stay

Most hotel prices vary considerably between the low season (November to February), the regular (March to mid-July and September to October), and the high (mid-July to August and Jewish holidays). The further you are from the sea, the less you tend to pay, as well. Netanya has a large German-Jewish population and most of the hotels seem to be run by them. Empty rooms may mean that the low season prices quoted here will apply in the high season too.

Places to Stay - bottom end

The *Landa Motel* (look for the sign 'Motel – Rooms to Rent') (tel 22634), 3 Jabotinsky Blvd has doubles from US$25, with breakfast. Close to the beach, it's to the south of Atzma'ut Square. *Beit Orit*, 21 Hen St, nearby (ask for directions) is a delightful hotel run by Swedish Christians. Nicely decorated and very comfortable, it is often full with Scandinavian groups. US$12 per person in twin-bedded rooms, US$18 for a single, breakfast included.

Places to Stay - middle

Netanya has over 30 listed hotels, most of which fall into the middle bracket. As usual, bargain hard, but expect higher prices in the high season.

In Atzma'ut Square is the *Hotel Atzma'ut* (tel 22562) to the south on the corner at 2 Ussishkin St, singles/doubles

from US$15/20, and on the north side the more modern *Hof Hotel* (tel 22825), with singles/doubles from US$20/32.

To the south of the square, Gad Machnes St starts by the tourist office and is just across from the seafront. At No 9, the *Hotel Margoa* (tel 624434) has singles/doubles US$30/40, with breakfast; at No 17, the *Grand Metropol Hotel* (tel 38038) is higher class, with singles/doubles US$35/55, with breakfast. It has a lower-grade sister hotel, the *Metropole* (tel 624777) behind it, with cheaper rooms.

The *Palace Hotel* (tel 620222), 33 Gad Machnes St, has singles/doubles from US$25/50. Behind the Palace, the small *Daphna Hotel* (tel 23655), 29 Rishon-le-Zion St, has sparse, cramped double rooms for US$30. The nearby *Mizpe-Yam Hotel* (tel 23730), 4 Karlebach St, has singles/doubles from US$30/35, with breakfast.

At 25 Ussishkin St the *Hotel Reuven* (tel 23107), has a pool, pleasant gardens and typically gruff management, for US$25/34 for singles doubles. Prices double in the high season.

North of Atzma'ut Square, on King David St, the hotels include the *Ginot Yam* (tel 341007), with singles/doubles from US$25/40, with breakfast. Two blocks from the square, the *Topaz Hotel* (tel 624555), has kitchen facilities available at extra cost; singles/doubles cost from US$45/60, with breakfast.

Places to Stay - top end

The luxury *Dan Netanya* (tel 30044), on Nice Blvd is the resort's top hotel with pool, sauna and tennis. Singles/doubles start at US$85/110, breakfast included.

Places to Eat

Budget visitors are not really catered for, and the cheapest options are the Egged self-service restaurant at the bus station, and the felafel stalls. There is a street market near the bus station on and around Zangwill St.

On Atzma'ut Square and along Herzl

St are several uninspiring cafés and restaurants. *Pundak Ha Yam Grill* Bar at 1 HaRav Kook St, off Herzl St by the square, seems to be a bit better than most. Hummus, spaghetti and grilled meats; good portions and you can eat well from US$5.

Entertainment
Netanya is proud of its reputation for providing visitors with a wide programme of organised events. Most of it is geared towards older tourists – younger travellers tend not to be so enthusiastic about bingo, bridge, chess or lawn bowls.

During the summer months in particular, the range of activities available is wide and the crowds of visitors obviously appreciate it. The Netanya Orchestra plays free concerts each Tuesday evening in Atzma'ut Square and there is also free Israeli folk dancing in the square on Saturday evening. In the amphitheatre in King's Park, there are free films and concerts.

All year round, the Cinematheque, Ohel-Shem Hall, 4 Raziel St, shows a film at least once a week.

Getting There & Away
Bus There are buses about every 10 minutes to and from Tel Aviv, a mere 20 minutes' drive away. Services to Haifa, Jerusalem and Ben-Gurion Airport run every 30 minutes and there are infrequent buses for Beersheba and Eilat.

To reach Caesarea, Meggido, Afulla, Nazareth or Tiberias, take a bus from Netanya to Hadera and change for the required destination.

Taxi Sherut services operate from Herzl St by Zion Square to Tel Aviv and Haifa.

Train The commuter Haifa-Tel Aviv and the less frequent Haifa-Jerusalem services stop at Netanya.

Getting Around
Most of the the areas of interest can be reached on foot as they are centred around Atzma'ut Square, the beach and the bus station. Arriving by train you will need to take a bus to the city centre.

Haifa & the North Coast

HAIFA

With a population of 224,700, Haifa is Israel's third-largest city, the country's main port and industrial centre, and home to two major universities. It is also the world centre of the Baha'i faith. Set on the wooded slopes of Mount Carmel overlooking the sea, the upper section of the city includes some delightful residential areas. The panoramic views to the east across Carmel National Park and the city lights at night are enchanting.

Haifa's beaches are among the country's best and there are also excellent museums, art galleries and venues for music and theatre. In addition Haifa boasts some of the best Israeli fast-food – the bakeries and felafel stalls are particularly good. Despite these attractions, few travellers spend much time in the city. However, there are quite a few places nearby which are well worth a brief visit and the city can be a useful base.

History

The city's name first appeared in 3rd century Talmudic literature and although its origin remains obscure, it has been related to the Hebrew words *hof yafe* (beautiful coast). The Crusaders called the city 'Caife', 'Cayfe' and sometimes 'Caiphas', which suggests that the name Haifa may have evolved from Caiaphus, the high priest of Jerusalem at the time of Jesus, who was was born in the city.

In earlier biblical times, the prophet Elijah was here, as were the Phoenicians.

There is evidence that one of the earliest known Jewish communities came from this area. Their exposure to foreign influences eventually led them to speak Hebrew in a way different from their fellow Jews. As a result of their mispronunciation of many important words and their inability to differentiate between gutterals, the rabbinical authorities decided that they should not be permitted to officiate in synagogues or to serve as readers of the Torah.

Haifa was an important Arab town during the Middle Ages, but early in the 12th century it was destroyed in battle when the Arabs teamed up with the small number of Jews to defeat the Crusaders. Nearby Akko superseded the town in importance, and when the Ottoman Turks took control of Palestine, Haifa was an insignificant village. Strangely, the Jews did not consider Akko part of the Holy Land, and the community used to come to Haifa to bury their dead.

By early in the 19th century, Haifa's Jewish community had begun to increase. With the growth of political Zionism the town expanded quite dramatically, although early in the 20th century the population was still only 10,000. Its port area was marshland, sand dunes dominated the coastline and the slopes of Carmel were used to graze sheep.

In 1898, Theodor Herzl, the founder of political Zionism, visited Haifa and visualised what lay ahead for modern Haifa: 'huge liners rode at anchor ... serpentine road to Mount Carmel', and at the 'top of the mountain there were thousands of white homes and the mountain itself was crowned with imposing villas'. His predictions have proved amazingly accurate.

The construction of the Hejaz Railway between Damascus and Medina in 1905 and the later development of lines to Zemach, Akko and the south of the country, started Haifa's modern revival. During the British Mandate the modern port was constructed – a major task which involved reclaiming from the sea the land now occupied by the warehouses, port offices, railway lines and adjoining streets. Haifa then began its rapid transformation, becoming the country's

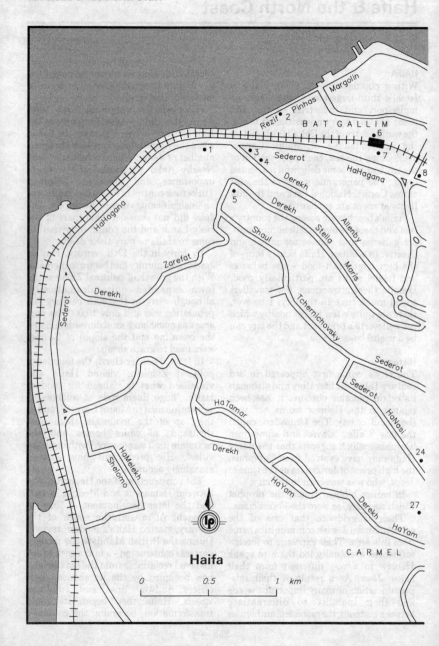

Haifa

0   0.5   1 km

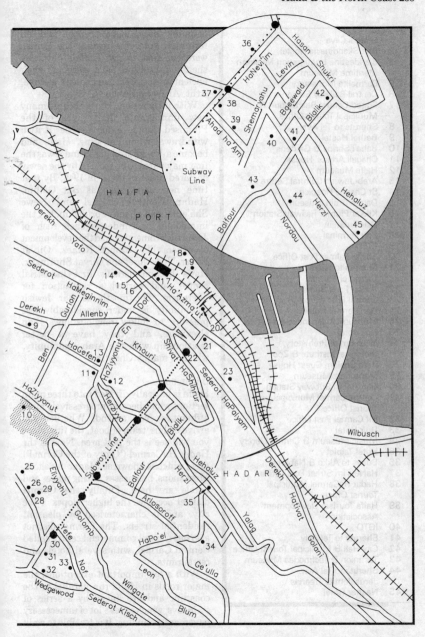

1 Elijah's Cave
2 Beit Skandinavia Hostel
3 Clandestine Immigration Museum
4 Maritime Museum
5 Carmelite Monastery
6 Central Railway Station
7 Egged Central Bus Station &
  Municipal Tourist Office
8 Sheruts to Tel Aviv
9 Bethel Hostel
10 Baha'i Shrine & Gardens
11 Chagall Artists' House
12 Haifa Museum
13 Arab-Jewish Cultural Centre
14 St Charles' Hospice
15 Dagon Grain Museum
16 Kikkar Plumer Railway Station
17 Beit Erdstein
18 Port Terminal
19 IGTO
20 Sha'ar Palmer Post Office
21 Sheruts to Isfiya &
   Daliyat el Karmel
22 Kikkar Paris Subway
23 Central Post Office
24 Dan Carmel Hotel
25 Museum of Japanese Art
26 Nof Hotel
27 Museum of Prehistory,
   Biological Institute & Zoo
28 Beth Shalom Guest House
29 Mane Katz Museum
30 Gan HaEm Subway Station
31 Central Carmel Municipal
   Tourist Office
32 Mt Carmel Post Office
33 Duir Hotel
34 Music Museum & Central Library
35 Hotel Talpiot
36 Buses to Akko & Nahariya
37 HaNevi'im Street Post Office
38 Hadar HaCarmel Municipal
   Tourist Office
39 Haifa Tourism Development
   Association
40 IGTO
41 Sheruts to Tel Aviv
42 City Hall & Municipal Tourist Office
43 Technion & Technodea Museum
44 Sheruts to Tel Aviv,
   Jerusalem & Tiberias
45 Nesher Hotel

shipping base, naval centre and oil terminal. For some reason, the British were the first to use Haifa's naturally sheltered position as a harbour; their ancient predecessors had chosen Caesarea, Atlit, Ahziv and Akko.

With its new port, Haifa became many new immigrants' first sight of the Promised Land. Prior to the British withdrawal from Palestine, Haifa had become a Jewish stronghold and it was the first major area to be secured by the newly declared State of Israel in 1948. By that time new areas such as Bat Gallim, Hadar, Central Carmel and Newe Sha'anan had already sprung up, but the immediate post-independence rush of Jewish newcomers spurred the development of others like Ramot Remez, Qiryat Elizer, Newe Josef and Qiryat Shprinzak. Haifa became Israel's first industrial centre, and earned a reputation for liberalism. The mostly secular Jewish community is under considerably less pressure to follow religious laws than elsewhere, and they have a better relationship with the Arab community, which is mainly Christian.

Orientation
Haifa is basically divided into three main sections which become progressively more affluent as you ascend. Whether you arrive by bus, train or boat, the first place you will see is the port area. Next is the Hadar HaCarmel ('Glory of the Carmel') area, which is known as 'Hadar' for short. Most shops, businesses, eating places and hotels are here. Finally the Carmel district occupies the higher slopes of the city, and is characterised by pleasant residential streets. The Carmel district also has a small commercial centre called Central Carmel, with several hotels and restaurants.

With a few important exceptions, the major roads in Haifa run parallel to the coastline and are linked by a series of stairways, which saves a lot of unnecessary pavement-pounding. It is feasible to walk

Top: Haifa panorama with the gold dome of the Baha'i Shrine (NT)
Bottom: The port, Akko (NT)

Top: View towards Capernaum, on the shore of the Sea of Galilee (NT)
Left: The Hula Valley & the Golan Heights from near Tel Hai (RE)
Right: Simlat Alsheih, Safed (NT)

between some sections of the port area and Hadar, but the tiring slopes encourage you to use public transport to and from Central Carmel.

Information

Tourist Offices Haifa has two IGTO offices – the one at the port (tel 63980) is usually open to coincide with the arrival of ferries and cruise ships, while the main office (tel 666521/3) is at 18 Herzl St in Hadar, open Sunday to Thursday 8.30 am to 5 pm, Friday 8.30 am to 3 pm, closed Saturday.

Municipal Tourist Offices are at four locations: the central bus station, open Sunday to Thursday 9 am to 4 pm, Friday 9 am to 1 pm, closed Saturday; in Hadar (tel 663056), 23 HaNevi'im St, open Sunday to Thursday 8 am to 7 pm, Friday 9 am to 1 pm, closed Saturday; in Hadar in City Hall (tel 645359), 14 Hassan Shukri St, open Sunday to Friday 8 am to 1 pm, closed Saturday; and in Central Carmel (tel 83683), 119 HaNassi Ave, open Sunday to Thursday 9 am to 1 pm, Friday 8 am to 1 pm, closed Saturday.

Haifa Tourist Development Association (tel 671645) is at 10 Ahad Ha'Am St, just off HaNevi'im St in Hadar. There is also a VTS office here. Open Sunday to Thursday 10 am to 12 noon, closed Saturday.

Post Offices & International Telephones The main post office, poste restante and international telephones are at 19 HaPalyam in the port area. Open Sunday to Thursday 8 am to 8 pm, Friday 8 am to 2 pm, closed Saturday. A more central branch is in Hadar at the corner of HaNevi'im and Shabtai Levi Sts, open Sunday to Thursday 9 am to 7 pm, Friday 8 am to 2 pm, closed Saturday.

Banks & Moneychangers Haifa's port area is a popular haunt for black marketeers, who offer a better rate than the banks – but they change cash only and there's a definite risk of being ripped off. Banks are easily found on Jaffa Rd, and in Hadar on and around HaNevi'im St.

The American Express office is in the port area at Meditrad Ltd (tel 642267), 2 Khayat Square. The entrance is in the alleyway near Steimatzsky's off Ha'Atzma'ut St, just west of Khayat St. Open Sunday to Tuesday and Thursday 8.30 am to 4 pm, Wednesday and Friday 8.30 am to 1 pm, closed Saturday.

Society for the Protection of Nature in Israel SPNI is at 8 Menahem St (tel 664135), near Nordau St. Open Sunday, Monday, Wednesday and Thursday 8.15 am to 3.45 pm, Tuesday 9.15 am to 4.45 pm, Friday 8.15 am to 12.30 pm, closed Saturday.

Student Travel ISSTA and ISIC are at 28 Nordau St, Hadar (tel 660411) – I found the staff to be consistently rude. Open Sunday to Tuesday and Thursday 8.30 am to 1 pm, 4 to 6 pm, Wednesday and Friday 8.30 am to 1 pm, closed Saturday.

Other Steimatzsky's bookshops are in the central bus station's arcade and at 82 Ha'Atzma'ut St, near Khayat St in the port area, and at 16 Herzl St, near the tourist office in Hadar. Also in Hadar, Beverly Book (tel 933217), 7 Herzl St, has a good selection of cheap new and used books, and old comics; open Sunday, Monday, Wednesday and Thursday 9 am to 1 pm, 4 to 7 pm, Tuesday, Friday 9 am to 1 pm, closed Saturday. In Carmel, Studio 5, 5 HaYam Rd; open the same hours.

The swimming pools are all in Carmel. The Maccabee pool (tel 80100) in Bikurim St is heated in winter, and admission is US$4, less for students. Galei Hadar pool (tel 667854) is at 9 HaPoel St, admission is around US$3. Both open daily, closing early Friday afternoon. The Dan Carmel Hotel's pool is open to non-residents for about US$7.

The central police station is at 28 Jaffa Rd in the port area (emergency tel 100).

Tours

The Haifa Tourism Development Association organises a free guided walking tour every Saturday at 10 am. Meet at the signposted observation point at the corner of Sha'ar HaLevenon and Ye'fe Nof Sts. The guide leads you down to the Haifa Museum, taking in most of the sights en route and pointing out various aspects of the city. Not mind-blowing, but it's one way to get your initial bearings in Haifa.

Egged Tours offer a half-day tour of the city for US$15, which seems a lot to pay for something you could do just as well on your own. They also offer tours to nearby Caesarea, Tel Aviv, Akko, Rosh Hanikra and the Druze villages.

Beaches

Haifa has some good beaches, most of which are to the north and the west – most of them are pay beaches, charging about US$2 per person per day. Closest is Shaqet beach, reached on Egged bus No 41 from Hadar. Bat Gallim beach is near the central bus station, and is rocky and not very attractive, although there is a free sandy stretch nearby. Egged bus No 41 also brings you here, or it is within easy walking distance from the central bus station. Carmel beach is the best free beach in Haifa and worth the longer ride on Egged bus No 44 or 45 from Hadar. Zamir and Dado beaches are south of Carmel beach.

Cable Car

This runs from near Bat Gallim Promenade up the Carmel's slopes to near the Carmelite Monastery. A recorded commentary in Hebrew or English gives a few facts about the surroundings en route but the ride is short and leads from one unexciting place to another. Open Sunday to Thursday 9 am to 11 pm, Friday 9 am to 3 pm, Saturday 4 to 11 pm. Return trip US$3.

To reach the lower station, you can walk the few blocks from the central bus station: take Ha'Aliya HaSheniya St. Egged bus No 45 speeds along Haganah Blvd; keep a lookout for the lower station to your right, there is a bus stop just past it.

Clandestine Immigration & Navy Museum

This museum in a boat deals with the Zionists' illegal immigration during the British Mandate. The boat is the *Af-Al-Pi*, one of the many which attempted to run the British blockade. It's across the busy Haganah Blvd from the lower cable car station at 204 Allenby Rd (tel 536249). Open Sunday and Thursday 9 am to 4 pm, Monday to Wednesday 9 am to 3 pm, Friday 9 am to 1 pm, closed Saturday. Admission is 70c.

National Maritime Museum

Just up the street at 198 Allenby Rd (tel 536622), this museum deals with the history of shipping in the Mediterranean area. There are some interesting archaeological finds in the collection. It's open Sunday to Thursday 10 am to 4 pm, Saturday 10 am to 1 pm. Closed Friday. Admission is US$2.50, students US$1.80 – free on Saturday.

Elijah's Cave

Just across Allenby Rd from the National Maritime Museum, this is where Elijah is believed to have hidden from King Ahab and Queen Jezebel after he slew the 450 priests of Ba'al (I Kings:17-19). There is also a Christian tradition that the Holy Family once sheltered here, and Elijah in the guise of Khadar 'the green prophet' is recognised by Muslims, so it's a holy place. Pilgrims of each of these three faiths come here to pray, and Arabs in particular enjoy it as a picnic site. The cave is also believed to provide relief for nervous disorders.

The cave is open in summer Sunday to Thursday 8 am to 6 pm, Friday 8 am to 1 pm, winter Sunday to Thursday 8 am to 5 pm,

Friday 9 am to 1 pm, closed Saturday. Admission is free. It is possible to climb up the hill from here to reach the Carmelite Monastery.

Carmelite Monastery

This monastery on Stella Maris Rd belongs to the Carmelites, a Catholic order that originated in the area, taking its name from the mountain. In the late 12th century, some Crusaders settled on the western slopes of Mount Carmel, wanting to live a hermit lifestyle in the caves here, just like the prophet Elijah. Later they became a part of the Jerusalem diocese and were eventually named the Carmelites.

Over the centuries they have suffered from Muslim persecution, twice having to abandon their monasteries. The current site is built over what they believe to be a cave where Elijah lived. The ruins of a medieval Greek church, St Margaret's Abbey, and an ancient chapel, probably Byzantine, had to be cleared from the site first.

The monastery was used by Napoleon's forces as a temporary hospital during his unsuccessful campaign in 1799. When he retreated, the Turks massacred the wounded and the Carmelites were again driven out. When they were eventually allowed to return, they buried the dead in a garden tomb, and erected a memorial monument in the form of a pyramid.

The monastery was destroyed in 1821 by Abdallah, Pasha of Akko, and a new church and monastery was opened in 1836, and named Stella Maris (Star of the Sea). Today the complex houses an extension of the International College of Theology of the Carmelites in Rome; the old building is now a hospice for pilgrim groups.

Paintings in the chapel's dome portray Elijah and the famous chariot of fire, King David with his harp, the saints of the order, the prophets Isaiah, Ezekiel and David, and the Holy Family with the four evangelists below. The cupola's base bears two texts from the Old Testament used in the mass service. The stained-glass windows portray Elijah in the desert, elevated in the chariot. The statue of Mary was made in two parts – the head in Genoa, Italy, in 1820, and the body about 100 years later, from Lebanese cedar.

A small adjoining museum contains ruins of former Mount Carmel cloisters dating from Byzantine and Crusader times. Open daily 8.30 am to 1.30 pm, 3 to 6 pm. Admission is free. Egged bus Nos 25 and 26 from Hadar and No 31 from Central Carmel stop nearby. To walk down to Elijah's Cave, cross the car park to the left of the coastguard/military installation and follow the track. The convent of the Carmelites' female order is on Tchernichovsky St, around the corner from the monastery, and is closed to the public.

Sculpture Garden

This garden, by the junction of HaZiyonut Blvd, features bronze sculptures by Ursula Malbin.

Baha'i Shrine & Gardens

Haifa's most impressive attraction is the golden-domed Shrine of the Bab which is in the middle of the beautifully manicured Persian Gardens. It contains the tomb of the Bab, the man who is called the 'Martyr-Herald' and the 'Forerunner' of Baha'ism.

The shrine, completed in 1953, combines the style and proportions of European architecture with designs inspired by the Orient. It is constructed of Chiampo stone cut and carved in Italy, with monolithic columns of Rose Baveno granite. The 12,000 eye-catching fish-scale tiles were made in the Netherlands by a process of fire glazing over gold leaf.

Take Egged bus No 22 from the central bus station or Nos 23, 25, 26 and 32 from HaNevi'im or Herzl Sts in Hadar stop outside. The shrine is open daily 9 am to 12 noon, with the gardens remaining open

Baha'i building

until 5 pm. Admission is free. Remove your shoes before entering.

Universal House of Justice

On the other side of HaZiyonut Blvd and higher up the hill, this impressive white marble building with a colonnade of 58 Corinthian columns, houses the nine Baha'is who form the co-ordinating body of all the faith's activities. They are elected by secret ballot every five years by members of the National Spiritual Assemblies of the Baha'is worldwide. Closed to the public, the building faces the Shrine of Baha'u'llah in Bahje, near Akko across the bay, and in its garden stand four Carrara marble monuments erected over the tombs of some of Baha'u'llah's relatives.

The International Baha'i Archives Building

Another attractive construction in the Ionic style of classical Greek architecture, this is a private museum of Baha'i relics and historical material. Built of Chiampo stone from Italy with green roof tiles from the Netherlands, it, too, is closed to the public.

Mane Katz Museum

Mane Katz, an influential artist of the Paris Jewish Expressionist group, left his studio, works and collection to the city of Haifa where he spent the last years of his life. The museum (tel 83482), at 89 Yafe Nof St, near the Dan Carmel Hotel, is open Sunday to Thursday 10 am to 1 pm and 4 to 6 pm, 10 am to 1 pm Saturday, closed Friday. Admission is free.

Tikotin Museum of Japanese Art

This museum (tel 383554), at 89 HaNassi Ave, was established in 1959 after Felix Tikotin of the Netherlands donated his private collection of Japanese art to the city of Haifa. Exhibits include over 7000 items such as paintings, woodblock prints, drawings, lacquer work, metals and ceramics of both ancient and modern Japan. Open Sunday to Thursday 10 am to 5 pm, Saturday 10 am to 2 pm, closed Friday. Admission is US$2.50, students US$1.80 – free on Saturday.

Gan Ha'em (Mother's Park), Zoo & Museum

With a small amphitheatre and an arcade of cafés, bars and shops, the park is particularly popular with the locals on Saturday. At its northern end is the zoo and museum complex (tel 337833).

The zoo features animals indigenous to Israel, and the M Stekelis Museum of Prehistory, the Natural History Museum and the Biological Institute deal with aspects of the area's history, flora and fauna. The complex is open Sunday to Thursday 8 am to 4 pm, Friday 8 am to 1 pm, Saturday 9 am to 4 pm (July to August – Sunday to Thursday 8 am to 6 pm). Admission is US$2, less for students and children.

Haifa Museum
The Haifa Museum (tel 523325), at 26 Shabtai Levi St Hadar, is three museums in one:

Museum of Ancient Art This includes sculpture, Egyptian textiles, Greek pottery, decorated oil lamps, terracotta figurines and coins from the time of the First Revolt against the Romans, items recovered from the sea off Haifa and various exhibits from excavations.

Museum of Modern Art Includes late 18th century collections and contemporary Israeli paintings, sculptures, graphics and photographs; also graphic works by world-renowned artists from Europe, America and South-East Asia.

Museum of Music & Ethnology Changing exhibitions display musical instruments clothing, crafts and jewellery.

All three are open Sunday, Monday and Wednesday 10 to 1 pm, Tuesday, Thursday and Saturday 10 am to 1pm and 6 to 9 pm, closed Friday. Admission is US$2.50, students US$1.80 – free on Saturday.

Chagall Artists' House
Works of contemporary Israeli artists are exhibited here, at 24 HaZiyonut Blvd on the corner of Herzlia St in Hadar (tel 522355). Open Sunday to Thursday 10 am to 1 pm, 4 to 7 pm, closed Friday, Saturday 10 am to 1 pm. Admission is free.

Beit HaGefen Arab-Israeli Cultural Centre
This centre sponsors joint Arab-Jewish social activities, and could be worth a visit – check to see if there are any social events or lectures during your stay. It's in Hadar on the corner of HaGefen St and HaZiyonut Blvd (tel 525252).

Technodea Museum
Its full title is the National Museum of Science & Technology. On Balfour St in Hadar (tel 671372), it specialises in

interactive displays mainly aimed at the younger generation. Open Monday, Wednesday and Thursday 9 am to 5 pm, Tuesday 9 am to 7 pm, Friday 9 am to 1 pm, Saturday 10 am to 2 pm, closed Sunday. Admission is US$3.20, students US$2.50. Walk uphill on Balfour from Herzl St and it's on the right, opposite No 15.

Technion
The Technodea Museum is on the old campus of the Technion, Israel's leading technological institute. Built in 1912, this was the first building in Hadar, which was initially known as the Technion quarter. The Turkish-style building houses the school of architecture, while Technion City in Newe Sha'anan comprises other departments such as electrical and soil engineering, chemistry, building research, aeronautics and physics. The Coler-California Visitors' Center presents the history and achievements of the institute. There are films and exhibits of the institute's work, including the Lavi fighter plane, a laser disc video module, a laser hologram and a robot.

Just before WW I the Technion saw a bitter controversy over the usage of modern Hebrew. Some of the school's German founders insisted that German was the only language suitable for teaching science. The students disagreed, refused to study, and eventually won. It's open Sunday to Thursday 8.30 am to 2 pm, Friday 8.30 am to 12 noon, closed Saturday (tel 293863, 210664). Take Egged bus No 17 or 19 from the central bus station, No 19 from Herzl St Hadar, or No 31 from Carmel to reach Technion City.

Haifa University
On the summit of Mount Carmel with the best views of Haifa and far beyond, the modern university campus is dominated by the 25-storey Eshkol Tower. Designed by the renowned architect Niemeyer, it features a top-floor observatory and a

museum in the basement. The Reuben & Edith Hecht Museum houses a fine collection of archaeological artefacts relating to Jewish history before the Diaspora. Open Sunday to Thursday 10 am to 1 pm, Tuesday also 4 to 6 pm, Saturday 10 am to 1 pm, closed Friday. Admission is free, and free guided tours of the museum are given Sunday to Thursday at 12 noon, on Tuesday also at 5 pm and on Saturday at 11.30 am. Free guided tours of the campus are available Sunday to Thursday between 8 am and 1 pm. On arrival dial 2093 or 2097 on the internal telephone system to speak with the Public Affairs Department.

Take Egged bus No 92 from the Central Bus Station, or No 24 or 37 from Herzl St, Hadar. Or walk the steep 20-minute climb from downtown.

Dagon Grain Silo

Not quite what most people come to Israel to see, but this grain silo is worth a visit. The distinctive fortress-like construction at Pulmer Square on Ha'Atzma'ut St near the port is the country's tallest industrial building. You can take a free guided tour of the plant to learn something about the other oldest profession: the cultivation, handling, storing and distribution of grain. There is also a small archaeological exhibit which is open to visitors only when the tours are given, which is Sunday to Friday at 10.30 am. Closed Saturday. Take Egged bus No 10, 12 or 22.

Railway Museum

Housed in the old Haifa East Railway Station (tel 531211 Ext 2347), opposite 40 Hativat Golani Rd in Ottoman buildings, the new museum features a collection of stamps, photographs, tickets, timetables and artefacts connected with the railways of this region. Rolling stock on display includes a 1922 saloon car and an 1893 coach brought from Egypt at the end of WW I and used as an ambulance by the British. Old timetables remind you that you could at one time travel from here by

train to Cairo via Qantara on the Sinai peninsula, or head off to Beirut, Damascus or Amman. The museum is open Sunday to Thursday 9 am to 12 noon, closed Friday and Saturday. Admission is free.

Carmel National Park

Israel's largest national park covers the scenic southern slopes of Mount Carmel; it's known to locals as *Shveytsaria HaK'tana* (Little Switzerland). Renowned for its fertility, vineyards covered the area in ancient times and the name Carmel is derived from the Hebrew *Kerem-El* (Vineyard of God). For some pleasant walking or for a picnic, take Egged bus No 92 from the Central Bus Station, Herzl St in Hadar or Central Carmel – when you see a nice spot, tell the driver that you want to get off.

Places to Stay – bottom end

The only real budget choice in Haifa is the pleasant *Bethel Hostel* (tel 521110), 40 HaGeffen St, west of Ben-Gurion Blvd. Take Egged bus No 22, get off at the first stop on HaGeffen and walk back, past Ben-Gurion, and it's on your right. It's quiet, comfortable and very clean, with a strong Christian emphasis. Dorm beds cost US$5, and there's a nice lounge with tea/coffee-making facilities (but no kitchen), and a garden with basketball and table tennis. There's a 7 am wake-up call, and everyone has to be out of the dorms by 9 am. The hostel stays closed until 5 pm (4.30 pm Friday), although the lounge and garden remain open. Check-in 5 to 9 pm (Friday 4.30 to 7.30 pm). Strict 10 pm curfew.

The *Carmel Youth Hostel – IYHA* (tel 531944), at the south-western approach to the city, has the usual set-up and prices. You might find it too isolated from the city, but it is just across from the free beach. Other factors not in its favour are the frequency of muggings in the area after dark, the absence of food shops or eating places nearby and its proximity to a cemetery. Egged bus No 43 goes right to the hostel from the Central Bus Station about every hour and the equally frequent No 45 will drop you off on the main road nearby. No curfew.

Primarily aimed at Scandinavian kibbutz and moshav volunteers is *Beit Skandinavia* (tel 512470), at 49 Pinchas Margolin St, by the Bat Gallim Promenade a few blocks west of the Central Bus Station. It is run by a Christian couple, a Norwegian ex-seaman and his wife, who provide a lovely place to stay in their house overlooking the sea. It's free for Scandinavians. No set curfew.

The *St Charles Hospice* (tel 523705), now run by the Carmelite Order, offers basic but comfortable accommodation near the port at 105 Jaffa Rd. Dorm beds are US$13, singles US$15, and doubles US$14.50 per person, all with breakfast. Curfew 10 pm.

Places to Stay – middle
Haifa's more expensive hotels are mostly spread between Hadar and Central Carmel. The latter provides the more pleasant surroundings, which compensates for being further away from the central area. Once again, bargaining can do wonders.

Hadar The *Nesher Hotel* (tel 640644), 53 Herzl St, has singles/doubles from US$22/33, with breakfast. It is basic but comfortable and has pleasant management. Nearby, the *Hotel Talpiot* (tel 673753/4), 61 Herzl St, has more basic and slightly less comfortable singles at US$14 to US$16 and doubles at US$20 to US$25.

The *Eden Hotel* (tel 664816), 8 Shemaryahu Levin St, corner of HeHalutz St, is on the dingy side. Singles/doubles cost from US$20/25. Better rooms, though still basic, are available at the *Hotel Aliya* (tel 663918), 35 HeHalutz St – singles/doubles are US$17/28.

The *Hotel Carmelia* (tel 521278/9), 35 Herlia St, corner of HaZiyonut Blvd, is a nice looking place, with a bar, dining room

and patio. Singles/doubles cost from US$45/55.

Central Carmel The *Dvir Hotel* (tel 389131), 124 Yafe Nof St, (Panorama Rd) is run by the Dan hotel group's training department and so the service is better than usual. The views are pleasant and the surroundings comfortable – prices double in the high season, though. Low season singles/doubles are US$35/60, with breakfast. Cheaper at all seasons is the *Beth Shalom Guest House* (tel 337481/2), at 110 HaNassi Ave. It's a comfortable German Protestant-run 'evangelical guest house'. Open to all, it provides good hotel-style facilities and is usually full. Singles/doubles from US$30/45, with breakfast, plus 15% service charge.

Vered HaCarmel (tel 389236) is at 1 Heinrich Heine Square, which is four blocks south of the Haifa Auditorium, along Moriah Blvd – turn down HaMayim, the small street on the right. It's nice, in a quiet location and has a pretty garden terrace. Singles/doubles are US$32/40.

Going up a bit in style and price, the *Shulamit Hotel* (tel 242811), 15 Qiryat Sefer St, is further along Moriah Blvd. Singles/doubles cost from US$35/75, with breakfast.

The *Marom Hotel* (tel 254355), 51 HaPalmach St, is further away from the centre of things; singles/doubles are US$32/45, with breakfast.

Places to Stay – top end
The *Dan Panorama Hotel* (tel 352222) with its twin towers, dominates HaNassi Ave and offers singles/doubles from US$72/85, with breakfast. They charge more for rooms with views.

The *Dan Carmel* (tel 386211), 87 HaNassi Blvd, is the city's top luxury hotel, with singles/doubles from US$85/100, with breakfast. At 101 HaNassi Ave, the *Nof Hotel* (tel 354311) provides four star comforts in the shadow of its five star competition. Singles/doubles are US$45/55, breakfast included.

Places to Eat

Markets & Food Stores For the cheapest fruit and vegetables, shop at the market on Nahum Dobrin St, between HaAtzma'ut and Nathenson Sts in the Wadi Nisnas Arab quarter west of Hadar. It operates Monday to Saturday and is closed Sunday. There's a small Jewish market near Paris Square, between Nahum and Nathan Sts, open Sunday to Friday, closed Saturday.

Khouri St in Wadi Nisnas has a couple of Arab groceries selling a wide range of foodstuffs. They're open Monday to Saturday, closed on Sunday.

Felafel & Bakeries Apart from the Baha'i Shrine & Gardens, one of Haifa's major attraction must be its street food, which is cheap, delicious and readily available. In particular, head for the corner of HaNevi'im and HeHalutz Sts where the country's best felafel is sold, alongside bakeries producing some delicious ring doughnuts, sticky buns and other sweet delights. The bakery right on the corner seems to be the best of all.

Cafés There are several pleasant *konditereis* (pastry shops and cafés combined) around Hadar. The *Ritz Conditoria*, 5 Haim St near Herzl St, is different to the rest. It serves draught beer and provides complimentary newspapers, and there is an art gallery on the premises. Open Sunday to Thursday 7.30 am to 11 pm, Friday 7.30 am to 3 pm, closed Saturday. Another nice spot for coffee and cake is the *Bank Café*, across from Gan Ha'Em on HaNassi Ave, Central Carmel; open daily.

For juice, check out the popular *Bet HaPri* (House of Fruit) on Shemaryahu Levin St, corner of Herzl (no English sign so look for the snowflake sign). This juice bar whisks up a variety of tasty shakes for about US$1.20, although you could sometimes die of thirst waiting to be served.

Restaurants - cheaper The Egged self-service restaurant at the central bus station provides the usual value for money, and there are several fast food outlets at the station, too. In the market area by Paris Square are two fairly decent and inexpensive restaurants. At *Naim's*, 6 Eliyahu HaNavi St, you can eat well for about US$3 on soup and hummus, and spend a little more on grilled meat and offal. Open Sunday to Thursday till 6 pm, Friday till 3 pm, closed Saturday. *Restaurant Shichmona*, 3 Nahum Dourin St, has more of the same.

In Hadar, head for 30 Herzl St and *Haim Tzimhonia Vegetarian Restaurant – Dairy Farm Food*, only the latter part of which is written in English. Here you will find plain but tasty vegetarian dishes served in a fairly busy though unexciting atmosphere. You can eat for as little as US$2. Open Sunday to Thursday 8 am to 9 pm, Friday 8 am to 2 pm, closed Saturday.

The *Balfour Cellar & Restaurant*, 3 Balfour St, up from Herzl St is an old favourite, serving Ashkenazi dishes. A self-service snack bar keeps prices down, but you can eat in the restaurant for US$4 to US$10. Open Sunday to Thursday, 12 noon to 6 pm, Friday 12 noon to 3 pm, closed Saturday.

Benny's, 23 HeHalutz St, is a sparse but clean Oriental restaurant with hummus and other salads, US$3, grilled meats from US$6.

In one of Hadar's nicest spots, *Beiteinu*, 29 Jerusalem St, inside the William Green Cultural Centre, is a self-service restaurant providing salads and Ashkenazi fare. Open Sunday to Thursday, 12 noon to 9 pm, Friday 12 noon to 2 pm, closed Saturday. You can eat well for US$5.

Up in Central Carmel, *Bagel Nash* at the intersection of HaNassi Ave and Wedgewood St, provides some decent options in the US$3 to US$5 range. Open daily 8 am to 10 pm.

Check out the two Technion campuses and Haifa University for the cheap food in their student cafeterias.

Restaurants - more expensive The port area has some decent food joints. The popular *Shmulik & Dany Restaurant* (tel 514411), 7 HaBankim St, off Jaffa Rd about four blocks north-west of Paris Square, is one of the better places. Interestingly decorated with Israeli art, it serves roasts and grills. Open for lunch only, Sunday to Friday, closed Saturday. About US$12 per person.

Closer to Paris Square are a few Arab restaurants. Perhaps the best of these is *Abu Yusuf's* (tel 663723) on the corner. The sign is only in Arabic and Hebrew, so look for the large windows and arches. Open daily, 7 am to 12 midnight, you can eat a little or a lot: hummus, foul, kubbe, grilled meat, offal or fish. People tend to spend anything from US$6 to US$12 here for a full meal.

In Hadar, another decent Arab establishment, though more expensive, is the *Peer Amran Brothers Restaurant* (tel 6657070) at 1 Atlit St, the third street to the left down HaNevi'im St from Masaryk Square. Luckily the food tastes a lot better than the attempt to create plush surroundings might suggest and you can expect to pay about US$15 per person. Open daily 7 am to 12 midnight.

The best of Haifa's Romanian restaurants is *Leon & Ioji Gratar Romanesc* (tel 538073) at 31 HaNevi'im St, on the corner of Emek HaZetim. It doesn't look much, but it deserves its reputation and you can eat well here for about US$12 per person. Open daily for lunch and dinner until 11 pm.

The *Dvir Hotel* (tel 389131), up in Central Carmel at 124 Yefe Nof St serves a good set dinner for US$17 in its dining room (except on Friday). Being the Dan hotel group's training school, the food and service are of a high standard and you can

enjoy the view of the city lights as you eat.

Bars

A pleasant little bar is the pub-like establishment on Herzlia St, corner of HaNevi'im – no English sign. This is one of the cheapest places to drink in Haifa, and you are given free pretzels to munch. Nearby is the *Studio 46* bar at 46 Pevsner St. Another pleasant drinking spot I found was up in Gan Ha'Em at the *Garden* restaurant-bar-café (no English sign) in the arcade there.

Among the bars in the port area are the *London Pride*, 85 H'Atzma'ut Rd; *The Pub*, 102 H'Atzma'ut Rd, and *Al-Pasha*, on Hammam al-Pasha St which also features energetic live music on some evenings.

Entertainment

Haifa is not renowned for its entertainment scene, however, there are usually a few things to do. Get a copy of the free leaflet, *Events in the Haifa & Northern Region*, from the tourist office. You can also dial 640840 after 4 pm for a recorded message listing that evening's events and the *Jerusalem Post* will include some of those details.

As anywhere else in Israel, people come out in the evening to stroll around. In Haifa, Panorama Rd-Ye'fe Nof St, enjoys a great view of the city and harbour lights. Also in Central Carmel, Gan Ha'em usually attracts a crowd, as do the shops further up Hanassi Ave. Bat Gallim Promenade, along the seafront, is popular for an evening stroll and the felafel and ice cream parlours along HaNevi'im and HeHalutz in Hadar are busy.

Cinemas Most of Haifa's cinemas feature the current crop of American and other imports, with a few Israeli productions.
Amphitheatre
43 HeHalutz St, Hadar (tel 664018)

Armon
  18 Hanevi'im St, Hadar (tel 664848) – just below the fountain
Atzmon
  30 Hanevi'im St, Hadar (tel 663003)
Chen
  7 Shabtei Levi St, Hadar (tel 666272)
Cinemateque
  142 Hanassi Ave, Central Carmel (tel 347424) in the Haifa Auditorium with a good selection of movie classics and oddities
Karen Or Hamehudesh
  67 Herzl St, Hadar (tel 663443) entrance on Sokoloff St around the corner
Moriah
  Moriah St, Central Carmel (tel 242477)
Orah
  41 Herzl St, Hadar (tel 664017)
Orly
  4 Mahayanim St, Central Carmel (tel 381868)
Peer
  Atlit St, Hadar (tel 662232) – off HaNevi'im St.
Rav Gat 1 & 2
  Solel Boneh Square, Hadar (tel 646969) – bottom of HaNevi'im St.
Ron
  67 HeHalutz St, Hadar (tel 669069)

Theatres The Haifa Municipal Theatre, at the intersection of Pevsner, Trumpeldor and Yehoshua Sts in Hadar, presents regular performances in Hebrew. The nearby Zafit Café-Theatre (tel 253641), 23 Jerusalem St, corner of Haim St, is another drama venue. There is also usually a chamber music concert here at 5 pm Saturday.

Music & Dance The Haifa Auditorium, 142 HaNassi Ave, Central Carmel, is where the Israel Philharmonic perform in Haifa, and other classical concerts and opera are also staged here. The Al-Pasha (tel 671309), Hammam al-Pasha St just south of the main post office on Ha'Atzma'ut St in the port area, regularly features Israeli folksingers and can be a lively spot – dancing on the tables and all that. In Central Carmel, the Rothschild Centre (tel 382749), next door to the Haifa

Auditorium, has folk dancing some evenings, as does the Newe Sha'anan campus of the Technion and the Haifa University. The students here also have regular film shows and discos.

Of the nightclubs, *Club 120* (tel 382979), 120 Ye'fe Nof St, Central Carmel, seems to be the most popular. There is usually a cover charge (around US$3), and on Friday and Saturday it's packed. Women are admitted free Monday and Wednesday. Dado Beach is often a venue for free disco dancing from 8 pm until midnight on summer evenings.

What to do on Shabbat in Haifa

Timing a visit to Haifa to coincide with Shabbat is not a bad idea, as it is still possible to 'do' many of the sights. This is mainly due to the city's liberal approach to Jewish religious law, highlighted by the fact that some Egged buses actually operate on Shabbat.

Haifa In the city itself, you have plenty of options, several of them free, to keep you busy on Saturday. The Baha'i Shrine & Gardens and the Haifa, Mane Katz, Japanese Art and National Maritime museums are all open in the morning – admission free. Then there is the free guided walking tour. Or take Egged bus No 23 from Ha'Nevi'im St in Hadar up to Central Carmel where Gan Ha'Em, the zoo, the museums and the café and restaurants are all open. In good weather the beaches are packed – Egged bus No 40 runs from Hadar.

The Arab market and grocers in Wadi Niswas stay open, as do some of the felafel merchants, bakeries and café along HaNevi'im and HeHalutz in Hadar.

There are also a couple of options for a Shabbat excursion from Haifa: to Akko, about 40 minutes away, and to the villages of Isfiya and Daliyat al-Karmel. Shabbat is the busiest day of the week for these two Druze villages with crowds of Israelis and foreign visitors coming along to see the locals, their market and the nearby

Mukhraqa Monastery. Sheruts operate from Eliyahu St, north of Paris Square in the port area.

Getting There & Away

For thousands of ferry and cruise-ship passengers, Haifa is the first port of call on a visit to Israel. Most of the city's other visitors arrive from Tel Aviv, Jerusalem or Tiberias, although there are bus services to several other areas. Haifa is also the original home of the country's railway network.

Bus The central bus station, on Jaffa Rd in the Bat Gallim neighbourhood of the port area, has inter-urban buses arriving and departing on the north side, and local buses operating from the south side.

The Jerusalem bus costs US$5, takes about two hours and departs every hour; every half hour at peak times. The Tel Aviv bus costs US$3, takes about an hour and departs at least every hour and more frequently at peak times.

Buses for Akko and Nahariya depart from Daniel St, Hadar as well as from the central bus station. Egged bus No 271 goes to Nahariya via Akko; No 251 goes to Akko only. The fare to Akko is US$1.25 and the bus takes 40 minutes; to Nahariya is US$1.80 and a 55 minute ride.

Egged bus No 331 leaves from the central bus station while the more frequent Arab bus No 331 leaves from Paris Square.

For bus information, try phoning 515221. The 'Department of Losses & Belongings Keepings' is opposite platform 10 in the Central Bus Station – it's open Sunday to Thursday 8 am to 3 pm, Friday 8 am to 1 pm, closed Saturday.

Sherut Amal (tel 66234, 522828) sheruts to Tel Aviv depart from 157 Jaffa Rd, next to the Central Bus Station and from HeHalutz, up from HaNevi'im, from 6 am to late at night each day. Aryeh (tel 673666) run a service to Tel Aviv from 9 Beerwald St in Hadar and Aviv (tel 666333) from 10 Nordau St in the same suburb; both cost around US$3.

Aviv and Amal both run services to Jerusalem, but you need to book.

Kavei HaGalil (tel 664442) to Akko and Nahariya depart from 16 HaNevi'im St in Hadar and from Kikkar Plumer by the Dagon grain silo in the port area. The trip should cost about US$2.50.

The trip to Isfiya and Daliyat al-Karmel should cost around US$1.25 and sheruts (tel 664640) depart from the corner of Shemaryahu Levin and Herzl Sts and from Eliyahu St, down from Paris Square near the corner of Derekh Ha'Atzma'ut in the port area. There are frequent services except on Fridays when most shops and businesses in the Druze villages are closed.

The sherut to Nazareth also departs from Eliyahu St near the intersection with Ha'Atzma'ut and costs around US$2.50. Departures are not as frequent as those to Tel Aviv, Akko and the Druze villages.

Trains Haifa has three railway stations. Bat Gallim, the central railway station, is adjacent to the central bus station – take the underground passage next to bus platform 33. The old or Plumer Square railway station is between the ferry port entrance and the Dagon Grain Silo. The east railway station is further east along Derekh Hativat Golani. For train information, telephone 521211. The Jerusalem train leaves the central railway station at 7 am Sunday to Friday, and services to Tel Aviv leave almost every hour.

Air Arkia depart from the airport in the east of Haifa, in the industrial zone. Flights connect directly with Eilat, with further connections to Tel Aviv and Jerusalem.

Hitch-hiking For Tel Aviv, stand on Haganah Blvd at the intersection outside the central bus station. For Akko, stand on Histadrut Blvd at the intersection with Yisrael Bar-Yehuda Rd, on the way out of the city centre towards the industrial zone. For Nazareth and the Galilee, stand by the same intersection but on Yisrael Bar-Yehuda Rd.

Getting Around

Haifa has Israel's only subway system, the Carmelite, which makes an interesting, albeit limited, contrast to the bus service. It's due to re-open after renovations in 1990.

Carmelite Subway Opened in 1959, the subway was built by a French company – Paris Square was named in their honour. Only 1800 metres long with six stations, its one line runs from Paris Square in the port area, straight up through Hadar to Central Carmel along the line drawn by HaNevi'im St, a rise of 275 metres.

Running about every 10 minutes in both directions, the Carmelite costs about 45c and is quicker than the bus. It operates Sunday to Thursday 5.30 am to 12 midnight, Friday 5.30 am to one hour before sunset, Saturday sunset to 12 midnight. Stations are:

1 Paris Square – lower station, port area.
2 Solel Boneh – near Khouri and Hasan Shukri Sts.
3 Hanevi'im – Shabtei Levi St, Hadar.
4 Massada – Massada St.
5 Eliezer Golomb – Eliezer Golomb St.
6 Gan Ha'Em – upper station, Central Carmel.

Bus The main city bus routes (all Egged) are:

Baha'i Shrine & Gardens
22 from the central bus station, 23, 25 and 26 from Hanevi'im and Herzl St, Hadar
Beaches
44 from Allenby Rd, near the Bethel Hostel to the free Carmel beach
Bethel Hostel
22 from the central bus station

Central Carmel
24 from the central bus station and Herzl St, Hadar, and 37, also from Herzl St
Hadar
6, 19, 21, 24, 28 and 51 from the central bus station to Herzl St
University
From the central bus station 24 via Herzl and Arlosoroff, Hadar, and 37 via Arlosoroff, Hadar and Central Carmel

DRUZE VILLAGES

The villages of Isfiya and Daliyat al-Karmel, on the slopes of Mount Carmel, are a popular attraction for Israelis as well as foreign visitors, providing an opportunity to observe and meet the Druze people and to wander around and shop in their village. The Druze have a reputation for being incredibly friendly and hospitable, and being invited into a house for tea or coffee and a bite to eat is not unusual.

The male elders are instantly recognisable by their thick moustaches, distinctive robes and Fez-style hat covered by a turban. Other religious Druze often sport a moustache, cropped hair and a flat, coloured hat. There are many Druze men, however, who choose to wear western-style clothes, and look no different from Arabs or Oriental Jews. Most of the women still wear the traditional long dark dress and white headscarf.

Isfiya (population 6600)

Built on the ancient Jewish village of Huseifa, Isfiya is the nearest of the two villages to Haifa (21 km). Although the town houses the now rather unimpressive remains of a 5th to 6th century synagogue, the main interest in Isfiya is the Druze themselves. Rosh HaCarmel, the mount's highest peak, is nearby, and scenic views can be enjoyed in most directions.

Place to Stay

The *Stella Carmel Hospice & Christian Conference Centre* (tel 22269, 22500), is on the outskirts of the village. Originally built as an Arab hotel, it is in an idyllic setting and provides clean and comfortable accommodation in a quiet atmosphere. Dorm beds US$8 (with breakfast), US$12 (half board), US$16 (full board); rooms cost from US$12 (with breakfast), US$16 (half board), US$20 (full board). It is often full, so it is advisable to make a reservation. The sherut from Haifa will drop you off on request.

Daliyat al-Karmel (population 8800)

A few minutes' drive from Isfiya, Daliyat al-Karmel is the larger of the two towns and the last stop for buses and sheruts from Haifa. Although the market attracts a large number of visitors, I was disappointed by the high prices and the lack of locally produced goods on sale.

Beit Oliphant At the end of the main street, this was the home of the Christian Zionists Sir Lawrence Oliphant and his wife between 1882 and 1887. The Oliphants were among the few non-Druze to have a close relationship with the sect, and did much to help the community. In the garden is a cave where they hid insurgents from the authorities. The house was recently renovated and is now a

memorial to the many Druze members of the IDF.

Mukhraqa About four km south of Daliyat al-Karmel is one of the country's most renowned viewpoints, the Carmelite Monastery of St Elijah, built to commemorate Elijah's showdown with the 421 prophets of Ba'al (I Kings 17-19). Climb to the roof of the monastery to enjoy the great views across the patchwork of fields of the Jezreel Valley. The monastery is open Saturday to Thursday 8 to 11.45 am and 1 to 4.45 pm, Friday 8 to 11.45 am only. Admission is 45c. There is no public transport so you have to walk/hitch-hike from Daliyat al-Karmel. Bear left at the signposted junction or else you will end up miles away and be part of the view that you are meant to be admiring.

Getting There & Away

The Druze villages are a convenient day trip from Haifa. Egged bus Nos 92 and 93 run infrequently Sunday to Thursday from the central bus station and go via Herzl St, Hadar and Central Carmel, taking about 40 minutes to do the journey.

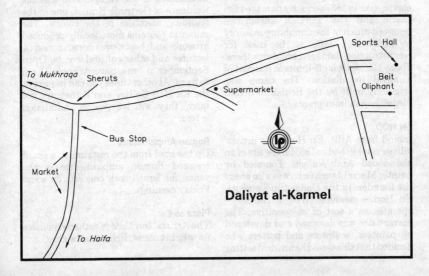

Daliyat al-Karmel

However, the sheruts are far more frequent, run on Saturday, are more comfortable, take half the time and are even a bit cheaper. They leave continually all day till about 5 pm from Eliyahu St, on the corner of Ha'Atzma'ut St, in the port area. Returning to Haifa, the sheruts become less frequent after about 5 pm and you run the risk of either a long wait for a stretch-Mercedes to fill up, or of being forced to pay more for a special taxi. The last bus back to Haifa leaves Daliyat al-Karmel at about 3.15 pm. Buses and sheruts pass through Isfiya en route between Haifa and Daliyat al-Karmel.

ATLIT

The old Haifa-Hadera coastal road passes Atlit and its Crusader ruins about 16 km from Haifa – in fact in 1291 this was the last Crusader castle to fall to the Arabs.

Known in Latin as *Castrum Pergrinorum* and in French as *Château Pelerin*, the Pilgrims' Castle, Atlit was built by the Crusaders around 1200. British-sponsored archaeologists excavated the site in 1930 and uncovered not only Crusader relics but others from the Persian, Hellenistic and Phoenician periods as well. An earthquake in 1837 seriously damaged the castle and the Turkish authorities removed much of the crumbling masonry to Akko and Jaffa to be used for reconstructing damaged buildings there. Today the castle is off-limits as it is part of a naval installation. The camp was originally built by the British to detain illegal Jewish immigrants.

EN HOD

Inland from Atlit, En Hod is an artists' village established in 1953 on the site of an abandoned Arab village. Founded by painter Marcel Janco (who was also one of the founders of the Dadaist movement), En Hod – meaning 'Well of Beauty' – operates as a sort of co-operative. The current site was designed and developed by painters, sculptors and potters who decided that this would be an ideal setting

in which to live and work. They succeeded in turning it into an established artists' colony although many would say that today's products are disappointing. There are various working studios and Israelis come here to learn such skills as ceramics, weaving and drawing. The studios are mainly closed to casual visitors but there are some things to see.

En Hod Gallery

This exhibits works by the residents – open daily 9.30 am to 5 pm, admission 45c.

Janco-Dado Museum

This museum mainly exhibits works by Marcel Janco but other residents of the colony are also represented. From the top floor porch you can appreciate the view down towards Atlit; it was views such as this that inspired Janco to settle here. Open Saturday to Thursday 9.30 am to 5 pm, Friday 9.30 am to 4 pm. Admission is 80c, students 40c.

Beit Gertrude

Next to the restaurant, a blue gate marks this small museum and memorial to past inhabitants of the village. This was the residence of Gertrude Krause, one of the founding members of the colony. The museum contains more locally produced artwork and hosts occasional concerts, lectures and other cultural events. Open September to June, Saturday only 11 am to 2 pm. At other times you can inquire at the En Hod Gallery and if they are not busy, they will let you in. Admission is free.

Roman Amphitheatre

Up the road from the restaurant, a small restored Roman amphitheatre is the venue for Israeli rock concerts on some Friday evenings.

Place to Eat

The *Artists' Inn Café* is rather expensive for what it offers. Bring sandwiches.

Getting There & Away

Egged bus Nos 202, 222 and 922 go past the En Hod junction on the Haifa-Hadera coastal road. Buses are fairly frequent and the trip takes about 20 minutes from Haifa. From the junction, walk up the hill for about 10 minutes, the village is on the right.

AROUND EN HOD
Yamin Orde

Just up the road past En Hod the settlement of Yamin Orde commands pleasant views over the surrounding countryside and the sea.

Carmel Caves

These caves can be seen from the Haifa-Hadera road in a rocky gorge just to the north of Habonim ('the Builders'), a settlement founded by South African Jews.

In the 1930s British and American excavations uncovered relics indicating that the caves were inhabited during the Stone Age.

DOR

Still on the coast road, about 29 km south of Haifa, Dor is a modern settlement mainly populated by Greek Jews. It is next to the site of an ancient town and near the lovely sandy beach of Tantura.

Tel Dor

At the northern end of the beach, the ancient ruins of Dor are on a hill. The town probably dates as far back as the 15th century BC. It was mentioned in an ancient Egyptian papyrus and was well known during King Solomon's reign. You can just about distinguish the ancient harbour and the fortress by the shore. There are Roman and Hellenistic remains and also the ruins of a 6th century Byzantine church.

Beach

One of the country's loveliest and most peaceful beaches, it has four small, rocky islands which act as bird sanctuaries.

Places to Stay

The area is an ideal camping spot and there are many appealing places to pitch a tent. Nearby is a camp site run by the Dor Moshav.

Getting There & Away

Take any of the several Egged buses going along the Haifa-Hadera road and ask the driver to drop you off at Dor.

ZICHRON YA'ACOV (population 5200)

About five km south-east of Dor and renowned for its role in Israel's wine industry, Zichron Ya'acov (Jacob's Memorial), was established in 1882 by Romanian Jews and is one of the first modern Zionist settlements.

Carmel Winery

From the bus station walk north (go out opposite the place the buses enter) and turn left down Jabotinsky St, then turn right on HaNadiv St and the winery is signposted at the bottom of the slopes. Telephone 063-90105 to arrange a guided tour of the winery and a tasting session. Admission is 80c.

Aaronsohn House Museum

Aaron Aaronsohn was a noted agronomist and botanist who lived in Zichron Ya'acov, but he and his family were also leaders of the NILI network which spied on the Turks in WW I. Thus the museum not only houses his collection of Palestinian plants, but also tells the story of NILI. It's open Sunday to Thursday 9.30 am to 1 pm, closed Friday and Saturday. Admission is US$1.25, students 80c. Following Jabotinsky St down from the bus station, a paved pathway leads up to the left – the museum is up here on the right.

Rothschild Family Tomb

A beautifully designed garden surrounds the family tomb where the bodies of Baron and Baroness de Rothschild lie, having been brought over from France in 1954 aboard an Israeli warship and given a state funeral. The setting is most appropriate: there are views across the Sharon Plain and the bordering mountains, the areas where their financial support helped establish several Jewish settlements, many of which are named after members of the Rothschild family. The tomb lies to the left just before the road approaches the town from the coast road.

Place to Eat
There is a small Egged restaurant at the bus station.

Getting There & Away
From Haifa take Egged bus No 202 or 222; from Netanya, No 707 or 708; and from Tel Aviv, No 872, 876 or 877.

CAESAREA
Now one of the country's most important

archaeological sites, Caesarea was the Roman capital of Judea for almost 600 years. During this time it became one of the Roman Empire's great trading ports, and was later a Crusader city. It was renowned for the splendour of its buildings and today you can visit the remains, which include the Roman amphitheatre, aqueduct and hippodrome, and the Crusader city.

Archaeologists have learnt much about Caesarea's colourful history. For many years, the ancient accounts of the construction of Caesarea's Roman harbour had been treated with scepticism because of the high standard of engineering that would have been required to build it. Until recently no trace of the 20 hectare harbour could be found and historians refused to believe that it existed. Today we know that those ancient accounts were accurate, and that Caesarea is indeed one of the greatest engineering achievements of all time.

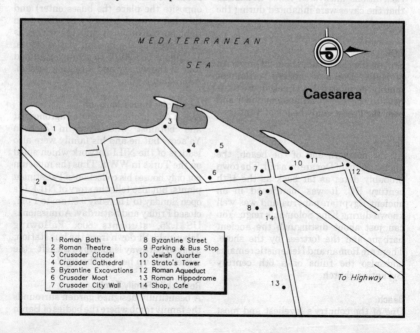

1 Roman Bath	8 Byzantine Street
2 Roman Theatre	9 Parking & Bus Stop
3 Crusader Citadel	10 Jewish Quarter
4 Crusader Cathedral	11 Strato's Tower
5 Byzantine Excavations	12 Roman Aqueduct
6 Crusader Moat	13 Roman Hippodrome
7 Crusader City Wall	14 Shop, Cafe

To Highway

History

Herod the Great established the city of Caesarea in about 22 BC on the site of a 3rd or 4th century BC Phoenician settlement called Strato's Tower. Naming it after the Roman Emperor Augustus Caesar, Herod apparently set out to create the most advanced city imaginable. Recent archaeological research suggests that in the pursuit of this desire he became increasingly tyrannical. It is highly likely that Herod's despotic behaviour was further reinforced by remorse at having executed his first wife and his suffering from a painful disease. Those who even questioned, let alone disobeyed, his orders were often executed.

For several years, hundreds of builders and divers worked round the clock to complete the project. To create the two lofty breakwaters which stretched for 540 metres on the south side and 270 metres on the north, stones of 230 cubic metres were lowered into the open sea, a technique not too dissimilar to that used to construct Mulberry Harbour in the Allied invasion of Normandy in WW II. Towers bearing colossal statues marked the entrance, and there was a massive oil-fuelled lighthouse. On land, the city enjoyed an advanced sewage system and a grid street pattern as well as a temple dedicated to Caesar, a palace, a theatre and the amphitheatre. The exact size of Herod's city is not certain because no outer wall has yet been discovered.

Archaeologists are still diving in the area and the coins and artefacts they recover amid Caesarea's sunken ruins continue to increase our knowledge of the Roman Empire. Pottery fragments indicate the volume of trade, and the coins with their emperor's face and dates show how long the city continued as a trading centre in competition with the better known Alexandria.

Caesarea became the local Roman capital after Herod's death, with Pontius Pilate residing here as prefect from 26 to 36 AD; an inscription bearing his name was found in the ruins of the theatre. Acts 10 in the Bible deals with Cornelius, a centurion of the Roman garrison here, who was the first Gentile converted to Christianity by Peter. Paul passed through the port several times on his missionary journeys and Acts 23-6 deal with these events.

A major cause of the First Revolt (66 to 70 AD) was the desecration of the synagogue here. Thousands of Jews were executed in Caesaria's amphitheatre when the Romans defeated the revolt. Later, after the defeat of the Bar Kochba Rebellion the Romans used the amphitheatre to kill 10 Jewish sages.

At the beginning of the 3rd century a leading rabbinical school was founded which produced some of the top Talmudic intellectuals. In the 4th century a leading Christian theologian, the Greek Eusebius, was Bishop of Caesarea. He was the author of *Onomasticon*, the first biblical geography, invaluable in identifying many of the biblical sites.

After the city fell to the Arabs in 640 it fell into disrepair. The harbour was allowed to silt up but the coastal plain's

Porphyry statue of a Roman Emperor, found in Caesarea

fertility continued to make this one of the area's richest cities. In 1101 the Crusaders took Caesarea from the Muslims, and found what they believed to be the Holy Grail: a hexagonal green glass bowl which was supposedly the vessel from which Jesus had drunk at the Last Supper. Under the Crusaders, whose principal ports were at Akko and Jaffa, only a part of Herod's Caesarea was rehabilitated.

The city was to change hands between Arabs and Crusaders four times until King Louis IX of France captured it in 1251. That same year he added most of the fortifications visible today but he was defeated by the Mameluke Sultan Baybars in 1261. The inhabitants had hidden from their attackers in the citadel on the southern breakwater and escaped to Akko under the cover of darkness during peace negotiations. In an apparent fit of pique at being deceived, Baybars destroyed the city. It remained deserted until 1878 when refugees from Bosnia (soon to become part of Yugoslavia) were installed here by the Turks. Their village was destroyed during the 1948 War of Independence with only the small mosque remaining beside the harbour.

In 1940 Kibbutz Sdot Yam was established nearby and during its first decade its members unearthed some remains of ancient Caesarea as they began to farm the land. Their initial discoveries led to a series of archaeological digs which continue today.

Orientation

Caesarea's remains are spread along a three km stretch of the Mediterranean coast about 3½ km from the old Haifa to Hadera road. Kibbutz Sdot Yam is at the southern end. North of here is the Roman amphitheatre, followed by the walled Crusader city with its citadel and harbour a half km further up the road. North of the Crusader city is Caesarea's oldest structure, Strato's Tower, and about a km beyond that on the beach is the Roman aquedect. Just inland from the Crusader

city is the Byzantine street, behind the café and car park. Further inland, beside the road, is the ruined Roman hippodrome. You will probably start from either the Roman amphitheatre or the Crusader city.

Caesarea's archaeological sites are maintained and operated by the National Parks Authority. Entrance to the Roman amphitheatre and the Crusader city is on the same ticket and there are ticket booths at both entrances. They open Saturday to Thursday 8 am to 4 pm, Friday 8 am to 3 pm. Admission is US$1.55, students 80c. The other sites have free access.

Roman Amphitheatre

Just beyond the ticket booth is a replica of the Pontius Pilate inscription. The original Herodian structure was modified and added to over the years: the semi-circular platform behind the stage was added in the 3rd century and the great wall with the two towers is part of a 6th century Byzantine fortress built over the amphitheatre's ruins. Unearthed in 1961, the amphitheatre is now used for concert performances.

Crusader City

Excavation continues here, as does the commercialisation of the complex, with a growing number of souvenir shops and restaurants.

To your right as you approach the ticket booth, you'll see that part of the guard tower has fallen into a moat, the work of Louis IX. Other visible defences include an L-shaped gate designed to slow down a charge, and the windows above where archers were stationed.

The cathedral was built over the site of Caesar's temple and was destroyed by the Arabs in 1291. Nearby are some Byzantine remains. Down by the harbour is the 19th century mosque and the Crusader citadel.

Jewish Quarter & Strato's Tower

Immediately to the north of the Crusader city wall is the Jewish quarter with its 3rd to 5th century synagogue remains. Foundations of houses from the Hellenistic period (4th to 2nd century BC) were found at the lowest level. The large wall in the sea below may have been part of the harbour.

Although it may seem logical to continue northwards up the beach to see the Roman aqueducts, it is easier to backtrack via the road past the Roman hippodrome and take the road to the left from there.

Byzantine St

In amongst the trees to the east of the Crusader city's entrance, behind the café and car park, is an excavated Byzantine street with two 2nd or 3rd century statues. Some steps lead down to the street where an inscription in the mosaic floor attributes it to Flavius Strategius, a 6th century mayor. The statues originally belonged to temples and were unearthed by the ploughs of local kibbutzniks. The white marble figure is unidentified but the red porphyry one is perhaps Emperor Hadrian holding an orb and sceptre.

Hippodrome

About one km east (inland) from the Crusader city is the rectangular ploughed field which is the neglected hippodrome. The best way to find it is to look for the modern arch by the roadside. Possibly built by Herod (Caesarea's horse races were apparently world-famous in the 4th century), the racetrack could accommodate 20,000 spectators.

It is best to reach the Roman aqueducts by continuing eastwards (inland) from here and taking the next turning to the left which takes you north to the section of beach where the aqueducts are located, saving you a more difficult walk along the beach from the Crusader city.

Roman Aqueduct

Although most of it has been buried by sand, the aqueduct is about 17 km long. Built by the Romans in the 2nd century, it carried water from mountain springs to Caesarea.

Beaches

There's a free beach south of the amphitheatre near the Kayet U'shait holiday village. Watch out for the 'No Bathing' signs – here the water is dangerously polluted by the kibbutz's factory. Even in the safe area you should watch out for tar from the oil tankers. Swimming at the beach near the amphitheatre costs around US$3.

Places to Stay

Accommodation here is expensive and while free camping is possible on the beach, theft is common.

The *Kayit U'shait* (tel 063-61161, 62928) holiday village and guest house at Kibbutz Sdot Yam provides comfortable accommodation in rooms with private bathroom for US$40/65 for singles/doubles, with breakfast. There is also a camp site – about US$5 per person, no tents provided.

The *Dan Caesarea* (tel 063-62266) offers five star luxury and service, with singles/doubles from US$70/90, with breakfast. Facilities include a pool, tennis, health club, sauna and golf.

Place to Eat

The café across from the Crusader city serves basic snacks and drinks.

Getting There & Away

From Haifa or Tel Aviv and Netanya take any Egged bus going along the coastal road to Hadera. Get off at the Caesarea intersection which is about 3½ km from the excavations. Unfortunately the local Egged bus No 76 is not that frequent and so you will often have to choose between a long wait or a long walk to reach the site.

AROUND CAESAREA
Moshav Beit Hananya
Near Moshav Beit Hananya on the coast north of Caesarea are Roman aqueducts. Continue north to Tel Mevorah where archaeologists are still uncovering Roman remains.

Kibbutz Ma'agan Michael
There are archaeological finds to be seen here, and it's one of the more pleasant kibbutzim to visit.

Places to Stay The kibbutz guest house has comfortable rooms with private bathroom for about US$25 per person, with breakfast. Cheaper is the nearby *SPNI Field Study Centre* (tel 063-99655) at the Beit Safer Sadeh Nature Preserve, but it's usually full. If there is room you will usually be able to stay for about US$6 per person.

BEIT SHE'ARIM
About 19 km south-east of Haifa, the archaeological site of Beit She'arim features a network of burial caves and a few ruins from the 2nd century. It does not justify a major detour, but if you are in the area with time on your hands it's worth a visit.

History
An important town in ancient Israel, Beit She'arim was the meeting place of the Sanhedrin, the supreme court, during the 2nd century. It was also the home of Rabbi Yehuda Hanassi, compiler of the Mishnah, and he was one of the many famous and learned Jews buried here. Later, when Hadrian closed the area around Jerusalem to Jews, making it impossible for them to bury their dead on the Mount of Olives, Beit She'arim became the ideal alternative because of the reverence with which Rabbi Yehuda Hanassi was held. For over 100 years Jews from Palestine and the Diaspora brought their dead here for burial. During the 4th century the town was destroyed by the Romans, presumably

in the process of suppressing a Jewish uprising.

Over the centuries the many tombs here have been destroyed: the caves were looted and the catacombs gradually covered by layers of earth and rock, becoming hidden as the town and the burial grounds were forgotten. It was not until 1936 that archaeologists first discovered some of the town's remains, and more extensive exploration resumed after Israel's independence. Today's site is basically in two parts – the town's remains on the crest of the hill, and the tombs below.

Ancient Synagogue
Coming down the hill from the Haifa-Nazareth road, the ruins of this 2nd century synagogue are on the left. Destroyed by the Romans around 350 to punish unrest, it was probably one of the largest synagogues in the country. A hoard of some 1200 4th century coins was found in the two-storey building between the synagogue and the road.

Olive Press
About 100 metres further on are the ruins of a 4th century olive press. Olives were stacked between two uprights on the circular stone and a heavy horizontal beam let into a notch in the wall acted as a lever to press out the oil which flowed from the circular groove into a plastered basin in the rock floor.

Basilica
Further up the slope from the road, the 2nd century basilica's ruins show a basic rectangle divided by two rows of columns with a raised platform at the end opposite the doors, which opened onto a wide court.

Alexander Zaid Statue
Alexander Zaid was the guardian of the surrounding area in the 1930s. He was killed during the 1936 uprisings.

Museum & Catacombs

There are 31 catacombs here, and a small museum in an ancient rock-cut reservoir. The catacombs are slightly spooky caves – cool chambers filled with now-empty stone coffins. Open Saturday to Thursday, 8 am to 5 pm, Friday 8 am to 4 pm. Admission is US$1.80, students 80c.

Place to Eat

A café adjacent to the museum and car park is open when the site is, and charges very high prices.

Getting There & Away

Egged bus No 338 from Haifa to Qiryat Tivon is about a 30 minute ride. Get off by the King Garden Chinese restaurant and walk back up the hill to the side road on the left, then take the first left (Hashomrin St), then Shikonella St, then right following the signs downhill.

AKKO (ACRE)

Akko's picturesque Old City is an understandably popular tourist attraction, with its minarets and domes, and Crusader remains dominating the labyrinth of alleyways and the small Arab market.

History

Akko's history is long and colourful. One of the world's oldest towns, it was first mentioned in Egyptian sacred texts of the 19th century BC when it was located on a mound, Tel el Fukhar, 1½ km north-east of the present Old City wall. Judges 1:31 mentions that in the 13th century BC the town remained in Phoenician control although the Israelites had conquered most of the country. It stood on the border of the Jewish tribe of Asher, which managed to take it a few hundred years later. Always an important port, in the 4th century BC it assumed the stature that Tyre and Sidon had earlier enjoyed. This was probably due to Alexander the Great having established a mint here in 333 BC, which operated for 600 years. The name Akko is perhaps derived from the Greek word *Aka* (cure), as the hero Hercules found herbs here to cure his wounds.

After Alexander's death, Akko was

Akko

taken by the Egyptian Ptolemites, who called it Ptolemais. In 200 BC they lost it to the Syrian Seleucids who struggled to keep it until the Romans, led by Pompey, began two centuries of rule. As Ptolemais the city is mentioned in the account of Paul's travels in Acts 21:7. At this time it was in decline as Caesarea developed.

In 636 the Arabs conquered Akko and, as Caesarea's port had silted up through neglect, Akko's regained its position as Palestine's leading port. When the Crusaders took the city they named it Jean D'Acre, because it housed the HQ of the Knights of St Jean. It soon became the main link between the Latin kingdom and Europe, with the new rulers arriving in their ships from Genoa, Pisa, Venice and Amalfi.

In 1187 Akko surrendered to Saladin without a fight, but four years later Richard the Lionheart and Philip of France retook it, and it remained the capital of the Latin kingdom for another 100 years. During this time the city grew outside its original walls and the new walls enclosed an area three times the size of today's walled city. St Francis of Assisi and Marco Polo were among the VIPs who passed through, and Akko became more important as a trading port.

Due to this growth in trade, disputes arose over the succession of the king here and eventually open war erupted between factions living in the individually fortified quarters. Venice and Genoa fought sea battles within sight of the city, and in 1259 the Mongols, and in 1265 the Mamelukes attacked unsuccessfully. The Mamelukes attacked again in 1291, outnumbering the defenders 10 to 1. After a two-month siege, with over 30,000 inhabitants escaping to Cyprus, Akko fell.

The city lay in ruins and was neglected for the next 450 years until a local Arab sheikh took advantage of the weak and corrupt Ottoman administration to establish a virtually independent fiefdom. Trade was encouraged and the port again developed. An Albanian mercenary,

known as 'el-Jazzar' (the Butcher) because of his cruelty, took over and continued the city's development. In 1799 Napoleon invaded Palestine and attempted to take Akko, but was repulsed by the English fleet under Sir Sidney Smith.

In 1832 Ibrahim Pasha, leading an Egyptian army, took Akko from the Turks and ruled Palestine and Syria from Akko until the British intervened on Turkey's behalf in 1840, and the Turks ruled until Britain captured Palestine in 1917. The British set up their HQ in Haifa and Akko's importance dwindled. They did establish Akko's Citadel as their main prison in Palestine, and many Jewish resistance fighters were executed here. During the 1930s Akko became a hotbed of Arab hostility towards increased Jewish immigration and the notion of a Zionist state. Jewish forces captured Akko fairly easily in 1948.

Today the city has a large new town, but it is the Arab Old City which attracts visitors. Akko is often given as an example of how Jews and Arabs can live together in relative harmony. Foreign women, however, may still be subjected to sexual harassment.

Orientation

Because all the places of interest are in or near the Old City, you only need to get to know a small, albeit confusing, area. From the bus station it's a short walk to the Old City: turn left as you leave the station, walk one block to the traffic-lights and turn right at Ben-Ami St. After four blocks turn left at Weizmann St and you will see the walls of the Turkish fortress in the distance. You can choose where to enter the Old City. Either turn right after the moat and head for el-Jazzar St, with the el-Jazzar Mosque and the subterranean Crusader city, or walk straight ahead to explore the market or the port.

Information

Tourist Offices The Municipal Information Office is in the Municipality building, 35

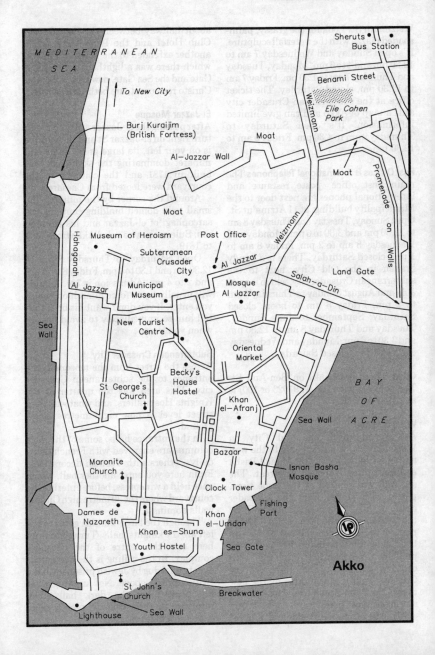

MEDITERRANEAN SEA

To New City

Burj Kuraijim
(British Fortress)

Al-Jazzar Wall

Moat

Moat

Benami Street

Elie Cohen
Park

Sheruts •
Bus Station

Moat

Promenade on Walls

Museum of Heroism

Subterranean
Crusader
City

Municipal
Museum

Post Office

Al Jazzar

Land Gate

Salah-a-Din

Mosque
Al Jazzar

Oriental
Market

New Tourist
Centre

Becky's
House
Hostel

St George's
Church

Khan
el-Afranj

BAY
OF
ACRE

Sea Wall

Maronite
Church

Bazaar

Isnan Basha
Mosque

Clock Tower

Dames de
Nazareth

Khan
el-Umdan

Fishing
Port

Khan es-Shuna

Youth Hostel

Sea Gate

Akko

St John's
Church

Sea Wall

Breakwater

Lighthouse

Hahaganah

Al Jazzar

Sea
Wall

Weizmann

Weizmann St. Look for the grassy, palm-shaded piazza with the waterfall sculpture. It's open Sunday and Wednesday 7 am to 12.30 pm and 4 to 6 pm, Monday, Tuesday and Thursday 7 am to 1.30 pm, Friday 7 am to 12.30 pm, closed Saturday. The ticket office at the subterranean Crusader city sells a map of Akko and can give limited information. It's open Saturday to Thursday 9 am to 4.30 pm, Friday 9 am to 12.30 pm.

Post Offices & International Telephones The main post office, poste restante and international phones are next door to the Municipality building, at 11 Atzma'ut St. Open Sunday, Tuesday and Thursday 8 am to 12.30 pm and 3.30 to 6 pm, Monday and Wednesday 8 am to 2 pm, Friday 8 am to 1 pm, closed Saturday. There is a handy branch in the Old City, next to the subterranean Crusader city, which is open July and August Sunday to Thursday 8 am to 2 pm, Friday 8 am to noon, closed Saturday; September to June Sunday, Tuesday and Thursday 8 am to 12.30 pm and 3.30 to 6 pm, Monday and Wednesday 8 am to 1 pm, closed Saturday.

Other There are banks on Ben-Ami St. The police station (tel 04 91023 or 100) is at 2 Ben-Ami St.

Walls & Gates
As you approach the Old City on Weizmann St, you first come to the wall and moat built in 1799 by Ahmed Pasha el-Jazzar after Napoleon's retreat. The sea wall was refaced at the same time, partly with stones from the Crusader castle at Atlit. It was originally built by the Crusaders in the 12th century. Other parts of the Crusader wall can be seen on both sides of Weizmann St, and were probably incorporated into the 18th century defences. The 13th century Crusader wall is now hidden by the new town – the Palm Beach Club Hotel marks its easternmost point.

A medieval mole extended to a point about halfway between the Palm Beach Club Hotel and the Land Gate, while another extended to the Tower of Flies on which there was a lighthouse. The Land Gate and the Sea Gate, now part of the Abu Christo restaurant, are both 12th century.

El-Jazzar Mosque
After passing the el-Jazzar wall and moat, turn right on el-Jazzar St and the mosque is on your left, its large green dome and minaret dominating the skyline. It was built in 1781 and the columns in the courtyard were looted from Caesarea.

Around the corner by the minaret, the small twin-domed building contains the sarcophagi of el-Jazzar and his adopted son, Suleiman, who ruled Akko from 1804 to 1819.

Open Saturday to Thursday 8 am to 12.30 pm and 1.30 to 4 pm, Friday 8 to 11 am and 2 to 4 pm. Admission is 70c. A guide will usually try to force himself on you as you enter. If you don't want his brief tour tell him so immediately to avoid hassles when you leave.

Subterranean Crusader City
Across the street from the mosque is the entrance to the subterranean Crusader city. This area was the quarter of the Knights Hospitallers, and what was their street level is now eight metres below ground.

In the entrance halls, some of the huge columns are engraved with French fleur-de-lys, others with Turkish decorations. From here you enter another hall, which once held a winepress, before entering the courtyard where the 30 metre high Citadel walls dominate.

Through the large Turkish gates to the left are the knights' halls. Turn right from here into the centre of the Crusader complex. In the ceiling is the cemented-over tunnel dug by Jewish prisoners in the British prison above. Not knowing what lay beneath in the dark halls they returned to their cells to plot a more successful mass escape.

Today the halls are occasionally used for concerts and the annual Akko Underground Theatre Festival is aptly staged here.

Back through the courtyard you come to the Grand Meneir, the centre of the Crusader government. A narrow passage leads to the knights' dining hall – the Refectory (or Crypt) of St John. Next to the crypt's third column is a stairway leading to a long underground passage. It's not known what its original purpose was, but el-Jazzar planned to use it as an escape route if Napoleon captured the city. Following the passage you come to the rooms and courtyard of the Crusaders' Domus Infirmorum, or hospital. The Turks used the area as a post office so it's also known as Al-Bosta.

The subterranean Crusader city is open Saturday to Thursday 9 am to 4.30 pm, Friday 9 am to 12.30 pm. Tickets are normally valid for both the subterranean Crusader city and the Municipal Museum. Admission is US$2, students US$1.50.

Municipal Museum

Turn right out of the subterranean Crusader city, follow el-Jazzar St around to the left, and the museum is on the right. It occupies what was originally a Turkish bath, Hammam el Pasha, built by el-Jazzar in 1780 for the people of Akko. The exhibits include drawings, lithographs and engravings relating to Akko during the Napoleonic wars, and artefacts found locally, such as Crusader weapons. The museum generally has the same operating hours as the subterranean Crusader city, and the same ticket is valid for both.

Tourist Center & Market

Continuing along the alley from the museum you come to the Tourist Center, a renovated area now occupied by art studios and the inevitable souvenir stalls.

The actual market occupies a few narrow streets and is positively tiny compared with its counterparts in other old cities. Nonetheless, its selection of shops makes it a popular distraction.

Khan el-Umdan

This is the most attractive of Akko's caravanserais which once served the camel caravans bringing grain from the southern Golan to the port. Its name means 'Inn of the Pillars' and it was built by el-Jazzar in 1785. You can easily find it by its tall clock tower which was erected in 1906 by the Ottoman sultan.

The ground floor housed the animals, and the people slept upstairs. The pillars are another example of the looting of Caesarea. The courtyard is now Akko's unofficial soccer stadium.

Fishing Port

South of Khan el-Umdan lies the fishing port. Especially in summer it is possible to take a boat trip to enjoy the view of the city. Ignore the imaginative prices suggested by your would-be skipper – about US$1.80 per person is the going rate.

Citadel & Museum of Heroism

On HaHaganath St, the Citadel houses the Museum of Heroism, dedicated to the Jewish resistance fighters during the British Mandate.

Built by the Turks in the late 18th century on 13th century Crusader foundations, the inmates of the prison included Bahu'a'llah, founder of the Baha'i faith, and Ze'ev Jabotinsky, a leader of the Jewish underground in the 1920s. Eight members of the Irgun were hanged here and other members staged a successful mass breakout in 1947. That scene in the movie *Exodus* was filmed here. The Citadel also houses a mental hospital.

The museum is open Saturday to Thursday 9 am to 5.30 pm, Friday 9 am to 12.30 pm. Admission is US$2, students US$1.50.

Burj Jurajim

Although usually called the British Fortress, Burj Jurajim means 'Fortress of the Vineyards' and it was built by the Turks on the Crusaders' foundations. From here you can follow el-Jazzar's wall and moat across to the centre to make your way back to the bus station.

Beaches

Akko's nicest beach is Purple Beach (Hof Argaman), so named because of the dye that could be obtained from the snails that frequented the area in ancient times. With wonderful views of the Old City on the horizon, the beach is very popular with Israelis, who are happy to pay the 70c admission.

To reach Purple Beach, either get off the bus from Haifa when you see the Palm Beach Club Hotel and the Argaman Motel, or walk east from Land Gate along Yonatan HaHoshmonai St – about a 10 minute walk.

The free but unattractive Walls Beach is just down from Land Gate, and is popular with windsurfers. There is a changing room near the entrance to the beach.

Tours

Egged Tours have a half-day tour to Akko and Rosh Hanikra which departs from Haifa. It costs US$20.

Places to Stay – bottom end

Most travellers visit Akko for the day from Haifa, or en route between Galilee and Tel Aviv, but there are some affordable accommodation options here.

A couple of private Arab hostels provide the cheapest accommodation – basic but clean enough and friendly, and without a curfew. From the clock tower of Khan el-Umdan, turn left away from the port and around the first corner on the left is the *Clock Tower Guest House* (tel 916159). This has a kitchen and comfortable mattresses on the floor. *Becky House* has cavernous dorm rooms in an old building,

with a TV and a kitchen. Follow el-Jazzar St past the mosque, the Municipal Museum and the New Tourist Center, and it is straight ahead.

Akko Youth Hostel – IYHA (tel 911982) is on the west side of the Old City, not far from the lighthouse, in a pleasant building which was the Turkish Governor's residence. It can be a bit difficult to find, despite signs here and there. When entering the Old City from the bus station head for HaHaganath St and walk down to the lighthouse. From here take the alley to the left, and the hostel is on the left. Beds are US$8 in dorms or double rooms, with breakfast. Closed 9 am to 5 pm, curfew 11 pm.

Places to Stay – middle

The two most noticeable places to stay in Akko are on Purple Beach. The *Argaman Motel* (tel 916691-7) is a modern complex with free access to the beach and that great view. Singles/doubles cost from US$35/45, with breakfast. The adjacent *Palm Beach Club Hotel* (tel 912891) has superior facilities, including a pool, sauna, tennis and water sports. They have singles/doubles from US$45/60 with breakfast.

On the north-eastern outskirts of Akko, *Nes Ammin* (tel 922566) is a Christian-run guest house whose aim is to promote understanding between Christians and Jews. They have some quite cheap hostel-style accommodation and singles/doubles from US$37/52, with breakfast. It's off the Akko to Nahariya road about five km north of Akko.

Places to Eat

There are a few felafel and shwarma places along Ben-Ami St and in the Old City, where there is also a bakery.

The fishing port is the most popular place for a sit-down meal. Fish is the obvious thing to order, and it is served simply cooked, with salad. The best of an average bunch is probably *Abu Christo*, which costs around US$10 for one. It's

Haifa & the North Coast 283

open daily from 11 am to about midnight.

Getting There & Away
Various Egged buses from Haifa, including No 271 which runs to Nahariya, stop at Akko and provide a frequent service. There is also a bus about every 30 minutes to and from Safed. Don't forget that buses run between Haifa and Akko on Saturday.

AROUND AKKO
Bahje House & the Baha'i Gardens
The holiest site for followers of the Baha'i faith, this is where Baha'u'llah, the founder, lived after his release from prison in Akko and where he died in 1892. His tomb is in a lovely garden, similar in style to the one in Haifa. You can visit the garden daily, between 9 am to 5 pm. Bahje House, which contains a small museum, is open Friday to Sunday 9 am to noon. Admission is free.

Take Egged bus No 271 from Haifa, Akko or Nahariya. Unless you're a Baha'i, you'll have to use the entrance about ½ km up the side road to the north of the main gate.

Turkish Aqueduct
On your right as you travel north on the Akko/Nahariya road is a long, arched, Roman-style aqueduct. Built by el-Jazzar in about 1780, it supplied Akko with water from Galilee's mountains.

Kibbutz Lochamei Hagetaot
Just north of the aqueduct, this kibbutz was established in 1949 by former resistance fighters from the ghettos of Germany, Poland and Lithuania. Their museum, Ghetto Fighter's House (tel 920412), has artefacts related to Jewish communities in those countries prior to the holocaust, and to the Jewish resistance movement. Open Sunday to Thursday 9 am to 4 pm, Friday 9 am to 1 pm, Saturday 10 am to 5 pm. Admission is free, but donations are requested. Ask the

bus driver to let you off – it's a short distance from the main road.

Nahal Shagur/Nahal Beit Hakerem
Known by either name, this small river runs through an attractive valley. The SPNI have marked out a pleasant and only slightly arduous 12 km hike which follows the river bed, and it makes a good day trip from Akko. Note that the walk is not possible when the river is flowing.

The hardest part is negotiating a couple of steep drops which become waterfalls in season. With these in mind, it is inadvisable to go alone in case you twist an ankle or worse. Also, be sure to take plenty of water.

Take Egged bus No 361 which leaves Akko for Gilon about every 30 minutes, and get off at the intersection for Gilon. It's marked by the Spanish-Jewish sign for Nahal Beit Hakerem. Take the steps by the sign down to the river bed and head right (west). For a short hike take the path to the left to head back to Gilon when you reach the first steep drop. Otherwise, follow the river bed to the path which leads up to the road between Yasur and Alihud. Turn left to hitch back to Akko.

NAHARIYA (population 28,600)
One of Israel's quietest seaside resorts, Nahariya is particularly popular with Jewish honeymooners on the Lag B'Omer holiday in spring, as this is the only day a Jew can marry during the six weeks between the Passover and Shavuot holidays.

Established in 1934 by German Jews escaping Nazism, Nahariya was Western Galilee's first Jewish settlement. In the town itself there is nothing much of interest except the pleasant beach, but it is close to the grottoes of Rosh Hanikra, the beach and national park at Ahziv, the Crusader castle at Montfort, and Peqi'in.

Orientation
A small place, Nahariya is centred around its main street, the two-lane HaGa'aton

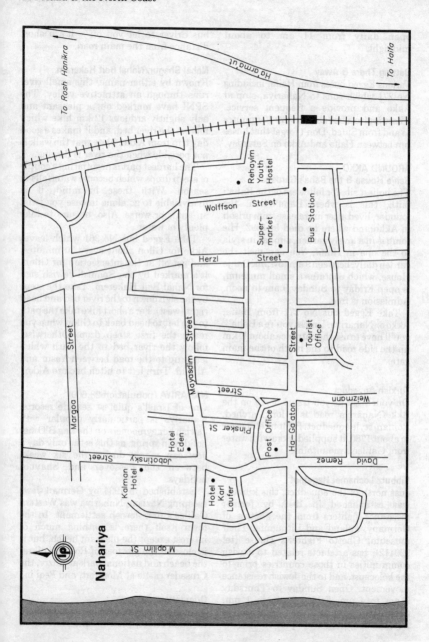

Nahariya

Blvd, which has an unimpressive stream running down the middle of it. Here are the bus and railway stations, tourist office, shops, banks, cafès and restaurants, cinema, and, at the western end, the beach. Most of the hotels are towards this end of town.

Information

Tourist Office The IGTO (tel 922126) is on the ground floor of the Municipality Building just west of the bus station on HaGa'aton. It's open Sunday to Thursday 9 am to 1 pm and 4 to 7 pm, Friday 9 am to 3.30 pm, closed Saturday.

Post Office & International Telephones These are at 40 HaGa'aton (tel 925355), west of the bus station on the opposite side. Open Sunday, Tuesday and Thursday 7.45 am to 12.30 pm and 3.30 to 6 pm, Monday and Wednesday 7.45 am to 2 pm, Friday 7.45 am to 1 pm, closed Saturday.

Police The police station (tel 920344, emergency 100) is on Ben Zvi St, just off HaGa'aton, east of the railway station on the opposite side.

Beaches

Follow HaGa'aton westwards and it leads to Nahariya's sandy beaches. Galei Gallil is the main beach, and is sectioned off with a swimming pool and a few amusements. Admission is US$2.50. Head south or further north for a pleasant and free stretch of sand and sea.

Canaanite Temple

Not really worth the 20 minute walk, the 4000-year-old remains of a Canaanite temple can be seen to the north of Galei Gallil.

Museum

Also uninspiring, this small collection of local archaeological finds, seashells and modern art is on the 5th floor of the Municipality building, near the bus station. Open Sunday to Friday 10 am to 12 noon, Sunday and Wednesday 4 to 6 pm, closed Saturday. Admission is free.

Places to Stay – bottom end

The only real choice for budget travellers (apart from sleeping on the theft-ridden beach) is the dingy *Rehayim Youth Hostel* (tel 920557), 6 Wolffson St. From the bus station, cross HaGa'aton Blvd and the hostel is one block north on the right. It has a kitchen, lounge and tables in the garden and could be a really nice place if they cleaned up their act. It costs US$5.50 for a bed and US$10 a double in the small, musty rooms. Bicycles are available for hire here. No curfew.

The other cheaper options cost considerably more. The *Motel Arieli* (tel 921076), 1 Jabotinsky, corner of HaGa'aton, has singles/doubles from US$12/23 in rooms with showers and the use of a kitchen.

Nahariya has several private homes where people let rooms. Look for the signs on Jabotinsky in particular, or ask at the tourist office. Prices hover around US$12 per person, but can be higher depending on the season, or lower depending on your bargaining skills.

Places to Stay – middle

Prices tend to go up by about 35% for July and August and Jewish holidays, while in winter you can get a reduction if you bargain hard. All rates include breakfast, and the rooms have private bathrooms.

Hotel Eden (tel 923246), on Mayasdim St at the corner of Jabotinsky, is modern and slick-looking which makes it stand out from the rest. It's pleasant and has singles/doubles from for US$36/50. *Kalman Hotel* (tel 920355) at 26-27 Jabotinsky St is a sparse place with singles/doubles from US$30/50. Next door, the *Hotel Beit Erna* (tel 920170) is a nice place with singles/doubles from US$25/35.

Hotel Rosenblatt (tel 923469) at 59 Weizmann St has singles/doubles from $US30/40.

Panorama Hotel (tel 920555), at 6

Ma'apilim St, one block north of HaGa'aton, is a nice, modern hotel with sea views and a rooftop terrace. Singles/doubles are US$35/45. *Pallas Athene Hotel* (tel 922381), 28 Ma'apilim St, is more expensive but has a rooftop sundeck, sauna, billiard table. Singles/doubles cost from US$60/75.

Hotel Frank (tel 920278), 4 HaAliyah St, off Ma'apilim, has balconies, sea views and friendly staff. Singles/doubles cost from US$35/47, although they climb steeply in the high season.

Places to Stay - top end

The *Carlton Hotel* (tel 922211), HaGa'aton Blvd, west of the bus station is Nahariya's top hotel. It's modern and attractive with some tasteful interior design and a pool, solarium and jacuzzi. Singles/doubles cost from US$53/75, with breakfast.

Places To Eat

There is the Supersol supermarket on HaGa'aton, corner of Herzl, and the bus station's Egged self-service restaurant. Elsewhere, the standard felafel or hummus is average at best. Nahariya lives up to its 'typical Israeli seaside resort' tag by having a shortage of decent eating places. HaGa'aton Blvd has cafés and restaurants which attract the crowds, but the food and service are usually mediocre. An exception is the *Donan Restaurant* (tel 923956), 32 HaGa'aton Blvd, which is a pleasant little Romanian grill with tables indoors or out on the pavement. It serves dishes such as grilled meats and fish for about US$12 per person.

The only other places I could recommend here are both Chinese. The *Singapore Chinese Garden* is one block north of HaGa'aton on Mayasdim, corner of Jabotinsky and across from the Yarden and Eden hotels. Nice decor and good service. It costs about US$15 per person for a full meal, but you could eat for less. The *Chinese Inn Restaurant*, 28 HaGa'aton is on the 2nd floor and you enter by the stairway at the rear. It's cheaper at about

US$7 per person. Both places are open for lunch and dinner.

For draught beer there are a few identical places along HaGa'aton and its off-shoots.

Getting There & Away

There are buses to and from Akko and Haifa every 30 minutes and an irregular train service to Haifa.

Getting Around

Although the beach and all accommodation is within walking distance of the bus and railway stations, it makes sense to hire a bicycle from the Rehayim Youth Hostel (see Places to Stay). This costs US$2.50 per day, which is about what you would pay in bus fares to reach Ahziv and Rosh Hanikra, and you are not dependent on the irregular local buses. On Shabbat it is the only way to travel!

An expensive alternatives to the bus and bicycle are the horse carts which presumably provide a living for their owners, although the unhealthy-looking horses don't seem to benefit from the deal. It costs US$8 for a 15 minute ride.

AROUND NAHARIYA
Ahziv

The short stretch of coastline between Nahariya and Rosh Hanikra is known as Ahziv. Once one of the towns of the Asher tribe in ancient Israel, it was also a Phoenician port, and remains dating from the Bronze Age have been found here.

Ahziv Beach About four km north on the road to Rosh Hanikra, this pleasant beach with its changing facilities, sunshades, showers and snack bar is free, although you do pay for car parking.

Ahziv National Park Just a little further north, this area of parkland is on the site of an 'abandoned' Arab village. You can see traces of a Phoenician port and use the beach. The beach has changing facilities and there is a snack bar but there is an admission charge of US$2.75, students US$1.40. It's open April to September Saturday to Thursday 8 am to 5 pm and Friday 8 am to 4 pm, October to March Saturday to Thursday 8 am to 4 pm and Friday 8 am to 3 pm.

Ahzivland In 1952 Eli Avivi settled in an old Arab house by the beach just north of the national park and declared his land to be an independent state which he called 'Ahzivland'. Since then he has established a museum housing his varied collection of artefacts found nearby, some of which date from the Phoenician, Roman and Byzantine periods. He opens daily, April to September 8 am to 5 pm, October to March 8 am to 4 pm. Admission is US$1.70.

Eli also has a dirty and very basic hostel with unpleasant looking slabs of foam rubber on the floor at US$7 and ground space outside for US$4.65. However, judging by the visitors' book, there are people who are happy to stay here. Passport stamp collectors may want to get an Ahzivland stamp.

Camp Site Across the road from Ahzivland is a camp site (tel 921792, off-season 923366), with small, basic two-person cabins for US$18 and four-person cabins for US$30. If you have your own tent you pay US$5 per person. There is a supermarket here and showers and toilets.

Yad Le Yad In 1946 14 Haganah soldiers were killed trying to blow up the railway bridges on this stretch of the line in order to cut British communication links. A monument to them stands by the road and the nearby IYHA hostel (tel 921343), is named *Yad Le Yad* (Memorial for the 14). Despite the bloody local history, the hostel is a pleasant place to stay, across the road from a popular beach. Members pay US$7, non-members US$8, with breakfast. Meals are available and there is

a kitchen for the guests' use. No curfew – you have your own key.

Kibbutz Gesher HaZiv Named after the bridge incident, this settlement (tel 927711) was established in 1949 by a group of Americans and Israelis. It was one of the first kibbutzim to raise its children at home with their parents rather than in separate accommodation. There is a guest house with comfortable rooms with private bathroom which costs from US$60/90, with breakfast. There is also a restaurant open to non-residents. Look for the signpost at the intersection on the coastal road.

Rosh Hanikra
On the sensitive Israel-Lebanon border (photography could be risky), the caves at Rosh Hanikra ('Cave of the Grotto') are a popular tourist attraction. Carved by the sea at the base of the tall white cliff, this series of caves was enlarged by the British for a railway and by the Israelis to improve access for visitors. They are at their most interesting in bad weather when the sea is wild.

Think twice about swimming here – it is illegal and dangerous. There are strong currents and the strictly out-of-bounds Lebanese territorial waters (along with shoot-first Lebanese border guards) are close by.

The only practical way to reach the caves is by cable car, which operates Saturday to Thursday 8.30 am to 6 pm, Friday 8.30 am to 4 pm. The US$4.75 fare is as steep as the cliff.

Places to Eat There are two cafeterias, one by the car park, down from the border and the other at the top of the hill, by the cable car.

Getting There & Away Only a couple of the buses from Nahariya go direct to the site (stopping at the foot of the hill), and normally you have to walk the three km from the junction. This is another good reason for renting a bicycle, although that last stretch is an uphill struggle.

Peqi'in

A predominantly Druze village, Peqi'in has had a Jewish community for many centuries which, according to tradition, has never been exiled from the Holy Land. In 1936, though, the political situation forced them to leave the area and only a small number returned after Israel's independence. There is also an Arab community here.

The village is believed to be where Rabbi Shimon Bar Yochai and his son,

Eliezer, hid from the Romans in the 2nd century to escape a decree which made it illegal to study the Torah. The tradition is that they stayed in a cave here for 13 years, during which the rabbi compiled the Zohar, the most important book in Jewish mysticism. Outside the cave a fresh-water spring and a carob tree miraculously appeared. The two are said to have fed on the fruit from the tree, drunk from the spring and embedded themselves in the sand up to their necks while they spent all their time studying the Torah.

The traditional cave of Rabbi Shimon

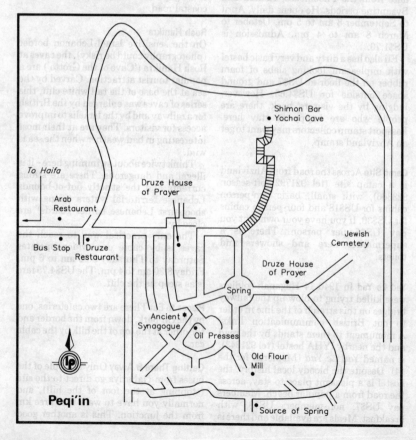

Peqi'in

Bar Yochai is now holy to religious Jews. Also to be seen are the spring (unattractively trickling through a modern-day pipe into a pool), an ancient synagogue now housing a museum, the Jewish community's old cemetery, and an old flour mill and oil presses. The village is a maze of twisting streets and it is hard to find these visually disappointing sites. To save time, stop off at the Druze café next to the bus stop by the entrance to the village for a free map, directions and a friendly chat.

A seal of the Crusader Kings

Places to Eat Peqi'in's food speciality is *pitta-eem-leben*. This is wafer-thin pitta bread served with a soft, sour, white cheese which is mixed with olive oil and dill. Two cafés opposite each other compete to serve you. The *Jewish Community Restaurant* on your left as you arrive from Nahariya was here first. Despite its name, it is owned by Arabs, and the old lady has been baking the pitta for over 30 years. Across the street by the bus stop, the friendly Druze man set up his operation about eight years ago, with his sister doing the baking. The Arabs charge less, about US$1.20, but the Druze man does give out that free map which, although in Hebrew and somewhat confusing, is just a bit better than nothing. You can also order hummus and some very good coffee at both cafés.

Getting There & Away Egged bus No 44 runs about every hour from Nahariya (45 minutes). You should get off at the old village Peqi'in Atika, not the modern settlement of Peqi'in Hadasha the stop before.

Beit Jan

The highest village in Israel at 940 metres above sea level, this is another friendly Druze community, and the views of the surrounding countryside are lovely. Take Egged bus No 44 from Nahariya and stay on after Peqi'in then get off three km later at the Beit Jan junction. From here the village is a 2½ km walk or hitch-hike.

Montfort

Montfort is not the most impressive of Israel's Crusader castles, but it is interesting and a visit here involves a pleasant hike.

Originally built in 1226 by the French Courtenays, its name changed from Montfort (Strong Mountain) to Starkenburg (Strong Castle) when they sold it to the Teutonic knights, the Templars and the Hospitallers. They modified the castle, which became their central treasury, archives and Holy Land HQ, although it had no real strategic value. In 1271 the Muslims, led by Baybars, took the castle after an attempt five years earlier had failed. The Crusaders retreated to Akko and the castle was razed.

Today there is little to see. To the right of the entrance is the governor's residence, with the tower straight ahead. The two vaulted chambers to the right are the basement of the knights' hall; next to them is the chapel. It's open Saturday to Thursday 8 am to 5 pm, Friday 8 am to 4 pm. Admission is US$1, students 70c.

Getting There & Away From Nahariya take a bus to Goren and ask for the park. From here you will see the castle in the distance, about a 1½ hour walk.

Gadin

This is another ruined Crusader castle, eight km west of Yehiam. There are two buses a day from Nahariya.

Galilee & the Golan

Taken from the Hebrew word *Galil* (district), Galilee is probably the most popular area of the country with visitors, as well as locals, due to its rich combination of beautiful scenery and religious heritage. This is Israel's lushest region, with green valleys and slopes, forests, farmland and, of course, the Sea of Galilee itself. Spring is a particularly good time to appreciate the area in all its glory.

Galilee is often labelled 'the land of the Bible' as here Jesus did most of his preaching and Jewish scholars produced the rabbinical texts, the Talmud, the Mishnah and the Kabbalah. However, this is also a land of conflict, in particular since Israel's independence, and you will see many war memorials on your travels here. Earlier battles were fought by the Egyptians, Canaanites, Greeks, Romans, Crusaders and Muslims.

Because of Galilee's fertility the Zionist pioneers first settled here, in particular around the Sea of Galilee and in the Jordan and Jezreel Valleys. Galilee's northernmost Jewish communities have had to exist under the continual physical threat of terrorist raids from Lebanon and Syria and until recently heavy artillery bombardments. It is often easy to forget that a large percentage of Israel's Arab residents still live here, although many were forced to leave before and during the 1948 War of Independence.

Jordan River

Despite its biblical background and status as Israel's longest river and major water source, the Jordan is often a disappointment. First-time visitors usually expect to find something more expansive than the small and muddy desert stream that it is for much of its length. Throughout the scenic Jordan Valley drive between Tiberias and Jerusalem,

the nearest you get to actually seeing the river is the trail of trees that cluster around its meandering course. The most attractive parts of the river are north of the lake, at Banyus in the Golan and Tel Dan in Uppeer Galilee.

There are three main sources of the Jordan: the Senir River (*Hasbani* in Arabic) which rises in Lebanon; the Banyus and the Dan River. The origin and meaning of the name 'Jordan' are not so clear. A 1300 map of Palestine shows the river with two sources: Jor and Dan. Another theory is that the name comes from the Hebrew *Yored Dan* (descends from Dan).

NAZARETH (population 46,300)

Generally believed to be the home of Mary and Joseph before the birth of Jesus, and where they returned to raise him after fleeing to Egypt, Nazareth usually fails to match the high expectations of pilgrims and tourists. The several important churches are unfortunately overshadowed by the unattractive and rapidly expanding town and its busy streets.

Today Nazareth is notable for its important Christian shrines and as a main centre of the Christian mission movement in the Holy Land with its many smaller churches, convents, monasteries, schools, orphanages and hospitals. Nazareth also stands out as a place where Sunday is the Sabbath and not Saturday, so be sure to check individual shops and businesses for opening hours.

One of the country's largest Arab towns, it is known in Arabic as *en-Nasra*, in Hebrew *Natsrat*. It now includes Nazareth Illit, or Upper Nazareth, the newer Jewish town. This started to develop in 1957 due to the establishment of factories, including textile and engineering plants.

Because of its large Arab population,

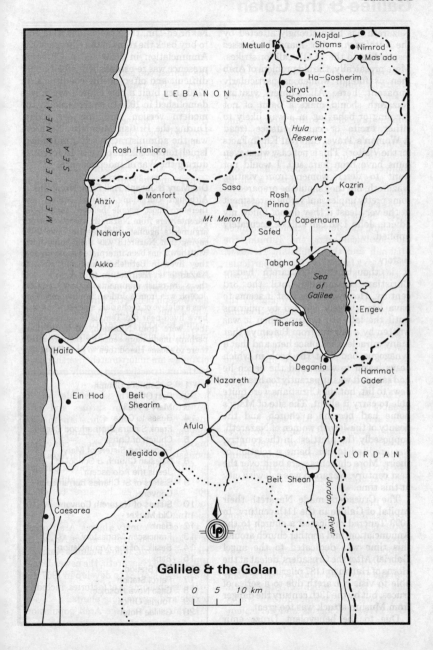

Galilee & the Golan

0   5   10 km

Nazareth has been strongly affected by the *intefadeh*, with many businesses responding to the PLO's call for strikes. More prosaically, the old problem of Arab men *vs* foreign women is particularly apparent here. All women visiting Nazareth should make a point of not dressing or behaving in a way likely to either excite or cause offence (read A Woman's Travel Survival Kit in Facts for the Visitor). This is not easy when even nuns have been harassed. I would not want to deter women from visiting Nazareth, but they should be prepared for some pretty unpleasant verbal harassment at the very least if they do not follow my advice. John 1:46 can still be accurately applied.

History

It is thought that Nazareth had a Christian community until the 3rd century. However, after that it seems to have been largely ignored by pilgrims until the late 6th century when it was written by a pilgrim from Piacimya that many miracles took place here and that a synagogue had kept the book in which Jesus learnt to write, and the bench he had sat on. It was apparently too heavy for Jews to lift, but the Christians were quite able to carry it about. The site of Mary's home had become a church and the beauty of the Jewish women of Nazareth, supposedly the prettiest in the country, was credited to her, being a relation of theirs. More churches were built over the next century. Nazareth was a Jewish city at this time.

The Crusaders made Nazareth their capital of Galilee in the 11th century. In 1099 Tancred dedicated a church to the Annunciation, and another church around this time was dedicated to the angel Gabriel. After the Crusaders' defeat at the Horns of Hattin in 1187 pilgrims were still able to visit Nazareth due to a series of truces, but by the 13th century the danger from Muslim attack was too great.

Due to the benevolent Druze emir Fakhr ed-Din, the Franciscans were able to buy back the ruins of the Church of the Annunciation in 1620 and a Christian presence was re-established; albeit under difficult and often hostile conditions. In 1730 they built a new church which was demolished in 1955 to be replaced by the modern version that you see today. During the British Mandate, Nazareth was the administration's HQ in Galilee. Israeli forces took the town on 16 July 1948 during the War of Independence.

Did Mary & Joseph Hail From Nazareth?

Although Christian tradition states, and therefore most people believe, that Jesus' parents were from Nazareth, there are strong arguments against this, despite Luke 2:4-5 saying that Nazareth was their home town. Matthew 2 has been interpreted as saying that they lived in Bethlehem and only went to Nazareth on their return from Egypt – and there are other arguments against tradition. Joseph was from a Judean family, and Mary was a relative of Zechariah, a priest who would have lived near the Temple in Jerusalem. If they were from Nazareth, it would have perhaps made more sense for them to return there to escape Herod then to go to Egypt. For

1   St Gabriel's Church
2   Post Office
3   Mary's Well
4   Buses to Cana
5   Frank Sinatra Brotherhood Centre
6   Church of Christ
7   Franciscan Sisters of Mary
8   Salesian Church & School of Jesus the Adolescent
9   Sisters of St Charles Borramaeus Convent
10   Sisters of Nazareth Convent
11   Old Market
12   Bank
13   Franciscan Monastery
14   Basilica of the Annunciation
15   Bank
16   Bus Station
17   Petrol Station
18   Casa Nova Hospice
19   Tourist Office
20   Galilee Hotel

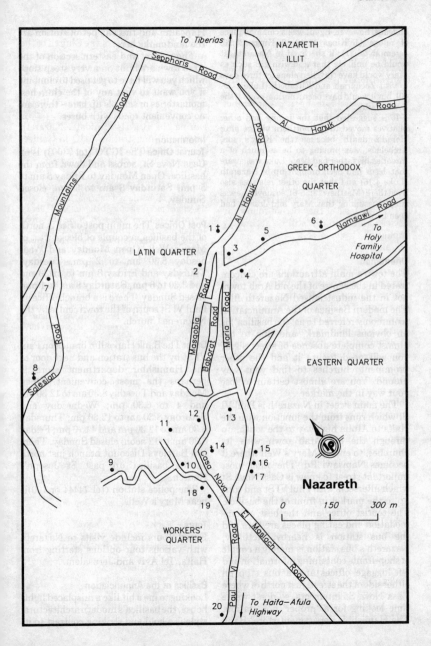

To Tiberias

NAZARETH ILLIT

Sepphoris Road

Al Hanuk Road

GREEK ORTHODOX QUARTER

Mountains Road

Namsawi Road

To Holy Family Hospital

LATIN QUARTER

Al Hanuk

1

5

6

3

2

4

7

Salesian Road

Masgobia Road

Baborat Road

Maria Road

8

EASTERN QUARTER

12

13

11

9

10

14

15

16

17

Casa Nova

Nazareth

0   150   300 m

18

19

WORKERS' QUARTER

El Maslach Road

Paul VI Road

20

To Haifa–Afula Highway

Judeans, however, Egypt was a common place of refuge (1 Kings 11:40, 2 Kings 25:26, Jeremiah 26:21). If she lived in Nazareth, it would be unlikely that a Jewish girl such as Mary would have travelled alone for three days to visit Zechariah and Elizabeth (Luke 1:39-40), but it would have been a normal event if she lived nearby.

It is suggested that the family and other relatives moved to the northern village after Herod's death because the King's son, Archelaus, was proving to be as much of a threat as his father had been. Luke was aware that Jesus had been brought up in Nazareth (Luke 4:16) and that the other relatives also lived there (Matthew 13:55-6), so maybe he was simply assuming that Mary and Joseph had been born here.

Orientation

The town's main attractions are concentrated in the centre of the old Arab town, not in the industrialised Nazareth Illit. The modern Basilica of the Annunciation (commonly referred to as 'the basilica') is an obvious landmark, and due to the almost complete absence of street signs, you will need to use it and the other prominent churches to find your way around. You are almost certain to lose your way in the market.

The main street in Nazareth is Paul VI St which runs from the junction with the Haifa to Afulla highway to the south, up through the old Arab town with its churches, to end by Mary's Well where it becomes Namsawi Rd. The other most important street to know is Casa Nova St which intersects with Paul VI St and runs up to the market in front of the basilica. The tourist office and the best accommodation and eating places are here and the bus station is nearby. Actually, Nazareth's bus station is merely a couple of shop-fronts containing information and left-luggage offices and a bus stop on either side of the street, just north of where Casa Nova St intersects, so don't waste time looking for a 'proper' bus station. The Hamishbir department store, Bank Hapoalim and the Paz petrol station are the landmarks here.

The market and eastern section of the Arab town are built on a very steep slope which you will have to get used to climbing if you want to visit any of the churches, monasteries or schools up here – there are no convenient roads with buses.

Information

Tourist Office The IGTO (tel 73003) is on Casa Nova St, across and down from the basilica. Open Monday to Friday 8 am to 5 pm, Saturday 8 am to 3 pm, closed Sunday.

Post Offices The main post office is north of the basilica, a couple of blocks west of Mary's Well. Open Monday and Wednesday 8.30 am to 2 pm, Tuesday, Thursday and Friday 8 am to 12.30 pm and 3.30 to 6 pm, Saturday 8 am to 1 pm, closed Sunday. There is a branch office on Paul VI St south of the town centre by the Nazarene Church.

Other The Bank Hapoalim branch on Paul VI St by the bus station and next door to the Hamishbir department store is perhaps the most convenient. Open Monday and Tuesday 8.30 am to 12.30 pm and 4 to 6.30 pm; Wednesday and Saturday 8.30 am to 12.30 pm; Thursday 8.30 am to 12.30 pm and 4 to 6 pm; Friday 8.30 am to 12 noon; closed Sunday. There is a Barclays Discount branch just north of the basilica up past St Joseph's Church.

The police station (tel 74444 or 100)is near Mary's Well.

Tours

Egged Tours include visits to Nazareth with various tour options starting from Haifa, Tel Aviv and Jerusalem.

Basilica of the Annunciation

Looking to me a bit like a misplaced lighthouse, the basilica's modern architectural style is a bold and striking contrast to its older environment. It is one of the world's most holy Christian shrines, as it is built on the traditional site of the Annunciation (Luke 1: 26-38), a cave or perhaps the house where Mary lived.

There are basically two churches in the complex incorporating the remains of the earlier one. Using the main entrance from Casa Nova St, you are on the lower level which contains archaeological excavations. The bronze doors are decorated with scenes from the life of Jesus. In the centre of the underground church is the apse of the 5th century Byzantine church. Behind it is the triple apse of the 12th century Crusader church. Also to be seen here are the square pre-Constantinian baptistery and, down a flight of steps, the mosaic floor which was the cave floor in the Byzantine period.

To reach the upper, modern level, use the stairs near the main entrance. The colours of the stained-glass windows here are highlighted against the bare stone. It is the basilica's collection of murals depicting Mary and the Baby Jesus, donated by Christian groups from all around the world, which is its most popular feature. My favourite is probably the Japanese one with Mary's kimono made from seed pearls. Leaving the upper level via the northern door you come out into a courtyard facing the Terra Sancta Monastery which houses the Franciscan monks who maintain the basilica. Under the courtyard lie more excavations of ancient Nazareth.

An interesting legend concerning the basilica says that when the Muslims captured Nazareth in 1263, they intended to convert the Crusaders' church into a mosque. However, angels appeared and carried the building across the sea to Italy. Today the Italian town of Loretto is known as the 'Nazareth of Italy' and contains the church mentioned in the legend, which was first heard of in the 15th century.

No visitors are allowed inside the basilica during services, otherwise it is open April to September, Monday to Saturday from 8.30 to 11.45 am and 2 to 5.45 pm, Sundays and holy days 2 to 5.45 pm; October to March, Monday to Saturday 9 to 11.45 am and 2 to 4.45 pm, Sundays and holy days 2 to 4.45 pm. Admission is free. Most of Nazareth's other churches operate the same visiting hours.

St Joseph's Church

Just up Casa Nova St from the basilica and monastery is St Joseph's Church, built in 1914 and occupying the traditional site of Joseph's carpentry shop. This belief probably originated in the 17th century and today's church was built over the remains of a medieval church. Down in the crypt you can see an underground cave used for grain storage in pre-Byzantine times.

Sisters of Nazareth Convent

Up the side street, across from the basilica with the Casa Nova Hospice on the corner, this convent is on the right. It operates a school for deaf and blind Arab children as well as providing accommodation for travellers in its hospice and hostel, and the convent boasts one of the best

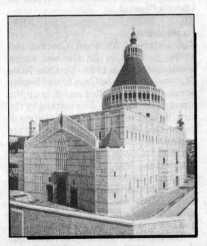
Basilica of the Annunciation

examples of an ancient tomb sealed by a rolling stone. It lies under the present courtyard and can only be viewed by appointment.

Market

At the top of Casa Nova St is the Arab market occupying a maze of steep and narrow, winding streets. Unfortunately, it is dominated, not by shops crammed with exotic bargains, but by an open drain running in the middle of the street and seemingly provided for the benefit of the donkeys which carry goods up and down the hill.

Greek Catholic Synagogue Church

In a prominent position in the market, this church is beside what is traditionally believed to be the synagogue where Jesus regularly prayed and later taught (Luke 4:15-30).

Mensa Christi Church

Built in 1861, this small Franciscan church contains a large rock known in Latin as *Mensa Christi* (Table of Christ). Tradition has it that Jesus dined here with his disciples after the Resurrection. It is north-west of St Charles Borramaeus, and the Maronite Church and the Ecumenical Christian Child Care Centre are nearby.

St Gabriel's Church & Mary's Well

The story surrounding this Greek Orthodox church and the nearby well conflicts with that of the basilica. According to this tradition, the angel Gabriel appeared before Mary while she was fetching water – not when she was in what is now the grotto in the basilica. The church was built in the late 17th century on the site of earlier churches and the crypt at the far end contains the source of the spring supplying the nearby well. The church is about a 10 minute walk north of the basilica, two blocks west of where Paul VI St ends.

Mary's Well, also known as the Virgin's Fountain, is now an unimpressive faucet down from St Gabriel's Church by Paul VI St. Some believe that the angel Gabriel appeared here and the water is said to have powers of healing.

Basilica & School of Jesus the Adolescent

Built in 1918 in 13th century style, this is probably the most beautiful of Nazareth's many churches. It belongs to the French Salesian Order and its attractive architecture, both inside and out, and the impressive views of the town below and surrounding countryside could justify your hiking up the steep slope to reach it. It's next door to the Salesian school.

Chapel of Fright

Luke 4:29-30 tells of when the people of Nazareth tried to throw Jesus off the top of a hill. In the southern part of the town, the Franciscan Chapel of Fright, or Notre Dame de l'Effroi, is built on the supposed site from where Mary watched this event. The nearby hill is known as 'The Precipice' or the 'Leap of the Lord'. Look for the signposted gate in the wall on Paul VI St, opposite the Galilee Hotel. The church is behind the wall, beyond St Claire's Convent.

Places to Stay

The *Sisters of Nazareth Convent* (tel 54304) provides by far the best cheap accommodation in town. Up Casa Nova St, turn left after the Casa Nova Hospice across from the basilica and it is up the street on the right, its door marked by the sign 'Religieuses de Nazareth – Sisters of Nazareth'. With beautiful architecture and a delightful cloistered courtyard, this is a peaceful haven and one of the cleanest places that you will find anywhere. There's a tastefully furnished lounge-dining room and kitchen; dorm beds cost US$4. There are also more expensive single, double and three-bedded rooms, and half and full board is available.

The dorms are open all year round, but the wing with the rooms is closed during late January and throughout February. For the rest of the year, peaking at Easter and in the summer, it is busy with pilgrim groups from Europe so you would be well advised to make a reservation if possible. The youth hostel is rarely full – check in after about 4 pm. You are expected to be out by 9 am and there is a strict 9 pm curfew. Although Nazareth may not be all that popular a place with visitors, the convent is such a nice place to stay that many choose to make it a base from which to visit other parts of Galilee. You are officially limited to a maximum stay of three nights in the youth hostel but this rule is sometimes waived.

The alternatives to the Sisters of Nazareth's hospitality are more expensive, and usually less friendly and comfortable. Coming a fairly close second, though, is the *Casa Nova Hospice* (tel 71367), across from the basilica on Casa Nova St. Belonging to the Franciscans, it is very popular with, and usually full of, pilgrim groups. It has the air of an exclusive club – but not for the right reasons. If you are not with one of those groups, you will be looked down upon by the unsmiling and officious staff who will often claim to be full when there are empty rooms – just to be awkward, it seems. Despite such setbacks, the hospice is excellent value providing pleasant rooms and serving good food, so make a point of asking for the priest in charge when checking in – regardless of what his local henchmen might say. US$16 with breakfast, US$20 full board per person. Curfew 10.30 pm.

There are other Christian institutions that provide accommodation, but they have limited facilities which are specifically for pilgrims. These include the *Frères de Betharram Monastery* (tel 570046) with singles/doubles for US$18 per person, including breakfast and lunch, and the *Sisters of St Charles Borramaeus Convent* (tel 54435), above the Carmelite Convent up on the western slopes. You may be able to get cheaper dorm beds at both these.

Nazareth also has three hotels to provide a secular but not very attractive alternative to the religious establishments. The modern *Hotel Galilee* (tel 571545) on Paul VI St about five minutes' walk south of the basilica, has singles/doubles for US$25/40 including breakfast, and is the most central and probably the nicest of the three. The *Nazareth Hotel* (tel 572045) is out of the way, on the edge of town at the intersection of the Haifa to Afulla highway. Singles/doubles are US$31/40, breakfast included. Further out towards Haifa is the *Grand New Hotel* (tel 73020/1, 73325) on St Joseph St, where singles/doubles cost US$32/42, with breakfast.

Places to Eat

The best places to eat in Nazareth are undoubtedly in the Christian hospices. Failing that, the next best thing is to cook for yourself.

The market is the place to buy fresh vegetables and fruit, and there are grocer shops along Paul VI St in both directions from Casa Nova St. Between the basilica and the bus station are several good felafel stalls, whilst a place for some hummus and/or a bottle of beer is the *Astoria Restaurant* on the corner of Casa Nova and Paul VI.

Just up the street, across from the basilica, *Mahroum's Sweets* enjoys a reputation as the best place in town for baclava and those other honey-soaked pastries. Several places have the same name, but the original is the one nearest to the basilica.

Getting There & Away

Bus Nazareth is a stop en route for several buses that cross Galilee. Remember that because the bus station here consists of an insignificant couple of bus stops, you could easily miss it and end up going past the town without realising it. Keep a lookout for the basilica, the Hamishbir department store, the Hapoalim Bank and the Paz petrol station.

There are buses about every hour to

Tiberias (34 km), Afulla (six km), Akko (14 km) and Haifa (35 km), and less frequently to Tel Aviv and just twice a day to Jerusalem. Stand outside the Hamishbir department store for the Tiberias bus; for all other destinations stand on the other side of the street.

The Egged information office is open Sunday to Thursday 4 am to 7 pm, Friday 4 am to 3 pm, closed Saturday. The left-luggage office next door is open Sunday to Thursday, 7.30 am to 5 pm, Friday 7.30 am to 1 pm, closed Saturday.

Sheruts Sheruts to Tiberias leave from in front of the Hamishbir department store. For Haifa and Tel Aviv, sheruts, go to the street by the side of the Paz petrol station. You will also get sheruts coming through Nazareth from Haifa, Tiberias and other places looking for extra passengers, so keep a lookout for them at the bus station.

Getting Around
All of the sights are within walking distance of the bus station, as are most of the places to stay.

AROUND NAZARETH & TIBERIAS
Cana
Also called Kafr Kanna, this town, seven km north-east of Nazareth on the road to Tiberias, is the purported site of Jesus' first miracle (John 2:1-11) when he changed water into wine at a wedding reception. It was also where he told the official that his son was cured (John 4:46-54) and it was the home town of the disciple Nathanael (John 21:2).

Franciscan Church This was built in 1881 on the traditional site of Jesus' first miracle. It contains an old jar of the type that contained the water he turned into wine. Under the church floor you can see a fragment of a mosaic pavement that bears an ancient Jewish Aramaic inscription.

St Nathanael Chapel Also belonging to the Franciscans and near their church, it is built on the traditional site of the disciple Nathanael's house.

Greek Church This contains ancient stone vats that some believe were involved in Jesus' first miracle. The painting on the wall, believed to date from 1849, portrays the miracle.

Getting There & Away Arab buses leave about every 45 minutes from near Mary's Well in Nazareth to go to Cana. Alternatively, Egged bus No 431 between Tiberias and Nazareth regularly passes the village – ask the driver to let you off. The Greek Church is nearest the main road, the Franciscan church and chapel are in the town centre.

Horns of Hattin
About 14 km east of Cana, heading towards Tiberias, the Horns of Hattin can be seen to the north. This long and low horn-shaped hill was where the Muslims, led by Saladin, defeated the Crusaders on 4 July 1187 and took control of most of the Holy Land in one of history's most important battles. There is nothing much to see here, but those with a keen interest might want to visit the summit, reached via a side road and a track two km from both Kibbutz Lavi and Zomet Poriyya.

At the foot of the Horns of Hattin is the traditional site of the Tomb of Jethro, holy to the Druze who make a pilgrimage here on 25 April.

Mount Tabor
With glorious views across the multi-coloured patchwork of fields of the Jezreel Valley, Mount Tabor is the traditional site of the Transfiguration of Jesus (Matthew 17:1-9, Mark 9:2-8 and Luke 9:28-36). This was when Jesus was seen by some of the disciples to be talking with the prophets Moses and Elijah. Two large churches on the summit, one Franciscan, one Greek, commemorate the event.

Neanderthal people came here from

80,000 to 15,000 BC to make flint tools, but because of the lack of water they were unable to settle; they worked here and lived elsewhere. The first Biblical mention of Mount Tabor is Judges 4:5-16, in relation to Deborah and Barak's victory over Hazor in 1125 BC. Judges 46:18 makes Mount Tabor a symbol of Nebuchadnezer's might. Hosea 5:1 relates to the altars built here to the heathen gods. In 218 BC the Egyptian soldiers stationed on the mount's summit were enticed down into the valley to be slaughtered by the Syrian forces of Antiochus III who were feigning retreat. In 67 AD the Romans under General Placidus did much the same to defeat the Jews who, led by Josephus, had fortified their position.

It is suggested that the Transfiguration was first linked to the site at the beginning of the Byzantine period. Mount Hermon in the Golan Heights was another contender, along with the Mount of Olives.

A Byzantine church was probably still standing when Benedictine monks were installed on the mount in 1099 by the Crusaders. They were massacred in a Turkish attack in 1113 that also saw their buildings destroyed. They later returned to build a new church and monastery which survived an attack by Saladin in 1183, but the nearby Greek church of St Elijah was destroyed. However, the Bendictines were forced to leave after the Crusaders' defeat at the Horns of Hattin in 1187.

The Muslims then built their own fortress on the mount and, as it was on the site of the Transfiguration, it inspired the 5th Crusade. Although a Crusader siege in 1217 failed, the Muslims dismantled the fortress because they realised that it would continue to be a serious provocation. Later in the 13th century a series of truces made it possible for Christians to return to the mount but in 1263 they were expelled by King Baybars.

Church of St Elijah Built in 1911, this church stands next to the Franciscan basilica although the access roads are some distance apart. The Cave of Melchizedek, its entrance marked by an iron door in the wall just after the turn-off for the Greek church, is where he received Abraham (Genesis 14:17-20), according to a medieval tradition.

Basilica of the Transfiguration The entrance to the Franciscan complex is through the main gate of the Muslim's 13th century fortress, restored in 1897. Its defence wall, including 12 towers, goes all the way round the summit. About 150 metres inside the gate to the right is a small chapel. Built on Byzantine foundations it commemorates the conversation between Jesus and his disciples after the Transfiguration (Mark 9:9-13). The cemetery to the north is medieval, the one to the south 1st century.

At the end of the drive is the basilica built in 1924, one of the Holy Land's most beautiful churches, both inside and out. Its highlight for me is the lovely mosaic of the Nativity. On the right of the piazza, in front of the basilica, stands the Franciscan monastery and hospice; on the left are remains of the Byzantine monastery. No visitors are allowed inside the basilica during services, otherwise it is open April to September, Monday to Saturday 8.30 to 11.45 am and 2 to 5.45 pm; Sunday and holy days 2 to 5.45 pm. October to March, Monday to Saturday 9 to 11.45 am and 2 to 4.45 pm; Sundays and holy days 2 to 4.45 pm. Admission is free.

Panorama With its height of 580 metres, Mount Tabor commands stunning views in all directions. To the north are the mountains of Upper Galilee with Mount Hermon slightly to the east, and in front of it the Horns of Hattin just above the Sea of Galilee further to the east. Nazareth can be seen clearly to the west, with Mount Carmel beyond, and the Samarian mountains blend in from the south round to the east.

Getting There & Away Mount Tabor can be reached by bus from Nazareth (50 minutes) stopping en route at Afulla, where you can connect with buses to most of the major destinations in Israel. However, the Mount Tabor bus is infrequent, so to avoid a long delay check the current schedule, especially for the return bus.

The bus will drop you off at the bottom of the steep and winding road that leads up to the summit; the climb takes about 30 minutes. At the top the turning to the left leads to the Greek church; carry straight on to reach the Franciscan basilica.

Megiddo

Megiddo is best known as Armageddon, the Biblical symbol for the last great battle on earth (Revelation 16:16). The name Armageddon is derived from the Hebrew *Har Megiddo* (Mount of Megiddo) and it is one of the most important cities in ancient history.

Today you can visit the archaeological site of Megiddo, maintained by the National Parks Authority, and see the remains of 20 distinct historical periods, from 4000 to 400 BC.

Due to its strategic location at the head of the ancient trade route from Egypt to Syria and Mesopotamia, Megiddo was the scene of important and bloody battles throughout the ages, right up to the 20th century.

Megiddo is first mentioned in the written records of an Egyptian king. Hieroglyphics on the wall of Karnak Temple in Luxor detail the battle that Thutmose III fought at Megiddo in 1468 BC. The account of his victory includes the capture of 924 enemy chariots. Megiddo remained a prosperous Egyptian stronghold for at least 100 years. Judges 1:27 tells of it being too strong for the invading Israelites to take and it probably

1	Museum
2	Staircase & Outer Gate
3	Gate – 15th Century BC
4	Gate – 18th Century BC
5	Gate – King Solomon's era
6	Holy Precinct
7	Chalcolithic Temple
8	Residence of Commander of King Solomon's Chariots
9	Observation Point
10	Building – King David's era
11	Palace – King Solomon's era
12	Grain Silo
13	'City of Chariots' – King Solomon's era
14	Water system
15	City Wall – Israelite Kingdom era

fell to David. Under Solomon, in the 10th century BC, it became one of the kingdom's major cities (1 Kings 9:15). Megiddo was known then as the 'chariot city' and excavations have shown relics of stables where Solomon kept thousands of chariots and horses.

Also known as the 'Way of the Sea', it later became the Roman Empire's 'Via Maris', a vital military zone. By the 4th century BC it had become uninhabited, inexplicably losing its importance as a city. Its strategic importance remained though, and among those armies who fought here were the British in WW I. On being awarded his peerage, General Allenby took the title Lord Allenby of Megiddo. More recently, Jewish and Arab forces fought here during the 1948 War of Independence.

The archaeological site, despite being signposted, is a bit confusing – a plan is available (about 35c) and the museum by the entrance contains a few exhibits that explain some of the site's history and how it used to look. One of the excavations is the preserved 9th century BC water system. This consists of a shaft sunk 30 metres through solid rock to a tunnel of 70 metres. This hid the city's water source

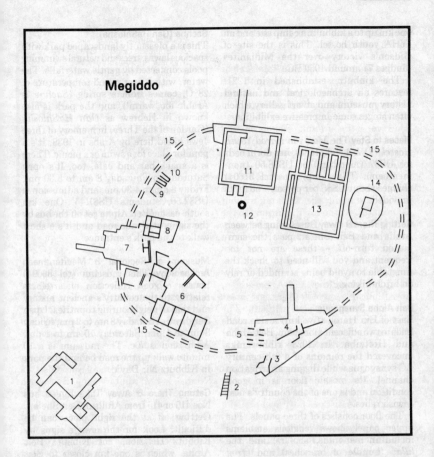

Megiddo

from invading forces, rather like Hezekiah's version in Jerusalem. There is no water to slosh through here, though. Save the tunnel till last as it leads you out of the site into the car park. The site is open Saturday to Thursday, 8 am to 5 pm, Friday 8 am to 4 pm. Admission is US$2, students US$1. There is a snack bar and café in the museum.

Getting There & Away The site is a 10 minute walk from the signposted intersection of the main road between Haifa

and the Afulla to Hadera highway. It is best reached from Nazareth, with buses regularly passing the intersection. If you want to combine visits to Megiddo and Mount Tabor from Nazareth, it makes sense to make an early morning start and head for Mount Tabor, then return to Afulla for a connecting bus to the Megiddo intersection.

Ein Harod
About 30 km east of Afulla on the road to Beit She'an, a side road on the left leads

one km up to a kibbutz, a camp site and an IYHA youth hostel. This is the site of Gideon's victory over the Midianites (Judges 7) around 1050 BC.

The kibbutz, established in 1921, features an archaeological and natural history museum and an art gallery which often stages some impressive exhibitions.

Places to Stay The *Ma'ayon Harod Youth Hostel – IYHA* (tel 31630), has dorm beds for US$7 (members) or US$6.50 (non-members). The camp site (tel 31604) charges about US$5 per person – no tents provided.

Getting There & Away Buses going between Afulla and Beit She'an pass the signposted turn-off – these are not too frequent and you will need to check the timetable to avoid being stranded or rely on hitch-hiking.

Beit Alpha Synagogue

East of Ein Harod (five km) a side road leads to two adjacent kibbutzim, Beit Alpha and Heftziba. In 1928 kibbutzniks uncovered the remains of a 6th century BC synagogue while digging an irrigation channel. Its mosaic floor is in good condition and is one of the country's best Jewish relics.

The floor consists of three panels. The upper panel shows religious emblems including menorahs, shofars, and the *lulav* (bundle of branches) and *etrog* (citrus fruit). A zodiac circle with the seasons symbolised in each corner makes up the central panel. Abraham's sacrifice is illustrated in the lower panel. It's open Saturday to Thursday 8 am to 5 pm, Friday 8 am to 4 pm. Admission is 90c, students 45c.

Members of the Makoya, a Japanese Christian sect, study Hebrew on the kibbutz, and their lovely little Japanese garden can be seen up the hill from the synagogue, beyond the swimming pool.

Sachne (Gan HaShlosha)

This is a pleasantly landscaped park with spacious lawns, trees and natural swimming pools connected by gentle waterfalls. The water, with a year round temperature of 28°C, comes from a spring (*Sachne* is Arabic for 'warm'), and the park is also known in Hebrew as *Gan HaShlosha* (Garden of the Three) in memory of three Jews killed here by Arabs in 1938. It's a popular place for a swim or a picnic. There is a snack bar and café, too. It's open Saturday to Thursday 8 am to 5.30 pm, Friday 8 am to 4.30 pm, and admission is US$2.50, students US$1.45. One km south-east of Beit Alpha get off the bus by the signposted side road and it's a short walk to the park's entrance.

Museum of Regional & Mediterranean Archaeology

This museum (tel 86094) houses a good collection of artefacts relating to the country's ancient history and that of neighbouring countries. Open Sunday to Thursday 8 am to 2 pm, Friday 8 am to 1 pm, Saturday 10 am to 1 pm. Admission is 70c. The museum is a 10 minute walk up the road behind the park in Kibbutz Nir David.

Getting There & Away Take Egged bus Nos 412 or 415 from Afulla or Beit She'an. Getting off at the right place can be difficult. Look for the orange signs by Kibbutz Heftziba, not Kibbutz Beit Alpha, which is one km closer to Beit She'an.

Beit She'an

The attractions here are the country's best-preserved Roman amphitheatre and an archaeological museum featuring a Byzantine mosaic floor. On a busy trade route, Beit She'an was an important ancient city and has been continuously occupied for over 5000 years. Excavations have revealed 18 superimposed cities on an 80 metre high section of ground.

Stone Age people settled here and the first real town was established circa

3000 BC; its name is mentioned in 19th century BC Egyptian texts. Proof of the Egyptian influence is provided by the excavations; this was one of the strongholds from which the country was controlled by the Pharaohs. In the 13th century BC, the Israelite tribe of Manasseh inherited the area (Judges I:27), losing it to the Philistines in the 11th century BC after the Israelites' defeat on nearby Mount Gilboa, when King Saul's body was hung on the city walls (I Samuel 31).

Jewish sages wrote 'If the Garden of Eden is in Israel, then its gate is at Beit She'an' (Eirubin 19a). Despite being subjected to the heat of the Jordan Valley, the nearby Harod River and the usually sufficient rainfall make this a highly fertile area with thousands of acres of crops. However, the modern day town of Beit She'an is not at all attractive.

Roman Amphitheatre & Tel Beit She'an

Turn left from the bus station and follow the road for some 800 metres, turn right by Bank Leumi and follow the road downhill to the site. The amphitheatre was built circa 200 AD with seating for 5000 people. Open Saturday to Thursday 8 am to 5 pm, Friday 8 am to 4 pm. Admission is US$1.75, students 90c.

Museum

Turn right from the bus station, left at the junction and follow the main road – the museum is on the left after some 150 metres where the main road curves to the right. The opening hours vary: Sunday to Thursday usually 8.30 am but sometimes 9.30 am to 3.30 pm, Friday 8.30 or 9.30 am to 12.30 pm, closed Saturday. Admission is 90c, students 45c.

Places to Eat

There is a snack bar in the bus station, and across the street are some cafés and felafel stands.

Getting There & Away

Beit She'an is a stop-off point for the Tiberias-Jerusalem bus and there are also regular services

between here and Afulla, making it accessible from Nazareth.

Belvoir

This is an attractive destination for a brief visit, with its 12th century Crusader castle ruins and great views over the Jezreel Valley, the Jordanian Gilead mountains and, on that clear day, even the Sea of Galilee and Mount Hermon.

The castle was built by the French Knights Hospitallers in 1168 in this strategic position on the trade route between Egypt and Damascus. Although they successfully fought off two attacks by Saladin in 1182-3, they were eventually defeated after the Muslim victory at the Horns of Hattin. From July 1187 to January 1191 Belvoir was under siege and the Crusaders were forced to surrender. Saladin permitted them to retreat to Tyre unharmed, in acknowledgement of their courage. Although his forces did not raze the castle, it was systematically destroyed in the early 13th century by the Sultan of Damascus who was afraid that the Crusaders would return. They did, in 1241, but did not stay long enough to do any rebuilding.

Today the ruins are still quite impressive, although it is the setting which is the main attraction. Open Saturday to Thursday 8 am to 5 pm, Friday 8 am to 4 pm. Admission is US$1.75, students 90c.

Getting There & Away

Buses running between Tiberias and Beit She'an will only drop you off at the signposted intersection with the road that leads up to the castle. From here it is a steep six km walk or hitch-hike. In the hot summer months it is best to make an early start, to cover your head, and to bring plenty of water.

TIBERIAS & THE SEA OF GALILEE

The Sea of Galilee is one of the most popular holiday destinations in Israel. The only town on its shores, Tiberias (population 29,500) is an ideal base from which to enjoy the surrounding beauty spots and holy sites. In summer the weather is particularly hot and humid, but the rule regarding acceptable clothing when visiting the holy places still applies.

History

Tiberias was established around 20 AD by Herod the Great's son, Herod Antipas, on the ruins of the ancient town of Rakkat. Named after his patron, the Roman emperor Tiberius, it included a stadium, a gold-roofed palace and a great synagogue. By the middle of the 1st century, Jews were in the majority, and after the Bar Kochba Revolt (132-5), Galilee became the country's Jewish sector with Tiberias its centre. Here the great sages came and the top academies of rabbinical studies were founded. The Mishnah was completed here around the year 200, the Palestinian Talmud around 400, and the vowels, punctuation and grammar were added to the Hebrew alphabet – achievements which made Tiberias one of the country's four cities holy to the Jews.

The Crusaders took Tiberias in 1099 but its capture by Saladin in 1187 provoked the battle at the Horns of Hattin which destroyed the Latin kingdom. After this, Tiberias went into decline, seriously damaged by the many battles fought here and by earthquakes.

In 1562 Suleiman the Magnificent gave Tiberias to a Jew, Don Joseph Nussi. Aided by his mother-in-law, Donna Grazia, he attempted to revive the town as a Jewish enclave. Historians disagree about his success: some say he made Tiberias flourish for 100 years, others that he failed completely. In the 18th century Daher el-Omar, an Arab sheikh, established an independent fiefdom in Galilee, and Tiberias was an integral part of it. He was assassinated in 1775 and an earthquake in 1837 demolished the town. The Jews of the First Aliyah at the end of the 19th century mostly settled in Tiberias, and with the expansion of the Zionist movement

many more immigrants have arrived, particularly since Israel's independence.

Following their 1948 defeat, Syrian troops positioned on the Golan Heights intermittently shelled Israeli targets to the north and east of Tiberias and Israel subsequently took the Heights in the 1967 Six-Day War. In the 1973 Yom Kippur War, Syria attacked the Israeli installations on the Heights but were eventually defeated again. As a result of these and other border incidents, it is only over the last decade that the area around the Sea of Galilee has been fully developed as a tourist attraction. Tiberias in particular has become more and more commercialised. Unfortunately this has meant a proliferation of gaudy buildings as hotels and eating places compete to win business. Tiberias is not a good-looking town, but the surrounding

1	Eden Hotel
2	Ministry of the Interior
3	Rambam's Tomb
4	Lamb & Goose Restaurant
5	Galil Hostel
6	Tourist Office
7	Scottish Hospice
8	Meyouhas Youth Hostel (IYHA)
9	Post Office
10	Cinema
11	Bus Station
12	Bicycle Hire
13	Hotel Toledo
14	Felafel shops
15	El Farsi Restaurant (shishlik)
16	Shipoday Restaurant (shishlik)
17	Supermarket & shopping area
18	Great Mosque
19	Terra Santa Hotel
20	Caramba Restaurant
21	Ferries
22	Aviv Hotel/Hostel
23	Maman Restaurant
24	Adina's Guest House
25	Pub Row
26	Maman Hostel
27	Nahum Hostel
28	Guy Restaurant
29	Plaza Hotel

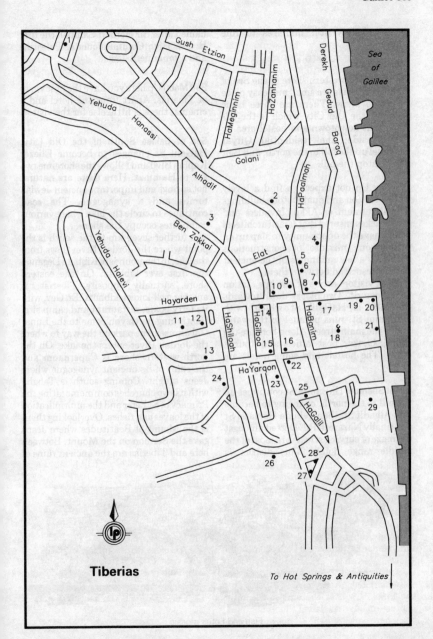

Tiberias

Sea
of
Galilee

To Hot Springs & Antiquities

natural beauty still manages to rule supreme.

Orientation

On the south-western shore of the Sea of Galilee, Tiberias is a small and easy place to get to know. There are three basic sections: the Old City which is the all-important downtown and hostel area by the lakeside; the residential Qiryat Shemuel up the hill to the north; and Beit Maon, atop the hill.

Old City Do not expect to find a lovely walled section and quaint stone buildings à la Jerusalem or Akko. Invaders and earthquakes ensured that Israeli architects would have the opportunity to slap up an incongruous mixture of constructions with only a few reminders of the ancient past interspersed between them.

Most visitors arrive at the bus station on Yarden St. Two blocks down towards the lake is HaGalil St which, with HaBanim St, runs parallel to the water and is the main street. Along here are the shops, banks, post office and tourist office. The hostels and some hotels are nearby.

Qiryat Shemuel HaBanim St continues up the hill to the north, changing to become first Alhadif St, then Yehuda HaNassi St and finally Nazareth Rd. Dotted amongst the maze of curving streets are most of the middle range hotels. This district is

named after Sir Herbert Samuel, the first British High Commissioner of Palestine and a prominent Jew.

Beit Maon Up here you have the best views of Tiberias. Apart from one hotel and a cinema, there is little else for the visitor.

Sea of Galilee South of the Old City, HaGalil St changes to become Eliezer Kaplan Blvd and follows the shoreline two km to Hammat. Here there are natural hot springs and important ancient Jewish tombs and a synagogue. The road continues to circle the lake where various camp sites occupy the shore.

A further seven km to the south is the point where the Jordan River flows from the lake, in the grounds of Kibbutz Degania, the first ever kibbutz. On the eastern shore, virtually opposite Tiberias, is another well-known kibbutz, En Gev, with its ferry boats, restaurant and camp site. Continuing north you come to the Luna-Gal amusement park on the way to where the Jordan River enters the lake. On the north-western shore is Capernaum and the ruins of its ancient synagogue where Jesus taught. Coming south is Tabgha with its two churches commemorating the Primacy of St Peter and the multiplication of the loaves and fishes. Overlooking them is the Mount of Beatitudes where Jesus gave the Sermon on the Mount. Between here and Tiberias are the ancient ruins of

Fish and Lotus mosaic

Migdal, the birthplace of Mary Magdalene, one of Jesus' followers.

Information

Tourist Office The IGTO is at 8 Alhadif St (tel 20992). Go up the hill from the intersection with HaYarden and HaBanim, on the right hand side. It's open Sunday to Thursday 8 am to 6 pm, Friday 8 am to 2 pm, closed Saturday.

Post Office & International Telephones HaYarden St (tel 21515), across from HaGalil and HaBanim. The entrance to the international telephone office is in Ha'Atzma'ut Square, the shopping arcade on the side of the building. Open Sunday, Tuesday and Thursday 7.45 am to 12.30 pm and 3.30 to 6 pm, Monday and Wednesday 7.45 am to 2 pm, Friday 7.45 am to 1 pm, closed Saturday.

Society for the Protection of Nature in Israel (SPNI) During the summer an information stand operates at the Beit She'an junction south of the lake. Enquire here about camp sites, hikes, and almost anything – the staff are very helpful.

Other Camping equipment can be hired from Gal-Cal (tel 20123), on Shiloah St in front of the bus station. They open Sunday to Thursday 7 am to 7 pm, Friday 7 am to 4.30 pm, closed Saturday.

Various bank branches are on and around HaGalil. Steimatzky's bookshop is on HaGalil, as is Blumfield's laundromat. For police, phone 92444, emergency 100.

Tours

Tiberias Although there is little to see of the town's historical past, there are a couple of free guided tours that go some way to pointing out the evidence.

On Wednesday and Saturday meet in reception at the Plaza Hotel for a 10 am start, with English and German spoken. On Sunday, also at 10 am, meet in reception at the Galei Kinneret Hotel for a guided tour of 'Biblical & Roman Tiberias'.

Check whether these tours are in operation during your stay in town – they normally take place only during summer.

Sea of Galilee, Upper Galilee & Golan With the distinct lack of public transport in Upper Galilee and Golan and even in some parts of the immediate area surrounding the Sea of Galilee, taking an organised tour often makes a lot of sense and can even be cheaper than doing it yourself. Most of them combine visits to sites in all of these areas.

Firstly, Egged Tours have a tour just of the Sea of Galilee. Called the 'Egged Minus 200 Line', it follows a route around the lake and its major sites and the driver provides a limited commentary in English. The coaches run every two hours from Tiberias bus station, Sunday to Friday 8.30 am to 4.30 pm, no service on Saturday. Ticket prices are around US$6 for the day, enabling you to get off at any of the stops to visit the sites, or US$9 for two days. Ticket holders are also entitled to discounts on admission prices to the sites en route and in some restaurants.

Very popular with travellers is Oded Shoshan and his taxi tour which takes in the Sea of Galilee, Upper Galilee and Golan. This amiable Tiberias-born Israeli knows the region very well and gives a more personal and humorous commentary than his competitors. Starting out from Tiberias at about 8.30 am and returning by about 5 pm, Oded manages to fit in most of the essential sites, usually including a dip in the Banyus waterfall, all for around US$16 which includes admission to Nimrod Castle and, if you're good, an ice cream. For those on a tight budget, this might seem out of reach but you will see in one day, and in comfort, what would take at least three days and a lot of hitch-hiking or waiting around for the infrequent buses to do by yourself. Oded visits the Tiberias hostels each evening to collect reservations, or you can telephone 21812.

Egged Tours cover much the same area

more or less for US$24, leaving from Tiberias bus station on Tuesday, Thursday and Saturday. It also has similar tours leaving from Haifa for US$33, and Tel Aviv for US$36.

The SPNI offers some guided camping hikes in the area. Although a bit more expensive, they do take you to some great out of the way places that you would not find on your own and that are usually inaccessible by bus or car.

Tomb of Rabbi Akiva
Above the Old City, beyond Qiryat Shemuel and the police station, a white dome covers the cave-tomb of Rabbi Akiva. Born in 50 AD, he was one of the great Jewish scholars, and was killed by the Romans for his role in the Bar Kochba Revolt in 135 AD.

Tombs of Rabbi Moshe Ben-Nahman & Rabbi Yohanan Ben-Zakkai
About two blocks on the right up Yohanan Ben-Zakkai St, a continuation of HaGalil north of HaYarden, these two tombs testify to the holy status of Tiberias.

Better known by his acronym 'Ramban', Ben-Nahman was born in Spain in 1135 and was one of the 12th century's highly regarded sages. He was also an Aristotelian philosopher, physician, scientist and astronomer. He died in 1204.

Ben-Zakkai founded the Yavne Academy and was Palestine's most eminent sage when the Romans destroyed Jerusalem in the 1st century. Near to his tomb are the tombs of Rabbi Eliezer the Great, a prominent 2nd century scholar; Rav Ammi and Rav Assii who lived in the 3rd century; and Rabbi Isaiah Horowitz, who died around 1630.

Old City Walls & Castle
Remnants of the black basalt wall, built by Daher el-Omar in 1738, can be seen in the Old City. The section now housing an art studio, gallery and restaurant, north of the tourist office on Alhadif St, is sometimes called the Crusader Castle. It

was possibly built later on in the 18th century by Daher el-Omar's son, Chulabi.

Great Mosque
In the middle of shopping arcades, this mosque was also built by Daher el-Omar in the mid-18th century. It is generally believed that its construction was partly paid for by the town's Jewish community, presumably grateful to the sheikh for being permitted to return.

St Peter's Church
This Franciscan church, commonly called 'Terra Sancta', was built in the 12th century by the Crusaders. The Muslims converted it into a mosque and the Turks used it as a caravanserai before it became a church again. In 1870 it was rebuilt, in 1903 enlarged and in 1944 restored. Its two main points of interest are the boat-shaped nave (relating to Peter's fisherman origins), and the courtyard built by the Polish soldiers stationed here during WW II. It's open daily 8 to 11.45 am and 3 to 5.30 pm and admission is free. There is also a hostel here.

Church & Monastery of the Apostles
South of the Plaza Hotel by the waterside, this Greek Orthodox complex is on the site of a Byzantine monastery that was destroyed by the Persians in the 7th century. It was replaced and then destroyed again several times over the years; today's building was restored in 1975. Three monks live here and are sometimes available to let you in when you ring the bell. There are four chapels beyond the pleasant walled courtyard. One is dedicated to St Peter, one to the disciples, one to Mary Magdalene and the one in the ancient round tower to St Nicholas.

Hot Springs
The hot springs, containing high amounts of sulphuric, muriatic and calcium salts, are believed to have excellent curative powers for such ailments as rheumatism,

arthritis, gout, and nervous and gynaeco-
logical disorders. The springs have been
known for thousands of years – in biblical
times a town called Hammath was built
around the springs (Joshua 19:35). Its
name was taken from the Hebrew *ham*
(hot), and it was part of the territory of the
Naphtali tribe.

Different legends surround origins of
the springs. Some believe that they were
formed during the great flood of the Bible
when the hot middle of the earth rose up;
others say that it was here that Jesus
cured many sick people. Perhaps the most
imaginative story credits King Solomon
with the springs' creation. This legend has
it that the king was approached by a group
of sick men who begged him to find a cure
for them. Solomon sent a group of demons
to heat the water at the springs, making
them deaf so that they would not hear the
news of his death and stop working. It
seems more likely, however, that the hot
springs were first enjoyed by Stone Age
people some 10,000 years ago.

In 110 AD, Roman emperor Trajan had
a coin struck dedicated to Tiberias, with
the image of Hygea, the goddess of health,
shown sitting on a rock enjoying the
water. The springs were also mentioned
by Idris, an Arab writer who lived during
the Crusades, and recommended by the
Ramban to his patients. Bathing and
therapy facilities in Tiberias date back to
these times and were much appreciated
by those well-known bath-lovers, the
Romans and the Turks.

Today there are two complexes. The
older one across the road from the lake,
Tiberias Hot Springs, is for people with
serious skin problems. The more modern
Young Tiberias Hot Springs nearby is
open to the general public. You don't need
to suffer from any particular ailment to
enjoy a good soak or massage. They open
Sunday to Thursday 8 am to 8 pm, Friday
8 am to 2.30 pm, Saturday 8.30 am to 8 pm.
There are various options at various
prices. For example, a dip in the thermal
pools costs US$6.50, a massage US$10,

pool and massage US$15. Prices are a
little higher on Saturday. Egged bus Nos 2
and 5 stop outside, or you can walk the two
km from the city centre.

Ancient Synagogue of Hammath

Behind the hot springs, away from the
lake, the Ernest Lehman Museum
displays the reconstructed ruins of the
ancient town of Hammath, the highlight
of which is the synagogue, dated to the
2nd or 3rd centuries, with its mosaic floor.
It's open daily 8 am to 5 pm and admission
is 90c.

Tomb of Rabbi Meir Ba'al Hanes

Up the hill from the museum and the hot
springs is one of Israel's holiest places for
Jews, the tomb of the 2nd century rabbi
who helped to compile the Mishnah.
A pupil of Rabbi Akiva, he became
renowned as 'the Miracle-Maker' due to
the legends telling of his miraculous
rescue of his sister-in-law, held captive by
the Romans.

The tomb is marked by two synagogues,
the one on the left Sephardic, and the
other Ashkenazi. In the courtyard of the
Sephardic synagogue is a pillar topped by
a large bowl. Four days before the Lag
B'Omer holiday a bonfire is lit here on the
Pesach Sheni (second Passover). Crowds
of religious Jews come throughout the
year to pray. It is a tradition that God will
answer the prayers of pilgrims who have
personal problems.

Sea of Galilee

A freshwater lake fed by the Jordan River,
the Sea of Galilee lies 212 metres below sea
level and in a good summer the lake can be
as warm as 33°C. Its length is
21 km and its width opposite Tiberias nine
km; its greatest breadth is 13 km, its
circumference 52 km and its depth about
49 metres – this can change depending on
the sometimes unreliable rainfall in the
region. Not just a natural beauty spot, it is
Israel's major water supply.

It has been known by several different names. The Old Testament calls it the Sea of Kinnereth (Numbers 34:11, Joshua 12:3, 13:27) which is linked to the Hebrew word *kinnor* (harp). Some say that the lake is shaped like a harp, others that its waves make the sound of a harp. Arab poets called it the 'Bride', the 'Handmaiden of the Hills' and the 'Silver Woman'. The New Testament calls it the Sea of Galilee (Matthew 4:18, 15:29, Mark 1:16, 7:31), the Sea of Tiberias (John 6:1, 21:1), the Sea (Mark 2:13) and the Lake (Luke 8:22). Josephus, the 1st century Jewish historian, called it the Lake of Gennesar. In Israel today, it is popularly known as the Kinneret.

There are over 20 species of fish found in the lake and fishing is still an important industry. The unique St Peter fish is enthusiastically recommended in Israeli restaurants although most now comes from fish farms rather than the lake.

Prehistoric tribes are known to have lived by the lake, in the Amud Caves south-west of Tabgha. The oldest human skull found in the country was discovered here in 1925. It was that of a man who lived in the Palaeolithic period, circa 100,000 BC. Bet Yerah, north of Kibbutz Degania, was an important Canaanite city 5000 years ago. Capernaum became the lake's most important site when Jesus made what was then a fishing village the centre of his ministry in Galilee. With the destruction of Jerusalem and Galilee's emergence as the new centre of Jewish life, the lakeside saw the establishment of schools of religious study and synagogues went up at Capernaum, Hammath Tiberias and Hammat Gader. The Byzantine period saw Christians flock here, and new churches were built in Heptapegon (Tabgha), Capernaum, Bet Yerah, and, on the east shore, Kursi and Susita.

Since the Syrian defeat in the Yom Kippur War, the lake has seen many new developments, particularly in the area of tourism with a proliferation of camp sites and amusement parks featuring giant water-slides.

Beaches Although the best things in life may be free, the best beaches on the lake are not. However, if you don't like the idea of paying US$1 to US$3 for a well-maintained stretch of shore with pleasant facilities, then you should either head for the harbour wall to the south of the Plaza Hotel, or leave Tiberias altogether and either walk, hitch-hike or take a bus further south, beyond the hot springs, and stop when you see an appealing site. The popular pay beaches are just to the north of Tiberias:

Lido Kinneret	Water-skiing facilities.
Shell Beach	Canoe hire.
Quiet Beach	Swimming pool and amusements.
Blue Beach	Swimming pool, canoe hire and water-skiing.

Kibbutz Ginnosar

In 1986, with the water level of the lake at its lowest for years, an ancient boat was found buried under an exposed section of the lake bed by the Kibbutz Ginnosar. It has been dated to somewhere between the 1st century BC and the 1st century AD. The wooden boat had become porous after the centuries spent in its muddy grave and it is now being subjected to a nine-year restoration programme, and a museum is being established to house it.

To get here, take Egged bus Nos 459, 841 or 963 from Tiberias bus station and get off at the orange signpost reading 'Nof Ginnosar Guest House'. Walk one km along the side road towards the lake and the boat is in the shack behind the monument and museum building.

Migdal

The lakeside road, six km north of Tiberias, passes ancient Megdal, or Magdala, birthplace of Mary Magdalene. Its name is Hebrew for 'tower', and it was named after the defence tower which dominated the important fishing village.

A tiny, white-domed shrine marks the site.

Minya

Following the lakeside road, one km north from Migdal, a side road leads eastwards to Minya. Here you will find the ruins of a 7th century palace. There are remnants of a western room with a mosaic floor, and on the south-eastern side a mosque with its *mihrab* (niche) facing Mecca. This is the most ancient Muslim prayer place in Israel.

Tabgha & the Mount of the Beatitudes

Generally considered to be the most appropriately beautiful and serene of the Christian holy places in the country, this site has managed to escape much of the commercialisation of modern Israel. Tradition locates three of the New Testament's most significant episodes here: the Sermon on the Mount, the multiplication of the loaves and fishes and Jesus' post-Resurrection appearance where he conferred the leadership of the church on Peter.

Tabgha is an Arab version of the Greek name *Heptapegon*, (Seven Springs), and it is given to the small valley that lies east of the main road 12 km north of Tiberias. A side road branches off to the right towards the lake and runs through the valley and past Capernaum to continue the circuit of the water, while the main road continues north towards Rosh Pinna.

Church of the Multiplication of the Loaves & Fishes

This pleasant complex belongs to the German Benedictine Order and includes an adjacent monastery and pilgrims' hospice as well as the church. Today's church building dates back only to 1936 and the monastery to 1956. These modern additions were constructed on the site of a 5th century Byzantine church whose well-preserved mosaic floor is probably the most beautiful in the country. Underneath the present floor are the remnants of a 4th century church. The

larger mosaic depicts a variety of flora and fauna, nearly all of which was found locally at the time it was made. The exception is the lotus flower which appears in several scenes. Along with the round tower, representing a Nilometer used to measure the water level of the lake, these touches show the influence of the Nilotic (Nile-like) landscapes that were popular in Hellenistic and Roman art.

The mosaic immediately in front of the altar depicts two fish flanking a basket of loaves. As the name implies, the churches were built on the traditional site where it is believed Jesus fed 5000 people with five loaves of bread and two fish (Mark 6:30-44). The church is open daily April to September 7.30 am to 6 pm, October to March 8 am to 5 pm. Admission is free.

Church of the Primacy of St Peter

This is where it is believed that Jesus appeared for the third time after his Resurrection (John 21). The modest black basalt church was built in 1933 by the Franciscans on the site of a late 4th century church that was destroyed in the 13th century. At the base of the newer walls, at the end furthest away from the altar, you can clearly see the ancient wall on three sides. The flat rock in front of the altar is believed to be the table at which Jesus and his disciples ate, and it was known to Byzantine pilgrims as *Mensa Christi* (Christ's Table).

Outside the church, by the water, are steps cut out of the rock. Some say that this was where Jesus stood when the disciples saw him, but they were possibly cut in the 2nd to 3rd century when this area was quarried for limestone. Six double, or heart-shaped, column bases lie below the steps, although they are sometimes under water if the lake level is high. These were probably taken from nearby buildings and intended to commemorate the 12 disciples. First mentioned in a text of 808 AD, they are known as the 12 Thrones. Open daily April to September 7.30 am to 5 pm,

October to March 8 am to 5 pm. Admission is free.

Church of the Mount of Beatitudes On the hill across the road from the entrance to the Heptapegon are the remains of a 4th century church. Abandoned in the 7th century, it was eventually replaced in 1937 by the present structure on top of the hill that is now known as the Mount of Beatitudes. It is believed that this is where Jesus gave the Sermon on the Mount (Matthew 5-7) and also where he chose his disciples (Luke 6:12).

Owned by the Franciscans, whose nuns live in the adjacent hospice, the church was built by the Italian dictator Mussolini. Its octagonal shape symbolises the eight beatitudes (Matthew 5:3-10), and the seven virtues (justice, charity, prudence, faith, fortitude, hope and temperance) are represented by symbols in the pavement around the altar. From the gallery you have some of the best views of the lake, particularly towards Tiberias to the south, and Capernaum, with the red domes of the Greek Orthodox monastery beyond, to the east. It's open daily 7 am to 12 noon and 2 to 5.30 pm. and admission is free.

Springs These powerful springs lie to the east of the Church of the Primacy and with a bit of searching you can locate a pleasant little waterfall for a refreshing shower on a hot sticky day.

Getting There & Away Egged bus Nos 459, 941 and 963 leave from Tiberias bus station and speed northwards, past Migdal and Minya. Just before the bus stop at the Tabgha turn-off on the right, the road passes an electric power plant on the right as you climb a steep slope. Watch out for this so that you have time to remind the driver that you want to get off at Tabgha. The Egged school of grand prix driving seems to teach its drivers to build up speed here to negotiate the approaching steep climb.

From this bus stop follow the side road

as it bends round to the left, with the Church of the Multiplication a few minutes' walk on the right. Continuing along the road above the lay-by is a rough path that leads up the slope to the Beatitudes Church. Alternatively, you can stay on the bus till the next stop, which is by the turn-off for the Beatitudes church. After the Tabgha turn-offf the road turns away from the lake and zig-zags up the steep hill before reaching the turn-off marked by the orange sign reading 'Hospice of the Beatitudes'. Follow this side road to the church. From here you can walk down the slope to reach the Church of the Primacy. Read on to learn how to reach Capernaum from here.

Capernaum
In Hebrew *Kfar Nahum* (Village of Nahum), Capernaum is a Greek rendering of this. Who Nahum was is not known. Medieval Jewish tradition suggests that the name refers to the prophet whose burial place was said to be here. However, it is as the home of Jesus when he started his ministry that Capernaum is best known (Matthew 4:12-17, 9:1, Mark 2:1). There are several other references to the town in the new Testament, including Jesus teaching in the synagogue (Mark 1:21), getting rid of a man's evil spirit (Mark 1:23-26), curing Peter's step-mother (Mark 1:29-31), the leper (Luke 5:12-16), the centurion's servant (Luke 7:1-10) and the paralytic (Mark 2:11-12, Luke 5:17-25), and walking on the water and discussing the bread of life (John 6:16-59).

The town's known history goes back to the 2nd century BC although evidence of its existence in the 13th century BC has been found. Jesus is believed to have decided to move from Nazareth because his first converts (Peter and Andrew) lived here. There seems to have been a strong Christian presence here in the 2nd century, according to both rabbinical texts and archaeological discoveries. By the 4th century the town had expanded towards the hills with the buildings

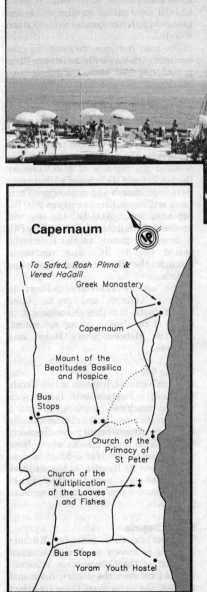

The Sea of Galilee

becoming more substantial. After the Arab conquest around 700 the town was destroyed and never again inhabited.

In 1894 the Franciscans purchased the site and set about restoring the ancient synagogue and other remnants found here.

Museum The Franciscans' open-air archaeological museum includes ruins which have enough detail to have permitted several precise drawings of how one of the buildings, a synagogue, might have looked – although each version is different. This is not the synagogue that Jesus frequented but its exact date of construction is debatable. There is a building that is believed to be the house of the disciple Peter, where Jesus may have stayed. Open daily 8.30 am to 4.15 pm. Admission is 45c. Modest dress is required – no shorts, bare shoulders, etc. There are toilets and a snack bar outside.

Greek Orthodox Monastery From the museum walk back to the road, turn right and walk about two km to the next turn-off. With its peeling paint it looks better from a distance and there is little to see here. The two monks may be around but they don't seem too keen on visitors.

Getting There & Away From the Beatitudes church you have a pleasant walk across the fields to Capernaum. Just follow the various tracks down the hill and aim for the red domes of the Greek Orthodox monastery. To reach the museum, walk down the signposted side road; it's at the end. From Tabgha just follow the road three km to the east to reach the turn-off for the museum, and keep going for the Greek Orthodox monastery.

Vered HaGalil

As the road to Rosh Pinna continues northwards from the Mount of Beatitudes, it steadily climbs to reach sea-level just before the intersection with the road to Almagor. Here an orange signpost directs you to Vered HaGalil (Rose of the Galilee) (tel 35785, 35609), a stud farm/riding stable which offers horse-riding and guest house facilities (see Places to Stay). The American-style complex enjoys a good reputation and is beautifully situated in great riding country. You can go on trail rides for US$10 per hour, US$28 half day or US$40 full day.

Korazim

Continue east along the road from Vered HaGalil and after four km you come to the ruins of ancient Korazim. There was a Jewish town here in the 1st century and along with Capernaum and Bethsaida its people were condemned by Jesus for their lack of faith (Matthew 11:20-24). Although it probably benefited from Galilee's influx of Jews after the destruction of Jerusalem (132-5 AD), with rabbis commenting on its excellent wheat, records show that the town was in ruins by the 4th century and occupation ceased in the 8th century.

Among the remains is a black basalt synagogue of the 3rd-4th century, similar in style to the limestone one at Capernaum.

Beyond Korazim to the east, the ground is covered with large basalt rocks. Many of

these are 'domens', large blocks of broad and flat stone placed on other stones and used as burial chambers between 6000 and 4000 BC.

The road continues to meet the road encircling the lake with the Jordan River meandering down through a marshy area nearby.

Beit Yerah & Kinneret Cemetery

Following the lakeside road some nine km south of Tiberias, just south of the Afulla junction you come to a hill where, up on the left by the water, excavations have revealed the remains of a 3rd century Roman fort and the ruins of a 5th century Byzantine church and synagogue. There was a settlement here as early as 4000 BC but after about 2000 BC the site was unoccupied until the late 6th century BC. It developed greatly in the Hellenistic period (332-63 BC) and continued through the Roman and Byzantine periods.

The nearby cemetery belongs to Kibbutz Kinneret and among those buried there are Berl Katsenelson, a leader of the Jewish labour movement, and the Hebrew poets Rahel and Elisheva.

Baptism Site

Kibbutz Kinneret, just east of Beit Yerah, has built a baptism site (along with vending machines, a snack bar and a souvenir shop) south of the bridge crossing the Jordan River where it leaves the Sea of Galilee. This is not the site where Jesus was baptised – that is at al-Maghtes near Jericho, but its location in the sensitive militarised zone near the West Bank-Jordan border puts it out of bounds to pilgrims.

Kibbutz Degania

The world's first kibbutz, Kibbutz Degania is known as *Em Hakevutsot* (Mother of the Co-operative Villages). Located between the Jordan River and the Beit She'an junction, there are in fact two kibbutzim here. The original, Degania A, is marked by a Syrian tank parked outside the main entrance just off the main road – a souvenir from the 1948 War of Independence when the kibbutzniks, armed only with molotov cocktails and rifles, defeated an enemy tank column.

Beit Gordon Dedicated to the memory of the father of the kibbutz movement, A D Gordon, this natural history and archaeological museum complex is in the grounds of Degania A, and is open Sunday to Thursday 9 am to 4 pm, Friday 8.30 am to 1 pm, Saturday 9.30 am to 12 noon. Admission is US$1.20. The entrance to the museum is on the lakeside road where there is a car park. On Saturday the entrance here is closed to cars (pedestrians and cyclists can still get through) and you should drive through the main entrance (marked by that tank).

Cemetery The Degania Cemetery is on the bank of the Jordan River and includes a section for the soldiers killed in action locally. Leading Zionists are also buried here, including A D Gordon, Otto Warburg, Arthur Roppin and Leopold Greenburg.

Hammat Gader

One of the highlights for many visitors to Galilee, and a regular attraction for locals, the Hammat Gader complex is eight km south-east of the Sea of Galilee (21 km from Tiberias). In a pleasant parkland setting along with Roman ruins, a crocodile park and amusements, hot sulphur springs provide a cheaper alternative to the indoor baths at Tiberias. Although the sulphur smell can be a bit pungent at times, this is a great opportunity to experience the sensation of a natural hot spring. The facilities include a modern pool with massage jets, a waterfall, and an area with black mud which is reputed to be good for the skin. The springs are first mentioned by the geographer Strabo (63 BC – 21 AD).

Hammat Gader is in the valley of the Yarmulk River on the sensitive border with Jordan and you will see lots of barbed-wire fences and sentry posts competing with the natural scenery. The Hebrew name Hammat Gader is derived from *ham* and the name of the nearby ancient city of Gadara, now a part of Jordan under the modern name of Umm Qeis. In Arabic it is called *El Hamme*.

The site was probably occupied as early as 3000 BC and again in the Roman and subsequent periods. The partially reconstructed Roman ruins are quite impressive and include various bathing areas, such as a smaller pool reserved for lepers and the hottest spring – 51°C – which is called in Hebrew *Ma'ayan HaGehinom* (Hell's Pool) and in Arabic *Ain Makleh* (Frying Pool). There is also a ruined 5th or 6th century synagogue just west of the Roman baths and past the picnic area. From the top of the excavation site you have a fine view of the valley crossed by the bridge that used to carry the Haifa to Damascus railway.

The alligator park was started off with denizens imported from Florida but they are now born and raised in the hot-house by the entrance to the pools.

The complex (tel 51039) is open Saturday to Thursday 8 am to 4 pm, Friday 8 am to 3 pm. Admission is US$8 which gives access to all the amenities, with some extra health and beauty facilities in the pool area at various prices. Egged buses from Tiberias bus station are not that frequent so you need to make an early start to get the most out of your admission fee. Buses from Tiberias depart Sunday to Thursday 8.30, 9 and 10 am, Friday 8.30 and 9.30 am. Departures from Hammat Gader are Sunday to Thursday 11 am, 12 noon, 1 and 2.15 pm, Friday 11.30 am and 12 noon. No buses run on Saturday. It's best not to miss the last bus back to Tiberias although you will normally find a refreshed Israeli family to give you a lift.

Kibbutz Ha'On

Its name meaning 'strength', this kibbutz was established in 1948. Next to the holiday village here is an ostrich farm which is open to visitors from 9 am to 6 pm in the high season (US$5, students US$3), and 9 am to 5 pm in the low season (US$3.75, students US$2).

Kibbutz Ein Gev

Established in 1937 by German and Czech pioneers, this kibbutz is renowned for its 5000-seat amphitheatre which is the setting for major music festivals. As well as its vineyards, banana plantations, date groves and fishing, the kibbutz makes a good living from tourism. They run the ferry service on the lake, and the 45 minute Tiberias to Ein Gev crossing is very popular with Israeli holidaymakers. At the kibbutz is an overrated restaurant, a swimming pool and a camp site.

Luna Gal

On the north-eastern shore of the Sea of Galilee this is the largest of the water-slide complexes. Open daily, the admission prices are steep: 9 am to 5.30 pm US$12; 2.30 to 5.30 pm US$8.25, or 7 pm to 12 midnight US$12. Take Egged bus No 18, 21 or 22 from Tiberias bus station.

Places to Stay

Tiberias and the Sea of Galilee offer a good selection of accommodation with some of the country's best inexpensive hostels and middle range hotels, including a couple of Christian hospices. You can choose between staying in Tiberias itself or in more peaceful and scenic surroundings on the shores of the nearby lake.

Due to fierce competition, especially among the cheaper places, you will often have touts greeting you as you get off the bus and prices are subject to dramatic changes – up during Jewish holidays when Israelis flock here and down immediately afterwards when nervous proprietors outbid each other to attract the travellers. It is best to ask around to see what the going rates are before agreeing to a price. Low season prices are quoted here – for high season add about 25%, but if things are quiet bargain hard.

Places to Stay – bottom end

Tiberias The town's cheap hostels are all within walking distance of the bus station.

The most popular hostel in town seems to be *Nahum Hostel* (tel 21505) on Tavor St. From the bus station bear right along HaShiloah St and follow it round to the left where it where it intersects with Tavor. Nahum Hostel is across the street to the right. It has a rooftop bar and terrace where videos are played in the evening, a kitchen and offers bicycle hire. Dorm beds/doubles US$4/15. Flexible midnight curfew.

En route to Nahum Hostel are some of the alternatives. The first you come to is the dingy *Shweitzer Hostel* (tel 21991) on the right as you head up HaShiloah St from the bus station. There's a kitchen, no curfew, and beds/doubles cost US$8.50/ 23. A little further along is the pleasant *Adina's Guest House* (tel 22507). Run by the ever-smiling Adina, an Orthodox Yemenite, this is a clean and comfortable family house with separate kitchen and bathroom facilities for guests, and a terrace. It's nice and quiet and you have a key so there's no set curfew. Beds/doubles cost US$7/28.

Following HaShiloah St round to the left and down the hill, you come to *Maman Hostel* (tel 92986) on the right. A nice-looking place with its front garden and terrace, it also has a kitchen and nice clean showers – although the food and beer prices are high. Beds/doubles cost US$5.75/20. Flexible midnight curfew and a popular alternative to Nahum.

From the bus station, walk down HaYarden St to the centre of town for the other hostels. Turn right on HaGalil St to find the *Aviv Hotel/Hostel* (tel 732311) on the corner of HaYarqon. This has to be Israel's longest building, but although busy during the Jewish holidays, business is not that good here generally, so you can usually bargain to get a lower price. There's a kitchen and lounge, and singles/doubles go from US$11/16, with breakfast. There's no set curfew.

A couple of hostels overlook the lake. *Terra Sancta* (tel 20516) is in the building adjacent to St Peter's Church. The entrance is on the other side, up the stairs on HaYarden St just up from the water. Although I met people who like the place, I found it a bit dingy. It has a kitchen and a terrace with nice views. Further south along HaBanim St, before the Plaza Hotel, is the *Castle Inn* or *Castle on the Lake Hostel* (tel 21175). It has a kitchen and is pleasant enough, but it has inflexible opening hours. Dorm beds cost from US$5. Closed 12 noon to 4 pm (1 to 4 pm Friday and Saturday), midnight curfew (1 am Friday and Saturday).

Back to HaYarden St and across from the supermarket is the *Meyouhas Youth Hostel* (tel 21775), one of the country's nicest IYHA hostels. It has a TV room, but no kitchen facilities for guests. Dorm beds cost US$7 for members, US$8 for non-members. Breakfast at US$3.40 is compulsory between April and September, and other meals are available. Reception is open 7 to 9 am and 4 pm to midnight. Between October and March there's a midnight curfew, April to September it's 1 am.

Tabgha Twelve km from Tiberias and in the peaceful vicinity of the important Christian holy places is the pleasant *Karei Deshe-Yoram Youth Hostel-IYHA* (tel 20601), which is well worth considering if you want to spend some time in the immediate area. Set in attractive grounds with eucalyptus trees, a rocky beach and a few peacocks, the rooms are clean and air conditioned, the management pleasant and the food good. Dorm beds are US$6 for members, non-members pay US$7.50. There's also a family-sized room, there's a kitchen and meals are available. There's

no curfew. Egged bus Nos 459, 841 and 963 stop on the main road nearby. Get off at the orange 'Tabgha' signpost and walk straight down the side road, past the turning to the left, and the hostel is at the end.

Places to Stay – middle
Unless stated otherwise, prices include breakfast.

Tiberias Just past the Meyouhas Youth Hostel towards the lake is the *Church of Scotland Hospice* (tel 90144-5). A lovely place: friendly management, comfortable furnishings, good facilities and a garden and private beach. Large rooms cost from around US$20/26 for singles/doubles. You may be lucky enough to get a bed in the dorm (US$4). Reception is open Sunday to Friday 7.45 am to 12.30 pm and 4 to 6 pm, Saturday 7.45 am to 12.30 pm. The main gate is locked at 10.30 pm but guests can get their own key.

Close to the bus station is the pleasant *Hotel Toledo* (tel 721649). Turn right up HaShiloah St and right again up HaRab Bibass St. It's a fairly new building, clean and comfortable with friendly owners. Singles/doubles are US$18/35 and lunch or dinner is US$7.

On HaGalil St, next to the petrol station, is *Beit HaGalil* (tel 792993). It caters more for Israelis than foreign travellers, and anyway it's less appealing than other places. Singles/doubles cost from US$35/52.

The *HaEmek Hotel* (tel 720308) at 17 HaGalil St, three blocks south of Ha'Atzmaut Square, is basically furnished and is clean enough, with singles/doubles from US$15/30. Next door is the *Panorama Hotel* (tel 720963), a little more basic with singles/doubles from US$17/23 – breakfast and other meals are extra and can be taken in the restaurant downstairs. Continuing south along HaGalil you come to the *Hagilad Hotel* (tel 720007) at No 4 above the Haroe Pub-Restaurant. Nice enough, with singles/doubles at US$24/36.

Many middle range hotels are a bit out of the way in Qiryat Shemuel. However, some of them do provide good value in nice surroundings and with great views across the lake.

The *Pe'er Hotel* (tel 791641), 2 Ohel Ya'acov St is one of the best in Tiberias, with well-equipped rooms, some with balconies facing the lake, and a restaurant and nightclub. Singles/doubles cost from US$35/50. Next door is the *Eden Hotel* (tel 790070), with similar facilities and singles/doubles from US$35/45. Further up the street on the corner with Naiberg St is the nice-looking and well-furnished *Astoria Hotel* (tel 722351), where singles/ doubles are from US$30/50.

Another of the better places is the small *Hotel Ron* (tel 720259), 12 Achad Ha'am St. It's modern and simple with good service, food and views, and singles/ doubles from US$23/45. The *Hotel Daphna* (tel 792261) is just off Yehuda HaNassi St on Ussishkin St. Another modern place that is well fitted out, with singles/doubles from around US$26/38.

Moving down the hill towards the Old City you come to the *Continental Hotel* (tel 20018) on Alhadif St, corner of Tabur HaAretz St. It's a small, older place, with a homely atmosphere and singles/doubles from US$26/41.

Hammat South of Tiberias, by the hot springs, are a couple more nice hotels. The first you come to is the swish-looking *Ganei Hammat Hotel* (tel 792890). Owned by the proprietors of the hot springs, it has four-star status and the rates, singles/doubles US$48/54, are justified. In addition to the nearby spa and sauna facilities there is a piano bar, nightclub and tennis courts. Further south is the pleasant *Ganei Menorah Hotel* (tel 792769), set in pleasant grounds with lovely lake views – peaceful and popular with retired people. Singles/ doubles US$40/72.

North Beaches Following Gedud Barraq

Rd north from the Old City there are some beachfront hotels. With its own stretch of private beach and a garden with a swimming pool, the *Quiet Beach Hotel* (tel 21441, 20602), is perhaps the best of these. Prices are in the singles/doubles US$40/50 bracket, varying a lot depending on the season.

Ginnosar The four-star graded *Nof Ginnosar Guest House* (tel 792161), run by the kibbutz, provides comfortable accommodation in its lakeside location. It offers gardens, a private beach and water sports facilities, and is very quiet and unhurried. Singles/doubles cost around US$40/60. Just south of Tabgha, the kibbutz is off the main road to Tiberias, marked by the orange 'Nof Ginnosar Guest House' sign.

Mount of Beatitudes A delightful place to stay for its peace and quiet, spotless rooms and lovely surroundings is the *Mount of the Beatitudes Hospice* (tel 20878) 12365 Doar Na, Hevel Korazim. Run by friendly Franciscan nuns who provide tasty food, rooms start around US$20 per person. The hospice overlooks the church and has fine views in all directions. Egged bus Nos 459, 841 and 963 pass by. Get off at the orange 'Hospice of the Beatitudes' sign and walk up the one km long drive. Down the hill are the churches of Tabgha and the ruins of Capernaum.

Vered HaGalil The 'guest farm' here (tel 935785), has lovely accommodation in Swiss-style chalets along with the horse-riding facilities. Singles/doubles cost from US$30/36 and there are some dorm beds at about US$15. The restaurant is very good and dinner costs about US$12. It is usually possible to camp out on the lawn for free and use the shower and toilet facilities if you go riding. Get off the bus from Tiberias at the signposted Korazim junction.

Places to Stay - top end

The long-established top hotel in Tiberias is the *Galei Kinneret* (tel 720018) at the southern end of the Old City overlooking the lake. Mentioned in books by Leon Uris, James D McDonald, Taylor Caldwell and Edwin Samuel, it has a touch of class not found elsewhere in town. The facilities include an outdoor pool, gardens and water sports. Singles/doubles start at US$80/100, with breakfast.

More obvious is the *Tiberias Plaza* (tel 792233) in the centre of the Old City with singles/doubles from US$90/105, with breakfast. Just to the south is the newer *Jordan River* (tel 92950) with a health club, pool and nightclub. Singles/doubles here start around US$70/85, with breakfast.

Camping

If you thought camping was an alternative to paying high prices, think again. The camp sites on the shores of the Sea of Galilee, mostly run by kibbutzim, are expensive. However, although there are still a few areas around the lake where you can camp for free, the camp sites are very popular.

The *Ein Gev Holiday Village* (tel 51177, 58027) is about 1½ km south of the kibbutz entrance. It is set amidst pleasant parkland and there is a rocky beach, boats and canoes for hire, crazy golf, cafeteria and restaurant. Prices go up considerably for the summer months and Jewish holidays. There are sites (US$14 per two people, US$6 per extra person), little bungalows and caravans/trailers fitted out with showers, toilets and kitchens that work out around US$28 per person.

Kibbutz Ha'On Holiday Village (tel 57555) is five km further south on the lakeside. With your own tent you pay from US$17. A caravan/trailer with shower, toilet and kitchen costs from US$60 for four, rising steeply during weekends, the summer months and Jewish holidays.

By the junction for Hammat Gader two km further south is the *Ma'agon Vacation Center* (tel 51360, 51172). There are no camping facilities here, just caravans/trailers. These cost from US$15. This is the top sailboard centre in Israel.

Places to Eat

There is a small food market on HaGalil St by the Aviv Hotel/Hostel with more stalls up the hill off HaRab Bibass St - open Sunday to Friday, closed Saturday. The most convenient supermarket is by the Great Mosque and is open on Saturdays. Its hours are Sunday to Thursday 7 am to 6.45 pm, Friday 7 am to 3.30 pm, Saturday 8 to 10 pm.

The place for felafel is HaYarden St between the bus station and HaBanim St. Several little shops compete here, and allow you to help yourself to salad. Take a look to see which has the best selection. These shops close by 7 pm during the week, 2 pm on Friday, and most stay closed on Saturday, although one or two sometimes open in the evening.

In the bus station the Egged self-service restaurant has the usual cheap choice.

For great shishlik sandwiches (in pitta bread with salad) go to *El Farsi*, the grubby kiosk (no English sign) on the corner of HaGalil and Harab Bibass. Closed Saturday, open Sunday to Friday for lunch until that day's meat supply runs out - very popular. Sandwiches cost about US$1.75, and soft drinks and beer are sold - eat here or take away. Across the street, opposite the Aviv Hotel/Hostel, is another place serving shishlik sandwiches. Beside the market stalls with low tables and chairs arranged out front, *Shipoday Himelreh* (no sign) charges US$2 for a sandwich and also serves soft drinks and beer. Open Sunday to Thursday 8 am to 11 pm, Friday 8 am to 3 pm, closed Saturday.

It's possible to enjoy decent hummus and other salads in a couple of the better middle category restaurants. *Maman* is an Oriental restaurant opposite the Aviv Hotel/Hostel on HaGalil St and further south is *Guy Restaurant*, a nicer looking place with hummus/salad for about US$2, and stuffed vine leaves or vegetables for US$3.50.

Restaurants – more expensive A St Peter fish dinner in Tiberias is not likely to be a gastronomic highlight. The Old City waterfront houses attractive fish restaurants where you pay about US$7 to US$9 for the fish, and US$12 to US$15 for a full meal.

At the northern end of the waterfront promenade is *Caramba*, a popular place with pleasant canework tables and chairs set outside amongst eucalyptus trees. Here you can enjoy soups or crepes (US$3.50), baked potatoes (US$4), vegetables au gratin (US$5), salads (US$5) and desserts (US$4.50). Open daily from about noon till very late.

On Donna Gracia St, up past the IYHA hostel with the Crusader castle wall as a backdrop, the *Lamb & the Goose* is a nice looking place open Sunday to Thursday, 12 noon to 1 am, Friday 12 noon to 3 pm, Saturday sunset to 1 am. Oriental dishes: salads US$1.50, and meat grilled 'on the fire' for US$7 to US$12.

For more Oriental food, visit *Guy Restaurant* on the right along HaGalil St as you head out of Tiberias to the south. Here you have the salads (US$2.50), soups, stuffed vegetables and vine leaves, and spiced meatballs (US$4), and grilled meats (US$7 to US$12). Sit inside or outside on the terrace. Open Sunday to Thursday 12 noon to 12 midnight, Friday 12 noon to sunset, Saturday sunset to midnight.

Also on HaGalil St, across from the Aviv Hotel/Hostel, is *Maman*, also with Oriental food at similar prices and hours.

Probably the best restaurant in town is *The House* (tel 20226) serving Chinese and Thai cuisine. It's on Gdud Barak Rd across from the beachfront hotels as you head north from Ha'Atzma'ut Square. A full meal can cost between US$20 to US$30 and it's open daily for dinner only, 5 pm to 12 midnight.

Bars 'Pub Row' is HaKishon St between HaGalil and HaBanim, with three popular watering holes, *Little Tiberias* and *Avi's Restaurant* open from 1 pm to 2 am and the *Studio Pub* open from 5 pm to 2 am. On Saturday they open later. Although very popular, the food is only so so and clever punters will just be here for the beer. To the north, by the Great Mosque arcade, are some cafés with tables outside. Open daily, *Big Ben* is a pleasant pub-style bar where you are given free olives/popcorn with your beer. Another nice place serving draught beer is the *Lamb & the Goose* restaurant and bar. Walk up the hill past the IYHA youth hostel, and it's on Donna Gracia St by the Crusader castle.

The rooftop bar at *Nahum Hostel* still has the cheapest beer and shows videos.

If you are up late, *Caramba* down on the waterfront is often still open at 3 am and is where the staff from other restaurants go for a nightcap. With its shaded garden of eucalyptus trees overlooking the lake it's nice here at any time.

At the southern end of HaGalil St is the *Haroe Pub-Restaurant*, underneath the Panorama Hotel.

Entertainment

The cafés and bars in and around the Great Mosque arcade and the waterfront promenade in the Old City are where the crowds form in the evening. Check the tourist office for special events – the *Ein Gev Music Festival* at Passover and the *Sea of Galilee Festival* in the summer attract a lot of attention.

With varying degrees of success there are a few discos/nightclubs, call them what you will. These include the *Castle Inn* on the waterfront, the *Blue Beach* (summer only), *Jordan River Hotel*, and the *Pe'er Hotel*. Admission varies between US$3 and US$7.

The *Luna-Gal* waterslide complex is open till midnight, although it's a long way to go from town and the buses stop well before closing time.

You'll find the *Gil* cinema on HaYarden St across the road from the felafel shops, the *Aviv* in Qiryat Shemuel on Bialik St, and the *Hen* up above the Old City in Beit Ma'on, near Jabotinsky St.

What to do on Shabbat in Tiberias
With no buses running, your mobility is limited but you do have a few decent options if you are not inclined to abide by the Jewish law.

Starting with the transport problem, it is possible to hire a bicycle on Friday to use during Shabbat. The roads around the lake are mostly flat, but do bear in mind the heat – go easy on yourself and drink plenty of water.

If the weather is fine then it may be too hot to do anything too energetic, so you will probably be happy just to lie in the sun or go swimming in the lake. Otherwise you can cycle up to Tabgha where the churches are all open and free. Capernaum is open too, for a small fee. In the other direction you can visit Kibbutz Degania and Beit Gordon, the museum. If you are really energetic you could cycle all the way around the lake.

If you don't mind hitch-hiking and risking a long wait, you can go to Hammat Gader for the day – if you do, make as early a start as possible to stand a better chance of getting a ride. Remember that Saturday sees the place packed with Israelis.

Finally, you can go on an organised tour – both Oded Shoshan and Egged Tours operate on Shabbat.

On the food front, the popular eating and drinking places open as usual on Friday evening for their busiest night of the week. However, stock up on food at the market and supermarket on Friday morning because on Saturday virtually everything is closed until the evening. The places that do open are unappealing.

Getting There & Away
Tiberias and the Sea of Galilee are usually reached via Nazareth, Safed or the Jordan Valley, with some visitors arriving from Jerusalem and Tel Aviv by bus.

Bus From the Tiberias bus station there are regular services to Safed, Nazareth, Beit She'an, Afulla, Haifa, Tel Aviv and Jerusalem. When leaving town, check the current timetable to avoid missing the last bus, as services stop comparatively early, eg Jerusalem 5 pm, Haifa and Tel Aviv 8 pm, and Safed 6.30 pm. The left luggage office is outside the bus station at the end of the row of offices as you turn right. It's open Sunday to Thursday 7.30 am to 3 pm, closed Friday and Saturday.

Although you can easily see it, getting to Upper Galilee and Golan is not so easy. From the bus station you have to take a bus to the Rosh Pinna junction and change there, which can involve a lot of waiting around.

Sheruts Outside the bus station and across the grass is where a few sheruts leave in the morning for Nazareth and occasionally Haifa. At other times you might find one looking for passengers to subsidise the journey back, but don't count on it.

Getting Around
In town you should be able to walk to most places, although if you stay up the hill in Qiryat Shemuel your legs would no doubt prefer you to use the bus. Bicycle hire is popular here and with good reason. As long as you can deal with the heat, go for it. It's 55 km all the way round the Sea of Galilee – a nice day out, but start early to beat the heat. You can rent bicycles from the *Nahum Hostel*, or from *Gal-Cal – Easy Wave Rent-a-Bike* (tel 20123) just outside the bus station – they open Sunday to Thursday 7 am to 7 pm, Friday 7 am to 4.30 pm, closed Saturday. They charge from about US$5 per day for a basic model, progressing to a 10-speed (US$6) and a tandem (US$8).

Another way to get about is by ferry. Kibbutz Ein Gev operates a service between their quay on the eastern shore and Tiberias. By special arrangement they also operate between Capernaum and Tiberias. Telephone 20248, 218131 in Tiberias or 58007/9 in Ein Gev, or check at the ticket office at each quay for current details.

Upper Galilee & The Golan

WARNING - UNEXPLODED MINES

Parts of the Golan Heights are still littered with undetonated Syrian land-mines. These areas have been sealed off with barbed-wire fences and warning signs – so stay away from them and any fenced-off areas. Unfortunately there have been people who ignored such warnings – some were killed and some lost limbs. Don't make the same mistake!

Unfortunately a distinct lack of regular public transport makes this area north and east of the Sea of Galilee much less accessible than other parts of Israel. However its outstanding natural beauty and historical sites should be more than enough to encourage you to make the effort.

The best way to visit the area depends on how much time and money you have, and whether or not you have your own car. This is one of the parts of Israel where it can be most advantageous to have your own vehicle. You can see a lot of the area in one day by car, but you would be rushed and would miss out on some great hikes with waterfalls and pools to swim in. A couple of days at least would be better to do it all justice.

Those who have limited time and money might decide to take one of the tours mentioned in the Tiberias section, and visit the area for a day with a guide to point out the major places of interest. Those with time but no money may want to spend at least two days in the area and

rely on buses and hitch-hiking to get around. The only inexpensive places to stay are in Qiryat Shimona and nearby Tel Hai, Metulla and Katzrin which does mean having to spend a fair bit of your time moving from place to place. For those with sufficient funds, there are some pleasant kibbutz guest houses in other areas.

ROSH PINNA

The busy junction at Rosh Pinna is the main point of entry to the region, with roads joining from Haifa, Akko and Safed from the west and Tiberias from the south. If you choose to travel by bus in the region you will often have to change here. Proceeding north from Rosh Pinna the road heads up to Metulla on the Israel-Lebanon border via Qiryat Shemona.

Up the hill just to the west of the junction, Rosh Pinna was the first settlement in Galilee, established in 1882. The discovery of wild wheat in the area by the leading Jewish botanist Aaron Aaronsohn in 1906 was an important development in the research of the origins of cultivated cereals. Galilee's major airport is nearby.

BENOT YA'ACOV - JORDAN BRIDGE

Just north of the Rosh Pinna junction, a side road leads to the east and Kibbutz Kfar Hanassi. A little further north, another side road leads to the east. Passing the small settlement of Mahanayim it comes to Mishmar HaYarden (Guard of the Jordan) after 11 km. This is Galilee's oldest moshav, established in 1890. It was captured and destroyed by the Syrians in 1948 and rebuilt after the area was returned to the Jews under an armistice agreement.

After another two km the road leads to a bridge over the Jordan River, called Benot Ya'acov, 'Daughters of Jacob', as this used to be the place where they crossed the river on their way to Canaan from Mesopotamia. This has also been the site of much conflict over the years. It marked the border between the Latin Kingdom of the Crusaders to the west, and the Muslims to the east and many battles were fought here during the 12th century. In 1799 Napoleon's forces were entrenched here to prevent Turkish reinforcements from reaching Akko which was under siege from the French. WW I saw the Turks in action here again, and in 1918 they were defeated in their campaign to liberate Syria. During the 1948 War of Independence there was severe fighting here between Syrian troops and Zionist groups. The Six-Day War saw Israeli troops cross the bridge on their way to capturing the Golan Heights and the surrounding area was regularly shelled.

From the bridge, the road leads up to the Golan Heights. A turn-off to the north leads through the scenic Hula Valley and after five km a turn-off to the south leads to Katzrin, the new 'capital' of the Golan.

HAZOR

Back on the Rosh Pinna to Metulla road, after nine km you come to the excavations of ancient Hazor. Mentioned in ancient Assyrian and Egyptian records from as early as the 19th century BC, it was the most important town in northern Canaan when the Israelites conquered the area (Joshua 11:10-13, 19:36) in the 13th century BC. In the late 10th century BC, Solomon made it one of his chariot towns (1 Kings 9:15). It was captured by the Assyrians around 732 BC (2 Kings 15:29) and they razed it to the ground.

Hazor Museum

Across the road from the tel (ancient mound), by the entrance to Kibbutz Ayelet HaShahar, is the Hazor Museum. This houses an exhibit of two pre-Israelite temples, a scale model of ancient Hazor and a selection of artefacts. It's open Sunday to Thursday 8 am to 4 pm, Friday 8 am to 1 pm, closed Saturday. Admission is US$1.20.

Place to Stay

The four star guest house at *Kibbutz Ayelet HaShahar* (tel 069-35364), is one of the nicest in the country with good facilities in pleasant gardens with a pool. There is a good restaurant, art gallery and free lectures on kibbutz life. It is not cheap, though – singles/doubles are around US$45/60, with breakfast.

HULA VALLEY & NATURE RESERVE

This beautiful valley between the Galilee and Golan mountains was once a huge malarial swamp dominated by Lake Hula, the northernmost and smallest of the three lakes fed by the Jordan. In order to provide rich, well-watered land for intensive agricultural development, the Israelis implemented a massive engineering project here in the 1950s to drain the lake and the surrounding swamps. In addition, there was a plentiful supply of peat to be dug out of the former lake bed.

However, another result of the Hula project was to endanger a unique plant and wildlife habitat. The Hula is the northernmost point in the world where papyrus reed grows wild, and the region's characteristic flowers are the white water lily and the yellow pond lily. These were threatened, along with great numbers of birds and animals, from small waders to pelicans, sea eagles, otters, jungle cats, boar and many other creatures. The valley is a migratory station for birds, with many coming from as far as Scandinavia, Russia and India.

This threat spurred a small group to form the *Society for the Protection of Nature in Israel* in 1953 which launched a campaign to retain an area of the swamp as a nature reserve. They were successful and their organisation continues to go from strength to strength. The result of their initial campaign is the Hula Nature Reserve (tel 069-37069), a unique wetlands reserve and wildlife sanctuary. There are free guided tours on Saturday, Sunday, Tuesday and Thursday between 9.30 am and 1.30 pm. It's open Saturday to Thursday 8 am to 4 pm, Friday 8 am to 3 pm and admission is US$2. Buses running between Rosh Pinna and Qiryat Shemona will drop you off at a junction about 2½ km from the entrance to the reserve – you have to walk or hitch-hike from there.

Kibbutz Kfar Blum

North of the Hula Nature Reserve and three km along a side road to the east of the main road is this kibbutz with its three star guest house (tel 069-43666). There is a pool, and opportunities for fishing, bird watching, and jogging. Singles/doubles cost around US$40/50, with breakfast.

QIRYAT SHEMONA (population 21,000)

This town's name is Hebrew for 'Town of the Eight' and it was so named after eight Jewish settlers were killed at nearby Tel Hai in 1920. The town was a more recent target for Palestinian terrorist attacks in the 1970s. This is Upper Galilee's 'big town' and its administrative and transport centre.

A standard Israeli new town, it has the familiar wide main boulevard, carefully laid out residential districts and bus station. Its most prominent feature is a children's playground made from three old army tanks that have been painted in bright colours.

Information

The post office is just south of the bus station on Tel Hai Rd and has international telephone facilities. Bank Hapoalim is nearby.

Places to Stay

There's only the expensive *Hotel North*, also called *HaTzafon* (tel 069-44703). Across the street from the bus station, it is a four star establishment with a bar, lounge and pool – singles/doubles are US$35/40, with breakfast.

Places to Eat

The choice is limited. There is an open-air market on Tel Hai Rd, north of the bus station and a supermarket to the south, behind Bank Hapoalim. Felafel and shwarma are sold nearby, there is a pastry and snack shop near the Hotel North and a basic Oriental-type restaurant near the petrol station to the south.

Getting There & Away

Qiryat Shemona is a major junction. Tel Hai, Metulla and the Israel-Lebanon border are to the north; the Hula Valley and Rosh Pinna to the south; and Hurshal Tal, Tel Dan, and such Golan attractions as Banyus, Nimrod Castle, Mount Hermon and Katzrin to the east. Check bus routes and timetables carefully before setting off, and stock up on food, especially for Shabbat.

TEL HAI

Just north of Qiryat Shemona, off the Metulla road, is Tel Hai. It was an incident here in 1920 that led to the naming of the nearby town and the status of Josef Trumpeldor as a Zionist hero.

Born in Russia in 1880, Trumpeldor served in the Czar's army where he lost an arm, and was decorated for gallantry. He later founded the HeHalutz Jewish pioneer movement. In 1912 he immigrated to Palestine and with his self-styled Zion Mule Corps fought with the British Commonwealth forces in the disastrous Gallipoli campaign. Back in Palestine after the war he established Tel Hai ('Hill of Life') in 1917 as a shepherds' camp. Three years later it was attacked by Arabs, and eight of the settlers were killed, including Trumpeldor, whose reported last words were, 'It is good to die for our country.'

Cemetery

The death of those eight settlers has since been made a symbol of political Zionism and Trumpeldor in particular is a model of courage and heroism – a sort of Jewish

Lord Nelson. A statue of the Lion of Judah, with Trumpeldor's famous last words inscribed on it, marks the military cemetery where the eight are buried. The 11th day of the month of Adar is 'Tel Hai Day' and Israeli youngsters make an official pilgrimage to the graves to honour the eight.

Museum

The original settlement's watchtower and stockade have been converted into a museum showing its history and purpose. A slide show in English will usually be screened for a small group on request. Open in summer Sunday to Thursday 8 am to 1 pm and 2 to 5 pm, closed Friday and Saturday; winter, Sunday to Thursday 8 am to 4 pm, Friday 8 am to 1 pm, Saturday 9 am to 2.30 pm. Admission is US$1.65, students US$1.20.

Place to Stay

The *Tel Hai Youth Hostel – IYHA* (tel 069-40043) is a cheap alternative to staying in Qiryat Shemona. It offers dorm beds for US$6.75, and rooms from $US20. Meals are available and reception is open 5 to 7 pm.

Getting There & Away

You can walk to Tel Hai from Qiryat Shemona or take Egged bus No 20 or 22 from either there or Metulla.

KIBBUTZ KFAR GILADI

One km to the north on the road to Metulla from the Tel Hai turn-off, Kibbutz Kfar Giladi has a museum and a guest house. It can also be reached via a track from the Tel Hai cemetery.

Museum

Just inside the gates to the kibbutz is Beit HaShomer (House of the Guardian), an IDF museum documenting the history of the early Zionist settlers' regiments in the British Army during WW I. Open Sunday to Thursday 8 am to 12 noon and 2 to 4 pm.

Friday and Saturday 8.30 am to 12 noon. Admission is 20c.

Place to Stay

The kibbutz guest house (tel 069-41414) is graded three-star with expensive singles/doubles from US$30/45, with breakfast.

METULLA

Established in 1896 with a grant from the Rothschild family, its name is Arabic for 'overlooking'. While the Jewish residents continue to farm, grow fruit and keep bees, it is their town's location that makes it important. It is right on the Israel-Lebanon border and, living up to its name, overlooks the barbed-wire and concrete fortifications and Iyon Valley on the other side.

Good Fence

Although Metulla has developed as a small-scale mountain resort with its slow pace and cooler climate, it is the 'Good Fence' that is the major attraction here (see History in Facts about the Country). Situated to the west of town you can see the checkpoint and, across the border, several Lebanese Christian villages. To the north-west is Beaufort Castle, once the Crusaders' but more recently a PLO artillery position.

Nahal Iyon Nature Reserve

Straight ahead on the main road, with the 'Good Fence' to the left, this is a small wood and picnic area. Further on, past the gate and down some stone steps, is a path leading to the Iyon Waterfall. Unfortunately it runs completely dry during the summer, bar a few stagnant pools.

Tanur Waterfall

East of the Qiryat Shemona to Metulla road runs the deep gorge of the Iyon River and two km before you enter the town there is an attractive 18 metre high waterfall surrounded by rocky walls. It is called Tanur, meaning 'oven', because the density of mist that it creates when in full flow supposedly resembles billowing smoke. The fall is reduced to a trickle during the summer months, although the deep pools below it are still good for a cool swim. The Iyon River continues to flow southwards where it later joins the Jordan. Egged bus No 20 will drop you at the turn-off if you ask; from there it's a few minutes' walk to the park.

Places to Stay

There is nowhere really cheap to stay in Metulla. The *Sheleg HaLevanon Hotel* (tel 069-944015) has tennis courts, two pools, a bar/restaurant and garden patio. Singles/doubles cost from US$26/40, with breakfast. There are similar prices at the smaller *HaMavri Hotel* (tel 069-40150) but without the facilities. Ask here about concerts at Kibbutz Daphna. The older-style *Hotel-Pension Arazim* (tel 069-44143) is perhaps more comfortable. Well-run and very clean, it too has a pool and tennis courts, bar and restaurant. Singles/doubles are $US37/80, with breakfast.

Places to Eat

There are snack bars serving felafel near the 'Good Fence' and a restaurant across from the HaMavri Hotel, where you pay about US$6 for a meal.

Getting There & Away

Egged buses run from Tiberias, Rosh Pinna and Qiryat Shemona.

HURSHAT TAL NATIONAL PARK

The road that heads eastwards from Qiryat Shemona crosses the Iyon River and crosses the Senir River, one of the principal sources of the Jordan River, to reach Hurshat Tal National Park after some five km.

A popular, and therefore often crowded, picnic spot, this forested area is famous for its ancient oaks. According to Muslim legend, 10 of Mohammed's messengers once rested here. With no trees around at that time to provide shade or a hitching post for their camels, they pounded sticks into the ground to fasten their mounts. Overnight the sticks grew into trees and in the morning the holy men awoke to find themselves in a beautiful forest. With some of them believed to be about 2000 years old, the oaks tower over the park with its lawns, pools and waterfalls. The Dan River has been diverted to create a series of pleasant but cold swimming pools. Open daily 8 am to 4 pm. Admission is US$2.30. Egged bus Nos 25, 26 and 36 from Qiryat Shemona will drop you off here.

Places to Stay

The *Horshat Tal Camping Ground* (tel 069-40400) is 100 metres up the road, on the banks of the Dan River. Tent space costs US$4.50 per person, and bungalows are available: three-bed US$25, four US$32 or five US$38. The guest house at nearby *Kibbutz HaGosherim* (tel 069-45231), established by Turkish Jews in 1948, is graded three-star, has a pool and singles/doubles from US$30/40.

TEL DAN

When the land of Israel was divided after Joshua's conquest, the Dan tribe received territory in the coastal plain near Jaffa (Joshua 19:40-6). Unable to hold it against the chariots of the Philistines, they headed north to occupy a Canaan city-state called both Leshem (Joshua 19:47) and Laish (Judges 18:27). Its name was then changed to Dan. Laish is mentioned in Egyptian Execration Texts of the 19th century BC, in the mid-15th century BC list of cities conquered by Thutmose III, and in documents from Mari across the desert on the Euphrates. In the Old Testament, 'from Dan to Beersheba' is the standard expression defining the northern and southern limits of the Promised Land (Judges 20:1, I Samuel 3:20, II Samuel 3:10, 17:11, 24:2).

The Arabs call the site Tal el-Kadi, 'Hill of the Judge', based on a legend that tells of the creation of the Jordan River. Before the Jordan existed, there were three streams, each flowing in a different direction. A quarrel broke out between them as to which was the largest and the most important. Unable to reach an agreement, the streams asked God to decide. God sat on a small hill between them and told them that he loved each of them and that they should join together to form the biggest river. This they did and the Jordan was the result.

There are excavations in a pleasant nature reserve – with some 40 hectares it is comparatively small. Many small springs nourish the dense forest, and it is an enchanting place to walk in and picnic. It's open daily, in summer 8 am to 5 pm, in winter 8 am to 4 pm. Admission is US$1.65 and an informative leaflet with a map of the site costs 25c. Egged bus No 25, 26 or 36 will take you to the nearby Kibbutz Dan; continue up the main road and turn left at the orange sign to the reserve which is a three km walk or hitch-hike.

KIBBUTZ DAN

Near to the Dan Nature Reserve, Kibbutz Dan houses the Beit Ussishkin Museum, named after the director of the Jewish National Fund and featuring exhibits covering the flora, fauna, geology, topography and history of the local area. Open Sunday to Thursday 9 am to 12 noon and 1 to 3 pm; Friday 9 am to 12.30 pm; Saturday 10 am to 2 pm. Admission is 70c, students 55c.

BANYUS

Just two km or so inside the Golan area, Banyus is an ancient cave sanctuary to Pan, the god of the countryside, flocks and herds. 'Banyus' is an Arabic corruption of the Greek word *Paneas*. A spring bursts from a crack below the cave and is one of the principal sources of the Jordan River. The water actually originates from the slopes of Mount Hermon.

In 200 BC the Seleucids of Syria defeated the Ptolemites of Egypt to take control of Palestine. In 20 BC the Roman

Emperor Augustus gave the area to Herod the Great and on his death it passed to his son Phillip, who built his capital here, Caesarea Phillipi. Matthew 16:13-20 tells of Jesus visiting the area when he told the disciples that the church would be built on Peter, the rock. In 1129 the Crusaders held Banyus, an important site as it controlled the road between Damascus and Tyre. The nearby Nimrod Castle was part of their fortifications. With the eventual defeat of the Crusaders the site reverted to its original significance. When the Israelis took it in 1967 there was only a village of some 200 inhabitants.

There is not really that much to see, although the Canaanites and later the Greeks built shrines and temples here. The niches in the cliff face next to the cave were cut during the Graeco-Roman period to receive statues and although there have not been any organised excavations here there are columns, capitals and blocks scattered around the site showing that this was an important 1st century city. To the north of the spring a room of an Herodian building can be seen, and above the cave to the north (left) is the Weli el-Khader (Tomb of St George), a Muslim saint, which is sacred to Muslims and Druze. Across the main road are some Crusader ruins.

Run by the National Parks Authority, the site is open daily 8 am to 6 pm. Admission is 75c. Along with the nearby Banyus Waterfall, this is the region's most popular site but the public transport situation is not brilliant.

Banyus Waterfall

About a km from the park is this lovely waterfall. Follow the path which starts near the stream in the park. Take the right fork just past the bakery, and you come to a pool built by the Syrian Army. Past the pool you come to three paths – take the middle or right paths to the waterfall. Although in winter the water crashes down with more ferocity it is too cold for most people to dive in, whereas in the summer it is most refreshing. Needless to say, it is a very popular site so try to come here early and avoid visiting on Shabbat and Jewish holidays.

Getting There & Away

Egged bus No 55 travels from Qiryat Shemona via Banyus to the Golan only twice a day with the last bus back to Qiryat Shemona leaving Banyus around 12 noon. An alternative, apart from hitchhiking, is to walk the five km west to Kibbutz Dan where bus Nos 25, 26 and 36 run a bit more often and until a bit later. Check the schedules.

NIMROD CASTLE

Less than two km north-east of Banyus, this is the biggest and best preserved of Israel's Crusader castles. Nimrod also enjoys some of the country's finest views from its prominent position, with the Hula Valley below and Mount Hermon to the north.

The castle was named after the biblical Nimrod (Genesis 10:8-10) to whom legend attributes its construction. In fact, Baldwin II had it built in 1129 by Reiner Brus to protect Banyus from an attack from Damascus. It took him three years, which was not bad going judging by the size of the stones that had to be hauled up the steep slopes. However, in 1132 the castle was lost to the Damascenes, who had it taken from them in 1137 by an Arab rival, Zengi, who wanted control of Damascus.

In 1140 the Crusaders and Arabs teamed up to win back the castle after a month-long siege but their alliance ended in 1154 when Zengi's son, Nur ed-Din, won control of Damascus. He twice attempted to take Nimrod in 1157 but had to retreat both times when a Crusader relief force impersonated the US Cavalry and appeared on the horizon just in the nick of time. He succeeded at his next attempt in 1164, with the garrison surrendering before the Crusader army could return from Egypt. During the 5th

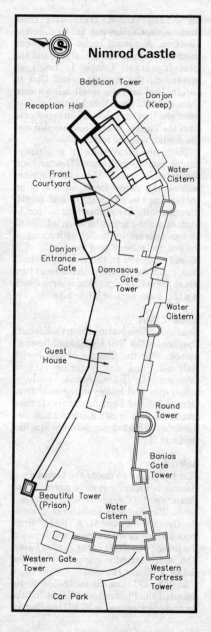

Nimrod Castle

Barbican Tower

Reception Hall

Donjon (Keep)

Front Courtyard

Water Cistern

Donjon Entrance Gate

Damascus Gate Tower

Water Cistern

Guest House

Round Tower

Banias Gate Tower

Beautiful Tower (Prison)

Water Cistern

Western Gate Tower

Western Fortress Tower

Car Park

Crusade (1217-21) it was dismantled but was later renovated by sultans of the Ayyub dynasty during the early 13th century. There are 10 Arabic inscriptions which tell of this work, and in fact most of the remains seen today are from this period. By 1260 the castle was under the Mameluke Sultan Baybars who constructed a citadel built from massive stones and decorated with inscriptions. From the 14th to the 16th centuries the castle served as a jail for political prisoners. After that it was abandoned and used as a cowshed and sheepfold by local farmers. In the Six-Day War it was first used by the Syrians as an observation post and a mortar position, and then by the Israelis. Both sides seemed keen to avoid damaging the impressive remains.

The site is open Saturday to Thursday 8 am to 5 pm, Friday 8 am to 4 pm. Admission is US$1.75, students 80c.

Getting There & Away

Egged bus No 55 running between Qiryat Shemona and Katzrin will drop you off nearby. You can also hike up the hill from Banyus – give yourself about 1½ hours each way, cover your head and take plenty of water. A footpath starts from just above the spring.

MOUNT HERMON SKI CENTRE

There are decent, albeit limited, skiing facilities here on the country's tallest mountain (2766 metres). The snow season is usually late December to early April and the slopes are pretty crowded on the weekend. There are four runs from the upper station, the longest being about 2½ km and all designed for the average to fairly good skier. Separate chair-lifts take skiers and onlookers up from the base station. A shorter chair-lift takes you up to a gentler run, with nursery slopes at the bottom of the hill.

Prices are as bad as you probably expect them to be. A round trip on the non-skiers' lift is about US$8. If you want to ski, the average daily cost of equipment hire, lift tickets and admission to the slopes is over US$50 per person. With most Israelis hiring their equipment, you need to get here early to ensure that your boots fit. It opens between 8.30 am to 3.30 pm, depending on the conditions – telephone (069) 981 341 to check.

Place to Stay

The *Moshav Neve Ativ Holiday Village* (tel 069-41744) is unique. Guests stay in members' homes and meals are served in the guest house dining room, a pleasant, country-style place complete with large fireplace and a great view down to Nimrod Castle and the Hula Valley. There is a disco/bar, billiard room and pool, and horse-riding is available. Rates with breakfast per person are US$35/70 for singles/doubles, rising on weekends and with mandatory half or full board at busy times. Guests get free admission to the slopes and chair-lift and free skiing lessons.

Getting There & Away

The infrequent Egged bus No 55 runs up here from Qiryat Shemona and Katzrin.

DRUZE VILLAGES

There are a number of Druze villages in the area. Unlike those on Mount Carmel, these Druze are fiercely anti-Israel and ever since Israel took the Golan Heights in 1967 they have protested against the occupation. Not only have they refused to accept Israeli citizenship, they actively support Syria and there have been several violent anti-Israeli demonstrations here over the years.

As well as their definite political differences, these Druze are also more traditional, having had less contact with the western world. However, they are just as super-friendly to visitors and although the ramshackle villages are not exactly attractive, the surrounding countryside is and the people themselves can be well worth a visit.

Majdal Shams (population 5900)

The name of this village means 'tower of the rising sun' in Arabic and it is the largest town in the Golan. It has a couple of inexpensive restaurants serving such things as felafel, hummus and grilled meats and salad. You'll find it two km below the ski facilities.

QUNEITRA VIEWPOINT

About 15 km south from Masada, the road heads towards Quneitra, the abandoned Syrian town, but skirts around it and reaches a high mound with an observation point. From here you can look across to Syria and the UN-patrolled border.

Quneitra was the Syrians' 'capital' of the Golan. It was mostly inhabited by Circassians, Muslim immigrants from the Caucasus. Captured by the Israelis in 1967, it was subsequently returned under the cease-fire agreement but has since remained a ghost town. Damascus is 70 km north-east of here.

KATZRIN (population 2500)

Established in 1977 and also known as Qazrin, Kazrin, etc, the name is Hebrew for 'forts', originally from the Latin *castra* (fortress). It's about four km down a road that heads south off the Rosh Pinna-Quneitre road. The new 'capital' of the Golan, Katzrin is as near to an ideal base from which to explore the area as you can get, especially for those on a tight budget.

Planned in the shape of a butterfly, with the wings as neighbourhoods and the body as the commercial district, it is far from fully grown, having a projected population of 10,000. Set amongst a bleak landscape it is not an attractive town, but its monotonous buildings and the decent facilities do provide a high standard of living by Israeli standards – further enhanced by government grants and allowances for those who live and work here.

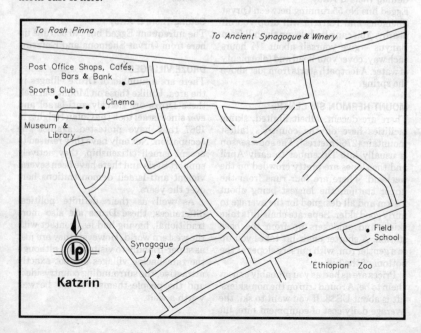

Orientation

The town lies to the south of the main road. The main street leads straight ahead past the shopping centre, which has a post office, bank, supermarket, eating places, cinema, museum and sports facilities to the southern edge of the town. To the left is the SPNI field school, the only accommodation in Katzrin.

Information

The post office is open Sunday, Tuesday and Thursday, 7.45 am to 12.30 pm and 3.30 to 6 pm, Monday, Wednesday and Friday 7.45 am to 2 pm, closed Saturday. The nearby Bank Leumi branch is open Sunday, Tuesday and Thursday 8.30 am to 12.30 pm and 4 to 6 pm; Monday, Wednesday and Friday 8.30 am to 12.30 pm; closed Saturday. The swimming pool is open daily 10 to 5 pm, admission US$2.70.

Things to See

The Golan Archaeological Museum has some interesting exhibits. Many of the artefacts on display come from the site of ancient Katzrin which was one of the original Jewish settlements in the Golan. Open Sunday to Thursday 9 am to 2 pm, Friday 9 am to 1 pm, Saturday 10 am to 2 pm. Admission is US$1.20, students 90c.

You can visit the site of ancient Katzrin, with its 3rd century synagogue. From the new town, return to the main road and head south (turn right). After about a 15 minute walk, it is on the opposite side of the road.

The turn-off to the north (left) passes the only petrol station in the Golan and leads to the new industrial area and the renowned Golan winery. At the time of writing, plans were being made to provide tours of the new outdoor winery where the prize-winning and much talked about Yarden wines are made. Telephone (069) 61841/8 for current information.

Back in town, a small zoo has been set up west of the field school by an Ethiopian resident.

Place to Stay

The SPNI's Golan-Katzrin Field Study Centre (tel 069-61352) has a modern, clean and comfortable guest house for US$16 per person. It is often full, so telephone to make a reservation. To the south it has a camp site with basic bungalows for around US$8 per person or tent sites for US$4. It is best to go straight to the main building of the field school regardless of where you want to stay. If no-one is around (not unusual), leave a note and your stuff. The staff are friendly and helpful to travellers who are keen to explore the area. They will happily tell you about natural beauty spots to visit, such as waterfalls, springs and rivers. Most of these places require a few hours hiking, but nothing too strenuous.

Places to Eat

In the shopping centre there are a few cafés serving felafel, salads and grilled meats; some serve draught beer. Their main trade is provided by the IDF, with soldiers from nearby positions pouring in. Most of the staff are Druze from nearby villages. The supermarket is open Sunday to Thursday 8 am to 6 pm, Friday 7 to 3.30 pm, closed Saturday.

Getting There & Away

Egged bus No 55 makes just two trips a day from Qiryat Shemona via Rosh Pinna.

ABBURA WATERFALL

The road from Katzrin heading north-east (left) joins the Benot Ya'acov Bridge to Quneitra road. Turn right to head towards Quneitra and a side-road after one km leads down to this attractive waterfall. Turn off after about two km. The Gilabon Nature Reserve between here and Hulata is another pleasant area of forest.

YA'AR YEHUDIYYA NATURE RESERVE

Stretching down to the Sea of Galilee from Katzrin, this lovely area includes some delightful waterfalls and rivers. Ask for specific directions at the Katzrin field school.

Berekhat HaMeshulim

One of the reserve's highlights is this pool with its unique hexagonally-shaped columns made of rock at the water's edge. These were formed when molten rock cooled slowly.

GAMLA

Well worth a visit is this spectacular site overlooking the Sea of Galilee, believed to be the ruins of ancient Gamla.

On 12 October 67 AD the Romans began the siege of Gamla, a Jewish city on the slopes of the Golan. With the Jewish Revolt against Rome, thousands of the rebels fled north to Gamla seeking refuge. Three legions of the Roman Army followed them and massacred 4000 Jews, while the remaining 5000 committed suicide by leaping over the cliff. As in the similar events at Masada, two women survived.

Our knowledge of Gamla is based on the account of its siege by the 1st century historian, Josephus. This includes descriptions of the location and layout of the city, and it was with this information that the site 15 km south-east of Katzrin was chosen. However, it is not certain that this is the right place – some archaeologists believe that a site near Jamle on the Syrian side of the current Golan border is more likely.

The name Gamla is derived from the word 'camel' and the chosen site here does bear a likeness to the ship of the desert. In accordance with Josephus' account, the ruins lie on a rock plateau (the camel's body) joined to the hillside by a narrow ridge (the camel's tail). One aspect of this site that clashes with Josephus' account is the citadel. Here it is west of the hump, but he wrote that it was south. Authentic or not, it is an impressive-looking place, particularly from the Golan looking south-west with the Sea of Galilee down below in the distance.

Getting There & Away

Not on a bus route, Gamla can only be reached by hitch-hiking, most easily done from Katzrin, some 15 km to the north.

SAFED (population 17,200)

Set high amongst the beautiful scenery of the Galilee mountains, the holy city of Safed, picturesque and peaceful with its maze of quaint cobbled streets, artists' quarter and a rich heritage of Jewish mysticism, is on most travellers' itineraries. It may be a day trip from Tiberias, a stop-off en route between Galilee and the coast, or somewhere to stay a little longer.

History

Safed was in the territory assigned to the Naftali tribe after Joshua's conquest of the land of Israel. During the First Temple period it was one of the hill-top towns and villages where *masu'ot* (beacons) were lit. Starting in Jerusalem, these fires acted as signals to let the country know about the beginning of a new month or holy day.

1	Ari Mikveh (ritual bath)
2	Ari Sephardi Synagogue
3	Ha Meir House
4	Banna Synagogue
5	Kikkar Abbo
6	Simtat Alsheik (blue-painted street)
7	Alsheik Synagogue
8	Abuhav Synagogue
9	Yosef Caro Synagogue
10	Ethiopian Folk Art
11	General Exhibition Hall
12	Printing Museum
13	Cave of Shem & Ever; Synagogue
14	Universal Felafel
15	Rehov Maalot Olei Hagaroom
16	Central Hotel
17	Davidka Memorial
18	Ari Ashkenazi Synagogue & Mikveh
19	Chernobl Synagogue
20	Former British Police Station
21	Post Office
22	Tourist Office
23	Hotels Tel Aviv, Hadar & HaGalil
24	Carmel Hotel
25	War Memorial
26	Israel Bible Museum

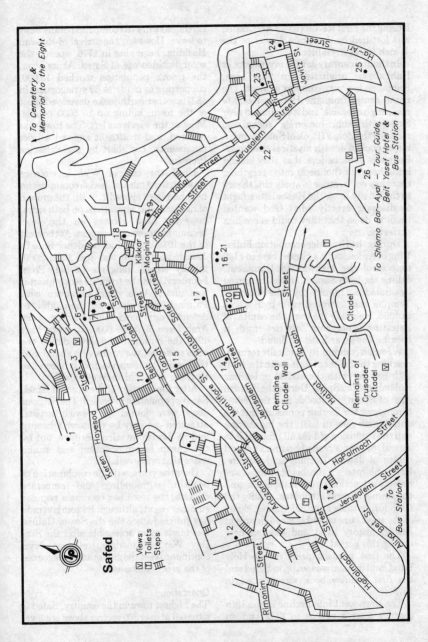

Safed

Views ☒
Toilets 🚻
Steps ⊞

To Cemetery &
Memorial to the Eight

To Shlomo Bar-Ayal – Tour Guide,
Beit Yosef Hotel &
Bus Station

To Bus Station

Ha-Ari Street

Ha-Ari Street

Javitz St

Jerusalem Street

Bar Yohai Street

Ha-Maginim Street

Kikkar
Maginim Street

Kikkar
Maginim Street

Yosef Street

Yosef Street

Tarpat Street

Sofer Street

Beit Street

Montifiore St

Jerusalem Street

Keren Hayesod Street

Yiplach Street

HaTam Street

Remains of Citadel Wall

Remains of Crusader Citadel

Citadel

HaLwzi Street

Aliyah Bet Street

HaPalmach Street

Rimonim Street

HaPalmach Street

Aliyah Bet Street

Jerusalem Street

During the First Revolt (66-73 AD), Safed was fortified by Josephus, leader of the Jewish forces in Galilee.

In the 2nd century Jewish mysticism, or Kabbalism, originated in this area. Kabbalah is a very complex subject. The name comes from the Hebrew root *kbl* meaning 'to receive' and it originated near Safed with Rabbi Shimon Bar Yochai who received the Zohar (Book of Splendour), a major book of Jewish mystical teachings. Religious Jews believe that they should bring *kedusha* (holiness) into everything that they do. In order to apply this theory to their daily lives, the Kabbalists sought to discover exactly what God wanted them to do so that they could serve him perfectly.

During the Crusader occupation Fulke, King of Anjou, built a citadel here in 1140 to control the highway to Damascus, calling the town Saphet. It was destroyed by Saladin, rebuilt by the Knights Templar and destroyed again by Baybars in 1266. He made the town the capital of Palestine's northern district and it became known as Safat or Safad.

A Jewish community gradually formed, reaching the height of its fame in the mid-16th century with the arrival of leading Kabbalists from Spain. During the 'Golden Age' of Spain, Kabbalah had flourished throughout the Iberian peninsula but the anti-Jewish riots in 1391, the Inquisition and the expulsion of 1492 all brought it to an end. Safed succeeded Spain as a world centre of Jewish learning and culture. Rabbi Shimon's tomb being nearby was Safed's attraction to the Kabbalists, and the town's natural attributes, chiefly the fresh air, became spiritual virtues. Some of the most famous and learned figures in Jewish history lived and studied here during this period.

The first printing press in the Holy Land, and in Asia, was set up in Safed and the first Hebrew book was printed in 1578.

The town went into decline in the 18th century after a plague in 1742 and an earthquake in 1769 compelled many Jews to leave. However, the arrival of Russian Hasidim, beginning in 1776, opened the second golden age of Safed. At its peak, the town's population reached 15,000, supporting as many as 69 synagogues. In 1837 another earthquake destroyed most of the town, killing up to 5000 people. Most of the survivors left. The town was restored, and in 1920 it enjoyed a brief renaissance, cut short by the Palestine Problem.

Until the end of WW I, violence between the Arab and Jewish communities here had been sporadic. With the growth of nationalistic aspirations on both sides, however, Arab attacks on the Jews became increasingly frequent. At the start of the 1948 War of Independence Safed's Jewish population was less than 2000, mainly elderly religious people. From February 1948 the town's Jewish quarter was under Arab siege and even with Palmach reinforcements those able to defend it numbered only a fraction of the Arab force of some 6000. In early May 1948 the outnumbered Jews defied the odds to defeat the Arabs who abandoned the town. The Jewish victory is referred to by them as the 'Miracle of Safed'.

After the creation of the State of Israel, Safed's population increased. The religious Jews were joined by Jewish artists, attracted not only by the town's beauty and its Jewish mystical heritage, but by the cheap accommodation and studio space that was available.

Over the years, with its combination of beautiful surroundings and temperate climate, the town has become a popular summer resort, although its tourist trade has suffered since the the Sea of Galilee was made more accessible after the Six-Day War. Meanwhile, religious Jews continue to visit the graves and synagogues of the great Kabbalists.

Orientation

The highest town in the country, Safed is situated at over 800 metres above sea level on a series of hilltops. Basically consisting of three main areas, there is the town centre on one hill, South Safed on another, and Mount Cana'an to the east.

Mount Cana'an is Safed's highest point at 950 metres above sea level. With its views and forest it is an attractive part of town and some middle range hotels are here along with picnic sites and observation points. South Safed has little to offer the traveller except the IYHA youth hostel and a swimming pool.

Most of your time in Safed will be spent in the town centre, which is small enough to cover on foot. The main thoroughfare is Jerusalem St which completes a circle right around the area. The central bus station is just below Jerusalem St, to the east. From here you can go either to the left or to the right to reach the sights. The centre can be split into three sections: Gan HaMetsuda, the park area with the remains of the Crusader fortress standing atop the hill and encircled by Jerusalem St; the Old City, or Synagogue Quarter, to the north-west, a compact cluster of narrow streets winding their way around the slopes and connected by a series of steep stairways; and the Artists' Quarter, immediately to the south of the Old City on the other side of Ma'alot Olei HaGardom St, the main stairway down the slope from Jerusalem St.

Lubavich school children, Safed

Information

Tourist Office The IGTO is at 23 Jerusalem St (tel 930633). Climb the stairs from the central bus station and turn right – it's up the hill and on the left after a few minutes. Open Sunday to Thursday 8.30 am to 12.45 pm and 4 to 6 pm; Friday 9 am to 1 pm; closed Saturday.

Post Offices A convenient branch office is at 37 Jerusalem St, and the main office and poste restante is on HaPalmach St. Look for the radar dish next door, visible from the corner of Aliyah Bet St. The main office is open September to June, Sunday, Tuesday and Thursday 7.45 am

to 2 pm and 4 to 6 pm; Monday and Wednesday 7.45 am to 2 pm; Friday 7.45 am to 1 pm. July to August, Sunday to Friday 7.45 am to 2 pm, closed Saturday. The branch office on Jerusalem St closes at 12.30 pm on Monday, Wednesday and Friday.

Other Bank branches are on Jerusalem Street west of the Citadel. They open Sunday, Tuesday and Thursday 8.30 am to 12.30 pm and 4 to 6 pm, Monday and Wednesday 8.30 am to 12.30 pm, Friday 8.30 am to 12 noon, closed Saturday.

The Emek Hatchelet Swimming Pool is east of the town centre, off Ha'Atzma'ut Rd just across from the central bus station. Open in the summer only, Sunday to Friday 7.30 am to 4 pm, Saturday 8.30 am to 4 pm. Admission is US$1.80, students US$1. In South Safed an indoor pool is open all year round. Take Egged bus No 6 or 7.

For police, telephone 930444 or 100.

Tours

Well worth considering for a deeper insight into Safed and its status as a holy city and the centre of Jewish mysticism are the walking tours offered by Shlomo Bar-Ayal. In the summer he gives three tours: Sunday to Thursday at 9.30 am, 1 pm and 4 pm; Friday 9.30 am only. In the winter Sunday to Friday 10.30 am only. Tours on Shabbat and in the evening are by prior arrangement only. Charging a reasonable US$5 per person, Shlomo gives a good two hours of interesting commentary on various aspects of Safed's history. He also offers a 'Bubbe Maise tour'. Popular mainly with Jewish visitors, this emphasises the many folk stories that have originated in Safed. For these, Shlomo charges US$25 for the tour (two hours minimum) which can be for any practical sized group. Based at the Hotel Beit Yosef, you can also contact Shlomo on Tel 974597.

Contact the information office at the central bus station for details of Egged Tours' local itineraries. They run tours to local Jewish religious sites and to the Golan Heights, the Sea of Galilee and Hammat Gader.

Israel Bible Museum

From the central bus station, climb the stairs to Jerusalem St, bear right up the hill and after the municipal offices on the left you come to the Israel Bible Museum (tel 973472) on the slopes of Gan HaMetsud, across from the smaller park to the north.

Once the home of a Turkish pasha, the 120 year old building is now home to the work of American Jewish sculptor and artist, Phillip Ratner. He has established a museum of his sculpture, painting, lithography and tapestry, which depict scenes from the Bible. There is also a collection of the sculpture of Henryck Glicenstein. It's open Sunday to Thursday 8 am to 6 pm, Friday 8 am to 2 pm, Saturday 10 am to 2 pm. Admission is free, donations accepted.

Gan HaMetsuda - the Citadel

This is the pleasant park and viewpoint at the summit of Mount Safed - the Citadel. It was here that the signal beacons were lit and where Josephus built his fortifications, but today it is the remains of the 12th century Crusader fortress that are evident. (Jerusalem St follows the line of the Crusaders' city wall). In 1986 pottery fragments were accidentally unearthed, which have been dated to the time of Abraham - a major excavation is planned once funds have been raised.

From the Citadel you can enjoy marvellous views, with the Sea of Galilee visible on that clear day. Around Safed is the largest forest planted by the Jewish National Fund - before 1948 there were hardly any trees in the area.

Synagogue Quarter

Along with the surrounding views, the Old City is Safed's major attraction. Resign yourself to losing your way amongst the network of narrow streets, courtyards and steep stairways.

The synagogue Quarter is centred on Defenders' Square, Kikar HaMaginim. In the good old days charcoal was sold here for heating; now it is Safed's main meeting place, known simply as 'the Kikar'. What is now the Tiferet Gallery was the HQ of the Haganah during the 1948 War of Independence. The Kikar is just off Jerusalem St, down the slope along HaMeginim St.

Safed's Kabbalist synagogues have their holy arks set in their southern rather than eastern walls so as to face Jerusalem. They are usually open throughout the day to visitors and admission is free but donations are requested. Suitable clothing must be worn and cardboard yarmulkas are provided.

Ha'Ari Ashkenazi Synagogue Just down from the Kikar, this is one of two synagogues dedicated to 'the Ari', one of the major figures of Jewish mysticism. 'Ari' (Lion) is an acronym of his name, Adoni (or Ashkenazi) Rabbi Itzhak Luria.

Born in Jerusalem in 1534, Rabbi Itzhak moved to Cairo where he quickly mastered conventional Jewish teachings and began to study Kabbalah. In 1569, after some 12 years of study, he brought his family to Safed so that he could study with the Ramak – Rabbi Moshe Cordeviero, the leading teacher of mysticism at the time. When he died, the Ari took over and taught the secrets of the Torah to a select group of students until his death in a sudden plague in 1572.

The Ha'Ari Ashkenazi Synagogue was built after his death on the site of the field (in those days it was outside the Old City) where the Kabbalists would gather to welcome Shabbat. There is no mezuzah on the synagogue entrance because the Ari had consecrated the area. The original building was destroyed in the 1852 earthquake.

The olive-wood ark was carved in the 19th century and represents over 10 years' work. It was painted about 30 years ago. The *bimah* (pulpit) bears a shrapnel hole from an Arab attack during the 1948 siege. The synagogue was packed at the time but nobody was hurt – the hole is now stuffed with messages to God à la Jerusalem's Western Wall.

In the small room at the rear of the synagogue is a chair carved at about the same time as the ark – Kisay Eliyahn, (Elijah's Chair). Legend has it that any Jewish couple who sit here will have a son within a year.

Caro Synagogue Rabbi Yosef Caro was another leading Kabbalist. He was born in Spain in 1488 and after the expulsion of the Jews in 1492 he moved to the Balkans, arriving in Safed in 1535. He later became the chief rabbi here, but he attained fame for his important written works which included the *Shulchan Aruch*, basically an extensive blueprint for living a Jewish life. So influential are his teachings and their interpretations of the Jewish Law that today's rabbis consider his opinions when dealing with contemporary questions.

Destroyed in the 1837 earthquake and rebuilt around 1847, the synagogue stands above Rabbi Caro's home where he produced his great works. The ark contains three ancient Torah scrolls: the one on the right is from Persia and is about 200 years old; the centre one, from Iraq, is about 300 years old; and the scroll on the left, from Spain, is over 500 years old.

Alsheikh Synagogue This is named after Rabbi Moses Alsheikh, another leading Kabbalist. The walls along this street are painted an attractive blue – a colour which represents royalty and heaven.

Abuhav Synagogue This synagogue is believed to have been built by followers of Rabbi Yitzhak Abohav in the 1490s, using a plan based on the Kabbalah. The four central pillars represent the four elements which, according to Kabbalists, make up all creation. The dome has 10 windows to represent the Commandments, pictures of the 12 tribes of Israel to represent Jewish unity, illustrations of the musical instruments used in the Temple, pomegranate trees (which traditionally have 613 seeds – the same number as the commandments in the Torah), and the Dome of the Rock, a reminder of the Temple's destruction. The silver candelabrum hanging opposite the central ark is a memorial to the holocaust victims.

Legend has it that when the 1837 earthquake struck, the entire synagogue was destroyed except for the wall next to, and the arch over, the ark which still houses the Torah scroll written by Rabbi Abohav. The large wooden ark is on your right as you enter, and the scroll is only used on Rosh HaShanah, Yom Kippur and Shavuot.

Banna Synagogue Named after Rabbi Yossi Banni (the Builder) who is buried here, this synagogue is also known as the Shrine of the White Saint – in Hebrew *Hatsadik Halavan*. This is based on a legend that tells of the time when an Arab governor of Safed ruled that the Jews had to use only white chickens for the Yom Kippur ceremony. The distressed Jews prayed at Rabbi Banna's tomb for a way out of the problem and the result was that all the black chickens turned pure white. Another version of the legend has it that the Jews were told to bring to the governor a certain number of white chickens, or face expulsion.

The synagogue contains the Torah scroll that is carried in the traditional procession to Meiron every Lag B'Omer.

Kikar Abbo This small square, marked by a Star of David made out of pine needles, is where the Hasidim start their procession to Meiron on Lag B'Omer. The square is named after the French ambassador of 1840 and his successors, Jewish or not, traditionally take part in the procession to Rabbi Shimon's tomb.

Ha'Ari Sephardic Synagogue On the lower slopes of the Old City, just up from the cemeteries, this synagogue is built on the site where Ari prayed. The small room on the left in the back is said to be where he learned the mystical texts with the prophet Elijah. In the 1948 siege, the synagogue was one of the key positions held by the Jewish defenders.

Cemeteries

Below the Old City on the western slopes, down from the Ha'Ari Sephardic Synagogue and facing Meiron, lie three adjoining cemeteries. The small building to the left of the path that leads down from the synagogue is its gents' mikveh (ritual bath).

The oldest of the cemeteries contains the graves of many of the famous Kabbalists who believed that Safed's pure air would benefit the souls of those buried here and fly them immediately to the Garden of Eden. Among those buried here are: the Ari; his teacher Cordoviero (Ramak), author of *Pardess Rimmonim* (Grove of Pomegranates); Shlomo Alkavets, composer of the hymn *Lecha Dodi*; Yosef Caro; Ya'acov Beirav, who attempted to re-establish the Sanhedrin (the Supreme Court) in Safed in 1538; and Moshe Alsheikh.

The domed tomb was built by the Karaites of Damascus and is believed by them to contain the body of the biblical prophet, Hosea. Legend has it that also buried on this hill are Hannah and her seven sons, martyred by the Greeks on the eve of the Maccabaean revolt. The sudden feeling of fatigue experienced when you climb the hill is apparently due to your walking over their graves.

The more recent cemeteries contain victims of the 1948 siege and, at the bottom of the slope, seven of the eight members of the Irgun and Lehi who were hanged by the British in Akko prison. The eighth is buried at Rosh Pinna, where he lived.

Hameira House

Just up the slope from the cemeteries and the Ari Sephardic Synagogue, this complex comprises a museum, a research institute and a 'center for educational tourism'.

The building dates back to 1517 when the Spanish Jews had begun arriving in Safed. They built it as a centre of Kabbalistic study. Partially destroyed in the earthquakes of 1759 and 1837, the house was restored between 1850 and 1860 by immigrants from Persia and North Africa. In the early 1900s the Sephardic Chief Rabbis and the Sephardic Law Court were based here. During WW I it served as accommodation for Jews made homeless or injured by the war and Safed's first Hebrew school was established here. During the Arab riots of 1929 and the late 1930s, parts of the building were destroyed, and the occupants killed, and it was eventually abandoned. The Jewish underground used it to store weapons and as a place to train between 1940 and 1948, and its ruins were a strategic Jewish position in the Arab siege.

Between 1959 and 1984 it was restored by Yehzkel Hameiri, a fifth generation Safedian, who has gradually transformed it into today's museum and institute which documents the town's history. Having collected material for some 30 years, Mr Hameiri has put together a variety of documents, papers, ancient books, utensils from homes and workplaces, clothes, furniture and holy objects from over the years – all of which show how Safed's Jewish community has lived. There are also photographs, recordings and video tapes of both sites and older residents – a wide variety of material for display and research.

Museum The aim of the museum is to give an understanding of Safed's Jewish community of the last century – the lifestyles of earlier generations and their struggle to survive. Open Sunday to Friday 9 am to 2 pm, closed Saturday.

Research Institute The institute provides a wide variety of material on the history of Safed's Jewish community and also publishes studies relating to the town's heritage.

Center for Educational Tourism Run in cooperation with the Ministry of Education, university research institutes and the IDF, the complex includes classrooms and a lecture hall with audio-visual facilities, all available for seminars and tour groups. Guest lecturers and accommodation can be arranged. For more details, contact Hameiri House (tel 971307), PO Box 1028, Safed.

Davidka Memorial

By a bus stop on Jerusalem St, across from the former British police station and overlooking the Old City, this war memorial incorporates an example of the Davidka, a primitive and unreliable mortar made by the Jews and used to great effect in 1948. Somewhat dangerous to use, it did little physical damage but the story goes that it made such a loud noise that it scared the living daylights out of the Arabs.

Ma'alot Olei HaGardom St

This is the wide stairway that separates the Synagogue Quarter to the north from the Artists' Quarter to the south. Its name is Hebrew for 'Men Who Were Hungry', referring to Safed's Jewish residents during the Arab siege. The stairway was built by the British after the 1929 Arab riots, to divide the town and keep the Arab and Jewish communities apart. Tarpat St, running from south to north along the slope, is the main street where the Arabs rioted in 1929. Note the ruins of 16th century Jewish houses which were built using stones removed from the Crusader wall up the hill.

Look across Jerusalem St from the steps towards Gan HaMetsuda – on the roof of the opposite building is a British gun position with a searchlight. Further north is the former British police station, riddled with bullet holes. This is now an income tax office and obvious jokes are made about the real reason for the bullets.

Artists' Quarter

South of Ma'alot Olei HaGardom St, this is the old Arab Quarter, now largely inhabited by artists. You may be disappointed with the work produced but I am told that the local art scene is going through a transitional period and is on the way up with new blood coming through.

The steepness of the slopes may soon wear out any enthusiasm for gallery-hopping. A few places that stand out, though not necessarily for the quality of their work, include the Ethiopian Folk Art Center & Gallery. Halfway down Ma'alot Olei HaGardom St and just to the north, it is housed in what was a synagogue established in the 1930s, not as a place of worship, but as a Palmach position to ward off future Arab attacks. The Ora Gallery at 1 Beit Joseph St, further north in the Synagogue Quarter, features work produced by religious artists, including some geometric acrylic paintings by Jacques Kaszemacher. This French Hasidic Jew, a fascinating character, is often here in the morning. Back in the Artists' Quarter, an abandoned mosque houses the General Exhibition which features a representative selection of Safed's art. Often run by the artists themselves, the galleries' opening hours vary.

Zvi Assaf Printing Museum

This houses exhibits of Jewish printing, and is open Sunday to Thursday 10 am to 12 noon and 4 to 6 pm, Friday and Saturday 10 am to 12 noon. Admission is free.

Shem Va'Ever Cave

Back on Jerusalem St, climb the stairs up to the bridge that carries HaPalmach St to reach this holy cave where Noah's son and great grandson supposedly studied the Torah.

According to Muslim tradition, it was here that a messenger told Jacob of the death of his son, Joseph. The Arabs therefore call the cave the 'Place of Mourning', and they believe that the messenger lies buried here.

Places to Stay

Safed's accommodation scene is not brilliant. There is a distinct shortage of cheap beds and hoteliers put up their rates by some 15 to 20% during summer. This is due to the climate being a pleasant cool alternative to the heat of the lowlands in the summer, but too cold for most people in the winter, when Safed does a good impersonation of a ghost town.

Places to Stay - bottom end

South Safed is where you will find the *Beit Binyamin IYHA Youth Hostel* (tel 973514). Take Egged bus No 2, 2A or 6 from the central bus station or walk the 25-odd minutes – it's near the Amal Trade School. Bed and breakfast (mandatory) is US$6.50 (non-members US$7.50). Other meals are normally provided only if a group is staying here.

In the town centre there are a few private homes with rooms to rent – usually around US$10/15 for singles/doubles. The tourist office has a list. Standards vary from those places that look as if they have remained untouched since the last earthquake to those that could be considered comfortable.

Shoshanna Briefer is a lady with distinct grey-black hair who rents out beds in a couple of dingy apartments with kitchen facilities south of the Artists' Quarter. She charges from US$5 which is the least you can expect to pay in town. Look for Shoshanna at the central bus station where she often waits to meet arriving travellers. If you don't see her or, even less likely, she doesn't see you, climb the stairs up to Jerusalem St, turn left and follow the road up to the bridge, climb the stairs and cross over the bridge heading south, away from Gan HaMetsuda. Take the first alley to your right, then take the alley that runs diagonally in the same general direction as the road. The apartments are towards the end – one is on the left, behind a large green metal door, the other is across the street on the right, with a grey door, about two-thirds of the way along.

Just down the slope from the Davidka memorial, *Nathan House* (tel 30121) at 50 Jerusalem St, is in a good location, clean, and with a kitchen and TV lounge. Unfortunately it's only open from July to mid-October. Singles/doubles are US$15/20.

Further on along Jerusalem St, past the park on the right, you come to Ridbaz St, a series of steps heading down the slope. Here are two hotels which offer pleasant rooms at a decent price – in the winter. *Hotel Hadar* (tel 930068) is on the left and opposite, *Hotel HaGalil*. Singles/doubles are US$20 per person with breakfast.Their prices shoot up in summer.

Places to Stay - middle & top end

The *Hotel Beit Yosef* (tel 930012), 2 Jerusalem St, is set in attractive grounds on the northern slopes of the town centre. Occupying what was once a Scottish-run Christian hospital and mission used by the Turks as their military HQ during WWI (the German air force used the airport at Rosh Pinna), it became the British military HQ during WWII after which the Haganah purchased it anonymously to run the hotel as a cover, with resistance fighters posing as bus boys. After Israel's independence it became a convalescent home for wounded soldiers. Now the hotel provides three-star standard accommodation, with singles/doubles US$30/45, with breakfast, and economy rooms with shared facilities at US$15 per person. Aimed primarily at religious Jews, the complex includes a tennis court, a restaurant with a value-for-money salad bar. The management also offer extensive facilities for tours of Safed with expert guides, and an audio-visual programme

on the town's history. Cultural events and evening programmes are staged in the amphitheatre.

Further up the hill and past the public garden on the right, you come to Javitz St, a series of steps leading down the slope. At No 8, the *Carmel Hotel* (tel 930053) is in a modernised old building. The rooms are plain but clean and comfortable, some with great views. Singles/doubles are US$25/38, with breakfast. *Hotel Hadar* and *Hotel HaGalil* on Ridbaz St, offer a higher standard, with singles/doubles US$30/45, with breakfast.

With modern-style asymmetrical public rooms decorated with local art and more conventional bedrooms, the *Central Hotel* (tel 972666) is at 37 Jerusalem St and has singles/doubles from US$35/50, with mandatory half board.

The *Hotel Yair* (tel 930245), 59 Jerusalem St, is a nice place – modern but folksy. The lobby is one flight up with the rooms up one more – no lift. Singles/doubles from US$25/35, with breakfast.

In the Artists' Quarter, the *Rimon Inn* (tel 930665) is rated four-star and facilities include an outdoor pool. Singles/doubles cost from US$35/45, with breakfast.

Over on Mount Cana'an there are a few hotels. These include the *David* (tel 930062), with singles/doubles for $US30/42, with breakfast; the *Ruckenstein* (tel 930060), with singles/doubles US$18/35, with breakfast; and the top of the range *Zefat*, with singles/doubles from US$40/50, with breakfast.

Places to Eat

Safed is no culinary centre, but there are a few places that are better than the rest.

For decent felafel, head straight for *Universal Felafel* at 54 Jerusalem St, adjacent to the steps of Ma'alot Olei HaGardom St.

There is a fruit and vegetable market on Monday and Tuesday morning in front of the main post office (cross the bridge and head south, away from the Citadel) and a supermarket on HaPalmach St (turn left from the central bus station).

The restaurant at the *Hotel Beit Yosef*, 2 Jerusalem St, features a help-yourself salad bar for US$5, with main dishes for US$7 to US$10.

In the Synagogue Quarter *HaKikar Restaurant*, upstairs in the Kikar, is a nice room decorated with local art – a pleasant place for a bottle of beer, a hot drink or a bite to eat. Hummus and other salads with pitta and pickles are about US$2.50, hot vegetarian dishes from US$3.

Back on Jerusalem St, the *Café California* sounds interesting but the *Restaurant Pinati* is better – it's also open during Shabbat. They serve hummus, etc (US$2.50) or more substantial meals from about US$6.

Entertainment

The *Wolfson Community Center*, on HaPalmach St near the market, is the venue for occasional chamber music concerts throughout the year, and a musical workshop in the summer. The *Hotel Beit Yosef*, 2 Jerusalem St also stages musical and other cultural events. Check the tourist office for the schedules of any current local events.

Some of the art galleries are open during the evening and a stroll around the Old City can be pleasant.

Getting There & Away

Safed is about one hour from Tiberias by bus with buses every hour until 5.45 pm (4 pm Friday). There are other services to Haifa and Akko every half hour (two hours) until 9 pm (5.45 pm Friday), only three a day to Tel Aviv (otherwise change at Haifa) and only one a day to Jerusalem (otherwise change at Rosh Pinna).

Getting Around

Safed's centre is close enough to the central bus station and compact enough to walk around. To reach Mount Cana'an

take local Egged bus No 1, 1/3, 1/4 or 3; take No 2, 2A or 6 to South Safed.

AROUND SAFED

Meiron

This small Orthodox Jewish settlement lies nine km north-west of Safed and is the site of the tomb of Rabbi Shimon Bar Yochai, second century author of the Zohar. His son, Eleazar, is also buried here.

On the eve of Lag B'Omer crowds of Orthodox Jewish pilgrims take part in a traditional procession that starts in Safed's Synagogue Quarter and ends here at the tomb in Meiron.

Ancient Synagogue In the north of the village is the almost intact facade of a 2nd century synagogue.

Tomb of Rabbi Yohanan Hassandlar Nearby is the tomb of another great 2nd century sage, the Shoemaker. Not far from the grave is a cave where he supposedly worked as a cobbler.

Hillel's Cave The path leads down to another cave where it is believed that Hillel the Elder, a famous Jewish scholar who lived in Jerusalem in the 1st century BC, is buried with his disciples. The cave is often mentioned by medieval pilgrims.

Throne of the Messiah Beside the tombs of Rabbi Shimon and his son and Hillel's Cave lies a deep gorge. Beyond it, on top of the hill, is the tomb of Rabbi Shammai and the rock known as the Throne of the Messiah. According to tradition, when the Messiah comes he will sit on this rock and Elijah will blow a trumpet to announce the event.

Jish

This Arab village four km north of Meiron is notable because most of its inhabitants are of the Maronite faith and originally came from Lebanon. This was an important town, known as Gush Halaav

(Abundance of Milk), in ancient times. Yohanan, a leader of the Jewish Revolt against the Romans in 66 AD came from here, and the town was renowned for its olive oil.

Tombs of Shamai'a & Avtalion On the outskirts of the village are the tombs of these famous Jewish sages who taught in Jerusalem at the beginning of the 1st century.

Ancient Synagogue Remains of a 3rd or 4th century synagogue can be seen in a small valley two km east of the village.

Bar'am
In this 'abandoned' Arab village are the oldest and perhaps most impressive remains of an ancient synagogue in the country. Dated to the 2nd century, legend has it that Queen Esther is buried in the grounds here.

The Dead Sea

INTRODUCTION

A unique natural phenomenon, the Dead Sea is a major attraction for visitors. Well-known for its high salt density that makes it impossible for bathers to sink, the water contains many minerals that, along with the climate, provide various health-giving properties.

Over recent years the region has been developed as a health resort with a slowly increasing number of spas, clinics and hotels.

There are plenty of other things to see and do as well as floating and feeling good. There are the archaeological sites at Qumran where the Dead Sea Scrolls were found, and Masada, Herod's mountain-top fortress and the Jewish zealots' last stronghold in their revolt against Rome. Going back to nature, there is the outstanding scenery in the barren mountains of the Judean Desert to the west, and the mountains of Moab in Jordan to the east. A direct contrast to their surroundings are the lush green oases of the Ein Feshka and Ein Gedi nature reserves.

History

Awareness of the Dead Sea's unique qualities goes back to at least the 4th century BC when the Nabateans collected bitumen with special boats which swept bitumen from the surface. This was sold to the Egyptians, who used it for embalming, and written records show that this industry continued well into the Roman period. Such luminaries as Aristotle, Strabo, Pliny, Tacitus, Pausanius and Galen all mentioned the sea's physical properties.

During the Byzantine and Crusader periods there was a lot of marine traffic here but subsequent legends (eg that no birds could fly over it) inspired by a 'Sea of the Devil' label, which meant that it was left alone until the US Navy explored it in 1848. Ancient times also saw various religious ascetics and political fugitives choosing to hide out among the caves and the isolated mountain tops that surround the Dead Sea. The future King David, King Herod, Jesus and John the Baptist were among them.

However, the Dead Sea remained desolate and unexploited until the 1920s, when mineral exploitation began. Soon two plants were producing half of Britain's and most of the Commonwealth's potash needs. During the 1948 War of Independence, the Qalya plant was destroyed as that area fell to the Jordanians. The Sodom plant remained in Jewish hands despite a siege that lasted some months until the IDF eventually arrived.

Despite the mass immigration and the programme of consolidating the areas gained by the new Jewish State, the first few years after independence were not good for Israel's development of the region. About 75% of the Dead Sea was in Jordanian hands, as were the freshwater supply, the roads and a considerable part of the evaporation pans at Sodom. It took time for a new road and a new supply of fresh water to be provided to the plant and it was not until 1952 that work there was resumed.

The Israelis have not yet fully exploited the enormous potential here for money-spinning tourist and health facilities. The luxuries of modern roads and air-conditioned vehicles make it easy to overlook the fact the region is a barren desert with an inhospitable climate and physically cut off from the rest of Israel by mountains. The heat and aridity and the political factors – half the area is in the occupied West Bank – have all played their part in making Israel's planners leave the area alone, with more attention focused on the coastal plain, the north, and even on the Negev.

Dead Healthy

Compared to regular sea water, the water of the Dead Sea contains 20 times as much bromine, 15 times as much magnesium and 10 times as much iodine. Bromine, a component of many sedatives, relaxes the nerves, magnesium counteracts skin allergies and clears the bronchial passages while iodine has a beneficial effect on certain glandular functions. Various cosmetic companies produce ranges based on Dead Sea products because of their reputation for health and beauty rejuvenation.

The hot sulphur springs and mud deposits provide treatment for a variety of ailments. The heat, the concentration of salts on the skin and the enforced relaxation are all helpful, particularly for muscular and joint conditions such as rheumatism and arthritis, fractures, several skin diseases and for those who simply want to unwind and be indulged.

The Dead Sea air is extremely dry, the temperatures are high all year round, and rainfall averages only five cm a year. Due to the low altitude, there is 10% more oxygen in the air than at sea level, and the lack of urban development has kept it free of pollution. All of this increases the body's metabolic rate and has a bracing effect. The misty evaporation haze over the Dead Sea contains large amounts of the water's bromine and this supposedly has a soothing effect.

Despite the high temperatures and around 300 cloudless days a year, the high atmospheric pressure filters the sun's burning ultra-violet rays which makes it harder to get sunburn. The intense, naturally filtered sunlight is used to help cure psoriasis, a severe skin disease.

Despite all the talk there are some who have found that the Dead Sea makes them feel ill rather than healthy. Certainly the water does have a few qualities that are not too appealing.

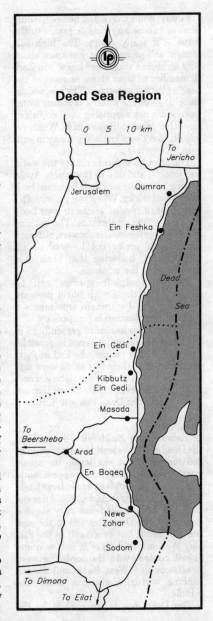

Firstly, don't shave just before bathing here, or expose any cuts or grazes to the water – it really stings. The high salt content will probably let you know about tiny scratches you never knew you had. Remember to wear shoes as most of the beaches have sharp stones. The magnesium chloride gives the water a revolting bitter taste – it's not surprising that no fish or any other organic life live in it. Whatever you do, don't swallow it or get any in your eyes.

The calcium chloride makes the water feel smooth and oily to the touch. Avoid getting your hair wet as it becomes both smelly and sticky. When you get out after your float, a residue sticks to your body that many find unpleasant. The bathing beaches have freshwater showers, although some locals prefer not to wash it off immediately, believing that their skin benefits from the minerals.

The hot sulphur springs can be dangerous to those with blood pressure problems and for certain treatments a medical examination is compulsory.

Although it is harder to get sunburn in the Dead Sea region, it is not impossible. I met a few pink people who had wrongly presumed that their fair skins were safe and didn't use a sunscreen – so be warned. Also, if you are even a little bit sunburned, don't go into the Dead Sea – it hurts.

Geography

In Hebrew *Yam HaMelah* – Sea of Salt, the Dead Sea is the world's lowest point at 386 metres below sea level. Its actual water level fluctuates but its approximate total size at present is 65 km in length and 18 km across at its widest point. After the 1948 War of Independence only about a quarter of the Dead Sea fell to the new State of Israel, but as a result of the Six-Day War, almost half of it is now under Jewish control, with the border between Israel/occupied West Bank and Jordan running virtually straight down the middle.

The Dead Sea is fed mainly by the Jordan River, supplemented by smaller rivers, underground springs and floods. With no outlet, the inflow of water is balanced by a high rate of evaporation due to the constant hot temperature. The water arrives with normal mineral concentrations (mainly magnesium, sodium, calcium and potassium chlorides) but the evaporation causes them to rise dramatically. The water's salt concentration is about 30% (compared to 4% for ordinary sea water) making it easy to sit up in and comfortably read this book.

The original lake was four or five times the size of today's Dead Sea and in the early 19th century it was about as low as it is now. Fluctuations in the water level were once due only to natural conditions, mainly the variation in the rainfall. With the construction of Israel's National Water Carrier system, the natural balancing act of the Dead Sea was disturbed. Inspired by the Israelis, the Jordanians built a similar project on the Yarmuk River, and together the two neighbours have deprived the Dead Sea of over 600 million cubic metres of water per year. This has resulted in the Dead Sea's southern basin drying up completely and the length of the sea has been shortened by over 25 km.

Today, all the water to the south of Masada is being pumped there by the Dead Sea Works Ltd on the Israeli side, and by the Arabic Potash Corporation on the Jordanian side – you will see the canals dug into the dried out sea-bed.

There are two very different sections of the Dead Sea. The northern basin is over three times the size of the southern one, and a lot deeper – about 400 metres. The southern basin is only about six metres deep and has a higher salt level which creates iceberg-like crystal formations. Now completely separating the two sections is the Lashon (Tongue) Peninsula which juts out from the Jordanian eastern shore.

Both the Israelis and the Jordanians exploit the Dead Sea's mineral wealth which supplies vast amounts of raw chemicals for industry, agriculture and medicine. Of the various minerals extracted here, potash (used as an agricultural fertiliser), is the most important, followed by bromine, magnesium chloride and industrial and table salts. More recent industrial developments here include solar energy power stations using salt ponds to absorb and store the sun's heat.

An ambitious project to build a Mediterranean Sea-Dead Sea Canal was proposed a few years ago. This involved digging a water conduit over 100 km long with a pumping station and a hydro-electric power station, powered by the steep descent down to the the Dead Sea. The aim of the project was to maintain the level of the Dead Sea, provide water to be used in further developing the Arava Valley and provide additional electricity. The project has been revised, and a Red Sea-Dead Sea Canal is now being planned.

Getting There & Away
Although you can reach the Dead Sea by direct bus from Haifa, Tel Aviv, Beersheba, Arad, Dimona and Eilat, the most comprehensive service is from Jerusalem's central bus station. Note that the buses stop on request at all the major sites. It is important, however, that you keep a sharp eye out for the place that you want. The Egged drivers speed along so fast that you can fly past Qumran or Ein Feshka, for example, without realising it.

In Jerusalem, the Old City tourist office is a better place to go for the current Dead Sea bus schedules than the hectic central bus station.

On Saturday no buses operate until the late afternoon. The only exception is a bus that runs from Beersheba for Ein Gedi at 7 am, stopping on the way at Arad at 7.45 am and Masada at 8.30 am.

'Doing the Dead'
Before setting off to visit the Dead Sea, there are several factors to be considered

that will greatly affect your enjoyment of the area.

Many travellers make the big mistake of regarding the Dead Sea as simply one place to visit. Instead, it covers a fairly large area with different things to see and do at various widespread points. Unless you have your own car or take an organised tour, you are dependent on the buses which do not run as frequently as you might like. Also, it is important to realise that with the area still in the early stages of development, there is a shortage of inexpensive places to stay and places to eat. Finally, the hot climate makes it even more essential that you arrange things so that you are not waiting endlessly for a bus, rushing around trying to cram in all the places that you want to visit, or having to pay more than you can really afford for accommodation and food.

Enjoying the sensation of floating in its water is the major attraction of the Dead Sea. The nicest place for this is the well-kept sandy beach at En Boqeq by the main hotel area, or at Hamme Zohar, a little further south. However, if you are short of time you may be better off using the beach at Ein Gedi.

After the obligatory float, the next popular thing to do is to visit Masada. Coming a close third is the Ein Gedi nature reserve. Those with only a day to spare can just about manage to fit it all in providing they plan ahead, start early and catch the right buses. Beat the heat and go to Masada first, then have a float before visiting the nature reserve.

Visits to Qumran and Ein Feshka come lower on the scale of 'musts' for most people, although they are worth a visit if you have the time.

You can help yourself to free Dead Sea mud when you go floating, otherwise you need more time and more sheqels to use the hot springs and clinics.

Deciding where to stay in the Dead Sea region or even whether to stay here at all is another dilemma, particularly for shoestring travellers. The IYHA youth hostels at Ein Gedi and Masada are by far the cheapest places, but they are over double the price of private hostels in nearby Jerusalem, so many choose to sleep rough, either on the beach at Ein Gedi or atop Masada à la zealot. Remember that by paying in US dollars, you save on the 15% VAT at IYHA hostels. Others choose to make day trips from Jerusalem, but the cost of the return bus fares and the extra travelling time should be taken into account. There are also camp sites at Ein Gedi and Newe Zohar but they are hardly cheaper than the hostels, nor is the Ein Gedi field school which is usually filled by SPNI members anyway. For those with good-hotel budgets, there are several choices at En Boqeq, Hamme Zohar, Newe Zohar, or the kibbutz guest house at Ein Gedi.

As with accommodation, there is a distinct shortage of inexpensive food in the Dead Sea region – to save a small fortune bring plenty of food. There are no supermarkets or grocery stores and the cheapest place to eat is the café at Hamme Zohar, hardly worth a special trip. Elsewhere, the self-service restaurants at the various sites provide unexciting snacks and meals from about US$4. By comparison, the basic but filling meals dished up by the IYHA hostels are excellent value.

Lastly, try to avoid the Dead Sea at weekends and holidays when it can be unpleasantly crowded.

Orientation

The entire west coast of the Dead Sea, about 90 km in length, is accessible from Israel. This is served by a single main road that starts in the north from the main Jerusalem-bound highway, and follows the shore line southwards to Sodom, continuing to Eilat, with intersections heading west to Beersheba via Arad and Dimona. Some of the distances you will travel are:

Jerusalem-Qumran	40 km
Qumran-Ein Feshka	3 km
Ein Feshka-Ein Gedi Nature Reserve	34 km
Ein Gedi Nature Reserve-Ein Gedi Kibbutz	2 km
Ein Gedi Kibbutz-Hamme Mazor	2½ km
Hamme Mazor-Masada	15 km
Masada-En Boqeq	15 km
En Boqeq-Hamme Zohar	3 km
Hamme Zohar-Newe Zohar	1½ km
Newe Zohar-Sodom	12 km
Sodom-Beersheba	78 km
Sodom-Eilat	185 km

The road from the Jerusalem-bound highway intersects with the shore-side road that runs down from the outskirts of Jericho from the east via Qalya, with its collection of crumbling remains of the old potash industrial plant, a Jordanian military camp and holiday centre. It now all belongs to the nearby Kibbutz Qalya and plans are afoot to develop it as a major resort. The road continues southwards towards Qumran and passes through a not particularly appealing section of shore. In the distance are black and red-hued mountains. Up here is the Qumran archaeological site with the excavations of the Essene settlement and caves. Continuing southwards, you come to the Ein Feshka nature reserve with its fresh-water pools and bathing beach.

Ein Gedi is the next major place of interest. The attractions are spread out over four km and they all answer to the name of Ein Gedi, so it is important to get off the bus at the right place to avoid a long, hot walk or wait. The nature reserves, field school and youth hostel are to the north, on the west side of the road. Next stop, one km further south, are the bathing beach, restaurant and camp site. Another 2½ km to the south is the turn-off for Kibbutz Ein Gedi, with the Hamme Mazor sulphur baths 2½ km beyond.

The archaeological site of Masada is at the end of a side road, overlooking the area where the Dead Sea is divided in two by the receding water level. There are restaurants and a youth hostel.

Back on the shore road and continuing south, you come to the pleasant En Boqeq area. Having the nicest beach on the Dead Sea, it is the region's most developed site, with hotels, restaurants and medical clinics. Another three km further south is the Hamme Zohar section. This features the top of the range Moriah Dead Sea Spa Hotel with its own beach and comprehensive medical and health facilities. Just south of the hotel are the Hamme Zohar Thermal Baths, the Kupat Holim Hot Springs and another nice beach.

Another 1½ km leads to Newe Zohar, a sparse, messy area with new and old buildings including a hotel and museum. Beyond here is the Arad junction, with the main road continuing to Sodom, past the Dead Sea Works Ltd plant.

QUMRAN

The Dead Sea Scrolls have been described as 'the most important discovery in the history of the Jewish people'. In early 1947, a Bedouin shepherd accidentally found them stored inside some earthenware jars in the caves here. They are now on display at the Shrine of the Book, part of the Israel Museum in Jerusalem.

Subsequent excavations revealed the community centre of the Essenes, a Jewish sect. They lived in the nearby caves (and in tents and underground chambers) from about 150 BC until 68 AD, when the Romans dispersed them. The area was inhabited as early as the 8th century BC by the Israelites, but was abandoned because of an earthquake. The Essenes lived communally, with a farm on the plain above the cliffs. Some of them worked the land and tended sheep, others made pottery or wrote. Most of their time was taken up by studying the Old Testament and other religious literature. They chose to settle here to get away from the Jewish establishment which was too liberal for them.

For a good view of the settlement, head for the tower. From here you can see the aqueduct, channels and cistern systems that ensured the water supply. Elsewhere is a refectory, a council chamber, the scriptorium where the Dead Sea Scrolls were probably written, ritual baths, a pottery workshop with kilns, and a cemetery.

The caves themselves are higher up and none of those in which the Dead Sea Scrolls were found are marked. If you interrogate the ticket office staff you might be given accurate directions. Give yourself about two hours for the return climb and take plenty of water.

The site is open Saturday to Thursday 8 am to 5 pm, Friday 8 am to 4 pm. Admission is US$1.75, students 80c. The bus stops on the main road; follow the turn-off up the hill. There is a self-service cafeteria at the site.

EIN FESHKA

Also known as Einot Zuqim (Spring of Cliffs), this nature reserve offers bathing in both freshwater pools and the Dead Sea, with a sandy beach nearby. Difficult to imagine, and often made to sound more attractive than it actually looks, Ein Feshka is an area of salt-encrusted reeds and grass, with several small pools of spring water, leading down to the Dead Sea shore. Various animals can be found here, from the fish in the pools to the ibex and hyrax that frequent the area. The pools tend to become a bit murky by the middle of the day and when there are crowds of people here there's not much room.

The reserve is open daily, April to October 8 am to 5 pm, November to March 8 am to 4 pm. Admission is US$3. There is a cafeteria and snack bar in the reserve.

EIN GEDI

One of the most attractive desert oases in the country, Ein Gedi (Spring of the Kid), has been developed by the Israelis into a major tourist site. There are two adjoining nature reserves that preserve the lush area of freshwater springs, waterfalls, pools and tropical vegetation to provide beauty spots and a haven for desert wildlife. Rich in biblical history as well, there are ancient remains of the early settlements here. The beach is one of the Dead Sea's most popular, although this is due more to its proximity to the oasis than to its own qualities – it's rocky rather than sandy.

The youth hostel, field school, camp site, restaurant and kibbutz all make Ein Gedi a popular base from which to enjoy the region.

Field School
Operated by the SPNI, this complex above the youth hostel features a small museum of local flora and fauna, a study centre and a hostel.

Nahal David Nature Reserve
This is the place that most people associate with Ein Gedi – a pretty canyon in the desert overlooking the Dead Sea, with lots of trees, plants, flowers, animals and David's Waterfall. Compared to some of the country's other great natural beauty spots, Ein Gedi can seem a little tame, with signposts and paths everywhere. What can really ruin it though, are the loud crowds of visitors at weekends and holidays.

The area was first settled during the Chalcolithic Age (3000 BC) when tribes just out of the Stone Age worshipped in a temple on the plateau just above the waterfall. I Samuel 24 tells of the encounter between David and Saul at Ein Gedi which suggests that the site was unoccupied at that time. Israelites did settle here later, at the end of the 7th century BC, and Ein Gedi is mentioned in Solomon's 'Song of Songs' (1:14). Occupation continued through the Persian, Hellenistic, Roman and Byzantine periods, up to the early Muslim period. The income provided by agriculture was supplemented by the sale of salt and bitumen extracted from the Dead Sea.

The entrance to the reserve is beyond

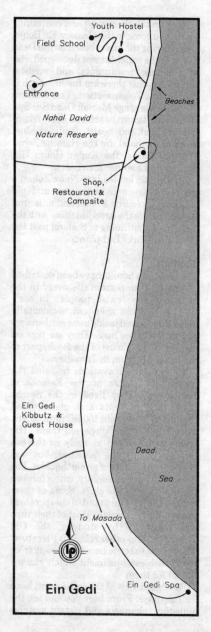

Youth Hostel

Field School

Entrance

Nahal David
Nature Reserve

Beaches

Shop,
Restaurant &
Campsite

Ein Gedi
Kibbutz &
Guest House

Dead

Sea

To Masada

Ein Gedi Spa

Ein Gedi

the car park at the end of the turn-off, past the road leading up to the youth hostel and field school. Once inside, follow signs to David's Waterfall – about a 15 minute walk. From here, follow the path around to head back towards the Dead Sea and pass another path leading up the slope. Climb up to reach the Shulamit Spring at the top of the cliff. Just past where the water bubbles out of the ground the path splits. To the right it leads to Dodim (Lovers') Cave, just above the waterfall in a lovely setting. Give yourself about 40 minutes to walk there and back. To the left, the steep path leads up to the fenced-in Chalcolithic Temple ruins – about a 10 minute climb.

Continuing down the slope, signs point to the Ein Gedi Spring. After about 25 minutes you come to it, surrounded by trees and reeds. Find your way through these to join another path. Go left to return to the main entrance, or go right to Tel Goren, the remains of the first Israelite settlement here. After another 20 minutes, you pass traces of ancient agricultural systems, including a watermill. Beyond Tel Goren is a ruined ancient synagogue (2nd or 3rd century BC). Continue down to the road and either turn right to reach the Nahal Arugot Nature Reserve by the car park or turn left to reach the main road, a 15 minute walk. From here it's a 10 minute walk northwards along the shore to the main entrance.

The Nahal David Nature Reserve is open daily 8 am to 4 pm. Admission is US$1.75. You can leave heavy bags at the entrance. Eating is not allowed in the reserve and you must keep to the paths.

Nahal Arugot Nature Reserve For those with more time and more energy, this adjacent site provides another lovely waterfall. Follow the road up to the car park for the start to the trail. Allow about 1½ hours for the hike. Admission is free.

Beach The public beach is beyond the petrol station and shops. The adjacent camping resort has a more pleasant private beach – non-residents can use it for US$2.75.

Hamme Mazor Further south, these therapeutic bathing facilities use hot sulphuric water from nearby mineral springs. There is a beach here, and a restaurant. Also called Ein Gedi Hot Springs, the complex belongs to the adjacent kibbutz whose guest house residents have the use of the facilities included in their room and board – non-residents pay from about US$7.

Places to Stay
You can sleep for free by the beach, otherwise the *Beit Sara IYHA Youth Hostel* (tel 84165) charges members/non-members US$10/12, with breakfast. Reception is open 7 to 9 am and 5 to 7 pm. Dinner costs about US$4 and is served from 7 to 8 pm.

The hostel at the field school (tel 84288, 84350) is usually full; reservations can be made here, or at SPNI offices.

Back by the beach, the *Ein Gedi Camping Resort* (tel 84347), has tent space for US$5.50 per person and cabins for doubles for US$42, plus $12.50 for each extra person.

The guest house at Kibbutz Ein Gedi (tel 84757/8) is one of the most popular around, with its combination of location and facilities. Surrounded by the patches of green trees and crops grown by the kibbutzniks, with gardens, a swimming pool and the Hamme Mazor hot springs all included in the price, it gives value for money. Terms are full board only, about US$50 per person. Note that guests clean out their own rooms.

Places to Eat
The best value, apart from self-catering, is the youth hostel. The self-service restaurant by the camping ground serves basic food at prices which are reasonable, but still too high for many travellers. A wide range of snacks and meals, hot and

cold, are available here. There is a similar establishment at the Hamme Mazor hot springs.

MASADA

Combining a spectacular setting with a dramatic history, the mountain-top fortress of Masada is well up on the list of 'musts' for visitors to Israel.

In Hebrew *Metzuda* (Stronghold), the summit was first fortified by Alexander Jannaeus (103-76 BC) to defend his southeastern border. Herod the Great took it in 43 BC and, inspired by his fears of either a Jewish revolt or Cleopatra of Egypt having him killed by Mark Anthony, he had this formidable and luxurious palace refuge built around 35 BC. It included a casement wall around the summit, defence towers, storehouses, an advanced water storage system, barracks, arsenals, public baths, and palaces with swimming pools. With its desert location, steep ascent, and elaborate fortifications, Masada is impressive.

Herod died without needing to call on it. In 66 AD the First Revolt started when a group of Jewish zealots captured the fortress from the Romans, who had occupied it since Herod's death in 4 AD. Masada played no major role in the revolt itself. Raids were carried out on surrounding villages, and it became a refuge with the original zealots joined by their families and other refugees from the fighting.

The revolt ended in 70 AD when the Romans captured Jerusalem. Masada, however, remained under the control of the zealots for another three years, not deemed an immediate threat to the authorities. Eventually the Romans advanced on the fortress, determined to capture what was now the last Jewish stronghold in Palestine. With eight camps around the base of the mountain and up to 15,000 men, Flavius Silva laid siege. There were 967 men, women and children atop Masada.

After the Romans had built a ramp on the western side and managed to reach the defence wall, the zealots knew that defeat was near and, rather than surrender, they chose to commit mass suicide. Taking lots, 10 were chosen to kill all the others, then nine of them killed themselves leaving the survivor to set fire to the palace before killing himself. Food had been stacked up in the courtyard to show that the zealots had not died because of starvation. When the Romans stormed the complex, they found two women and five children who had survived by hiding and were able to tell them what had happened. With all the other Jews expelled by Titus when he captured Jerusalem, this was the end of that era of the Jewish presence in Palestine. In the 4th to 5th centuries, Byzantine monks occupied the site.

Although there was a written record of the zealots' defeat, courtesy of the historian Josephus, Masada's location had been forgotten and it was not until the early 19th century that it was found again. In 1807 it was seen from a boat on the Dead Sea, but not identified, in 1838 it was seen from Ein Gedi and identified correctly, and in 1842 it was climbed for the first time. Various small excavations took place during the late 1950s, and in 1963 a major programme commenced. The site was not only excavated and preserved, but partially rebuilt – a black line distinguishes ancient from modern.

Masada today is used as a symbol for the modern State of Israel with the oath that 'Masada shall not fall again'. Israeli schoolchildren visit the site as a part of their curriculum and some units of the IDF hold their swearing-in ceremonies here.

The various remains are signposted; a detailed book is available and is good value. Depending on your level of interest in archaeology, you could be up here for hours.

To reach the top you can take the cable car or climb up either of the two footpaths. The cable car operates daily from 8 am with the last one returning from the top at

Eilat, Israel's toehold on the Red Sea (RE – top, NT – Bottom)

Top: The wilderness of Zin, Negev (NT)
Bottom: Makhtesh Ramon, Negev (NT)

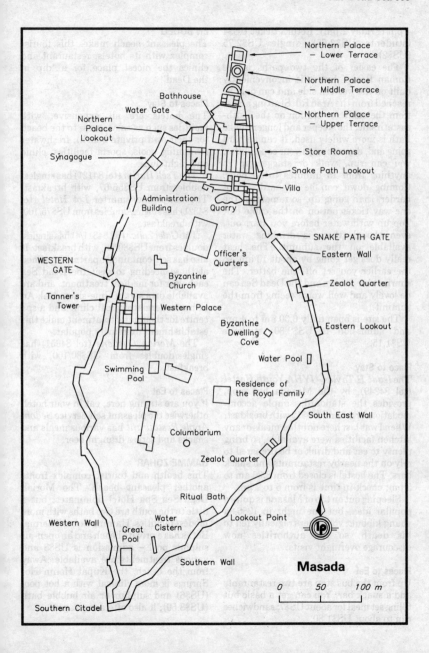

Masada

Northern Palace – Lower Terrace
Northern Palace – Middle Terrace
Northern Palace – Upper Terrace

Bathhouse
Water Gate

Northern Palace Lookout

Synagogue

Store Rooms
Snake Path Lookout
Villa

Administration Building

Quarry

SNAKE PATH GATE
Eastern Wall

Officer's Quarters

Byzantine Church

WESTERN GATE

Tanner's Tower

Western Palace

Zealot Quarter

Eastern Lookout

Byzantine Dwelling Cove

Water Pool

Swimming Pool

Residence of the Royal Family

South East Wall

Columbarium

Zealot Quarter

Ritual Bath

Water Cistern

Lookout Point

Western Wall

Great Pool

Southern Wall

Southern Citadel

0   50   100 m

4 pm (Friday 2 pm). Return ticket US$4 (students US$2.65), single US$2.75 (US$2).

The easier of the two paths is the Roman Ramp, but it is inconveniently built on the western side and can only be reached from the Arad Rd. Starting across from the cable car station on the southeastern side, the steeper and longer Snake Path is more widely used. It can be hard going and, depending on your capabilities, you can run, walk or stagger up in anything from 15 minutes to an hour. Coming down can be as hard, if not harder, than going up, so remember the one-way ticket option on the cable car. Top up with water before you start out, even though there is drinking water available on the summit. The heat really does get going by about 10 am, so the earlier you set off, the better. The sunrise over Jordan and the Dead Sea can be lovely and well worth seeing from the summit.

The site is open daily 6.30 am to 4 pm and admission is US$2.30, students US$1.15.

Place to Stay

The *Isaac H Taylor – IYHA Youth Hostel* (tel 84349), by the Masada bus stop, provides the standard, simple accommodation for around US$12 with breakfast. When I was last here no other meals or any kitchen facilities were available, so bring plenty to eat and drink or be prepared to rely on the nearby restaurants and snack bars. The hostel is closed from 8.30 am to 5 pm; check-in time is from 5 to 7 pm.

Sleeping out on top of Masada is quite a popular idea, but one night in 1986, a young kibbutz volunteer tragically fell to his death, so the authorities now discourage overnight visits.

Places to Eat

Up from the bus stop are two restaurants and a snack bar. You can get a basic but filling set meal for about US$7; sandwiches run to about US$1.80.

EN BOQEQ

The pleasant beach makes this tourist complex with its hotels, restaurant and clinics the nicest place for a 'dip in the Dead'.

Places to Stay

The hotels are all expensive, with facilities such as easy access to the beach (or their own private beach), freshwater swimming pools, sports facilities, clinic and nightclubs.

The *Tsell Harim* (tel 84121) has singles/doubles from US$56/67, with breakfast. The newer and smarter *Lot Hotel* (tel 84321) has singles/doubles from US$75/100, with breakfast.

The *Galei Zohar* (tel 84311/4) has singles/doubles from US$80/95, with breakfast. It also has self-contained apartments aimed at those needing to visit the Dead Sea each year for medical treatment, and are available on a sort of time-share deal. An in-house dermatological clinic and a spa centre for rheumatic treatment make this establishment extremely popular.

The *Moriah Gardens* (tel 84351) has singles/doubles from US$80/100, with breakfast.

Places to Eat

If you are staying here, eat in your hotel, otherwise the pleasant self-service *Sedom Apple Restaurant* has various meals and snacks and serves draught beer.

HAMME ZOHAR

This health and tourist complex fronts another pleasant beach. The Moriah Dead Sea Spa Hotel dominates, but a little to the south are two baths with more modest facilities. Hamme Zohar Thermal Baths has a private beach and an open-air sulphur pool – admission is US$3 and various treatments are available. Away from the beach, the Kupat Holim Hot Springs is more clinical with a hot pool (US$6) and sulphur or air bubble bath (US$8.50); it also offers massages.

Salt crystals, The Dead Sea

Place to Stay

The luxury *Moriah Dead Sea Spa Hotel* (tel 84221/2) is where many of the promotional photos for the Dead Sea are taken. The private beach with freshwater pool, indoor seawater pool and other spa facilities, along with the tennis court, cinema and nightclub all make this the place to stay on the Dead Sea. Singles/doubles go for US$80/100 plus.

Places to Eat

In direct contrast to the trappings of its five-star neighbour, the unassuming café next door is the cheapest on the Dead Sea. Nothing exciting, just snacks including sandwiches (75c) and bottled beer (90c).

NEWE ZOHAR

This messy development of buildings is the 'regional centre' for the Dead Sea with administration offices, emergency services, museum, camp site and hotel.

Bet HaYotzer Museum

Also known as the Dead Sea Museum, this was established under the auspices of the Dead Sea Works Ltd and shows the geographic make-up of the Dead Sea, its history and industrial development. At the time of writing, the museum was only open by appointment with the Dead Sea Works Ltd (tel 665111) but the management of the adjacent Dead Sea Hotel seemed to have access too, so you can ask there.

Places to Stay

Newe Zohar Camping (tel 84306) offers basic but friendly facilities and judging by the satisfied comments in the guests book those who stay here are not bothered by the relative isolation and the barren surroundings. Tent space is US$5 per person, and there are self-contained two-person caravans for around US$18. A restaurant and bar provide decent food and drink.

Extremely good value is the *Dead Sea Hotel* (tel 84248), which provides the cheapest hotel accommodation on the Dead Sea. The rooms and facilities are very pleasant – the only drawbacks are the unattractive surroundings and its distance from the beach. If you are relying on buses this is a problem, but the management will drive you to Hamme Zohar or En Boqeq in the morning on request. Singles/doubles cost from US$25/36 including breakfast, and there is a dining room.

SODOM

Dominated by the unsightly Dead Sea Works Ltd plant, this area is traditionally thought to be the site of Sodom and Gomorrah, the wicked biblical cities that God destroyed with fire and brimstone (Genesis 18, 19). However, they were probably located further east in what is now Jordan. The reasons for today's industrial activity are highlighted by the salty surroundings. The interesting sights are well off the beaten track, with only the infrequent Eilat buses passing by, so you either need to have your own car or to take an organised tour – the SPNI offer some of the best.

Sodom Mountain & Caves

This 11 km by three km mountain range is 98% salt. In most climates, salt dissolves and disappears, but in the dry Dead Sea region these salt rocks remain. The run-off water that collects on the surface cuts through to form a series of potholes that drain into a maze of caves. The largest of these is next to a noticeable salt rock formation that has been dubbed 'Mrs Lot' in reference to Lot's wife who was turned into a pillar of salt for looking back at God's destruction (Genesis 19:26). Access to these caves is only possible with a guide, due to the danger of avalanches – contact the SPNI or a tourist office.

Nahal Prazim & Flour Cave This is an interesting canyon carved out of soft limestone into a variety of shapes by water currents. The Flour Cave is so called because of its powdery chalk lining.

The Negev

The Negev Desert accounts for almost two-thirds of Israel's land area. Its name means 'dry land' and it is far from being simply an expanse of sand. Starting by the Dead Sea where the Judean Desert ends, the northern Negev is a region of low sandstone hills, steppes and fertile plains with canyons and wadis. Moving south, the central Negev is drier and more mountainous: an area of bare rocky peaks, lofty plateaus and more canyons and wadis. The most outstanding features are the world's three largest craters, caused by millions of years of erosion. The Arava Valley is an extremely parched stretch of land to the east on the Israel-Jordan border. At the Negev's southern tip are the grey-red Eilat Mountains and beyond is Egypt's Sinai Desert of which the Negev is, geographically speaking, a natural extension.

Most of the Negev remains largely uninhabited and there are only a handful of towns. However, the harsh environment is dotted with an increasing number of Jewish settlements, mainly kibbutzim and moshavim but also 'Nahal' military projects (military service combined with agricultural work in marginal areas). Established somewhat longer are the estimated 25,000 Bedouin who still live in tents and breed camels and livestock. The Israeli Government seems to be trying to lure them away from their nomadic traditions by providing permanent housing and welfare facilities. You will hear more, though, about the progress made by the Jewish settlers in their bid to make the desert 'bloom'.

David Ben Gurion, Israel's first prime minister and dubbed 'father of the Negev', was one of the first to publicly recognise the strategic importance and economic potential of the region. Under his leadership a development programme of sorts was launched with the basic aim of transforming a wilderness where nothing grows into much needed farmland. One of Ben Gurion's many popular quotes was, 'If the State does not put an end to the desert, the desert may put an end to the State.'

Settlements were established in the middle of nowhere and after much painstaking trial and error results have been achieved. As you travel around the desert you will suddenly come across agricultural oases where the water piped down from the Sea of Galilee has been put to good use.

The Negev is often ignored by visitors or simply seen through a bus window en route to Eilat. However, there are several places just a short distance away from the main roads that are well worth a visit – spectacular natural beauty spots, archaeological sites and the Black Hebrews' settlement in Dimona.

Major roads in the Negev are limited to two highways heading south to Eilat – the one from the Dead Sea is the most direct and the fastest, the other from Beersheba goes via Sde Boker, Avdat and Mitzpe Ramon. Linking the Dead Sea and Beersheba is a road via Arad and another via Dimona.

With the Sinai Desert back under Egyptian control, the Negev has become the 'playground' of the IDF. Military manoeuvres, both on the ground and in the air, regularly contribute to the scenery and soldiers are everywhere.

The Negev is a harsh desert, but due to its rapid development visitors can easily be lulled into a false sense of security and forget to follow guidelines for safety in a desert environment. It really is best to make an early start and to avoid physical exertion in the middle of the day (say 12 noon to 3 pm) – and be sure to cover your head and drink plenty of water. Presumably due to the demands of IDF personnel, bus

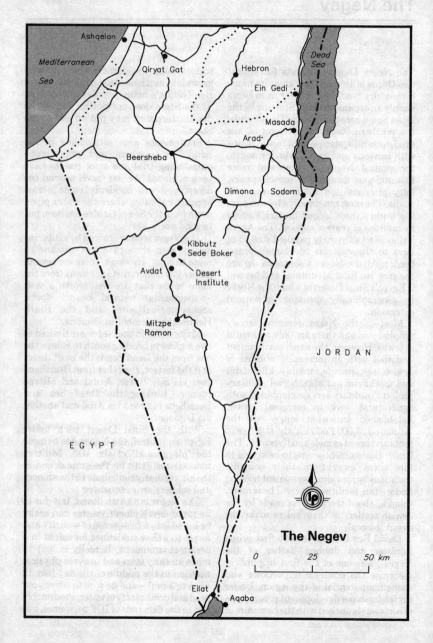

The Negev

0   25   50 km

services pass by most of the places of interest – check the timetables to avoid too much waiting around. Hitch-hiking is possible, if perhaps more dangerous than elsewhere in Israel.

ARAD (population 13,600)

On the road between Beersheba (48 km) and the Dead Sea (28 km), Arad is a new town even by Israeli standards. Established in 1961 after the discovery of natural gas, Arad is one of the more attractive of Israel's pre-planned towns, with pedestrian and motor traffic separated as much as possible in residential quarters. Situated on a high plateau (620 metres above sea level) it has commanding views of the desert and in the distance the Dead Sea.

Renowned for its cool, dry and pollen-free air, the town is promoted as an ideal health resort for those suffering from asthmatic and respiratory difficulties. However, Arad offers nothing much to either see or do and so most people limit any time spent here to changing buses en route to or from the Dead Sea.

Orientation

On Yehuda St, Arad's bus station is easy to miss as there is no actual building, just a hut. Look instead for the police station next door. Across the street is the pedestrianised commercial centre with shops, eating places, the tourist office, banks, post office and a cinema.

If you choose to stay overnight the youth hostel is just a five minute walk to the east, as is one of the hotels.

Information

Tourist Office The IGTO (tel 958144) is in the commercial centre, and is open Sunday to Thursday 9 am to 12 noon and 5 to 8 pm, Friday 9 am to 12 noon, closed Saturday.

Post Office & International Telephones These are in the commercial centre and are open Sunday to Thursday 7.45 am to 2 pm, Friday 7.45 am to 12 noon.

Other There are banks in the commercial centre. East of the commercial centre, off Yehuda St on HaSport St is an outdoor and an indoor pool. The police station (tel 957044 or 100) is next door to the bus station on Yehuda St.

Things to See

In Arad itself there are no real sights. In the industrial quarter to the south, the Abir Riding School (tel 954147) offers horse-riding facilities and there is a pleasant viewpoint at the far eastern end of Ben Yair and Moav St, by the Masada Hotel.

Opposite the tourist office, the Matnas Cultural Center hosts various activities including folk dancing, chess, bridge and a youth club. The Orion Cinema in the commercial centre is another possible source of entertainment.

Places to Stay

The IYHA's *Blau Weiss Youth Hostel* (tel 957150) is on the corner of HaPalmach and Atad Sts. From the bus station walk east (past the police station) up Yehuda St, and follow the signs to turn right on HaPalmach. It's clean and quiet with kitchen facilities and meals are available. Dorm beds cost US$9.50 and meals are available. It's closed 9 am to 5 pm but there's no curfew.

The nearby *Arad Hotel* (tel 957040) is basic but clean and comfortable – singles/doubles are US$25/42, with breakfast. Dinner costs US$10. There are a couple of more expensive hotels two km further east and each has a swimming pool: the *Nof Arad* (tel 957056/7) and the *Margoa* (tel 957014) which has a clinic for the climatic treatment of asthma.

Arad's top hotel is the four star *Masada* (tel 957140, 957260) which charges only about the same as its competitors. Singles/doubles cost from US$35/47, with breakfast.

Places to Eat

The commercial centre is where you will

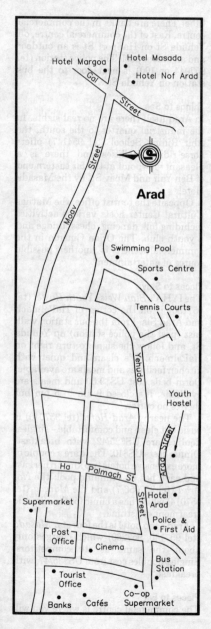

Arad

Hotel Margoa

Hotel Masada

Hotel Nof Arad

Gal Street

Moav Street

Swimming Pool

Sports Centre

Tennis Courts

Yehuda Street

Youth Hostel

Arad Street

Ha Palmach St

Supermarket

Hotel Arad

Police & First Aid

Post Office

Cinema

Bus Station

Tourist Office

Banks

Cafés

Co-op Supermarket

find what Arad has to offer. There are two supermarkets, the Co-op across from the bus station and Supersol across from the tourist office. Various unexciting places sell felafel, pizza, etc, or you can spend more and eat at one of the sit-down cafés.

Getting There & Away

With only a few buses connecting Beersheba to the Dead Sea, you will often have to change at Arad. From here there are fairly frequent buses to Masada (45 minutes), Ein Gedi (one hour) and Beersheba (45 minutes). Remember that on Saturday morning a special bus runs from Beersheba to Ein Gedi via Arad and Masada. Egged provide this service primarily for the locals who would otherwise be unable to benefit from the Dead Sea's health facilities.

AROUND ARAD
Tel Arad

Although this is the country's best example of an Early Bronze Age city, only the keen archaeologists will find Tel Arad worth a visit, due to its inconvenient location some 10 km west of modern Arad.

First mentioned in the Old Testament accounts of the Israelites' attempts to penetrate into the Promised Land from the south (Numbers 21:1-3, 33:40, Joshua 12:14), ancient Arad was an important fortress guarding the southern approaches to the country.

Covering several hectares, the excavations are clearly marked and an information leaflet is available (30c). They are open April to September, Saturday to Thursday 8 am to 5 pm, Friday 8 am to 4 pm, October to March Saturday to Thursday 8 am to 4 pm, Friday 8 am to 3 pm. Admission is US$1, students 65c.

Getting There & Away
Buses running between Arad and Beersheba pass the orange signposted turn-off for Tel Arad – from here it's a two km walk.

BEERSHEBA (population 114,300)
Not a particularly attractive town for
visitors, with little in the way of
impressive sights, Beersheba is the
'capital' of the Negev and the region's
transportation hub. It is a good example of
the progress made by Israel in developing
the desert. In 1948 this was just a village
with some 2000 inhabitants and in the
middle of nowhere. Today's urban sprawl
of drab apartment blocks surrounded by
dusty gardens belies the fact that this is a
'frontier town' in a truly harsh environment.

History
Beersheba is mentioned several times in
the Old Testament in its definition of the
limits of ancient Israel: 'from Dan to
Beersheba' (Judges 20:1, I Samuel 3:20, II
Samuel 3:10, 17:11, 24:2). It is an
important town because of its association
with the Patriarchs: the name is explained
by Genesis 21:25-33 as meaning 'the well
of the seven' or 'the well of the oath' in its
account of Abraham's treaty with Abimelek
the Philistine.

The Patriarchs lived and worked in the
surrounding area which was later assigned
to the tribe of Simeon. However, its history
goes further back, as far as 4000 BC and
the Chalcolithic Age. Excavations reveal
that these people, who had introduced
domesticated sheep to the Negev and
moved away in about 3000 BC, were
skilled at crafts.

David built a fortified town here, on the
site of a small fort erected by his
predecessor Saul, during his campaign
against the Amalekites (I Samuel 14:48,
15:29). The ancient site is almost five km
north-east of the modern town which was
first settled during the late Roman
period.

Until the late 19th century Beersheba
was just a collection of wells used by the
Bedouin. The Turks then established a
small town here which served as an
administrative centre for the Negev's
Bedouin tribes. In 1917 towards the end of
WW I it fell to Allenby's British forces as

they advanced north to win control of
Palestine. Part of Palestine's Arab section
in the UN Partition Plan, Beersheba was
captured by the Egyptian Army at the
very start of the 1948 War of Independence
but the Israelis took it on 21 October in
'Operation 10 Plagues'.

During the early years after Israel's
independence, Beersheba was compared
to a 'Wild West frontier town' due to its
stark location and the tough, adventurous
types it apparently attracted. Today,
however, you need a good imagination to
picture it as such a place.

Orientation
The downtown area, where you will find
most of the shops, eating places and
accommodation, is in the Turkish Old
Town about 15 minutes' walk south-west
of the central bus station. One of its main
streets is Keren Kayemet Le-Israel St,
more easily referred to as KKL St. The
rest of Beersheba is post-1948 and mainly
residential, with the Civic Center and
Ben-Gurion University to the north and
the market just south of the central bus
station. Tel Sheva, the ancient site of the
town, is five km outside to the east.

Information
Tourist Office The IGTO (tel 36001/2) is on
Nordau St, across from the entrance to
the central bus station. Open Sunday to
Thursday 8 am to 3 pm, Friday 8 am to
1 pm, closed Saturday.

Post Office & International Telephones The
main office is just north of the central bus
station at the corner of HaNessi'im and
Ben Zvi Sts. Open Sunday, Monday,
Wednesday and Thursday 7.45 am to
12.30 pm and 3.30 to 6 pm, Tuesday
7.45 am to 2 pm, Friday 7.45 am to 1 pm,
closed Saturday. There is a branch in the
central bus station.

Other Various bank branches are on and
around KKL St. The swimming pool at
the IYHA hostel is open daily 9 am to 4 pm

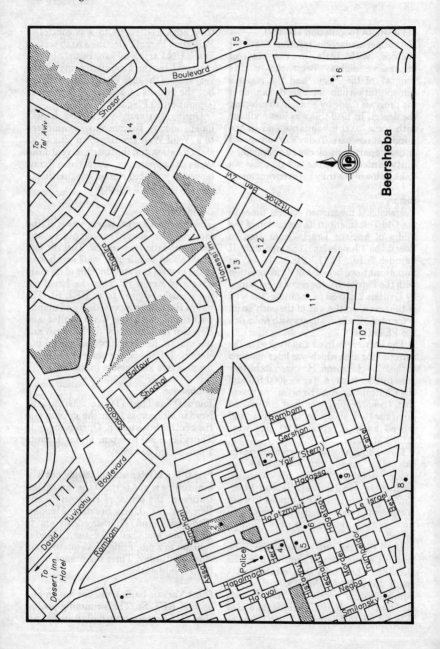

1	Beit Yatziv Youth Hostel (IYHA)
2	Negev Museum
3	Chinese Restaurant & Palachinta Créperie
4	Arava Hotel
5	Rol Hotel
6	KKL (main street – shops, cafés & sheruts)
7	Smilansky St (art galleries & cafés)
8	Abraham's Well
9	Hotel HaNegev
10	Bedouin Market
11	Bus Station
12	Tourist Office
13	Post Office
14	Konditory Bakery
15	Hotel Zohar
16	Negev Research Institute

and costs US$2 for guests, US$3 for visitors. The pool at the Desert Inn Hotel is open to non-residents (except on Saturday). Admission is US$3.

The police station (tel 37444 or 100) is on Herzl St in the Old Town.

Market

Thursday is the day for Beersheba's much talked-about Bedouin market. Traditionally this is when hundreds of the Negev's Bedouin Arabs come into town to buy and sell their livestock, food, carpets, clothes and jewellery to anyone who is willing to barter and buy, be they Israelis, tourists or each other.

It used to be truly authentic but it now has such things such as T-shirts and electronic goods, and an Israeli market sets up alongside. Only very early in the day can you really hope to capture a Bedouin scenario – the show starts about 6 am. The market takes place just south of the central bus station, across the main road where you can see the arched rooftops.

Negev Museum

In one of the more attractive areas of Beersheba, this museum (tel 39105) at 18 HaAtzma'ut St, Old Town, occupies an old Turkish mosque in a park – look for the minaret.

The exhibits include a history of the town itself as well as a series of archaeological artefacts from the whole Negev region. There is also a section on Bedouin culture, and a collection of medieval maps of the Holy Land and a 6th century mosaic floor depicting animals in its geometric design. You can climb the minaret for a view which shows where the town abruptly ends and the desert begins. You are not allowed to take photographs up here because of the adjacent military installation. It's open Sunday and Monday 8 am to 2 pm, Tuesday 8 am to 1 pm, Wednesday and Thursday 8 am to 5 pm, Friday 8 am to 1 pm and Saturday 10 am to 1 pm. Admission is US$1, students 70c.

Abraham's Well

At the southern end of KKL St, near the riverbed, this very unimpressive reconstruction is said to be the site where Abraham and Abimelech made their transaction. Open daily 8 am to 7 pm. Admission is free.

Town Hall

North of the central bus station along HaNessi'im St, the modern town hall dominates the skyline with its distinctive tower. Is it meant to resemble a clenched fist or a spanner? Due to suicide attempts the tower is only open to visitors by appointment.

Ben Gurion University of the Negev

The university's Research & Development Authority deals with the desert environment, so the subjects studied here include artificial rainmaking, desalinisation of water, solar energy, and the chemical and biological conditions necessary for desert life. The university campus is architecturally interesting, and guided tours of the main campus (tel 61111) and the desert studies facilities (tel 78382) can be arranged.

Negev Palmach Brigade Memorial

North-east of the town on a hill, this is a bizarre and confusing modern tribute to the Jewish soldiers killed whilst taking Beersheba from the Egyptians in 1948. Hebrew inscriptions explain the significance of the images, which include a tent, a well, battle maps, a narrow passage, a bunker, a bird, a watchtower, an aqueduct, and a snake that represents the evil enemy. Also known as the Andarta memorial, it is difficult to reach by public transport. Near the Arad road, you can get off Egged bus No 388 and walk the ¾ km, or take local bus No 4 to the railway station and cut across the tracks to reach the hill. Admission is free and there is a café at the site.

Tel Beersheba

The site of the ancient town, this is some five km north-east of modern Beersheba on the Jerusalem road. Here you can see remains of city walls and houses – it's a good idea to visit the Negev Museum first to have a better idea of what it's all about. Next to the ruins is a visitors' centre with a cafeteria, a restaurant and a small museum dealing with the Bedouin. The site is open daily 9 am to 5 pm and admission is free.

Nearby is a new Bedouin village, part of the Israeli programme to encourage the nomads to change to a more permanent address.

Places to Stay

Beersheba has a limited selection of places to stay. The IYHA *Beit Yatziv Youth Hostel* (tel 77444) is the cheapest and is a clean, modern complex with a swimming pool, pleasant gardens and no curfew. The hostel is in the Old Town, a 20 minute walk from the central bus station. From the main entrance turn left and left again on HaNessi'im St, go straight over the crossroads onto Herzl St (either of the two streets leads to the Old Town), and turn right on HaAtzma'ut St – the park on the corner contains the Negev

Museum and its minaret. The hostel is on the left-hand side of the street after HaTivat HaNegev St. Local bus No 13 stops nearby but only runs about every 45 minutes.

It's rarely full, and you have a choice of dorm beds for US$8.50 (members US$7.50) or US$9.60 (members US$8.60) in rooms with private bathroom. An adjoining guest house has singles/doubles for US$26/33. All prices include breakfast. Lunch and dinner are available; if you want them, make a point of telling the staff when you check in and don't be late. The US$5 meal is good value.

The hotels tend to offer a lot less of a deal than the youth hostel. Also in the Old Town, the *HaNegev* (tel 77026) at 26 HaAtzma'ut St is a scruffy old building, with basic singles/doubles for US$20/30, with breakfast. Some cheaper quality rooms are also available. Over on Histadrut St, near KKL St and one block down from the police station, the *Arava Hotel* (tel 78792) has singles/doubles US$17/34, with breakfast. At 48 Mordei HaGetaot St, corner of KKL St, the *Hotel Aviv* (tel 78059) has singles/doubles for US$20/25 – breakfast costs US$3.

Up past the Civic Center on Shazar Blvd is the more respectable *Zohar Hotel* (tel 77335/6). Modern and with decent facilities, it's a good deal at US$17/34 for singles/doubles, with breakfast.

Beersheba's top hotel is the *Desert Inn* (tel 74931/4) to the north of the Old Town in what is now a residential area but was once the town's outskirts. It has a pool and a tennis court. Singles/doubles cost from US$40/60, with breakfast.

Places to Eat

Apart from the Egged self-service restaurant at the central bus station and the felafel stalls at the Bedouin market, the Old Town is where you will find most of the places to eat. On and around KKL St are cafés that serve the standard versions of grilled meats and salads, and ice cream parlours and fast food outlets. Nowhere

here really stands out as being better than anywhere else.

For fruit and vegetables visit the market or the grocers' stores in the Old Town. Just behind the police station, the *Konditoria* bakery serves lovely pastries.

The *Sh'va Tea House-Restaurant* (tel 71454), 29 Smilansky St, is open daily from about 7.30 pm to 2 am or so. Set in a lovely old building decorated with art objects, this is a nice spot for a drink – there is a bar with draught beer – or a meal. There is live music some evenings.

The *Beersheva Chinese Restaurant* (tel 75375), 79 Histadrut St, corner of Yair St, is another of the nicer places in town – about US$15 for a full meal, but you could get away with less. Across the street is *Palachinta*, a crèperie with both savoury and sweet styles from about US$5.

Top of a limited range is the *Papa Michel Restaurant*, further north on Histadrut St, near Ramban St. It serves French-style food from about US$15 per person.

Entertainment
Most of the locals seem to congregate on and around KKL St with its street cafés and cinema. Smilansky St and its art galleries are another diversion.

The renowned local orchestra regularly performs at the S Rubin Music Conservatory and the Bet Ha-Am (tel 73478) often stages Beersheba Theatre productions. For these and any other happenings check the free *This Week in the South* leaflet available at the tourist office.

Getting There & Away
Bus Buses run almost continuously to and from Tel Aviv, about every 30 minutes to Jerusalem and almost hourly to Eilat. There are also frequent services to Dimona and Arad, with only the occasional through bus to the Dead Sea and also to Gaza. On Saturday morning an Egged bus leaves Beersheba for Ein Gedi, via Arad and Masada.

Sherut Ya'ed Daroma (tel 39144), 195 KKL St, operate sherut services to Tel Aviv (US$3.60, every hour), Jerusalem (US$3.50, every 45 minutes) Sunday to Thursday 6.30 am to 7 pm, Friday 6.30 am to 2 pm, no Saturday service, and Eilat (US$8, 10 am and 2 pm) Sunday to Thursday only. There may be Arab service taxis going to Gaza from near the central bus station (about US$4).

Getting Around
You can easily walk from the central bus station to the Old Town and the Market. Local buses leave from outside the main entrance to the central bus station.

AROUND BEERSHEBA
Kibbutz Lahav
Established in 1952 as a border settlement on the edge of the West Bank, occupied at that time by Jordan, Kibbutz Lahav now has one of the country's largest pig farms. Of more interest to visitors is the Joe Alon Center with its Museum for Archaeology and Bedouin Culture (tel 961597). It is the world's largest museum of its kind. Bedouin from the Negev, the Sinai and Saudi Arabia have donated a variety of traditional items such as clothes, household utensils, tools and jewellery. With the current push for modernisation, the nomadic existence of the Bedouin and all its traditional trappings is fading fast and it is the museum's aim to preserve and present it to the public. There is also an archaeological museum here. It is open Saturday to Thursday 9 am to 3 pm, Friday 9 am to 1 pm, admission US$2.

Getting There & Away The kibbutz is near Kibbutz Dvir, both off a side road that intersects with the Beersheba to Qiryat Gat road. From Beersheba, Egged bus No 369 to Tel Aviv passes the intersection quite often – from here it's an eight km hitch-hike to the kibbutz. Bus No 042 runs directly to the kibbutz, but once only, at 11.50 am, returning to Beersheba at 1.20 pm.

Shivta (Subeita)

Unfortunately not on the regular bus network, this is one of the Negev's most impressive archaeological sites. Some 58 km south-west of Beersheba in the middle of nowhere, the area was first settled in the 1st century by the Nabateans who are noted for their irrigation skills in an area where the average annual rainfall is less than 90 mm.

In the 4th century, Shivta had expanded to become an important Byzantine town on the caravan route between Egypt and Anatolia. Today's ruins include churches, houses, tiled streets, and water and drainage systems. In the 7th century the Arabs took the town and did not destroy any of the earlier Christian constructions. After a further two centuries, Shivta was abandoned due to problems with the water supply. Being so isolated, its ruins escaped being pillaged over the years by people on the lookout for ready-cut stone, which is why the buildings are in such good condition. The site is open Saturday to Thursday 8 am to 5 pm, Friday 8 am to 4 pm, October to March, the site closes one hour earlier. Admission is US$2, students US$1.

Getting There & Away You can take the infrequent Egged bus No 44 from Beersheba to Nizzana, get off at the 'Horvot Shivta' stop and walk the remaining 8½ km. With little traffic about, hitch-hiking can be a lengthy exercise. From the Nizzana road, the turn-off to Shivta has two lanes and is paved only for the first 2½ km. It then narrows considerably, passing a track to an army installation on the left after one km.

DIMONA (population 26,600)

Established in 1955 and named after the biblical town of the tribe of Judah (Joshua 15:22), Dimona is one of the better-known development towns. Its harsh desert location was the cause of considerable controversy as many thought that the climate would prove to be too fierce for

people to live and work here. However, the initial brave collection of tents has developed into today's bleak collection of apartment blocks. Dimona's original settlers worked at the nearby chemical plants of the Dead Sea Works, but now the town also has glass-making, ceramics and textiles as local industry, along with Israel's nuclear reactor.

Unless you're involved in espionage, the sole attraction in Dimona is the controversial Black Hebrew settlement. A visit is highly recommended – you can telephone 55400 or simply ask any of the staff in the Eternity restaurants or the Hebrews you meet selling jewellery. Otherwise simply go straight to the settlement. The Hebrews occupy what was originally an absorption centre where they live a virtually self-contained lifestyle. However, they welcome visitors to discuss how they live, their aims and beliefs. It is possible to stay overnight in the guest house and food is available – of the excellent vegetarian style unique to the group. When I was there last, there was no set price: it depended on the visitor's means.

Getting There & Away

With frequent buses from Beersheba (40 minutes) Dimona is not difficult to reach. There are also occasional buses from Arad and Mitzpe Ramon. From Dimona's central bus station, the Hebrews' settlement is only about 10 minutes' walk along Herzl St.

AROUND DIMONA
Mamshit

Another Nabatean, Roman and Byzantine city, Mamshit is less visually impressive than Shivta, but it is particularly renowned for the engineering skills used in its construction.

The Nabateans built their city here in the 1st century and it was later used by the Romans. Six km south-east of Dimona an abandoned British police station marks the site where the Romans built a series of dams to store rainwater to supply the town's inhabitants all year round. Razed by the Muslims in the 7th century, the site is dotted with explanatory signs and an information leaflet is available. The excavations include Nabatean remains, reservoirs, the dams, watchtowers, Roman military and Byzantine cemeteries, jewellery and coins, churches and mosaics. The site is open April to September, Saturday to Thursday 8 am to 5 pm, Friday 8 am to 4 pm, October to March, Saturday to Thursday 8 am to 4 pm, Friday 8 am to 3 pm. Admission is US$2, students US$1.

Getting There & Away Buses run from Dimona to the turn-off for the site.

KIBBUTZ SDE BOKER

One of the best known of the kibbutzim, Sde Boker was established in 1952 by pioneers who planned to breed cattle in the desert; its name is Hebrew for 'Ranchers' Field'. Although the initial aims have not been totally fulfilled, the kibbutz is often seen to be a success, judged by its appearance as a lush oasis in the middle of the desert with its fruit orchards and zoo. Its main claim to fame though, is that it was here that David Ben Gurion chose to live when he retired as prime minister in 1953. Only 14 months later he returned to the political scene and went on to serve a second time as prime minister, returning to kibbutz life in 1963. He died here in 1973.

South of the kibbutz and overlooking the Wilderness of Zin is the Sde Boker campus of the Ben Gurion University, with the graves of Ben Gurion and his wife and the En Avdat springs nearby.

You will see three separate turn-offs for Sde Boker: heading south from Beersheba you first come to the turn-off to the main entrance of the kibbutz, then the turn-off for the Ben Gurion Home (where he and his wife lived, now a museum) and finally the turn-off for the university campus, the Ben Gurion graves and En Avdat.

Ben Gurion Home

Only slightly more regal than their fellow kibbutzniks' quarters, the small hut where David and Paula Ben Gurion lived has been maintained as a museum. Kept basically as it was when they were here, there is a collection of letters, photographs and books on display in the simply furnished rooms. It's open Sunday to Thursday 8.30 am to 3.30 pm, Friday 8 am to 12 noon, Saturday 9 am to 1 pm. Admission is free. A café nearby serves meals and snacks, including fruit grown on the kibbutz.

Zoo

This small collection of animals is found near the Ben Gurion Home. From the museum and café, instead of turning right along the side road back to the main road, turn left past the tennis courts, turn right and the zoo is on your right. Feeding time is around 2 pm.

Ben Gurions' Graves

From the bus-stop outside the entrance to the university campus, the graves of Ben Gurion and his wife are reached by turning right then following the arrows to the left on the Hebrew signs. From here you have great views eastwards across the Wilderness of Zin, and southwards over to En Avdat.

Ben Gurion University

The Sde Boker campus of the Ben Gurion University, still in its initial stages of development, contains the Jacob Blaustein Institute for Desert Research, the Blaustein International Center for Desert Studies, and the Ben Gurion Research Institute. The latter boasts the most comprehensive archives dealing with Israel's first prime minister and therefore much of the country's history. However, it is the advanced level of knowledge of the desert achieved by the other institutes that is of most importance here. Phone 35333 for a guided tour of the campus, whose departments include desert hydrology, salinity & water engineering and desert meteorology. Much of the work carried out is unique and has international significance in its aims to solve the problems of desert development.

Sde Boker SPNI Field Study Centre

Also on the university campus, this field school is primarily responsible for nature conservation in the area. This includes Makhtesh Ramon (crater), En Avdat and other desert springs. For those interested in animal life, the field school staff are good people to meet. Extremely knowledgeable and enthusiastic once you have shown your interest, they will tell you all about the local wildlife and where and when to see it. This will include griffin vultures having their breakfast of raw meat provided by the field school, ibex and other animals coming to drink at a spring, and sooty falcons nesting in cliffsides. You should also inquire here about the various hikes in the desert where you can see a lot of this natural activity as well as some beautiful scenery. Although often filled by groups, the guest house here is sometimes available for travellers – it's worth asking about if you want to spend some time in the area.

EN AVDAT

One of the highlights of the Negev and missed by most visitors as it is hidden from the main road, En Avdat is one of those freaks of nature – a pool of icy water in the hot expanse of desert, fed by waters that flow through an intricate network of channels. Dominated by a steep, winding canyon, reaching it involves an exhilarating hike through the incredible scenery. At the very least, you should stop off for a few minutes to admire the view from the observation point.

Although the natural beauty of En Avdat attracts most visitors, the area on top of the cliffs is where prehistoric tribes camped for over 100,000 years. They lived in huts made from branches and the concentration of flint tools stands out from the soil here –

especially on the northern rim of the canyon. Here and nearby, archaeologists have found evidence of dwellings from the Upper Palaeolithic and Mesolithic periods (35,000 to 15,000 BC).

Nature Trail

Outside the main entrance to the Sde Boker campus of the Ben-Gurion University, an orange 'En Avdat' sign points the way. Follow the zig-zagging road down into the Wilderness of Zin until it ends at the car park. Follow the path that leads off beyond, and about 40 minutes' after leaving the campus you will see the large cave up on your left. Ibex and gazelles are often to be seen along here, too. Simply follow the water and after another five minutes you will come to a spring. Despite the warning sign, many enjoy a refreshing dip – if tempted, be aware of the danger caused by the extreme difference in temperature between the hot sun and the cold water.

This is a dead-end, so come back the way you came and on your left look out for steps cut into the rock leading up the cliff (hidden behind a tree). Climb the steps to a paved ledge with a great view.

Carry on walking and after another 10 minutes, having rejoined the water, you will reach another pool, surrounded by trees. In the winter the waterfall here is quite spectacular.

Some more steps have been cut into the rock to lead up the cliff to the right (not always easy to find – look for the caves up above). Quite a steep climb is involved to reach the spot where iron ladders enable you to get to the top of the canyon. I think the best views of all are from the ladders, so be sure to take a good look before reaching the top. A short distance away an observation point has been provided.

The whole hike usually takes two to three hours, allowing plenty of time for relaxing by the springs.

The main road is a 10 to 15 minute walk along a side road from the observation point. You come out south of the university campus – unfortunately there is no bus-stop here but you can usually hitch-hike to Mitzpe Ramon or Beersheba quite easily, or at least get a lift to Sde Boker or Avdat where you can catch a bus.

For those who just want to visit the observation point, look out for the signpost, north of the Avdat archaeological site, south of Sde Boker (no bus-stop, remember).

AVDAT
Not to be confused with En Avdat, this is the well-preserved Nabatean, Roman and Byzantine city perched atop a nearby hill that dominates the desert skyline. The rich combination of impressive ruins and incredible vistas makes the steep climb well worth the effort.

Built by the Nabateans in the 2nd century BC as a caravan stop on the road from Petra and Eilat to the Mediterranean coast, Avdat was taken by the Romans in 106 AD. Prosperous throughout the Byzantine period, the city was abandoned in 634 when it fell to the Muslims. The ruins include Nabatean burial caves, a pottery workshop and a road, a Roman camp, and a Byzantine bath-house, wine press, house, church, monastery and castle. It's open Saturday to Thursday 8 am to 5 pm, Friday 8 am to 4 pm, and admission is US$1.75, students 90c.

Desert Run-Off Farms Unit
Some would say that the achievements of the Israelis in developing the desert pale by comparison with those of the Nabateans who, about 2000 years ago, managed to create great cities in the same harsh environment but with a lot less in the way of technical knowledge and equipment. Their systems of desert agriculture inspired the establishment in 1959 of an experimental farm which can be seen below the archaeological site. It's closed to the general public, but you can phone 88484 if you are interested in the work being done here.

Part of the Ben-Gurion University's Desert Farms Unit, the work carried out includes studying the Nabateans' farming techniques. Basically these involved the 'run-off' rain water that has not been absorbed by the soil. The chosen catchment area was divided into sections by low walls built at an angle across the sloping sides of the wadi. As well as dividing the run-off into manageable quantities, this enabled the farmers to direct it into specific fields. They also collected the stones on the slopes into heaps, which increased the run-off from light rains by as much as 40%.

The overall effect was that a specific field could receive the water equivalent to an annual rainfall of 300 to 500 mm (comparable to the Jerusalem region) despite the average annual rainfall in the Negev being less than 90 mm.

Place to Eat
The large and dirty roadside restaurant down from the entrance to the archaeological site serves a set three-course meal for a pricey US$7, but sandwiches and snacks are also available – and the beer's cold.

Chalcolithic copper 'wand'

Getting There & Away

On the Beersheba to Mitzpe Ramon road, Avdat lies 10 km south of the Ben Gurion Home, 23 km north of Mitzpe Ramon. Buses pass by in each direction about every hour or so, with some continuing to Eilat.

MITZPE RAMON

The word *mitzpe* is Hebrew for 'lookout' and this small town, which began in 1956 as a camp for a 17-member roadbuilding co-operative, is named after the nearby cliff that looks over the massive Ramon Crater – the Makhtesh Ramon.

Intended to be part of the desert development programme, the town failed to take off as planned due to the lack of employment opportunities, and scores of apartments lie empty despite various incentive schemes. In 1986 the government announced that Mitzpe Ramon would be a free trade zone (ie no VAT) in a bid to attract new businesses and residents. Other plans involve promoting the area's unique geological, ecological and archaeological sites and its clear, dry air as tourist attractions.

The Makhtesh is the centre of attention for most visitors to Mitzpe Ramon. A few would also be interested in Tel Aviv University's astronomical observatory which lies to the north-west of the main street. Telephone 88133 to inquire about access.

Mitzpe Ramon makes a good base from which to visit the adjacent Makhtesh, Avdat, En Avdat and Sde Boker.

Orientation

Standing on the northern edge of the Makhtesh, the town is very small with little in the way of sights and amenities for the visitor. Leading from the Beersheba to Eilat road, the main street is a wide dual carriageway passing the small collection of shops, a bank, swimming pool and cultural centre, with side roads connecting with the residential quarters. The new youth hostel and the visitors' centre are to the south, overlooking the Makhtesh. The town's only hotel is a little further west. All these places are within easy walking distance of each other.

Information

There is no tourist information office here, but the staff at the visitors' centre and the

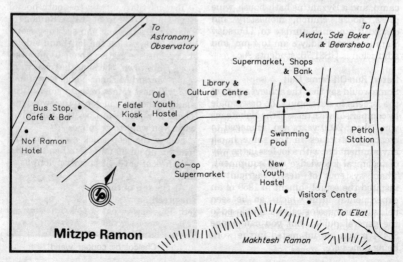

manager at the youth hostel are usually able to help out with general queries.

Post Office It's across from the library and the cultural centre in a residential block - look for the blue sign. It opens Sunday, Tuesday and Thursday 7.45 am to 12.30 pm and 3.30 to 6 pm, Monday and Wednesday 7.45 am to 2 pm, Friday 7.45 am to 1 pm, closed Saturday.

Other Bank Hapoalim, in the arcade beside the swimming pool, is open Sunday and Tuesday 8.30 am to 12 noon and 4.30 to 6.30 pm, Monday, Wednesday and Friday 8.30 am to 12 noon, Thursday 8.30 am to 12 noon and 4.30 to 6 pm, closed Saturday.

The library is on the main street, west of the shops, the indoor swimming pool and cultural centre. It's open Sunday, Monday, Wednesday and Thursday 3 to 7 pm, Tuesday and Friday 9 to 11.30 am, closed Saturday.

For police, phone 100.

Visitors' Centre

Perched right on the edge of the Makhtesh, this attractive modern structure houses a museum whose aim is to explain everything you want to know about the massive and intriguing crater. It does the job quite well with a slide show and an exhibition of charts, illustrations, photographs, models and samples.

Admission is US$2.50, which is worth spending to learn something about this natural phenomenon that, while difficult to describe without going overboard, is said to remind visitors a little of the Grand Canyon and the moon. The centre is open Sunday to Thursday 9.30 am to 4.30 pm, Friday 9 am to 1.30 pm, closed Saturday.

Makhtesh Ramon

The crater's vital statistics are: 300 metres deep, eight km wide, 40 km long. Known in Arabic as *Wadi Ruman*, it offers you a unique opportunity to walk through the successive stages of the earth's evolution in reverse, a unique and strange experience with a mass of different colours and shapes. Although the ceramics and cement industries are represented by a mine or two and there are plans to further exploit the area's mineral wealth, the crater remains largely unspoilt. A few nature trails have been marked out which lead through some of the most attractive and interesting sections. At the time of writing, the only maps of the crater were in Hebrew but plans are afoot to publish versions in English and other languages. For current details ask at the visitors' centre.

Mezard Mishhor - Nahal Gewanim This nature trail in the Makhtesh Ramon was recommended to me by the staff at the visitors' centre as the best one to do. The sights along the way of the various rock formations and the variety of colours are simply awe-inspiring. Taking about 4½ to 5½ hours, the walk covers an occasionally steep rocky terrain in very hot conditions. Do not over-estimate your stamina - take along plenty of water, wear a head covering and start as early in the day as possible.

To reach the trail, take the south-bound Egged bus No 392 from Mitzpe Ramon (to Eilat). Get off when you see the second orange signpost on the left-hand side of the road in the crater. About 10 minutes' drive from town, the sign that you want reads 'Mezard Mishhor-Nahal Gewanim'. You will pass mines on both sides of the road just before you get to the two signs. There is no bus-stop, so tell the driver when you want to get off.

Follow the jeep track away from the road for about 30 minutes, then take the right fork after the electricity pylon on the left.

At the top of the steepish slope follow the green-on-white trail markers to your left. This narrow path takes you along the ridge, giving you excellent views across the crater to your left. There is a pleasant shaded spot for that necessary drink and

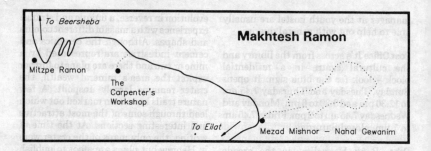

Makhtesh Ramon

To Beersheba

Mitzpe Ramon

The Carpenter's Workshop

To Eilat

Mezad Mishnor – Nahal Gewanim

rest after about 10 minutes – climb up to your right here. It should have taken you about an hour to reach this spot from the road. After a further five minutes, the path splits in two, but both the high and the low paths go the same way. Scramble up the rock face briefly to the top of the ridge for a commanding view in all directions. Here you can see all at once the variety of contrasting rock formations and colours with the maze of wadis and canyons winding through them. If you took the high path, climb down after about 20 minutes to join the low path to save an even steeper descent later. It's possible to take either of the three paths here as they all join up eventually to lead down to a wadi.

Follow the wadi to the right and around to the left. After 25 minutes it narrows considerably with large and small caves on both sides of the canyon. Another 15 minutes and you come to a Hebrew signpost. Follow the track just past it to the left, leading away from the wadi. The track forks after five minutes; take the left track leading to the sign with the coloured trail markers. Go straight ahead following the blue-on-white trail markers. After 20 minutes you should reach another signpost; again go straight ahead and then follow the path to the left. Follow the wadi for 20 minutes and you will come to a couple of water holes. Follow the track to the left 10 minutes from here – there is a blue-on-white sign. After five minutes you will come to a jeep track going left to right

with a signpost. Go to the left and after 25 minutes you will reach the electricity pylon that you passed at the start of the walk. Go to the right here and the road is 30 minutes away.

Hitch-hike back to Mitzpe Ramon – it shouldn't take too long.

Carpenter's Workshop Shortly after the road from Mitzpe Ramon zig-zags down into the crater, an orange signpost points to this site of geological interest, a half km to the right. To be honest I wasn't over-impressed by what I saw, but a couple I met were – perhaps they were keen geologists. Looking like wood, this unique rock formation has been shaped by pressure. Eventually the rock breaks into pieces, but amongst the rubble you can see unbroken parts.

Follow the jeep track from the road that ends with a car park. From here take the path up the hill to the left (past the refuse bins). This leads you around the hill to a wooden observation platform which gives you a close-up look at the rocks in question. You can either take the Eilat bus or hitch-hike from Mitzpe Ramon, or stop here on your way back from the hike.

The Negev's other two craters are just south of Dimona and not accessible by public transport. HaMakhtesh HaQatan is the smallest. Roughly circular in shape, it looks more like it was caused by a massive meteor than the slow process of erosion. HaMakhtesh HaGadol is the easier of the two to reach. Both are worth a visit if you can get to them.

Places to Stay

The new IYHA *Beit Noam Youth Hostel* (tel 88443) is in a great location near the edge of the Makhtesh. There are dorm beds and singles/doubles for US$15/33, with breakfast. With kitchen facilities available enabling travellers to provide their own meals, and a pleasant manager, this is a more popular place to stay than its Beersheba rival.

The only alternative is the *Nof Ramon Hotel* (tel 88255, 88253), 7 Nahal Meishar. With a pleasant German-speaking proprietor, this offers self-contained apartments with kitchen and bathroom facilities. Singles/doubles are US$25/30, with breakfast.

Places to Eat

Two supermarkets provide a range of inexpensive provisions for self-caterers. The Co-op across from the old youth hostel building is open Sunday, Monday, Wednesday and Thursday 8.30 am to 1 pm and 4 to 6 pm, Tuesday and Friday 8.30 am to 2 pm, closed Saturday. Its larger competitor, in the arcade beyond the bank, is open Sunday to Thursday 9 am to 1 pm and 4 to 7 pm, Friday 8.30 am to 1 pm, closed Saturday.

Eating out is restricted to the kiosk selling felafel between the old youth hostel building and the main bus stop, closing at about 6 to 7 pm, and the dreary café by the main bus stop. Serving basic Oriental dishes, it also has draught beer.

Getting There & Away

Mitzpe Ramon lies 23 km south of Avdat and 136 km north of Eilat, via the Gerofit crossroad. Egged bus No 392 stops here en route between Beersheba and Eilat. Other buses run between the town and Beersheba, with stops at Avdat, Sde Boker and occasionally Dimona. Arkia flights link the town with Tel Aviv and Eilat.

EILAT (population 18,800)

Inspired by the hot climate and the Red Sea location, the Israelis have developed what was less than 40 years ago a tiny desert outpost into their southernmost town and a major resort.

For many visitors to Israel, Eilat is a must on the itinerary. Promoted as a centre of hedonism, it is one of the few places in the country where religion does not occupy centre stage. Instead of synagogues, mosques and churches, it is sun-worshipping, watersports and nightlife that dominate. Unfortunately, Eilat is not all that it is cracked up to be. As a result of its speedy development the town is a mass of hastily built and unattractive constructions that fail to blend in with each other and with the beautiful natural surroundings. Even when you look out to sea, the horizon is usually dominated by oil tankers waiting to dock at nearby Aqaba. Another Eilat turn-off is the large number of entrepreneurs attracted by the 'boomtown' image. Too often in Eilat you will find yourself paying out and feeling hard done by.

In 1985 Eilat became a free trade zone. As a result, VAT was abolished and many items are cheaper than elsewhere in the country. However, the average visitor will not feel too much benefit as accommodation and food prices are not all that different and only luxury goods offer any real savings.

History

Mentioned in the Old Testament as Elath or Eloth, the Israelites stopped here on their way from Egypt back to the Promised Land (Deuteronomy 2:8). It was the port used by King Solomon as his gateway to the Far East trade routes (I Kings 9:26), the Queen of Sheba landed here when she journeyed to Jerusalem to see Solomon, King Jehoshophat of Judah built his unsuccessful navy here and King Uzziah rebuilt the town (2 Chronicles 26:2) which later fell to the Syrians (2 Kings 16:6), after which the town was to

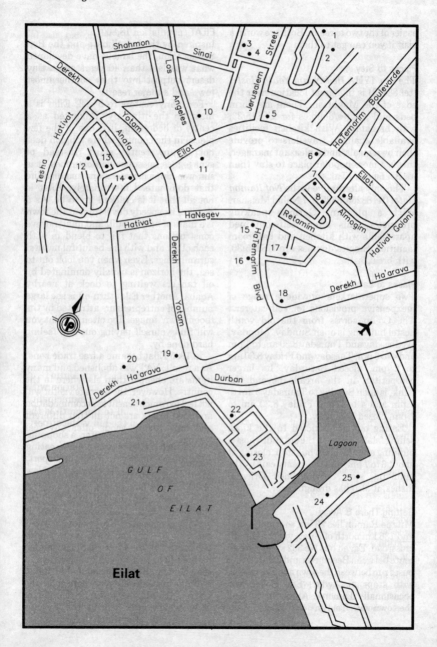

Eilat

1	Sinai Hostel
2	Simon's Place
3	Patio 830 Hostel
4	689 Hostel
5	Corinne's Hostel
6	Supermarket
7	Felafel Boutique
8	Max & Merran's Welsh Australian Hostel
9	Peace Bar, Old Kent Rd & Mercury Restaurants
10	Melony Club Hotel
11	The Shelter
12	Egyptian Embassy
13	Esther's Apartments
14	MOR Centre Tower Apartments
15	Municipality Building (Ministry of the Interior for Visas)
16	Tourist Office
17	Bus Station
18	Shalom Centre
19	New Tourist Center
20	Eilat Youth Hostel (IYHA)
21	Red Rock Hotel
22	Neptune Hotel
23	Moriah Hotel
24	Laguna Hotel
25	King Solomon's Palace Hotel

change hands several times over the centuries.

In 1116 the Crusaders conquered the town, losing it to Saladin some 50 years later. With the development of the port of Aqaba by the Turks, Eilat's importance declined and it became a backwater. Right up until the end of the British Mandate it was simply a small police outpost in the desert. Captured by the Israelis on 10 March 1949 in the last military operation of the War of Independence, it was deemed by the new state as a vital port, with its strategic location on the Red Sea and its access to the eastern routes.

There are a few things that travellers visiting Eilat should be aware of. Firstly, the high rate of thefts here. You will probably meet or hear of people who have had valuables or even whole backpacks stolen. This happens mostly to those who sleep on the beach, but also in hostels. Therefore be very security conscious at all times.

Eilat's police have something of a reputation for unfriendly behaviour. Be sure not to be caught jay-walking – easily done with the absence of traffic lights at key junctions between the beach and the town. Fines are often slapped on ignorant tourists, especially in the vicinity of the bus station. It would seem prudent to avoid behaving in any way that could be interpreted as unlawful. Despite their tough image, the police still tolerate the crowds who sleep on the beach and who congregate in the bars of the New Tourist Center at night. A few brawls have occurred here so perhaps in the eyes of the police, all travellers are the same as the rowdy minority.

Finally, beware of offers to change money. A few travellers have been robbed of their cash by sharp operators, so only change money with a bank or a hostel manager.

Orientation

There are five basic areas in Eilat: the town itself on the slopes leading down to the sea, the hotel area with the lagoon, marina and main beaches, and to the south the port, Coral Beach and Taba.

Town The main street is HaTemarim Blvd – here you will find the bus station with the Commercial Center and municipality opposite. Up the hill to the north is the sherut rank, down the hill is the airport. Nearby is the Shalom Center, a shopping plaza which includes some popular eating and drinking places. South of the airport, before you reach the hotel area, the New Tourist Center is a plaza of cafés, restaurants and bars. Further north, up the hill amongst the residential streets, you will find the hostels.

Hotel Area East of the airport, the hotel area is spread around a purpose-built lagoon and marina with the most accessible beaches nearby, known collectively as the North Beach. There are also various eating, drinking and dancing places to be found here amongst the middle and top end hotels.

Coral Beach This is a marine reserve, a stretch of protected beach five km south of the town, where you find the underwater observatory and aquaria, glass-bottomed boat trips, a mock Wild West town, camp sites, hotels and restaurants.

Taba Another two km further south, this stretch of the coast was the subject of a diplomatic tug-of-war which the Egyptians won.

Information

Tourist Office The IGTO (tel 72268, 76737) is in the Commercial Center across from the bus station and is open Sunday to Thursday 8 am to 6 pm, Friday 8 am to 1 pm, closed Saturday.

Post Office & International Telephones In the Commercial Center. Open Sunday, Tuesday and Thursday 7.45 am to 12.30 pm and 4 to 6.30 pm, Monday and Wednesday 7.45 am to 2 pm, Friday 7.45 am to 1 pm, closed Saturday.

Banks Bank Leumi is on HaTemarim Blvd across from the bus station by the municipality building, and is open Monday to Friday 8.30 am to 12 noon, Sunday, Tuesday and Thursday 5 to 6.30 pm, closed Saturday. There is an Israel Discount Bank at the Shalom Center by the airport, and it's open Sunday to Thursday 8.30 am to 12 noon, Sunday, Tuesday and Thursday 4 to 5.30 pm, closed Saturday.

Egyptian Consulate This is at 34 Deror St (tel 76115) in a residential area. Head south on Eilot St, turn right at the Moore Center, then first left and it's at the end of the dead-end street (look for the flag). It's open Sunday to Thursday 10 am to 2 pm, closed Friday and Saturday. Visa applications can be made here and collected the next day.

Other Steimatzsky's bookshop is in the bus station, and is open Sunday to Thursday 9 am to 7 pm, Friday 9 am to 2 pm, closed Saturday. Bronfman sell used books in the Commercial Center, across from the bus station near the tourist office, and open Sunday to Thursday 8 am to 1 pm and 5 to 7.30 pm, Friday 8 am to 1 pm, closed Saturday. Book Bar, 15 Almogim St, next to the Peace Bar, is open Sunday to Thursday 9 am to 1 pm and 5 to 8 pm (winter 4.30 to 7.30 pm), Friday 9 am to 1.30 pm, closed Saturday.

The library is in the Philip Murray Cultural Center, across from the corner of HaTemarim Blvd and Hativat HaNegev St. It's open Sunday, Monday, Wednesday and Thursday 10 am to 6.45 pm, Tuesday 1 pm to 6.45 pm, Friday 9 to 11.45 am, closed Saturday.

The Gill laundromat, corner of Eilot St and HaTemarim Blvd, is open Sunday to Thursday 8 am to 1 pm and 4 to 7 pm, Friday 8 am to 1 pm, closed Saturday.

The police station (tel 72444/5 or 100) is on Avdat St, at the eastern end of Hativat HaNegev St. This is where many travellers end up going to report a theft.

Beaches

Eilat's hot climate and seaside location are its main attraction, and most visitors spend their time lying out in the sun and cooling off in the water. Not to be missed is a glimpse of the underwater scenery of colourful coral and fish – either by visiting the observatory, taking a trip on a glass-bottomed boat, hiring a snorkel, mask and flippers or going all the way with scuba equipment.

The most convenient beaches are those by the hotel area but they are also the most crowded and do not have much in the way of coral and fish. Head south to Coral Beach for these or to Taba for a more pleasant spot.

Coral Beach Nature Reserve

Beyond the well-kept stretch of sand and

under the clear blue water, lie coral and fish whose beauty has to be seen to be fully appreciated. The reserve is open daily 8 am to 6 pm and admission is US$2.25. Snorkelling and scuba gear is available for hire here and nearby. Officially certified diving courses are also available and are very popular – shop around for current prices. Take local bus No 5 or 15.

Glass-bottomed boats operate from the marina and from a pier just to the north of Coral Beach. Itineraries can vary, but a 45 minute cruise costs about US$4.50.

South of the Coral Beach Nature Reserve, the Coral World Underwater Observatory & Aquarium is another opportunity to see the sea. A pier leads 100 metres out and 4½ metres below the water to a glass-walled chamber. The complex also includes aquaria and a museum which tell you all about the fish that are to be seen. It's open Saturday to Thursday 8.30 am to 4.30 pm, Friday 8.30 am to 3 pm.

Across the street from the nature reserve, Texas Ranch is an unimpressive mock Wild West town inspired by the debatable resemblance of the local terrain to that of American cowboy country. The complex offers horse-riding facilities (40 minutes US$12, half day US$40) and has apparently been used as a film set. It's enough to make John Wayne turn in his grave. Admission is US$1.

To get to Coral Beach take local bus No 5 or 15.

Taba

In Egyptian territory since early 1989, this pleasant beach has freshwater showers and the luxury Sonesta hotel. You don't need an Egyptian visa, just a passport, but you will probably have to change money – the hotel will do it. To get to Taba take local bus No 15.

International Birdwatching Centre

Eilat is the best place in the world to watch the migration of birds. The peak migration periods are in spring and autumn. In particular, migrating birds of prey are an impressive attraction and over a million raptors of about 30 different species can be seen in season. In addition, some 400 varieties of song birds, sea birds and waterfowl have been recorded migrating through here.

Based at the King Solomon's Palace Hotel by the lagoon, the International Birdwatching Centre (tel 77236, 71506) co-ordinates all activities of research, surveys, tours and educational work in the area with the ultimate aim of promoting interest in the conservation of birds. The centre offers visitors a variety of activities, regardless of their depth of knowledge. Observation points and hiking trails have been established and guided hiking tours include the observation of the various birds and a visit to a ringing station. Lasting for two hours, the tours are good value for US$3.50. Other facilities include the rental of field glasses, literature and background material, participation in the migration surveys, lectures and nature films.

The observation points, ringing stations and hiking trails are in the vicinity of the salt ponds to the east of the town and in the northern fields of Kibbutz Eilot. Inquire at the centre for details.

Israel Palace Museum

Only those suffering from sunstroke or parents with easily satisfied children will find this place worth a visit. It uses dioramas with little dolls to present a history of the Jews. It's next to the Caesar Hotel by the lagoon and is open Saturday to Thursday 9.30 am to 12.30 pm and 4.30 to 8.30 pm, Friday 9.30 am to 1 pm. Admission is US$2.50, students US$1.25.

Desert Hikes

Overshadowed by the activities on the beach and underwater, there are some marvellous hiking possibilities in the Eilat region. The colourful mountains and valleys just outside the town have been enthusiastically explored by SPNI

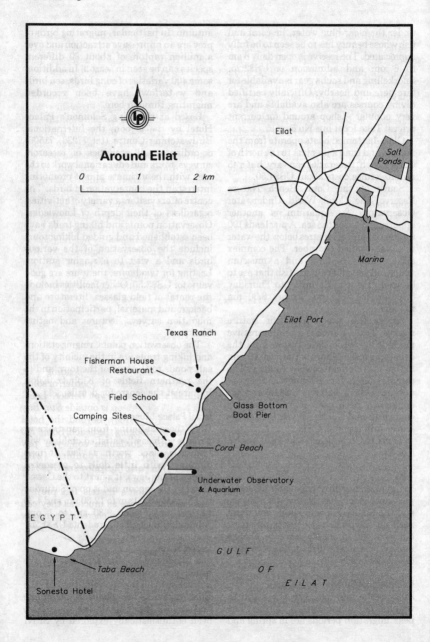

Around Eilat

0   1   2 km

Eilat

Salt Ponds

Marina

Eilat Port

Texas Ranch

Fisherman House
Restaurant

Field School

Camping Sites

Glass Bottom
Boat Pier

Coral Beach

Underwater Observatory
& Aquarium

EGYPT

GULF

OF

EILAT

Taba Beach

Sonesta Hotel

personnel, and marked nature trails enable visitors to see the most interesting of the beauty spots. *Self-Guided Tours & Walks in the Eilat Region* by Jacob Dafni is due for publication by the SPNI and is an excellent guide (the published title may be different). Alternatively, contact the staff at the Coral Beach Nature Reserve for details about recommended hikes. Most of these are best reached by car, but those relying on public transport can still enjoy some of them.

When you go hiking in the desert be sure to abide by the safety guidelines: follow a marked path, take sufficient water, cover your head, beware of flash floods and avoid the Israel-Egypt border area and army installations – do not take photographs or hike at night near here.

Tours

There are several tours available from Eilat which explore the southern Negev and the Sinai. Egged Tours, Neot Hakikar on HaTemarim Blvd and Johnny Desert Tours in the Shalom Center are among the larger operators. It's worth shopping around for the best deal as none are particularly cheap.

Places to Stay

Although Eilat is often referred to as a winter resort, its season actually lasts all year long. From November to March, the coolest months with an average daytime temperature of 24°C, the town is at its busiest and reaches an unbelievable peak of overcrowding at Passover. At this time it seems that most Israelis head south. You would do well to stay away from Eilat for that week, and the week before and after as well. From April to October, with the average temperature zooming up to 36°C, the town is filled mainly with Israelis, and reaches another peak at Sukkot. Not only is it hard to find a place to stay, but when you do, you will usually find that the price has been doubled or trebled. Other Jewish holidays can present the same problems.

Places to Stay – bottom end

Like most resort towns, it is the big-spending tourist that Eilat welcomes the most. Large hotels dominate the main beaches and there are restaurants and bars aplenty.

Unlike most resort towns, Eilat also encourages the budget traveller with several hostels and by allowing them to doss on the beach – this liberal approach to the use of its beaches has given Eilat a permanent community of 'beach people'.

For those tempted to join them, remember that there is a high theft rate on Eilat's beaches and if you sleep near the beach-front hotels you will also share your bed with the rats who are attracted by the refuse areas. Avoid the rodents but not necessarily the thieves by heading east of Sun Bay Camping or south of the Red Rock Hotel. There are toilets and tent pitching is allowed.

Once you could head south to Taba Beach, where the risk of theft was said to be less, and pitch a tent and use the showers and toilets. Check it out to see how the new Egyptian owners feel about beach camping.

Those who wish to pay for a camping site can choose between heading east towards the Israel-Jordan border, or south towards the Israel-Egypt border. Local bus No 1A's last stop is outside *Sun Bay Camping* (tel 73105), beyond the hotel area and overlooking the beach. Some 750 metres from Jordanian soil, you pay US$15/20 for singles/doubles (with breakfast) in basic bungalows or US$3 for pitching your own tent.

Some of Eilat's hostels fall prey to owners who charge as much as they can get away with. Prices, therefore, can vary considerably from time to time. Arriving travellers are often greeted at the bus station by hostel touts who have been known to fight over prospective guests. Private room renters may also approach you. Be sure to see any accommodation before deciding to stay there.

Max & Merran's – the Welsh &

Australian Hostel (tel 71408) on Ofarim St is an old favourite, although this is partly due to a lack of competition. It's clean, with a lounge and kitchen, although it could do with another bathroom to reduce the long queues. A bed costs US$5, with a few doubles for US$10. It's closed from 9 to 1 am, with a 12 midnight curfew. From the bus station, turn right up HaTemarim Blvd, cross Hativat HaNegev St and Retamim St, turn right across the 'grass' area to the end of the dead-end street that is Ofarim. The hostel is at the other end on the left.

Nearby is the *Village Youth Hostel* (tel 71311) at the end of Retamim St. It looks pleasant enough, although the prices could be lower. Beds in the dorm are US$7, and singles/doubles are US$20/23. There's no curfew.

One of the better places is *Corinne's Room* (tel 71472), 413/4 Eilot St, corner of Jerusalem St. From the bus station turn right up HaTemarim Blvd to Eilot St, turn left and turn right on Jerusalem. The hostel is on the right across some waste ground. It's clean and comfortable with pleasant staff and a kitchen. Dorm beds are US$5.50, and rooms (up to three people) are US$16 with bathroom. No curfew.

Another of the favourite places to stay in Eilat is *Patio 830* (tel 76611, 77629). A comfortably furnished apartment turned into a hostel, this is run by a friendly husband and wife team, Ruffi and Dalia. Super clean, with a well-equipped kitchen and bathroom, it's like staying at a friend's place. Not easy to find at first, it's near the Esidor Center. If arriving with heavy bags it's worth forking out the US$2 for a taxi, otherwise it's a 10 minute walk from the bus station: turn right up HaTemarim Blvd, left on Eilot St, right up Jerusalem St, left on Pharan St then right, and the apartment is on the ground floor on the right behind a gate on the left. Their prices haven't risen for years – a sunbed in the garden costs US$4, indoors US$5, doubles US$14. You are given your own key so there is no curfew.

On Roded St, *Sinai Hostel* (tel 72826) is over-priced with singles/doubles from US$20 per person.

Eilat's *IYHA Youth Hostel*, south of the New Tourist Center, is best avoided, as is the adjacent *Nophit Hostel* which may well have made way for a new building by now, and the *Masada Hotel* on Almogim St.

Opposite Coral Beach by the Hotel Caravan, *Carolina's Camping* (tel 71911) has bungalows for US$9 per person, doubles US$13, the cleanest bathrooms and showers around, and a basic cafeteria. It may appeal to those who plan to spend time on Coral Beach where guests get a 50% reduction off admission. US$3 per person with your own tent. Local bus No 15 stops nearby, or stay on to the observatory stop where the more basic *Yigal's Bedouin Village* has bungalows from around US$20 per person – or you can pitch your tent for US$3 per person. There is a small pool, kitchen and bar. Look for the sign reading 'Bedouin Bazaar 30 m'. Remember that Coral Beach and Taba are some distance away from the town if you plan to spend your evenings enjoying the nightlife.

Places to Stay – middle

Apartments The *Melony Club Apartotel* (tel 31181) at 6 Los Angeles St, north of the Municipality building, has apartments with kitchens and bathrooms: singles/doubles cost from US$30/45. At the MOR Center, *Tower Apartments* (tel 751336) have doubles with kitchen and bathroom for US$35, extra bed for US$15. *Esther's Apartments* (tel 74575, 75206), at 41 Nesher St, is an agency with various properties on their books varying from about US$40 for a two-bedroom villa for up to four people.

Hotels Eilat's hotels, unlike the hostels, are answerable to the Ministry of Tourism and so prices are more regulated. However, they can still go up by over 30%

for the winter and Jewish holidays. Tariffs include breakfast.

Next to the tourist office, the *Red Sea Hotel* (tel 72171/2) has a small pool, and small rooms from US$25/35 for singles/doubles – these prices can double when it's busy. The *Etsion Hotel* (tel 74131/3) has a sauna, pool and nightclub, with singles/doubles from US$45/55.

At the eastern end of HaTivat HaNegev St, behind the bus station, the *HaDekel Hotel* (tel 73191) is a nice place; modest, but clean and friendly. Singles/doubles cost from US$22/35.

Up the hill and behind the New Tourist Center off Yotam Blvd, the *Adi Hotel* (tel 76151/3) is fairly well hidden; look for the red and white 'ADI' sign on its wall. They have singles/doubles at US$40/53.

In the expensive hotel area by the lagoon, there are some more moderately priced beds available. Near to the Galei Eilat Hotel, the *Dalia Hotel* (tel 75127/8) has singles/doubles from US$38/56. With the same prices is the *Bel Hotel* (tel 76121/3), behind the Moriah Hotel. The *Americana Hotel* (tel 75176/9) has a pool, nightclub and tennis with singles/doubles from US$50/60.

Further east, the *Blue Sky Holiday Village* (tel 73953/4) has caravans equipped with a bathroom and kitchenette for US$27/36 for singles/doubles.

Back in the hotel area by the lagoon, the *Queen of Sheba Hotel* (tel 72121/6) has singles/doubles overlooking the sea from US$45/68. Facilities include pool, tennis and water sports.

Out by Coral Beach, the *Caravan Sun Club Hotel* (tel 71345) is moderately priced considering its facilities, including a pool, skin-diving, sailboarding, boating, cycling, tennis and horse-riding. Singles/doubles start around US$30/40, breakfast extra.

Places to Stay - top end

Eilat's top hotels are geared towards the holiday market and are generally of large and brash design, with swimming pools, nightclubs and various sports and social activities. They deal mostly with the travel trade and you will end up saving money by booking through an agent rather than by checking in as an individual. Most are in the US$75 and above bracket, but there are few that offer better deals.

Sport Hotel (tel 33333) has singles/doubles from US$50/70, with breakfast. The *Red Rock Hotel* (tel 73171), south of the main beach, has singles/doubles from US$60/80, with breakfast.

Back out by Coral Beach, *Club Inn* (tel 75122/3) is a complex of villa apartments set around a pool with sports facilities along with other luxury hotel trappings. With two bedrooms, lounge, kitchenette and bathroom prices are US$80 to 100 for two, US$180 for four.

Places to Eat

Eilat's food scene is simply diabolical – good eating places are as hard to find as a rainy day. With the heat, appetites tend to be smaller anyway and many people are happy to buy food from a supermarket and prepare their own snacks or sandwiches. A convenient Co-op supermarket is on Eilot St, corner of HaTemarim Blvd. In the Commercial Center, near to the tourist office, the Mini-Supermarket is more expensive but is open for longer hours, including Shabbat.

Eilat's bakers win the prize for baking Israel's smallest pitta bread. When you order felafel here, the pitta is so tiny that there is hardly any room for the salad. The best and some of the cheapest felafel I tasted in town was from a little stall called *Felafel Boutique* on HaTemarim Blvd, up the hill from the bus station and just below Almogim St. Open Sunday to Thursday 10 am to 10 pm, Friday 10 am to 2 or 3 pm, closed Saturday.

The bus station's Egged self-service restaurant provides the usual great value, which is even more appreciated in Eilat.

At the corner of Eilot and Jerusalem Sts, *Pat Bar* is a bakery and dairy restaurant with good prices. They even serve the large bottles of Nesher beer for about 65c.

Near Max & Merran's Hostel, the *Mercury* and *Old Kent Rd* cafés provide basic snacks and meals at basic prices.

At the bottom of the hill that is HaTemarim Blvd turn left by the airport, and across Ha'Arava Rd in the Paz petrol station building is the *Jade Garden Chinese Restaurant*. It's open for lunch and dinner, and you can eat well for US$8 to US$12.

More upmarket are the *Lotus Chinese Restaurant* (tel 76161) by the Caesar Hotel near the lagoon and *Mandy's Chinese Restaurant* (tel 72238) at Coral Beach – about US$15 here.

The *Oasis Restaurant* (tel 72414), to the left of the western end of the footbridge across the lagoon, provides decent salads for US$5, and meat or fish dishes from US$9. Neither the Shalom Center nor the New Tourist Center have a truly recommendable eating place. Ice cream and blintzes dominate here, along with pizzas and cafés serving shishlik and kebab.

The *Fisherman House* (tel 71330), across from the glass-bottomed boats' pier at Coral Beach, offers a self-service meal of fish, chips, salad and bread. Average quality at best, but you can eat as much as you like for US$6.

The *Aviya-Sonesta Beach Hotel* at Taba has a very good restaurant serving French cuisine at about US$15 to US$35 per person. *La Coquille* (tel 73461) behind the lagoon is similar.

Bars

With the temperature usually so high it is just as well that the beer prices here are Israel's lowest. Not surprisingly, the bars are popular both after dark and during the day when the hot sun can be too much to handle.

In the Shalom Center, *Tropicana* serves cheap draught beer and shows free videos. It's especially popular during the day with its 'happy hour' prices.

The crowds tend to congregate in the New Tourist Center, especially at night. Two British-style pubs are very popular here, the *Red Lion* and *The Tavern*, but can be too crowded and rowdy for some. The *Cuckoo's Nest* further along shows free videos.

Over on the corner of Almogim and Agmonim Sts are some more drinking spots. The *Peace Bar* is a hangout for tougher locals and unemployed builders. Come here early in the morning to try for a job on a building site, or later for a cheap beer. Next door, the *Old Kent Rd* and the *Mercury* are a little better. Down the hill a little on Retamin St, *Chaplin's* can be a nice place.

Teddy's, behind the lagoon, is more sedate, as is *The Yacht Pub*, part of the King Solomon's Palace Hotel complex. West of the footbridge across the lagoon and next to the marina is the *Yatush-Ba-Rosh*, a popular bar whose name translates literally to 'Mosquito on the Head'.

For most eating and drinking places, Shabbat is just another day and they are open as usual.

Entertainment

Eilat's evenings are based around the bars and eating places of the Shalom Center, the New Tourist Center and the hotel area. Pick up the free *Events in Eilat* leaflet from the tourist office to find out what else is happening. Some of the big hotels regularly put on free happenings such as Hebrew lessons, belly dancers, films and videos, dancing lessons and lectures.

The Cinemateque at the Philip Murray Cultural Center shows a usually good choice of films, and concerts and shows are staged here, too. Alternatively, the Cinema Eilat is next to the post office.

There are several nightclubs, or discos, and opinions differ as to which is the best. The cheapest is at the Americana Hotel –

it's free. Others regularly mentioned are at the Shulamit Gardens Hotel and the nearby *Godfathers*.

Getting There & Away

Bus Eilat has express bus links with Jerusalem via the Dead Sea (4½ hours), Tel Aviv via Beersheba (five hours) and Haifa (6½ hours). It is often necessary to make reservations at least two days in advance – if you are unable to get on a Jerusalem bus, go to Beersheba and change there.

If you want to stop off in the Negev en route, Beersheba buses pass through Mitzpe Ramon and will also drop you at Avdat and Sde Boker. All buses pass by the Timna Valley National Park, Hai Bar Biblical Wildlife Reserve and Yotvata visitors' centre.

If you are heading to or from the Sinai, local bus No 15 runs between Eilat's central bus station and Taba. The Israeli border checkpoint is open daily from 7 am to 9 pm. Don't forget the US$8 (approximately) departure tax, to be paid in Israeli currency. If you are only visiting the Sinai, no Egyptian visa is necessary, just a valid passport; you will have to buy some Egyptian currency.

You must get a visa from the Eilat consulate or the Tel Aviv embassy if you want to visit any other part of Egypt. There are irregular Egyptian buses running from the border to Sharm el Sheikh and St Catherine's Monastery – only one or two a day. Ask around for the current rough schedule and aim to get there in plenty of time as they are reliably unreliable.

Sherut Yael Daroma, (tel 72279) run a good value sherut service from Almogim St, up the hill from the bus station; it's faster and with fares only slightly higher than Egged. Cars regularly speed up to Jerusalem and Tel Aviv via Beersheba. You will usually have to make reservations at least two days in advance.

An alternative to the unreliable and uncomfortable Egyptian buses in the Sinai are Arab service taxis. You will normally have to bargain hard to get an acceptable price, but that's not impossible.

Air Arkia flights depart from the central airport, connecting to Jerusalem, Tel Aviv and Haifa.

Getting Around

Bus Local bus No 15 is the most used service, running every day between the bus station and Taba via the hotel area and Coral Beach. Distances within the town are not so great and many people walk. If you don't want to, bus Nos 1, 2 and 3 run between the town and the hotel area, with No 1A running between the town and Sun Bay Camping, towards the Israel-Jordan border.

Taxi Especially when there are two or more of you, Eilat's taxis can be an inexpensive and comfortable way to get around. Although distances are short much of the town is on a hill and, worn out by the heat, you could well decide to take a smart Mercedes ride rather than walk. Fares tend to be about US$2 to US$4.

Bicycle The heat may prove to be too much of a deterrent, but you can hire a bicycle for the day for about US$6 from in front of the Queen of Sheba Hotel by the lagoon, or at the Red Sea Sports Center.

AROUND EILAT

Unfortunately most of the many wonderful places of natural beauty near Eilat can only be reached by private transport, and with the high temperatures and infrequent traffic, hitch-hiking is impractical. However, you can reach some marvellous places by bus.

The area's incredible landscape is due to the Great Syrian-African Rift which terminates here with the Arava Valley. The result is a desert environment with glorious colours and a surprising variety of flora and fauna.

Of the Negev's 1200 recorded plant species, only 300 exist in this southern, more arid, area. These include palms, acacia, tamarisk, pistachio and the very rare horseradish tree. The animals found here include gazelles, wolves, foxes, ibex and Israel's largest bird, the almost extinct lappet-faced vulture.

There are also many archaeological sites in the area which show that ancient people managed not only to live here, but also dug copper mines in these harsh surroundings.

Places that should be seen if you have a car or decide to take a tour include En Netafim, a small spring at the foot of a 30 metre waterfall which attracts many animals who come to drink; the Red Canyon, one of the area's most beautiful sights, 6000 metres long, one to three metres wide, and some 10 metres at its deepest; and Moon Valley which is Egyptian territory, but can be seen from the Red Canyon.

Here are some places that can be reached by public transport:

Timna Valley National Park

A popular excursion 30 km north of Eilat, this area of the desert measures some 60 square km. Timna Valley is the site of biblical copper mines (mining began here around 4000 BC) and some really stunning desert landscapes with multi-coloured rock formations.

Among the things to see are the ancient copper mines, which now consist of sandstone arches and caves, underground shafts and galleries. About three km away are some Egyptian and Midianite rock drawings. Other signs of ancient life include copper smelting camps and the ruins of the 14th century BC Temple of Hathor.

More striking, though, are the natural phenomena here. King Solomon's Pillars are a series of sandstone ridges caused by gradual erosion on a 50 metre high cliff face. The Mushroom is an aptly named rock formation, again caused by erosion.

Information about walks is available at the park's entrance. A lot of km are involved in walking around the park, although you can sometimes hitch a ride from other visitors. Open Saturday to Thursday 8 am to 4 pm, Friday 8 am to 3 pm. Admission is US$2.25.

Getting There & Away Any bus heading to or from Eilat passes the turn-off for Timna Valley. From the main road it is a 2½ km walk to the park's entrance. Make as early a start as possible to beat the heat and, as usual, take plenty of water and cover your head.

Hai-Bar Biblical Wildlife Reserve

Hai-Bar is Hebrew for 'wild game' and this wildlife reserve on 8000 acres of salt flats was created to establish breeding groups of wild animals threatened by extinction. Although inspired by the desire to re-introduce animals mentioned in the Bible, other creatures are also found here.

Visitors can only tour the reserve by car, so if you arrive by bus wait by the entrance for a ride. The reserve is open daily 7.30 am to 1.30 pm, but it is best to be here 8 to 10.30 am for feeding time. Admission is US$1.50, students 75c.

Getting There & Away The reserve is some 40 km north of Eilat and any bus heading north from Eilat goes past the turn-off.

Yotvata Visitors' Centre

The main source of information on the entire Eilat area, this new visitors' centre (tel 76018) features a sound and light presentation that describes the region's natural assets and an exhibition of maps, diagrams and photographs on the zoology, botany, geology, archaeology and history of the settlement here. It's open Sunday to Thursday 9 am to 4 pm, Friday 9 am to 2 pm, Saturday 10 am to 2 pm. Admission is US$2.50.

Top: Arab children, Hebron (NT)
Bottom: Arab men, Hebron (NT)

Top: Nablus from Mount Gerizim (NT)
Left: St George's Monastery, Wadi Qelt (NT)
Right: Arab girls, Hebron (NT)

Place to Eat A cafeteria, run by the adjacent kibbutz, serves some of the local dairy produce.

Getting There & Away The centre is less than two km north of the Hai-Bar Biblical Wildlife Reserve and all buses to and from Eilat pass by.

The Occupied Territories

WARNING

The *intefadeh* may mean that some areas of the Occupied Territories are out of bounds to travellers, or they may be affected by strikes, curfews, road-blocks and even riots. Find out as much as you can about the current situation before travelling here, and remember that things can change dramatically from day to day. Where possible take Arab rather than Egged buses, and remember that it is extremely dangerous to voice pro-Israeli opinions here. If there is trouble, get away quickly – wherever your sympathies lie, rocks and bullets are notoriously indiscriminate in their victims.

As used here, the term Occupied Territories refers to the areas commonly known as the West Bank and the Gaza Strip.

The Occupied Territories are more rural and less developed than the rest of Israel and the scenery is superb. There are more of the clichéd everyday scenes of the Middle East to see here, with Arab women balancing their shopping on their heads, donkeys managing to convey even heavier loads (note that the donkey handlers are nearly always young boys or old men), and the ever-present stretch Mercedes and Peugeots sounding their horns.

These areas were occupied by Israel during the Six-Day War and ever since have remained in political limbo, neither annexed outright by Israel (as were East Jerusalem and the Golan Heights), nor granted autonomy. The military administration set up by the Israelis in 1967 is based on regulations first introduced by the British during the Mandate, against which the Zionists had themselves rebelled. IDF patrols are a constant aggravation to the Arab population and you will sense the tension just below the surface.

Since the 1970s the Israelis have permitted Arab elections, although only for local government. Not surprisingly, these have been highly controversial, with Arab critics arguing that only those without pro-PLO views are allowed into office, and Zionist critics arguing that giving power to the Arabs is leading to Israel's self-destruction. Little real progress has been made by these elections. The main issues of the Occupied Territories do not revolve around local government but national government and this is the stumbling block.

The Occupied Territories are seen by the vast majority of Palestinians as land that rightfully belongs to them. Most Israelis believe that the occupation of the West Bank and the Gaza Strip has resulted in greater security for the Jewish State, creating a buffer zone between them and hostile neighbours. Since 1967 the number of terrorist raids here has fallen, and many Israelis feel that to return these areas to Arab control would recreate a situation that would lead to a major war.

Some Israelis support the Jewish occupation, not for defence reasons but because they believe that the land historically belongs to them and not to the Arabs. These extremists are in favour of annexation, while those who agree with the occupation for defence purposes are divided. Some would prefer to grant a degree of autonomy to the Arabs while maintaining control over the military and foreign policy aspects of such a state. A small number support a fully autonomous Arab state.

Since the Arab *intefadeh* began in late 1987, and especially since Yassar Arafat's PLO was recognised by the US, Israeli attitudes to the Occupied Territories have polarised. Those who are thankful that the US and the PLO are at last talking are willing to consider trading land for peace, while others feel betrayed by their American allies and are more determined than ever that the land will stay under Israeli control. The *intefadeh* also means that many Arab businesses, including hotels and restaurants, have responded to the PLO's call for strikes and operate for restricted hours, if at all.

West Bank

An integral part of any visit to the Holy Land, this region includes such familiar place names as Bethlehem, Jericho and Hebron. Amidst dramatic landscapes you will find the birthplace of Jesus, the Mount of Temptation and the Tombs of the Patriarchs.

Covering an area of less than 6000 square km, the West Bank consists of a diverse range of geographic regions. Starting from the edge of the Jezreel Valley in the north, the Samarian Mountains are a range of green and brown peaks with a distinct red soil, with olive and fruit trees, tobacco, livestock and the occasional Arab village on the terraced slopes. Nablus is the major town here. The Judean Hills are dominated by Jerusalem. Descending eastward towards the Dead Sea, the Judean Hills become the savage scenic splendour of the Judean Desert. Moving down into the Jordan Valley you come to Jericho, a lush oasis with a distinctly hotter climate. Often overlooked is the fact that the shore of the Dead Sea, almost as far south as Ein Gedi, is part of the West Bank. This includes Qumran, where the Dead Sea Scrolls were found, and Ein Feshka, the freshwater spring. These areas are covered in detail in the Dead Sea Chapter. To the west, the Judean Hills end where the Negev Desert begins, and you find Bethlehem and Hebron, surrounded by hillsides of lush vineyards, orchards and olive trees set amongst the rocky brown terrain.

The Israelis officially designate the West Bank by the biblical names Judea and Samaria in the linguistic war. As you travel around you will see the fortified Jewish settlements, military installations, periodic road-blocks and refugee camps that only begin to indicate the reality of the situation here. These aspects cannot be ignored, but do not allow them to deter you from visiting the region.

Most travellers base themselves in Jerusalem and make day trips to destinations in the West Bank. Because of the *intefadeh* the hotels in Ramallah and Nablus have been closed to foreigners from time to time.

Unless otherwise stated, telephone area codes in the West Bank are the same as Jerusalem - 02.

JERUSALEM TO JERICHO

The main attraction on the road between Jerusalem and Jericho is the change in the scenery and temperature as you experience the rapid descent from 820 metres above sea level to 250 metres below sea level in less than an hour. You also pass by Bethany and the Inn of the Good Samaritan with their New Testament connotations; the Wadi Qelt, a nature reserve with a natural spring where you can bathe in a pool under a waterfall, hike along an aqueduct to a monastery built into the cliff face of a canyon and end up walking to Jericho; and Nebi Musa, the tomb of Moses according to Muslim tradition. Arab buses to Jericho leave East Jerusalem via the western slopes of the Mount of Olives and pass through Bethany. Egged buses leave the central bus station and head around the Mount of Olives to the north to join the Jericho road beyond Bethany.

Bethany

On the western slopes of the Mount of Olives, Bethany is renowned as the site of the resurrection of Lazarus (John 11:1-44). A Franciscan church commemorates the traditional site of the miracle performed by Jesus. Bethany is also named as the

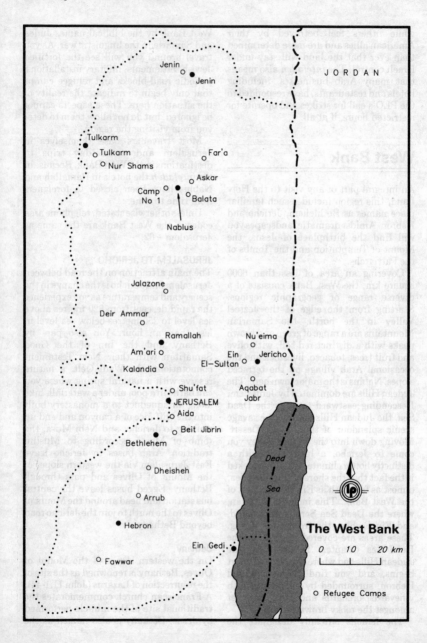

The West Bank

place where Jesus was anointed, much to the disapproval of his disciples (Matthew 26:6-13, Mark 14:3-9, John 12:1-8). The church features some impressive mosaics, one of which illustrates the resurrection. Built in 1954, this is the fourth church to occupy the area. The first was constructed in the mid-1st century, the second in the Byzantine period and the third by the Crusaders.

A Greek Orthodox church stands by the Tomb of Lazarus. In the 16th century Muslims built a mosque here and Christians later dug their own entrance to enable them to worship. Local guides are often on hand and do a decent job of telling their interesting version of the local history. If you listen, you should tip a couple of sheqels. It's open daily 8 am to 12 noon, 2 to 6 pm and admission is 30c.

The church itself is only open to the public on the Feast of Lazarus, usually in early April. The Greek Orthodox convent, a 10-minute walk away from Jerusalem, boasts the rock upon which Jesus sat while waiting for Martha to arrive from Jericho. Ring the bell to enter.

To reach Bethany you can take either of two Arab buses – the Bethany service, No 36 (there are two No 36 services, ask for *El-Azariya* – Lazarus – before boarding) or No 28 to Jericho and get off on the way through. Another option is to walk. If it's not too hot (or too wet), you can walk up and over the Mount of Olives and around the side to Bethany, or choose other routes. You can't really get lost, and you're never far from a busy road on which to hitch-hike or hail a service taxi.

Inn of the Good Samaritan
After Bethany the Jericho road winds its way eastward through a suddenly barren landscape. You will usually see one or two Bedouin camps here. About 10 km from Bethany the road climbs the mountain called Ma'ale Adumim, Red Ascent, after the soil's reddish tint. In ancient Israel this marked the tribal border of Judah to the south with Benjamin to the north.

On the right-hand side of the road is a 16th century Turkish building called the Inn of the Good Samaritan by Christians who believe that this is the site of the inn of Jesus' parable (Luke 10:25-37). There is little to see here and the sight of the signpost as you speed by will probably be enough.

Atop the nearby hill are the ruins of a Crusader fortress, Tour Rouge. It overlooks the Judean wilderness and what was an ancient caravan route where the Romans later built a road.

Nebi Musa
Beyond the turn-off for the Wadi Qelt and, eight km from Jericho, a side road to the right leads 1½ km to Nebi Musa, which is revered by the Muslims as the tomb of Moses. Some see this belief as being more politically than spiritually inspired, claiming that the site has changed from being a place where Moses and his unknown tomb were venerated to 'become' the tomb itself, due to a combination of simple peasants mis-interpreting its status and the political rivalry between the Muslim and Christian hierarchy.

Nebi Musa stands on an old road from Jerusalem where Muslims used to come to venerate the prophet because Mount Nebo can be seen across the Jordan Valley (now in Jordan). According to Deuteronomy 34 it was there that Moses was shown the Promised Land by God and where he died. In 1269 the Mameluke Sultan Baybars built the mosque here which was later joined by accommodation quarters for pilgrims. The complex was extended in the 1470s to the spacious dimensions seen today.

Around 1820 the Turks launched a major restoration project and instigated an annual pilgrimage. It is claimed that this was done to compete with the Easter ceremonies staged by the Orthodox Christian churches. It became the custom for thousands of Muslim pilgrims to arrive in Jerusalem for a seven-day pilgrimage that coincided with Holy Week. This started on the Friday with prayers at El Aqsa Mosque, after which came a day-long march to Nebi Musa followed by five days of prayers, feasting and games before a return procession. It grew to become one of Palestine's most popular and colourful events, but with the rise of Arab nationalism during the Mandate it was carefully controlled by the British and was eventually stopped by the Jordanians.

In the belief that this is the tomb of Moses, many Muslims choose to be buried here. Tradition also identifies two of the tombs in the large cemetery as those of Moses' shepherd, Hassan er-Rai, and of Aisha, Mohammed's favourite wife.

With the landscape of the Judean Desert an impressive backdrop, Nebi Musa is worth seeing. Getting inside is dependent upon the watchman being here and in the mood to let you in. During Easter you will not normally be allowed in, and with a tradition of political demonstrations being staged here at this time you probably won't want to be.

WADI QELT & ST GEORGE'S MONASTERY
The hike through the Wadi Qelt to Jericho, stopping off at St George's Monastery along the way, is popular. If you don't fancy the long trail through the canyon there is a more direct road leading past the monastery on its way to Jericho.

A wadi is a rocky watercourse that is dry except in the rainy season, and the Wadi Qelt runs through a steep canyon surrounded by limestone and chalk cliffs, the barren terrain dotted with clumps of trees and foliage.

Wadi Qelt Hike
Taking about four hours, this hike involves some straightforward walking over slightly rough ground with a bit of scrambling over rocks here and there. Regular sports shoes are suitable footwear – sandals are not. In winter it is often muddy underfoot in places and you can also end up getting your feet wet wading through shallow water. Flash floods are a danger at this time, with a sudden downpour being followed by a rush of water. Keep an eye on the weather and be ready to climb to higher ground.

Take plenty of water and cover your head. Also remember to take suitable clothes for the visit to the monastery. Although the monks will usually provide some unflattering rags for you to cover your legs and arms, you will show more respect by providing your own. The Wadi Qelt is much warmer than Jerusalem though, so you might prefer to carry them to slip on when you get there.

At the turn-off on the Jerusalem-Jericho road, follow the sign to the monastery. After five minutes the road forks at another sign for the monastery pointing to the right. This is the direct route that avoids the wadi, so go to the left and after 100 metres turn right onto the dirt track that winds down to the valley, with a marvellous view before you. After 25 minutes you arrive at the spring, Ein Qelt, and the nature reserve. The aqueduct here carries spring water from Ein Fuwwar, a few km west of here, to Jericho. It was restored by the British, but note the ruins of the Herodian aqueduct.

Further along the wadi to the left you will find some picturesque bathing possibilities; climb up the opposite bank and turn right though for the monastery and Jericho. Following the path beside the aqueduct you will see occasional red on white painted trail markers showing the way. The paint must have been in short supply as they often appear at intervals lengthy enough to make you wonder whether you are still heading in the right direction.

After following the aqueduct for about 40 minutes the trail leads down to the wadi; this can be tricky if there is a lot of water. After another 45 minutes you'll pass under the ruined arches where the Herodian aqueduct crossed the canyon.

Follow the wadi a little further and around the next bend you will see the monastery.

After visiting the monastery stay on the same side of the wadi, with the trail climbing high above the bed. Look out for the first sight of the Jordan Valley after about 25 minutes as you pass caves once used by hermits and the ruins of other monasteries. The trail later splits; you can either follow the wadi or climb up the other side.

If you choose the latter route, you find yourself by a largely abandoned refugee camp where young children insist that they be paid for saying 'shalom – baksheesh'. Head for the road that passes the mosque (look for the minaret) and follow it through the melon and banana fields to the main road by the restaurant and military camp.

Follow the wadi to the main road and you will pass the Tulul Abu el-Alaiq excavations. On both sides of the wadi and very easy to miss (well, they were for me), these are the remains of Hasmonean, Herodian and Roman winter palaces and villas.

At the main road, which is Jerusalem Rd, turn left to enter Jericho.

St George's Monastery

The more direct route to the monastery is the right fork on the turn-off from the Jerusalem-Jericho road, as directed by the orange signposts. Look out for the metal cross that marks the monastery's location. Steps lead down into the canyon and the road continues and eventually passes the previously mentioned refugee camp and mosque, intersecting with Jerusalem Rd by the restaurant and military camp.

The monastery, named after St George of Koziba, was first built in the late 5th century, based on a small oratory built by hermits in the early 4th century. The Wadi Qelt's numerous cave-dwelling hermits would attend the divine liturgy on Saturday and Sunday. It was virtually abandoned after the Persians swept through the valley and massacred the 14 monks, but it was restored in 1179. A pilgrim in 1483 wrote that he only saw ruins here, and reconstruction began in 1878 and was completed in 1901 by the Greek Orthodox Church.

The traditions surrounding the monastery include St Elijah stopping here en route to the Sinai, and St Joachim weeping here because his wife Anne was sterile and then having an angel announce to him the news of the Virgin Mary's conception.

The oldest part of the building is the 6th century mosaic floor of the church of St George and John which features a black, white and red double-headed Byzantine eagle. The skulls of the martyred monks are kept here and a niche contains the tomb of St George. Most of the paintings and icons date from the latest reconstruction but the doors at the centre of the iconostasis date back to the late 12th century.

It's open Monday to Saturday 8 am to 5 pm, but the hours can be flexible. Admission is US$1.

Place to Eat

Top up with water at the monastery, after which the *Wadi el-Kalt Cafeteria & Restaurant* at the Jerusalem Rd intersection serves draught beer and soft drinks to thirsty hikers. Prices are higher than average. Towards Jericho on Jerusalem Rd, the *Alwaha Restaurant* is clean and serves various snacks, meals and drinks. It also has a pleasant swimming pool – admission US$3 but half price for customers.

Getting There & Away

Take Arab bus No 28 from East Jerusalem or any Egged bus that is heading for the Dead Sea or Jericho from Jerusalem's central bus station. Tell the driver that you want the Wadi Qelt and/or the monastery and keep an eye out for the orange signpost after about 25 minutes.

JERICHO (population 7000)

Reputedly the world's oldest town, Jericho is best known for the biblical account of Joshua and the tumbling walls. A popular destination for visitors, especially in the winter when its warm climate is a pleasant alternative to the cold and rain in Jerusalem, its ancient ruins are surpassed by the shabby beauty of their surroundings. Often compared to Egypt, Jericho is a lush oasis of colour, with fruit and flowers abundant amongst the greenery; quite a contrast to the desert valley setting which, at 250 metres below sea level, makes it the world's lowest town.

History

The Old Testament Book of Joshua tells how Jericho was the first town captured by the Israelites when, after their years in the wilderness, they sent in spies, crossed the River Jordan nearby, laid siege and caused the walls to collapse by the sound of their priests' trumpets.

Prior to the arrival of the Israelites around 1200 BC the climate and the perennial spring of Ein es-Sultan had attracted prehistoric nomads to the area. They settled at the adjacent Tel es-Sultan, or ancient Jericho, where archaeologists have uncovered remains of the town built around 7000 BC, making Jericho one of the known places where people changed from being wandering food gatherers to settled food producers. The tel was abandoned as a result of the Babylonian exile around 586 BC.

Becoming a centre of administration for the Persians in the late 6th century BC, there is a settlement of some sort still to be located in the area where those who worked the plantations were housed. During Alexander the Great's rule (336 to 323 BC), Jericho became the private estate of the ruling sovereign.

Mark Anthony gave the oasis to Cleopatra and after their suicide in 30 BC it was awarded to Herod the Great by Octavian, the new Roman leader. Herod had been leasing it from the Queen of Egypt, and he now put in new aqueducts to supply his winter palace by the Wadi Qelt at Tulul Abu el-Alaiq. The Byzantine period saw the area heavily populated, with synagogues built at Na'aran and near ancient Jericho, and monasteries such as St George's in the Wadi Qelt. The 8th century Hisham's Palace is an impressive remnant from the Arab period, whilst the Middle Ages saw the cultivation of sugar cane and Crusader sugar mills, and the construction of churches on the Mount of Temptation.

When Saladin defeated the Crusaders in 1187, Jericho was left undefended against Bedouin raids and what was a thriving town became a desolate village. It wasn't until the British Mandate that Jericho's natural resources were again used effectively with the development of fruit production. As a result of the 1948 War of Independence, Jordan gained control of the town which had been flooded by Arab refugees from the new State of Israel. Refugee camps, amongst the largest on the West Bank, were hastily built to house them. During the Six-Day War most of the refugees crossed the Jordan River to escape the Jewish occupation, but a few hundred still remain.

Orientation & Information

With all the 'oldest town in the world' talk, visitors usually have the wrong impression of what to expect when they arrive in Jericho. The archaeological site that is ancient Jericho lies on the northern outskirts of the present-day Arab town. The other popular sights are also quite a distance away, and this makes it difficult to see everything in one visit.

Coming from Jerusalem the Egged buses continue through the town and pass by ancient Jericho on their way to Tiberias; the Arab buses' last stop is downtown. Here you will find the main square with its police station (tel 92251), municipality building, service taxi rank

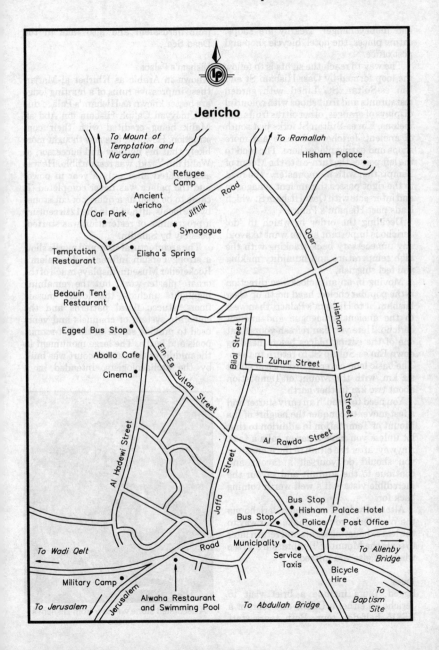

Jericho

To Mount of
Temptation and
Na'aran

To Ramallah

Hisham Palace

Refugee
Camp

Jiftlik Road

Ancient
Jericho

Car Park

Synagogue

Qasr Hisham Street

Temptation
Restaurant

Elisha's Spring

Bedouin Tent
Restaurant

Egged Bus Stop

Bilal Street

Abollo Cafe

El Zuhur Street

Cinema

Ein Es Sultan Street

Al Hadewi Street

Al Rawda Street

Jaffa Street

Bus Stop

Hisham Palace Hotel

Bus Stop

Police

Post Office

To Wadi Qelt

Municipality

Service
Taxis

To Allenby
Bridge

Military Camp

Road

Bicycle
Hire

Jerusalem

To Jerusalem

Alwaha Restaurant
and Swimming Pool

To Abdullah Bridge

To
Baptism
Site

and moneychanger. Nearby are shops, eating places, the hotel, bicycle shop and post office.

The way to reach the sights is to follow the loop formed by Qasr Hisham St and Ein es-Sultan St. Lined with garden restaurants and fruit shops with colourful displays of oranges, other citrus fruits and melons, Ein es-Sultan St forks just south of ancient Jericho and there are more shops and eating places here. The road to the left passes the turn-off to the Mount of Temptation with its monastery; the road to the right passes the ancient synagogue and intersects with Qasr Hisham St which leads past Hisham's Palace.

Deciding the order in which to 'do' Jericho is important as you want to avoid any unnecessary back-tracking with the high temperature and humidity making you feel sluggish.

Moving in an anti-clockwise direction is the popular choice: head north up Qasr Hisham St to Hisham's Palace, then west to the ancient synagogue and ancient Jericho. Here you can refresh yourself at one of the eating places before heading down Ein es-Sultan St to return to town. The basic loop covers a distance of about six km, with the Mount of Temptation about two km further north.

You need to be both an early starter and a fast mover to conquer the heights of the Mount of Temptation in addition to that lot unless you have a car or take a taxi. Anyway, after the climb to the monastery you should do yourself a favour and continue to the summit and savour the incredible vista – it's well worth coming back for.

Alternatively, if you reach Jericho via the Wadi Qelt, you can make your way to the less exhausting sights and return later to scale the Mount of Temptation and see whatever else you missed.

Tours

Egged Tours include a brief visit to Jericho on either a US$35 day tour, or a US$15 half-day tour. Both tours start from Jerusalem and also take in the Dead Sea.

Hisham's Palace

Known in Arabic as Khirbet al-Mafjar, these impressive ruins of a hunting lodge are better known as Hisham's Palace due to Umayyad Caliph Hisham ibn Abd al-Malik being credited with their construction. However, it is now thought more likely that his nephew and successor, al Walid ibn Yazid, was responsible. He was assassinated after only a year in power and the palace was never completed. It came to be used as a quarry of cut stones by the locals, although in the 12th century a programme of restoration was started, possibly by Saladin.

The architectural style and motifs show a strong Persian influence. Jerusalem's Rockefeller Museum displays much of the ornate plaster-work, but the remaining highlights include the lovely mosaic floors, stucco floral patterns and the elaborate system of channels and vents used to provide steam to the hot-rooms, pools and baths. The large monument in the middle of the central court was built by the archaeologists. Intended as a

A decorated stone window from Hisham's palace

window, it shows how the Umayyads adapted the motifs they found in the places they conquered. This star is Roman.

Hisham's Palace is open Saturday to Thursday 8 am to 5 pm, Friday 8 am to 4 pm. Admission is US$1.75, students 90c.

Ancient Synagogue

An orange signpost points to the modern building at the end of the gravel road. Inside is the mosaic floor of a 5th or 6th century synagogue. This pictures a menorah with the Hebrew inscription *Shalom al Israel* (Peace Upon Israel).

It's open daily, although the attendant's hours are erratic. While appearing to be absent, he will often arrive as if from nowhere to unlock the door and think of a suitable fee. Pay no more than US$1.50.

Ancient Jericho

Only archaeology buffs are likely to be impressed by the sight of the Tel es-Sultan excavations. The fact that they reveal the remains of a stone tower constructed around 7000 BC is interesting, as it is the only known structure from the Stone Age.

Imagination is required to put together a picture of the ancient town whilst taking in the signposted trenches and mounds of dirt. The tel grew to its present height due to successive towns being built on top of the previous one. The mud-brick wall at the tel's summit is not one of those brought down by Joshua's trumpets as initially believed. It has now been dated to a thousand years before the Israelites' arrival.

The site is open 8 am to 5.30 pm, Friday 8 am to 4.30 pm. Admission is 80c, students 45c.

Ein es-Sultan

Across the street from ancient Jericho is Ein es-Sultan, also known as Elisha's Spring, as opposed to Sultan's Spring. This will only quench your thirst, not your appetite for impressive sights: there is little to see except a shabby building and a

UN sign barring admission. This is the spring traditionally associated with 2 Kings 2:19-22 which tells of Elisha purifying the water with salt. Producing 76 litres per second, the spring's water is distributed around Jericho's fields by a complex gravity-flow irrigation system.

Mount & Monastery of Temptation

For a simply knockout view of Jericho and the Jordan Valley, with the Dead Sea to the south and the Mount of Olives to the west, you should risk bringing on a heart attack and climb to the top of this mountain. It is traditionally associated with the first and third temptations of Jesus by the Devil (Matthew 4: 1-11). The Crusaders called the mountain Mont Quarantana – 'Mount of Forty' – which the Arabs modified to Qarantal.

Similar in style to St George's in the Wadi Qelt, the Greek Orthodox monastery clings to the cliff. Rebuilt around the same time (1874-1904), it dates back to the 12th century when two churches were constructed, one here and the other on the summit. Both are known to have been in ruins by the 14th century. The monastery is built around the original church which is believed to be the cave where Jesus fasted and refused to turn stones into bread. The stone on which he supposedly sat during the confrontation with the Devil is here.

Construction of a replacement church was started on the summit in 1874 with only the surrounding wall being completed. On this site in the 2nd century BC the Syrian General Baccides built the Castle of Dok and it was here that Simon Maccabaeus was assassinated by his son-in-law Ptolemy, the governor of Jericho, in 134 BC.

The mount is deceptively further north of ancient Jericho than it looks, so give yourself plenty of time if walking or cycling. The summit is officially out of bounds but if you ask nicely (a sheqel usually does the trick) the attendant will let you through the back door of the monastery. It's well worth the extra 20-minute hike to the top. The combination of the view and the quiet stillness is superb. You may well feel like staying up here for a while; ignore the attendant if he tells you 'five minutes, five minutes'. It's open Monday to Saturday, summer 8 am to 5 pm, winter 7 am to 2 pm and 3 to 4 pm, closed Sunday. The cave-church is usually closed after 11 am.

Na'aran

About two km beyond the Mount of Temptation are the scanty remains of an ancient Jewish settlement. Close to the springs of Ein Duq, the 4th or 5th century synagogue's mosaic floor is the highlight of the site.

Places to Stay

The *Hisham Palace Hotel* (tel 922414) on Ein es-Sultan St is usually the sole choice of accommodation in town. A large, shabby place, it offers small rooms for about US$8 per person with showers, US$5.50 without. For about US$4 you can have a bed on the verandah. Bargaining is usually necessary to get these prices and be sure to get an electric fan. If you make the initial effort, the staff can be friendly and hospitable. The *Park Hotel*, north of the town centre between Ein el-Sultan St and Qasr Hisham St, is sometimes open in the winter with similar prices when the Palace fills.

Places to Eat

In the town itself there are a few cafés and felafel/shishlik joints, but nothing outstanding. The best deal is at the *Temptation Restaurant* near ancient Jericho. Here you can help yourself from a good selection of salads (US$4) or meats (US$6) in pleasant and cool surroundings. *The Steak House* across the road is also a nice place. Draught beer is served in chilled glasses and the felafel sandwiches, while not cheap, are large and delicious.

The *Alwaha Restaurant*, south of the town centre on Jerusalem Rd, has a pleasant swimming pool (admission US$2.70, half price for customers) and serves various snacks and meals.

The garden restaurants on Ein es-Sultan St rarely seem to have enough trade to survive but in winter especially, they are popular with both Arabs and Jews, serving Palestinian meat specialities and salads. Look out for the *Bedouin Tent Restaurant* with its bizarre water-wheel based on a Drott mechanical digger.

The prices of the fruits attractively displayed here are much higher than those in Jerusalem.

Getting There & Away

Arab bus No 28 runs daily from the Suleiman St station in East Jerusalem about every 20 minutes. The last bus leaves Jericho at about 4.30 pm. The faster Egged buses operate from Jerusalem's central bus station to pass through Jericho en route to Beit She'an and Tiberias. They can drop you off near the ancient archaeological site as they head north on Ein es-Sultan St. The returning buses can be flagged down here until late in the evening.

Service taxis operate from the rank opposite Jerusalem's Damascus Gate – US$2 for the pleasant 30-minute drive. In Jericho they operate from the town square, usually until about 5.30 pm. You can find taxis after this time but with a shortage of passengers you may have to fork out for a higher fare.

Getting Around

With the distance involved between the town and the sights, cycling is a popular mode of transport. The roads are relatively flat and free of traffic so decide for yourself whether the heat is easier to bear on foot or on the saddle of a rented boneshaker. The bicycle shop is on al-Madaras St, just off the town square. Bargaining hard, you should pay about US$3 for the day. A passport or another suitable document will be asked for as security.

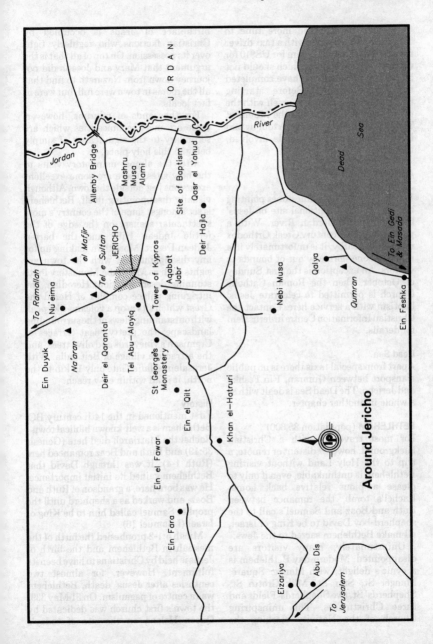

Around Jericho

You can devote even more time to bargaining and arrange with a taxi-driver for a tour of the sights – aim for US$10 for up to seven passengers, which should not be paid in full until you have completed the agreed circuit. Before starting negotiations familiarise yourself with the town's layout and include the Mount of Temptation in the itinerary. A tour by taxi is often not worth the hassle involved, though.

AROUND JERICHO
Jesus' Baptism Site
You will see old-style milestones pointing the way to the traditional site of Jesus' baptism on the Jordan River. With a picturesque 19th century Greek Orthodox monastery nearby, it is unfortunately in a military zone normally out of bounds to visitors. An exception is the first Sunday of October when the Roman Catholic Church is permitted to celebrate Jesus' baptism with a service here. Contact the Christian Information Centre in Jerusalem for details.

Dead Sea
Apart from special taxis there is no public transport between Qumran, Ein Feshka and Jericho. The Dead Sea is dealt with as a whole in another chapter.

BETHLEHEM (population 35,000)
For most travellers with a Christian background, however distant or remote, a trip to the Holy Land without visiting Bethlehem is unthinkable, even if only to please a pious relative back home. Rachel's tomb, the romance between Ruth and Boaz and Samuel's call to the shepherd-boy David to be King of Israel, all make Bethlehem sacred to the Jews.

Unfortunately, many visitors are disappointed. Modern-day Bethlehem is a cynic's delight, with Manger Square, Manger St, Star St, Milk Grotto St, Shepherds' St, two Shepherds' Fields and three Christmases. The uninspiring Church of the Nativity marking the

birthplace of Jesus is occupied by Christian factions who regularly fight over its possession. On top of all that is the argument that Mary and Joseph did not journey down from Nazareth to find that all the rooms in town were full, but were in fact locals.

For thousands of pilgrims, however, these are mere technicalities which are secondary to the significance of simply being in this holy place.

After the almost mandatory visits to the holy sites, there are some excellent excursions just outside the town. Although visually disappointing itself, Bethlehem is set amongst some of the country's most spectacular scenery on the edge of the fertile Judean Hills and the barren Judean Desert. More than making up for any disappointment with the town are sights such as Mar Saba Monastery in its stunning desert location; Herodian, the intriguing palace complex of Herod the Great which sits atop a volcano-like peak with outstanding views of the surrounding landscape; the pretty, neat terraces of Cremisan's vineyards and olive trees; and the attractive village of Beit Jalla. With Jerusalem's Jaffa Gate only 10 km to the north, it is all within easy reach.

History
First mentioned in the 14th century BC, Bethlehem is a well-known biblical town – Rachel the Matriarch died here (Genesis 35:19) and Ruth and Boaz romanced here (Ruth 1-4). It was through David that Bethlehem gained its initial importance. He was born here, a grandson of Ruth and Boaz, and worked as a shepherd until the prophet Samuel called him to be King of Israel (I Samuel 16).

Micah 5:1-2 prophesied the birth of the messiah in Bethlehem and the birth of Jesus is held by Christians to have been its fulfilment. However, for almost two centuries after Jesus' death, Bethlehem was a centre of paganism. On 31 May 339, the town's first church was dedicated by Queen Helena on the site of today's

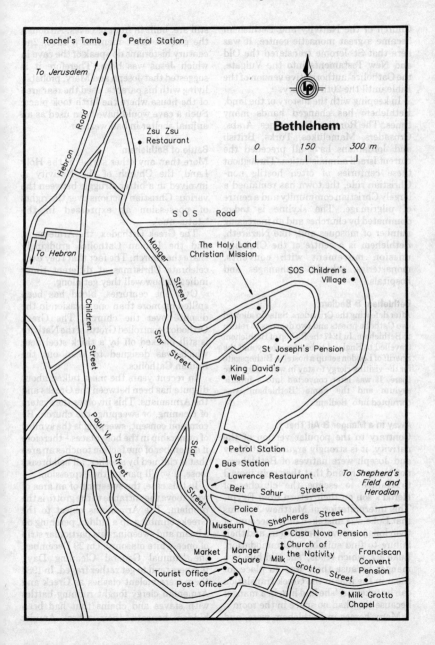

Bethlehem

0   150   300 m

Rachel's Tomb
Petrol Station
To Jerusalem
Hebron Road
Zsu Zsu Restaurant
To Hebron
SOS Road
Manger Street
Children Street
Star Street
The Holy Land Christian Mission
SOS Children's Village
St Joseph's Pension
King David's Well
Paul VI Street
Star Street
Petrol Station
Bus Station
Lawrence Restaurant
Beit Sahur Street
To Shepherd's Field and Herodian
Police
Shepherds Street
Museum
Casa Nova Pension
Church of the Nativity
Market
Manger Square
Milk Grotto Street
Franciscan Convent Pension
Tourist Office
Post Office
Milk Grotto Chapel

Church of the Nativity and Bethlehem became a great monastic centre. It was here that St Jerome translated the Old and New Testaments into the Vulgate, the Catholics' authoritative version of the Bible until the 20th century.

In keeping with the history of the land, Bethlehem has changed hands many times. The Romans, Byzantines, Arabs, Crusaders, Mamelukes, Turks, British and Jordanians have all preceded the current Israeli administration. Throughout these centuries of often hostile non-Christian rule, the town has remained a largely Christian community and a centre of pilgrimage. The skyline is today dominated by churches and an increasing number of mosques and, like Nazareth, Bethlehem is a centre of the Christian mission movement with convents, monasteries, schools, orphanages and hospitals.

Bethlehem & Bedlam

After defeating the Crusaders, Saladin allowed two Catholic priests and two deacons to return to Bethlehem. In 1247 the Bishop of Bethlehem travelled to England to beg for money and the Sheriff of London set up a hostel in Bishopsgate for the visiting clergy to stay in while they were there. It was later converted into a lunatic asylum and the name 'Bethlehem' was corrupted into 'Bedlam'.

Away in a Manger & All That

Contrary to the popular version of the nativity, it is strongly argued that Mary and Joseph were natives of Bethlehem, not Nazareth, and that they only moved to Galilee to escape the clutches of Herod's son on their return from Egypt. This interpretation of Matthew 2 claims that Luke was mistaken in his account of their long journey to Bethlehem, and their failure to find suitable accommodation. Luke 2:7, which reads, 'she laid him in a manger because there was no place for them in the inn' in the Greek translation can be taken as, 'she laid him in a manger because they had no space in the room'.

Many homes in Bethlehem were, and

still are, built in front of caves. Although the gospels don't mention a cave, 2nd century historians do speak of the cave in which Jesus was born. Therefore it is suggested that Joseph and Mary, probably living with his parents, used the rear area of the house where the birth took place. Such a cave would have been used as an animal shelter in bad weather.

Battle of Bethlehem

More than any other shrine in the Holy Land, the Church of the Nativity is involved in a bitter struggle between the various Christian factions over the rights of possession as expressed in the 'status quo'.

The Greek Orthodox, the Armenians, and the Roman Catholics grudgingly share the church. The fact that they each celebrate Christmas at different times indicates how well they get along.

Over the centuries, blood has been spilled on more than one occasion in the dispute over the church. The Greek Orthodox-controlled Grotto of the Nativity is still blocked off by a thick steel door which was designed to keep out the Roman Catholics.

In recent years the most talked about dispute has been between the Greeks and the Armenians. This involves the system of cleaning, or sweeping, the church. By common consent, sweeping is the symbol of ownership in the holy places – therefore if a member of one faction touches an area that is claimed by another, all hell breaks loose, if you'll pardon the expression.

In this case, the sweeping of an area of wall above the entrance to the grotto is the problem. The Armenians object to the Greeks climbing up a ladder, perching on a beam and sweeping this particular strip of once-white masonry. On 29 December, the 'Annual General Cleaning Day', tempers tend to get rather frayed. In 1984 there were violent clashes as Greek and Armenian clergy fought running battles with staves and chains that had been hidden beneath their robes. Amidst

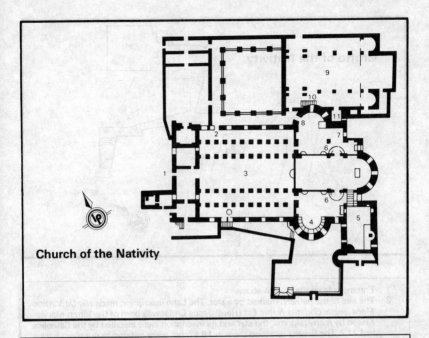

Church of the Nativity

1   The main entrance to the church is through a small door. This is one of three 6th century entrances, the others have been blocked up. The Crusaders first reduced its size to prevent attackers from riding in. Later, either during the Mameluke or the Ottoman period, it was made even smaller to prevent looters from driving their carts inside.

2   If there is a long queue of visitors slowly working its way through the tiny main entrance, you can save time by taking the entrance to the left and turning right as you come out onto the cloistered courtyard. The door here leads into the church.

3   The red limestone pillars here may date back to the original 4th century church. They were decorated by individual Crusaders with paintings of saints. Wooden trapdoors are usually left open to reveal the original 4th century mosaic floor.

4   Exit to the Greek Orthodox monastery.

5   Greek Orthodox monastery.

6   Entrances to the Grotto of the Nativity.

7   Armenian chapel.

8   Entrance to St Catherine's Church.

9   The Franciscan St Catherine's Church was built in 1881. It is here that the Midnight Mass is held on 24 December and broadcast around the world.

10 Entrance to the caves.

11 Statue of St Mary.

accusations and counter accusations of 'bully boys' being hired for the day to take part in the violence, the Jewish authorities frantically tried to find a diplomatic solution.

The result was that the Greeks were

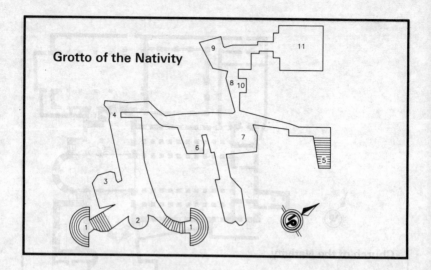

Grotto of the Nativity

1. Entrances from the church above.
2. The site of the nativity, marked by a star. The Latin inscription reads *Hic De Virgine Maria Jesus Christus Natus Est* (Here Jesus Christ was born of the Virgin Mary). Kissed by many pilgrims, the star and its inscription were installed by the Catholics in 1717. The Greeks removed them in 1847, but were ordered to put them back by the Turkish authorities in 1853. The quarrel over the star was one of the causes of the Crimean War (1853- 56) when Russia fought against Turkey, Britain and France.
3. Here is where Jesus supposedly 'laid in a manger'. The actual manger believed to have been used is now kept in the Church of Santa Maria Maggiore in Rome.
4. Normally the gate here is locked. To reach the nearby caves, head back up the stairs to the church and use the other entrance in the Church of St Catherine.
5. These steps inside the Church of St Catherine lead down to caves which tradition, with little historical evidence, associates with various figures and events.
6. St Joseph's Cave, where Joseph had a dream in which an angel warned him to flee to Egypt (Matthew 2:13).
7. Chapel of the Holy Innocents, in memory of the children slaughtered by Herod (Matthew 2:16).
8. Tombs of St Paula and her daughter Eustochia. A noble Roman woman, Paula led the sisterhood founded here by St Jerome. She died in 404, her daughter in 419.
9. Tomb of St Jerome, who died in 420. His remains were transferred to the Church of Santa Maggiore in Rome.
10. Tomb of Eusebius, who succeeded Jerome as head of the local monastic community.
11. The room where Jerome translated the Bible.

able to sweep, but without actually walking along the beam. The Greek Patriarch was not happy and wrote a stiff letter of protest to the Israeli Governor of Judea and Samaria – the 'status quo' continues to be a cause of controversy.

Orientation

Bethlehem lies just to the east of the Jerusalem-Hebron road. Manger St intersects here, with Rachel's Tomb opposite, to wind south to Manger Square. This is the the town centre, dominated by parked cars, tour buses and taxis, and here you will find the Church of the Nativity, tourist office, police station, post office, shops, hotels and eating places. Milk Grotto St heads off to the south-east, past the Milk Grotto Chapel. Paul VI St heads uphill to the north-west, with the museum, outdoor market and more shops and hotels along the network of winding streets.

The two Shepherds' Fields are almost two km east of the town, beyond the village of Beit Sahur. The monasteries of Theodosius and Mar Saba lie seven km and then another seven km further east, with Herodian eight km to the south. The village of Beit Jalla lies west of Hebron Rd, with Cremisan beyond it, up the steep hill.

Information

Tourist Office The IGTO (tel 742591) is on Manger Square, on the west side, next to the post office. Their information is consistently inaccurate. It's open Monday to Friday, summer 8 am to 5 pm, winter 8am to 4 pm, Saturday 8 am to 1 pm, closed Sunday. During Ramadan, Saturday to Thursday 9 am to 2.30 pm, closed Friday.

Post Office & International Telephones These are on the west side of Manger Square, next to the tourist office, and open Monday to Saturday 8 am to 5 pm, closed Sunday, during Ramadan Monday to Thursday and Saturday 9 am to 3 pm, closed Friday and Sunday.

Other There are banks on Manger Square and on Paul VI St and Manger St. The police station (tel 741581 or 100) is on Manger Square too.

Church of the Nativity

Probably even more of a disappointment to visitors than the Church of the Holy Sepulchre, this is, nonetheless, generally agreed to be the likeliest site of the nativity. One of the world's oldest churches, it is built like a citadel over the cave where it is believed that Jesus was born.

Emperor Constantine's 4th century church was altered considerably by Emperor Justinian around 530. His aim was to create a major shrine that would overshadow all others, including those in Jerusalem. Apart from the roof and the floor, which have been replaced several times, the basic structure of his church has remained in use to the present day.

On 6 June 1099 the Crusaders captured the church, a major prize. They crowned their kings here and between 1165 and 1169 and embarked on a major restoration programme, renewing the interior decoration and replacing the roof. Under Saladin the church was respectfully preserved, but with his defeat by the Mamelukes in the 13th century came the start of a long period of abuse which lasted right through to the end of the Ottoman period at the beginning of the 20th century. Infrequent repairs and systematic looting, along with an earthquake in 1834 and a fire in 1869 that destroyed the cave's furnishings, all took their toll.

The church is open daily, 8 am to 5 pm in winter, and in summer 7 am to 6 pm. Admission is free. The adjoining Church of St Catherine and the underground caves are closed daily 12 noon to 2 pm.

Milk Grotto Chapel

A few minutes walk along Milk Grotto St on the south side, this Franciscan chapel is where tradition has it that the Holy Family sheltered on their way to Egypt. It is said that while Mary was breast-feeding the baby Jesus, some of the milk fell to the floor. According to some versions of the tradition, this caused the rock out of which the cavern is built to turn chalky white. Women come here to pray in the belief that the white stone helps their lactation, and packets of the powdered stone are sold to pilgrims. The chapel is open daily 8 to 11.45 am and 2 to 5 pm. Admission is free, ring the bell in the courtyard to enter.

Bethlehem Museum
On Paul VI St, just up from Manger Square and on the north side, this small museum has exhibits of traditional Palestinian crafts and costumes. It's open Monday to Saturday 10 am to 12 noon and 2.30 to 5.30 pm, closed Sunday. Admission is 80c.

Market
Across from the Syrian Orthodox Church on Paul VI St, a short way up from Manger Square, the market is a small affair with stalls catering to the everyday needs of the locals rather than the tourists.

King David Cinema & King David's Well
On Star St, about ½ km north of Manger Square, the King David Cinema presents a film, *Jesus*, which is a virtual word-for-word dramatisation of Luke's gospel. Poorly acted and directed, it is not the wonderful experience that the Christian organisation responsible for it would have you believe. Even more of a non-event are the three restored water-cisterns in the parking lot outside the cinema. They are associated with 2 Samuel 23:13-17 which tells of the thirsty David offering the water to God as a sacrifice.

Rachel's Tomb
One of Judaism's most sacred shrines, also revered by Muslims and Christians, this is the tomb of the matriarch Rachel, wife of Jacob and mother of Benjamin (Genesis 35:19-20). Inside a plain, white-washed building built by Sir Moses Montefiore in 1860, the tomb attracts people who pray for fertility and a safe birth. You will often find Sephardic Jewish women here weeping and praying.

It's at the intersection of Hebron Rd and Manger St and all buses between Jerusalem, Bethlehem and Hebron pass by. It opens Sunday to Thursday 8 am to 5 pm, Friday 8 am to 1 pm, closed Saturday. Admission is free; cardboard yarmulkas are provided.

Places to Stay
Bethlehem's accommodation choice is somewhat limited (some things never change) and at Christmas and Easter you will need to plan ahead to be sure of a place to stay. Most people prefer to remain in Jerusalem with its wider choice and often lower prices.

Along Milk Grotto St, beyond the chapel, the *Franciscan Convent Pension* (tel 742441) is run by pleasant nuns who provide basic but clean and comfortable accommodation. Dorm beds are US$6, when they're full floor space is US$3.50. Singles or doubles are US$15 per person, with breakfast. Curfew is 9 pm for men, 8 pm for women.

Near the King David Cinema, *St Joseph's Pension* (tel 742483) on Manger St is run by friendly Syrian Catholics. Singles or doubles are about US$10 per person, floor space when full can be negotiated for about US$3.50. Curfew 11 pm.

Part of the Church of the Nativity complex is the recently renovated Franciscan *Casa Nova Hospice*. This lovely place is the nicest looking in town but you will often have to deal with the holy bureaucracy of the staff to get in. Great facilities and good food make it worth the effort. It costs US$23 for half board, US$26 full board plus 15%. Curfew 11 pm.

The *Al-Andalus Hotel* (tel 741348) is upstairs on Manger Square. It has clean rooms and facilities but it's a bit depressing. Singles/doubles US$18/32, with breakfast. Curfew 11 pm. Expect to pay about 25% more at Christmas.

On Manger St, just down from the Church of the Nativity, the *Palace Hotel*

(tel 742798) was built by the Greek Orthodox. It's a bit run-down but is clean, and has singles/doubles for US$22/32. In the quiet summer months you can bargain for less.

There are some more hotels among the narrow streets north-west of Manger Square off Paul VI St. The *Bethlehem Star* (tel 743249) on Al Baten St, has singles/doubles for US$18/32, with breakfast. The *Handal* (tel 742494) has singles/doubles US$18/30, with breakfast. Add 20% for Christmas and Easter.

Places to Eat
Bethlehem in Hebrew is *Beit Lechem* (House of Bread), and in Arabic *Beit Lahem* (House of Meat).

A few felafel merchants compete on the steps leading up from Manger St to Manger Square. Try the market or the various grocer stores nearby for provisions. The *Reem Restaurant*, down the side street past the bakery on Paul VI St, is inexpensive with hummus and other salads for about US$1.50.

For cheap draught beer head north along Manger St to the *Hamburger House*; the proprietor is a Palestinian who recently returned from Chile. Between the bus station and Manger Square, the *Lawrence Restaurant* serves good home-made burgers with salad and chips for US$2.50. The beer glasses are chilled, never a bad sign. Lawrence is an artist who specialises in mother-of-pearl and has had exhibitions of his work.

One of the best meat restaurants anywhere is *Zsu Zsu*, next to the Nissan Store on Manger St, down from Rachel's tomb. Named after the extrovert proprietor, you can enjoy here some of the tastiest shishlik and kebabs around. Look at spending US$6-12 per person.

Getting There & Away
Arab bus No 22 runs frequently from East Jerusalem and stops outside Jaffa Gate en route. Service taxis from outside Damascus Gate take half that time. The last bus leaves Bethlehem at about 6 pm; taxis can be found after this time but you will often have to pay a special price due to a lack of fellow passengers.

Arab bus No 23, running between Jerusalem and Hebron, passes by Rachel's Tomb, as do Egged buses that go to Hebron and Qiryat Arba.

Being so close, walking from Jerusalem to Bethlehem is a popular option. At Christmas there is an official procession, but the two to 2½ hour, downhill-all-the-way hike is pleasant all year round. Follow Hebron Rd out past the Jerusalem railway station and eventually you will emerge into the countryside. Pass the Greek Orthodox Elias Monastery and you will see Bethlehem in front of you.

Getting Around
With the exception of Rachel's Tomb, the sights are within easy walking distance of the bus station and taxi rank. If you want to visit the tomb, it is perhaps best, if coming from Jerusalem, to stop here, rather than stay with the bus or taxi to the town centre. With the frequent bus service, you can then easily continue to the centre to see the other places of interest.

AROUND BETHLEHEM
Beit Jalla, Gillo & Cremisan
Past Rachel's Tomb in the direction of Hebron, a road heads west up the hill to the pleasant Christian Arab village of Beit Jalla. The road continues to the summit of Har Gillo, believed to be biblical Gillo, the home of King David's counsellor, Anhithophel. With great views of Jerusalem it is a popular picnic site. Back down the slope, a side road leads to the attractive Salesian monastery of Cremisan (tel 742605), renowned for its wine and olive oil.

Getting There & Away Arab bus No 21 runs from Jerusalem to Beit Jalla. From here it is a steep walk to either the summit or the monastery.

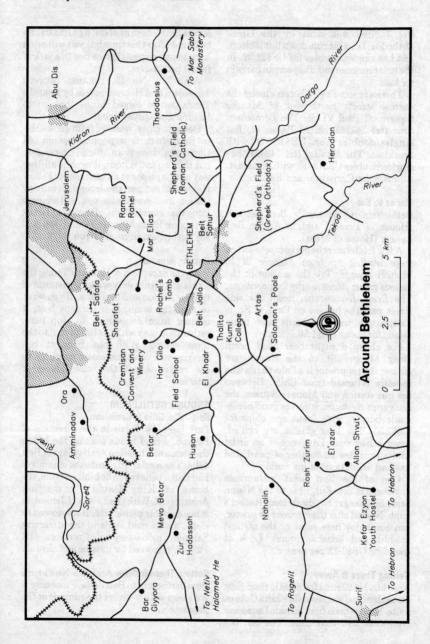

Around Bethlehem

Ruth's & Shepherds' Fields

The village of Beit Sahur stands one km east of Bethlehem. Nearby, the Field of Ruth is traditionally associated with the events of the Old Testament Book of Ruth. In Hebrew, Beit Sahur means 'Village of the Watching' and both the Roman Catholics and the Greek Orthodox have a Shepherds' Field associated with the shepherds mentioned in Luke 2:8-18.

The Roman Catholic site features a Franciscan chapel built in 1954. There are ruins of a Byzantine monastery nearby, destroyed by the Persians in 614. The Greek Orthodox site features a 5th century church built over a cave with a mosaic floor.

Getting There & Away Arab bus No 47 leaves from Manger St by the police station for Beit Sahur. The respective fields are about a 20 minute walk further east from the village, beyond the fork in the road. Take the right fork for the Greek Orthodox field, left for the Roman Catholic. Alternatively, you can walk the three or four km from Bethlehem.

Mar Saba Monastery

Simply one of the most impressive buildings in the Holy Land due to the combination of architecture and location, this Greek Orthodox monastery is strictly closed to women, but the outside alone is worth a visit.

The monastery is on the steep bank of the Kidron River in the proverbial middle of nowhere, which in this case is the Judean Desert. Unless you have your own car, you will have to walk the eight km from where the bus stops in the village of Abusiye.

Just before the last stop is another monastery. Overlooking Abusiye, the large Monastery of Theodosius or Deir Dosi is built over a cave where the three wise men supposedly rested on their way home from Bethlehem. It was founded by St Theodosius and accommodated 400

monks by the time he died in 529. Restored in 1893, only one monk and a nun live here now (they are genuinely brother and sister, I am told), and they will often refuse access. There is little to see anyway; some 7th century mosaics and skulls of monks massacred by the Persians are stored underground.

The Mar Saba Monastery was founded in 482 by St Sabas (439-532). He had been living in a cave (look for the cross and letters A and C on the opposite side of the wadi), but with an increasing number of disciples he needed more room. The Persians massacred the occupants in 614 but the monastery managed to continue, with its 'golden age' occurring in the 8th and 9th centuries. However, until as recently as the 19th century the monks were still subjected to hostility, occasionally resulting in murderous attacks. After an earthquake in 1834 caused considerable damage the buildings were almost completely reconstructed, hence their impressive appearance today.

The body of St Sabas is displayed in the main church. It had been removed by the Crusaders but was returned by Pope Paul VI in 1965. More skulls of monks massacred by the Persians can also be seen. The adjacent Tower of St Simeon, built in 1612, is sometimes open to women and a path runs past here down into the wadi, which is rather smelly courtesy of the Jerusalemites who use the river as a sewer. You should make a point of crossing over to the other side for the superb view of the monastery. It is mainly this that makes the hot hike worthwhile. There were some 5000 men living over here in the caves before the monastery was built.

To enter the monastery, pull the bell chain by the blue door. To enter, you must be suitably dressed (and of acceptable sex) – with the heat it's best to bring long pants to slip over shorts when on arrival. There are no set opening hours and the monks will normally let you in. However, on Sundays and at mealtimes your rings may be ignored. Saturdays are relatively busy with other visitors, so a morning visit during the week is best.

Getting There & Away Take Arab bus No 60 from Bethlehem bus station to the last stop, or get off by the Monastery of Theodosius. The last bus back to Bethlehem leaves Abusiye at about 4 pm. From here follow the road east. After a km it forks; take the left branch. You will be hassled by children demanding baksheesh until you leave the outskirts of the village. The walk takes 1½ to two hours each way. Bring plenty of water – you can get a refill from the monastery. Hitch-hiking is possible, although there is little traffic, and you will be especially grateful of a ride for the steep climb back from the monastery.

Herodian

Built by Herod the Great between 24 and 15 BC, the Herodian palace complex occupies the top of a hill reshaped as part of the construction programme. About 100 metres above the surrounding area and looking rather like a volcano, it offers more great views and the remains of the citadel.

A lavish and luxurious place in its day, a stairway of white marble led up to the ring of round towers enclosing apartments, baths and a garden. It is not certain whether Herod was buried here as he had instructed. During the First Revolt (66 to 70 AD) the Jewish rebels attacked the Herodian and sheltered here. During the Second Revolt (132-5) they used it as an administrative centre. In the 5th century Byzantine monks established a monastery among the ruins.

The site is open Saturday to Thursday 8 am to 5 pm, Friday 8 am to 4 pm. Admission is US$1.50, students 75c.

Getting There & Away Although the Bethlehem tourist office will only tell you about the taxi service, you can use the bus system although it is infrequent. Ask a few locals and use the most popular answer to

determine which bus and when. No 52 was the one I caught, but on a previous visit I took No 47 from Manger St to Beit Sahur and changed there. Egged bus No 66 also stops nearby. Another alternative is simply to walk and hitch-hike. The Herodian stands about eight km south of Beit Sahur – take the right fork past the Greek Orthodox Shepherds' Field.

Wadi Khareitun

Two km south-west of the Herodian the road crosses a wadi where you can see some prehistoric caves – follow the path on the right-hand side to get a good view as the wadi deepens. Continue for three km to the end of the path and you will come across the ruins of a Byzantine monastery established in the 4th century by St Chariton and remaining in use up to the 12th or 13th century.

Still occupied by Bedouin, the first cave was home to prehistoric families from around 80,000 BC. The second cave has not been excavated, but the third cave is the most important. This provides archaeologists with the earliest evidence of the use of fire in Palestine and was first occupied in the Lower Palaeolithic period (500,000 to 120,000 BC).

BETWEEN BETHLEHEM & HEBRON
Solomon's Pools

Eight km south of Beit Jalla, a turn-off to the east leads to these large reservoirs and a Turkish fort. The trees and shrubs help to make this a popular picnic site and there is a café. Legend associates the pools with Solomon (Ecclesiastes 2:6); others date them to Herod. The aqueducts supplied Jerusalem with water right up to the early years of the State of Israel. The fort was built around 1540 to defend the water supply.

Getting There & Away From Manger St, Bethlehem, take Arab minibus No 1 to Dashit, the nearby Arab village. You could also take Arab bus No 23 or the

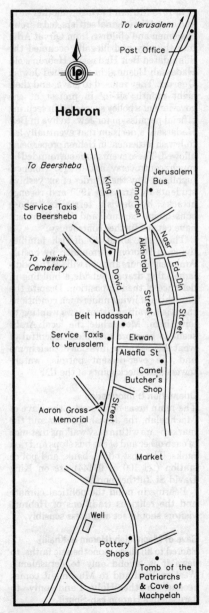

Hebron

To Jerusalem

Post Office

To Beersheba

King

Omar ben

Jerusalem Bus

Service Taxis to Beersheba

Alkhatab Street

Nasr Ed-Din Street

To Jewish Cemetery

David Street

Beit Hadassah

Service Taxis to Jerusalem

Ekwan

Alsafia St

Camel Butcher's Shop

Aaron Gross Memorial

Market

Well

Pottery Shops

Tomb of the Patriarchs & Cave of Machpelah

Egged buses which run between Jerusalem and Hebron.

Kfar Etzion
Continuing south to Hebron, after seven km a side road to the right leads to Kfar Etzion, a Jewish settlement. First established by religious Zionists in 1943, it was destroyed by the Arabs in 1948 and most of the settlers were killed. In 1967 the settlement was re-established, with some of the new settlers being the children of those killed almost 20 years before.

Halhoul
Just outside Hebron, the main road passes through the small village of Halhoul with the Tombs of Nathan and Gad (I Chronicles 29:29).

HEBRON (population 70,000)
As the burial place of Abraham, Isaac and Jacob, the city of Hebron is holy to Jews, Muslim and Christians. The Cave of Machpelah/Tomb of the Patriarchs, the main focal point for locals and visitors alike, plays no small part in making the predominantly Arab city a centre of fierce opposition to the Jewish occupation in general and to Jewish settlement in Hebron in particular. As well as this important shrine, Hebron is worth a visit for its interesting old quarter with one of the country's most colourful and authentic markets. Unfortunately, due to the controversial re-establishment of a Jewish community in Hebron, along with the problems of Jews and Muslims having to share such a major shrine, tensions in the city are worse than in, say, Bethlehem or Jericho.

History
Evidence has been found of a settlement in Hebron around 2000 BC making it one of the oldest cities in the world. It was at Hebron that God made a covenant with Abraham that he would be the father of the chosen people (Genesis 17). When his wife Sarah died, Abraham purchased the

Cave of Machpelah and the field in which it stood from Ephron the Hittite as a burial place, paying 400 silver sheqels (Genesis 23). When Abraham died, his sons Ishmael and Isaac buried him here as well. Isaac and his wife, Rebecca, were also buried here, as were Jacob and his wife Leah (Genesis 49:29-32; 50:7-9, 12-14).

Numbers 13:17-33 tells of the spies sent by Moses who came to Hebron and returned carrying grapes and other fruits from the region, and 2 Samuel tells of David's consecration and reign as king in Hebron and of Absalom's rebellion.

The Cave of Machpelah dominates Hebron's history and the succession of conquerors have left their mark. Throughout the centuries a small Jewish community had existed in relative peace amongst the Arabs. However, the late 19th century saw the start of political Zionism and Hebron's Jewish population increased with the arrival of immigrants from Eastern Europe. In the wave of Arab riots that swept Palestine in August 1929 the violence in Hebron was especially fierce. Most of the Jews were killed and the few survivors were forced to abandon the city and were evacuated to Jerusalem.

After the Israeli victory in the Six-Day War, some religious Jews were keen to re-establish a Jewish presence in Hebron, regardless of the fierce opposition from fellow Jews as well as Arabs.

The Israeli government banned Jews from settling in Hebron, not wanting to cause further upheaval, but this served merely to make these religious Jews even more determined. Unable to live in the city, they eventually reached a compromise with the government and in 1972 established Qiryat Arba, a large settlement right on the edge of Hebron, a km from the Cave of Machpelah. Not surprisingly, this development did not go down at all well with the Arabs. The Jewish settlers were also far from satisfied with this situation – they still wanted to live in Hebron proper, regardless of the obvious danger of violent resistance from the Arabs.

In 1979 Miriam Levinger, mother of 11 and one of the original settlers, led a group of women and children from Qiryat Arba into the city and illegally occupied the dilapidated Beit Hadassah, Hebron's old Hadassah Hospital in the ruined Jewish Quarter. They refused to leave, and their eight month 'sit-in' in protest at the government's policy succeeded in securing official permission for Jews to live in Beit Hadassah, a decision that eventually led to Jewish settlement in Hebron proper being allowed. These events were surrounded by much controversy and tragic violence, highlighted by the murder of six yeshiva students by Arabs in 1980 and revenge attacks by Jewish terrorists, whose subsequent capture and imprisonment have caused further controversy.

There are about 40 Jewish families living in Hebron, surrounded by hostile Arab neighbours and you will see the odd – Israeli flag draped outside a building in defiance of their opposition. Despite the hardships of living under such conditions there is a waiting list of Jews wanting to join them. Meanwhile the local Arabs seem to be more and more resentful of what they see as an invasion of their home and the ever-present patrols, watch-towers and checkpoints of the IDF.

Orientation & Information

The main areas of interest – the Cave of Machpelah, the Jewish Quarter and the market – are within easy walking distance of each other and of the bus stops and taxi ranks. The post office, bank, and police station (tel 100 or 97144) are on King David St, further north.

Bearing in mind the political climate and the religious traditions of Hebron, visitors should act and dress sensibly.

Cave of Machpelah (Haram el-Khalil)

Sacred to all three monotheistic faiths, to Jews it is second only to Jerusalem's Western Wall and to Muslims it comes second in the Holy Land only to Jerusalem's Haram esh-Sharif.

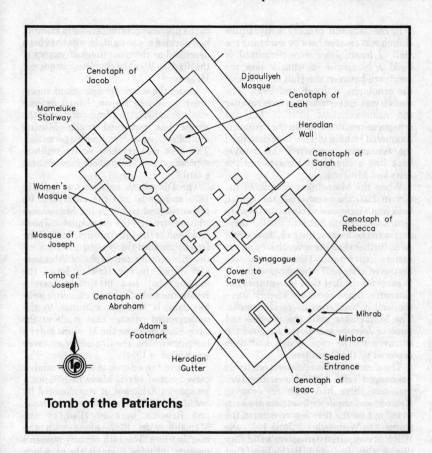

Tomb of the Patriarchs

Labels in figure:
- Cenotaph of Jacob
- Mameluke Stairway
- Women's Mosque
- Mosque of Joseph
- Tomb of Joseph
- Cenotaph of Abraham
- Adam's Footmark
- Herodian Gutter
- Djaouliyeh Mosque
- Cenotaph of Leah
- Herodian Wall
- Cenotaph of Sarah
- Cenotaph of Rebecca
- Synagogue
- Cover to Cave
- Mihrab
- Minbar
- Sealed Entrance
- Cenotaph of Isaac

Meaning 'double-cave', the name Cave of Machpelah leads visitors into expecting something quite different from the large, imposing structure that resembles a fortress. It stands over the cave purchased by Abraham because according to tradition he learned through divine inspiration that Adam and Eve were buried here. His wife, himself, his sons and their wives (except Ruth) were also buried here.

Around 20 BC, Herod the Great sealed off the cave and built the haram. Legend has it that King Solomon, assisted by jinns (Muslim genie-like spirits) did the work. You can see the chiselled borders of the massive Herodian stones. The original building had no roof, and by the southern wall of the Hall of Isaac you can see the Herodian rain-gutter carved into the stone floor.

The exact location of the cave underneath the shrine is not known. The stone cenotaphs were only designed to represent the tombs and do not necessarily reflect their true location. A popular theory is that they lie underneath the cenotaph of Abraham.

In the late 6th century a Byzantine church was created here by enclosing the Hall of Isaac. Jews were permitted to build a synagogue in what is now the courtyard between the Hall of Isaac and the cenotaphs of Jacob and Leah. The church was converted into a mosque after the Arab conquest of 638, but the synagogue remained. When the Crusaders conquered Hebron in 1100 they destroyed the synagogue, converted the mosque back into a church and massacred the Jews and Muslims.

When the Mamelukes conquered the city in 1260 they converted the church back into a mosque and permitted Jews to return to Hebron, but still denied them access to the haram. Instead, Jews could go no further than the seventh step on the eastern outer wall. This stairway was destroyed after 1967 when Jews were able to enter for the first time in centuries but you can still just about see where it was – the wall is blackened by candle smoke. The Mamelukes built the mosque and tomb of Joseph, and closed for good the entrance to the cave which had been explored by the Crusaders.

The shrine's status remained relatively unchanged until 1967. Since the 1929 massacre there had been no Jews in Hebron, and the Jewish settlers are keen to tell of how the first Jew re-entered the shrine. On Wednesday 7 June 1967, the IDF had conquered Jerusalem's Old City during the day, and Bethlehem that evening. They camped at Kfar Etzion in readiness to advance onto Hebron. At dawn, the army's chief chaplain, Rabbi Goren tried to find the officer who would lead the troops into the city, wanting to be the very first Jew to return to Hebron. Unable to find him, the rabbi ordered his driver to proceed ahead of the army. They arrived in Hebron to find the streets deserted with white flags of surrender hanging from most of the windows. The Arab population, presumably in view of the Jewish victories elsewhere and the likelihood of a fierce and bloody battle due

to the previous confrontations in Hebron, had decided not to fight. In what has been described as the most unusual victory of the Six-Day War, the chaplain 'conquered' Hebron.

Under the surrender agreement supervised by Moshe Dayan, Israeli defence minister in 1967, the administration of the shrine has remained under Muslim control, with equal Jewish access permitted. The area still remains under military supervision with IDF soldiers on permanent guard.

The Djaouliyeh mosque was built in 1320 and leads into the courtyard. Its present layout is due to the Mamelukes who constructed the cenotaphs of Jacob and Leah in the 14th century. In 1967 the Israelis installed the synagogue separating the 9th century cenotaphs of Abraham and Sarah. In the Hall of Isaac, the mosque that had previously been a Byzantine and a Crusader church, a well-like hole is the sole entrance to the underground passage that is above the cave. Each morning the Muslims lower a lamp down here. The Crusaders' entrance was sealed in 1394.

Next to the mihrab is a lovely minbar carved out of wood. Made in 1091 for a mosque in Ashkelon, it was donated by Saladin in 1191. The cenotaphs of Isaac and Rebecca were installed by the Mamelukes in 1332, along with the marble frieze. The 14th century women's mosque includes a small shrine where Arab legend has it that Adam prayed so much that his foot left a mark in the stone. Nearby, another mosque contains Joseph's cenotaph.

The site is open Saturday to Thursday 11 am to 7 pm, closed Friday (except for Muslims). Admission is free, cardboard yarmulkas are provided and suitable clothing must be worn. During the daily Muslim prayers, the times of which vary, access to the mosques is limited to Muslims only, though free access to the rest of the building remains.

Jewish Community of Hebron

The religious Jews so keen to re-establish the Jewish presence in Hebron are labelled extremists, warmongers and worse by their critics, many of whom are fellow Jews. They are certainly well organised, as shown by their success in establishing Qiryat Arba and reversing the government's policy regarding Jewish presence in Hebron. The Jewish Community of Hebron is their representative body whose basic aim is to promote and develop their cause. An active public relations department publishes a newsletter, *Hebron Today*, and offers tours of the city to show what they are trying to achieve. They also lobby politicians and prospective supporters in the Diaspora for financial, political and spiritual support.

Whether you are Jewish or not and whether you agree, disagree or have no opinion at all on the subject, it is well worth going on their guided tour of the Cave of Machpelah and the Jewish Quarter in Hebron to hear the settlers' argument and see for yourself the places involved. When I was last here the tour was free, but a small charge may have been introduced since. Phone 963057/8/9 for details.

The re-established Jewish community is centred on four main areas within the city centre:

Beit Hadassah Complex On King David St, this was the Hadassah Hospital, forced to close in 1929. It has been restored and converted into JCH offices, a museum and residential apartments. Next door to the left, Beit Chason was until 1929 the home of Ben-Zion Gershon, the pharmacist-doctor of the hospital who had the downstairs apartment, and Rabbi Chason, former Chief Rabbi of Hebron, who lived upstairs. This, too, has been renovated and converted into new apartments. To the right, Beit Hashisha is a new building erected in memory of the six yeshiva students killed by terrorists in

1980. Next door is the Beit Shneerson building.

Jewish Quarter Centred around the 16th century Avraham Avinu Synagogue, the Jewish Quarter, abandoned after the 1929 massacre and destroyed by the Jordanians in 1948, is now being restored.

Beit Romano Constructed in 1867 as a rest-home for elderly Jews, this later became a yeshiva. The Jordanians used it as a girls' school. Today it is the home of the Shavei Hebron Yeshiva, also established in memory of Jewish victims of Arab terrorists. Families as well as students now live here.

Admot Yishai Near the ancient Jewish cemetery, this is the latest settlement in Hebron. Believed to be the site of the original Jewish settlement in the city, its name is derived from the belief that Yishai, David's father, was buried nearby.

Market

Hebron's market is made special by the authentic Middle East scenes that can be observed here. With the marvellous backdrop of Crusader and Mameluke facades, vaulted ceilings, tiny shops and narrow alleyways, are crowds of Arabs, many in traditional clothes, doing their everyday shopping. Among the most unusual/revolting things to see/avoid is the butcher's shop selling camel meat. The ship of the desert can be seen moored to a meat hook, still with that expression of nonchalance on his face, hanging upside down while his intestines and feet are arranged on the shop floor to be sold separately.

Birket el-Sultan

An unattractive well or reservoir just west of the Cave of Machpelah, the 'Pool of the Sultan', is believed by some to be where David hanged the assassins of Saul's son (2 Samuel 4:12). It is now empty of water

Arab market

and has become an unofficial rubbish dump.

Places to Eat
Take your pick from the various establishments around the market and the felafel and foul carts.

Those who are interested can eat camel meat. Ask the butcher which restaurant he has recently sold meat to – don't ask the restaurants themselves as they will say anything to make you buy.

Getting There & Away
Arab bus No 23 operates regularly between Jerusalem and Hebron via Rachel's Tomb at Bethlehem. Egged also have less regular buses which go via Qiryat Arba. For only a little more, service taxis operate between Hebron and Jerusalem (opposite Damascus Gate) and are quicker and more comfortable. They also operate less frequently to and from Beersheba.

AROUND HEBRON
Qiryat Arba (population 5000)
The name of this controversial Jewish settlement just north of the city centre means 'Town of the Four', referring to the four couples who are believed to be buried in Hebron: Adam and Eve, Abraham and Sarah, Isaac and Rebecca, Jacob and Leah. There is little to see here except the contrast between the crowded city and the settlement's modern apartment blocks, wide streets and gardens behind a barbed-wire perimeter. Egged buses stop here between Jerusalem and Hebron.

Oak of Abraham
An oak tree two km west of Hebron marks the legendary site where Abraham pitched his tent (Genesis 18:1). In the Middle Ages pilgrims used to remove pieces from the tree for good luck charms, so there is not a lot to see now and the trunk is protected by steel braces, wire and nails. A nail in the coffin of the tree's authenticity is its probable age of only 600

years. The Russian Orthodox Church owns the site and its monastery is nearby.

BETWEEN JERUSALEM & RAMALLAH

Heading north from Jerusalem, the road passes over Mount Scopus towards Ramallah, first coming to the village of Shu'fat. Today this is dominated by a refugee camp with a population of over 5000 displaced Palestinians. Across to the west, with the mountains in the distance, you can see Samuel's Tomb just above the modern suburban developments. In the Middle Ages, Jews came here for solemn religious celebrations and it is where the Crusaders had their first glimpse of Jerusalem – they called it Mount Joy.

Shu'fat is the site of biblical Gilbeah, Saul's capital. King Hussein of Jordan started to build a villa here but its construction was interrupted by the Six-Day War – it's now used by the IDF. Several other pleasant homes can be seen in what was a cool summer retreat for wealthy Arabs.

El-Bireh

After passing Jerusalem airport and Tel Nashe, biblical Mizpeh, you drive under the 'Welcome to El-Bireh' archway just south of Ramallah and 14 km north of Jerusalem. Perhaps the first caravan stop on the ancient Jerusalem-Galilee route, there is little to see in this relatively affluent Arab suburb. An exception is the headquarters of the Inash El Usra Society.

Inash El Usra Society Established in 1965, this is a Palestinian women's charity organisation whose aims include improving women's general standing in the local community, helping the needy and preserving and developing Palestinian culture such as folklore and handicrafts. These aims have been put into practice by setting up vocational training centres. The society also has production centres which provide employment in these

trades for Palestinians, with profits going to charity. There is a wide range of other activities including an orphanage, child care, sponsorship of students otherwise unable to afford university education and other financial support schemes.

Perhaps of most interest to travellers is the society's Palestinian Folklore & Research Centre. Initiated in 1972 with the aim of preserving, studying and developing Palestinian folklore, this facility produces publications including the *Society & Heritage* journal, studies of villages, and books on such subjects as traditional costumes, architecture and food. It stages folkloric festivals in El-Bireh and is compiling an archive of materials. Worth a visit is its museum in the society's El-Bireh headquarters.

The society has no official political role or policy and its general aim is to improve the lot of Palestinian women. However, the inevitable view of its membership is that Israel's occupation of the West Bank and the Gaza Strip is unjust and that there should be an independent Palestine free of Jewish rule. For more information and to arrange a visit to the society's headquarters and museum, contact the Inash El-Usra Society, El-Bireh, PO Box 3549, West Bank (tel 952876, 952544). To get there it is most convenient to take a special taxi from Ramallah (about US$2.50).

RAMALLAH (population 25,000)

Arabic for 'Heights of the Lord', Ramallah and its environs are among the more affluent areas of the West Bank region, as can be seen by the houses and gardens. Before the Israeli occupation it was a summer resort popular with wealthy Jordanians. Calling it the 'Switzerland of Jordan', they came here to escape the heat of Amman.

Things to See

There are no real sights in Ramallah. However, it is a jumping-off point for other places of interest and while here a

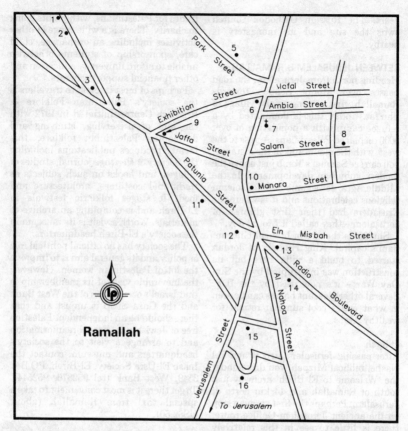

Ramallah

To Jerusalem

brief walkabout is worthwhile to get a glimpse of another Arab town in the Occupied Territories. As you check out the various shops, buildings and eating places, you will often be approached by locals curious to know where you are from and keen to talk about life in the West Bank. Next to the bus station is the small market, with the Abu Nasser Mosque nearby. Non-Muslims are not at all welcome here so don't be surprised at the grumpy reaction of the attendant if you get too close.

Places to Stay

Note that Ramallah's hotels may be closed to foreigners. Anyway, with Jerusalem and its superior choice of accommodation nearby, it is unlikely that you would choose to stay in either of Ramallah's hotels. It's not that they are so undesirable, they just fail to compete in terms of cost, cleanliness and facilities. Both on Jaffa Rd, the *Pension Miami* (tel 952808) has singles/doubles for US$11/22, the *Plaza Hotel* (tel 952020) has singles/ doubles US$8/14. These prices are negotiable, depending on your bargaining skills.

1	Pension Miami
2	Plaza Hotel
3	Na'oum Restaurant
4	Al-Rashid & Abukhader Restaurants
5	Post Office
6	Rukab's Ice Cream
7	Quaker Church
8	El Kana Restaurant
9	Mais al Reem Restaurant
10	Service Taxis
11	Special Taxis
12	Jerusalem Bus Stop (arrival)
13	El Iktisad Restaurant
14	Bus Stop (for University)
15	Bus Station
16	Mosque

Places to Eat

Ramallah has some good eating places, mostly inexpensive. On Jaffa St, the *Al-Rashid* and the *Mais al Reem* restaurants both serve excellent felafel (served stuffed with spiced onion), shwarma and kubbé. Their colourful and fancy salad displays show up their sloppy competitors elsewhere. For some reason, Ramallah's felafel is finger-shaped.

Two establishments compete for the 'best hummus in town' award. They provide other choices, too. The *El-Iktisad Restaurant* (no English sign) on Radio Blvd is a slightly grubby eatery dishing up hummus, pitta and pickles for about US$1.50, with meat US$4.50. Also available are soup and hot main dishes such as kebabs in tehina, and *okra* (a beef stew served with rice and vegetables). The cleaner *El Kana Restaurant* on Salam St does a great plate of hummus and also specialises in shishlik and kebab.

Renowned as one of the best Arab restaurants in the country, *Na'oum Restaurant & Bar* on Jaffa St is worth a splurge. Set in a pleasant garden, it has managed to continue successfully despite losing many Jordanian patrons after 1967. The menu is limited to meat dishes such as liver, 'grilled meat', steak and chicken. The speciality, *mousakhan*, should be tried. This is chicken cooked with herbs, spices and pine nuts on bread. It tastes a lot more delicious than it sounds. One person can expect to spend US$12 to US$20.

Getting There & Away

Arab bus No 18 runs from the Nablus Rd station in East Jerusalem and takes about 40 minutes. The service taxis from opposite Damascus Gate take only 10 minutes. The last bus leaves from Ramallah for Jerusalem at about 6 pm with service taxis running till about 9 pm.

BETWEEN RAMALLAH & NABLUS
Beit-El (Bethel)

On the road to Nablus, this is biblical Bethel ('House of God'), the site of Jacob's dream about a ladder (Genesis 28:10-17), and the home of Deborah (Judges 4:4-6). Bethel offers little for the visitor. There is a hill called Jacob's Ladder but you will need to have it pointed out for you to find it.

The nearby Jewish settlement of Beit-El might be of interest if you want to know more about the religious and political ideals of the West Bank settlers. Egged bus No 70 runs here from Jerusalem.

Shiloh (Seilun)

Continuing north, you come to the Arab village of Sinjil. The name comes from the original Crusader settlement here, called St Giles. After five km you come to the sparse ruins of ancient Shiloh. It was here that the Tabernacle and the Holy Ark rested before the conquest of Jerusalem (Joshua 18:1-9; I Samuel 1:3; I Samuel 4; Jeremiah 7:12; Psalm 78:60).

NABLUS (population 75,000)

Another centre of violent Palestinian opposition to Israel, Nablus is the largest West Bank town. Beautifully situated between the scenic mountains of Gerizim and Ebal, it has the typical appearance of a modern-day Arab town with a mix of old and new lifestyles, highlighted by the

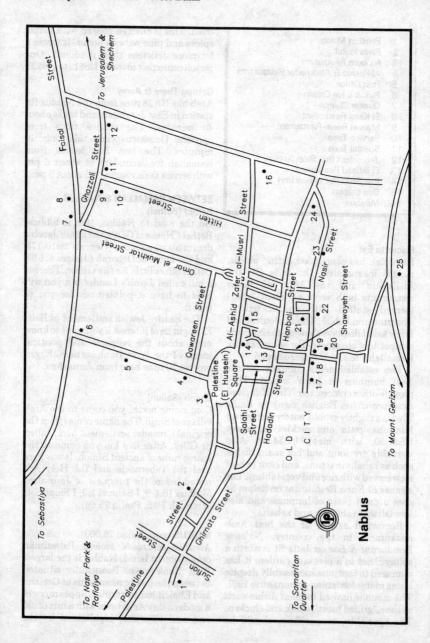

1	Palestine Hotel
2	Foul Hamis Restaurant (no sign)
3	Bank Leumi
4	Service Taxis – Sebastiya
5	Buses
6	Petrol Station
7	Post Office
8	Police Station
9	Municipality
10	El-Istiklal Pension
11	Pension Ramses
12	Mini Market
13	Aj Aj (Busy Busy) Restaurant & Carpenter's Shop opposite
14	& 15 Service Taxis – Jerusalem & Tel Aviv
16	Aker Sweets
17	Turkish Bath
18	Abdul Arafat's Herbal Medicine Shop
19	El Beik Gate
20	Touqan Castle
21	Nasir Mosque & El Aqsa Sweets
22	Soap Factory
23	Al Qutub Bakery
24	Kabir Mosque
25	Roman Amphitheatre

contrast between the tall office blocks and the narrow streets of the casbah.

As in Hebron, travellers should always bear in mind the strong anti-Israeli sentiments of the local population. For most Jews, these have made Nablus a 'no-go' area.

History

First settled around 4500 to 3100 BC by Chalcolithic people, Nablus stands adjacent to another of the world's oldest towns. Mentioned in early biblical times when it was called Shechem, it was here that Abraham came in about 1850 BC and received the promise of the Land of Israel (Genesis 12:6-7), Jacob purchased a field (Genesis 33:18-19), Joshua gathered his people to renew their covenant (Joshua 8:30-35, 24:1-29), and Joseph was buried (Joshua 24:32). Ancient Shechem lies to the east, just outside the Arab town of

Nablus. However, Israel officially calls Nablus by the biblical name of Shechem.

In the 9th century BC, the town's importance lessened when the northern kingdom's capital moved from Shechem to Samaria, near the Arab village of Sebastiya. The name Nablus is derived from Flavia Neapolis, the Roman colony built here in 72 AD.

The New Testament tells of Phillip, Peter and John spreading Christianity in the region (Acts 8:4-25). The Byzantine period saw churches built on the site of ancient Shechem and on Mount Gerizim. Evidence of the Crusader presence was obscured by an earthquake in 1927 which virtually wiped out the town, and by the removal of the cut stones by the locals for building purposes.

Nablus became a main centre of industry and commerce in Palestine with several soap factories, goldsmiths and other businesses and farmers coming into town to sell their products.

Orientation & Information

The main road runs east-west through Nablus, and the town centre is to the south, based around Palestine/El Hussein Square. Buses and service taxis arrive and depart from near here. The police station (tel 100) and post office (open Saturday to Wednesday 8 am to 1 pm and 3 to 5 pm, Thursday 8 am to 1 pm, closed Friday) are across from the Municipality building to the north, with the hotels nearby.

Just south of Palestine/El Hussein Square is the Old City. Nasir St, running east-west, is the main thoroughfare here. Behind it are the slopes of Mount Gerizim, holy to the Samaritans. Mount Ebal stands to the north. On the eastern outskirts of Nablus, about three km from the town centre, is the site of ancient Shechem, Tel Balata, and Jacob's Well and Joseph's Tomb.

Everywhere you go in Nablus you will see posters and pictures of Zafer al-Musri, the town's late mayor who was assassinated in the winter of 1986. A memorial outside the Municipality marks the spot where he was gunned down – probably by fellow Palestinians who felt that he was too friendly with the Israeli authorities, although his killers are still not known.

The spectre of the occupation hangs over the town in other ways, with IDF patrols, anti-Israel graffiti and the general air of discontent. However, the visitor can still experience something of the authentic Arab Palestine in Nablus, especially in and around the Old City.

Being predominantly Muslim, the market, shops and businesses are closed on Friday afternoon. Saturday is a particularly busy day with crowds of Arabs who live in Israel coming to shop.

Old City

Besides the colourful market there are other interesting sights to look out for as you wander through the labyrinth of narrow streets and alleyways in the Old City. Other signs of the troubled times are the barricades that block off some of the alleyways, put up by the IDF to help suppress disturbances.

Markets & Shops Markaz el-Tujari is the goldsmiths' market, just north of the Nasir Mosque. At 82 Nasir St, between Salahi St and el-Beik Gate, Abdul Arafat's little shop sells herbal medicine. Down on Salahi St you can see the carpenter's workshop where the green-painted handcarts are made.

Soap Factories Nablus is the centre of the Arab soap-making industry with over 40 factories and it is usually possible to visit one and see how the soap is made. Although some modern technology is now used, the production process is still traditional. One of the more interesting factories is also the most convenient. Al-Bader (Full Moon) Soap at 20 Nasir St has been here for over 250 years and exports to other Arab countries via Amman. The soap's basic ingredients are caustic soda and olive oil. They once used local olive oil but the quality is very good and therefore too expensive; it is more economical to buy Italian. By the way, the soap is particularly good for dandruff.

Turkish Bath At 70 Nasir St is Hamam Lesjid, the oldest working Turkish bath in the country. Built around 1480 at the start of the Ottoman period, it is one of six in Nablus. It isn't in very good condition but it is worth a look. The old man who works here speaks only Arabic but there may be someone else around who can explain to you how it all works. Open daily from about 7 am to 2 pm, it still has a few regular customers. At one time most of the town would have used a public bath such as this.

Touqan Castle One of the grandest buildings in the Old City is this Turkish mansion. It is now a private home but visitors are usually welcome to have a look at the architecture and garden. Whilst not brilliantly maintained, you can still appreciate something of its former glory. From Nasir St walk south through el-Beik Gate and the entrance is up the slope on your left.

Mosques

There are something like 30 minarets that dominate the Nablus skyline. Nasir Mosque is in the centre of the market; Kabir Mosque is the largest with its beautiful arch at the corner of Nasir St and Jame' el Kabir St. Non-Muslims are not normally permitted inside.

Amphitheatre

On the slopes, tucked away behind the markets and houses, is an excavated Roman amphitheatre. Presumably plans are afoot to develop the site for visitors. At the time of writing there were no explanatory signs.

Samaritan Quarter

Nablus is home to the Samaritans (see Population & People and Religion in Facts about the Country). They live in a small western section of the town and their synagogue houses what they claim to be the world's oldest Torah scroll, dated to the 13th year of the Israelites' settlement in Canaan.

Shechem

To reach Shechem, take the main road three km east from the town centre and follow the signposts. It's possible to walk or take a taxi. The bus will drop you nearby.

Tel Balata The remains of biblical Shechem, dated to between 1650 and 1550 BC, are not that impressive to non-archaeologists.

Jacob's Well A little further east is the Greek Orthodox convent of Jacob's Well. A Byzantine church was first built here in 380, but it was destroyed in 529. The Crusaders erected a replacement and in 1914 the Russian Orthodox Church began to rebuild it. WW I stopped them and the Greeks took control of the building, which remains uncompleted. In its crypt is the deep well believed to be the one where Jesus met the Samaritan woman (John 4) on the land purchased by Jacob (Genesis 33:18-20). It's open Monday to Saturday 8 am to 12 noon and 2 to 5 pm, closed Sunday, and admission is free.

Joseph's Tomb Just north of Jacob's Well is the traditional site of Joseph's Tomb. The simple white-domed building, similar in style to Rachel's Tomb in Bethlehem, is believed to be where Joseph's remains were carried to from Egypt (Joshua 24:32). Holy to Jews and Muslims, it used to be controlled by the Muslims but the Israeli authorities took it over and now IDF soldiers are on guard. Open daily 6 am to 6 pm. Admission is free.

Mount Gerizim

Sacred to the Samaritans, Mount Gerizim (881 metres above sea level) offers a superb panoramic view of the town and the surrounding countryside.

The Samaritans spend the 40 days of their Passover up here, living in the houses just below the summit. The highlight of their celebrations is the bloody sacrifice of sheep. You can see where the ceremony takes place, just to the south of the road.

Following the instructions given in Exodus 12, they kill the sheep, pour water over them, strip off the fleece, extract the fat, and burn both. Each sheep's forefoot is then cut off and given to the priests. After being cleaned and salted, the sheep are put on a spit and roasted. After prayers, the sheep are eaten by the Samaritans who must be fully clothed and wearing shoes. The meat bones must not be broken, and everything that is edible has to be eaten quickly. When they have finished eating they gather up the bones, hooves, horns and spits, in fact everything that came in contact with the sacrificial altar, and solemnly burn it all. This deeply religious event now attracts a crowd of bemused tourists.

Further north is where the Samaritans believe Abraham sacrificed Isaac, disputing the tradition that it took place on Mount Moriah in Jerusalem.

No buses go up the mountain, so you either have to walk (say two hours) or take a taxi (say US$8).

Places to Stay

Because of the *intefadeh*, the hotels here are usually closed to foreigners. They aren't very good anyway; cheapest is the *El-Estiklal Pension* near the municipality building. Beds in the large rooms cost US$4.50. Nearby is the slightly less inviting *Pension Ramses* with beds for US$5.

Although intended as a step up, the *Palestine Hotel* (tel 053-70040) on Shwetereh St offers little more in the way of cleanliness or comfort. Despite a distinguished past with a guest-book signed by the President of Tunisia and the

King of Jordan, its price of US$15 per person is over the top due to the musty state of the large, bare rooms.

Places to Eat

Along with soap, the Nablus speciality is sweets. These include all the various pastries, halvah and Turkish Delight, but in particular *kanafe* (cheese topped with orange wheat flakes and soaked in honey). The best bakery at which to try this rich delicacy is *El Aqsa*, next to Nasir Mosque and across from the soap factory on Nasir St in the Old City. *Aker Sweets* on Hitten St has its followers, too. A decent sized slice costs about 70c.

In the heart of the Old City market, on Salahi St across from the carpenter's workshop, is an unobtrusive plain-looking restaurant. Called *Aj-Aj* which means 'Busy-Busy' (no English sign), it serves great hummus, and also *laban*, a delicious cheese salad dip and omelettes. *Juma Saih* (no English sign) on Ghirnata St, near Atimad Taxis, also serves great hummus. For the best foul in Nablus, head for *Foul Hamis* (no English sign), on 39 Palestine St. It's on the right towards the end as you walk from the square.

Self-caterers can choose from the produce available in the market. For bread, the best bakery is *Al Qutub* (no English sign) at 20 Nasir St.

Although inconveniently situated away from the town centre, the Christian area of Rafidya to the west boasts some of the better places to eat. *Quick Meal* on Rafidya St serves various versions of fast food and is popular with the locals. *Abu-Bedou* is said to have the best shwarma in town, while *Arz 14* wins the prize for its ice cream.

Due to Islamic law, beer and other alcohol is not sold in the cafés and eating places, although a few stores do stock it. If you buy some, be sure not to upset the locals by drinking in public. A good place to head for is *Mini-Market Abbud* on Faisal St, a few hundred metres east of the municipality building. Specialising in American and British 'luxury imports' ranging from confectionery and cigarettes to cosmetics and toiletries, it also stocks cold beer and the manager is a friendly host to thirsty travellers who are welcome to sit, sip, chat and listen to music.

Getting There & Away

Arab buses run to Nablus from East Jerusalem (Nablus Rd Station) via Ramallah. The journey takes two to 2½ hours which makes the service taxi option (1¼ hours) very appealing. Buses also run to and from Jenin and Afulla in the north, and service taxis also run to and from Jaffa.

AROUND NABLUS

Sebastiya

This quiet little Arab village stands about 15 km north-west of Nablus up on the scenic slopes of the Samarian hills. Just above it on the summit of the peak lie the impressive ruins of Samaria, the capital of the ancient Israelite kingdom.

Omri, King of Israel, established the city here in 876 BC (I Kings 16:24). It was greatly improved by his son Ahab, who constructed various great buildings and fortifications. In 724 to 722 BC the Assyrians invaded and destroyed the Israelite kingdom. Samaria's citizens were deported and it became a provincial capital under the Persians. Razed in 108 BC and restored in 57 BC, it came to Herod in 30 BC who renamed it Sebaste (Greek for Augustus) and initiated a new construction programme. It eventually declined with the development of Nablus. The Israelite, Hellenistic and Roman ruins include an amphitheatre, temple, palace, towers, columns and a hippodrome. They are open Saturday to Thursday 8 am to 5 pm, Friday 8 am to 4 pm. Admission is US$1.35, students 75c.

In the village itself is a 12th century Crusader church that was converted into a mosque by Saladin. Built on the site of a ruined 5th century church, it contains two tomb chambers. The prophets Elisha and

Obadiah are believed to be buried here, along with the head of John the Baptist – the prophet Yahya to the Muslims. Named after him, the Nabi Yahya Mosque is on the east side of the square.

Places to Eat There is a café outside the archaeological site, and another in the village square.

Getting There & Away No buses run direct to Sebastiya. Instead, take a service taxi from near Palestine/el-Hussein Square (70c). You could take the Jenin bus and get off at the turn-off for the village, but you then have a steep two km climb.

Gaza Strip

The Gaza Strip is just that, a narrow stretch of land on the Mediterranean coast south of Ashdod, with the Negev Desert to the east and the Sinai Desert to the south. Only about 50 km long and as little as 6 km wide, it cannot boast the holy places or natural beauty spots found elsewhere, standing out instead as a largely ignored and tragic consequence of the Palestine Problem. Rather than fascinating ruins and lovely views, you are confronted with an area of squalid and overcrowded living conditions with crumbling towns and refugee camps having to cope with one of the world's highest birthrates. The Strip's population doubles each generation and by the year 2000 it is expected to reach 900,000.

The Gaza Strip has three main towns, of which Gaza is the largest (often called Gaza City or Gaza Town to avoid confusion). The others are Khan Yunis and Rafah. There are also eight refugee camps and about 20 Jewish settlements.

There is a very different quality to the Gaza Strip than to the West Bank and it is not just the desert terrain and climate. It is a quality of neglect and helplessness and the hatred towards Israel for its role in the events that have caused this situation. Over 60% of the residents here are refugees, representing about 20% of the whole Palestinian refugee population.

All of the Strip's residents, natives and refugees, are stateless. They have no passport from the Israeli administration, just as they had none from the Egyptians. West Bank residents are Jordanian citizens and are basically able to travel to and from Jordan and then beyond. Strip residents, on the other hand, are usually unable to enter Egypt, and need a difficult-to-obtain *laissez-passer* document from the Israelis to travel abroad.

The Strip has been dubbed 'the Soweto of Israel' for its unofficial role as a source of cheap labour. At least half of the region's labour force works in Israel and virtually all of those who stay behind are ultimately dependent on the Israeli economy for their livelihood as well. This dependence will increase as local agriculture declines because of a falling water table that has begun to dry up orchards. Palestinian critics say that with Gaza workers in Israel earning 40% lower wages than Israeli workers, Israel is content to keep the situation as it is. All of these factors serve only to make the residents of the Strip cling even more desperately to the Palestinian identity.

Due to an upsurge of terrorism here in recent years, followed by the *intefadeh*, most Israelis would not think of visiting the Strip. Non-Jews, however, are often made welcome, although women should be prepared for the usual hassles. The tension in the air is very evident, as is the IDF presence with patrols, barbed wire and watchtowers in the towns and the road-blocks in the rural areas.

Note that all the hotels in the Strip are officially (and usually actually) closed to foreigners, and that the IDF may prevent you from entering. Ask around to find out the current situation – both Israeli and Arab viewpoints are essential. The UNRWA used to organise tours – at the moment they may have their hands full

Gaza Strip

0   5   10 km

○ Refugee Camps

with other matters, but check. In Jerusalem, contact Mohammed H Jarallah (tel 282451, Nablus Rd PO Box 19149), in Gaza phone 861196/7/8.

GAZA (population 125,000)
Although there is little left to show for it, Gaza is one of the world's oldest towns. Well established by 2000 BC, it stands on what was in ancient times the 'Way of the Sea', the main route between Egypt and Assyria. Of great economic and strategic importance, Gaza was one of the Philistines' five great cities. It was then

called Aza, probably derived from the Hebrew word *Az* (strong) and was called Gaza (treasure), by the Arabs after the Islamic conquest of Palestine in the 7th century. They renamed the town 'Gaza of Hashim' after Hashim ibn Abd Munaf, grandfather of the prophet Mohammed, who died here on his way back to Hijaz on the Arabian peninsula.

It is said that Gaza has been taken and destroyed in war more often than any other town in the world. Certainly some well-known events took place here, mostly in biblical times. First mentioned by the Bible as a Canaanite city (Genesis 10:15-19), the Israelites managed to get a foothold only to lose it to the Philistines (Deuteronomy 2:18-23). Samson was imprisoned and died here (Judges 16) and the city was condemned by Amos for its slave trade with Edom (Amos 1:1-7), and by Zephania for its opposition to the Judean kingdom (Zephania 2:1-6). The last biblical reference to Gaza is in connection with Phillip and the spread of Christianity (Acts 8:25-29).

Continuing as a prosperous station between Palestine and Egypt, Gaza was taken by all the powers who succeeded each other in the region: the Greeks, Romans, Muslims, Crusaders, Mamelukes, Turks, British, Egyptians and now the Israelis. In 1779 Napoleon Bonaparte camped here on his Egyptian campaign and called Gaza 'the Guardian of Africa, the Gate of Asia'. During WW I, as one of the main military bases of the Turks and their German allies, it was the scene of heavy fighting as the British forces battled to conquer Palestine.

During the British Mandate, Gaza again prospered as the main centre of the southern Palestine region. At this time a small Jewish community settled in the town, but with the rising tide of Arab nationalism making Gaza one of the centres of opposition to a Jewish State they were obliged to leave. The Egyptian Army made Gaza their main military base during the 1948 War of Independence and the area of land that they held at the end of the fighting became the Gaza Strip. This was when today's problems really started.

Prior to the war, Gaza Town and the surrounding villages had a population of about 60,000. Now it was flooded with some 150,000 refugees who had left their homes in the north and were unable either to return or to go anywhere else. Making this terrible situation even worse was the sudden isolation of the region caused by the politics of being under the Egyptian administration. With Israel bordering it

to the north and east and the barren and mostly uninhabited Sinai Desert to the south, the Gaza Strip was forced to adapt itself to a new and harsh reality of the sudden tripling of its population and the loss of most of its revenue sources, as links to the new State of Israel were cut.

The UN sponsored the setting up of refugee camps, but the lack of employment and access to the outside world, along with many related factors, made it virtually impossible for the region to develop even to the limited extent that the West Bank did. In 1956, Israel briefly occupied the Strip as a result of the Sinai or Suez War, took it again in the Six-Day War and has held it ever since. The Israeli authorities are blamed for running down what little agricultural and industrial life there was in Gaza by prohibiting exports and limiting sales in Israel. During your visit to the town, conversations with the locals are likely to centre on the politics and economics of the area.

Orientation & Information

Gaza is a fairly easy town to get to know, centred as it is on one long main street. Running about four km from Gaza/el Shajaria Square westwards to the seafront, Omar el-Mukhtar St is lined with shops and businesses and passes by or near to the town's main facilities and places of interest.

Gaza/el Shajaria Square is a messy junction that marks the start of downtown Gaza. Down to the south is the disused railway station, built by the British at the start of the century. East, towards Beersheba, is Gaza's 'East End slum', el-Shajaria. The police station (tel 100) is on the north side of the square, and around the corner is the post office (open Saturday to Thursday 8 am to 2.30 pm, closed Friday). Service taxis for Tel Aviv-Jaffa operate from nearby.

About a km west, Omar el-Mukhtar St crosses busy Palestine Square. The bus station and the rank for service taxis

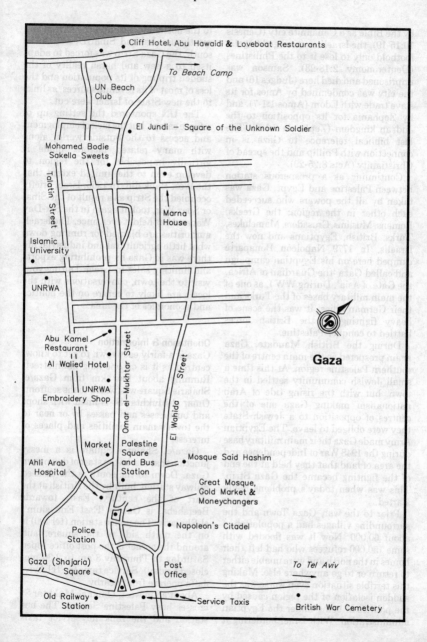

Cliff Hotel, Abu Hawaidi & Loveboat Restaurants

To Beach Camp

UN Beach Club

El Jundi – Square of the Unknown Soldier

Mohamed Bodie Sakella Sweets

Talatin Street

Marna House

Islamic University

UNRWA

Abu Kamel Restaurant

Al Walied Hotel

UNRWA Embroidery Shop

Omar el-Mukhtar Street

El Wahida Street

Gaza

Market

Palestine Square and Bus Station

Mosque Said Hashim

Ahli Arab Hospital

Great Mosque, Gold Market & Moneychangers

Napoleon's Citadel

Police Station

Gaza (Shajaria) Square

Post Office

To Tel Aviv

Old Railway Station

Service Taxis

British War Cemetery

running to and from Jerusalem and the West Bank are here.

There are few reminders of Gaza's colourful ancient history to be seen. Sadly, a visit to the town is dominated instead by the harsh effects of the more recent political developments.

Your attention will be focused on the refugee camps that surround Gaza town and dominate the Strip, and on the slums and the general aura of neglect, decay and hopelessness. You can find much worse scenes of hardship in the world, but it is the stark contrast between the conditions in Gaza and those you have seen in Israel that makes such an impact.

As in most Muslim Arab communities, the biggest social event in Gaza is the wedding. With the lack of most other possible diversions here, it takes on an even greater importance as one of the rare occasions for celebration. Especially in view of the economic situation in the Strip, they are lavish affairs with scores of guests, plenty of food, and singing and dancing through the night.

Many Gaza residents have relatives who work in the Gulf countries to provide for the folks back home. These 'ex-pat' Palestinians tend to return for summer and this is the busy wedding season. Every night along the seafront and on Omar el-Mukhtar St you will see processions of cars bedecked with ribbons, loaded with bewildered couples and happy guests and accompanied by the shrill sound of screaming that is a sort of verbal confetti in the Middle East. Out of season, Friday night is wedding night.

Also to be seen are bicycles, brightly decorated with stickers, transfers, lights and, in competition with the many cars, a fancy electric horn.

The UNRWA

The organisation's Field Office is the pastel blue building on Talatin St which runs parallel with Omar el-Mukhtar St. Phone 861196/7/8 to see if they can

arrange arrange a visit to the Strip's refugee camps. At least a weeks' notice is normally required and it is best to call between 8 and 10 am, Saturday to Thursday.

Islamic University

Across from the UNRWA complex is Gaza's university, the largest in the Occupied Territories. Funded mostly by Saudi Arabia, the study of Islamic fundamentalism is mandatory here. The students can be a lot less open to foreigners than those on the West Bank, but it may still be worth a visit.

Beach

Due to a combination of the security situation and the local males' lack of self-control at the sight of a woman's knee, beach life in Gaza is not what it could be. The wreck of a ship just off-shore and the oil from tankers near Ashkelon also detract from the stretch of sand. If you fancy a swim, go to the UN Beach Club, just south of where Omar el-Mukhtar St

UN Checkpoint

meets the seafront. Although the facilities are only for UN staff and soldiers, you can use the well-kept private beach.

El Jundi – Square of the Unknown Soldier
This unkempt common on Omar el-Mukhtar St was dedicated by the Egyptian Army who buried one of their dead here and erected the monument in his honour. Shelled by the Israelis in 1956 it has remained in disrepair.

UNRWA Embroidery Shop
East of the Al Walied Hotel on Omar el-Mukhtar St, this shop sells traditional Palestinian embroidery pieces with profits going towards the refugees' welfare. Open Saturday to Thursday 6.30 to 11.45 am and 1.30 to 3.45 pm, closed Friday.

Markets & Shops
The town's main food market is on the south-west side of Palestine Square, under the corrugated iron roof. There are more stalls across the square to the north-east, on the back street that runs parallel with Omar el-Mukhtar St and behind the Great Mosque. 'Goldsmiths' Alley' (dating from Herodian times, it is said) runs alongside the mosque. At the eastern end a crowd of moneychangers stand around with fists full of dollars and other local currencies.

You can watch cane furniture being made in the workshops at various places in town. Carpets are traditionally made in el-Shajaria, just past Gaza/el Shajaria Square, and if you ask around you may be led to see an artisan at work.

Mosque Said Hashim
This mosque was erected on the grave of the prophet Mohammed's grandfather. A merchant who travelled a great deal between the Arabian peninsula and Damascus, he died in Gaza on one of those journeys.

To reach the mosque, head north from Palestine Square to reach El Walhida St, which runs parallel with Omar el-Mukhtar St. Head west (left, towards the sea) and the mosque is down the second turning to the north (right).

Greek Orthodox Church
East of Palestine Square (away from the sea) is the town's Christian Quarter. Follow Rassel Talia St south and you come to this church on the right. With its dome and Arabic signs it resembles a mosque, but a church it is. It was built on the ruins of a 4th century Byzantine church, but there is little to see. Someone may be available to show you around.

Great Mosque
The Jammal al-Ikbeer, commonly called the Great Mosque, is probably the town's most distinguished building, with its tower dominating the market skyline. Built on the remains of a 13th century Crusader church dedicated to John the Baptist, it contains a pillar from a 3rd century synagogue which bears a carving of a menorah with a Hebrew and Greek inscription. Some say that the Crusader church was itself built on the site of a 4th century church erected by Queen Helena. An underground tunnel that leads from the mosque to the beach was supposedly dug as an escape route in times of siege. Muslims argue that before the Crusaders arrived it was a mosque during the time of Omar ibn el Khattab, second Kalef of Islam.

Non-Muslims are usually allowed to enter the mosque in between the daily prayers.

Napoleon's Citadel
During his Egyptian campaign Napoleon Bonaparte camped in Gaza in 1799 to replenish supplies, and this building was commandeered as his HQ. It stands on El Wahida St, east of the Mosque Said Hashim, and has some attractive ornamental stonework from the Mameluke period. It's now a girl's school and to get a close look you normally need to be persistent and ask the caretaker to let you

into the school compound after 4 pm when the lessons are over.

Samson Monument

Continue eastwards along El Wahida St and you come to this arched monument about 200 metres on the north side (left). Called Abu el Azim ('Father of Strength'), it commemorates Samson. One tradition has it that he lies buried under the Great Mosque.

British War Cemetery

Both world wars saw heavy fighting in the region. In 1917 British and Commonwealth forces, mainly Australian, attacked and took Gaza. During WW II the British base hospital in Gaza received many of the wounded from the desert campaign. The British War Cemetery is about three km from town on the north-bound road that leads from Gaza/el Shajaria Square towards Tel Aviv-Jaffa, on the east side (right) across from the 7-Up factory.

Places to Stay

Gaza's hotels have been officially closed to foreigners since the *intefadeh* began, so the prices listed here are a couple of years old, but the lack of business has probably kept prices down anyway.

Across from the municipal gardens on Omar el-Mukhtar St, the *El Walied Hotel* (tel 861230) is the cheapest option in town. Although the management are a bit straight-faced and serious, it is a neat, clean and quiet place to stay. A bed in a twin room costs US$6 and you will not normally see many, if any, other guests. There is a 10 pm curfew and check-out time is 9 am. As there is little to do after dark in Gaza this is not much of a problem.

On the seafront, to the left from where Omar el-Mukhtar St intersects, the *Cliff Hotel* (tel 861353) has singles/doubles US$15/25, with breakfast.

Marna House (tel 86225) is a comfortable private establishment. In a quiet residential street and with a large front garden,

terrace and lounge, it is a faded reminder of pre-1948 Gaza. Singles/doubles are US$25/45, with breakfast. It's off the main drag, so use the cheap taxi service to find it. Otherwise, head towards the sea along Omar el-Mukhtar St, take the second right past the cultural centre, then take the first right and it's about 50 metres along the street on your left. Most locals know it, so don't hesitate to ask the way.

Places to Eat

Cheap prices abound for fruit and vegetables in the markets, especially if you bargain hard. Felafel is sold on the street and in cafés at prices considerably lower than in Israel, although travellers with sensitive stomachs may not feel that it is really such a bargain. Some of the best hummus is served at *El Khuzinder* (no English sign). It's east of the El Walied Hotel on Omar el-Mukhtar St; look for the orange table-tops and chairs outside. Nearer the hotel and towards the sea, on the corner before the prison, the *Abu Kamel* restaurant serves tasty salads and kebabs.

Despite the spelling, *Borgerland*, north of the Square of the Unknown Soldier, is a surprisingly clean and pleasant place, serving decent fruit shakes, shwarma and salads.

Gaza disputes Nablus' status as the best place for sweets, and there are several bakeries producing honey-soaked delicacies to keep the many dentists in business. Arguably the town's best bakery is *Mohammed Bodie Sakalla* (no English sign – look for the white on green Arabic script) on the south side (left) of Omar el-Mukhtar St just before the Square of the Unknown Soldier. A particular specialty here is *gataieff*, a type of pancake filled with either cheese or nuts, and soaked in honey. Other favourites to ask for are kanafe Arabia and kanafe beljibna.

Fish is another local speciality and restaurants on the seafront compete to attract the bigger spenders. The *Loveboat* and *Abu Hawaidi* restaurants, owned by the Cliff Hotel, are typical with a meal running to about US$10-15 per person.

Getting There & Away
The bus links between Gaza and Israel are limited, irregular and unreliable, but fortunately there is an efficient service taxi system that makes the trip comfortable, quick and inexpensive. The service taxis operate from two different places in Gaza: just north of Gaza/el Shajaria Square for Jaffa via Tel Aviv (one hour) and Palestine Square for Jerusalem (1¾ hours) and West Bank destinations (Bethlehem, Hebron, Ramallah, Nablus, etc).

The Arab bus station is also on Palestine Square, with services to Ashkelon (No 20 – three times daily) and Beersheba (No 40 – twice daily). Local services operate to and from Rafah, Khan Younis, and other destinations on the Strip.

Getting Around
With Gaza having a four-km-long main street, the unofficial local taxi set-up is great. Instead of walking, stand by the roadside and, by pointing your index finger, hail a taxi. It seems like half of the

cars in town act as pirate taxis and everyone uses them. Wherever you along Omar el-Mukhtar St you only pay about 30c. If you want to go off the main road, to UNRWA HQ for example, you normally need to pay double.

AROUND GAZA
Along with the refugee camps, the Strip's other towns are worth a visit on days when the colourful Bedouin market sets up shop. This means Wednesday and Thursday in Khan Younis and Saturday and Sunday in Rafah. Apart from the hectic trading there is little to see, unfortunately, except more overcrowded slum conditions. Get there on Arab buses from Palestine Square in Gaza Town.

Rafah's is a particularly sad situation because the town was divided by the border drawn up under the Camp David Agreement. When the Sinai was returned to Egypt in 1979, part of the town went with it. This resulted in a local version of the Berlin Wall separating families and friends. Unable to visit each other, they can be seen sadly shouting across the fenced-off no-man's land.

Index

Map references in **bold** type

Abbura Waterfall 331
Absalom's cave (see Avshalom)
Abu Gosh 198
Abusiye 407
Acre (see Akko)
Admot Yishai 413
Ahziv 286
Ahziv Beach 286
Ahziv National Park 286
Akko 58, 277-283, **279**
Arad 45, 359-360,**360**
Arava, the 26
Ashdod 242
Ashkelon 243-247, **244**
Atlit 270
Avdat 369
Avshalom 198

Banyus 327
Bar'am 343
Bat Yam 236-238
Beersheba 59, 361-365, **362**
Beit Guvrin 248
Beit Jalla 398, 405
Beit Jan 289
Beit She'an 302
Beit She'arim 276
Beit Yerah 314
Beit-El (Bethel) 417
Belvoir 303
Benot Ya'acov 322
Bethany 387
Bethlehem 66, 398-405, **399, 406**
Birket el-Sultan 413-414
Bnei Brak 240

Caesarea 272-275, **272**
Cana 298
Canada Park 200
Capernaum 312-314, **313**
Carmel Caves 271
Carmel National Park 262
Cave of Machpelah 410
Cremisan 405

Daliyat al-Karmel 269 **269**
Dead Sea 26, 344-356, **345**
Dimona 35, 36, 65, 366
Dor 271

Eilat 373-383, **374, 378**
Ein Feshka 395
Ein Gedi 349-352, **350**
Ein Harod 301-302
Ein es-Sultan 395

El-Bireh 415
Elisha's Spring (see Ein es-Sultan)
Emmaus 199
En Avdat 368
En Boqeq 348
En Hod 270
En Kerem 174

Gadin 289
Galilee & the Golan 26,
    290-343, **291**
Gamla 332
Garden of Gethsemane 28, 164
Gaza 423, 424-430, **426**
Gaza Strip 18, 423-430, **424**
Gillo 405

Hai-Bar Biblical Wildlife
    Reserve 384
Haifa 35, 55, 253-268, **254-5**
    Baha'i Shrine 259
    Elijah's Cave 258
Halhoul 409
Hammat 318
Hammat Gader 315
Hamme Mazor 351
Hamme Zohar 354
Haram el-Khalil
    (see Cave of Machpelah)
Haram esh-Sharif 138-141, **137**
Hebron 409-414, **409, 411**
Herodian 408
Herzlia 238
    Sydney Ali Beach 238
Hillel's Cave 342
Hinnom Valley 162
Horns of Hattin 298
Hula Valley 26, 323-324
Hurshat Tal National Park 326

Isfiya 268

Jaffa 59, 228-236, **229**
Jericho 387, 392-396, **393, 397**
Jerusalem 60, 66, 121-200,
    122, 126-127
    Armenian Quarter 157-159, **158**
    Christian Quarter 151-157, **151**
    Church of the Holy Sepulchre
    152-155, **154**
    City of David 161-162
    Dome of the Rock 123
    East Jerusalem 121, 124,
    165-166, **131**
    Jewish Quarter 143-145, **143**
    Mea Shearim 167-168
    Mount of Olives 162-163

Mount Scopus 165
Mount Zion 159-161
Muslim Quarter 146-151, **146**
New City 121,124, 166-176
Old City 121, 123, 124, 130-165, **131**
Via Dolorosa 147-149
Western Wall 142
Temple Mount/Haram esh-Sharif
138-141, **137**
Jesus' Baptism Site 398
Jezreel Valley 26, 387
Jish 342
Jordan Bridge (see Benot Ya'acov)
Jordan River 26, 27, 290, 398
Jordan Valley 26, 290, 387
Judean Desert 26, 387
Judean Hills 387

Katzrin 330-331, **330**
Kfar Etzion 409
Khan Yunis 423
Kibbutzim
    Dan 327
    Degania 68, 314
    Ein Gev 316
    Gesher HaZiv 287
    Ginnosar 310
    Ha'On 316
    Kfar Blum 324
    Kfar Giladil 325
    Lahav 365
    Lochamei Hagetaot 283
    Ma'agan Michael 276
    Ramat Rachel 175
    Sde Boker 367
    Sdot Yam 274
Kidron River 407
Kidron Valley 162
Korazim 314

Latrun 104, 199

Majdal Shams 330
Makhtesh Ramon 370-371, **372**
Mamshit 366
Mar Saba Monastery 407
Masada 353-354, **353**
Megiddo 300, **301**
Meiron 64, 342
Metulla 25, 325
Migdal 245, 310
Minya 311
Mitzpe Ramon 370-371, **370**
Montfort 289
Moshav Beit Hananya 276
Mount & Monastery of
    Temptation 395

Mount Gerizim 421
Mount Hermon 26
Mount Hermon Ski Centre 329
Mount Herzel 173
Mount Tabor 298
Mount of the Beatitudes 311, 318
Mukhraga 269

Na'aran 396
Nablus 387, 417-422, **418**
Nahal Arugot Nature Reserve 351
Nahal David Nature Reserve 350
Nahal Iyun Nature Reserve 325
Nahal Prazim 356
Nahal Shagur/
    Nahal Beit Hakerem 283
Nahariya 283-286, **284**
Nazareth 290-298, **293**
Nebi Musa 387, 389
Negev, the 26, 27, 28, 357-385, **358**
Netanya 104, 249-252, **250**
Newe Zohar 355
Nimrod Castle 58, 328-329, **328**

Occupied Territories
    (see West Bank, Gaza Strip)

Peqi'in 288-289, **288**
Petah Tiqwa 240

Qirat Shemona 324
Qiryat Arba 414
Qiryat Gat 248
Qumran 349, 387
Quneitra Viewpoint 330

Rafah 423, 430
Ramallah 387, 415-417, **416**
Ramla 241-242
Ramon Crater
    (see Makhtesh Ramon)
Rehovot 240-241
Rift Valley 26
Rishon Le Zion 240, **240**
Rosh Hanikra 287
Rosh Pinna 322

Safed 332-342, **333**
Samarian Mountains 387
Sea of Galilee 303-322
Sebastiya 422
Shechem 421
Shiloh (Seilun) 417
Shivta (Subeita) 366
Shoresh Junction 198
Shu'fat 415
Sodom 356
Solomon's Pools 408
St George's Monastery 390-391

Taba 377
Tabgha 311, 317
Tanur Waterfall 325
Tel Arad 360
Tel Aviv 60, 61, 201-236,
    202-203, 235
Tel Balata 421
Tel Beersheba 364
Tel Dan 326
Tel Dor 271
Tel Hai 324
Tel Lakhish 248
Tel Maresha 248
Tiberias 303-322, **305**
Timna Valley National Park 384

Vered HaGalil 314

Wadi Khareitun 408
Wadi Qelt 387, 389
West Bank 387-423, **388**

Ya'ar Yehudiyya Nature Reserve 331
Yad Le Yad 287
Yad Vashem 173
Yamin Orde 271

Zichron Ya'acov 104, 271

MAPS

Akko	279	Jerusalem *cont*	
Arad	360	Egged Bus Route 99	176
Ashkelon	244	Jewish Quarter	143
Beersheba	362	Municipal Boundaries	122
Bethlehem	399	Muslim Quarter	146
Around Bethlehem	406	Temple Mount	137
Grotto of the Nativity	402	The Citadel	134
Church of the Nativity	401	Katzrin	330
Caesarea	272	Makhtesh Ramon	372
Capernaum	313	Masada	353
Daliyat al-Karmel	269	Megiddo	301
Dead Sea	345	Mitzpe Ramon	370
Eilat	374	Nablus	418
Around Eilat	378	Nahariya	284
Ein Gedi	350	Nazareth	293
Galilee & the Golan	291	Negev	358
Gaza	426	Netanya	250
Gaza Strip	424	Nimrod Castle	328
Haifa	254-5	Peqi'in	288
Hebron	409	Ramallah	416
Tomb of the Patriarchs	411	Rail Network	117
Jaffa	229	Rishon Le Zion	240
Jericho	393	Safed	333
Around Jericho	397	Tel Aviv	202-203
Jerusalem	126-127	Central Bus Station	235
Armenian Quarter	158	Around Tel Aviv	237
Christian Quarter	151	Tiberias	305
Church of the Holy		West Bank	388
Sepulchre	154		
East Jerusalem &			
the Old City	131		

Temperature

To convert °C to °F multiply by 1.8 and add 32

To convert °F to °C subtract 32 and multiply by ·55

Length, Distance & Area

	multiply by
inches to centimetres	2.54
centimetres to inches	0.39
feet to metres	0.30
metres to feet	3.28
yards to metres	0.91
metres to yards	1.09
miles to kilometres	1.61
kilometres to miles	0.62
acres to hectares	0.40
hectares to acres	2.47

Weight

	multiply by
ounces to grams	28.35
grams to ounces	0.035
pounds to kilograms	0.45
kilograms to pounds	2.21
British tons to kilograms	1016
US tons to kilograms	907

A British ton is 2240 lbs, a US ton is 2000 lbs

Volume

	multiply by
Imperial gallons to litres	4.55
litres to imperial gallons	0.22
US gallons to litres	3.79
litres to US gallons	0.26

5 imperial gallons equals 6 US gallons
a litre is slightly more than a US quart, slightly less
than a British one

Guides to Africa

Africa on a shoestring
From Marrakesh to Kampala, Mozambique to Mauritania, Johannesburg to Cairo – this guidebook gives you all the facts on travelling in Africa. It provides comprehensive information on more than 50 African countries – how to get to them, how to get around, where to stay, where to eat, what to see and what to avoid.

East Africa – a travel survival kit
Whether you want to climb Kilimanjaro, visit wildlife reserves, or sail an Arab dhow, East Africa offers a fascinating pastiche of cultures and landscapes. This guide has detailed information on Kenya, Uganda, Rwanda, Burundi, eastern Zaire, Tanzania and the Comoros Islands.

West Africa – a travel survival kit
This book has all the necessary information for independent travel in 16 countries – Benin, Burkino Faso, Cape Verde, Gambia, Ghana, Guinea, Guinea Bissau, Ivory Coast, Liberia, Mali, Mauritania, Niger, Nigeria, Senegal, Sierra Leone and Togo.

Swahili phrasebook
Swahili is widely spoken throughout East Africa – from the coast of Kenya and Tanzania through to Zaire.

Morocco, Algeria & Tunisia – a travel survival kit
A blend of African, Islamic, Arab and Berber cultures make this a fascinating region to visit. This book takes you from bustling souks to peaceful oases and is packed with all the information you'll need.

Central Africa – a travel survival kit
Central Africa offers the visitor incomparable wildlife and scenery, and the essence of African culture. Countries covered include Cameroon, Central African Republic, Chad, The Congo, Equatorial Guinea, Gabon and Zaïre.

Guides to the Middle East

Egypt & the Sudan – a travel survival kit
The sights of Egypt and the Sudan have impressed visitors for more than 50 centuries. This guide takes you beyond the spectacular pyramids to discover the villages of the Nile, diving in the Red Sea and many other attractions.

Jordan & Syria – a travel survival kit
Roman cities, ancient Petra, Crusader castles – these sights, amongst many others, combine with Arab hospitality to make this undiscovered region a fascinating and enjoyable destination.

Turkey – a travel survival kit
Unspoilt by tourism, Turkey is a travellers' paradise, whether you want to lie on a beach or explore the ancient cities that are the legacy of a rich and varied past. This acclaimed guide will help you to make the most of your stay.

West Asia on a shoestring
A complete guide to the overland trip from Bangladesh to Turkey. Information for budget travellers to Afghanistan, Bangladesh, Bhutan, India, Iran, Maldives, Nepal, Pakistan, Sri Lanka, Turkey and the Middle East.

Yemen – a travel survival kit
One of the oldest inhabited regions in the world, the Yemen is a beautiful mountainous region with a unique architecture. This book covers both North and South Yemen in detail.

Lonely Planet Guidebooks

Lonely Planet guidebooks cover virtually every accessible part of Asia as well as Australia, the Pacific, Central and South America, Africa, the Middle East and parts of North America. There are four main series: 'travel survival kits', covering a single country for a range of budgets; 'shoestring' guides with compact information for low-budget travel in a major region; trekking guides; and 'phrasebooks'.

Australia & the Pacific
Australia
Bushwalking in Australia
Papua New Guinea
Papua New Guinea phrasebook
New Zealand
Tramping in New Zealand
Rarotonga & the Cook Islands
Solomon Islands
Tahiti & French Polynesia
Fiji
Micronesia

South-East Asia
South-East Asia on a shoestring
Malaysia, Singapore & Brunei
Indonesia
Bali & Lombok
Indonesia phrasebook
Burma
Burmese phrasebook
Thailand
Thai phrasebook
Philippines
Pilipino phrasebook

North-East Asia
North-East Asia on a shoestring
China
China phrasebook
Tibet
Tibet phrasebook
Japan
Korea
Korean phrasebook
Hong Kong, Macau & Canton
Taiwan

West Asia
West Asia on a shoestring
Trekking in Turkey
Turkey

Mail Order

Lonely Planet guidebooks are distributed worldwide and are sold by good bookshops everywhere. They are also available by mail order from Lonely Planet, so if you have difficulty finding a title please write to us. US and Canadian residents should write to Embarcadero West, 112 Linden St, Oakland CA 94607, USA and residents of other countries to PO Box 617, Hawthorn, Victoria 3122, Australia.

Eastern Europe
Eastern Europe

Indian Subcontinent
India
Hindi/Urdu phrasebook
Kashmir, Ladakh & Zanskar
Trekking in the Indian Himalaya
Pakistan
Kathmandu & the Kingdom of Nepal
Trekking in the Nepal Himalaya
Nepal phrasebook
Sri Lanka
Sri Lanka phrasebook
Bangladesh

Africa
Africa on a shoestring
East Africa
Swahili phrasebook
West Africa
Central Africa

Middle East
Egypt & the Sudan
Jordan & Syria
Yemen

North America
Canada
Alaska

Mexico
Mexico
Baja California

South America
South America on a shoestring
Ecuador & the Galapagos Islands
Colombia
Chile & Easter Island
Bolivia
Peru
Argentina

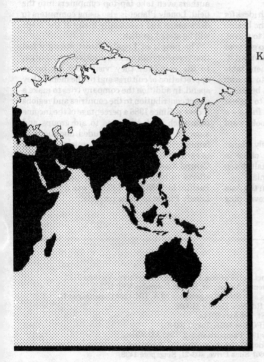

Lonely Planet

Lonely Planet published its first book in 1973. Tony and Maureen Wheeler had made a lengthy overland trip from England to Australia and, in response to numerous 'how do you do it?' questions, Tony wrote and they published *Across Asia on the Cheap*. It became an instant local best-seller and inspired thoughts of a second travel guide. A year and a half in South-East Asia resulted in their second book, *South-East Asia on a Shoestring*, which they put together in a backstreet Chinese hotel in Singapore in 1975. The 'yellow book', as it quickly became known, soon became *the* guide to the region and has gone through five editions, always with its familiar yellow cover.

Soon other writers came to them with ideas for similar books – books that went off the beaten track with an adventurous approach to travel, books that 'assumed you knew how to get your luggage off the carousel,' as one reviewer put it. Lonely Planet grew from a kitchen table operation to a spare room and then to its own office. It's international reputation began to grow as the Lonely Planet logo began to appear in more and more countries. In 1982 *India – a travel survival kit* won the Thomas Cook award for the best guidebook of the year.

These days there are over 70 Lonely Planet titles. Over 40 people work at our office in Melbourne, Australia and another half dozen at our US office in Oakland, California.

At first Lonely Planet specialised in the Asia region but these days we are also developing major ranges of guidebooks to the Pacific region, to South America and to Africa. The list of walking guides is growing and Lonely Planet now has a unique series of phrasebooks to 'unusual' languages. The emphasis continues to be on travel for travellers and Tony and Maureen still manage to fit in a number of trips each year and play a very active part in the writing and updating of Lonely Planet's guides.

Keeping guidebooks up to date is a constant battle which requires an ear to the ground and lots of walking, but technology also plays its part. All Lonely Planet guidebooks are now stored and updated on computer, and some authors even take lap-top computers into the field. Lonely Planet is also using computers to draw maps and eventually many of the maps will be stored on disk.

The people at Lonely Planet strongly feel that travellers can make a positive contribution to the countries they visit both by better appreciation of cultures and by the money they spend. In addition the company tries to make a direct contribution to the countries and regions it covers. Since 1986 a percentage of the income from each book has gone to aid groups and associations. This has included donations to famine relief in Africa, to aid projects in India, to agricultural projects in Nicaragua and other Central American countries and to Greenpeace's efforts to halt French nuclear testing in the Pacific. In 1988 over $40,000 was donated by Lonely Planet to these projects.

Lonely Planet Distributors

Australia & Papua New Guinea Lonely Planet Publications, PO Box 617, Hawthorn, Victoria 3122.
Canada Raincoast Books, 112 East 3rd Avenue, Vancouver, British Columbia V5T 1C8.
Denmark, Finland & Norway Scanvik Books aps, Store Kongensgade 59 A, DK-1264 Copenhagen K.
India & Nepal UBS Distributors, 5 Ansari Rd, New Delhi – 110002
Israel Geographical Tours Ltd, 8 Tverya St, Tel Aviv 63144.
Japan Intercontinental Marketing Corp, IPO Box 5056, Tokyo 100-31.
Netherlands Nilsson & Lamm bv, Postbus 195, Pampuslaan 212, 1380 AD Weesp.
New Zealand Transworld Publishers, PO Box 83-094, Edmonton PO, Auckland.
Singapore & Malaysia MPH Distributors, 601 Sims Drive, #03-21, Singapore 1438.
Spain Altair, Balmes 69, 08007 Barcelona.
Sweden Esselte Kartcentrum AB, Vasagatan 16, S-111 20 Stockholm.
Thailand Chalermnit, 108 Sukhumvit 53, Bangkok 10110.
Turkey Yab-Yay Dagitim, Alay Koshu Caddesi 12/A, Kat 4 no. 11-12, Cagaloglu, Istanbul.
UK Roger Lascelles, 47 York Rd, Brentford, Middlesex, TW8 0QP
USA Lonely Planet Publications, PO Box 2001A, Berkeley, CA 94702.
West Germany Buchvertrieb Gerda Schettler, Postfach 64, D3415 Hattorf a H.
All Other Countries refer to Australia address.